SUNDAYS AND SEASONS

YEAR A 2014

Sundays and Seasons
2014, Year A
Guide to Worship Planning

The Sundays and Seasons family of resources

Worship Planning Calendar, 2014, Year A (978-1-4514-2562-8)

Words for Worship, 2014, Year A (978-1-4514-2566-6)

Church Year Calendar, 2014, Year A (978-1-4514-2563-5)

Church Year Calendar, 2014, Year A PDF (978-1-4514-2564-2)

Calendar of Word and Season 2014 (978-1-4514-2568-0)

Bread for the Day: Daily Bible Readings and Prayers 2014 (978-1-4514-2565-9)

www.sundaysandseasons.com

www.newproclamation.com

Acknowledgments

Copyright © 2013 Augsburg Fortress. All rights reserved. Except as noted herein and for brief quotations in critical articles or reviews, no part of this book may be reproduced in any manner without prior written permission from the publisher. Write to: Permissions, Augsburg Fortress, Box 1209, Minneapolis, MN 55440-1209.

Unless otherwise indicated, scripture quotations are from the New Revised Standard Version Bible © 1989 Division of Christian Education of the National Council of the Churches of Christ in the United States of America. Used by permission. All rights reserved.

Revised Common Lectionary © 1992 Consultation on Common Texts. Used by permission.

The prayers of intercession (printed in each Sunday/festival section) may be reproduced for onetime, non-sale use, provided copies are for local use only and the following copyright notice appears: From Sundays and Seasons, copyright © 2013 Augsburg Fortress.

Evangelical Lutheran Worship (Augsburg Fortress, 2006) and Evangelical Lutheran Worship Pastoral Care (Augsburg Fortress, 2008): seasonal worship texts for the Three Days, opening acclamations (Lent and Summer), offering prayers, sending of communion prayers, and dismissals (except Advent and Time after Epiphany).

Celebrate God's Presence (The United Church of Canada): trinitarian formula (Advent).

Wonder, Love, and Praise (Church Publishing, Inc., 1997): invitation to communion, alt. (Easter).

Susan R. Briehl, Come, Lord Jesus: Devotions for Advent, Christmas, Epiphany (Augsburg Fortress, 1996): Lighting the Christmas Tree 1, Blessing for a Home at Epiphany.

Washed and Welcome: A Baptism Sourcebook (Augsburg Fortress, 2010): Baptismal Anniversary Greeting, Celebrating a Baptismal Anniversary.

Go Make Disciples: An Invitation to Baptismal Living (Augsburg Fortress, 2012): Accompanying Adults Preparing for Baptism, Accompanying Newly Baptized Adults.

This Far by Faith: An African American Resource for Worship (Augsburg Fortress, 1999): Blessing of Lectors.

Evangelical Lutheran Worship Occasional Services for the Assembly (Augsburg Fortress, 2009): Remembering Those Who Have Died.

Annual and seasonal materials

A Case for the Revised Common Lectionary: Christian Scharen

The Gospel of Matthew: Erma S. Wolf

Preparing for the Season: Clint A. Schnekloth

Seasonal Worship Texts: Jon Niketh and Martin A. Seltz, incorporating texts from Evangelical Lutheran Worship resources as noted in the acknowledgments.

Seasonal Rites: Melissa Moll (Midweek Advent Series, Midweek Lenten Series, Service of Word and Song for Summer); John Roberts (scripts for Matthew Passion, John Passion, and Day of Pentecost); Ryan Marsh (Lighting the Advent Wreath, Welcome to the Waiting Room)

Weekly materials

Prayers of Intercession: Jennifer Baker-Trinity, Gwenn Bazajou, Lynn Bulock, Shelley Cunningham, James Hugh Drury, Erik Haaland, Barbara Larsen, Christine Marie Merkel Nessel, Kyle Schiefelbein, Kevin Shock

Images in the Readings and Connections with the Liturgy: Gail Ramshaw

Ideas for the Day: Pari Bailey, Erik Christensen, Michael Coffey, Anne Edison-Albright, Pam Fickenscher, Bryon Hansen, Zebulon Highben, Dirk Lange, Rebecca Schlatter Liberty, Justin J. Lind-Ayres, Stephen G. Marsh, Anastasia McAteer, Craig M. Mueller, Joel Nau, Patrick Shebeck

Let the Children Come: Liv Larson Andrews, Melissa Bergstrom, Amanda Grell, Mary C. Lindberg, Erin Martinson, Joy McDonald Coltvet

Music materials

Assembly Song: Scott Rohr (hymns), Cheryl Dieter (psalmody), Tom Witt (global), Will Sappington (praise)

Music for the Day: Tom Leeseberg-Lange (choral), Gwen Gotsch (children's choir), Sarah J. Hawbecker (keyboard/instrumental), Michael Glasgow (handbell)

Art and design

Cover art: Nicholas Wilton

Interior art: Claudia McGehee, Tanja Butler

Book design: Laurie Ingram, Jessica Hillstrom

Development staff

Suzanne Burke, Martin A. Seltz

Manufactured in the U.S.A.

978-1-4514-2561-1

Introduction

Advent

Christmas

Time after Epiphany

LENT

THE THREE DAYS

EASTER

TIME AFTER PENTECOST — SUMMER

TIME AFTER PENTECOST — AUTUMN

Time after Pentecost — November

Index of Seasonal Rites

Lectionary Conversion Chart
Time after Pentecost, Year A, 2014

If today is . . .	. . . it falls within this date range.	The "lectionary" number assigned to this date range in *Evangelical Lutheran Worship* is . . .	. . . which is equivalent to "proper ___" in other printed lectionaries.	In 2014, this Sunday is the "___ Sunday after Pentecost."
Sunday, June 22	Sunday between June 19 & June 25 (if after Holy Trinity)	Lectionary 12	7	2nd
Sunday, June 29	Sunday between June 26 & July 2	Lectionary 13	8	3rd
Sunday, July 6	Sunday between July 3 & 9	Lectionary 14	9	4th
Sunday, July 13	Sunday between July 10 & 16	Lectionary 15	10	5th
Sunday, July 20	Sunday between July 17 & 23	Lectionary 16	11	6th
Sunday, July 27	Sunday between July 24 & 30	Lectionary 17	12	7th
Sunday, August 3	Sunday between July 31 & Aug 6	Lectionary 18	13	8th
Sunday, August 10	Sunday between Aug 7 & 13	Lectionary 19	14	9th
Sunday, August 17	Sunday between Aug 14 & 20	Lectionary 20	15	10th
Sunday, August 24	Sunday between Aug 21 & 27	Lectionary 21	16	11th
Sunday, August 31	Sunday between Aug 28 & Sept 3	Lectionary 22	17	12th
Sunday, September 7	Sunday between Sept 4 & 10	Lectionary 23	18	13th
Sunday, September 14	Sunday between Sept 11 & 17	Lectionary 24	19	14th
Sunday, September 21	Sunday between Sept 18 & 24	Lectionary 25	20	15th
Sunday, September 28	Sunday between Sept 25 & Oct 1	Lectionary 26	21	16th
Sunday, October 5	Sunday between Oct 2 & 8	Lectionary 27	22	17th
Sunday, October 12	Sunday between Oct 9 & 15	Lectionary 28	23	18th
Sunday, October 19	Sunday between Oct 16 & 22	Lectionary 29	24	19th
Sunday, October 26	Sunday between Oct 23 & 29	Lectionary 30	25	20th
Sunday, November 2	Sunday between Oct 30 & Nov 5	Lectionary 31	26	21st
Sunday, November 9	Sunday between Nov 6 & 12	Lectionary 32	27	22nd
Sunday, November 16	Sunday between Nov 13 & 19	Lectionary 33	28	23rd
Christ the King, November 23	Sunday between Nov 20 & 26	Lectionary 34	29	Last

Lectionary Color Chart
Year A, 2014

Advent

Dec 1	First Sunday of Advent	Blue
Dec 8	Second Sunday of Advent	Blue
Dec 15	Third Sunday of Advent	Blue
Dec 22	Fourth Sunday of Advent	Blue

Christmas

Dec 24/25	Nativity of Our Lord	White
Dec 29	First Sunday of Christmas	White
Jan 5	Second Sunday of Christmas	White
Jan 6	Epiphany of Our Lord	White

Time after Epiphany

Jan 12	Baptism of Our Lord	White
Jan 19	Second Sunday after Epiphany	Green
Jan 26	Third Sunday after Epiphany	Green
Feb 2	Presentation of Our Lord	White
Feb 2	Fourth Sunday after Epiphany	Green
Feb 9	Fifth Sunday after Epiphany	Green
Feb 16	Sixth Sunday after Epiphany	Green
Feb 23	Seventh Sunday after Epiphany	Green
Mar 2	Transfiguration of Our Lord	White

Lent

Mar 5	Ash Wednesday	Purple
Mar 9	First Sunday in Lent	Purple
Mar 16	Second Sunday in Lent	Purple
Mar 23	Third Sunday in Lent	Purple
Mar 30	Fourth Sunday in Lent	Purple
Apr 6	Fifth Sunday in Lent	Purple
Apr 13	Sunday of the Passion	Scarlet/Purple
Apr 14	Monday in Holy Week	Scarlet/Purple
Apr 15	Tuesday in Holy Week	Scarlet/Purple
Apr 16	Wednesday in Holy Week	Scarlet/Purple

Three Days

Apr 17	Maundy Thursday	Scarlet/White
Apr 18	Good Friday	None
Apr 19/20	Resurrection of Our Lord	White/Gold

Easter

Apr 27	Second Sunday of Easter	White
May 4	Third Sunday of Easter	White
May 11	Fourth Sunday of Easter	White
May 18	Fifth Sunday of Easter	White
May 25	Sixth Sunday of Easter	White
May 29	Ascension of Our Lord	White
June 1	Seventh Sunday of Easter	White
June 8	Day of Pentecost	Red

Time after Pentecost

June 15	The Holy Trinity	White
June 22	Lectionary 12	Green
June 29	Peter and Paul, Apostles	Scarlet/Red
June 29	Lectionary 13	Green
July 6	Lectionary 14	Green
July 13	Lectionary 15	Green
July 20	Lectionary 16	Green
July 27	Lectionary 17	Green
Aug 3	Lectionary 18	Green
Aug 10	Lectionary 19	Green
Aug 17	Lectionary 20	Green
Aug 24	Lectionary 21	Green
Aug 31	Lectionary 22	Green
Sept 7	Lectionary 23	Green
Sept 14	Holy Cross Day	Scarlet/Red
Sept 14	Lectionary 24	Green
Sept 21	Lectionary 25	Green
Sept 28	Lectionary 26	Green
Oct 5	Lectionary 27	Green
Oct 12	Lectionary 28	Green
Oct 13	Day of Thanksgiving (Canada)	Green
Oct 19	Lectionary 29	Green
Oct 26	Reformation Sunday	Red
Oct 26	Lectionary 30	Green
Nov 2	All Saints Sunday	White
Nov 2	Lectionary 31	Green
Nov 9	Lectionary 32	Green
Nov 16	Lectionary 33	Green
Nov 23	Christ the King (*Lect. 34*)	White/*Green*
Nov 27	Day of Thanksgiving (USA)	Green

WELCOME

Dear partners in ministry,

Welcome to the 2014 edition of *Sundays and Seasons*. There is something about beginning another three-year lectionary cycle that always renews my energy around keeping this resource fresh and useful each year. In our editorial conversations here at Augsburg Fortress we evaluate the scope, format, and quality of the content provided in these pages every year, and especially when year A rolls around again. Your feedback, collected from you firsthand at events around this church, from postings in various forms of social media, from phone calls and emails to our customer care representatives, and from surveys, helps us make decisions about how to tweak content so it is even more helpful, or, frankly, to leave it alone because it is doing its job.

What's new or different?

While the basic form and content of *Sundays and Seasons* continues from previous years, you will notice a few additions and some reorganization of familiar content.

Within the weekly materials are three new content sections: **images in the readings**, **connections with the liturgy**, and **let the children come**. All of these sections work together with **ideas for the day**, which has been tightened up a bit.

This year's weekly suggestions include additional musical options for **psalmody**. Do you sing the psalm the same way each week? Using different methods of singing the psalms can revitalize the assembly's singing and allow the psalm texts to be heard in new ways. Does your choir always sing the psalm while the assembly listens? Although occasional singing of the psalm by the choir again allows it to be heard in different ways, the primary voice in worship is the assembly's voice, and the singing of the psalm as a response to the first reading belongs primarily to them.

The music listings have been reorganized into the categories of **assembly song** and **music for the day**. Psalmody/ acclamations, praise songs, and global song suggestions have been moved into the assembly song category with the hymn suggestions so that all suggestions intended for assembly singing are in one place. Music for the day offers suggestions for choirs and instrumentalists.

Claudia McGehee has created beautiful new **seasonal art** for this three-year cycle of *Sundays and Seasons*. You may recognize her scratchboard style from our Washed and Welcome series of baptismal preparation resources, which she also illustrated. Learn about her and see more of her work at claudiaillustration.blogspot.com. This edition also features the familiar artwork of Tanja Butler within the weekly materials. You may already be using Tanja's black and white icons from Sundays and Seasons.com. We plan to colorize her icons and make a first set available online in time for Advent 2013.

Many new **seasonal rites** appear in this edition, including resources for Advent and Lent, and scripts for dramatic readings of the gospels for Passion Sunday and Good Friday and the Acts reading for the Day of Pentecost. We will also be experimenting for the first time in September 2013 with posting expanded components of the Advent series "Welcome to the Waiting Room" on Sundays and Seasons.com, including leader scripts and detailed activity descriptions.

Seasonal **greetings** are not included in the seasonal worship texts this year. Presiders are encouraged to use familiar liturgical greetings that can be spoken confidently and graciously, by heart, to the assembly.

The **seasonal checklists** at the end of each seasonal introduction were feeling recycled and a little worn. If you miss these terribly, let us know. Or, if you have an idea for presenting some kind of seasonal checklist, let us know that, too.

With the whole church

This resource could not be published without the creative talents of many people across the church. Those who create content for *Sundays and Seasons* are people just like you. They are pastors, musicians, associates in ministry, members of worship committees and altar guilds, seminary professors, visual artists, diaconal ministers, and deaconesses. They work full time, part time, or are volunteers in their churches. They serve large and small congregations and campus ministries in rural areas, small towns, cities, and suburbs in the United States, Canada, and abroad. They come from various cultural contexts, and with different approaches to worship in word and sacrament. In nineteen years literally hundreds of people have contributed to *Sundays and Seasons*. Here's this year's group.

Visual images

Claudia McGehee (annual and seasonal images) contemplates and illustrates from her home-studio in Iowa City, Iowa. A personal business motto, "Illustration for all seasons," was aptly applied while working on the *Sundays and Seasons* pieces. The project was a wonderful reminder of the rich rhythm of life we derive from our spiritual calendar. **Tanja Butler** (weekly images) has been teaching visual arts at Gordon College in Wenham, Massachusetts, since 2000. She is interested in finding ways to create collaborative artwork within the context of community. Liturgical art, illustration, and community service projects are the focus of her artistic activity. In creating the cover art for *Sundays and Seasons*, **Nicholas Wilton** believed that symbols of things were needed as, like poetry, we are trying to express something about the spiritual. Working metaphorically, for him, is far more universal and engaging than literally depicting something specific.

Annual and seasonal materials

Christian Scharen teaches worship and practical theology at Luther Seminary in St. Paul, and is a regular columnist on faith and pop music in *The Cresset*. **Erma S. Wolf** is the pastor at Hawarden American Lutheran, Hawarden, Iowa in the Western Iowa Synod of the ELCA. She also writes for LivingLutheran.com. **Clint A. Schnekloth** (www.clintschnekloth.com) serves as lead pastor at Good Shepherd Lutheran, Fayetteville, Arkansas. If all goes according to plan, he will walk for his D.Min. at Fuller Theological Seminary in the summer of 2013. **Jon Niketh** serves as pastor of First Lutheran in Lynn, Massachusetts on Boston's north shore, and chairs the worship team of the New England Synod. **Melissa Moll** is an organist and librarian who lives in Lincoln, Nebraska. **Ryan Marsh** leads Church of the Beloved, a creatively Lutheran worshiping community in Edmonds, Washington. **John Roberts** is associate pastor of Unity Evangelical Lutheran in Chicago.

Prayers of intercession

Kyle Schiefelbein is lecturer in liturgical and theological studies at Pacific Lutheran Theological Seminary in Berkeley, California, and a member of St. Mark's Lutheran in San Francisco. **Jennifer Baker-Trinity** is a church musician and writer in the areas of theology and music. She resides in Middleburg, Pennsylvania, with her spouse and three children. **Erik Haaland**, of St. Paul, Minnesota, has degrees from St. Olaf College and Luther Seminary. He is a member of Christ Church Lutheran in Minneapolis. **Lynn Bulock** is a diaconal minister and program director for Lutheran Social Services of Southern California. She is part of New Hope Lutheran, serving as a Stephen Leader. **Barbara Larsen** lives in Princeton, Minnesota, and is an acute care social worker with a masters degree in counseling. She is a church musician/composer, writes litanies for worship, and contributes to *Bread for the Day*. **Shelley Cunningham** lives in Rochester, Minnesota, with her three school-age children. She is a pastor at Zumbro Lutheran and a writer for Luther Seminary's communications office. **Gwenn Bazajou** is pastor of New Hope Lutheran in Alvarado, Minnesota. **Christine Marie Merkel Nessel** is a writer, mom, baker, preacher, friend, advocate, and crafter. She loves long walks on the beach and has a silly sense of humor. **Kevin Shock** enjoys many ministry opportunities with seniors, Penn State students, and others, but especially feels blessed as pastor for the people at St. Mark Lutheran in Pleasant Gap, Pennsylvania. **James Hugh Drury** is an Air Force brat; has lived in eight states and Japan; and has been a Lutheran pastor for more than 35 years, serving congregations in California, Texas, Alaska, and Utah.

Images in the readings, connections with the liturgy

Gail Ramshaw is a scholar of liturgical language and professor of religion at La Salle University. She served on the Revised Common Lectionary design committee and on the Church's Year task force for the Renewing Worship project of the ELCA.

Ideas for the day

Pastor **Rebecca Schlatter Liberty** has served in congregations and campus ministries in the western United States and now lives in Maine. Pastor **Anne Edison-Albright** serves Redeemer Lutheran and lives in Stevens Point, Wisconsin, with husband Sean, son Walter, and dog Hank. She recommends getting a pine branch and flicking baptismal water at your congregation as often as possible! **Pam Fickenscher** is a pastor at Edina Community Lutheran in Minnesota. She lives in Minneapolis with her husband, two children, and a 90-pound Labrador Retriever. She blogs regularly about the lectionary, parenthood, and ministry at www.pastorpam.typepad.com. **Zebulon Highben** is a church musician, conductor, and associate in ministry in the ELCA. He serves on the music faculty of Muskingum University, a college of the PC-USA in southeastern Ohio. The Rev. **Stephen G. Marsh** is currently serving as co-pastor of Lake Edge Lutheran in Madison, Wisconsin. He has a passion for the justice agenda of Jesus, as well as the missional focus of the church. **Erik Christensen** is pastor to St. Luke's Lutheran of Logan Square. He lives in Chicago with his partner, Kerry, and takes guitar lessons at the Old Town School of Folk Music. **Joel Nau** is pastor of St. Paul Lutheran in Winterset, Iowa. **Justin J. Lind-Ayres** serves as pastor at Bethany Lutheran in Minneapolis, a congregation committed to prophetic witness, the Lutheran liturgical tradition, and the wide welcome of God. **Anastasia McAteer** writes on a variety of topics, from alternative liturgy to foodie spirituality. She holds an M.Div. from Fuller Seminary and lives in San Diego with her family. **Bryon Hansen** is pastor of Bethlehem Lutheran in Auburn, located in the foothills of Northern California. He is passionate about worship and preaching and its potential for shaping lives. **Dirk Lange**'s ministerial experience has covered a wide spectrum of activities, but all under one umbrella: liturgy in the lives of people. During the early 1990s as brother of Taizé he was engaged with the prayer and songs of Taizé. He is currently associate professor of worship at Luther Seminary. **Patrick Shebeck** is pastor of Prince of Peace Lutheran in Chicago Heights, Illinois, and convener of the Metropolitan Chicago Synod Liturgy Team. Prior to serving as a pastor, he was a church musician in Roman Catholic, Episcopal, and Lutheran parishes in the Twin Cities. **Craig M. Mueller** is pastor of Holy Trinity Lutheran in Chicago. He is finishing a D.Min. in liturgy, contrasting declining church attendance and the effects of consumerism and technology with what the liturgy holds up as what is essentially human. The Rev. **Pari Bailey** has spent fifteen lovely years in rural southwestern Minnesota, growing disciples and petunias. She also is an officer with the Minnesota Police Pipe Band. **Michael Coffey** currently serves as pastor of First English Lutheran in Austin, Texas. He enjoys writing, blogging, cooking, liturgical and ritual experimentation, Old Testament studies, and exploring spiritual formation.

Let the children come

Erin Martinson is a part time pastor, part time writer/healer and a full time mom. She lives in Ventura, California, with her husband, Tim, and their super energetic preschooler, Dara. **Liv Larson Andrews** is an ELCA pastor serving in the West Central neighborhood of Spokane, Washington. Her Sunday worship is enlivened by her toddler son, Arlo, and spouse, Casey. **Melissa Bergstrom** serves as Edina Community Lutheran's organist and choir director and chairs the music department at Anoka-Ramsey Community College, both in the Minneapolis-St. Paul area. **Amanda Grell** lives in Fayetteville, Arkansas, with her husband and three small children. She is a librarian by profession and has previously contributed to the Washed and Welcome series for Augsburg Fortress. **Joy McDonald Coltvet** is a pastor and parent residing in St. Paul, Minnesota. She belongs to a multicultural family with roots in Africa, Europe, and North America. **Mary C. Lindberg** is a mom, writer, and

pastor who lives in Seattle, Washington. She has contributed to many Augsburg Fortress resources, including *Spark Story Bible* and *Living the Promises of Baptism*.

Music suggestions

Scott Rohr (hymns) has served as a musician at several Lutheran and Episcopal congregations in Montana and Minnesota, and is currently cantor of University Lutheran Church of Hope, Minneapolis. **Cheryl Dieter** (psalmody) is minister of worship and music at Trinity Lutheran in Valparaiso, Indiana, and business manager for the Association of Lutheran Church Musicians. **Tom Witt** (global song) is a church musician and worship planner living in Minneapolis. He is co-founder of Bread for the Journey (www. bfjmusic.com) and leads worship retreats as a member of the Living Liturgy team (www.livingliturgy.com). **Will Sappington** (praise songs) is proud to be a husband and dad and he knows why there are so many songs about rainbows. **Tom Leeseberg-Lange** (choral) has been a Lutheran church musician for 44 years in Missouri, Indiana, and Maryland. His passions are hymnody and iTunes. **Gwen Gotsch** (children's choir) directs choirs for children and teens at Grace Lutheran Church and School in River Forest, Illinois, where she also serves as Communications Coordinator. She blogs at perverselutheran.blogspot.com and publishes her hymn texts at gwengotsch.com. **Sarah J. Hawbecker** (keyboard/instrumental) is a full time musician at Lutheran Church of the Redeemer in Atlanta, and active in the American Guild of Organists and the Association of Lutheran Church Musicians. Now an honorary Carolinian, **Michael Glasgow** (handbell; www.michaeljglasgow.com) grew up in Michigan. He is an award-winning composer, with works published for handbells, organ, orchestra, and choir. Michael is an engaging, energetic conductor and self-proclaimed "theory geek."

You make it happen

Sundays and Seasons is truly a collaborative endeavor. You make this resource happen. I love hearing from you, whether it is ideas for future content, suggesting potential contributors (maybe you!), or offering feedback. Thank you for the trust you place in the changing roster of contributors who offer their time and talent to the whole church through *Sundays and Seasons* each year. Even more, thank you for the many and various ways in which *you* care for the church's worship and for those who gather weekly around the word, the bath, and the meal in Christ's name.

Suzanne K. Burke, general editor

A CASE FOR THE REVISED COMMON LECTIONARY

The Revised Common Lectionary (RCL) has been taking quite a beating in some quarters of the church. A senior pastor of a large church told me he'd recently read a book titled *The Big Idea*. His take-away? "We give people too many things; we confuse them. I get the lectionary, but people don't." Making a similar argument, a seminary colleague described the RCL as "reading the biblical story in a disjointed, unconnected, seemingly random fashion." Many pastors claim the new post-Christian mission context in the United States *requires* something simpler, more narratively driven, so newcomers can learn the basics of the Christian story.

In response to the new mission context in North America, I make the case for the need to *deepen* rather than *abandon* our engagement with the RCL. By "our" in the last sentence, to be clear, I mean lay ministers of all sorts who are involved in worship planning and leading, along with rostered leaders who do the same. I challenge those who plan and lead worship to reclaim the Revised Common Lectionary as a "big idea." After all, it points us to the very heart of the Christian story: our participation in the paschal mystery of Christ's death and resurrection! The following three points might serve well as points of study and conversation with your worship planning team.

I. Proclaiming the Living Word

Some object that lectionaries leave out sections of the Bible. Right! All lectionaries—meaning a list of choices to be read—*edit* the Bible, you might say. Christians gather to celebrate the paschal mystery of our participation in Christ's death and resurrection each Sunday, and most centrally, in the great Three Days of Maundy Thursday, Good Friday, and the Easter Vigil. That we do so means necessarily highlighting some texts, and leaving other texts for study in contexts other than worship (in Sunday school or Bible study, for example). Take, just as an example, the strange story in Genesis 6:1-4 where "the sons of God went to the daughters of humans and had children by them." The logic of the lectionary, then, suggests Sunday's texts are not for "teaching the Bible" but proclaiming the Living Word, Jesus Christ. The readings are paired so as to foster a rich and full proclamation of this Living Word throughout the year, drawing on the fullness of the revelation of Jesus Christ

in and through the Bible. So: the "big idea" of scripture in worship is for the gathered assembly to be confronted with the Word, Jesus Christ, who comes as law and gospel, and thereby learn the good news of Jesus Christ. Such is our confessional claim about the church, the assembly where the word is rightly proclaimed and the sacraments administered according to the gospel.

2. Richer Fare

Some view the complex interrelation of the texts on Sunday as a burden. These leaders worry the diverse images and stories found in four readings—from the Old Testament (or Acts during the Easter season), the Psalms, the Epistles, and the Gospels—simply confuse hearers. Here, it is important to know and then capitalize upon the logic of the RCL. First, despite a common view to the contrary, the Psalm is not "another reading." It is meant to be the assembly's sung response to what it hears of God's merciful salvation in the first reading.

In addition, the first reading (usually from the Old Testament) and the gospel are intentionally paired based upon scripture's own basic principle of intertextual interpretation—scripture interpreting scripture. Jesus does this continually, as for example in his teaching in Matthew 5 on fulfilling the law: "You have heard it said . . . But I say to you . . ." Take a careful look at any Sunday texts. The coming Sunday as I write is November 11, 2012. The first reading, from 1 Kings 17, recounts Elijah's encounter with the widow of Zarephath who gave the prophet the last of her oil and meal to eat. God promised to provide for her and the jug of oil did not fail and jar of meal was not emptied. This text is set next to the gospel reading from Mark 12, where Jesus observes a poor widow putting two small copper coins in the temple treasury, and declares she has contributed more than the rich since she gave all she had to live on. Set side by side, the texts help portray the abundance of God's manna and mercy, but also contain a sharp critique of how our possessions may keep us from trusting God.

Lastly, the second reading either complements the gospel (during the festival season from Advent through Trinity Sunday) or is read in a continuous fashion, week by week, through various books of the Bible. This can offer opportunity for a preaching series, say, on the book of Romans (which comes up in year A during the time after Pentecost). Even here, however, the richness of intertextual interplay can make for lovely and powerful juxtaposition. Take as an example Sunday, July 13, 2014 (lectionary 15), which has Romans 8:1-11 as its epistle reading. Paul uses the images of "flesh" and "spirit" to speak about how we are to live "alive in Christ." Set next to the gospel from Matthew 13, the parable of the sower, we see powerful interplay between God's prodigal love, sowing seeds of mercy in every direction, in every sort of soil, and the work of the Spirit within each of us, transforming flesh into spirit so that Christ might live in us to the glory of God.

The richness of the juxtaposition of the texts is a gift to worship leaders as they plan for the multiple ways proclamation happens throughout the liturgy: in scripture and preaching, to be sure, but also in prayer and praise, in bread and wine, and in sending to live as Christ's body in daily life. The texts set side by side say the Living Word into our lives, and allow for an overflowing of points of connection for the diversity of worshipers and their spiritual needs on a given day.

3. Shared Practice

Some congregations view the lectionary as an unnecessary constriction on worship that fits their mission context. They want the freedom to do preaching series, to focus the service either in length or in theme. It can be a gift to inhabit a deeply shared and ecumenical pattern of proclaiming scripture in worship, however. The lectionary represents decades of hard-won ecumenical agreement, a shared practice of the church as body of Christ. In following its pattern, congregations participate in a shared practice connecting them with brothers and sisters in Christ not only across town (helpful for shared scripture study and worship planning) but also around the world. Noting this (in projected or printed service notes) allows a congregation to say clearly that we gathered in this place are not unto ourselves but are joined to Christians of every time and every place, members of one,

holy, catholic and apostolic church. The RCL is, whether we name it or not, a way we live these ancient "marks of the church." It saves us, truth be told, from merely presenting the gathered assembly with our own tastes and preferences, or those of the worship leadership team.

In conclusion, it is important to say the RCL is not perfect, nor will it endure forever. Many different lectionaries have served the church well in the past, and a diversity serve the church now. Yet the creation of a 3-year lectionary in the 1960s, the Common Lectionary in 1983, and its revision (the RCL) in 1992, binds us together by offering a shared practice of hearing the Word of God, Jesus Christ, proclaimed in law and promise, for us. This common practice, when engaged with wisdom and imagination, strengthens our common ability to be drawn into God's great mission of loving and redeeming all creation.

Christian Scharen
Assistant Professor of Worship and Theology
Luther Seminary, St. Paul

Helpful Reading

Ramshaw, Gail. *Treasures Old and New: Images in the Lectionary.* Minneapolis: Fortress Press, 2002.

———. *A Three-Year Banquet: The Lectionary for the Assembly.* Minneapolis: Augsburg Fortress, 2004.

The Revised Common Lectionary: Twentieth Anniversary Annotated Edition. Consultation on Common Texts. Minneapolis: Fortress Press, 2012.

West, Fritz. *Scripture and Memory: The Ecumenical Hermeneutic of the Three-Year Lectionaries.* Collegeville, MN: The Liturgical Press, 1997.

www.commontexts.org/rcl/index.html
lectionary.library.vanderbilt.edu
www.textweek.com
www.elca.org/Growing-in-Faith/Worship/Lectionary.aspx
www.workingpreacher.org/default.aspx

THE GOSPEL OF MATTHEW

The year of Matthew, year A in the cycle of readings of the Revised Common Lectionary, is an opportunity for extended reflection on what traditionally was considered the earliest written gospel. While that designation has been discredited by scholars (with the honor going to the Gospel of Mark), the Gospel of Matthew still occupies a privileged position, being listed as the first of the four gospel books in the New Testament. In terms of the biblical ordering of books, it picks up the story of God's interaction with the chosen people of Israel with its introduction of the Jewish Messiah, Jesus, a descendant of King David and the founding patriarch, Abraham. Quickly, however, the reader learns that this Jesus is to be understood as greater than any other descendant of Abraham, like Moses but greater than Moses, a son of David who is yet Lord of David. This Jesus is the fulfillment of what was promised through the prophets: Immanuel, "God with us." This year in the lectionary cycle brings that theme home as the year winds from Advent through the Easter season and into the long summer and fall of the Sundays after Pentecost.

It is a good idea to read through the entire gospel before the new year begins on the first Sunday of Advent. Each gospel has a distinctive "voice," and Matthew is no exception. The author of Matthew, while drawing on what is found in the Gospel of Mark and sharing much with that writing as well as with the Gospel of Luke, has sharp differences in how stories are developed and important points emphasized. Matthew also contains material that is unique to this book, some of which is included in the lectionary assignments for the coming year. Whether this gospel is being used for preaching, teaching, or in other ways, getting a "refresher course" in it will enliven your encounter with its message and themes.

It is important to note, however, that quite a bit of Matthew does not make its way into any of the lectionary selections. Out of twenty-eight chapters, only five are used in their entirety during the course of the year (those being chapters 2–5 and 25). All lectionaries must make choices regarding what is included and what is left out. Some of the more notable omissions in this year of Matthew include the Matthean Lord's Prayer, along with the second half of the Sermon on the Mount (6:22—7:29); the call of Matthew in chapter 9; Jesus' instructions to his disciples to not go among the Gentiles, but only to "the lost sheep of the house of Israel" (10:5-6); and Jesus' extended and heated diatribe against the scribes and Pharisees, along with his withdrawal from the temple in chapter 23.

Disturbing Side to the Gospel

The omission of that final long discourse of Jesus, along with some other shorter passages scattered throughout the gospel, points out one of the most disturbing aspects of Matthew: the intense antagonism within the book between Jesus and the scribes and Pharisees, which at times is broadened to include all of Israel, or at least all of its leaders. A reading of the entire book quickly reveals that, in this account of the good news, the leaders of Israel are opposed to Jesus from beginning to end, from the story in chapter 2 of the magi seeking the newborn king in the palace of Herod the Great to the recounting in chapter 28 of the priests bribing the soldiers who guarded the tomb into spreading the lie that the body of Jesus had been stolen by his followers. Preaching and teaching this gospel definitely does not require Christians of today to re-enter and adopt the antagonisms and growing divisions that existed between the community of the author of Matthew and the non-Christian Jewish community of the later first century. However, it is important to recognize this tension within the gospel, even if this tension is not, for the most part, dealt with within worship.

One place, however, where this tension clearly surfaces within the lectionary is in the assigned reading for Passion Sunday. Whether one chooses the long reading or the shorter option, both include the notorious verse in which the people cry, "His blood be on us and on our children!" (27:25). The Matthean passion, while not as notoriously anti-Jewish as the passion account in John, still emphasizes the role of the chief priests, elders and scribes in stirring up the crowds against Jesus and in mocking him during his crucifixion. In a year in which both the Matthew and the John passion stories are scheduled to be read within a week of each other, preachers and other worship leaders need to prepare themselves and the faith community for the cumulative effect of these readings.

The Good News in Matthew

The good news is that there is much good news in Matthew. The lectionary year quickly brings the first good news theme, that Jesus is identified with the promised Immanuel of the prophet Isaiah, on the fourth Sunday of Advent with the story of Joseph's vision in a dream regarding his fiancée Mary's unplanned pregnancy. That this Jesus is "God with us" will be emphasized over and over throughout the year, including in the reading for Trinity Sunday in June. Then the lectionary provides the closing verses of Matthew, including the reassurance from the risen Lord that "I am with you always, to the end of the age" (28:20). As the gospel makes the connections between Jesus' story and various important persons and events in the story of Israel (such as the Exodus and Jesus' own flight to Egypt followed by his return to his home country), it also makes clear that Jesus is much more than yet another prophet-king in the long line of prophets and kings of Israel.

This is reflected in the readings for both the Advent season and the time after Epiphany. In Advent, just as John the Baptist has proclaimed, Jesus is the one giving evidence of "good fruit." At the beginning of Epiphany the account of the wise men coming to worship the child Jesus, along with the signs and warnings, support the claim that Jesus is more entitled to the honor due a king than the puppets of the Roman Emperor. (With the feast of the Epiphany falling on a Monday, worship leaders might give serious thought to transferring its observance to the Sunday before.) Due to the number of Sundays between the Epiphany of Our Lord and Lent, the entire first chapter of the Sermon on the Mount gets presented. Besides the familiar Beatitudes, the community hears Jesus' voice of authority declare, "You have heard it said . . . but I say to you . . ." This culminates on Transfiguration (March 2) when Jesus is not only the disciples' object of worship (as he had been for the wise men on January 6) but also is raised above Moses and Elijah when the divine voice from the cloud orders the disciples to listen to Jesus, the beloved Son.

After the readings from Matthew on Ash Wednesday and the first Sunday in Lent the lectionary turns to the Gospel of John for an extended period. With the exceptions of Passion Sunday and possibly Easter Sunday (when the resurrection account in Matthew 28 is one of the options for the gospel reading), the worshiping community will not hear from Matthew from the second Sunday in Lent until the feast of Holy Trinity. Then we hear the return of the "God with us" theme, and in the Sundays to come launch into the heart of Matthew's gospel.

Teachings for the Church

The lectionary selections that occupy the Sundays of the summer through September include parables that are unique to Matthew, as well as accounts of Jesus' ministry with his disciples. The emphasis on the importance of bearing fruit is challenging to many Christians today, and especially within the Lutheran tradition with its emphasis on grace and faith alone apart from human works. But the gospel wishes to impress on the followers of Jesus, then and now, that living the life of faith is more about what one does than what one says. As with the parable of the sower at the beginning of chapter 13, the abundant harvest is evidence of the seed having fallen into good soil.

Whether it is the response of those who sell all they have to obtain the treasure in the field, or the twelve baskets of leftovers following the feeding of the 5000, or the declaration that Peter's confession will be the foundation for the church numbering far beyond the twelve or so who follow Jesus now, all these are the fruits that come bursting forth from the good tree, the good seed, the good soil of the kingdom of heaven.

This gospel is the only one in which the word for "church" is used. The church is described in chapter 16 as the solid house built on the rock, which even the storms of hell cannot destroy; but in chapter 18 the church is the place for sheltering the little ones, finding the lost sheep, and bringing sinners to repentance through acts of grace and forgiveness. That also is the fruit of the good tree, the evidence the good news has taken root. Most of the Sundays in October and November are filled with one parable after another in which the importance of the community bearing good fruit is portrayed. Whether it is the disobedient son who changes his mind and goes to work as his father asked, or the bridesmaids who are prepared with extra oil, or finally the "sheep" who discover to their surprise that they have been doing good works all along, it is made clear that good fruit comes from the planting of the gospel seed even though those fruits seem to appear almost by accident!

The Gospel of Matthew isn't content with a church that is satisfied with only saying the right words, or ensuring that the proper teachings are proclaimed. While those things do matter, and in fact it is critically important that they be said by the church, having the correct words without following through with the actions bearing good fruit only means that the church is judged with the same woes which Jesus hurled at those he declared to be hypocrites. And that is true whether those words are "Salvation is by grace alone through faith alone," or "All are welcome," or even "Jesus is Lord!"

A Call to Action

At the end of the Gospel of Matthew in chapter 28, as in the parable of the king judging the nations (chapter 25), Jesus issues a call to action. "Make disciples," he says. Disciples (the brothers and sisters in the community of the church) are to go to the nations and teach all people what obeying Jesus looks like: forgiving others over and over; feeding and clothing and visiting; making peace and showing mercy; spending every moment awake and watchful for the return of the Son of Man. The command, while daunting, is accompanied by two promises. The first is that the seed of the good news *is* being planted and *is* bearing good fruit even in the most surprising of places. And the second is that Jesus is still with us, with his church, with his gathered followers and his restored lost sheep, meeting us on the road and accompanying us as we go in the way of baptizing and teaching and worshiping and living as Jesus has taught us.

Erma S. Wolf
Hawarden American Lutheran
Hawarden, Iowa

ADVENT

PREPARING FOR ADVENT

May the God of hope fill you with all joy and peace in believing,
so that you may abound in hope by the power of the Holy Spirit.
— *Romans 15:13*

There is little distance between hope and desperation, yet the space between them makes all the difference in the world. Entering the Advent season primarily in one mode or the other means the difference between awaiting the Messiah with patience and faith, or awaiting the Messiah with anxiety and uncertainty. It is quite likely, in the buzz that is the holiday season, that each of us brings with us a substantial mix of each. During this season, in our worship and Advent devotional practices, we explore resources to dampen the desperation and hop up the hope. And we put Christ at the center of it all.

Lectionary

Scripture assigned for this season is our friend. Perhaps no Advent in the three-year lectionary cycle has texts that express so profoundly the depth of the hope we have in Christ Jesus. We return for our gospel readings to the first of the four gospels. We begin this Advent season exclaiming, "Welcome back, Matthew!"

Additionally, three of the four epistle readings are drawn from the first and longest of the epistles in the New Testament: Romans. Romans will come back around this year as a continuous series in the summer. Romans has quite a lot to say about hope. We are to "Rejoice in hope" (12:12). We boast in our hope (5:2). In hope are we saved (8:24). Hope is a dominant motif in Romans. The overall flow of the texts from Romans assigned for Advent follows a pattern familiar to those experienced in the "shape" of Advent. The first Romans text, 13:11-14, emphasizes advent as "second" coming, Christ's immanence, and the kind of life those who anticipate this coming are called to live in the light of this coming. The second text, 15:4-13, is our central hope text. It is simply full of hope. The scriptures were given that we might have hope (15:4). The Romans community is blessed by hope (15:13).

Two aspects of how Romans approaches hope warrant our attention. First of all, Romans repeatedly claims that the scriptures were given for our instruction, that we might have hope. It is a common thread in 15:4-13 as well

as Romans 1:1-7, both of which are readings for the Advent season. Paul understands the gospel of God to have been "promised beforehand through his prophets in the holy scriptures" (1:2). In other words, scripture as prophetic voice anticipating the gospel of Jesus Christ is to be celebrated because it is given as a gift that inspires and instills hope.

Second, and this aspect is central, Romans understands hope to be grounded in endurance. It may not be the primary way most of us would like hope to be grounded and shaped. We might prefer that hope simply be given as a pure and surprising gift. But apparently for Paul hope happens another way. Suffering produces endurance, and endurance produces character, and character produces hope—and hope will not disappoint us (Rom. 5:1-5). This understanding of hope and how to comprehend it is shared by the Letter of James as well. He writes, "Be patient, beloved, until the coming of the Lord" (James 5:7). James even believes, again in a way comparable to Romans, that patience itself is learned by the example and writing of the prophets (James 5:10). James considered blessed those who show endurance and patience. Make sure to find faithful ways to include this insight in your gospel proclamation. Hope proclaimed in the Advent season in a way detached from endurance and patience may actually be no hope at all, but precisely the kind of desperation that is the near opposite of true hope.

Also, the Old Testament readings themselves are primarily drawn from what we might call the proto-gospel, the gospel before the gospel—Isaiah. Isaiah is simply steeped in hope. What other kind of writer can imagine swords turned into plowshares, except for one studied in endurance and hope (Isa. 2:4). "Say to those who are of a fearful heart, 'Be strong, do not fear!'" (Isa. 35:4).

These prominent themes in Isaiah, Romans, and James can provide the warp and woof of a garment to wrap around the readings from Matthew. First, remember that although we do not read aloud chapter one of Matthew during the Advent season, Matthew is grounded completely and utterly in the historical narrative of God with God's people outlined in the genealogy of the first chapter. Matthew, of all the gospels (though not exclusively so), cares about the connection between the gospel he is proclaiming and the prophetic and historical context that has come prior.

Matthew's serious and often dramatic *evangel* also makes more sense when contextualized within this larger horizon and swaddled in these additional texts. Matthew 24:36-44, for example, comes across as apocalyptic, even shocking—and it is. But its rhetorical goal is to massage endurance and hope in the listening community. Stay awake. Be watchful. Endure. Be ready. Always as a message not of despair or desperation, but of hope and grounded faith. Matthew 3 similarly prepares hearers, with the narrative of John the Baptist. The third reading from Matthew for the season, 11:2-11, helps distinguish between the messenger, the last of the prophets given to instruct toward hope, and the content of the hope itself, which is the one who comes after the Baptist. And then, unique to year A, the birth of the Messiah is actually proclaimed during the Advent season and prior to Christmas Day. Be ready indeed.

For those who add a commentary to their collection at the beginning of each church year, consider O. Wesley Allen's *Matthew* in the new Fortress Biblical Preaching Commentaries series (2013). It is a commentary series keyed toward preaching as well as developing teaching resources for congregational ministry and tied to the lectionary readings.

Liturgical Arts

Although hope and endurance are highly conceptual, there are ways to express them artistically. Sit down with a liturgical arts planning team, and ask these questions: *What does hope look like? Which word pictures in the texts especially catch our attention? How can patient endurance be practiced in the assembly? Are there ways to illustrate the movement in these texts from prophets, through John the Baptist, to the coming Messiah, in our worship arts? How can our desire to decorate for Advent stay grounded in the proclamation and hope of the Messiah, and not just tied up in liturgical ideas about the color and themes for the season?*

If you do not have a liturgical arts planning team, maybe this is the year to form one. Remember that many teams (like in sand volleyball) can play a great game with just two members. Consider the following three ideas as seed ideas for your own brainstorming session on liturgical arts for the season. Or use them as is. They're yours now.

1. Select art, signs, paintings, sculpture, drama, or banners that create a flow in the worship space from the hope-filled Old Testament scriptures; through the middle texts on endurance, patience, and John the Baptist; all the way to the content of our hope: Christ. So, for example, create four banners with names on them. In the back of the worship space, a banner reads *Isaiah*. In the middle of the worship space on both sides, banners read *endurance* and *John the Baptist*. In the front, a banner reads *hope* or *Christ*. Place candle stands in front of or near these banners. Perhaps even have these four candles be the Advent candles for the season, in which case the banners would create both a flow—from *Isaiah* to *endurance/John the Baptist* to *hope/Christ*—and would surround the worshiping assembly with these words and images in a kind of Advent wreath. Each banner could also be replaced with actual art that depicts each of these themes.

2. How can the worship environment actually help in the practice of endurance and patience? Perhaps the assembly needs to encounter those things that require our patience in the gathering space prior to entering the worship space. Set up a table, stand, or prayer wall at which worshipers can encounter the written and public prayers of others. The more we encounter the needs of others for prayer, the more we practice the struggle of faith on behalf of and for others. Place reminders in the bulletin or worship folder encouraging everyone to return to the gathering space and truly pray on behalf of someone else before starting worship, emphasizing in this way that "preparation for worship" is itself part of worship.

3. In the labor-intensive and kind of wacky category, consider building four freestanding doors that the assembly is invited to pass through into worship each Sunday. Paint all four doors blue, and decorate the door frames with seasonally appropriate decorations. Paint one word on the front of each door. On the first: Scripture. On the second: The Baptist. On the third: Hope. On the fourth: Born. The fourth door would open onto a crèche. On the fourth Sunday of Advent, place a large baby Jesus in the center of the crèche. If it is not possible to build four freestanding doors, decorate four doors leading into the worship space progressively in this manner, such as two doors into the building, a doorway into the gathering space, and a door into the worship space.

Finally, one important question to ask of this liturgical arts team: What can we reasonably accomplish that will bring joy and help us and our congregation know the hope of Christ, but will not bring us to the point of despair and desperation because it is too much work during a very busy season?

Music

The beginning of another church year is a good opportunity to take the long view on liturgy and worship music. Review the previous year in two different categories. First, list which settings of the liturgy have been your primary resource over the course of the year. What music have you been using for those parts of the worship service that ground the overall movement? Many, but not all, congregations include in their pattern for worship things like the Kyrie, hymn of praise, gospel acclamation, offering song, and song after communion.

Now consider an overall strategy. What will you repeat in the coming year either because it is the beloved musical setting of the liturgy in your congregation, or because you introduced it recently and want to strengthen the assembly's grasp of it? What will you introduce new this year to expand the musical horizons of the assembly? What music in *Evangelical Lutheran Worship* and elsewhere are you personally interested in exploring as a worship leader? Sit down with music planners and look through all ten settings of the liturgy, as well as the Service Music section (#151–238). Advance work now can simplify worship planning for the remainder of the year.

Next, review what you have been doing for the music that varies from week to week. In most congregations, these are the hymns, praise songs, canticles, and anthems. Musical tastes are so highly subjective that even in a very homogeneous congregation, there are probably widely varying desires for what the assembly might sing from week to week. Although your assembly might have a core mode or style, make sure to review options so that your music might represent, as much as possible, the breadth of Christian tradition in its rich variety. Notice that even just in the Advent section there are hymns representing Yiddish folk tunes (ELW 240), twentieth-century liturgical renewal (ELW 242), Lutheran pietism (ELW 241), plainsong (ELW 245), and Cameroon (ELW 253). Representing the gift of the diversity of Christian tradition in song is a core value of our church, if our hymnal is any indication. Take time this Advent season to exercise and flex this core value.

In addition to the hymns available for Advent, *Evangelical Lutheran Worship* includes a section on Hope, Assurance (#618–639). Although many faith communities will be attracted to the carols sung so ubiquitously during the holiday season, some of these hymns might be intriguing companions during the Advent journey, especially as hymns to be sung as the hymn of the day.

Finally, if you have never done so, this is the year to purchase the *Hymnal Companion* and *Indexes to Evangelical Lutheran Worship*. The first offers story and historical background to the text and tune of every hymn in the hymnal. The second offers a wider array of hymn suggestions keyed to each Sunday of the church year than is represented here in *Sundays and Seasons*.

WORSHIP TEXTS FOR ADVENT

Confession and Forgiveness

All may make the sign of the cross, the sign marked at baptism, as the presiding minister begins.
Blessed be the holy Trinity, ✛ one God,
our life, our mercy, our might.
Amen.

As we await the day of the Lord, let us confess our sin.

Silence is kept for reflection.

Great and Holy One,
in this time of waning daylight,
we confess the shadows of sin in our lives.
We build ourselves up at the expense of others.
We rely on our own efforts to make our lives secure.
Yet you, O Lord, are the potter, and we are the clay.
Come to restore us in your image,
remake us into your people,
and rebuild what sin has broken,
that we and the whole creation may rejoice. Amen.

Fear not, people of God:
the Almighty has done great things for us.
God casts away our sin from us
and makes of us a new creation.
In ✛ Jesus Christ, God comes to set you free.
Take heart in the tender compassion of our God.
Amen.

Offering Prayer

God of abundance,
we bring before you the precious fruits of your creation,
and with them our very lives.
Teach us patience and hope as we care for all those in need
until the coming of your Son, our Savior and Lord.
Amen.

Invitation to Communion

Come to the table
where Christ comes to make a home in you.

Prayer after Communion

God of wonder,
we give thanks that you have fed us once again
with this foretaste of the feast to come.
Strengthen us through this gift
to serve our neighbor with joy,
that all may come to see your glory
reflected in the lives of your people;
through Jesus Christ, our Savior and Lord.
Amen.

Sending of Communion

Gracious God,
whose mercy endures from generation to generation:
As Mary set out to visit Elizabeth
before she gave birth to her son,
bless those who go forth to share your word and sacrament
with our sisters and brothers who are
sick/homebound/imprisoned.
In your love and care, nourish and strengthen
those to whom we bring this communion,
that through the body and blood of your Son
we may all know the hope of your promised coming
in Jesus Christ our Lord.
Amen.

Blessing

The God of hope,
through Christ our peace,
in the power of the Holy Spirit,
✝ bless you now and forever.
Amen.

Dismissal

Go in peace. Bring good news to the poor.
Thanks be to God.

SEASONAL RITES FOR ADVENT

Lighting the Advent Wreath

*Written for two leaders (**L1** and **L2**) and assembly.*

Week 1
Song

O Come, O Come, Emmanuel   ELW 257, st. 1

Litany

L1: At every beginning there is a yearning
for the one who is coming.
O Emmanuel,
Wake us up to your coming.

L2: We gather together to expect the unexpected
and imagine the unimaginable.
O Emmanuel,
Wake us up to your coming.

L1: We wait for the day
when God will recycle tanks into tractors
and transform minefields into soccer fields.
O Emmanuel,
Wake us up to your coming.

L2: We stay awake by telling stories
that offer a glimmer of a future
and agitate dormant hope within us.
O Emmanuel,
Wake us up to your coming.

L1: Jesus, we welcome your presence now
with the lighting of this candle,
whose flame brings warmth to winter
and fills this place with the glow of hope.
Amen.
Light the first candle.

Song

O Come, O Come, Emmanuel   ELW 257, st. 3

Week 2
Song

O Come, O Come, Emmanuel   ELW 257, st. 1

Litany

L1: At every beginning there is a yearning
for the one who is coming.
O Emmanuel,
Prepare us for your coming.

L2: We gather together to get ready for what?
Only heaven knows.
O Emmanuel,
Prepare us for your coming.

L1: We wait for the day
when God will create a prevailing peace on the earth,
and natural-born enemies turn into newborn friends.
O Emmanuel,
Prepare us for your coming.

L2: We get ready for God to come close
by laying our lives open to Jesus,
asking him to sort through all our mixed motives.
O Emmanuel,
Prepare us for your coming.

L1: Jesus, we welcome your presence now
with the lighting of these candles,
whose flames bring warmth to winter
and fill this place with the glow of hope.
Amen.
Light two candles.

Song

O Come, O Come, Emmanuel   ELW 257, st. 6

Week 3

Song

O Come, O Come, Emmanuel   ELW 257, st. 1

Litany

L1: At every beginning there is a yearning
for the one who is coming.
O Emmanuel,
Open us up to your coming.

L2: We gather together to allow our deeply held hopes
to be reshaped by God's promises.
O Emmanuel,
Open us up to your coming.

L1: We wait for the day
when God will make for us a future
that is no longer predicated on our fear.
O Emmanuel,
Open us up to your coming.

L2: We find a new receptivity within us
that desires God's will over our own will
and relies on God's justice and mercy to accomplish it.
O Emmanuel,
Open us up to your coming.

L1: Jesus, we welcome your presence now
with the lighting of these candles,
whose flames bring warmth to winter
and fill this place with the glow of hope.
Amen.

Light three candles.

Song

O Come, O Come, Emmanuel   ELW 257, st. 4

Week 4

Song

O Come, O Come, Emmanuel   ELW 257, st. 1

Litany

L1: At every beginning there is a yearning
for the one who is coming.
O Emmanuel,
Surprise us by your coming.

L2: We gather together to let God's good news
reorient our lives.
O Emmanuel,
Surprise us by your coming.

L1: We wait for the day
when all the world will see the sign
that God is with us.
O Emmanuel,
Surprise us by your coming.

L2: We are shocked by how God comes close,
even at this very moment.
O Emmanuel,
Surprise us by your coming.

L1: Jesus, we welcome your presence now
with the lighting of these candles,
whose flames bring warmth to winter
and fill this place with the glow of hope.
Amen.

Light all four candles.

Song

O Come, O Come, Emmanuel   ELW 257, st. 5

Adapted from the Clayfire Collection, "What Happens When God Comes Close," by Ryan Marsh, Church of the Beloved, Edmonds, Washington.

The Gifts of Advent
A Midweek Series for Advent

A gift is given freely and offered in love. In the weeks before Christmas, we often race around finding just the right gifts for friends and family. The season of Advent is itself a gift—a time set apart to prepare our hearts for the coming of Christ. We give thanks for God's gift to us in the baby of Bethlehem.

This series highlights four aspects of Advent that become blessings and gifts in our lives: patience, speech and silence, hope, and family.

Consider adding a visual aspect to the worship space in the form of large boxes decorated in blue wrapping paper. The boxes could contain a representation of each week's theme: for instance, an Advent calendar to represent patience; a megaphone and earplugs for speech and silence; a single candle for hope; and a sculpture or photograph showing a family or friends.

Overview

Week 1: The Gift of Patience
Waiting is hard. We eagerly anticipate the desires of our hearts and want them to come soon. We wait for the first day of school or the first snowfall. We wait to see a loved one or to hear a doctor's news. Just as the farmer waits for crops or the fig tree waits for summer, we are reminded to be patient until the coming of the Lord.

Week 2: The Gifts of Speech and Silence
Encountering the angel of the Lord, Zechariah was struck speechless. His imposed silence became a time to reflect on the wonders of God. Like Zechariah, we are called at times to be silent and listen, at other times to shout with joy.

Week 3: The Gift of Hope
Hope is a word on which our future rests. We cannot know what will come, but with faith we place our hope in Christ. Like Zechariah, we hope for the tender mercy of our God, light in the midst of darkness and death, and the knowledge of salvation by the forgiveness of our sins.

Week 4: The Gift of Family
The Gospel of Matthew begins with a family tree from Abraham to Jesus. Between the recitation of names, we also hear the story of God at work in our world from generation to generation. The Advent and Christmas seasons highlight the significance of family and friends in our lives. We witness Mary and Joseph, Elizabeth and Zechariah, and the shepherds together tending their flocks. As God's children, we become part of the family tree.

Opening Dialogue

Week 1 *(Ps. 37:7; Heb. 12:9)*
"Patience is a virtue," we hear it said.
But the wait is long; we cannot see the end.
"Rome wasn't built in just a day."
We rest in the Lord, and wait patiently for him.
"Patience is also a form of action."
So we run with endurance the race set before us.
"How poor are they that have not patience!"
We are rich in our hope of the promised Messiah.
Come, Lord Jesus!

Week 2 *(Eccles. 3:1, 6; Ps. 62:1; Ps. 40:10; Ps. 19:14)*
For everything there is a season:
A time to keep silence, and a time to speak.
For God alone my soul waits in silence;
from God alone comes my salvation.
I will not hide God's saving help within my heart.
I will speak of God's faithfulness and steadfast love.
May the words of our mouths
and the meditations of our hearts
be acceptable to God, our rock and our redeemer.

Week 3 *(Isa. 42:16, 30:26, 11:6, 35:1, 7:14)*
Hope is a candle that flickers yet offers warmth and life.
The darkness will turn into light,
the moon shine as bright as the sun.
Hope is a hand that grasps and reaches out in peace.
The wolf will live with the lamb,
the leopard lie down with the kid.

Hope is a song that grows and fills the world with joy.
The wilderness and dry land will be glad,
the desert rejoice and bloom.
Hope is a promise of a baby to be born in a manger stall.
A woman will bear a son and name him Immanuel.

Week 4 *(Matt. 1)*
Mothers, fathers, grandparents, and friends,
aunts, uncles, sons, and daughters,
people who reach out to nurture and love,
people who live by water and word—
God adopts us and names us and claims us.
God renews us, uplifts and restores us.
Generations from Abraham to David to Joseph,
to Jesus, son of Mary, Son of God;
our generations too, and all those to come:
We are joined in the family of God.

Gathering Song

Week 1: Wait for the Lord   ELW 262
Week 2: Open our eyes, Lord   W&P 113
Week 3: Blessed be the God of Israel   ELW 250
Week 4: Savior of the nations, come   ELW 263, LBW 28

Greeting

The grace of our Lord Jesus Christ, the love of God,
and the communion of the Holy Spirit be with you all.
And also with you.

Prayer

Week 1 *(Luke 2:30-32)*
O God for whom we long,
we thank you for the gift of patience.
Grant peace in our hearts as we wait with hope,
that we may sing with Simeon:
My eyes have seen your salvation,
a light to reveal you to the nations
and the glory of your people Israel.
We pray in the name of our Savior, Jesus Christ,
your gift to all the world.
Amen.

Week 2 *(Luke 2:68-69, 72)*
O God for whom we long,
we thank you for the gifts of speech and silence.
Teach us to listen from our hearts and speak of your love,
that we may shout with Zechariah:
Blessed be the Lord God of Israel,
who has remembered his holy covenant
and raised up a mighty Savior.
We pray in the name of our Savior, Jesus Christ,
your gift to all the world.
Amen.

Week 3 *(Isa. 40:31)*
O God for whom we long,
we thank you for the gift of hope.
Be our light in the darkness,
that we may proclaim with Isaiah:
Those who hope in the Lord will renew their strength.
They will soar on wings like eagles;
they will run and not grow weary,
they will walk and not be faint.
We pray in the name of our Savior, Jesus Christ,
your gift to all the world.
Amen.

Week 4 *(Luke 1:46, 49, 50)*
O God for whom we long,
we thank you for the gift of family and friends.
Strengthen the ties that bind us together,
that we may sing with Mary:
My soul magnifies you, and holy is your name.
You shower mercy from generation to generation.
We pray in the name of our Savior, Jesus Christ,
your gift to all the world.
Amen.

Psalmody

Week 1: Psalm 37:1-9
Week 2: Psalm 19
Week 3: Psalm 33:13-22
Week 4: Psalm 96

Reading

Week 1: James 5:7-11
Week 2: James 1:17-21
Week 3: Romans 8:18-25
Week 4: 1 John 3:1-3

Song

For each perfect gift of thine,
peace on earth and joy in heav'n;
for thyself, best gift divine,
to our world so freely giv'n:

Praise we sing to Christ the Lord,
Virgin's son, incarnate Word!
To the holy Trinity
praise we sing eternally!
Tune: *NUN KOMM, DER HEIDEN HEILAND* (ELW 879, st. 5; ELW 263, st. 6)

Gospel

Week 1: Mark 13:24-37
Week 2: Luke 1:5-25, 57-66
Week 3: Luke 1:67-79
Week 4: Matthew 1:1-17

Reflection

The reflection may include brief commentary, non-biblical readings, or interpretation through drama or other art forms.

The reflection may conclude:
God has given us eternal life,
and this life is in Jesus, God's Son.

Hymn

Week 1: Son of God, eternal Savior   ELW 655, LBW 364
Week 2: Let all mortal flesh keep silence   ELW 490, LBW 198
Week 3: All earth is hopeful   ELW 266, WOV 629
Week 4: Once in royal David's city   ELW 269, WOV 643

Prayers

For this time of waiting and watching
for the coming of our Savior,
we give you thanks, O Lord.
When the Spirit intercedes with sighs too deep for words,
we cry to you, O Lord.
For the hope that shines through the darkest night,
we turn to you, O Lord.
For the gift of friends and family
who walk with us through life,
we praise your name, O Lord.
Here other prayers may be offered.
Gather us all under the promise of your Son,
who taught us to pray: **Our Father . . .**

Lord's Prayer

Blessing

The peace of God accompany your waiting,
the light of Christ warm your hearts,
and the joy of the Spirit fill you with hope.
Amen.

Sending Song

Week 1: Come, thou long-expected Jesus   ELW 254, LBW 30
Week 2: Awake! Awake, and greet the new morn   ELW 242, WOV 633
Week 3: Rejoice, rejoice believers   ELW 244, LBW 25
Week 4: People, look east   ELW 248, WOV 626

Dismissal

Go in peace. Christ is coming soon.
Thanks be to God.

Additional Resources

Selected poetry on the series themes from *Spiritual Literacy: Reading the Sacred in Everyday Life* by Frederic and Mary Ann Brussat (New York: Touchstone, 1998).
On patience: "How to Stuff a Pepper" by Nancy Willard.
On speech and silence: "Listening" by William Stafford.
On hope: "I was just thinking" by Macrina Wiederkehr.
On family: "Reflection" by Mitch Finley.

ACKNOWLEDGMENTS

"Patience is a virtue…": Traced to William Langland, *Piers Plowman* (1377).
"Rome wasn't built…": English translation (from the French) included in *The proverbs, epigrams, and miscellanies of John Heywood* (1906).
"Patience is also…": Auguste Rodin.
"How poor are they…": William Shakespeare, *Othello*, Act 2, Scene 3.
"Savior of the nations, come" (ELW 263): Text © 2006 Augsburg Fortress.

Welcome to the Waiting Room
A Worship Series for Advent

A series summary is presented here. The series reflects the themes in the Revised Common Lectionary texts for Advent, year A. Expanded weekly resources, including more detailed descriptions of each waiting room and experiential station, leader scripts, and other resources for this series will be available to Sundays and Seasons.com subscribers in early September 2013.

Series Overview

Advent is a season of hoping, waiting, yearning, and preparing, but for *what* or *whom* and *how*? These are some of the themes explored in this Advent series. During these four weeks, the future and the past mingle together as we celebrate the Christ who came and is yet to come. Memories, inherited through scripture and tradition, are sparked in order to feed tomorrow's hope.

Advent is a season largely forgotten by our culture of immediate gratification, and likewise we've forgotten what it means to wait well. In all of this waiting, God is creating desire within us. And we trust it's worth the wait. Along the way, there are a few things for which we're not yet ready, because when God comes close it's almost always accompanied by surprise or scandal.

Advent 1: Surprise
Salvation always comes as a surprise. It's what happens when God does for us what we could never do for ourselves. So when God comes close it is always unimaginable, yet God asks us to expect it.

Advent 2: Prepare
Hope might sound passive, but it's the farthest thing from it. Christian hope won't let you just sit on your hands. There are preparations to be made and roadwork to be straightened out because *God is coming.*

Advent 3: Expectations
How do we know when God has come close? What if it's not what we were expecting? Advent asks us to adjust some of our hopes and expectations.

Advent 4: Scandal
More often than not, when God comes close it results in a major scandal. Our sensibilities are offended and misunderstandings fly about. When "God is with us" it's likely that public disgrace and secret dismissals will soon follow, because, essentially, when God comes close life gets disrupted.

Pattern for Worship
Gathering

- Waiting Room
- Entrance
- Lighting the Advent Wreath (see p. 24–25)
- Confession and Forgiveness

Word

- First Reading
- Second Reading
- Gospel
- Sermon
- Experiential Station/s
- Peace

Meal

- Offering
- Great Thanksgiving
- Communion

Sending

- Song
- Blessing

Preparing the Environment: The Waiting Room

For this series, you will need two distinct spaces: the worship space and the "waiting room." You might make the narthex, gathering space, or fellowship hall into the waiting room. Each week, the community waits together in the waiting room before entering the worship space. The environment helps to create the tone for Advent while introducing the community to the theme of each service. The tension and release of having to wait to enter the worship space is a significant part of this experience.

The basic setup could look like a typical waiting room in a doctor's office with rows of chairs back to back, lamps, and some magazines. Near the door to the worship space, a table is set with different materials each week (see the weekly materials lists, just below). In contrast to the brightly lit waiting room, the worship space for this series calls for a warm, dark, and cozy atmosphere, like a bear's den.

Week 1 Waiting Room: Alarms
Materials: Four or more alarm clocks set to go off a few minutes *after* worship is scheduled to begin.

Week 2 Waiting Room: Now Turning
Materials: A lazy Susan (revolving tray); two open containers that fit on top of it, one labeled "Turning Toward," the other "Turning Away"; a numbered pad of sticky notes (so that people can "take a number" as though waiting in line); pens; and slips of paper for writing prayers.

Week 3 Waiting Room: Expecting the Boil
Materials: A heating element (such as a single stove-top burner that can be plugged into the wall); a large pot of water; pens; and slips of paper for writing prayers.

Week 4 Waiting Room: You're Expecting!
Materials: A TV monitor hooked up to a DVD player or laptop playing either the "Scandal of Incarnation" loop (to be available on Sundays and Seasons.com) or the *I Love Lucy* episode, "Lucy Has Her Baby" (http://www.amazon.com/gp/product/B007MHJ2CGI); and a few volunteers willing to walk around and "congratulate" people for "expecting."

Before Worship (Weekly)

As people arrive for worship, ask them to wait before going into the worship space, directing them to the waiting room. A leader introduces and/or instructs the waiting activity. Following or during the activity, people are welcomed into the worship space.

Experiential Stations

Each week of this series provides one or more experiential "stations" to which worshipers are invited for prayer, reflection, or another guided activity. Fuller descriptions and leader scripts will be available on Sundays and Seasons.com.

Week 1: News Prayers
At a glance: Worshipers use current local, national, and/or international newspapers to write and offer prayers for the people and places in the articles. The world enters our worship in order that our worship might enter the world.

Week 2: Turning Ritual
At a glance: This experience consists of four prayer stations—Stones, Water, Fire, and Fruit—whose themes are drawn from the day's gospel reading, Matthew 3:1-12.

Week 3: Wailing Wall
At a glance: Worshipers are invited to write prayers on the theme of unmet hope and then tuck them into a temporary wailing wall constructed of bricks or stones.

Week 4: Cradle Our Hopes
At a glance: Worshipers are invited to write down their hopes for the world, the church, their family and friends, and their lives, and then place them in a baby cradle.

Adapted from the Clayfire Collection, "What Happens When God Comes Close," by Ryan Marsh, Church of the Beloved, Edmonds, Washington.

December 1, 2013
First Sunday of Advent

The new church year begins with a wake-up call: Christ is coming soon! In today's readings both Paul and Jesus challenge us to wake from sleep, for we know neither the day nor hour of the Lord's coming. Isaiah proclaims the day when God will gather all people on the holy mountain and there will be no more war or suffering. Though we vigilantly watch for the promised day of salvation, we wait for what we already have: Christ comes among us this day as the word and meal that strengthens our faith in the promises of God.

Prayer of the Day

Stir up your power, Lord Christ, and come. By your merciful protection save us from the threatening dangers of our sins, and enlighten our walk in the way of your salvation, for you live and reign with the Father and the Holy Spirit, one God, now and forever.

Gospel Acclamation

Alleluia. Show us your steadfast ¹ love, O Lord,* and grant us ¹ your salvation. *Alleluia.* (Ps. 85:7)

Readings and Psalm

Isaiah 2:1-5

The visionary message presented in this reading focuses on a future day when God establishes a universal reign of peace. Divine decisions will make war obsolete, and the worshiping community responds: "Let us walk in that light of that Lord now!"

Psalm 122

I was glad when they said to me, "Let us go to the house of the Lord." (Ps. 122:1)

Romans 13:11-14

Paul compares the advent of Christ to the coming of dawn. We live our lives today in light of Christ's coming in the future.

Matthew 24:36-44

Jesus describes his second coming as a sudden, unexpected event that will bring salvation or judgment upon people caught up in the usual affairs of daily life. He urges people to be alert and expectant.

Preface Advent

Color Blue

Prayers of Intercession

The prayers are prepared locally for each occasion. The following examples may be adapted or used as appropriate.

In hope and anticipation, we pray for the church, those in need, and all of God's creation.

A brief silence.

Gather all people into your house, O Lord, and open our eyes to your presence among us. Send us as witnesses, that others may see and be drawn to you. Hear us, O God.

Your mercy is great.

Unite our voices to the great song of praise sung by mountains and rivers, fields and trees. Join our voices with theirs in announcing your promised coming throughout all creation. Hear us, O God.

Your mercy is great.

Transform our tools of war and destruction into instruments for cultivation and growth. Plant peace in places of conflict (*especially*). Hear us, O God.

Your mercy is great.

Be attentive to all who wait expectantly for your mercy in times of crisis, illness, fear, and grief (*especially*). Answer them when they cry out to you. Hear us, O God.

Your mercy is great.

Heal all who live with HIV/AIDS. Reveal your creative power through those who seek a cure, and give us compassion to bear our neighbors' burdens. Hear us, O God.

Your mercy is great.

Here other intercessions may be offered.

You have clothed the saints in the light of Christ. Teach us to live in his ways until the great day when he comes to make all things new. Hear us, O God.

Your mercy is great.

Almighty God, we entrust to you all for whom we pray, confident that you fulfill your promises through Christ our Savior and Lord.

Amen.

Images in the Readings

The apocalyptic imagery of **the end of the world**, like the flood sweeping all things away, echoes from the Old Testament into the preaching of Jesus, and continues in contemporary disaster movies and terrorist activity. For Christians, fear about the end always comes to rest in trust in the presence of God. When all is over, at our end, is God.

The readings we hear expand on and challenge our society's welcome of God arriving as only baby Jesus, for God comes as **judge** and calls us into a life of justice for all, evoking in us both anticipation and fear. Often in classical art, Justice is a towering robed woman who judges right from wrong.

Frequently in the Bible God meets with humankind on a **mountain**. Our language even calls "a mountain-top experience" one so overwhelming that it changes one's future. Sinai, Horeb, Jerusalem, the Mount of Jesus' sermon, the Mount of Transfiguration, the Mount of Olives, Golgotha, Zion: all are superimposed on our church buildings, for the Christian mountain is wherever we receive the word and sacraments.

In English, the phrase "**swords into plowshares**" indicates the hope for world peace, a hope for which Christians pray to God.

Ideas for the Day

◆ Today's gospel reading is a lesson in emergency preparedness. Jesus instructs his disciples to do what seems impossible: to be ready for the coming of the Son of Man, an event whose timing not even the Son himself knows (Matt. 24:36). Jesus highlights the difficulty of such preparation with his illustration of the thief and the homeowner. Consider the ways we prepare for various contingencies in our lives—the spare tire in a car's trunk; the emergency flashlight in a home's kitchen; the first-aid kit at the back of a church sanctuary. Likewise, how might we become and remain spiritually prepared for Christ's return, even though we know not the day or the hour? The reading from Romans 13 provides some possible answers.

◆ The emphasis in today's texts on Christ's coming and the judgment that accompanies it suggests not only a connection to the Apostles' Creed but also to Luther's explanation of it in the Small Catechism (see *Evangelical Lutheran Worship*, p. 1162). His explanation of the second article is particularly relevant, with its compact description of who Christ is and what Christ means for the individual believer and the community of the faithful. Allow Luther's explanation of the creed to influence your Advent worship. Print it in the worship folder, incorporate it into the gathering rite, or verbally profess it with the creed.

◆ The words *justice* and *judgment* have common roots. Our 24/7 media-driven culture seems quicker than ever to judge (think of the term "snap judgment") and to point out apparent lapses in justice—while often ignoring systemic injustice that threatens the poor and the oppressed. How can Christians refrain from this shallow form of judgment while actively working toward the promised justice of God's kingdom? How does the church's worship at Advent and Christmas—perhaps best represented by its songs, such as the Magnificat and the Gloria—call us to this same goal?

Connections with the Liturgy

The Apostles' Creed anticipates the coming of the judge: I believe in Jesus Christ, who "will come to judge the living and the dead."

Let the Children Come

Advent is beginnings and endings all mixed together. It is the beginning of the church year and the ending of the calendar year. It is the beginning of Jesus' story accompanied by readings about the end of the world. We begin this season of shadowy anticipation by lighting a candle to end the darkness. Today is the first day of the twelfth month. Sunday is the first day of the week but the last day of the weekend. The winter solstice (Dec. 21) is the first day of winter but the beginning of longer days anticipating spring. Look for visual reminders of the unending presence of God in the worship space: images in paraments, windows, artwork, architecture, advent wreaths, bulletin covers, hugs, and more!

Assembly Song
Gathering

Wake, awake, for night is flying   ELW 436, LBW 31
Rise, O Sun of righteousness   ELW 657
O Lord, how shall I meet you   ELW 241

Psalmody and Acclamations

Farrell, Bernadette. "I Rejoiced" from PS1.
Haas, David. "Psalm 122: I Was Glad." Cant, assembly, kybd, gtr. GIA G-4133.
Harbor, Rawn. "Let Us Go Rejoicing (Psalm 122)." TFF 17.
Pishner, Stephen. "Advent Gospel Acclamation" from *Psalm and Gospel Acclamation for Advent*. SATB, cant, assembly, kybd. GIA G-5259.

Hymn of the Day

Awake! Awake, and greet the new morn   ELW 242,
   WOV 633   *REJOICE, REJOICE*
Come now, O Prince of peace   ELW 247   *OSOSO*
Soon and very soon   ELW 439, TFF 38, W&P 128, WOV 744
   VERY SOON

Offering

Creator of the stars of night   ELW 245
My soul proclaims the greatness of the Lord   ELW 235

Communion

O God of love, O King of peace   ELW 749

Christ, Be Our Light   ELW 715

Lord our God, with praise we come   ELW 730

Sending

My Lord, what a morning   ELW 438, TFF 40, WOV 627

Fling wide the door   ELW 259, LBW 32

Additional Assembly Songs

I want to be ready   TFF 41

Stir up your power   ASG 38

❂ Come to be our hope, O Jesus   GS2 18

✿ Crouch, Andraé. "Soon and Very Soon" from CCLI.

✿ Herms, Bernie/Mark Hall. "East to West" from WT.

✿ Houston, Joel. "Salvation Is Here" from WT.

✿ Mark, Robin. "Days of Elijah" from CCLI.

✿● Smith, Martin/Stuart Garrard/Tim Hughes. "Wake Up" from CCLI.

✿ Walton, Greg. "Come to Us" from CCLI.

Music for the Day
Choral

● Bankson, Jeremy. "Come Now, O Prince of Peace." SATB, kybd, fl, perc, opt assembly. AFP 9780806698243.

Dusek, Dennis/arr. Kimberley Denis. "When He Comes on That Day." SSAB, a cappella. AFP 9781451424089.

Hobby, Robert. "My Lord, What a Morning." SATB, sop solo, pno. MSM 50-6059.

Miller, Aaron David. "Rejoice, Rejoice." 2 pt, kybd. AFP 9780800678555.

Nelson, Ronald. "A Vision of Peace." SAB, pno. GIA G-7007.

Children's Choir

Ellingboe, Bradley. "We Light the Advent Candles." U. AFP 9780800674243.

Lindh, Jody. "An Advent Carol." U, kybd. CG CGA648.

Zimmer, Dennis. "What Is This Crying at Jordan?" 2 pt, opt 3 pt. CPH 98-4052.

Keyboard / Instrumental

Bach, J. S. "Wachet auf" from *Schübler Chorales*. Org. Various editions.

● Chapin, Rachel. "Awake! Awake, and Greet the New Morn" from *Greet the New Morn*. Pno. CPH 97-7273.

● Schrader, Jack. "Soon and Very Soon" from *Amazing Grace*. Pno. HOP 8138.

● Sedio, Mark. "Rejoice, Rejoice" from *Augsburg Organ Library: Advent*. Org. AFP 9780800658953.

Handbell

● McChesney, Kevin. "Soon and Very Soon." 3-5 oct, L3. FB FBBGH1008.

Prins, Matthew. "Come, Emmanuel." 3-5 oct, L4. MSM 30-755.

● Sternowski, Carolyn. "Awake! Awake, and Greet the New Morn." 3 oct, L3. GIA G-7085.

Tuesday, December 3

Francis Xavier, missionary to Asia, died 1552

Francis Xavier (SAYV-yehr) was born in the Basque region of northern Spain. Francis's native Basque language is unrelated to any other, and Francis admitted that learning languages was difficult for him. Despite this obstacle he became a missionary to India, Southeast Asia, Japan, and the Philippines. At each point he learned the local language and, like Martin Luther, wrote catechisms for the instruction of new converts. Another obstacle Francis overcame to accomplish his mission work was a propensity to seasickness. All his travels to the Far East were by boat. Together with Ignatius Loyola and five others, Francis formed the Society of Jesus (Jesuits). Francis spoke out against the Spanish and Portuguese colonists when he discovered their oppression of the indigenous people to whom he was sent as a missionary.

Wednesday, December 4

John of Damascus, theologian and hymnwriter, died around 749

Born to a wealthy family in Damascus and well educated, John left a career in finance and government to become a monk in an abbey near Jerusalem. He wrote many hymns as well as theological works. Foremost among the latter is a work called *The Fount of Wisdom*, which touches on philosophy, heresy, and the orthodox faith. This summary of patristic theology remained influential for centuries.

Friday, December 6

Nicholas, Bishop of Myra, died around 342

Though Nicholas is one of the church's most beloved saints, little is known about his life. In the fourth century he was a bishop in what is now Turkey. Legends that surround Nicholas tell of his love for God and neighbor, especially the poor. One famous story tells of Nicholas secretly giving bags of gold to the three daughters of a father who was going to sell them into prostitution because he could not provide dowries for them. Nicholas has become a symbol of anonymous gift giving.

❂ = global song
✿ = praise song
● = relates to hymn of the day

Saturday, December 7

Ambrose, Bishop of Milan, died 397

Ambrose was a governor of northern Italy and a catechumen when he was elected bishop of Milan. He was baptized, ordained, and consecrated a bishop within one week's time. While bishop he gave away his wealth and lived in simplicity. He was a famous preacher and is largely responsible for the conversion of Augustine. He is also well known for writing hymns. On one occasion, Ambrose led people in a hymn he wrote while the church in which they were secluded was threatened by attack from Gothic soldiers. The soldiers turned away, unwilling to attack a congregation that was singing a hymn. Ambrose is credited with authorship of three hymns in *Evangelical Lutheran Worship,* including "Savior of the Nations, Come" (ELW 263).

December 8, 2013
Second Sunday of Advent

At the heart of our Advent preparation stands John the Baptist, who calls us to repent and make a new beginning. As the darkness increases we turn toward the light of Christ's coming. For Christians he is the root of Jesse, the righteous judge who welcomes all, especially the poor and meek of the earth. We wait with hope for that day when the wolf will dwell with the lamb, and there will be no more hurt or destruction. From the Lord's table we are sent in the spirit of John the Baptist to proclaim that in Christ the kingdom of God has come near.

Prayer of the Day

Stir up our hearts, Lord God, to prepare the way of your only Son. By his coming nurture our growth as people of repentance and peace; through Jesus Christ, our Savior and Lord, who lives and reigns with you and the Holy Spirit, one God, now and forever.

Gospel Acclamation

Alleluia. Prepare the way │ of the Lord.* All flesh shall see the salva- │ tion of God. *Alleluia.* (Luke 3:4, 6)

Readings and Psalm

Isaiah 11:1-10

In today's reading the prophet describes the ideal ruler who will come in the future as a green shoot springing from a dead stump (David's royal line) of Jesse (David's father). Gifted by the Spirit, this messiah will seek justice for the poor, and the reign of this monarch will be experienced as paradise regained.

Psalm 72:1-7, 18-19

May the righteous flourish; let there be an abundance of peace. (Ps. 72:7)

Romans 15:4-13

God's promise to include Gentiles within the circle of God's blessed people has been fulfilled in Jesus Christ. Christians live out their unity by welcoming and encouraging each other just as Christ has welcomed them into God's family.

Matthew 3:1-12

Just before Jesus begins his public ministry, John the Baptist appears, calling people to mend their ways and speaking of a powerful one who is to come.

Preface   Advent

Color   Blue

Prayers of Intercession

The prayers are prepared locally for each occasion. The following examples may be adapted or used as appropriate.

In hope and anticipation, we pray for the church, those in need, and all of God's creation.

A brief silence.

Renew us in the covenant of your Son, O Holy One, and revive us by the outpouring of your Spirit, who leads us to wisdom, understanding, and faithfulness in you. Hear us, O God.

Your mercy is great.

Establish harmony in all creation, that all living things may work according to your loving and generous purpose. Fill the earth with your goodness and glory. Hear us, O God.

Your mercy is great.

Send your Spirit to those who hold power and authority among the nations. Lead them to tend to those who are poor and meek with your righteousness and justice. Hear us, O God.

Your mercy is great.

By your word and your people encourage and give heart to those who have lost hope in the face of depression, disease, and death (*especially*). Give them faith in your promises. Hear us, O God.
Your mercy is great.

Shape this faith community into a place of welcome and support for all people. Feed and strengthen us by your gifts of grace, that we may share them with others. Hear us, O God.
Your mercy is great.

Here other intercessions may be offered.

You have gathered the saints into your holy and eternal presence. Make us steadfast in the faith until we are all made one in your new creation. Hear us, O God.
Your mercy is great.

Almighty God, we entrust to you all for whom we pray, confident that you fulfill your promises through Christ our Savior and Lord.
Amen.

Images in the Readings

Ancient Near Eastern iconography often depicted the monarch as a **tree of life**, whose successful reign insured a vibrant life for the people. Both first and second readings rely on this ancient imagery when they refer to the "root of Jesse." In Israelite history, Jesse, the father of the shepherd boy David, is described as the root of the tree that was King David. John the Baptist warns that some trees will be cut down to make way for Christ, who is our tree of life.

The gospel reading situates John the Baptist in the **wilderness**, baptizing in the Jordan River, the **river** that the Israelites crossed on their way into the promised land. Led by Jesus, our Joshua, who entered the wilderness of our lives, Christians too cross a river in baptism, and so enter into the kingdom of God.

The lion and the lamb has become a beloved symbol of peace between natural enemies. The toddler is playing with the adder, a poisonous snake. In Christ is the promise of this extraordinary hope for the world.

Ideas for the Day

◆ The introduction of John the Baptist in today's gospel provides an opportunity to focus on what it is the season of Advent is preparing us *for*. Advent is about readying ourselves for the kingdom of God; through our baptisms, we are made inheritors of that kingdom and, like John, tasked to share the news of the coming Christ with the world. Highlight this connection between Advent and baptism in today's worship. Begin with a thanksgiving for baptism (see *Evangelical Lutheran Worship*, p. 97, for an example) rather than a confession. Sing a baptismal hymn (ELW 442–459) as the canticle of praise, hymn of the day, or elsewhere in the service.

◆ There is a vivid contrast between our traditional ideas or images of *wilderness*—where John lives and where people come to hear him preach—and our ideas or images of *kingdom*. The former might suggest ruggedness, danger, and volatility, while the latter suggests order, safety, and stability. Another comparison: If a wilderness is a place in which people survive, a kingdom is a place in which citizens dwell. How do these contrasting images interact in the readings and the broader narrative of Advent? How do they interact in our lives? If we are metaphorically in the wilderness with John, how does the coming of Christ transform our existence into the kingdom where God dwells?

◆ Today's passage from Isaiah is full of familiar paradoxes—the wolf living with the lamb, the child playing with the adder—but there are less obvious ones in verses 3 and 4. Here we are told that Christ will not judge using human senses (how else does one judge?) but with righteousness, and that the breath of God (which gives life) will destroy what is wicked. Contradictions are the very essence of Advent: The world's expectations and the incomplete justice dispensed by our human systems are subverted by God's kingdom. This is made even clearer in the Magnificat (Luke 1:46-55), which is an option to be proclaimed and sung next Sunday.

Connections with the Liturgy

A prayer of confession echoes the preaching of John the Baptist: "Turn us again to you, and uphold us by your Spirit, so that we may live and serve you in newness of life through Jesus Christ, our Savior and Lord."

Let the Children Come

Repentance can be a tough vocabulary word for all ages, but what about the physical translation of "turning away from" or "turning toward God." If an order of confession and forgiveness is used today, perhaps the assembly could literally redirect their vision from the back of the worship space to the front as the words of forgiveness are proclaimed. This could be a powerful kinetic experience of John's call. Alternatively, during the gospel, invite the assembly to turn each time they hear the words *repent* or *repentance*. Connect the circular nature of this movement with last week's introduction to Advent's seasonal symbolism.

Assembly Song
Gathering

Prepare the royal highway   ELW 264, LBW 26
Come now, O Prince of peace   ELW 247
Hark! A thrilling voice is sounding!   ELW 246

Psalmody and Acclamations

Gelineau, Joseph or Michel Guimont. "Second Sunday of Advent / A" from LP/W4.

Haas, David. "In the Time of God (Psalm 72)." Choir, cant, assembly, kybd, gt, opt hb, 2 C inst. GIA G-5657.

Haugen, Marty. "Every Nation on Earth." Cant, assembly, opt SAB, kybd, gtr, perc. GIA G-5241.

Pishner, Stephen. "Advent Gospel Acclamation" from *Psalm and Gospel Acclamation for Advent*. SATB, cant, assembly, kybd. GIA G-5259.

Hymn of the Day

On Jordan's bank the Baptist's cry   ELW 249, LBW 36
  PUER NOBIS
Awake, O sleeper, rise from death   ELW 452, WOV 745   *AZMON*
Christ, Be Our Light   ELW 715   *CHRIST, BE OUR LIGHT*

Offering

Light one candle to watch for Messiah   ELW 240, sts. 1, 2; WOV 630
My soul proclaims the greatness of the Lord   ELW 235

Communion

O day of peace   ELW 711, WOV 762
Come now, O Prince of peace   ELW 247
There's a voice in the wilderness   ELW 255

Sending

Jesus shall reign   ELW 434, LBW 530
Rejoice, rejoice, believers   ELW 244, LBW 25

Additional Assembly Songs

Come by here   TFF 42
Night of Silence   W&P 101, sts. 1, 2
⦿ Who will set us free?   SP 44
⦿ In the Lord I'll be ever thankful   SP 18
✿ Camp, Jeremy. "Walk by Faith" from WT.
✿ Gungor, Michael. "The Earth Is Yours" from WT.
✿ Hall, Charlie. "Make Straight" from CCLI.
✿ Leonard, David/Leslie Jordan. "All the Poor and Powerless" from CCLI.
✿ Reeves, Jesse/Kristian Stanfill/Matt Maher/Christy Nockels/Daniel Carson. "Lord, I Need You" from WT.
✿ Tomlin, Chris/Jesse Reeves/Martin Smith. "Waiting Here for You" from WT.

Music for the Day
Choral

Hopp, Roy. "And a Little Child Shall Lead Them." SATB, org, opt assembly. AFP 9780800674007.

Horn, Richard. "A Shoot Shall Come Forth." SAB, org. MSM 50-0200.

Nelson, Ronald A. "Rejoice, Rejoice, Believers." SAB/3 pt mxd. AFP 9781451424027.

Organ, Anne Krentz. "There's a Voice in the Wilderness." 2 pt mxd, kybd. AFP 9780800676537.

Rowan, William. "Prepare the Way of the Lord." SATB/2 pt or SAB. HOP A596 or C5696.

Smith, Alan. "Come, Jesus, Come." SATB. AFP 9781451423952.

Children's Choir

Biery, Marilyn. "A Little Child Shall Lead Them." U or 2 pt, kybd, opt C inst. AFP 9780806695914.

McRae, Shirley W. "Carol of Prophecy." U, hb. CG CGA720.

Owens, Sam Batt. "Sing and Rejoice." U, org, hb. GIA G-5529.

Phillips, Craig. "There's a Voice in the Wilderness Crying." 2 pt, kybd. SEL 422-903.

Keyboard / Instrumental

● Davenport, Rudy. "Puer nobis" from *Darkness and Light*. Pno. MSM 15-839.

Henkelmann, Brian. "Savior of the Nations, Come" from *Instruments for All Seasons, Vol. 1*. Kybd, fl. CPH 97-7227.

Manz, Paul. "Bereden väg för Herran" from *Augsburg Organ Library: Advent*. Org. AFP 9780800658953.

● Miller, Aaron David. "Puer nobis" from *Augsburg Organ Library: Advent*. Org. AFP 9780800658953.

Handbell

● Childers, Brian. "Celebration on 'Azmon.'" 3-6 oct, L2+. LOR 20/1628L.

● Philips, Judy. "Advent Fantasy." 3-6 oct hb, opt 2 oct hc, opt perc, L3. CG CGB751.

Tucker, Margaret. "Light in the Darkness (Light One Candle to Watch for Messiah)." 3-5 oct hb, opt 3 oct hc, opt fc, L2+. CG CGB501.

Friday, December 13

Lucy, martyr, died 304

Lucy was a young Christian of Sicily who was martyred during the persecutions under Emperor Diocletian. Apparently she had decided to devote her life to God and her possessions to the poor. Beyond that, however, little is known for certain about Lucy. However, her celebration became particularly important in Sweden and Norway, perhaps because the feast of Lucia (the name means "light") originally fell on the shortest day of the year. A tradition arose of a girl in the household, wearing a crown of candles, bringing saffron rolls to her family early in the morning on the day of Lucia.

⦿ = global song
✿ = praise song
● = relates to hymn of the day

Saturday, December 14

John of the Cross, renewer of the church, died 1591

John was a monk of the Carmelite religious order who met Teresa of Ávila when she was working to reform the Carmelite Order and return it to a stricter observance of its rules. He followed Teresa's lead and encouraged others to follow her reform. He was imprisoned when he encountered opposition to the reform. His writings, like Teresa's, reflect a deep interest in mystical thought and meditation. In one of John's poems, "The Spiritual Canticle," he cried, "Oh, that my griefs would end! Come, grant me thy fruition full and free!"

December 15, 2013

Third Sunday of Advent

A note of joyful expectation marks today's worship. Isaiah announces that the desert shall rejoice and blossom. Jesus points to signs of God's reign: the blind see, the lame walk, lepers are cleansed, the deaf hear. We wait with patience for the coming of the Lord, even as we rejoice at his presence among us this day: in word and holy supper, in church and in our homes, in silent reflection and in works of justice and love. We pray that God would open our eyes and ears to the wonders of Christ's advent among us.

Prayer of the Day

Stir up the wills of all who look to you, Lord God, and strengthen our faith in your coming, that, transformed by grace, we may walk in your way; through Jesus Christ, our Savior and Lord, who lives and reigns with you and the Holy Spirit, one God, now and forever.

Gospel Acclamation

Alleluia. I am sending my messen- | ger before you,* who will prepare your | way before you. *Alleluia.* (Matt. 11:10)

Readings and Psalm

Isaiah 35:1-10

The prophet describes the return from the Babylonian captivity as a joyous procession to Zion. God's coming reign will bring a renewal of creation in which health and wholeness will be restored. There is no need for fear, for God is coming to save.

Psalm 146:5-10

The Lᴏʀᴅ lifts up those who are bowed down. (Ps. 146:8)

or Luke 1:46b-55

My spirit rejoices in God my Savior. (Luke 1:47)

James 5:7-10

In anticipation of the Lord's coming, Christians are called upon to cultivate patience rather than discontent.

Matthew 11:2-11

John the Baptist expects the Messiah to bring God's judgment upon the earth. From a prison cell, he wonders whether Jesus is the one who will do this.

Preface   Advent

Color   Blue

Prayers of Intercession

The prayers are prepared locally for each occasion. The following examples may be adapted or used as appropriate.

In hope and anticipation, we pray for the church, those in need, and all of God's creation.

A brief silence.

Stir up in our hearts an eagerness for your coming. Grant us patience in our waiting, and while we wait, strengthen us to persevere in ways of justice and righteousness. Hear us, O God.

Your mercy is great.

In this season, nurture dry and dormant lands so that they will blossom in the coming months. Spread your abundance throughout all lands, that every living thing may be filled. Hear us, O God.

Your mercy is great.

Draw near to all who are oppressed or neglected. Lift up all who are cast down. Deliver those in the captivity of loneliness and poverty into your freedom. Hear us, O God.

Your mercy is great.

Strengthen those who are made weak by the heavy burdens that they carry (*especially*). Surround them with messengers who announce your presence with them. Hear us, O God.

Your mercy is great.

Raise the expectations of all who seek you in this season. Turn us from material things, and open us to a life full of healing and renewal, where all people receive good news. Hear us, O God.

Your mercy is great.

Here other intercessions may be offered.

Remembering the saints who have entered into your eternal reign, sustain us through their witness to your everlasting faithfulness until we are united in the fullness of your kingdom. Hear us, O God.

Your mercy is great.

Almighty God, we entrust to you all for whom we pray, confident that you fulfill your promises through Christ our Savior and Lord.

Amen.

Images in the Readings

The **flowering wilderness** is the image presented in both the first reading and the gospel. Often the Bible uses imagery from nature to celebrate the presence of God. All of nature rejoices in God's continuing creation. We are called to ecological care for God's good earth, making literal the symbol of a flowering wilderness.

The **healing of the blind and lame** is a recurring image in the Old Testament to describe the effect of the presence of God. The gospels say that Jesus healed people who were blind, who were crippled, who suffered from leprosy, and those who were deaf; he raised the dead; and he preached to the poor—thus enacting all the miracles that are cited in the ancient poems.

In the ancient Near East, conquerors built massive **highway**s to allow for civic processions so as to display their power. The Bible cites and then transforms this image: there will be a highway on which the people will return in safety into their own city. Might is changed into right.

Ideas for the Day

◆ Through a messenger, John asks: "Are you the one . . . ?" In a world where many meetings happen online, questions about true identity are common. How do we establish an identity, online or otherwise? How do we determine whether the people we meet in different contexts are who they claim to be? What are the markers of a Christian identity, and how do we communicate that online, in person, overtly and indirectly?

◆ Jesus calls John a prophet, and identifies what a prophet is *not*—a prophet isn't rich, wearing soft robes; a prophet isn't easily broken. How would you describe a modern-day prophet? What does a prophet look like? What is a prophet *not* like? Explore organizations that claim the name prophet, like Green Prophet, a source for news on the green movement in the Middle East (www.greenprophet.com).

◆ Isaiah describes a desert blossoming. Search the Web or YouTube for descriptions and pictures of both flash floods and blooming flowers in Israeli deserts. Why would Isaiah choose this image to describe the return to Jerusalem after exile? Explore the dangerous, powerful, and miraculous occasion of water in the desert. How are John, the baptizer, and Jesus, the source of living water, similarly dangerous, powerful, and miraculous?

◆ Invite worshipers to spend time looking at and reflecting on Leonardo da Vinci's painting of John the Baptist (on the Web, search for Leonardo and John the Baptist). What do they see? What do they notice? John is shown pointing at Christ on the cross. Talk together about what that pointing means, how John's life and work pointed to Jesus, and how we are called in our life and work to point to Jesus. Ask children and others to point to where they can see Jesus in the church building (crosses, communion elements, baptismal font, stained-glass windows, one another, and so forth). Where can they see and point to Jesus outside the church building?

Connections with the Liturgy

Recalling the promises of the miraculous presence of God, we pray in the intercessions "for the poor, oppressed, sick, bereaved, lonely, and for all who suffer in body, mind, or spirit," for the ancient poems to be realized today.

Let the Children Come

Magnificat. Magnify. A young woman enlarging (both physically and metaphorically) sings a song to magnify God's love for creation. Mary's song is one option for today's psalmody. Have magnifying glasses (almost always circular) to enlarge words in hymnals and Bibles or details in art and architecture. Magnification helps us see details more clearly. Through her role, her trust, and her song, Mary helps us to experience the promise of God-made-flesh—clear, in focus, magnified. How can our souls magnify the Lord?

Assembly Song
Gathering

All earth is hopeful   ELW 266, TFF 47, WOV 629

People, look east   ELW 248, WOV 626

He comes to us as one unknown   ELW 737, WOV 768

Psalmody and Acclamations

Chepponis, James. "Psalm 146." 2 cant, assembly, opt SATB, kybd, gtr, C inst, hb. GIA G-4227.

Haugen, Marty. "Psalm 146," Refrain 3, from PSCY.

Makeever, Ray. "Sing unto the Lord (Psalm 146)" from DH.

"My Soul Proclaims Your Greatness." ELW 251.

Smith, Alan. "Magnificat" from PS1.

Pishner, Stephen. "Advent Gospel Acclamation" from *Psalm and Gospel Acclamation for Advent*. SATB, cant, assembly, kybd. GIA G-5259.

Hymn of the Day

Come, thou long-expected Jesus   ELW 254, LBW 30   JEFFERSON

Open your ears, O faithful people   ELW 519, TFF 715
YISRAEL V'ORAITA

Light dawns on a weary world   ELW 726   TEMPLE OF PEACE

Offering

We come to the hungry feast   ELW 479, WOV 766

My soul proclaims the greatness of the Lord   ELW 235

Communion

Wait for the Lord   ELW 262

Lost in the night   ELW 243

He came down   ELW 253, TFF 37

Sending

Joy to the world   ELW 267, LBW 39

Praise the Almighty!   ELW 877

Additional Assembly Songs

For all people Christ was born   DH 52

◉ Tenemos esperanza. Argentina.   GS3 38, LLC 458

◉ Bena tune, arr. Austin C. Lovelace. "Christ the Savior Has Appeared" from *Set Free: A Collection of African Hymns*. SATB. AFP 9780806600451.

✿ Hughes, Tim/Martin Smith. "God Is Coming" from WT.

✿ Leonard, David/Don Chaffer/Leslie Jordan. "Wake Up" from CCLI.

✿ McClarney, Chris/John Hartley/Katie Gustafson/Miriam Webster. "Who Is This Love Amazing" from CCLI.

✿ Nockels, Nathan/Charlie Hall/Stuart Townend. "Sending" from WT.

✿ Redman, Matt. "Here Is Love" from WT.

✿ Wesley, Charles. Arr. Chris Eaton/John Hartley/Gareth Robinson "Come Thou Long Expected Jesus" from garethrobinson.net.

Music for the Day
Choral

Costello, Michael. "Canticle of the Turning: Magnificat." SATTBB, org, trb, opt assembly. AFP 9781451401615.

Gibala, Richard. "Advent Carol." SATB, opt hb. MSM 50-0100.

Keesecker, Thomas. "Waiting." SAB, kybd. AFP 9781451401769.

● Kosche, Kenneth. "Prepare the Royal Highway." SATB, kybd. MSM 50-0038.

Pelz, Walter L. "Magnificat." SATB, org. AFP 9780800677350.

Pfautsch, Lloyd. "Go and Tell John." SATB, SAB, SSA, a cappella. HOP CY3334, CY3342, CY3345.

Children's Choir

● Blersch, Jeffrey. "Come, O Long Expected Jesus" from *Children Rejoice and Sing*. U, perc, C instr. CPH 97-7074.

Schram, Ruth Elaine. "Magnificat." U/opt desc, kybd, fl. AFP 9780800676681.

Shute, Linda Cable. "Stir Up Your Power and Come." 2 pt trbl, kybd, fl, opt assembly. AFP 9780800675271.

Keyboard / Instrumental

Leavitt, John. "Oh, Come, Oh, Come, Emmanuel" from *Silent Night, Wondrous Light*. Pno. CPH 97-6970.

● Organ, Anne Krentz. "Jefferson" from *Advent Reflections: For Piano and Solo Instrument*. Pno, inst. AFP 9780800657284.

● Phillips, Craig. "Yisrael v'oraita" from *Augsburg Organ Library: Autumn*. Org. AFP 9780800675790.

● Powell, Robert J. "Come, Thou Long-Expected Jesus" from *Four Advent Pieces for Flute and Organ*. Org, fl. MSM 20-061.

Handbell

● Biggs, Susan. "Come, Thou Long-Expected Jesus." 3 oct, L2. AFP 9780800659875.

Bigham, Veronica and Derek Hakes. "Light of Peace." 3-6 oct, L3. FTT 20178.

● Delancy, Lauran. "Come, Thou Long-Expected Jesus." 3 or 5 oct, L3. CPH 97-9316.

Friday, December 20

Katharina von Bora Luther, renewer of the church, died 1552

Born to an impoverished nobleman, when Katharina (Katie) was five her mother died and she was sent to live in a convent. She later took vows as a nun, but around age twenty-four she and several other nuns who were influenced by the writings of Martin Luther left the convent. Six children were born to Katie and Martin. Though initially Luther felt little affection for Katie, she proved herself a gifted household manager and became a trusted partner. She was so influential that Luther took to calling her "my lord Katie."

◉ = global song
✿ = praise song
● = relates to hymn of the day

December 22, 2013
Fourth Sunday of Advent

Today Isaiah prophesies that a young woman will bear a son and name him Emmanuel. The gospel is Matthew's account of the annunciation and birth of the one named Emmanuel, God-with-us. During these final days of Advent we pray, "O come, O come, Emmanuel," a beloved hymn based on ancient prayers appointed for the seven days preceding Christmas. On this final Sunday in Advent we prepare to celebrate the birth of the one born to save us from the power of sin and death.

Prayer of the Day

Stir up your power, Lord Christ, and come. With your abundant grace and might, free us from the sin that hinders our faith, that eagerly we may receive your promises, for you live and reign with the Father and the Holy Spirit, one God, now and forever.

Gospel Acclamation

Alleluia. The virgin shall conceive and ¹ bear a son,* and they shall name ¹ him Emmanuel. *Alleluia.* (Matt. 1:23)

Readings and Psalm

Isaiah 7:10-16

An Israelite and Aramean military coalition presented a serious threat to King Ahaz of Judah. In response, Ahaz decided to secure his throne and kingdom by seeking refuge in Assyrian help. Isaiah reminds Ahaz that human attempts to establish security will fail. The prophet gives the sign of Immanuel that is the only source of true safety: God is with us!

Psalm 80:1-7, 17-19

Let your face shine upon us, and we shall be saved. (Ps. 80:7)

Romans 1:1-7

Most of the Christians in Rome do not know Paul. In this letter's opening he introduces himself as an apostle divinely appointed to spread God's gospel. The gospel's content is the promised coming of Christ, and Paul's mission is to bring about the obedience of faith among all nations, including his Roman audience.

Matthew 1:18-25

Matthew's story of Jesus' birth focuses on the role of Joseph, who adopts the divinely-begotten child into the family of David and obediently gives him the name Jesus, which means "God saves."

Preface   Advent

Color   Blue

Prayers of Intercession

The prayers are prepared locally for each occasion. The following examples may be adapted or used as appropriate.

In hope and anticipation, we pray for the church, those in need, and all of God's creation.

A brief silence.

Continually restore and give life to the people of your covenant established in Christ. Use our presence in the world to reveal your salvation for all people. Hear us, O God.

Your mercy is great.

Reveal your light to those who dwell in darkness during this season. Awaken all creation to the hope of new life through your promised coming. Hear us, O God.

Your mercy is great.

Secure your grace and your peace among the nations. Lead us in ways of unity and justice to work with one another for the sake of all people. Hear us, O God.

Your mercy is great.

Deliver the hope of Emmanuel, God with us, to all who suffer loneliness and despair. Send your Spirit to accompany those who long for your healing (*especially*). Hear us, O God.

Your mercy is great.

Prepare a way of safety and security for children to grow up free from fear or threat. Establish prosperity in every land, that no child may go hungry. Hear us, O God.

Your mercy is great.

Here other intercessions may be offered.

We give thanks that you welcome the saints into your eternal dwelling place. Train us to look forward to the day when you come to dwell among all your people for all time. Hear us, O God.

Your mercy is great.

Almighty God, we entrust to you all for whom we pray, confident that you fulfill your promises through Christ our Savior and Lord.

Amen.

Images in the Readings

In Matthew's narratives, an **angel** figures in the stories of Jesus' birth and resurrection. In our society, many depictions of angels are unfortunately quite cutesy, not very helpful as images of the might of God. The angel is the divine messenger, the extension of the power and mercy of God, and in the Bible often the way that believers encounter the Almighty.

The **pregnant woman** can be a symbol of the life that comes from God. In the Bible, many women, from Eve in Genesis 4:1 on, conceive and bear children with the help of God. When we acclaim God as creator, we attest that God is continually creating life on this earth.

This Sunday it is **Joseph** who hears and receives the word of God. The history of art often depicted Joseph as an old man as a technique to convey that he was not instrumental in Mary's pregnancy. However, often in the scriptures a woman's pregnancy is seen as a gift from God. We are now Mary, and God is in us. We are now Joseph, receiving from God a gift we cannot have achieved on our own.

Ideas for the Day

◆   When the narrator of John Irving's *A Prayer for Owen Meany* (New York: Harper Collins, 1989) is chosen by his friend to play Joseph in the Christmas pageant, he's angry: "For what an uninspiring role it is; to be Joseph, that hapless follower, that stand-in, that guy along for the ride" (p. 164). Over the course of the novel, he begins to strongly identify himself as "just a Joseph"—a man who never speaks and who does what he's told, a witness to miraculous events. What does the character of Joseph suggest and symbolize to you? If your congregation puts on a pageant, how is Joseph chosen?

◆   Do an online image search for "angels" (make sure safety settings are on). Try a search for "seraphim," then compare and contrast those results. Do any of the images look to you like you imagine the angel who appeared to Joseph in his dream? How would you draw that angel?

◆   Emmanuel means "God is with us." Mary and Joseph had a unique experience of "God with us" during the course of her pregnancy. Ask a couple who have recently had a baby to share their individual experiences of their growing awareness of the baby as it developed in the womb. When did Mom feel the first flutter? When did Dad get the first good kick to his hand? How did their sense of connection grow and change throughout the pregnancy?

◆   The Gospel of Matthew records two angel appearances coming to Joseph in dreams; one with the news that Mary's child is the Son of God, another with the news that the infant Jesus is in danger (Matt. 2:13). Imagine Joseph's experience by creating a dream journal for him. A dream journal is kept next to the bed so dreamers are ready to write down anything they remember from their dreams immediately upon waking. The writing style is usually stream of consciousness and fragmented, with an emphasis on key, vivid images or words that seem important to the dreamer.

Connections with the Liturgy

In the Nicene Creed we acclaim: Jesus Christ, "the only Son of God, . . . was incarnate of the Holy Spirit and the virgin Mary."

Let the Children Come

So many people help to bring the good news of Jesus: John, Isaiah, Mary, Joseph, angels. God comes to us today, too, in word and sacrament. Who is helping to announce, to proclaim, to magnify, and to obey? Look around! Ushers, readers, preachers, presiders, pray-ers, choir members, acolytes, and all who are gathered to share in God's presence are part of this grand story today and every time we worship. How can children be prepared to participate in worship leadership?

Assembly Song
Gathering

Awake! Awake, and greet the new morn   ELW 242, WOV 633
Savior of the nations, come   ELW 263, LBW 28
As the dark awaits the dawn   ELW 261

Psalmody and Acclamations

Gelineau, Joseph. "Psalm 79 (80)" from *Thirty Psalms and Two Canticles.* Cant or SATB, assembly, kybd. GIA G-1430.
Haugen, Marty. "Lord, Make Us Turn to You." SATB, cant, assembly, kybd, gtr. GIA G-2884.
Wold, Wayne L. "Psalm 80," Refrain 1, from PSCY.
Pishner, Stephen. "Advent Gospel Acclamation" from *Psalm and Gospel Acclamation for Advent.* SATB, cant, assembly, kybd. GIA G-5259.

Hymn of the Day

Creator of the stars of night   ELW 245
   CONDITOR ALME SIDERUM
O come, O come, Emmanuel   ELW 257, LBW 34
   VENI, EMMANUEL
Of the Father's love begotten   ELW 295, LBW 42
   DIVINUM MYSTERIUM

Offering

People, look east   ELW 248, WOV 626
My soul proclaims the greatness of the Lord   ELW 235

Communion

Love divine, all loves excelling   ELW 631, LBW 315

That boy-child of Mary   ELW 293, TFF 54

The angel Gabriel from heaven came   ELW 265, WOV 632

All earth is hopeful   ELW 266, WOV 629

Sending

He comes to us as one unknown   ELW 737, WOV 768

The King shall come   ELW 260, LBW 33

Additional Assembly Songs

Emmanuel   TFF 45

⊕ Ya viene la Navidad   LLC 282

⊕ Bell, John. "Carol of the Advent" from *Innkeepers and Light Sleepers: Seventeen New Songs for Christmas.* SATB. GIA G-3835.

✿ Card, Michael. "Immanuel" from musicnotes.com.

✿● Neale, John Mason/Thomas Helmore. "O Come, O Come, Emmanuel" from CCLI.

✿ Norman, Bebo/Jason Ingram. "The Only Hope" from CCLI.

✿ Thomas, Dylan/Rueben Morgan. "With Us" from WT.

✿ Tomlin, Chris/Daniel Carson. "My Soul Magnifies the Lord" from CCLI.

Music for the Day
Choral

Benson, Robert. "Savior of the Nations, Come." SATB, org. AFP 9780806698298.

Jean, Martin. "Advent Hymn." SATB. AFP 9780800656621.

Manz, Paul/arr. Nancy Raabe. "Peace Came to Earth." U, opt assembly, kybd, ob. MSM 60-1007.

Pearson, Donald. "An Advent Processional." U/2pt mixed, hb, perc. AUR AE63.

Raabe, Nancy. "Creator of the Stars of Night." 2 pt mixed, kybd. AFP 9781451401622.

Sedio, Mark. "Once He Came in Blessing" from *Augsburg Easy Choirbook, Vol. 1.* 2 pt, org, fl. AFP 9780800676025.

Sirett, Mark. "Thou Shalt Know Him." SATB. AFP 9786000175962.

Children's Choir

Burkhardt, Michael. "He Came Down." 3 pt trbl, caller, desc. MSM 50-9423.

Horman, John. "Psalm 80" from *ChildrenSing Psalms.* U, org. AFP 9780800663872.

● Tucker, Margaret. "O Come, O Come, Emmanuel." U/2 pt trbl/mxd, assembly, org, opt ob/fl, opt hb. CG CGA917.

Keyboard / Instrumental

● Carter, Andrew. "Toccata on Veni Emmanuel" from *A Carter Organ Album.* Org. OXF 9780193753228.

● Larkin, Michael. "Creator of the Stars of Night" from *Hymn Meditations for the Church Year.* Pno. MSM 15-837.

● Phillips, Craig. "Divinum mysterium" from *Joy to the World: Three Preludes for Christmas.* Org. SEL 160-815.

● Schaefer, Marty. "Divinum mysterium" from *Quiet Carols: Ten Piano Settings.* Pno. AFP 9781451401905.

Handbell

● Gramann, Fred. "Change Ring Prelude on Divinum Mysterium." 2-3 oct, L3+. LOR 20/1537L. 3-6 oct, L3+. LOR 20/1239L.

● Malinowski, John. "Emmanuel Bell Carol." 4-5 oct, L3. FTT 20350.

● Moklebust, Cathy. "Creator of the Stars of Night." 2-3 oct hb, opt wch, L1+. CG CGB268.

⊕ = global song
✿ = praise song
● = relates to hymn of the day

CHRISTMAS

PREPARING FOR CHRISTMAS

During Christmas, more than any other season, preachers and worship leaders can rely on widespread and considerable familiarity with the assigned texts, as well as the hymns. This is a blessing, in the sense that with little work or fanfare, worship can evoke (and invoke) deep emotion and memory. It is at the same time a challenge, in the sense that the familiar and memorized sometimes becomes rote. We are called in this season to surprise the assembly with the familiar, and comfort them with the surpassing strange. Part of the work of worship is simply to open eyes and hearts to see what has already always been there—afresh.

Lectionary

You say Christmas and Incarnation, and the first texts that come to mind are Sirach and Wisdom, right? The Revised Common Lectionary offers readings from the deuterocanonical texts as options (on the second Sunday of Christmas this includes Sirach 24:1-12 and Wisdom 10:15-21). It is worth just a moment of our attention to ponder whether and why we will read these optional lectionary texts in our assemblies. Although many Protestant communities consider these texts extrabiblical—and thus on a level with Christian devotional writings rather than scripture itself—Lutherans have tended to have a slightly more moderate view. Because of our continuing commitment to full communion dialogues, including ongoing dialogue with the Roman Catholic communion, we explore ways to share a common lectionary with these traditions. As a result, some readings from these texts make it into our lectionary as well.

However, there is a different historical and theological reason why we might wish to include readings from the deuterocanonical texts in our worship assembly. These texts represent the intertestamental period—from Malachi (roughly 420 B.C.) to the birth of Christ. It is also roughly the entire period of Second Temple Judaism. Sometimes Christian communities give the impression that God, not to mention the faith community, were basically silent during this 400 year period, when in fact worship in Jerusalem and Israel (not to mention God) were all alive and kicking.

Additionally, at least one of the four gospels, John, understands the birth of Christ as the fulfillment and full restoration of the temple in the body of Christ himself, and so this gospel and others make even more sense as scripture in relation to a robust understanding of Second Temple Judaism. Daring preachers willing to experiment a bit with references to texts outside of where they typically tread may find that these pericopes offer an even wider and appropriate context for proclaiming the incarnation of the *logos* during the Christmas season.

That being said, the main texts for Christmas are still the main texts, and the beating heart of the Christmas season are Luke 2:1-20 and John 1:1-14. Had we but world enough and time, these two chapters could be the basis for an entire year's worth of sermons. They are genuinely that rich and inexhaustible. Preachers and worship leaders coming at these by now very familiar texts are presented with a variety of challenges. One temptation is to retrieve old material and simply say again what has already been said in previous years. An opposite but equal temptation is to try and find something completely unique and out of the ordinary to say, thus abandoning the matchless familiarity of the text.

Instead, find the middle way. Do the hard work of studying something old long enough and deep enough to find it new again. Insight often comes from engaging great literature or poetry. Having your nose in a good work of systematic theology through the preceding season can be a great inspiration for fresh preaching come Christmas, too. Consider St. Athanasius's *On the Incarnation of the Word of God* (available in many fine translations), or St. Maximus the Confessor's *On the Cosmic Mystery of Jesus Christ* (St. Vladimir's Press Popular Patristics Series), both of which offer ample and substantive reflection on the incarnation.

Also, let the pattern of the three services for Christmas Eve and Christmas Day work to your advantage. You can spread your attention between them, adapted to local context. The historical development of the three services is of interest here:

In the fourth century there was one mass celebrated by the pope on Christmas day, at nine o-clock in the morning. In the fifth century a midnight mass in the Basilica of St. Maria Maggiore (or St. Mary Major) was added, and in the sixth century a third mass was introduced in the Church of St. Anastasia, December 25 being her feast day. Since then, in the Roman tradition Christmas is celebrated with three masses: the midnight mass of the angels' announcement of the birth of the Savior, the dawn mass of the shepherds meeting the child in the manger, and the mass during the day, the mass of the faithful, proclaiming the theological meaning of the feast, the mystery of the incarnation, set out in the prologue to St. John's Gospel (Philip H. Pfatteicher, *New Book of Festivals and Commemorations: A Proposed Common Calendar of Saints* [Minneapolis: Fortress, 2008], 623).

Liturgical Arts

Hands down the best thing you can do to create a powerful environment for Christmas Eve is to make use of the **Proclamation of the Birth of Christ** at the beginning of the assembly's worship. The proclamation should be understood as the announcement of the incarnation within human history rather than a literal counting of years.

Many ages after God created the heavens and the earth,
　　when man and woman were formed
　　　in God's own image;
long after the great flood, when God set the rainbow
　　in the clouds as a sign of the covenant;
twenty-one centuries from the time of Abraham and Sarah;
thirteen centuries after Moses led God's people to freedom;
eleven centuries from the time of Ruth and the judges;
a thousand years from the anointing of David as king;
in the sixty-fifth week as Daniel's prophecy takes note;
in the one hundred ninety-fourth Olympiad;
the seven hundred fifty-second year
　　from the founding of the city of Rome;
in the forty-second year of the reign of Octavian Augustus;
in the sixth age of the world,
　　all earth being at peace,
Jesus Christ, eternal God, Son of the eternal Father,
　　willing to hallow the world by his coming in mercy,
　　was born of the virgin Mary in Bethlehem of Judea.
Today is the birth of our Lord Jesus Christ,
　　God made flesh.

The proclamation may be read or sung on one note by a leader standing at the entrance to the church. (A more involved musical form is provided in *Music Sourcebook for All Saints through Transfiguration* [Augsburg Fortress, 2013].) The drama can be enhanced by printing the proclamation on, and reading it from, a large scroll, visually illustrating the text as a proclamation. No other services of the church year are quite like Christmas. Anticipation and drama have been built almost to fever pitch. The church will be as full as it gets. Christmas decorations have in all likelihood transformed the sanctuary into a hall of wonders. The assembly needs someone to stand up and name the formal beauty of it all.

Music

These are the most familiar hymns of the church year. There are typically more Christmas hymns worship leaders hope to sing than there is even space for in the regrettably brief Christmas season. Some communities have decided to creatively extend the Christmas season out into Epiphany somewhat in order to sing more of these great carols. Others sing Christmas hymns even before the Christmas season. These hymns are beloved for a reason. They are theologically rich, and bear up the gospel and the biblical narrative nicely. Sing lots of them.

Consider doing an informal survey of the congregation in order to select hymns you are sure represent the interests of the people. Count how many Christmas carols you will need. Then hand a hymnal to that number of people after Advent worship some Sunday morning, and say, "Before you leave, would you page through these hymns and tell me which is your absolute favorite Christmas carol, so we can make sure and sing it?" This simple act has many benefits. It honors those you are asking. It heightens the chance that they will attend those services because they will want to sing their hymn. And it spreads hymn selection out in a simple and effective way beyond the pastor, church musicians, and worship planning team. It might even be a practice worth repeating for each season of the church year.

Careful planning for the music for the first and second Sundays of Christmas is equally important. The death of innocent children memorialized in Matthew 2:13-23 calls for lament. In spite of the overall festivity of the Christmas season, select hymns that offer space to remember and reflect. Given that so many people in our assemblies bring their grief and horror to worship with them, the remembrance of the tragedy of the death of those many children at the hands of Herod actually offers space for grieving in a time many feel little permission to do so. Susan Palo Cherwien's "In deepest night" (ELW 699), part of a collection of lament hymns in *Evangelical Lutheran Worship*, is haunting and appropriate. Given that we have just recently heard the angelic songs proclaiming the birth of the Messiah, her text sings the lament as appropriate counter-melody: "In deepest night, in darkest days, when harps are hung, no songs we raise, when silence must suffice as praise, yet sounding in us quietly there is the song of God."

Epiphany

Then there is Epiphany itself. Because Christmas is so full, and the season so short, if worship planners have not thought through a plan for whether and how to observe Epiphany, they may need to hold off for another year. However, observing Epiphany on the actual day, or on the Eve of Epiphany, has many merits. Consider in 2014 an Epiphany Eve vespers or eucharist in the late afternoon or early evening, followed by a Twelfth Night celebration. Since it does not fall on a Sunday morning this year, it also provides an opportunity for ecumenical partners to gather and share a mix of preachers and worship leaders. Take just two non-Sunday festivals, Epiphany and Ascension, and you have two opportunities for joint worship with two or more full communion partners.

WORSHIP TEXTS FOR CHRISTMAS

Confession and Forgiveness

*All may make the sign of the cross, the sign marked at baptism,
as the presiding minister begins.*
Blessed be the holy Trinity, ✛ one God,
the Maker of heaven and earth,
the Word made flesh,
the Lord and giver of life.
Amen.

Let us come into the light of Christ,
confessing our need for God's mercy.

Silence is kept for reflection.

God of peace,
**we confess that we are not at peace—
with others or with ourselves.
We bring to you all that tears us apart:
discord in our families,
violence in our world,
our own conflicted hearts.
In your mercy, mend us.
Reconnect us to one another and to you.
Let peace reign over all the earth,
through the Prince of peace,
our Savior Jesus Christ. Amen.**

In the Word who has come to dwell with us,
God has given us grace upon grace:
forgiveness that is stronger than our sins,
love that can heal every broken heart.
Hear this word of God's pardon and peace:
in the name of ✛ Jesus our Savior,
you are free from all your sins.
Rise, shine, for your light has come.
Amen.

Offering Prayer

Good and loving God,
we rejoice in the birth of Jesus,
who came among the poor to bring the riches of your grace.
As you have blessed us with your gifts,
let them be blessing for others.
With the trees of the field, with all earth and heaven,
we shout for joy at the coming of your Son,
Jesus Christ our Lord.
Amen.

Invitation to Communion

The mystery hidden for the ages
is revealed for us in this meal.
Come, behold and receive your God.

Prayer after Communion

We give you thanks, O God,
that in this bread and cup of Christ's very life,
you give us food for our journey.
As you led the magi by a star,
as you brought the holy family home again,
guide us on the way unfolding before us.
Wherever we go, may our lives proclaim
good news of great joy in Jesus Christ our Lord.
Amen.

Sending of Communion

O God,
whose grace and truth are revealed
in the Word-made-flesh,
bless those who go forth to share your word and sacrament
with those who are *sick/homebound/imprisoned*.
Nourish and strengthen
those who receive this holy communion,
that through the body and blood of your Son
all may rejoice at his birth
and in his presence among us now and forever.
Amen.

Blessing

May the Word that Mary brought to birth
carry you into new and abundant life.
Amen.
May the Word that Joseph cradled in his arms
enfold you with love and strength.
Amen.
May the Word that angels proclaimed in song
bring harmony to our world.
Amen.
And the blessing of almighty God,
the Father, the ☩ Son, and the Holy Spirit,
be upon you and remain with you always.
Amen.

Dismissal

Go in peace. Christ is with you.
Thanks be to God.

SEASONAL RITES FOR CHRISTMAS

Lighting the Christmas Tree 1

Use this prayer when you first illumine the tree or when you gather at the tree.

God our Creator,
we praise you for this Christmas tree.
It is a sign of your everlasting, evergreen presence.
It is a sign of the reign of heaven,
sheltering the creatures of the earth under its open arms.
It is a sign of the cross,
shining with the light of your grace and mercy.

Gracious God,
let your blessing come upon us
as we illumine this tree.
Send us your Son,
the tender shoot of Jesse,
who brings us light and life.

May all who stand in its light
eagerly welcome the true Light which never fades.
We ask this through Christ our Lord.
Amen.

From Come, Lord Jesus: Devotions for Advent, Christmas, Epiphany (Augsburg Fortress, 1996).

Blessing of the Nativity Scene 1

This blessing may be used after the sermon or after the communion of the people on Christmas Eve.

O Lord our God, with Mary and Joseph, angels and shepherds, and the animals in the stable, we gather around your Son, born for us. Bless us with your holy presence and inspire us to help those who have no place to dwell. Be with us that we might share Christ's love with all the world, for he is our light and salvation. Glory in heaven and peace on earth, now and forever. **Amen.**

Lighting the Christmas Tree 2

Use this prayer when you first illumine the tree or when you gather at the tree.

Let the heavens rejoice, and let the earth be glad;
let the sea thunder and all that is in it;
let the field be joyful and all that is therein.
Then shall all the trees of the wood shout for joy
at your coming, O LORD,
for you come to judge the earth.
You will judge the world with righteousness
and the peoples with your truth. (Ps. 96:11-13)

Be praised, O God,
for the blessings around us that point to you.
Be praised, O God,
for the signs of this holy season
that awaken in us wonder.
Praise for the steadfast green of this tree,
like your love, enduring all seasons.
Praise for the light that illumines our darkness,
like Christ, who brings light to the world.
Join our voices with those of the tree and of all creation,
who sing at your coming:
Glory to God in the highest,
and peace to God's people on earth.
Amen.

Blessing of the Nativity Scene 2

This blessing may be used when figures are added to the nativity scene throughout the days of Christmas.

O God, bless us who gather around this stable. As we celebrate Christ's birth into the world, may we receive the Christ child into our hearts with gratitude and song. **Amen.**

Lessons and Carols for Christmas

This service may be used during the twelve days of Christmas.

Gathering Song

Once in royal David's city   ELW 269, WOV 643
Love has come   ELW 292
O come, all ye faithful   ELW283, LBW 45

Dialogue

The people who walked in darkness have seen a great light.
The light shines in the darkness,
and the darkness has not overcome it.
Those who dwelt in the land of deep darkness,
on them light has shined.
We have beheld Christ's glory,
glory as of the only Son from the Father.
To us a child is born, to us a Son is given.
In the Word was life,
and the life was the light of all people.

Opening Prayer

Almighty God, you have filled us with the new light of the
Word who became flesh and lived among us. Let the light of
our faith shine in all we do; through your Son, Jesus Christ
our Lord, who lives and reigns with you and the Holy Spirit,
one God, now and forever.
Amen.

Lessons and Carols

Isaiah 9:2-7   *God promises a king*
Lo, how a rose e'er blooming   ELW 272
Emmanuel   TFF 45, W&P 36

Micah 5:2-5a   *The king will come from Bethlehem*
O little town of Bethlehem   ELW 279, LBW 41
Midnight stars make bright the sky   ELW 280

Luke 1:26-35, 38   *The annunciation to Mary*
Sing of Mary, pure and lowly   WOV 634
The angel Gabriel from heaven came   ELW 265, WOV 632

Luke 2:1-7   *The birth of Jesus*
Infant holy, infant lowly   ELW 276, LBW 44
I wonder as I wander   WOV 642, TFF 50

Luke 2:8-16   *The shepherds go to see the Savior*
Angels, from the realms of glory   ELW 275, LBW 50
On Christmas night   ELW 274

Luke 2:21-36   *Jesus receives his name*
That boy-child of Mary   ELW 293, TFF 54
Jesus, what a wonderful child   ELW 297, TFF 51

Matthew 2:1-11   *The magi follow the star*
The first Noel   ELW 300, LBW 56
What child is this   ELW 296, LBW 40

Matthew 2:13-18   *The slaughter of the holy innocents*
Oh, sleep now, holy baby WOV 639
Your little ones, dear Lord   ELW 286, LBW 52

John 1:1-14   *The mystery of the incarnation*
Of the Father's love begotten   ELW 295, LBW 42
He came down   ELW 253, TFF 37

Responsive Prayer

Glory to God in the highest,
and peace to God's people on earth.
Blessed are you, Prince of peace.
You rule the earth with truth and justice.
Send your gift of peace to all nations of the world.
Blessed are you, Son of Mary.
You share our humanity.
Have mercy on the sick, the dying,
and all who suffer this day.
Blessed are you, Son of God.
You dwell among us as the Word made flesh.
Reveal yourself to us in word and sacrament
that we may bear your light to all the world.

Lord's Prayer

Blessing and Dismissal

Let us bless the Lord.
Thanks be to God.

May you be filled with the wonder of Mary,
the obedience of Joseph,
the joy of the angels,
the eagerness of the shepherds,
the determination of the magi,
and the peace of the Christ child.
Almighty God, Father, ☩ Son, and Holy Spirit,
bless you now and forever.
Amen.

Sending Song

Love has come   ELW 292
Hark! The herald angels sing   ELW 270, LBW 60
Go tell it on the mountain   ELW 290, TFF 52, LBW 70

NOTES

Choral anthems or other hymns may be substituted for the congregational carols.

Each lesson may be read by a different reader. At the end of the lesson, the reader may pause and then say, "The word of the Lord," and all may respond, "Thanks be to God."

Blessing for a Home at Epiphany

Matthew writes that when the magi saw the shining star stop overhead, they were filled with joy. "On entering the house, they saw the child with Mary his mother" (Matt. 2:10-11). In the home, Christ is met in family and friends, in visitors and strangers. In the home, faith is shared, nurtured, and put into action. In the home, Christ is welcome.

Twelfth Night (January 5) or another day during the season of Epiphany offers an occasion for gathering with friends and family members for a blessing of the home, using the following as a model. Someone may lead the greeting and blessing, while another person may read the scripture passage. Following an eastern European tradition, a visual blessing may be inscribed with white chalk above the main door; for example, 20 + CMB + 14. The numbers change with each new year. The three letters stand for either the ancient Latin blessing Christe mansionem benedica, which means, "Christ, bless this house," or the legendary names of the magi (Caspar, Melchior, and Balthasar).

Greeting

May peace be to this house and to all who enter here.
By wisdom a house is built
and through understanding it is established;
through knowledge its rooms are filled
with rare and beautiful treasures.
See Proverbs 24:3-4.

Reading

As we prepare to ask God's blessing on this household,
let us listen to the words of scripture.

In the beginning was the Word,
and the Word was with God, and the Word was God.
He was in the beginning with God.
All things came into being through him,
and without him not one thing came into being.
What has come into being in him was life,
and the life was the light of all people.

The Word became flesh and lived among us,
and we have seen his glory,
the glory as of a father's only son, full of grace and truth.
From his fullness we have all received, grace upon grace.
John 1:1-4, 14, 16

Inscription

This inscription may be made with chalk above the entrance:
20 + C M B + 14
The magi of old, known as
C   Caspar,
M   Melchior, and
B   Balthasar
followed the star of God's Son who came to dwell among us
20   two thousand
14   and fourteen years ago.
+   Christ, bless this house,
+   and remain with us throughout the new year.

Prayer of Blessing

O God,
you revealed your Son to all people
by the shining light of a star.
We pray that you bless this home and all who live here
with your gracious presence.
May your love be our inspiration,
your wisdom our guide,
your truth our light,
and your peace our benediction;
through Christ our Lord.
Amen.

Then everyone may walk from room to room, blessing the house with incense or by sprinkling with water, perhaps using a branch from the Christmas tree.

Adapted from Come, Lord Jesus: Devotions for the Home *(Augsburg Fortress, 1996). See also "Blessing for a Home" in* Evangelical Lutheran Worship Pastoral Care, *pp. 337–353.*

December 24, 2013

Nativity of Our Lord
Christmas Eve

On a long winter evening we gather to proclaim the coming of the light. Isaiah announces that the people who walked in darkness have seen a great light. Paul reminds us that the grace of God has appeared, bringing salvation to all. In the familiar account of Christ's birth, the evening sky is bright with the heavenly host singing, "Glory to God in the highest." Amid our broken world we proclaim that the prince of peace is born among us. God comes to us in human flesh—in Christ's body and blood—so that we may be bearers of divine light to all the world.

I
Particularly appropriate for Christmas Eve

Prayer of the Day

Almighty God, you made this holy night shine with the brightness of the true Light. Grant that here on earth we may walk in the light of Jesus' presence and in the last day wake to the brightness of his glory; through your Son, Jesus Christ our Lord, who lives and reigns with you and the Holy Spirit, one God, now and forever.

Gospel Acclamation

Alleluia. I am bringing you good news of great joy for ¹ all the people:* to you is born this day in the city of David a Savior, who is the Messi- ¹ ah, the Lord. *Alleluia.* (Luke 2:10-11)

Readings and Psalm

Isaiah 9:2-7

This poem promises deliverance from Assyrian oppression, a hope based on the birth of a royal child with a name full of promise. While Judah's king will practice justice and righteousness, the real basis for faith lies in God's passion for the people: The zeal of the Lord of hosts will do this!

Psalm 96

Let the heavens rejoice and the earth be glad. (Ps. 96:11)

Titus 2:11-14

The appearance of God's grace in Jesus Christ brings salvation for all humanity. Consequently, in the present we live wisely and justly while also anticipating the hope of our Savior's final appearance.

Luke 2:1-14 [15-20]

God's greatest gift comes as a baby in a manger. Angels announce the "good news of great joy" and proclaim God's blessing of peace.

Preface   Christmas

Color   White

Prayers of Intercession

The prayers are prepared locally for each occasion. The following examples may be adapted or used as appropriate.

In joy and wonder, we pray for the church, those in need, and all of God's creation.

A brief silence.

Increase the joy of your people who gather this night to celebrate the arrival of your Anointed One. Send us out to announce all that you have done for your people. Hear us, O God.

Your mercy is great.

Raise our voices in the song of all creation. With earth and heavens, seas, fields, and trees, lead us in proclaiming your salvation and declaring your glory throughout the world. Hear us, O God.

Your mercy is great.

Bring glad tidings of peace to every nation. Break the rod of the oppressor. Cover the global community in the compassionate authority of your Son, our Sovereign. Hear us, O God.

Your mercy is great.

Give birth to hope in the lives of those who are lost or helpless. Send your Spirit of healing and comfort to all who are in need (*especially*). Hear us, O God.

Your mercy is great.

As you made yourself manifest in Christ, our Savior, make your salvation known also through us, his body. Shape us into a people who are zealous for good and righteous deeds. Hear us, O God.

Your mercy is great.

Here other intercessions may be offered.

All the saints rejoice in the eternal light of your salvation. Inspire us to rejoice in all things, trusting in your promises fulfilled, until you come among your people again. Hear us, O God.

Your mercy is great.

Almighty God, we entrust to you all for whom we pray, confident that you fulfill your promises through Christ our Savior and Lord.

Amen.

Images in the Readings

Luke's gospel presents images of **the poor**: those oppressed by Roman government, a woman giving birth in a place that houses both people and barn animals, a newborn wrapped only in strips of cloth, the socially despised and religiously unclean shepherds. In our society where Christmas suggests unrestricted spending and continual feasting, Luke's image of the poor is striking.

Both the gospel and the first reading suggest the image of the **mother** bearing new life. Often in the Bible, childbirth is credited to God's power. All Christians are now Mary, bearing Christ for the world.

The Hebrew word **Bethlehem** means house of bread. From this historic city famous for its connection to King David comes the one who will feed the people forever. In the liturgy, we enter that house of bread and eat.

Ideas for the Day

◆   Upside-down artificial trees were the rage a number of years ago. They were hung from the wall or ceiling and were perfect for crowded urban living spaces. Sound sinister? The tree is to point to heaven, you say? How surprising, then, to learn that—at least according to legend—in seventh- or eighth-century Germany, St. Boniface used an upside-down triangular tree to explain the holy Trinity. If you think about it, with Jesus down is up, and up is down. Though many of us seek the path of upward mobility, the recipients of Jesus' ministry were the downtrodden. Christ comes down, spiritually speaking, and joins us in the most lowly of places and circumstances. Then—in baptism—raises us up with him.

◆   Many of our Christmas crèches are stables for barnyard animals. It's a reminder that there is no stable, no place in our world or in our lives that is too poor, too remote, too messy for Christ to be born. And if you think about it, at Christmas our emotions can at times seem a bit un-*stable*. Our war-torn and complex world may seem unstable as well. Yet we are filled with wonder as we ponder what is revealed in that stable. As Oscar Romero wrote, "No one can celebrate a genuine Christmas without being truly poor. . . . Without poverty of spirit there can be no abundance of God."

◆   Many churches have late-night, or even midnight, Christmas Eve services on one of the longest nights of the year. George Herbert wrote that "life is half spent before we know what it is." We don't know the day or time when Jesus was born. Yet a beloved carol says it was "when half-spent was the night." Midnight is a liminal, transitional time and has many scriptural allusions. Maybe that explains some of our fascination with the darkness and light of this holy night.

◆   When setting up the nativity scene, one church discovered that the baby Jesus was missing! Though there is plenty of talk about putting Christ back in Christmas, the missing Jesus gave them an opportunity to reflect on where Christ is born and revealed in our world today. Almost certainly in places no less surprising than the manger in Bethlehem.

Connections with the Liturgy

The standard canticle of praise quotes today's gospel: "Glory to God in the highest, and peace to God's people on earth." Every time that we sing this canticle, we join with the angels at the birth of Jesus.

Let the Children Come

Sometimes it is important to review the vocabulary we casually use each year in carols and prayers. Noël can be used interchangeably with Christmas and comes from *natalis*, the Latin word for birth. Gloria or glory refers to greatness in a variety of ways: great praise, great beauty, great importance, even great light. Can we *give* glory for the great things God has done and *reflect* God's glory in our lives? "Hark!" we sing lustily: "Listen!" Perhaps there are points in today's worship to invite people's attention with a commanding, "Hark!" (before the scripture readings, in the prayers, or to begin the communion liturgy).

Assembly Song
Gathering

O come, all ye faithful   ELW 283, LBW 45

Joy to the world   ELW 267, LBW 39

Of the Father's love begotten   ELW 295, LBW 42

Psalmody and Acclamations

Alonso, Tony. "Today Is Born Our Savior" from TLP:S. Cant, assembly, C inst.

Gerike, Henry. "Psalm 96." SATB, assembly, org, opt br. CPH 983732WEB.

O'Brien, Francis Patrick. "Today Is Born Our Savior (Psalm 96)." SAB, assembly, kybd, fl, tpt. GIA G-5920.

Chepponis, James. "Festival Alleluia." Cant, opt SATB, assembly, opt br, hb. MSM 80-847A.

Hymn of the Day

On Christmas night ELW 274 *SUSSEX CAROL*

Peace came to earth ELW 285, WOV 641 *SCHNEIDER*

In the bleak midwinter ELW 294 *CRANHAM*

Offering

Midnight stars make bright the skies ELW 280

I am so glad each Christmas Eve ELW 271, LBW 69

Communion

Silent night, holy night! ELW 281, LBW 65

Away in a manger ELW 277, 278

Lo, how a rose e'er blooming ELW 272, LBW 58

Sending

Hark! The herald angels sing ELW 270, LBW 60

All my heart again rejoices ELW 273, LBW 46

Additional Assembly Songs

I wonder as I wander TFF 50, WOV 642

⊕ Pastores: a Belén LLC 305

✿ Cantelon, Ben. "Love Came Down" from CCLI.

✿ Cash, Ed/Chris Tomlin. "Emmanuel (Hallowed Manger Ground)" from WT.

✿ Getty, Keith/Stuart Townend. "Joy Has Dawned" from CCLI.

✿ Hutson, Wihla/Alfred Burt. "Some Children See Him" from musicnotes.com.

✿ Mohr, Joseph/Matt Maher. "Silent Night (Emmanuel)" from WT.

✿ Rice, Chris. "Welcome to Our World" from CCLI.

Music for the Day
Choral

Ferguson, John. "What Is This Lovely Fragrance?" SATB div, fl, hb/kybd. AFP 9781451401783.

Halley, Paul. "Infinite Light." SATB, org. Pelagos 2039.

⊕ Kwami, Robert M. Ghana. "Krismas dodzi vo/Christmas Time Is Here" from *World Carols for Choirs*. SATB. OXF 9780193532311.

● Manz, Paul/arr. Nancy Raabe. "Peace Came to Earth." U, opt assembly, kybd, ob. MSM 60-1007.

● Miller, William. "Sussex Carol." SATB, kybd, hb. AFP 9780800678180.

Robb, J. D./arr. Richard Proulx. "A la ru." SATB, fl, ob, cello. GIA G-6466.

Van, Jeffrey. "Child of Peace." SATB, gtr/pno. HAL HL.41903014.

Children's Choir

Berg, Ken. "While Shepherds Watched." U/2pt, opt fl, opt ob, pno. CG CGA1276.

● Culli, Benjamin M. "In the Bleak Midwinter." SSA, kybd. CPH 98-4072.

Langlois, K. "Midnight Stars Make Bright the Skies." U, Orff inst, perc. AFP 9780800679309.

Keyboard / Instrumental

Carter, John. "I Am So Glad Each Christmas Eve" from *Christmas Jazz: Suite for Piano*. Pno. AFP 9780806698007.

● Cherwien, David. "On Christmas Night All Christians Sing" from *The Bethlehem Collection*. Org. MSM 10-165.

● Maynard, Lynette L. "In the Bleak Midwinter" from *All Earth Is Hopeful: Piano Preludes for the Christmas Season*. Pno. AFP 9780806697987.

Callahan, Charles. "A Christmas Prelude for Flute and Organ." Fl, org. MSM 20-160.

Handbell

● Sherman, Arnold. "News of Great Joy." 3-6 oct, L3. HOP 2273.

● Thompson, Martha Lynn. "In the Bleak Midwinter." 3-5 oct hb, opt 3-5 oct hc, L3. ALF 23157.

Wagner, Douglas. "Dona Nobis Pacem." 3-5 oct, L2. BP HB54.

⊕ = global song
✿ = praise song
● = relates to hymn of the day

December 25, 2013
Nativity of Our Lord
Christmas Day

On this Christmas morning the people of God gather to celebrate the birth of the Word made flesh, Christ our Lord. Luke recounts the familiar story of shepherds and angels; John's gospel tells of the Word that dwells among us, full of grace and truth. The meaning of Christmas is made clear: the light shines in the darkness. It is in the liturgy that we encounter the Word made flesh—in the people of God gathered together as the body of Christ, and in the meal around the holy table. We go forth to be bearers of light as we proclaim this good news to all the ends of the earth.

II
Particularly appropriate for Christmas Day

Prayer of the Day

All-powerful and unseen God, the coming of your light into our world has brightened weary hearts with peace. Call us out of darkness, and empower us to proclaim the birth of your Son, Jesus Christ, our Savior and Lord, who lives and reigns with you and the Holy Spirit, one God, now and forever.

Gospel Acclamation

Alleluia. A holy day has dawned upon us. Come, you nations, and a- | dore the Lord.* For today a great light has come up- | on the earth. *Alleluia.*

Readings and Psalm
Isaiah 62:6-12

The prophet invites the people to give God no rest until God reestablishes Jerusalem. In turn, they will receive names full of promise: Holy People, the Redeemed of the Lord, a City Not Forsaken.

Psalm 97

Light dawns for the righteous, and joy for the honest of heart. (Ps. 97:11)

Titus 3:4-7

God saves us not because of what we do. Rather, God is a God of mercy and salvation who graciously cleanses us in baptism and renews our lives through the Holy Spirit.

Luke 2:[1-7] 8-20

The world's deep night is shattered by the light of God's new day. The glory of God is revealed to poor shepherds, who share the good news with others.

III
Particularly appropriate for Christmas Day

Prayer of the Day

Almighty God, you gave us your only Son to take on our human nature and to illumine the world with your light. By your grace adopt us as your children and enlighten us with your Spirit, through Jesus Christ, our Redeemer and Lord, who lives and reigns with you and the Holy Spirit, one God, now and forever.

Gospel Acclamation

Alleluia. I am bringing you good news of great joy for | all the people:* to you is born this day in the city of David a Savior, who is the Messi- | ah, the Lord. *Alleluia.*
(Luke 2:10-11)
or
Alleluia. A holy day has dawned upon us. Come, you nations, and a- | dore the Lord.* For today a great light has come up- | on the earth. *Alleluia.*

Readings and Psalm
Isaiah 52:7-10

A messenger races home to Jerusalem with the marvelous words: "Your God reigns!" In comforting the people, God proves to be the best brother or sister (redeemer) they have ever known. Everyone will witness the victory (salvation) of God.

Psalm 98

All the ends of the earth have seen the victory of our God. (Ps. 98:3)

Hebrews 1:1-4 [5-12]

This letter opens with a lofty declaration of Jesus' preeminent status as the Son through whom God created the world and through whom our sins are cleansed. God speaks to us now through the Son, who is exalted even above the angels.

John 1:1-14

The prologue to the Gospel of John describes Jesus as the Word of God made flesh, the one who reveals God to be "full of grace and truth."

Preface Christmas

Color White

Prayers of Intercession

The prayers are prepared locally for each occasion. The following examples may be adapted or used as appropriate.

In joy and wonder, we pray for the church, those in need, and all of God's creation.

A brief silence.

Sustain the church by your Word made flesh among us. Feed us with your gracious gifts of the written word, the proclaimed word, and the visible word of the body and blood of Christ. Hear us, O God.

Your mercy is great.

Shine your new dawn on all creation. Restore health to polluted rivers and seas, to hills and plains destroyed by natural disaster. Reveal your glory in all that you have made. Hear us, O God.

Your mercy is great.

Enter into the places of darkness in this world, where pride and abuse of power threaten right relationships among peoples. Overcome the darkness with your light. Hear us, O God.

Your mercy is great.

Pour out your mercy and righteousness on all your people, and by your Spirit bring renewal to those who long for wholeness and health (*especially*). Give them the hope of abundant life. Hear us, O God.

Your mercy is great.

Now that we have seen your salvation, keep us diligent in seeking your presence among us, and make us eager to proclaim good news to those in need. Hear us, O God.

Your mercy is great.

Here other intercessions may be offered.

Rejoicing for the gift of the saints, whose lives announced your salvation, we pray that you would mold our lives to always bear witness to the goodness you show your people. Hear us, O God.

Your mercy is great.

Almighty God, we entrust to you all for whom we pray, confident that you fulfill your promises through Christ our Savior and Lord.

Amen.

Images in the Readings
II

Luke writes that **angels**, messengers from heaven, a link between God and humankind, announce Christ and sing praise to God. It is a challenge to describe and, especially, to depict angels in a worthy manner. Contrary to popular notions, Christian doctrine does not teach that dead Christians become angels, but rather that angels are mighty supernatural beings that signify and convey the power of God. In Luke, the angels proclaim the meaning of the incarnation.

Although in some places in the Bible cities are described as evil and filled with temptations, in Isaiah 62 the city **Jerusalem** symbolizes God's protection, God's very presence on earth. Throughout history, the church has used the image of Jerusalem as a picture of itself: we are like Jerusalem, a magnificent city, protected by the arms of God, thriving on word and sacrament. This imagery might not be clear to all worshipers, who might think that we are referring to the actual city of the twenty-first century, for sometimes in our worship "Jerusalem" is a metaphor for the church, and sometimes the name of a current city filled with international religious conflict.

On a day that we think about the **birth** of Jesus, we recall also the water of our rebirth in baptism.

III

During the fourth century, Christians chose the festival at the winter solstice as an appropriate time to celebrate the birth of Jesus. The prologue of John praises the Word of God as this **light** come to illumine the world. What has been born into the darkness on the earth is its light—an image especially appropriate for Christians in the Northern Hemisphere. The light of Christmas awaits the light of the resurrection.

Too often the church speaks about **creation** as if it were the task of only God the Father. However, the prologue of John and the introduction to Hebrews see the fullness of God as having created the world. Jesus Christ, the Son of God, "the exact imprint of God's very being," is lauded as creator of all things. For Christians, God is triune.

The Gospel of John demonstrates its Greek context in its reliance on the imagery of Jesus as the **Son of God**. Christian theologians stressed that calling Jesus the Son of God does not mean what it commonly signified in

Greco-Roman polytheism, where superhumans were born from a human mother who had been impregnated by a god like Jupiter. Rather, the image is supreme metaphor. John claims that Jesus, as the Father's only Son, makes all believers into children of God.

For John, Christ is the **Word**, and when he speaks, we hear God. When God speaks, we encounter Jesus. An important image in John's gospel, this image is not easy to depict.

Ideas for the Day

◆   How many weeks before Christmas did you hear your first Christmas carol or see your first Christmas tree? If you look down alleyways tomorrow, you will find discarded trees. No twelve days of Christmas; it's over until next year. Some cities may seem to keep Christmas alive all year long: North Pole, Alaska; Christmas, Florida; Santa Claus, Indiana; Bethlehem, Pennsylvania. If Christmas is about the incarnation—God sharing our humanity in Jesus Christ— then we could say that the true meaning of Christmas is year-round. When we think that being spiritual means rising above our fleshly existence, we share bread and wine at the Lord's table. The Word becomes flesh and dwells among us. Or as Eugene Peterson translates that verse, the "Word moved into the neighborhood." Christmas all year long.

◆   Is the phrase "no crying he makes" in the beloved Christmas song "Away in a manger" theologically problematic? If Jesus were truly human he must be fully one of us: crying and all. Consider the ways the world cries out in pain this Christmas morning. Jesus, the one who wept over Jerusalem and at the grave of his friend Lazarus, is born among us not to make everything better, but to take on our crying, to enter fully our very human, messy, and sometimes tearful lives.

◆   A Bette Midler song declares that "God is watching us / from a distance." Though God is certainly transcendent and beyond our comprehension, the mystery of Christmas is that the Word is very near—dwells among us full of grace and truth. The birth accounts from Matthew and Luke invite us to ponder God's presence in the infant Jesus. John writes of the incarnation in beautiful, poetic language. How might we reflect on God coming near to us in the joys and sorrows of our lives?

Connections with the Liturgy
II

For the dismissal today, we call out, "Go in peace. Share the good news. Thanks be to God." We are the shepherds.

III

In the Nicene Creed we confess that our one Lord, Jesus Christ, is "the only Son of God, eternally begotten of the Father, God from God, Light from Light, true God from true God."

Let the Children Come

Today's gospel from John shines with the very Light it speaks. Plan a simple but dignified gospel procession. Instruct four older children, grades four and above, to carry substantial pillar candles, two preceding the book bearer and presider and two following. Another child could hold the book. Depending on the shape of your worship space, there may be room for a "wreath" of flame around the word, the light no darkness can overcome.

Assembly Song
Gathering

Good Christian friends, rejoice   ELW 288, LBW 55

Hark! The herald angels sing   ELW 270, LBW 60

Let all together praise our God   ELW 287, LBW 47

Psalmody and Acclamations

Alonso, Tony. "A Light Will Shine on Us This Day" from TLP:S.

Manalo, Ricky. "Be Glad in the Lord." Cant, assembly, kybd, C inst, gtr. GIA G-4363.

Trapp, Lynn. "All the Ends of the Earth." SATB, assembly, kybd, tpt, 2 C inst. GIA G-5623.

Chepponis, James. "Festival Alleluia." Cant, opt SATB, assembly, opt br, hb. MSM 80-847A.

Hymn of the Day

Of the Father's love begotten   ELW 295, LBW 42
DIVINUM MYSTERIUM

The bells of Christmas   ELW 298, LBW 62
DET KIMER NU TIL JULEFEST

Light dawns on a weary world   ELW 726   *TEMPLE OF PEACE*

Offering

Your little ones, dear Lord   ELW 286, LBW 52

'Twas in the moon of wintertime   ELW 284, LBW 72

Communion

In the bleak midwinter   ELW 294

Around you, O Lord Jesus   ELW 468, LBW 496

Infant holy, infant lowly   ELW 276, LBW 44

Sending

Go tell it on the mountain   ELW 290, LBW 70, TFF 52

Jesus, what a wonderful child   ELW 297, TFF 51

Additional Assembly Songs

The virgin Mary had a baby boy   TFF 53

✷ Gloria en las alturas   LLC 297

✷ Bell, John. Scotland. "I Am for You" from *Heaven Shall Not Wait.* SATB. GIA G-3646.

✿ Avery, Brad/David Carr/Mac Powell/Mark Lee/Tai Anderson, Jr. "Born in Bethlehem" from CCLI.

✿ Brown, Brenton/ Jason Ingram. "Joyful (The One Who Saves)" from WT.

✿ Crocker, Matt/Scott Ligertwood. "Born Is the King (It's Christmas)" from CCLI.

✿ Fieldes, Mia. "O Rejoice" from CCLI.

✿ Longfellow, Henry Wadsworth/Jean Baptiste Calkin. "I Heard the Bells on Christmas Day" from CCLI.

✿ Tomlin, Chris/Ed Cash/George Frederic Handel/Isaac Watts/Matt Gilder. "Joy to the World (Unspeakable Joy)" from CCLI.

Music for the Day
Choral

Busarow, Donald. "The Best of Rooms." SATB, pno. Coronet 392-41997-C.

Carter, John. "While Shepherds Watched Their Flocks." 3 pt, pno. AFP 9781451401653.

Miller, Aaron David. "Joy to the World" from *The New Gloria Deo.* 2 pt, pno. AFP 9781451401653.

Peeters, Flor. "In Excelsis Gloria." SATB, kybd. AFP 9786000175757.

Spurlock, William. "Christ Was Born on Christmas Day." SATB, pno. AFP 9781451423945.

Stewart, H. C. "On This Day Earth Shall Ring." SATB, org. OXF 9780193501362.

Children's Choir

Jacobson, Borghild. "Oh, Mary, Rock the Word Made Flesh" from *Five Christmas Songs, Set I.* U. MSM 50-1800.

Pergolesi, Giovanni Battista. "Glory to God." 2 pt, 2 opt C inst, kybd. MSM 50-1450.

Schultz, Donna Gartman. "Cold December's Winds Were Stilled." 2 pt trbl, pno. AFP 9780800675912.

Keyboard / Instrumental

● Haan, Raymond H. "Divinum mysterium" from *O Come, Emmanuel: Six Advent and Christmas Hymns for Cello or Viola and Organ.* Cello or DB, org. MSM 20-168.

● Held, Wilbur. "Divinum mysterium" from *Augsburg Organ Library: Advent.* Org. AFP 9780800658953.

Petersen, Lynn L. "Once in Royal David's City" from *In Royal David's City: Carols for Piano.* Pno. AFP 9780800663865.

Willcocks, David. "Postlude on 'Hark, the Herald Angels Sing'" from *The Oxford Book of Christmas Organ Music.* OXF 9780193751248.

✷ = global song
✿ = praise song
● = relates to hymn of the day

Handbell

● Buckwalter, Karen. "The Bells of Christmas." 4-5 oct hb, opt 3 oct hc, L3. BP HB240. Opt fl and vln. BP HB240A.

Glasgow, Michael. "Carol of the Drum." 3-6 oct hb, opt 3, 5, 6, or 7 oct hc, opt drm, L4. JEF JHS9462.

● Mathis, William. "In Dulci Jubilo" from *Three Favorite German Carols.* 4-5 oct hb, opt 2 or 4 oct hc or C inst, opt perc, L3. AFP 9780800674939.

Thursday, December 26
Stephen, Deacon and Martyr

Stephen was a deacon and the first martyr of the church. He was one of those seven upon whom the apostles laid hands after they had been chosen to serve widows and others in need. Later, Stephen's preaching angered the temple authorities, and they ordered him to be put to death by stoning, with Saul (later Paul) as one of the observers. As he died, he witnessed to his faith and spoke of a vision of heaven.

Friday, December 27
John, Apostle and Evangelist

John, the son of Zebedee, was a fisherman and one of the Twelve. John, his brother James, and Peter were the three who witnessed the light of the transfiguration. John and James once made known their desire to hold positions of power in the kingdom of God. Jesus' response showed them that service to others was the sign of God's reign in the world. Tradition has attributed authorship of the gospel and the three epistles bearing his name to the apostle John. John is a saint for Christmas through his proclamation that the Word became flesh and lived among us, that the light of God shines in the darkness, and that we are called to love one another as Christ has loved us.

Saturday, December 28
The Holy Innocents, Martyrs

The infant martyrs commemorated on this day were the children of Bethlehem, two years old and younger, who were killed by Herod, who worried that his reign was threatened by the birth of a new king. Augustine called these innocents "buds, killed by the frost of persecution the moment they showed themselves." Those linked to Jesus through their youth and innocence encounter the same hostility Jesus encounters later in his ministry.

December 29, 2013
First Sunday of Christmas

As we celebrate the Twelve Days of Christmas, our gospel today confronts us with the death of innocent children at the hands of Herod. The birth of Christ does not remove the power of evil from our world, but its light gives us hope as we walk with all the "holy innocents" of past generations and today who have suffered unjustly. In our gathering around word and meal, God continues to redeem us, lift us up, and carry us as in days of old.

Prayer of the Day

O Lord God, you know that we cannot place our trust in our own powers. As you protected the infant Jesus, so defend us and all the needy from harm and adversity, through Jesus Christ, our Savior and Lord, who lives and reigns with you and the Holy Spirit, one God, now and forever.

Gospel Acclamation

Alleluia. Let the peace of Christ rule ˈ in your hearts,*
and let the word of Christ dwell ˈ in you richly. *Alleluia.*
(Col. 3:15, 16)

Readings and Psalm

Isaiah 63:7-9

God does not delegate divine intervention to a messenger or angel. God's own presence brings salvation. The prophet and all who read these words join in celebrating God's gracious deeds. God trusts that God's people will not act falsely.

Psalm 148

The splendor of the Lord is over earth and heaven.
(Ps. 148:13)

Hebrews 2:10-18

Through Jesus' suffering and death, the trail to eternal salvation has been blazed for us. We do not fear death, because he has conquered the power of death. Thus Christ, our merciful and faithful high priest, has the final say over the destiny of our lives.

Matthew 2:13-23

Matthew relates the slaughter of babies in Bethlehem as one example of evil in the world. Jesus has been born into this world to manifest God's presence and save his people from their sins.

Preface   Christmas

Color   White

Prayers of Intercession

The prayers are prepared locally for each occasion. The following examples may be adapted or used as appropriate.

In joy and wonder, we pray for the church, those in need, and all of God's creation.
A brief silence.
Shine your favor on your people, and uphold us with the abundance of your steadfast love. Send us out from our assembly, trusting in your presence, to announce your gracious deeds. Hear us, O God.
Your mercy is great.

Fill all who hunger with your gracious provision. Establish justice in the ways that food is grown and distributed. Work through agencies, such as the World Hunger Appeal, to feed all people. Hear us, O God.
Your mercy is great.

Make your ways known to all the nations. Join all people together, young and old, rich and poor, in order to work your righteous acts among them. Hear us, O God.
Your mercy is great.

Ease the suffering of all who live with chronic illness, addiction, or distress (*especially*). Surround them with family and friends who bring assurance of your compassion and care. Hear us, O God.
Your mercy is great.

Draw near to all children, the sisters and brothers of Jesus. Free the young and vulnerable ones who are in the chains of abuse, poverty, or neglect. Give them abundant life. Hear us, O God.
Your mercy is great.

Here other intercessions may be offered.

Remembering your covenant that draws the saints into one community, join our voices with theirs in praise of all the good things you do for your people. Hear us, O God.
Your mercy is great.

Almighty God, we entrust to you all for whom we pray, confident that you fulfill your promises through Christ our Savior and Lord.
Amen.

Images in the Readings

The image that recurs in the three readings is **the child**. Jesus is the child of God; the children of Bethlehem are slaughtered; God has treated Israel like beloved children; the sacrifice of Jesus makes believers into children of God. The challenge in our culture is to keep this image from shallow sentimentality.

The gospel reading contrasts the protected child with **the victim**. All three readings speak their good news against the backdrop, not of joyous Christmas celebration, but of horrific human suffering. Many medieval churches displayed life-sized depictions of the slaughter of the innocents, with weeping mothers holding bleeding infants. This art hinted at what is to come: Mary weeping over the dead Jesus. Christianity is not for the squeamish.

God, like **a loving parent**, a father, a mother, is carrying the toddler to safety.

Ideas for the Day

◆ Jesus was a refugee. The phrase is sometimes a tagline for refugee ministries such as Lutheran Immigration and Refugee Service (www.lirs.org). Today would be a good day to include a story or example from LIRS or RefugeeOne (www.refugeeone.org). In today's gospel the holy family, fleeing for their lives, escape to Egypt. At one point Jesus describes himself as "the Son of Man [who] has nowhere to lay his head" (Luke 9:58). How can we hear the familiar Christmas narratives anew and reach out to those who live with danger, risk, or homelessness?

◆ An Eric Clapton song says it's Christmastime "but it's raining in my heart." Tears can fall this time of year for many reasons: a touching memory, an aching loss, a response of gratefulness, a painful encounter. Imagine the tears of the families grieving their children killed by King Herod, or Rachel weeping for her children. And perhaps our lives only have meaning when we realize that we too will die and that every moment we live is a gift of God. As an ancient proverb says: "When we are born into this world there are tears of joy, so let me live my life so that when I die the tears of joy will be the same."

◆ We hear of the holy innocents killed by Herod, and we remember all the innocent children and adults killed through the ages. Christmas in 2013 will mark one year since the tragedy at Sandy Hook Elementary School in Newtown, Connecticut. The movie *Of Gods and Men* (Sony Classics, 2010) tells the true story of eight Cistercian monks in Algeria who learn of extremist guerillas in the area who have murdered a number of innocent people. On Christmas Eve the terrorists break into the monastery and demand medical supplies for wounded members of their group. Later the monks must decide whether, in the face of certain death by the terrorists, they will leave or stay put. They

declare: "We're martyrs out of love, out of fidelity. Our mission is to be brothers to all. We had to resist the violence and we discovered what Christ calls us to: to be born again and again."

Connections with the Liturgy

In the thanksgiving for baptism we hear, "By water and your Word you claim us as daughters and sons," and in the prayers of intercession, we pray for "the poor, oppressed, sick, bereaved, lonely, and all who suffer in body, mind, or spirit."

Let the Children Come

Ask children to listen for the words *child*, *children*, *brothers*, *sisters*, *mother*, and *father* in today's readings. If you print the readings in your worship folder, older children could underline or circle these words. Pre-readers could hold up a finger each time they hear one. This is a hard gospel in the midst of our Christmas celebration. It is true that in this unsafe world innocents die and refugees roam in search of safety. The wonder of God's promise provides the sanctuary, the safe place that allows us to move within our broken world. Assure children of God's never-ending presence with them.

Assembly Song
Gathering

All my heart again rejoices   ELW 273, LBW 46
Once in royal David's city   ELW 269, WOV 643
Let all together praise our God   ELW 287, LBW 47

Psalmody and Acclamations

Ogden, David. "Let All Creation Sing" from PS1.
Krentz, Michael. "Psalm 148" from PWA.
Makeever, Ray. "Praise and Exalt God (Psalm 148)" from DH.
Chepponis, James. "Festival Alleluia." Cant, opt SATB, assembly, opt br, hb. MSM 80-847A.

Hymn of the Day

'Twas in the moon of wintertime   ELW 284, LBW 72
   UNE JEUNE PUCELLE
Your little ones, dear Lord   ELW 286, LBW 52
   HER KOMMER DINE ARME SMÅ
That boy-child of Mary   ELW 293, TFF 54   *BLANTYRE*

Offering

What feast of love   ELW 487, WOV 701
Your little ones, dear Lord   ELW 286, LBW 52

Communion

What child is this   ELW 296, LBW 40
Love has come   ELW 292
Of the Father's love begotten   ELW 295, LBW 42

Sending

Cold December flies away   ELW 299, LBW 53

The first Noel   ELW 300, LBW 56

Additional Assembly Songs

Hush, little Jesus boy   TFF 56

⊕ María, pobre María   LLC 310

⊕ Loh, I-to. Taiwan. "Child of Christmas Story" from *Sound the Bamboo*. U. GIA G-6830.

✿ Hughes, Tim. "When the Tears Fall (I've Had Questions)" from CCLI.

✿ Ingram, Jason/Reuben Morgan. "Forever Reign" from WT.

✿ Keyes, Aaron/Johnny Parks/Matt Maher/Michael Gungor. "Hope Is Dawning" from CCLI.

✿ MacIntosh, Sarah/Vicky Beeching. "Deliverer" from CCLI.

✿ Maher, Matt/Ike Ndolo/Tam Le. "Kyrie" from WT.

✿ Morgan, Reuben. "Yahweh" from WT.

Music for the Day

Choral

Arnatt, Ronald. "A Great and Mighty Wonder." SAB. ECS 7068.

Callahan, Charles. "A Manger Carol." U, org. MSM 50-1300.

Eckhardt, A. Royce. "The Lovingkindness of the Lord." SATB, org. AFP 9781451424065.

⊕ Grau, Alberto. Venezuela. "Niño lindo/Lovely baby" from *World Carols for Choirs*. SATB. OXF 9780193532311.

Keesecker, Thomas. "God So Loved the World." SAB, kybd, opt gtr, opt assembly. AFP 9780806697635.

Paulus, Stephen. "How Far Is It to Bethlehem?" SATB, kybd or harp, ob. AFP 9780800645373.

Warland, Dale. "Coventry Carol." SATB. CPH 98-1928.

Children's Choir

Cool, Jayne Southwick. "A Prayer for Peace." U/2 pt, pno, opt assembly. AFP 9780800664114.

● Reeves, Jeff. "'Twas in the Moon of Wintertime." U, pno, opt fl, opt fc, opt drm. CG CGA1064.

Stroope, Z. Randall. "Sans Day Carol." 2 pt trbl, hp or pno. CG CGA549.

Keyboard / Instrumental

● Carter, John. "'Twas in the Moon of Wintertime" from *More Carols for Piano*. Pno. HOP 1508.

● Ferguson, John. "'Twas in the Moon of Wintertime" from *A Christmas Triptych, Set 1*. Org. MSM 10-103.

Maynard, Lynette L. "Un Flambeau" from *Sing We Now of Christmas: Joyous Piano Music for the Season*. Pno. AFP 9780800677619.

Pelz, Walter L. "Vom Himmel hoch" from *Augsburg Organ Library: Christmas*. Org. AFP 9780800659356.

Handbell

● McChesney, Kevin and Julie Turner. "Gloria Hodie." 3-6 oct, L3. JEF JHS9482.

● Moklebust, Cathy. "'Twas in the Moon of Wintertime." 2-3 oct hb, opt fc, opt tamb, opt wch, L2. CG CGB155. 3-5 oct hb, opt fc, opt tamb, opt wch, L2. CG CGB402.

● Prins, Matthew. "Born Is the King of Israel." 3-5 oct hb, opt 2 oct hc, L4+. GIA G-7089.

Wednesday, January 1, 2014

Name of Jesus

The observance of the octave (eighth day) of Christmas has roots in the sixth century. Until the recent past, Lutheran calendars called this day "The Circumcision and Name of Jesus." The emphasis on circumcision is the older emphasis. Every Jewish boy was circumcised and formally named on the eighth day of his life. Already in his youth, Jesus bears the mark of a covenant that he makes new through the shedding of his blood on the cross. That covenant, like Jesus' name, is a gift that marks the children of God. Baptized into Christ, the church begins a new year in Jesus' name.

Thursday, January 2

Johann Konrad Wilhelm Loehe, renewer of the church, died 1872

Loehe (approximate pronunciation: LAY-uh) was a pastor in nineteenth-century Germany. From the small town of Neuendettelsau, he sent pastors to North America, Australia, New Guinea, Brazil, and the Ukraine. His work for a clear confessional basis within the Bavarian church sometimes led to conflict with the ecclesiastical bureaucracy. Loehe's chief concern was that a congregation find its life in the holy communion, and from that source evangelism and social ministries would flow. Many Lutheran congregations in Michigan, Ohio, and Iowa were either founded or influenced by missionaries sent by Loehe.

⊕ = global song
✿ = praise song
● = relates to hymn of the day

January 5, 2014
Second Sunday of Christmas

Within the gospel reading's profound words lies the simple message that God is revealed in a human person. Though we may try to understand how the Word existed with God from the beginning of time, the wonder we celebrate at Christmas is that the Word continues to dwell among us. Christ comes among us in the gathered assembly, the scriptures, the waters of new birth, and the bread and the wine. Through these ordinary gifts we receive the fullness of God's grace and truth.

Prayer of the Day

Almighty God, you have filled all the earth with the light of your incarnate Word. By your grace empower us to reflect your light in all that we do, through Jesus Christ, our Savior and Lord, who lives and reigns with you and the Holy Spirit, one God, now and forever.

or

O God our redeemer, you created light that we might live, and you illumine our world with your beloved Son. By your Spirit comfort us in all darkness, and turn us toward the light of Jesus Christ our Savior, who lives and reigns with you and the Holy Spirit, one God, now and forever.

Gospel Acclamation

Alleluia. All the ends ¹ of the earth* have seen the victory ¹ of our God. *Alleluia.* (Ps. 98:3)

Readings and Psalm

Jeremiah 31:7-14

God promises to bring Israel back to its land from the most remote parts of exile. In Zion Israel will rejoice over God's gift of food and livestock. Young women will express their joy in dancing; God will give gladness instead of sorrow.

or Sirach 24:1-12

The figure of Wisdom played a major role in early discussions of Christology. Wisdom is the divine word, coming from the mouth of God, and ruling over all of creation. Wisdom, created at the beginning of time, made her dwelling place in Jerusalem among God's people.

Psalm 147:12-20

Worship the Lord, O Jerusalem; praise your God, O Zion. (Ps. 147:12)

or Wisdom 10:15-21

We sing, O Lord, to your holy name. (Wis. 10:20)

Ephesians 1:3-14

In Jesus, all of God's plans and purposes have been made known as heaven and earth are united in Christ. Through Jesus, we have been chosen as God's children and have been promised eternal salvation.

John 1:[1-9] 10-18

John begins his gospel with this prologue: a hymn to the Word through whom all things were created. This Word became flesh and brought grace and truth to the world.

Preface   Christmas

Color   White

Prayers of Intercession

The prayers are prepared locally for each occasion. The following examples may be adapted or used as appropriate.

In joy and wonder, we pray for the church, those in need, and all of God's creation.

A brief silence.

Dwell among your people, and fill the church with your wisdom. Guide us in ways of righteousness, that we may show others the witness of your goodness. Hear us, O God.

Your mercy is great.

May every season work for your good purpose. Send sun and rain, warmth and chill, in due measure to draw forth your bounty from the earth. Hear us, O God.

Your mercy is great.

Journey with all refugees and displaced peoples. Lead them in safety to a place where they will find security, that they rejoice in the care you have provided them. Hear us, O God.

Your mercy is great.

Be a sure defense to all whose lives are threatened by pain, personal crisis, or persistent fear (*especially*). Give them shelter from hardship and rest when they are weary. Hear us, O God.

Your mercy is great.

Shine your light through this faith community into the wider community. Make us a beacon for all who hunger and thirst for righteousness and who are in need of mercy. Hear us, O God.

Your mercy is great.

Here other intercessions may be offered.

Giving thanks that the saints now dwell with you in the fullness of your kingdom, we ask you to keep us faithful to your truth revealed in Christ until you make all things new. Hear us, O God.

Your mercy is great.

Almighty God, we entrust to you all for whom we pray, confident that you fulfill your promises through Christ our Savior and Lord.

Amen.

Images in the Readings

Once again this Sunday, **light** is a primary image for the power of God to transform the earth and us in it. Even the smallest light shines through a field of darkness.

Again, becoming **children of God** recurs in the readings. Although many contemporary people think of God as being naturally father of humankind, this was not a cultural idea in the first century, and the Bible understands this extraordinary claim only as a consequence of the incarnation. God is not, as many people imagine, the alien and uncaring other. Rather, God loves us as children.

The church is a **watered garden**. A garden is more personal, more beautiful, than a field of crops. We think ahead to Good Friday and the Easter Vigil, when according to John's gospel Jesus is buried and raised to life in a garden.

Ideas for the Day

◆   Though the incarnation of Jesus Christ is a central part of our faith, in much of Christian history spirit has been elevated above the body. The poet Edwin Muir expressed the dualism in the worship of his Calvinistic childhood: "The Word made flesh is here made word again." We encounter the gospel in our bodies through the water of baptism and the bread and wine of the eucharist. How is the liturgy in your congregation multisensory, and/or in what ways could it become more so?

◆   At age fifteen Marcia Mount Shoop was raped. Though church was a comforting and familiar place for Marcia, she found little solace there; she mostly sensed language about exalted souls and sinful bodies. Now a Presbyterian minister, Marcia feels called to mend the rift between body and mind, soul and spirit. With an emphasis on incarnational theology, she helps people put the body back into the body of Christ. Though her experience is related to healing from sexual violence, she wants people to see the importance of

their bodies in relation to their Christian faith ("A Rape Survivor Now Ministers Body and Soul," *New York Times,* June 29, 2012).

◆   Many of us exchanged gifts at Christmas, and since then many of us have tried to exchange some of those gifts for ones that fit us better. A hymn with rich theological and poetic language is "Let all together praise our God" (ELW 287). Stanza 5 names the "wonderful exchange" of Christmas: God taking on our flesh and giving us divine grace. Martin Luther spoke of the joyous exchange in this way: "Lord Jesus, you are my righteousness, just as I am your sin. You have taken upon yourself what is mine and given me what is yours. You have taken upon yourself what you were not and have given to me what I was not." As the twelve days of Christmas come to a close and a new year has just begun, reflect on the great Christmas exchange in which God shares our humanity that we may share in God's divinity.

Connections with the Liturgy

Christians are enlightened at baptism. In the words of the baptismal welcome, "Whoever follows me will have the light of life."

Christians are watered at baptism. In the words of the presentation of candidates for baptism, "By water and the Holy Spirit we are reborn children of God."

Let the Children Come

On this second Sunday of Christmas we gather to celebrate the Word-made-flesh even as the world-of-flesh has already moved on to a new year. What a wonderful time to retell the Christmas story, to revisit the carols of the season, to have young and old share their musical renditions of familiar holiday tunes to capture the still-celebratory spirit of these twelve days. Additional votive candles, strings of white Christmas lights added to furniture or windows throughout the worship space—how can you make real the light shining in the darkness?

Assembly Song
Gathering

Word of God, come down on earth   ELW 510, WOV 716

The first Noel   ELW 300, LBW 56

Angels, from the realms of glory   ELW 275, LBW 50

Psalmody and Acclamations

"O Praise the Lord, Jerusalem" *Psallite* A-203.

Woehr, Roland. "Psalm 147:12-20," from PSCY.

Pavlechko, Thomas. "Psalm 147:12-20" from SMP.

Chepponis, James. "Festival Alleluia." Cant, opt SATB, assembly, opt br, hb. MSM 80-847A.

Hymn of the Day

Let our gladness have no end   ELW 291, LBW 57
NARODIL SE KRISTUS PÁN

Of the Father's love begotten   ELW 295, LBW 42
DIVINUM MYSTERIUM

What feast of love   ELW 487, WOV 701   *GREENSLEEVES*

Offering

Of the Father's love begotten   ELW 295, st. 4, LBW 42

Midnight stars make bright the skies   ELW 280

Communion

'Twas in the moon of wintertime   ELW 284, LBW 72

God extends an invitation   ELW 486, LLC 397

Jesus, what a wonderful child   ELW 297

Sending

Praise the Lord, rise up rejoicing   ELW 544, LBW 196

The bells of Christmas   ELW 298, LBW 62

Additional Assembly Songs

There's a star in the east   TFF 58

Holy child   DH 54

☻ Gloria en las alturas   LLC 297

☻ Bell, John. Scotland. "Word of the Father" from *Come, All You People: Shorter Songs for Worship*. SATB. GIA G-4391.

✿ Galanti, Gio/Jorim Kelly. "The Father's Heart" from CCLI.

✿ Gordon, Adoniram Judson/William R. Featherston. "My Jesus I Love Thee" from CCLI.

✿ Herms, Bernie/Jason Mcarthur/Mark Hall/Roger Gildwell. "Until the Whole World Hears" from WT.

✿ Houston, Joel. "Point of Difference" from CCLI.

✿ Hughes, Tim. "Here I Am to Worship" from CCLI.

✿ Redman, Matt/Chris Tomlin. "Wonderful Maker" from WT.

Music for the Day

Choral

● Albrecht, Mark. "Let Our Gladness Have No End." SAB, kybd, perc. KJO 5762.

Burkhardt, Michael. "Let Our Gladness Banish Sadness." SATB, kybd, fl. MSM 50-1290.

Hyslop, Scott. "O Son of God, Eternal Lord of Might." 2 pt, org. AFP 9781451401073.

Langlais, Jean. "Grace to You" from *Three Short Anthems*. SATB. HIN HMC423.

Micheelsen, Hans Friedrich. "Let All Together Praise Our God" from *Four Chorales for the Christmas Season*. SAB. MSM 50-1825.

Pelz, Walter L. "And the Word Became Flesh." SATB, org. AFP 9780800620172.

Children's Choir

Bach, Johann Sebastian. "Beside Thy Manger Here I Stand" from *The Morning Star Choir Book*. CPH 97-6287.

Lindner, Jane. "O Love, How Deep." U, C inst, kybd. GIA G-6253.

Sensmeier, Randall. "A Hymn for the Days after Christmas." U, desc, org. GIA G-4028.

Keyboard / Instrumental

Marohnic, Chuck. "Go Tell It on the Mountain" from *Christmas Jazz: Five Carols for Piano, Set. 2*. Pno. MSM 15-820.

Phillips, Craig. "Toccata on Antioch" from *Joy to the World: Three Preludes for Christmas*. Org. SEL 160-815.

● Purvis, Richard. "Prelude on 'Greensleeves'" from *The Oxford Book of Christmas Organ Music*. Org. OXF 9780193751248.

● Weston, Matthew. "Of the Father's Love Begotten" from *Hymns of the Holy Child*. Pno. MSM 15-821.

Handbell

● Coe, Michael. "Fantasy on 'Greensleeves.'" 3-5 oct, L3. LOR 20/1333L.

● McChesney, Kevin. "Of the Father's Love Begotten." 3-5 oct, L3+. BP HB206.

Mitchell, Kirtsy. "Sing and Dance." 3-5 oct, L3. JEF JHS9392.

☻ = global song
✿ = praise song
● = relates to hymn of the day

January 6, 2014
Epiphany of Our Lord

Epiphany means "manifestation." On this day we celebrate the revelation of Christ to the Gentiles—that is, to all nations. Some Christian traditions celebrate three great epiphanies on this day: the magi's adoration of the Christ child, Jesus' baptism in the Jordan River, and his first miracle in which he changes water into wine. The word and sacraments are for us the great epiphany of God's grace and mercy. We go forth to witness to the light that shines brightly in our midst.

Prayer of the Day

O God, on this day you revealed your Son to the nations by the leading of a star. Lead us now by faith to know your presence in our lives, and bring us at last to the full vision of your glory, through your Son, Jesus Christ our Lord, who lives and reigns with you and the Holy Spirit, one God, now and forever.

or

Almighty and ever-living God, you revealed the incarnation of your Son by the brilliant shining of a star. Shine the light of your justice always in our hearts and over all lands, and accept our lives as the treasure we offer in your praise and for your service, through Jesus Christ, our Savior and Lord, who lives and reigns with you and the Holy Spirit, one God, now and forever.

or

Everlasting God, the radiance of all faithful people, you brought the nations to the brightness of your rising. Fill the world with your glory, and show yourself to all the world through him who is the true light and the bright morning star, your Son, Jesus Christ, our Savior and Lord, who lives and reigns with you and the Holy Spirit, one God, now and forever.

Gospel Acclamation

Alleluia. We have observed his star ¹ at its rising,* and have come to ¹ worship him. *Alleluia.* (Matt. 2:2)

Readings and Psalm

Isaiah 60:1-6

Jerusalem is assured that nations will make a pilgrimage to her, because the light of God's presence is in her midst. The bountiful food of the sea and the profits of international trade will come streaming to Jerusalem and thereby declare God's praise.

Psalm 72:1-7, 10-14

All kings shall bow down before him. (Ps. 72:11)

Ephesians 3:1-12

What had been hidden from previous generations is now made known through the gospel ministry of Paul and others. In Christ both Jews and Gentiles participate in the richness of God's promised salvation.

Matthew 2:1-12

God's promise shines bright in the night as magi follow a star to honor a new king. Strangers from a faraway land, they welcome the long-awaited messiah of Israel.

Preface   Epiphany of Our Lord

Color   White

Prayers of Intercession

The prayers are prepared locally for each occasion. The following examples may be adapted or used as appropriate.

Guided by the light of Christ, who has been made known to the nations, we offer our prayers for the church, the world, and all people in need.

A brief silence.

For the church throughout the world and all servants of the gospel, that the mystery of God's justice and righteousness be revealed to all, let us pray.

Have mercy, O God.

For all plants and animals, seas and skies, snow and rain, and all natural resources, that all creation may grow and thrive and that we do our part as stewards of creation, let us pray.

Have mercy, O God.

For all nations of the world, their rulers and authorities, places torn apart by war and strife (*especially*), that peacemakers be raised up to establish justice throughout the earth, let us pray.

Have mercy, O God.

For the sick and those who care for them, prisoners and those who guard them, victims of oppression and violence and those who serve them as advocates, and those who have no helper (*especially*), that God's all-sufficient grace turn darkness into light, let us pray.

Have mercy, O God.

For the members of the body of Christ in this place, for those returning to school from break, for those continuing their holiday travels, that we be thrilled and rejoice at the coming of Christ, let us pray.

Have mercy, O God.

Here other intercessions may be offered.

In thanksgiving for the faithful departed (*especially*), that their witness to the gospel inspire our confidence in the boundless riches of Christ, let us pray.

Have mercy, O God.

Radiant God, hear the prayers of your people, spoken or silent, for the sake of the one who has made his dwelling among us, your Son, Jesus Christ our Savior.

Amen.

Images in the Readings

The main image is **light**. The star symbolizes a new light in the cosmos. The dawn pierces the thick darkness that has obscured our vision. During January, the Northern Hemisphere experiences a gradual lightening of the darkest time of the year, an appropriate time for the church to praise Christ as the light. This light shines again at the Easter Vigil.

Made popular in hymns, pageants, and crèche sets are the gifts of the magi: **gold, frankincense, and myrrh**. Gold denotes Jesus as a king. Frankincense and myrrh are sweet-smelling resins that were used in offerings to a god and at status burials. These are symbolic gifts for the divine king who has come to die. The birth narratives contain in them the death of Christ.

The ancient political idea was that monarchs were supposed to ensure safety for their subjects. Christ, not Herod, is the true **king** who gives life, rather than death, to the people.

Ideas for the Day

◆ Do you have one of those talking GPS gadgets in your car? A cheerful voice says "in one hundred yards turn left" or "recalculating." The magi looked up and followed the star for their directions, and it involved some detours before it led them to Bethlehem. We may need to change directions on our journey through the twists and turns of life. What will be the star that leads us to Christ?

◆ The magi may have been exotic astrologers bringing strange gifts to a child in a strange land. The whole story is filled with strange incidents, strange gifts, and strangers encountering one another. The movie *The Best Exotic Marigold Hotel* (Fox Searchlight, 2012) tells of a group of seniors who head off to an inexpensive retirement home in exotic India. As unfamiliar and sometimes frustrating as the experience is, when one character asks why he likes it so much, he replies, "The lights, the colors, the vibrancy. The way people see life as a privilege, not as a right." Perhaps Epiphany will open our eyes as well to the holy revealed in what we may have previously thought of as strange, foreign, outside our experience.

◆ What kind of gift bearers have you seen the past several weeks? Folks loading up presents in their car before heading off to spend Christmas with family members? Much has been written about the spiritual significance of the magi's gifts of gold, frankincense, and myrrh. Yet the feast of Epiphany reveals a gift of even greater magnitude and scope. God comes among us in Jesus, bringing gifts of grace, mercy, and forgiveness. God's love is graciously revealed not to a few but to all the world. Let your light shine! You are now "gift bearers" of divine grace for all the world.

◆ *Star light, star bright, first star I see tonight. / Wish I may, wish I might have the wish I wish this night.* Some say that whatever will be is in the stars, or that life just happens. How will the star of Epiphany shine on us during our baptismal trek beyond the manger, to Christ's death and resurrection?

Connections with the Liturgy

Even when today's churches encourage parish contributions via automatic withdrawals from individuals' bank accounts, the liturgy hopes to make clear that at every service, whenever believers celebrate God's gift of grace, they make donations for those in need. Our offerings to help those in need and to pay for the ministries of the church are like the magi's gold, frankincense, and myrrh: they are gifts of financial value that come in symbolic praise to God and in recollection of the death of Christ.

Let the Children Come

What a day for bringing forth our gifts, opening our treasure chests, and paying this King of kings homage! Perhaps a portion of today's offering can be given to a specific global or local cause that benefits children particularly. Or in this season of resolutions, perhaps today is a day of time and talent reflection, making commitments to support outreach, social justice, or other ministerial projects within your community. Are there opportunities for your children to serve with gratitude?

Assembly Song
Gathering

Hail to the Lord's anointed   ELW 311, LBW 87

Arise, your light has come!   ELW 314, WOV 652

O Morning Star, how fair and bright!   ELW 308, LBW 76

Psalmody and Acclamations

Haas, David. "In the Time of God (Psalm 72)." Choir, cant, assembly, kybd, gt, opt hb, 2 C inst. GIA G-5657.

Haugen, Marty. "Every Nation on Earth." Cant, assembly, opt SAB, kybd, gtr, perc. GIA G-5241.

Chepponis, James. "Lord, Every Nation on Earth." SATB, cant, assembly, kybd, gtr, C inst, perc. GIA G-6894.

Chepponis, James. "Festival Alleluia." Cant, opt SATB, assembly, opt br, hb. MSM 80-847A.

Hymn of the Day

What child is this ELW 296, LBW 40 *GREENSLEEVES*

Rise, shine, you people! ELW 665, LBW 493 *WOJTKIEWIECZ*

I want to walk as a child of the light ELW 815, WOV 649 *HOUSTON*

Offering

Bright and glorious is the sky ELW 301, LBW 75

Songs of thankfulness and praise ELW 310, LBW 90

Communion

In the bleak midwinter ELW 294

Come, beloved of the Maker ELW 306

This little light of mine ELW 677, TFF 65

Sending

Shine, Jesus, shine ELW 671, TFF 64, W&P 123, WOV 651

Angels from the realms of glory ELW 275, LBW 50

Additional Assembly Songs

Jesus, the Light of the World TFF 59

Sister Mary TFF 60

☻ Los magos que llegaron a Belén LLC 317

✿ Brown, Brenton. "I Will Remember You" from WT.

✿ Brown, Brenton/Doug Bacon. "Wonderful" from WT.

✿ Doerksen, Brian/Steve Mitchinson. "The Jesus Way" from briandoerksen.com.

✿ Morgan, Rueben/Edward Mote/Jonas Myrin/Eric Liljero. "Cornerstone" from WT.

✿ Reeves, Jesse/Laura Story. "Indescribable" from CCLI.

✿ Sampson, Marty/Lincoln Brewster. "Son of God" from WT.

Music for the Day
Choral

☻ Aguiar, Ernani. Brazil. "Acalanto para o Menino Jesus/Carol for the Baby Jesus" from *World Carols for Choirs.* SATB. OXF 9780193532311.

Averitt, William. "Star in the East." SATB. ECS 7777.

Hopson, Hal. "I Am the Light of Nations (Yo soy la luz del mundo)." SATB, pno, opt fl, tamb. AFP 9780800675868.

How, Martin. "Arise, Shine, for Your Light Has Come." U/2 pt, org, opt assembly. Ionian Arts CH-1009.

Marshall, Jane. "Pondering Mystery." SATB. ECS 7846.

Schalk, Carl F. "A Carol for Epiphany." SATB, org, ob, fc, drm. CPH 98-4097.

Willan, Healey. "Arise, Shine, for Your Light Has Come." SATB, org. CPH 98-1508.

Children's Choir

Cool, Jayne Southwick. "Bright Morning Star." U, kybd. AFP 9780800664213.

Raabe, Nancy. "Epiphany Carol" from *Nativity Triptych.* U, kybd. AFP 9780800678364.

● Vaughan Williams, Ralph. (Stultz, Marie, ed.) "What Child Is This?" 2 pt/3 pt trbl, kybd. MSM 50-9911.

Keyboard / Instrumental

Buxtehude, Dietrich. "Wie schön leuchtet der Morgenstern." Org. Various editions.

● Callahan, Charles. "A Prelude on 'Greensleeves' for Flute and Organ." Fl, org. MSM 20-162.

● Organ, Anne Krentz. "Houston" from *Woven Together: Reflections for Piano and Solo Instrument.* Pno, inst. AFP 9780800658168.

● Young, Jeremy. "Greensleeves" from *A Pianoforte Christmas: Christmas Carols for Piano Solo.* Pno. AFP 9780800655709.

Handbell

Gross, William. "The Star of the Wisemen." 3-5 oct, L4. FLG FLHB317.

● Krug, Jason. "What Child Is This?" 2-3 oct, L2. SF 274746.

● Tucker, Sondra. "I Want to Walk as a Child of the Light." 3-5 oct, L3. AFP 9780800658861.

☻ = global song
✿ = praise song
● = relates to hymn of the day

TIME AFTER EPIPHANY

Preparing for the Time after Epiphany

This is ordinary time, this is no ordinary time. Although the paraments return for a brief time to green, reminiscent of the time after Pentecost, the time after Epiphany is different on two levels. First, although it is not properly the Epiphany season, it still includes many texts evocative of the Epiphany itself, including Jesus' baptism, his presentation at the temple, and his transfiguration. Second, it is a transitional time between the two great feasts of the church year—Christmas and Easter. Many liturgical traditions, including the catechumenate (rites of Christian initiation for adults), although emphasized especially during the Lenten season leading up to Easter, initiate some of their activity during this season. So we consider the season according to these two themes, that of epiphany, and that of transition/preparation.

Lectionary

The central, not-to-be-missed, lectionary emphasis in this season is Jesus' Sermon on the Mount. Gather everything else you do during this season around these texts. Prepare well in advance. Read around in the literature on the sermon. Some of the best resources to assist in your reflections on the sermon include Han Dieter Betz's classic text in the Hermeneia series, *The Sermon on the Mount* (Fortress Press, 1995), and Frederick Dale Bruner's *The Christbook: Matthew 1–12* (Eerdmans, 2007). Either of these volumes will take you deep into the sermon and its relationship to the Gospel of Matthew as a whole.

The lectionary sets the assembly up to hear the Sermon by first offering Jesus' call of the disciples as the text for the third Sunday after Epiphany (Matt. 4:12-23). He calls the disciples, but also proclaims the good news among the people. Then, beginning with the fourth Sunday after Epiphany and continuing the next three Sundays, the gospel is taken from the fifth chapter of Matthew.

One potential problem presents itself—the Presentation of Our Lord falls on a Sunday this year (Feb. 2), thus coinciding with the option of reading Matthew 5:1-12 on that Sunday. As important as our observance of the lesser festival is, if you are going to do a series on the Sermon on the Mount, use the fourth Sunday after Epiphany texts this year rather than the Presentation of Our Lord texts. You

could still use the prayer of the day for Presentation after the Epiphany 4 prayer and sing Simeon's song ("Now, Lord," the *Nunc dimittis*) after communion.

Then to the Sermon on the Mount itself. The four-Sunday structure is as follows:

- February 2/Epiphany 4: Matthew 5:1-12; the beatitudes, also read on All Saints
- February 9/Epiphany 5: Matthew 5:13-20; salt and light, the law and the prophets
- February 16/Epiphany 6: Matthew 5:21-37; concerning anger, adultery, divorce, and oaths
- February 23/Epiphany 7: Matthew 5:38-48; concerning retaliation and love of enemies

It is worth keeping in mind that although Epiphany 7 is the last Sermon on the Mount text in this round of the year A lectionary, the actual sermon continues for two more chapters. In the structure of Matthew's gospel, Jesus ascends, offers this expansive and rich teaching, and then descends the mountain at the conclusion of the sermon. There are more than enough rich resonances, in other words, between the *movement* of the Sermon on the Mount, and the *movement* of the other texts for Epiphany. For example: the ascent and descent of the Transfiguration, the ascent and descent for the Presentation, and even in a parallel manner, Jesus going out to the disciples in their vocations and calling them away to discipleship with him.

One of the most intriguing parallels comes in the gospel reading for January 26. In the context of the beginning of Jesus' public ministry, Matthew indicates that Jesus' ministry happens where it does so that "the people who sat in darkness have seen a great light, and for those who sat in the region and shadow of death light has dawned" (Matt. 4:16). In other words, the epiphany is much more than the first epiphany, the star to the magi and the light of Christ to the shepherds and others. The epiphany is also Jesus' public ministry, his transfiguration on the mount, his presentation at the temple, and his teaching and preaching itself. All of this is Epiphany.

There is much more to be said about the Sermon on the Mount. There is necessary work that needs to be done to ensure that the sermon is not preached as trite moralism, or dismissed away as the impossible ethical imaginings of an ethereal Jesus. Engage a good commentary or three as part of your sermon preparation. For the overall shape of this season, consider the precise way in which the Sermon on the Mount is an epiphany. Then gather all the other epiphanies of this season around it.

Liturgical Arts

Given that ascent and descent are such intrinsic aspects of this season (even the central event of Epiphany, the visit of the wise men, is at least an arrival and return, and given who they are arriving to see, and what they return to, it is easily argued that this too is ascent and descent), the liturgical arts ought to consider how to practice ascent and descent—going up and coming down—in the liturgy.

This can be done in a variety of ways, many of which depend on the architectural opportunities or limitations of your place of worship. Here are a few ideas.

- At least on the festival days (Baptism, Presentation, and Transfiguration), increase the formality of the processional and recessional, or introduce processional or recessional movement if this is not normally done.
- In modular worship spaces, add floor squares to lift the altar higher.
- In simple or spare worship spaces, create a progression of visual movement by adding a bit more green to the worship space each week in the form of draped fabric, ribbon, or plants with trailing vines. Or plan a growing progression of hanging stars, translucent globes, mirrors, or other objects that catch and reflect light over the course of the season.

Ascent and descent also has to do with intellectual content and emotional response. Design the overall flow of worship so the gathering and sending reflect the regularity of daily life (often this is already the case in places where announcements are made at the beginning or conclusion of service). At the two central places in the service, the word and the eucharist, elevate the language, increase the actual volume of the audio system, ring bells, burn incense, do whatever it takes to make those particular moments brighter, more mysterious, awe-inspiring.

Design these liturgical actions and the worship space itself in the right ways, and you will be well served throughout the time after Epiphany. You will be all set to observe the Epiphany, Baptism, Presentation, and Transfiguration of Our Lord, as well as make the most of the texts from the Sermon on the Mount. Signpost this somehow in your worship resources, and the assembly will see how each of these special observances resonates with the others and offers a cohesive sense of what it means to "go up on the mount with the Lord."

Music

Evangelical Lutheran Worship contains many hymns with connections to the Sermon on the Mount. See if you can sing all of them in this season. They include: "Blest are they" (ELW 728), "Rejoice in God's saints" (ELW 418), "Go, make disciples" (ELW 540), "Christ, Be Our Light" (ELW 715), "This little light of mine" (ELW 677), and "We Are Called" (ELW 720). Additionally, three hymns are especially evocative of the call of the disciples: "Come, follow me, the Savior spake" (ELW 799), "Jesus calls us; o'er the tumult" (ELW 696), and "You have come down to the lakeshore" (ELW 817).

Then there are hymns especially designated for these days. Of the hymns for the time after Epiphany, the ones that especially evoke the ascent/descent motif include: "As with gladness men of old" (ELW 302), "When Jesus came to Jordan" (ELW 305), "Come, beloved of the Maker" (ELW 306), "O Lord, now let your servant" (ELW 313), "How good, Lord, to be here!" (ELW 315), and "Jesus on the mountain peak" (ELW 317).

Rites of Christian Initiation

Many Christian communities, having already offered a period of inquiry for those new to the faith, begin their formal process of welcome and exploration during this season. For rich, practical resources to assist in the planning, see *Go Make Disciples: An Invitation to Baptismal Living* (Augsburg Fortress, 2012).

One reason why attention to rites of Christian initiation is so vital during the time after Epiphany has to do with the presence of so many rites of initiation in the biblical texts themselves. In this season we commemorate Jesus' baptism in the Jordan river and his presentation in the temple, not to mention the rite of initiation of the disciples as they are called by their Lord. Even many of the secondary texts read during this season mark various kinds of initiation, including the initiation of the Gentiles into the church (Acts 10:34-43), the call of the Servant (Isa. 49:1-7), and the call of Paul and clarification about who and through whom God calls (1 Cor. 1:1-18). Thus, especially in congregations where a catechumenal formation process is in place, the lectionary itself offers ample opportunity for deepened reflection on what it means to live as a disciple of Jesus.

WORSHIP TEXTS FOR THE TIME AFTER EPIPHANY

Confession and Forgiveness

*All may make the sign of the cross, the sign marked at baptism,
as the presiding minister begins.*

Blessed be the holy Trinity, ✢ one God,
who forgives all our sin,
whose mercy endures forever.
Amen.

Let us come into the light of Christ,
confessing our need for God's mercy.

Silence is kept for reflection.

Holy and faithful God,
**we so often choose our own way instead of yours.
We think we can evade your commandments.
We have spoken in ways that kill,
strayed with our hearts,
betrayed friends, and hated enemies.
We have broken our promises.
Search us deeply and create us anew.
Lift the heavy burden of our sin
and free us to follow your way of life.**
Amen.

"Call upon me," says the Lord, "and I will answer."
Our God has come among us to loose every bond
and set us free from all that weighs us down.
Receive the forgiveness of all your sins
in the name of ✢ Jesus Christ,
our crucified and risen Savior.
Amen.

Offering Prayer

God of all creation,
all you have made is good,
and your love endures forever.
You bring forth bread from the earth
and fruit from the vine.
Nourish us with these gifts,
that we might be for the world
signs of your gracious presence
in Jesus Christ, our Savior and Lord.
Amen.

Invitation to Communion

Behold the Lamb of God
who takes away the sin of the world!
Blessed are all who are called to the supper of the Lamb.

Prayer after Communion

Lord, it is good for us to be here,
for we have tasted your glory in this holy meal.
Continue your goodness as we go out from here.
Open our eyes to see your face shining in every person,
and send us to be your servants in every place,
for you are the life and light of all,
both now and forever.
Amen.

Sending of Communion

Compassionate God, as Jesus called disciples to follow him,
bless those who go forth to share your word and sacrament
with those who are *sick/homebound/imprisoned.*
May these gifts be signs of our love and prayers,
that through the sharing of the body and blood of Christ,
all may know your grace and healing
revealed in Jesus Christ our Lord.
Amen.

Blessing

May the God of glory dwell in you richly,
name you beloved,
and shine brightly on your path;
and the blessing of almighty God,
the Father, the ☩ Son, and the Holy Spirit,
be upon you and remain with you always.
Amen.

Dismissal

Go in peace. Christ is your light.
Thanks be to God.

SEASONAL RITES FOR THE TIME AFTER EPIPHANY

Celebrating a Baptismal Anniversary

This order may be given to a family on the baptismal day with instructions to keep it with the baptismal candle. For other suggestions on celebrating a baptismal anniversary, see "10 Ways to Celebrate Your Child's Baptismal Anniversary" and "Ways to Celebrate Your Godchild's Anniversary" in Washed and Welcome: A Baptism Sourcebook, *and* Living the Promises of Baptism: 101 Ideas for Parents *(both Augsburg Fortress, 2010), both part of the Washed and Welcome family of baptismal resources.*

Gather around a table where you usually share a meal, or at some other quiet place in your home, with a bowl of water and the baptismal candle. As the candle is lighted, the leader begins.

In the name of the Father, and of the ✚ Son,
and of the Holy Spirit.
Amen.

We remember and give thanks for the baptism of *name*.
Thanks be to Jesus for the saving waters of baptism.

A hymn may be sung. One of these from Evangelical Lutheran Worship *or another favorite may be used:*

451   We are baptized in Christ Jesus
456   Baptized in water
459   Wade in the water
613   Thy holy wings
781   Children of the heavenly father
815   I want to walk as a child of the light

One of these or another passage of scripture is read.
Genesis 1:1-2   *The Spirit moved over the waters*
Genesis 8:1-5   *God saves Noah and his family*
Exodus 14:21—15:1   *The Israelites come safely through the sea*
Exodus 17:1-7   *Water gushes from the rock*
2 Kings 5:1-14   *Naaman's leprosy is washed clean*
Isaiah 55   *Isaiah calls all who thirst*
Matthew 3:13-17   *Jesus is baptized*
Acts 2:37-47   *The newly baptized are added to the church*
Acts 8:26-40   *Philip baptizes a new Christian*

The group joins together in reading and discussing one of the following.
The Lord's Prayer *(ages 1-5)*
The Apostles' Creed *(ages 4-8)*
The Ten Commandments *(ages 7-12)*

These foundational baptismal texts and their explanations can be found in Evangelical Lutheran Worship, *along with Luther's explanations, on pages 1160 and following. They encompass the three pillars of faith that parents and sponsors committed to teach their child at the time of his or her baptism.*

Rejoice in sharing memories and stories of the baptismal day.

The leader continues.
Let us bless the Lord.
Thanks be to God.

Almighty God bless us and keep us,
by the Holy Spirit guiding our days, our thoughts,
and our actions,
in the grace of Jesus Christ.
Amen.

All join in dipping their hands in the water and making the sign of the cross on their own or one another's forehead.

Baptismal Anniversary Greeting

Congregations that mark baptismal anniversaries of their members in any way may wish to send the following message, or something similar, on a note card, postcard, or in an electronic message.

Happy baptismal anniversary!

As you celebrate another year in the life of Christ and his church on *date*, we invite you to reflect on your baptism and how it guides you in your daily life and work. Our *congregation/pastoral leadership* will be remembering you in prayer as you celebrate this anniversary.

Jesus said, I am the light of the world.
Whoever follows me will have the light of life. (John 8:12)

Almighty God, who gives us a new birth by water and the Holy Spirit and forgives us all our sins, strengthen us in all goodness and by the power of the Holy Spirit keep us in eternal life through Jesus Christ our Lord.

Week of Prayer for Christian Unity

The Week of Prayer for Christian Unity is January 18–25. Resources for observing this week of prayer may be obtained from the Graymoor Ecumenical and Interreligious Institute, 475 Riverside Dr., Room 1960, New York, NY 10115; email: lmnygeii.org@aol.com; phone: 212/870-2330; or at www.geii.org. Resources on the website include a brief history of the Week of Prayer for Christian Unity, an ecumenical celebration of the word of God, music suggestions, bulletin announcements, and more.

Blessing of the Candles

On the feast of the Presentation of Our Lord (Candlemas), February 2, some traditions dedicate the candles to be used in worship during the following year. The candles may be brought forward with the offering, or they may be placed on a table near the altar prior to the service.

The presiding minister may lead this prayer before the offering prayer.
Let us pray.
Blessed are you, O Lord our God, ruler of the universe.
You have enriched our lives
with every good and perfect gift;
you have commanded us
to show your splendor to our children
and to praise you with lives of love, justice, and joy.
Accept these candles which we offer in thanksgiving;
may they be to us a sign of Christ,
the Light of the world,
the light no darkness can overcome.
Bring us all at length to your perfect kingdom,
where you live and reign with the Son and the Holy Spirit,
now and forever.
Amen.

January 12, 2014

Baptism of Our Lord
Lectionary 1

In the waters of the Jordan, Jesus is revealed as the beloved Son of God. Through this great epiphany, Jesus fulfills all righteousness and becomes the servant of God who will bring forth justice and be a light to the nations. In the waters of baptism we too are washed by the Word, anointed by the Spirit, and named God's beloved children. Our baptismal mission is to proclaim good news to all who are oppressed or in need of God's healing.

Prayer of the Day

O God our Father, at the baptism of Jesus you proclaimed him your beloved Son and anointed him with the Holy Spirit. Make all who are baptized into Christ faithful to their calling to be your daughters and sons, and empower us all with your Spirit, through Jesus Christ, our Savior and Lord, who lives and reigns with you and the Holy Spirit, one God, now and forever.

Gospel Acclamation

Alleluia. A voice from heaven said, "This is my Son, ¹ the Beloved,* with whom I ¹ am well pleased." *Alleluia.* (Matt. 3:17)

Readings and Psalm

Isaiah 42:1-9

God's servant Israel is endowed with the Spirit in order to bring justice to the nations. The servant will not exercise authority boisterously or with violence, nor will weariness ever prevent the fulfilling of the servant's task. God's old promises have been fulfilled; the new assignment of the servant is to bring light to the nations.

Psalm 29

The voice of the Lord is upon the waters. (Ps. 29:3)

Acts 10:34-43

Peter crosses the sharp religious boundary separating Jews from Gentiles and proclaims the good news of God's inclusive forgiveness in Jesus' name to Cornelius, a Roman centurion. As a result of Peter's preaching, Cornelius and his family become the first Gentiles to be baptized in the name of Jesus Christ.

Matthew 3:13-17

Before Jesus begins his ministry, he is baptized by John, touched by the Spirit, and identified publicly as God's child.

Preface Baptism of Our Lord

Color White

Prayers of Intercession

The prayers are prepared locally for each occasion. The following examples may be adapted or used as appropriate.

Guided by the light of Christ, who has been made known to the nations, we offer our prayers for the church, the world, and all people in need.

A brief silence.

For the community of the baptized throughout the world and its leaders, that justice and forgiveness be proclaimed to all, let us pray.

Have mercy, O God.

For the beauty of creation, trees and animals, clean water, and favorable weather, that all creatures live abundantly on our fragile planet, let us pray.

Have mercy, O God.

For all in authority at the local, state, national, and international levels, that they rule with equity and sincerity of heart; for relief workers and those who support them, let us pray.

Have mercy, O God.

For the oppressed, the imprisoned, the sick, those living with HIV/AIDS, and all who call out for help (*especially*), that all who dwell on the earth find comfort, peace, and redemption through Christ, let us pray.

Have mercy, O God.

For this congregation and all who have been washed in the waters of baptism (*especially those who celebrate their baptisms today*), for those inquiring about the gift of baptism and life in Christ, and for those who are absent from this gathering, let us pray.

Have mercy, O God.

Here other intercessions may be offered.

In thanksgiving for those who have died in the faith (*especially*), that the grace of Christ in their lives guide us in our vocation as Christians throughout the world, let us pray.

Have mercy, O God.

Radiant God, hear the prayers of your people, spoken or silent, for the sake of the one who has made his dwelling among us, your Son, Jesus Christ our Savior.
Amen.

Images in the Readings

There can be no life as we know without **water**. Christians see in the waters of baptism the matrix of our new life in Christ. The font is like the Jordan, a river of water that leads us to the new land of promise.

The **dove** functions in several biblical stories as a symbol of the presence of God's Holy Spirit. The white color matches the baptismal garment. Secular culture connects the dove especially with peace, which Acts cites as the message of Jesus' preaching.

The gospel reading uses the image of **Son** to describe Jesus' identity; the first reading uses the image of **servant**; and the second reading speaks of Jesus as **the anointed one**. Each of these images conveys something of the meaning of Jesus for believers. It is instructive to think about "Son" and "Christ" as metaphors before these words became literalized as part of Jesus' name.

Once again **light** is an image for the power of God. Early Christians referred to baptism as enlightenment.

Ideas for the Day

◆   On this day when the readings before us each in its own way give testimony and witness to what God has done, is doing, or will do through Jesus Christ, the theme of testimony and witness is an apt one. Both testimony and witness are a public profession or affirmation of one's religious faith or experience. Lutherans and other mainline Protestants are known for not being very verbal, expressive, or public about their personal religious faith or experience. Encouraging the opening and closing of every leadership and small-group meeting with prayer led by different members of the group could be a way to open up conversations with God and conversations with others about God. A commitment to be more verbal and expressive about one's own faith—in preaching, teaching, and conversation—could model some different ways of expression for others.

◆   Disturbed water creates ripples, concentric circles that continue to move out from the center of the disturbance until they lose their power, or run into something that stops them. John the Baptist literally disturbed the waters of the Jordan River as he baptized Jesus of Nazareth. The figurative ripples made in that baptismal water have neither lost their power nor run into something that could stop them. Or have they? Have your own baptismal waters stopped being disturbed? Have the ripples in the baptismal waters of your congregational leaders seemingly lost their power or focus? Has your stated congregational mission or vision run into something that has stopped its baptismal ripples from flowing into your wider surrounding community?

◆   The passages from both Isaiah (". . . a light to the nations") and Acts (". . . everyone who believes in him . . .") emphasize that the good news and the kingdom of God are inclusive and not only for the covenant community. What is the temperature in your congregation regarding the fostering of ecumenical or interfaith relationships? How can you use these texts to encourage such relationships? How are you providing leadership in this important arena of ministry? Consider introducing yourself to an ecumenical or interfaith neighbor in your church community whom you have not yet met.

Connections with the Liturgy

In the thanksgiving for baptism, we praise God with these words: "At the river your Son was baptized by John and anointed with the Holy Spirit," which Spirit now has anointed us for service.

Let the Children Come

This is the first of four major baptismal festival days in the church year. The Vigil of Easter, Pentecost, and All Saints day will follow. On these days, let the children come to the font during the hymn of the day. They can carry the things needed for baptism: the candle, robe, towel, shell, and oil. Have an older child carry a pitcher of water that can be poured into the font during the thanksgiving for baptism, connecting sight and sound and word. The children will have a great view of the action and maybe they will be splashed a little during this great bath.

Assembly Song
Gathering

All who believe and are baptized   ELW 442, LBW 194
Christ, when for us you were baptized   ELW 304
God, whose almighty word   ELW 673, LBW 400

Psalmody and Acclamations

Hopson, Hal H. "Psalm 29" from TP.
Smith, Geoffrey Boulton. "Give Strength to Your People, Lord" from PS1.
Mummert, Mark. "Psalm 29," Refrain 1, from PSCY.
Ferguson, John. *Gospel Acclamations for Advent–Transfiguration.*

Hymn of the Day

When Jesus came to Jordan   ELW 305, WOV 647   *KING'S LYNN*
I bind unto myself today   ELW 450, LBW 188
   ST. PATRICK'S BREASTPLATE
Crashing waters at creation   ELW 455   *STUTTGART*

Offering

Wash, O God, our sons and daughters   ELW 445, TFF 112,
WOV 697

What child is this   ELW 296, LBW 40

Communion

Light shone in darkness   ELW 307

O living Breath of God   ELW 407, LLC 368

Spirit of God, descend upon my heart   ELW 800, LBW 486

We have seen the Lord   ELW 869

Sending

Wade in the water   ELW 459, TFF 114

Oh, love, how deep   ELW 322, LBW 88

We have seen the Lord   ELW 869

Additional Assembly Songs

The virgin Mary had a baby boy   TFF 53

Sister Mary   TFF 60

⊕ Belihu, Almaz. Ethiopia. "When Jesus Worked Here on Earth"
from *Set Free: A Collection of African Hymns*. SATB. AFP
9780806600451.

✧ Cross, Henry/Marc James. "Everything That I Am" from WT.

✧ Doerksen, Brian/Brian Theissen/Michael Hansen. "The River" from
briandoerksen.com.

✧ Hall, Charlie/Kendall Combes/Todd Cromwell. "Chasing" from WT.

✧ Keyes, Aaron/Andy Lehman. "Not Guilty Anymore" from WT.

✧ Mann, Robin. "See Yourself" from CCLI.

✧ Rend Collective Experiment. "You Are My Vision" from WT.

Music for the Day
Choral

Bengtson, Bruce. "Behold My Servant." SATB, org. AFP
9780800659127.

Helman, Michael. "Christ, When for Us You Were Baptized." SAB,
kybd. AFP 9780800674052.

Moore, Bob. "Down Galilee's Slow Roadways." SATB, C inst, opt
bass. GIA G-5502.

Schalk, Carl F. "Baptized in Living Waters." SATB, br qrt, timp. GIA
G-6053.

Weber, Paul D. "When You Pass Through the Waters." U or 2 pt
mxd, pno. MSM 50-0501.

Children's Choir

Atteberry, John. "And the Glory of the Lord Shall Be Revealed." SA,
pno. GIA G-7709.

Bach, J. S. "The Only Son from Heaven" from *The Morning Star
Choir Book*. U/2 pt, kybd. CPH 97-6287.

Hildebrand, Kevin. "God's Own Child, I Gladly Say It." U/2pt, kybd,
trbl inst, opt assembly. CPH 98-3981.

Keyboard / Instrumental

• Biery, James. "King's Lynn" from *Contemplations on Four English
Hymn Tunes*. Org. MSM 10-621.

Oliver, Curt. "Variations on 'O Morning Star, How Fair and
Bright!'" from *Built on a Rock: Keyboard Seasons*. Pno. AFP
9780800654962.

Organ, Anne Krentz. "Baptized and Set Free" from *Come to Us,
Creative Spirit: Piano Reflections*. Pno. AFP 9780800659042.

• Peek, Richard. "Prelude on St. Patrick's Breastplate." Org. MSM
10-845.

Handbell

• Page, Anna Laura. "Praise Ye the Father." 2-3 oct, L1. ALF 19647.

Sherman, Arnold. "In the Beauty of Holiness" (based on Psalm
29:2). 3-6 oct hb, opt 3-4 oct hc, L3. RR HB0038.

Tucker, Margaret. "Shall We Gather at the River." 3-5 oct hb, opt 3-4
oct hc, L2. CG CGB298.

Wednesday, January 15

Martin Luther King Jr., renewer of society, martyr, died 1968

Martin Luther King Jr. is remembered as an American
prophet of justice among races and nations, a Christian
whose faith undergirded his advocacy of vigorous yet non-
violent action for racial equality. A pastor of churches in
Montgomery, Alabama, and Atlanta, Georgia, his witness
was taken to the streets in such other places as Birming-
ham, Alabama, where he was arrested and jailed while
protesting against segregation. He preached nonviolence
and demanded that love be returned for hate. Awarded the
Nobel Peace Prize in 1964, he was killed by an assassin on
April 4, 1968. Though most commemorations are held on
the date of the person's death, many churches hold commemorations near Dr. King's birth date of January 15, in
conjunction with the American civil holiday honoring him.
An alternate date for the commemoration would be his
death date, April 4.

Friday, January 17

Antony of Egypt, renewer of the church, died around 356

Antony was born in Qemen-al-Arous, Upper Egypt, and
was one of the earliest Egyptian desert fathers. Born to
Christian parents from whom he inherited a large estate,
he took personally Jesus' message to sell all that you have,
give to the poor, and follow Christ. After making arrangements to provide for the care of his sister, he gave away his

⊕ = global song
✧ = praise song
● = relates to hymn of the day

inheritance and became a hermit. Later, he became the head of a group of monks who lived in a cluster of huts and devoted themselves to communal prayer, worship, and manual labor under Antony's direction. The money they earned from their work was distributed as alms. Antony and his monks also preached and counseled those who sought them out. Antony and the desert fathers serve as a reminder that certain times and circumstances call Christians to stand apart from the surrounding culture and renounce the world in service to Christ.

Pachomius, renewer of the church, died 346

Another of the desert fathers, Pachomius (puh-KOME-ee-us) was born in Egypt about 290. He became a Christian during his service as a soldier. In 320 he went to live as a hermit in Upper Egypt, where other hermits lived nearby. Pachomius organized them into a religious community in which the members prayed together and held their goods in common. His rule for monasteries influenced both Eastern and Western monasticism through the Rule of Basil and the Rule of Benedict, respectively.

Saturday, January 18
Confession of Peter
Week of Prayer for Christian Unity begins

The Week of Prayer for Christian Unity is framed by two commemorations, the Confession of Peter (a relatively recent addition to the calendar) and the older Conversion of Paul. Both apostles are remembered together on June 29, but these two days give us an opportunity to focus on key events in each of their lives. Today we remember that Peter was led by God's grace to acknowledge Jesus as "the Christ, the Son of the living God" (Matt. 16:16). This confession is the common confession that unites us with Peter and with all Christians of every time and place.

January 19, 2014
Second Sunday after Epiphany
Lectionary 2

Today's gospel opens with further reflection on Jesus' baptism. He is the Lamb of God who takes away the sin of the world, and the one anointed by the Spirit. In the liturgy we come and see Christ revealed among us in word and meal. We go forth to invite others to come and worship the Holy One, and to receive the gifts of grace and peace made known among us.

Prayer of the Day

Holy God, our strength and our redeemer, by your Spirit hold us forever, that through your grace we may worship you and faithfully serve you, follow you and joyfully find you, through Jesus Christ, our Savior and Lord.

Gospel Acclamation

Alleluia. In the ¹ Word was life,* and the life was the light ¹ of all people. *Alleluia.* (John 1:4)

Readings and Psalm

Isaiah 49:1-7

Here the servant Israel speaks for herself and acknowledges herself as God's secret weapon. Called before her birth like Jeremiah and John the Baptist, the servant is not only to restore Israel itself. The servant's ultimate assignment is to bring news of God's victory to the ends of the earth. God in faithfulness has chosen Israel for this task.

Psalm 40:1-11

I love to do your will, O my God. (Ps. 40:8)

1 Corinthians 1:1-9

Though God's church in Corinth is a fractious congregation beset with many conflicts, Paul opens this letter by spotlighting the multiple ways God has enriched and sustained its life as part of the divine call into the fellowship of our Lord Jesus Christ.

John 1:29-42

John the Baptist's witness to Jesus initiates a chain of testimony as his disciples begin to share with others what they have found.

Preface   Sundays

Color   Green

Prayers of Intercession

The prayers are prepared locally for each occasion. The following examples may be adapted or used as appropriate.

Guided by the light of Christ, who has been made known to the nations, we offer our prayers for the church, the world, and all people in need.

A brief silence.

For the church throughout the world, that it proclaim salvation through Christ to the ends of the earth, let us pray.

Have mercy, O God.

For all coastlands and waters, for the well-being of creation, and for our proper stewardship of those gifts of God, let us pray.

Have mercy, O God.

For the leaders of the world at all levels, for those who bring about peace in war-torn areas (*especially*), and for all people of faith everywhere, that compassion and love thrive, let us pray.

Have mercy, O God.

For those who are suffering in mind, body, or spirit (*especially*), and for those who care for the suffering, that God's steadfast love and faithfulness through Christ bring about healing and wholeness, let us pray.

Have mercy, O God.

For the fellowship gathered in this place, for the spiritual gifts of each of our members, for those celebrating significant events in their lives, that the Holy Spirit guide us in our work and our journeys, let us pray.

Have mercy, O God.

Here other intercessions may be offered.

In thanksgiving for the saints who have died in Christ (*especially Henry, Bishop of Uppsala*), that the witness of their faithfulness inspire us in our Christian lives, let us pray.

Have mercy, O God.

Radiant God, hear the prayers of your people, spoken or silent, for the sake of the one who has made his dwelling among us, your Son, Jesus Christ our Savior.

Amen.

Images in the Readings

Once again we are given images of **water**, **light**, and **dove** (see Baptism of Our Lord).

The fourth gospel refers to Jesus as the **Lamb** of God. Several New Testament writers used this image to give salvific meaning to Jesus' execution. The lamb as apocalyptic conqueror, the lamb as suffering servant, and the paschal lamb are all possibilities of what the earliest Christians meant by the image. The medieval church stressed Christ as sacrificial lamb, whose blood takes away sin.

God calls. The scriptures include many **call** narratives, in testifying that this God is the kind of deity who knows us by name and who calls us into a new identity. All three readings refer to such a call. In the poem from Second Isaiah, the call comes to the prophet even before birth. The church has described baptism as our call to servanthood, and many churches use the imagery of the call in descriptions of their clergy.

Ideas for the Day

◆   The texts from both Isaiah 49 and John 1 bring to mind the mission of the Christian church: to make known God's love through Jesus Christ. How does your congregation understand mission? How can you help them understand it more clearly and more contextually? Consistent missional emphasis is needed from our pulpits and in all teaching/learning opportunities if mission is to be a priority. How do you incorporate a missional emphasis in your preaching? Are mission references and conversations reserved for special times of the year, or is mission incorporated into everything the congregation does?

◆   Many people tend to think of mission as something we support in other countries, or in varying settings in our own North American context. A sermon or teaching illustration that could help make mission a more local concept could be to identify the mission and purpose of some of the nonchurch institutions and businesses in your community. Note that even as necessary as their purposes might be in the community, none of them have the purpose of making known God's love through Jesus Christ. That is the unique mission of the Christian church. How can it be done more relationally and effectively in your local context? From a marketing perspective, what is it that you would be inviting your community to "come and see" (John 1:39)?

◆   One resource that could feed missional conversations is *Unbinding the Gospel: Real Life Evangelism,* by Martha Grace Reese (2nd ed., St. Louis: Chalice Press, 2011). She speaks clearly to pastors eager to foster a hopeful vision for what a missional church can be—and not with gimmicks. The *Unbinding the Gospel* series also offers other helpful resources. Another enjoyable and effective resource is *It: How Churches and Leaders Can Get It and Keep It,* by Craig Groeschel (Grand Rapids, MI: Zondervan, 2008). It is a well-written and humorous book about that seemingly unexplainable attraction that draws people to church, and some of the tried-and-true paradigms that undergird having "It."

Connections with the Liturgy

Many Christians sing "Lamb of God" when they come forward for communion to receive this blood of mercy and peace. Some pastors begin their sermons by quoting Paul, "Grace to you and peace from God our Father and the Lord Jesus Christ."

Let the Children Come

"Come and see." Before or after worship, invite the children to the place (or places) from which the Word is proclaimed and "fleshed out" in the readings and in preaching. Allow them to look, touch, and stand behind it. Show them where the Bible or lectionary is placed.

Assembly Song
Gathering

O day full of grace   ELW 627, LBW 161
O God of light   ELW 507, LBW 237
The only Son from heaven   ELW 309

Psalmody

"Here I Am." *Psallite* A-96.
Kelly/Weber. "Psalm 40" from TP.
Folkening, John. "Psalm 40:1-11" from PWA.

Hymn of the Day

Christ, Be Our Light   ELW 715   *CHRIST, BE OUR LIGHT*
He comes to us as one unknown   ELW 737, WOV 768   *REPTON*
You are holy   ELW 525   *DU ÄR HELIG*

Offering

This little light of mine   ELW 677, TFF 65
Have no fear, little flock   ELW 764

Communion

O Lamb of God/Oi, Jumalan Karitsa   ELW 197
Jesus, come! For we invite you   ELW 312, WOV 648
You are holy   ELW 525
Now behold the Lamb   ELW 341, TFF 128

Sending

Jesus calls us; o'er the tumult   ELW 696
Rise, shine, you people!   ELW 665

Additional Assembly Songs

The Lord is my light   TFF 61
You are my hiding place   W&P 160

⟐ Hamba nathi/Come, walk with us GS2 6
✿ Brown, Brenton/Don Williams. "Jesus You Are Worthy" from WT.
✿ Getty, Keith/Stuart Townend. "In Christ Alone" from CCLI.
✿ Gungor, Michael/Lisa Gungor. "Glory Is Here" from WT.
✿ Hall, Mark/Matthew West. "The Well" from CCLI.
✿ Houston, Joel/Matt Crocker. "Tear Down the Walls" from CCLI.
✿ Maher, Matt/Ike Ndolo/Tam Le. "Lamb of God" from WT.

Music for the Day
Choral

African American spiritual, arr. Mark Sedio. "We Believe That This Is Jesus" from *Global Choral Sounds*. SATB. CPH 98-3720WEB.

Behnke, John. "The Only Son from Heaven." 2 pt, kybd. CPH 98-3816.

Graun, Carl Heinrich. "Lamb of God." SATB, org. CPH 98-3995.

Helgen, John. "Spirit of God, Descend." SATB, kybd, cello. AFP 9780800676377.

Miller, Aaron David. "Jesus Is Calling." SATB. AFP 9780800623821.

Pelz, Walter L. "God Is Faithful." SATB, org. GIA G-3762.

Children's Choir

Christopherson, Dorothy. "Followers of the Lamb." U, pno, fl, xyl, tamb, fc. CG CGA672.

Horman, John D. "Behold the Lamb of God." U, fl, cello, pno. GIA G-7715.

Tucker, Margaret R. "Come to Me." U/2 pt, pno, opt fl. CG CGA1221.

Keyboard / Instrumental

Bach, J. S. "Herr Christ, du einig Gotts Sohn" from *Das Orgelbüchlein*. Org. Various editions.

● Callahan, Charles. "Repton" from *O God beyond All Praising: Seven Pieces for Organ on English Hymntunes*. Org. MSM 10-799.

● Mossing, Sally Drennan. "Christ, Be Our Light" from *Christ, Be Our Light: Music for the Church Pianist*. Pno. AFP 9780800663858.

Oliver, Curt. "Variations on 'Dearest Jesus, We Are Here'" from *Built on a Rock: Keyboard Seasons*. Pno. AFP 9780800654962.

Handbell

Gramann, Fred. "Lumière." 3-5 oct, L4. AGEHR AG35174.

McChesney, Kevin. "Arise, Shine, Thy Light Has Come." 3-5 oct, L4. JEF JHS9108.

Thompson, Martha Lynn. "I Waited for the Lord" (based on Psalm 40). 3-5 oct hb, opt C inst, opt vcs. GIA G-7364.

Sunday, January 19

Henry, Bishop of Uppsala, martyr, died 1156

Henry, an Englishman, became bishop of Uppsala, Sweden, in 1152 and is regarded as the patron of Finland. He traveled to Finland with the king of Sweden on a mission trip and remained there to organize the church. He was murdered in Finland by a man he had rebuked and who was disciplined by the church. Henry's burial place became a center of pilgrimage. His popularity as a saint is strong in both Sweden and Finland.

Tuesday, January 21

Agnes, martyr, died around 304

Agnes was a girl of about thirteen living in Rome, who had chosen a life of service to Christ as a virgin, despite the Roman emperor Diocletian's ruling that had outlawed all Christian activity. The details of her martyrdom are not clear, but she gave witness to her faith and was put to death as a result, most likely by the sword. Since her death, the church has honored her as one of the chief martyrs of her time.

Saturday, January 25

Conversion of Paul
Week of Prayer for Christian Unity ends

Today the Week of Prayer for Christian Unity comes to an end. The church remembers how a man of Tarsus named Saul, a former persecutor of the early Christian church, was turned around by God's grace to become one of its chief preachers. The risen Christ appeared to Paul on the road to Damascus and called him to proclaim the gospel. The narratives describing Paul's conversion in the Acts of the Apostles, Galatians, and 1 Corinthians inspire this commemoration, which was first celebrated among the Christians of Gaul.

⟐ = global song
✿ = praise song
● = relates to hymn of the day

January 26, 2014
Third Sunday after Epiphany
Lectionary 3

Jesus begins his public ministry by calling fishers to leave their nets and follow him. In Jesus the kingdom of God has come near. We who have walked in darkness have seen a great light. We see this light most profoundly in the cross—as God suffers with us and all who are oppressed by sickness, sin, or evil. Light dawns for us as we gather around the word, the font, and the holy table. We are then sent to share the good news that others may be "caught" in the net of God's grace and mercy.

Prayer of the Day

Lord God, your lovingkindness always goes before us and follows after us. Summon us into your light, and direct our steps in the ways of goodness that come through the cross of your Son, Jesus Christ, our Savior and Lord.

Gospel Acclamation

Alleluia. Jesus preached the good news ⎜ of the kingdom*
and cured every sickness a- ⎜ mong the people. *Alleluia.*
(Matt. 4:23)

Readings and Psalm

Isaiah 9:1-4

The northern tribes of Zebulun and Naphtali experienced the gloom of defeat by Assyrian military forces, but they are assured that their condition will be reversed when God makes a light-filled appearance. The joy they will experience will resemble celebrations of great harvests, because God will deliver them from everything that diminishes or oppresses them.

Psalm 27:1, 4-9

The LORD is my light and my salvation. (Ps. 27:1)

1 Corinthians 1:10-18

Paul calls on the Corinthians to end their dissensions and share the unified outlook of the gospel. Discord arises when we forget that we belong not to human leaders or institutions but to Christ. Indeed, the unifying word of the cross is the center of the gospel and the power of God's salvation.

Matthew 4:12-23

Jesus begins his public ministry shortly after John the Baptist is imprisoned by Herod. He proclaims the nearness of God's reign and calls four fishermen to be his first disciples.

Preface   Sundays

Color   Green

Prayers of Intercession

The prayers are prepared locally for each occasion. The following examples may be adapted or used as appropriate.

Guided by the light of Christ, who has been made known to the nations, we offer our prayers for the church, the world, and all people in need.

A brief silence.

For Christ's church on earth and for those who proclaim the good news of the kingdom, that all divisions cease, let us pray.

Have mercy, O God.

For sky and sea, fish and bird, and the beauty of the whole creation, that God's goodness be seen through our everyday surroundings, let us pray.

Have mercy, O God.

For our political and social leaders, that they use their power justly, and for all the nations of the world, that peace and understanding prevail, let us pray.

Have mercy, O God.

For all who call upon the Lord for help: those dealing with gloom or anguish, those who are afraid, those suffering from malaria or other illnesses (*especially*), and for those who seek shelter, that God provide them with compassionate caregivers and advocates, let us pray.

Have mercy, O God.

For the followers of Jesus Christ gathered here, that we be guided by the Holy Spirit to proclaim the cross as the power of God, let us pray.

Have mercy, O God.

Here other intercessions may be offered.

In thanksgiving for the faithful departed (*especially the biblical missionaries Timothy, Titus, and Silas*), that their witness to the spread of God's word inspire us in our doings, let us pray.

Have mercy, O God.

Radiant God, hear the prayers of your people, spoken or silent, for the sake of the one who has made his dwelling among us, your Son, Jesus Christ our Savior.

Amen.

Images in the Readings

The gospel describes the first disciples as catchers of **fish**. This may be a memory of the profession of some in the Jesus movement. As well, it grounds the early Christian imagery of baptism as water, believers as water-dwellers, the net as the gospel, and the boat as the church. The Greek of the early Christian creed, "Jesus Christ, God's Son, Savior," presents the acronym *ichthus*, meaning "fish," and fish show up in much Christian iconography.

The gospel introduces the image of "the **kingdom** of heaven." Arguably the most important image in the New Testament, the kingdom invoked Israelite memory of a time of political independence. Yet this kingdom is, according to Matthew, "of heaven," that is, of a realm beyond this earth and was probably, in accord with Jewish sensibilities, a circumlocution for "God." The designation of Jesus as Christ, that is, the one anointed by God for power to reign, relies on the kingdom imagery. It is not an image easily accessible for twenty-first century believers. In the New Testament, *basileia*—kingdom—is not solely a reference to either the church or an afterlife.

The poem in Isaiah mentions **Midian**. Israel remembered its oppression by the Midianites and then under the leadership of Gideon its victory over them. Invoking this memory, first Isaiah likens God's coming salvation to the military victory that set them free. Even the archetypal practice of warriors **plunder**ing the vanquished is offered as a positive image.

Ideas for the Day

◆ It has been said that North Americans are more likely to introduce themselves by sharing their name and occupation than any other personal characteristic. But Jesus called the first disciples away from their work as fishermen to follow him and "fish for people" (Matt. 4:19), suggesting that there is sometimes tension between the requirements of our careers and our calling as Christians. How do we deal with such conflicts when they arise, particularly in a culture that defines us by our work? How do we live out the truth that our baptismal identity has a greater claim on us than our jobs do? What if we introduced ourselves to each other this way: "Hello, my name is Simon, and I am a child of God"?

◆ Light and salvation are often connected in scripture, and this is especially true in the time after Epiphany and in today's readings. This connection, however, can be uncomfortable for persons who cannot see light (the visually impaired) or others for whom the word might have a negative connotation (such as persons of darker complexions who have suffered from discrimination). It is occasionally helpful to unpack the biblical relationship between light and salvation. Today's Isaiah text helps to do that—all of us walk in darkness, yet the light of Christ breaks our burdens and overthrows our oppressors.

◆ Factions and divisions occur in every community, and neither the church nor its individual congregations are immune. In keeping with the 1 Corinthians text, add petitions for church unity to the prayers of intercession today (find two fine examples in *Evangelical Lutheran Worship*, p. 73). While you're at it, include a petition for Christian mission—the mission that began with Christ's calling of Simon and Andrew (mission prayers begin on p. 75).

Connections with the Liturgy

Paul's comments remind us that all Christians are baptized either into the name of our Lord Jesus Christ or into the name of the Father, the Son, and the Holy Spirit. Baptism is into the Christian church as a whole, rather than into its denominational units, and nearly all branches and denominations of the church agree not to re-baptize anyone who has already received baptism.

Let the Children Come

Enhance children's hearing of the word by pointing out the connections between the readings. Children can tune in to a repeated word, image, or phrase. On some Sundays children may also be able to connect the readings to hymns, the sermon, and other parts of the service. In today's readings, children can listen for images of light. Children may want to keep a tally of how many times they hear the word light. To engage the youngest listeners, add a physical element such as, "Raise your finger in the air every time you hear the word light."

Assembly Song
Gathering

Thy strong word   ELW 511, LBW 233
Shine, Jesus, shine   ELW 671, TFF 64, W&P 123, WOV 651
We are marching in the light   ELW 866, W&P 148, WOV 650

Psalmody

Browning, Carol. "The Lord Is My Light/El Señor Es Mi Luz." SAB, cant, kybd, gtr, opt vln. GIA G-7256.
Berthier, Jacques/Hal H. Hopson. "Psalm 27" from TP.
Haas, David. "The Lord Is My Light" from PCY, vol. 1.

Hymn of the Day

Will you come and follow me   ELW 798, W&P 137   *KELVINGROVE*
Come, follow me, the Savior spake   ELW 799, LBW 455
   MACHS MIT MIR, GOTT
Lift every voice and sing   ELW 841, LBW 526, TFF 296
   LIFT EVERY VOICE AND SING

Offering

Light shone in darkness   ELW 307

Dearest Jesus, at your word   ELW 520

Communion

I love to tell the story   ELW 661

Here I Am, Lord   ELW 574

Let all mortal flesh keep silence   ELW 490, LBW 198

Sending

O Master, let me walk with you   ELW 818, LBW 492

I want Jesus to walk with me   ELW 325, TFF 66, WOV 660

Additional Assembly Songs

I heard the voice of Jesus say   TFF 62

The Lord is my light   TFF 61

Thy word is a lamp   TFF 132, W&P 144

⌖ Czech hymn tune. "The Lord Is My Light" from *Many and Great: Songs of the World Church.* SSATB. GIA G-3649.

✧ Cash, Ed/Jack Mooring/Leeland Mooring. "Follow You" from CCLI.

✧ Houston, Joel/Marty Sampson/Jonathon Douglass. "My Future Decided" from WT.

✧ Hughes, Tim. "Day after Day" from CCLI.

✧ Ingram, Jason/Kristian Stanfill/Rueben Morgan. "My Reward" from WT.

✧ Keyes, Aaron/Jack Mooring/Bryan Brown. "Sovereign over Us" from WT.

✧ Stanfill, Kristian. "Lead Us On" from WT.

Music for the Day
Choral

Chepponis, James. "We Are One in Christ." SATB or cant, assembly, opt br, gtr, perc, timp, hb. MSM 50-8313A.

Haugen, Marty/arr. Michael Burkhardt. "Lord, You Call Us." SATB, opt assembly and hb. MSM 50-7800.

Ickstadt, William. "They Cast Their Nets in Galilee." 2 pt, org. CPH 98-3980.

Keesecker, Thomas. "Jesus Said, Come, Follow Me." SATB a cappela, ob. AFP 9781451420746.

Scott, K. Lee. "Jesus Calls Us" from *Treasures in Heaven: Music for Two-Part Choirs.* 2 pt mxd, org. AFP 9780800679477.

von Kampen, David. "Breath of the Living God." 2 pt mxd, pno, opt C inst, tamb. CPH 98-4099.

Children's Choir

Coleman, Gerald Patrick. "Light of the World." U/2pt, kybd, fl, opt hb. CPH 98-3887.

Cool, Jayne Southwick. "Lumen Christi." U, kybd. CG CGA1098.

Kosche, Kenneth T. "The Lord Is My Light." 2 pt, kybd. CPH 98-4053.

Keyboard / Instrumental

Keesecker, Thomas. "Siyahamba" from *Piano Impressions for Epiphany.* Pno. CPH 97-6806.

Maynard, Lynette L. "This Little Light of Mine" from *Let It Shine: Worship Music for Solo Piano.* Pno. AFP 9780800677640.

• Miller, Aaron David. "Kelvingrove" from *Organ Preludes on Folk Songs.* Org. AFP 9780800677572.

• Walther, Johann Gottfried. "Machs mit mir, Gott, nach Deiner Güt" from *Orgelchoräle.* Org. BAR 9790006402236.

Handbell

• Nelson, Susan. "Will You Come and Follow Me (The Summons)." 3-5 oct hb, opt C inst, L3. AGEHR AG35289.

Rogers, Sharon. "Followers of the Lamb." 3-5 oct hb, opt drm or tamb, L3. AGEHR AG35202.

• Smith, Vicki. "Lift Every Voice and Sing." 3-5 oct, L3. CPH 97-6943.

Sunday, January 26
Timothy, Titus, and Silas, missionaries

On the two days following the celebration of the Conversion of Paul, his companions are remembered. Timothy, Titus, and Silas were missionary coworkers with Paul. Timothy accompanied Paul on his second missionary journey and was commissioned by Paul to go to Ephesus, where he served as bishop and overseer of the church. Titus was a traveling companion of Paul, accompanied him on the trip to the council of Jerusalem, and became the first bishop of Crete. Silas traveled with Paul through Asia Minor and Greece and was imprisoned with him at Philippi, where they were delivered by an earthquake.

Monday, January 27
Lydia, Dorcas, and Phoebe, witnesses to the faith

On this day the church remembers three women who were companions in Paul's ministry. Lydia was Paul's first convert at Philippi in Macedonia. She was a merchant of purple-dyed goods, and because purple dye was extremely expensive, it is likely that Lydia was a woman of some wealth. Lydia and her household were baptized by Paul, and for a time her home was a base for Paul's missionary work. Dorcas is remembered for her charitable works, particularly making clothing for needy widows. Phoebe was a *diakonos,* a deaconess in the church at Cenchreae, near Corinth. Paul praises her as one who, through her service, looked after many people.

⌖ = global song

✧ = praise song

• = relates to hymn of the day

Tuesday, January 28
Thomas Aquinas, teacher, died 1274

Thomas Aquinas (uh-ᴋᴡʏ-nus) was a brilliant and creative theologian of the thirteenth century. He was first and foremost a student of the Bible and profoundly concerned with the theological formation of the church's ordained ministers. As a member of the Order of Preachers (Dominicans), he worked to correlate scripture with the philosophy of Aristotle, which was having a renaissance in Aquinas's day. Some students of Aristotle's philosophy found in it an alternative to Christianity. But Aquinas immersed himself in the thought of Aristotle and worked to explain Christian beliefs in the philosophical culture of the day.

February 2, 2014
Presentation of Our Lord

The Presentation of Our Lord is referred to in some corners of the church as Candlemas because of an ancient tradition of blessing all the candles to be used in the church in the coming year at the mass celebrated on that day. It was a way of underscoring the truth of Simeon's confession that this baby Jesus was "a light for revelation to the Gentiles" and a light for glory to Israel. Let the light of every candle in church be a little epiphany of the love of God for all people in the person of God's son, Jesus, the light of the world.

Prayer of the Day

Almighty and ever-living God, your only-begotten Son was presented this day in the temple. May we be presented to you with clean and pure hearts by the same Jesus Christ, our great high priest, who lives and reigns with you and the Holy Spirit, one God, now and forever.

Gospel Acclamation

Alleluia. My eyes have seen ⎮ your salvation,* which you have prepared in the presence ⎮ of all peoples. *Alleluia.* (Luke 2:30-31)

Readings and Psalm
Malachi 3:1-4

This reading concludes a larger section (2:17—3:5) in which the prophet speaks of the coming of the God of justice. Malachi looks for that day when the wondrous power of God will purify the priestly descendants of Levi who minister in the temple at Jerusalem.

Psalm 84

How dear to me is your dwelling, O Lᴏʀᴅ. (Ps. 84:1)

or Psalm 24:7-10

Lift up your heads, O gates, that the King of glory may come in. (Ps 24:7)

Hebrews 2:14-18

Jesus shared human nature fully so that his death might be for all humans a liberation from slavery to death's power.

Here the writer uses the image of priestly service in the temple as a way of describing the life and saving death of the Lord Jesus. He is the high priest who offers his life on behalf of his brothers and sisters.

Luke 2:22-40

This story is a study in contrasts: the infant Jesus with the aged prophets; the joy of birth with the ominous words of Simeon to Mary; the faithful fulfilling of the law with the presentation of the one who will release its hold over us. Through it all, we see the light of God's salvation revealed to the world.

Preface   Christmas

Color   White

Prayers of Intercession

The prayers are prepared locally for each occasion. The following examples may be adapted or used as appropriate.

Guided by the light of Christ, who has been made known to the nations, we offer our prayers for the church, the world, and all people in need.

A brief silence.

For messengers of the gospel throughout the world, that the light of Christ be made present to all, let us pray.

Have mercy, O God.

For the well-being of the earth and all its inhabitants, and for those who advocate for the just use of resources, that all creation continue to thrive, let us pray.

Have mercy, O God.

For the nations of the world—the prosperous and the poor, the peaceful and the perilous (*especially*)—that leaders work toward the betterment of all, let us pray.

Have mercy, O God.

For the sick, the suffering, the imprisoned, and all who need help for any reason (*especially*), let us pray.

Have mercy, O God.

For those gathered in this house of worship, that we continue to praise God, rejoice at the salvation brought about through Christ, and be guided by the Holy Spirit, let us pray.

Have mercy, O God.

Here other intercessions may be offered.

In thanksgiving for those who died in the faith, that by their witness we live in confidence that Christ has destroyed death and brought about life eternal, let us pray.

Have mercy, O God.

Radiant God, hear the prayers of your people, spoken or silent, for the sake of the one who has made his dwelling among us, your Son, Jesus Christ our Savior.

Amen.

Images in the Readings

In the ancient Near East, some religious practice required parents to sacrifice their firstborn child to the deities, who would then reward the parents with many healthy children. Numbers 18:16 stipulates that instead parents should provide for the sacrifice of animals, the slaughter of which **redeems** the infant. This practice, so alien to us, is fundamental to the New Testament's explanation of the purpose behind the crucifixion of Christ. Kept alive as an infant—recall also Matthew's story of Jesus escaping Herod's slaughter of the innocents—Jesus as an adult will die as a sacrificed lamb in order to redeem us all. Thus the festival of the Presentation is really a meditation on Good Friday.

Simeon's poem about Christ being **light** to the Gentiles—that is, to most of us—led to the medieval practice of people bringing to the church on this day their year's supply of candles to be blessed: thus the popular naming of this day as Candlemas. Perhaps you can use up the remainder of your Christmas candles by having all worshipers hold their lighted candles during the reading of this day's gospel. These tiny lights remind us of the refiner's fire that Malachi anticipates.

The book of Hebrews expands the metaphor of Jesus being the sacrifice by naming him as the **high priest** who does the sacrificing. This reminds us that no image of Christ is profound enough, and so we sometimes turn the image around and use it backwards.

Here is part of today's gospel: that according to the oracle from Malachi, we become like **gold and silver**, precious, shining with the beauty of God.

Ideas for the Day

◆ The Nunc dimittis or Song of Simeon is one of the four "infancy canticles" in Luke's gospel. Like the others—the Magnificat (1:46-55), Gloria in excelsis (2:14), and Benedictus (1:68-79)—it is a powerful hymn of praise, rich with imagery. Yet some parishes rarely sing these profound words. Highlight the Song of Simeon on this day by singing it after communion (see *Evangelical Lutheran Worship*, pp. 113, 135, and 324; or hymns 200–202). Ask the musicians to prepare one of the many beautiful choral or solo vocal settings of this text. You may also incorporate Martin Luther's paraphrase "In peace and joy I now depart" (ELW 440) as one of the hymns for the day.

◆ A frequent programming goal for many congregations is "intergenerational activity" that brings together young, old, and middle-aged people. Today's gospel story provides a glimpse of such involvement: Mary and Joseph, the infant Jesus, and the aging Simeon and Anna participate in a "liturgy" of blessing, prophecy, and proclamation. Thus the Presentation of Our Lord provides a wonderful opportunity to connect different generations in worship leadership. Vary their roles: If youth normally serve as acolytes, ask older members to do so. If adults are usually lectors and assisting ministers, allow youth the responsibility and privilege to serve in these capacities, providing appropriate training so they may lead with confidence and grace. Integrate musical leadership rather than scheduling the adult or children's choirs to sing separately. Although Christian worship is by nature an intergenerational activity, on this day it is particularly worthwhile to have many generations involved in leading worship. Be certain that all worshipers understand that these generational switches relate to the gospel.

◆ A common thread in today's scripture texts might be the question: what is valuable to God, and what should be valuable to us? The reading from Malachi says Christ will purify us like gold and silver; Hebrews teaches that Christ took on our flesh and blood that he might thereby destroy death. Christ does these things because we are valuable and precious to God. Simeon's song and Anna's proclamation in Luke's narrative are borne out of their devotion—devotion that can itself be traced to their awareness of God's care for them and all of Israel. This festival, then, is about the value of right relationships. God cherishes us. We, in turn, are to cherish God and one another.

Connections with the Liturgy

When Simeon holds the child in his arms, he is ready to face death, and he sings praise to the light of God. Since at least 1531, Lutherans have sung Simeon's song after receiving communion (*Evangelical Lutheran Worship*, p. 113). As we hold out our hands, we receive in them the body of Christ, our salvation and the light of the world. We hold out our hands as if our palm is like a cradle for the infant, like a throne for the king. As well, in Night Prayer (p. 324), we join in the long tradition of singing Simeon's song each evening as we ready ourselves for the "death" that is sleep.

Let the Children Come

Children, like adults, may or may not be comfortable in front of a large group. Many churches invite children to come forward for a children's message. As a complement to that model, offer children regular opportunities to participate from their seats. One simple way to do this is by asking a question that children and parents can discuss together. This model puts the emphasis on parents as the primary spiritual teachers for their children, and it encourages the involvement of all children, not just those bold enough to go before the assembly. Children may appreciate not being in the spotlight as they hear and discuss the gospel.

Assembly Song
Gathering

In his temple now behold him   ELW 417
Angels, from the realms of glory   ELW 275, LBW 50
Let all together praise our God   ELW 287, LBW 47

Psalmody

Hopson, Hal H. "Psalm 84" from TPP.
Holland, M. Roger II. "Holy Family of Jesus, Mary and Joseph/ Optional C" from LP:LG.
Duba, Arlo D. "How Lovely, Lord, How Lovely" (MERLE'S TUNE) from PAS 94C.

Hymn of the Day

Now, Lord   ELW 202
In a lowly manger born   ELW 718, LBW 417   MABUNE
I want to walk as a child of the light   ELW 815, WOV 649   HOUSTON

Offering

What child is this   ELW 296, LBW 40
Thankful hearts and voices raise   ELW 206

Communion

Now, Lord   ELW 202
At last, Lord   ELW 203
Of the Father's love begotten   ELW 295, LBW 42

Sending

O Lord, now let your servant   ELW 313
In peace and joy I now depart   ELW 440

Additional Assembly Songs

The Lord is in his holy temple   TFF 143
In his temple now behold him   LBW 184
❋ Galbraith, Douglas. "I've Waited Long" from Common Ground: A Song Book for All the Churches. U. Saint Andrews Press, Edinburgh.
❋ Ascencio, Rudolfo. Mexico. "Yo soy la luz del mundo/I Am the World's True Light" from Halle, Halle: We Sing the World Round. U, gtr, perc. CG CGC41.
✿ Barnard, Shane. "Be Near" from WT.
✿ Houston, Joel. "Children of the Light" from WT.
✿ Lang, Braden/Rueben Morgan. "Open My Eyes" from CCLI.
✿ Redman, Matt. "Beautiful News" from WT.
✿ Rend Collective Experiment. "Second Chance" from WT.
✿ Tomlin, Chris/Ed Cash/Kari Jobe. "I'm Singing" from CCLI.

Music for the Day
Choral

Kosche, Kenneth. "How Lovely Is Your Dwelling Place." 2 pt mxd, kybd. MSM 50-6302.
● Langlois, Kris. "I Want to Walk as a Child of the Light." SAB, org. AFP 9780800678197.
Manz, Paul. "Peace Came to Earth." SATB, opt assembly, org. MSM 50-1020.
Schalk, Carl. "Simeon's Song: The Nunc Dimittis." SATB. AFP 9781451401721.

Children's Choir

Burkhardt, Michael. "There Shall a Star from Jacob Shine" from Part-Singing Global Style. 2 pt trbl, hb/hc, opt kybd. MSM 50-9811.
Hillert, Richard. "The Lord Is My Light and My Salvation." U, kybd, tpt/fl/ob/sax. GIA G-4951.
Schalk, Carl. "Lord, Now You Let Your Servant Go in Peace." U/2 pt, assembly, org, opt hb. CPH 98-3733.

Keyboard / Instrumental

Bach, J. S. "Mit Fried und Freud ich fahr dahin" from Das Orgelbüchlein. Org. Various editions.
● Manz, Paul. "I Want to Walk as a Child of the Light." Org. MSM 10-520.
● Wasson, Laura E. "Houston" from A Piano Tapestry, Volume 2. Pno. AFP 9780800658182.
● Sedio, Mark. "Houston" from Once Led to Your Font: A Keyboard Collection. Pno. AFP 9780800677855.

Handbell

Afdahl, Lee. "How Lovely Is Thy Dwelling Place" (based on Psalm 84). 3-7 oct, L4. AGEHR AG37003.
● Behnke, John. "I Want to Walk as a Child of the Light." 3 or 5 oct, L2. CPH 97-6611.
Sylvester, Susan. "The King of Glory." 3-6 oct hb, opt fl or vln, L3+. BP HB292.

❋ = global song
✿ = praise song
● = relates to hymn of the day

February 2, 2014
Fourth Sunday after Epiphany
Lectionary 4

Who are the blessed ones of God? For Micah, they are those who do justice, love kindness, and walk humbly with God. For Paul, they are the ones who find wisdom in the weakness of the cross. For Jesus, they are the poor, mourners, the meek, those who hunger for righteousness, the merciful, the pure in heart, the peacemakers. In baptism we find our blessed identity and calling in this countercultural way of living and serving.

Prayer of the Day

Holy God, you confound the world's wisdom in giving your kingdom to the lowly and the pure in heart. Give us such a hunger and thirst for justice, and perseverance in striving for peace, that in our words and deeds the world may see the life of your Son, Jesus Christ, our Savior and Lord.

Gospel Acclamation

Alleluia. Rejoice ¹ and be glad,* for your reward is ¹ great in heaven. *Alleluia.* (Matt. 5:12)

Readings and Psalm

Micah 6:1-8

With the mountains and the foundations of the earth as the jury, God brings a lawsuit against Israel. God has "wearied" Israel with a long history of saving acts. God does not want or expect lavish sacrifices to attempt to earn divine favor. Rather God empowers the people to do justice, to love loyalty to God, and to walk shrewdly in God's service.

Psalm 15

Lord, who may abide upon your holy hill? (Ps. 15:1)

1 Corinthians 1:18-31

According to the world's standards of power and might, the message of the cross seems stupid and offensive. Yet this word reveals the paradoxical way God has chosen to work power and salvation through weakness, rejection, and suffering. Hence the message of the cross becomes true wisdom and power for believers.

Matthew 5:1-12

Jesus opens the Sermon on the Mount by naming those who are blessed in the reign of God.

Preface   Sundays

Color   Green

Prayers of Intercession

The prayers are prepared locally for each occasion. The following examples may be adapted or used as appropriate.

Guided by the light of Christ, who has been made known to the nations, we offer our prayers for the church, the world, and all people in need.

A brief silence.

God, you call the church on earth to witness to the life we receive in Jesus. Help us to share your good news with the world. Lord, in your mercy,

hear our prayer.

All creation is holy. Lead us to restore the hills and valleys, lakes and rivers, forests and coastlands to the beauty you created. Lord, in your mercy,

hear our prayer.

Call those who are wise and powerful to use their gifts to do justice in a world longing for peace. Lord, in your mercy,

hear our prayer.

Comfort those who mourn, ease the suffering of all who are lonely or in pain, heal the sick (*especially*). Bring to your table all who hunger and thirst. Lord, in your mercy,

hear our prayer.

Continue to uphold this community of faith to proclaim Christ crucified and reach out to those who are poor, hungry, homeless, or easily overlooked. Lord, in your mercy,

hear our prayer.

Here other intercessions may be offered.

Protect us in our weakness until you gather us with all your saints upon your holy hill. Lord, in your mercy,

hear our prayer.

Radiant God, hear the prayers of your people, spoken or silent, for the sake of the one who has made his dwelling among us, your Son, Jesus Christ our Savior.

Amen.

Images in the Readings

Jesus preaches from the top of a **mountain**. In the Bible, significant religious events occur on a mountain because God was described as dwelling above the earth, and still today people climb mountains for an otherworldly experience. In worship, the mountain is here in the church building, on the ambo, in the pulpit, on the altar.

Especially intertestamental Jews wrote about Hokmah, the **wisdom** of God, personified as a goddess-like figure who accompanied, even governed, the activity of God. Yet Paul criticizes the cultural idea of wisdom as being quite other than the mercy of the cross.

The oracle from Micah includes the imagery of **sacrifice**, that is, burnt offerings of animals or children to prove veneration of the gods. Although Christians never authorized literal sacrifices, the imagery remains, both in the theological proposal that Christ's death was in some way a similar sacrifice and in the church's speech about a selfless life of giving for others.

Ideas for the Day

◆ The idea of the "mountaintop experience," inspired by the many significant biblical events that occur on significant heights, is a challenging one for Christians. Though the emotions and energy that accompany such moments can be profound, such feelings do not usually remain with us in our day-to-day lives. What to do? Paradoxically, in his Sermon on the Mount Jesus provides a useful tool: the beatitudes. These blessings may not seem needed during our mountaintop moments, but through the valleys of life they sustain our hope and remind us of Christ's resurrection promise.

◆ The book of Micah reminds us that the appropriate response to the mercy God has lavished on us is to do justice and love kindness (Micah 6:8), or—as Jesus and Martin Luther might put it—to love our neighbor. The Matthean beatitudes remind us that the world does not reward such love. The merciful, the peacemakers, and those who strive for righteousness are often reviled and persecuted on earth (Matt. 5:11), but will be rewarded in heaven. Yet we do not practice justice and kindness to obtain a heavenly reward; rather, secure in the knowledge of our salvation through Christ's death and resurrection, we are free to love our neighbor without fear of earthly consequences.

◆ Many of our familiar metaphors for God are masculine by definition or implication: Lord, king, shepherd. The personification of God's many qualities, including wisdom, as female provides less familiar but necessary female images. Although all metaphors and images are imperfect, balancing familiar and unfamiliar, male and female images can enrich our spiritual imaginations and our corporate worship. Hymnody is often a good place to begin. For example, the hymns "Mothering God, you gave me birth" (ELW 735) and "God, the sculptor of the mountains" (ELW 736) are replete with vibrant images for God. Both hymns would be appropriate on this day as gathering songs, communion hymns, or elsewhere in the service.

Connections with the Liturgy

In the oracle from Micah, the Lord asks, "O my people, what have I done to you? In what have I wearied you? Answer me!" These words are the inspiration for the Solemn Reproaches, an optional litany for Good Friday, in which Christ on the cross asks, "O my people, O my church, what have I done to you? How have I offended you? Answer me."

Let the Children Come

Today's gospel takes place on a mountain, signifying the importance of Jesus' words. Invite children to identify the "high places" in your worship space (altar, pulpit, choir loft). Why are they elevated? What are the practical reasons (younger children can provide some ideas here) and symbolic reasons (older children may have some ideas about this) that some places in church are elevated? Children can consider these questions as they listen to the readings and sermon. You may wish to ask children to share their answers with the congregation or their parents. Some children may like to write or draw their answers.

Assembly Song
Gathering

We Are Called   ELW 720, W&P 147

Oh, praise the gracious power   ELW 651, WOV 750

To be your presence   ELW 546

Psalmody

Nelson, Ronald A. "Psalm 15" from PWA.

Hopson, Hal. "Psalm 15" from TPP. (Note: verses may be spoken or improvised.)

Traditional, arr. Wendell Whalum. "Psalm 15" from PAS 15C.

Hymn of the Day

O God of mercy, God of light   ELW 714, LBW 425   *JUST AS I AM*

When the poor ones   ELW 725, LLC 508   *EL CAMINO*

Blest are they   ELW 728, WOV 764   *BLEST ARE THEY*

Offering

Jesus, the very thought of you   ELW 754, LBW 316

Let streams of living justice   ELW 710

Communion

Holy god, holy and glorious   ELW 637

Thee we adore, O Savior   ELW 476, LBW 199

Beloved, God's chosen   ELW 648

Sending

The Spirit sends us forth to serve   ELW 551, WOV 723

Let justice flow like streams   ELW 717, TFF 48, WOV 763

Additional Assembly Songs

Sing Out, Earth and Skies W&P 126

⚉ Bell, John, arr. "Hey, My Love" from *Heaven Shall Not Wait*. SATB. GIA G-3646.

⚉ Falam Chin traditional melody. "Lord of Region and of World" from *Sound the Bamboo*. GIA G-6830.

✿ Hughes, Tim. "God of Justice" from WT.

✿ Maher, Matt. "Unwavering" from CCLI.

✿ McClarney, Chris/Chris Eaton/John Hartley. "Immortal Invisible" from WT.

✿ McCracken, Sandra. "Justice Will Roll Down" from CCLI.

✿ Morgan, Rueben. "One Day" from WT.

Music for the Day

Choral

Miller, Mark. "What Does the Lord Require of You?" Solo, SATB, pno. Abingdon 9780687331543.

Leavitt, John. "Blessed Are They." U/2 pt mxd, kybd. AFP 9781451423938.

Roberts, William Bradley. "In All These You Welcomed Me" from *Augsburg Easy Choirbook, Vol 2*. 2 pt mxd, org, opt solo, inst. AFP 9780800677510.

Weber, Paul. "Blessed." SATB or U, org, opt assembly. MSM 50-0565.

Children's Choir

Bedford, Michael. "Blessed Are They." U/2 pt, org, fl. CG CGA1025.

Leavett, John. "Blessed Are They." U/ 2 pt mxd, pno. AFP 9781451423938.

Lowenberg, Kenneth. "Blessed Are the Poor in Spirit." U/2 pt, kybd. SEL 410-557.

Keyboard / Instrumental

Cherwien, David. "O God of Light" from *More Postludes on Well Known Hymns*. Org. AFP 9780800678425.

● Mann, Adrian. "Blest Are They" from *Blest Are They: Preludes for Low Instrument and Keyboard*. Inst, kybd. AFP 9780800679422.

Miller, Aaron David. "Light Dawns on a Weary World" from *Chorale Preludes for Piano in Traditional Styles*. Pno. AFP 9780800679033.

● Organ, Anne Krentz. "Blest Are They" from *In Heaven Above: Piano Music for Funerals and Memorials*. Pno. AFP 9781451401912.

Handbell

● Helman, Michael. "Blest Are They." 3-6 oct hb, opt 3-5 oct hc, opt fl, L3-. GIA G-7043.

Helman, Michael. "Variations on 'Gather Us In.'" 3-5 oct hb, opt 3 oct hc, L4. AFP 9780800674922.

● Lamb, Linda. "Just As I Am." 2-3 oct, L2. ALF 29950.

Sunday, February 2
Presentation of Our Lord

Forty days after the birth of Christ we mark the day Mary and Joseph presented him in the temple in accordance with Jewish law. There a prophetess named Anna began to speak of the redemption of Israel when she saw the young child. Simeon also greeted Mary and Joseph. He responded to the presence of the consolation of Israel in this child with the words of the Nunc dimittis. His song described Jesus as a "light for the nations."

Because of the link between Jesus as the light for the nations, and because an old reading for this festival contains a line from the prophet Zephaniah, "I will search Jerusalem with candles," the day is also known as Candlemas, a day when candles are blessed for the coming year.

Monday, February 3
Ansgar, Bishop of Hamburg, missionary to Denmark and Sweden, died 865

Ansgar was a monk who led a mission to Denmark and later to Sweden, where he built the first church. His work ran into difficulties with the rulers of the day, and he was forced to withdraw into Germany, where he served as a bishop in Hamburg. Despite his difficulties in Sweden, he persisted in his mission work and later helped consecrate Gothbert as the first bishop of Sweden. Ansgar had a deep love for the poor. He would wash their feet and serve them food provided by the parish.

Wednesday, February 5
The Martyrs of Japan, died 1597

In the sixteenth century, Jesuit missionaries, followed by Franciscans, introduced the Christian faith in Japan. But a promising beginning to those missions—perhaps as many as 300,000 Christians by the end of the sixteenth century—met complications from competition between the missionary groups, political difficulty between Spain and Portugal, and factions within the government of Japan. Christianity was suppressed. By 1630, Christianity was driven underground.

Today we commemorate the first martyrs of Japan, twenty-six missionaries and converts who were killed by crucifixion. Two hundred and fifty years later, when Christian missionaries returned to Japan, they found a community of Japanese Christians that had survived underground.

⚉ = global song
✿ = praise song
● = relates to hymn of the day

February 9, 2014
Fifth Sunday after Epiphany
Lectionary 5

Light shines in the darkness for the upright, the psalmist sings. Isaiah declares that when we loose the bonds of injustice and share our bread with the hungry, the light breaks forth like the dawn. In another passage from the Sermon on the Mount, Jesus, the light of the world, calls his followers to let the light of their good works shine before others. Through baptism we are sent into the world to shine with the light of Christ.

Prayer of the Day

Lord God, with endless mercy you receive the prayers of all who call upon you. By your Spirit show us the things we ought to do, and give us the grace and power to do them, through Jesus Christ, our Savior and Lord.

Gospel Acclamation

Alleluia. Jesus says, I am the light ˈ of the world;* whoever follows me will have the ˈ light of life. *Alleluia.* (John 8:12)

Readings and Psalm

Isaiah 58:1-9a [9b-12]

Shortly after the return of Israel from exile in Babylon, the people were troubled by the ineffectiveness of their fasts. God reminds them that outward observance is no substitute for genuine fasting that results in acts of justice, such as feeding the hungry, sheltering the homeless, and clothing the naked.

Psalm 112:1-9 [10]

Light shines in the darkness for the upright. (Ps. 112:4)

1 Corinthians 2:1-12 [13-16]

Though people such as the Corinthians are enamored with human philosophy and wisdom, Paul continuously presents God's hidden wisdom which is Jesus Christ crucified. True spiritual maturity involves judging ourselves and others in light of God's revelation in the cross.

Matthew 5:13-20

In the Sermon on the Mount, Jesus encourages his followers to be the salt of the earth and the light of the world, doing good works and keeping God's commandments.

Preface   Sundays

Color   Green

Prayers of Intercession

The prayers are prepared locally for each occasion. The following examples may be adapted or used as appropriate.

Guided by the light of Christ, who has been made known to the nations, we offer our prayers for the church, the world, and all people in need.

A brief silence.

Your light springs forth like the dawn. Call your church to share the mystery of your grace with a broken and searching world. Lord, in your mercy,

hear our prayer.

Increase our care for the earth and all its creatures. Help us reflect your light in our use of these good gifts. Lord, in your mercy,

hear our prayer.

You care for the weak and the strong, O God. Raise up leaders who will free the oppressed in all places (*especially*). Lord, in your mercy,

hear our prayer.

Quickly send your healing for all in pain (*especially*). Feed the hungry and shelter the homeless. Lord, in your mercy,

hear our prayer.

Give light and life to this gathering of faith, that we may delight to know your ways and share them with a world longing to know you. Lord, in your mercy,

hear our prayer.

Here other intercessions may be offered.

Satisfy our needs until we gather with all your saints from every time and place in your glorious light. Lord, in your mercy,

hear our prayer.

Radiant God, hear the prayers of your people, spoken or silent, for the sake of the one who has made his dwelling among us, your Son, Jesus Christ our Savior.

Amen.

Images in the Readings

Light is an image on many Sundays. The Sermon on the Mount speaks also of the **lampstand**. Paul would remind us that, contrary to the wisdom of the world, our lampstand is the cross.

Salt is necessary for human life. In recollection of this passage, some early Christian communities placed salt on the tongue of the newly baptized. In the early twentieth century, the British placed an embargo on salt, requiring the Indian people to purchase salt from them, and Gandhi's Salt March became a symbol of the right of Indians to manage their own survival.

The passage from Isaiah speaks about a **fast**. In many religious traditions, people limit or refrain from some necessary human activity as a symbol that their truest life comes only from the divine. In both the Jewish and Christian traditions, fasting must be accompanied with justice for the poor for God to acknowledge its value.

Ideas for the Day

◆   In 2002 the producer of BBC-London, Danny Wallace, gained a following when he issued an anonymous invitation in a London newspaper to "join him." After hundreds of replies the Karma Army was born, an online community commissioned to perform random acts of kindness every Friday, called "Good Fridays." Mike Breen and Steve Cockram, in *Building a Discipling Culture* (Pawleys Island, SC: 3DM, 2011, pp. 92–98), reflect on the impact a Christian community would have if it made a similar pledge, but for different reasons. Followers of Jesus act as salt and light because they have been seasoned and enlightened by the Spirit.

◆   Among salt's many uses in the Bible was as an element in sacrifice (Paul Sevier Minear, "The Salt of the Earth," *Interpretation*, Jan. 1997, pp. 31–41). As "salt," followers of Jesus are characterized by self-giving that leads to greater life. Betty Anne Waters is an example of such self-sacrifice. While raising two children and working as a waitress, she completed college and law school in order to exonerate her incarcerated brother (details at www.innocenceproject.org/Content/Kenny_Waters.php). Waters's story of personal cost and devotion to her cause are portrayed in the movie *Conviction* (Fox Searchlight, 2010). What does our focused devotion to God's kingdom look like? What are the costs? What are the rewards?

◆   A question often asked by lawyers in ancient Rome was *Cui bono?*—"Who benefits?" Who benefits from the Christian community? Answer: the world! Just as salt and light do not exist for their own benefit, the local community of disciples does not exist for itself but rather to model God's reign of forgiveness. Who benefits from your ministries? Be specific. List examples and give thanks to God for them. You may be surprised how many come to mind.

◆   Today Jesus upholds the law so that he may fulfill, not fossilize, the law. In the same way, musicians must first learn and master rudimentary skills and tunes before they can transcend the basic rules creatively without inflicting harm on the piece they are playing. Can you think of other examples of "mastering the rules" in order to move beyond them?

Connections with the Liturgy

At the welcome to the newly baptized (*Evangelical Lutheran Worship*, p. 231), we hear reminders of today's gospel reading. Option 1 connects Matthew's words about light with John's: our light comes from the Light that is Christ. Option 2 quotes Matthew 5:16: our light draws people not to ourselves, but to our Father in heaven.

Let the Children Come

The gospel for this Sunday may remind children of the hymn "This little light of mine" (ELW 677). Take this opportunity to involve children in leading the assembly in song. Enlist two or three older children who are willing to lead the actions. Give them time to prepare actions to accompany each stanza of the hymn, and then go over the stanzas and actions with them prior to worship. Invite other children to come up and join them as the hymn is sung.

Assembly Song
Gathering

Christ, whose glory fills the skies   ELW 553, LBW 265

Gather Us In   ELW 532, WOV 718

I want to walk as a child of the light   ELW 815, WOV 649

Psalmody

"Take Your Place at the Table." *Psallite* C-176.

Pavlechko, Thomas. "Psalm 112," Refrain 3, from PSCY.

Gelineau, Joseph or Michel Guimont. "Fifth Sunday in Ordinary Time/A" from LP:W4.

Hymn of the Day

Light shone in darkness   ELW 307   *LUX IN TENEBRIS*

This little light of mine   ELW 677, TFF 65   *THIS JOY*

We Are Called   ELW 720, W&P 147   *WE ARE CALLED*

Offering

Lord of light   ELW 688, LBW 405

Creating God, your fingers trace   ELW 684

Communion

Thee we adore, O Savior   ELW 476, LBW 199

Holy, holy, holy, holy   ELW 762, LLC 273, TFF 203, W&P 61

In the singing   ELW 466

Sending

Go, make disciples   ELW 540, W&P 47
Joyful, joyful we adore thee   ELW 836, LBW 551

Additional Assembly Songs

Listen! You nations of the world   LBW 14
Rejoice in the mission   W&P 120
❂ Loh, I-to. Taiwan. "Light of the World, Salt of the Earth" from *Sound the Bamboo*. U. GIA G-6830.
❂ Vas, Charles. India. "Give Us Light/Jyothi dho Prabhu" from *Love and Anger: Songs of Lively Faith and Social Justice*. U. GIA G-4947.
✿ Camp, Jeremy. "Speaking Louder Than Before" from CCLI.
✿ Fee, Steve. "You Are the Light" from CCLI.
✿ Hall, Charlie/Kendall Combes. "Breathe" from CCLI.
✿ Herbert, Nick/Ben Cantelon. "New Day" from WT.
✿ Redman, Matt/Jonas Myrin. "All That Really Matters" from WT.
✿ Redman, Matt/Tofer Brown/Bryan Brown/Chris Tomlin. "Not Ashamed" from WT.

Music for the Day
Choral

Eicker, Edward. "What You Have Done." SATB, cant, opt assembly, C inst, kybd. GIA G-7699.
Haugen, Marty. "Eye Has Not Seen." SATB, gtr, kybd, 2 inst, assembly. GIA G-2659.
Leavitt, John. "Lord, You Are Light." SATB, kybd. AFP 9780800679231.
Lovelace, Austin. "The Beginning of Wisdom." SATB, org. ECS 6637.
Miller, Aaron David. "We Will Shine." SATB, kybd. AFP 9780800678111.
Schalk, Carl. "Those Who Are Wise." SATB. MSM 50-9009.
Sedio, Mark. "Christ Comes Among Us." SATB, org, tpt. AFP 9780800678326.

Children's Choir

Carter, John. "We Are Called to Be His Servants." U/2 pt, pno. AFP 9780800675455.
Kemp, Helen. "Set the Sun Dancing." U, kybd, hb. CG CGA780.
Sullivan, Joseph B. "Not to Be Hidden." 2 pt, kybd, gtr. GIA G-5801.

Keyboard / Instrumental

Bach, J. S. "In dir ist Freude" from *Das Orgelbüchlein*. Org. Various editions.
● Childs, Edwin T. "This Joy" from *Spirituals for Organ: For Manuals Only*. Org or kybd. AFP 9781451401141.
● Hassell, Michael. "This Little Light of Mine" from *Jazz Sunday Morning: Piano Arrangements*. Pno. AFP 9780800655402.
● Maynard, Lynette L. "This Little Light of Mine" from *Let it Shine: Worship Music for Solo Piano*. Pno. AFP 9780800677640.

Handbell

Glasgow, Michael. "Lux Aeterna." 5-7 oct hb, 4 or 7 oct hc, L3+. National Music Publishers NMHB-661.
Keller, Michael. "From Darkness, Light." 5 or 7 oct, L5. AGEHR AG57015E.
● Moats, William. "This Little Light of Mine." 2-3 oct, L2+. CG CGB678.

Friday, February 14

Cyril, monk, died 869; Methodius, bishop, died 885; missionaries to the Slavs

These two brothers from a noble family in Thessalonika in northeastern Greece were priests and missionaries. After some early initial missionary work by Cyril among the Arabs, the brothers retired to a monastery. They were later sent to work among the Slavs, the missionary work for which they are most known. Since Slavonic had no written form at the time, the brothers established a written language with the Greek alphabet as its basis. They translated the scriptures and the liturgy using this Cyrillic alphabet. The Czechs, Serbs, Croats, Slovaks, and Bulgars regard the brothers as the founders of Slavic literature. The brothers' work in preaching and worshiping in the language of the people are honored by Christians in both East and West.

February 16, 2014
Sixth Sunday after Epiphany
Lectionary 6

In today's reading from Deuteronomy we are called to choose life by loving and obeying God. Much of today's gospel reading echoes portions of the Ten Commandments. Jesus' instructions to the crowd reveal a pattern of behavior that honors both God and the neighbor, resulting in life and health for the whole community. We, too, are invited to embrace these commandments, not out of fear of retribution, but because God has promised that to do so means life for us.

Prayer of the Day

O God, the strength of all who hope in you, because we are weak mortals we accomplish nothing good without you. Help us to see and understand the things we ought to do, and give us grace and power to do them, through Jesus Christ, our Savior and Lord.

Gospel Acclamation

Alleluia. You are the light | of the world.* A city set upon a hill can- | not be hid. *Alleluia.* (Matt. 4:14)

Readings and Psalm
Deuteronomy 30:15-20

The Lord sets before the people of God a clear choice. Life and prosperity will come to the faithful; loss of the land will be the consequence of disobedience. Choosing life entails loving and holding fast to the Lord. Life in God's presence presupposes the promise made to the ancestors.

or Sirach 15:15-20

Wisdom literature has a high estimation of human possibilities. We are God's trusted creatures. Wisdom invites people to choose to keep God's commandments. Contrariwise, God does not command people to be wicked or give them permission to sin.

Psalm 119:1-8

Happy are they who follow the teaching of the Lord. (Ps. 119:1)

1 Corinthians 3:1-9

Human leaders in the church are not the ones who control ministry. Rather they are fellow workers who belong to God, the one who truly controls and continuously empowers the ministry of the church.

Matthew 5:21-37

In the Sermon on the Mount, Jesus exhorts his followers to embrace standards of righteousness that exceed legal requirements and traditional expectations.

Preface   Sundays

Color   Green

Prayers of Intercession

The prayers are prepared locally for each occasion. The following examples may be adapted or used as appropriate.

Guided by the light of Christ, who has been made known to the nations, we offer our prayers for the church, the world, and all people in need.

A brief silence.

God, you are faithful all the time. Show us the way to live faithfully as your church on earth. Lord, in your mercy,
hear our prayer.

You give growth to all living things. Provide snow and rain in their season, and lift up all who plant and till your earth. Lord, in your mercy,
hear our prayer.

Help the leaders of the world to put aside jealousy and quarreling so that we see your peace. Lord, in your mercy,
hear our prayer.

Reconcile families with one another and give comfort to those who mourn. Send healing to those who are ill or in pain (*especially*). Lord, in your mercy,
hear our prayer.

Continue to raise up leaders in this and every community of faith so that your word will be shared and all will know life in you. Lord, in your mercy,
hear our prayer.

Here other intercessions may be offered.

Holy Spirit, comfort and sustain us until we gather with all the saints around the throne of God. Lord, in your mercy,
hear our prayer.

Radiant God, hear the prayers of your people, spoken or silent, for the sake of the one who has made his dwelling among us, your Son, Jesus Christ our Savior.
Amen.

Images in the Readings

According to Matthew, Jesus threatened immoral people with **hell**. The idea that God will punish sinners with eternal fire came into intertestamental Jewish tradition from their Zoroastrian neighbors and is included in some New Testament books. Matthew's literalism is seen in the phrases that one's "whole body be thrown into hell." Fear of hell was a central religious motivation during some pieties and periods of the church, and lurid descriptions of torment extended far beyond what many theologians propose: that hell is self-willed distance from God, through life and beyond death. From the second century to the present, some Christians have maintained that eternal punishment contradicts the primary description of a merciful God. The Apostles' and Nicene creeds speak only of judgment and an everlasting life of the world to come, although according to the later Athanasian Creed, "those who have done evil will enter eternal fire."

The word of God is **milk** to us, who are infants. As nursing mothers know, both the infant and the mother need the times of feeding. It is as if God needs to give us the milk we need.

The passage from Deuteronomy evokes the classic *The Pilgrim's Progress*, by John Bunyan, in which the Christian life is described as one **choice** after another. It is God's Spirit who inspires us to choose what God has already chosen for us: in Paul's words, life in God's field, God's building.

Ideas for the Day

◆ Think of the difference between something genuine (an orange, the sun, real cream in your coffee) and its imitation (artificial orange flavoring, a light bulb, powdered creamer). Can one be satisfied with the imitation after experiencing the real thing? Likewise, if the rhetorical figures in our gospel today seem harsh (trial before council, dismemberment, hellfire), yet they serve to bring out the true colors of the kingdom by contrast. God's reign of love and forgiveness is a world apart from our artificial fiefdoms ruled by retribution and violence.

◆ Trusting in God's reality, we are free to live the law of love in an imperfect world. Without fear, we can take to heart the words of Margaret Thatcher, portrayed in the film *The Iron Lady* (Weinstein Company, 2011): "Watch your thoughts, for they become words. Watch your words, for they become actions. Watch your actions, for they become habits. Watch your habits, for they become your character. And watch your character, for it becomes your destiny. What we think, we become."

◆ In the "but I say" antitheses of Matthew 5:21-32, Jesus urges his followers to go beyond the letter of the law to find its roots in compassion. The Charter of Compassion, inspired by religious scholar and popular writer Karen Armstrong, is an effort to encourage followers of all faiths to place compassion in the center of their prayer, teaching, and practice. Christians may remember the rule of St. Augustine: that any interpretation of scripture that does not build up love of God and neighbor misses the mark (*On Christian Doctrine*, 1.40). To sign the charter visit charterforcompassion.org.

◆ Jesus' words today serve as a check on the ways we justify our failures to love. Arbinger Institute's *Leadership and Self-Deception: Getting Out of the Box* (San Francisco: Berrett-Koehler, 2010) illustrates, in story form, the extent of our own self-betrayal when we consider and treat people as things. It calls our self-deceptions and self-justifications as "being in the box." We can say that to live in God's promises is to be "outside the box," a perspective from which we can better see our anger, lusts, and falsehoods for what they are—and to seek God's strength to live otherwise.

Connections with the Liturgy

In the order for Individual Confession and Forgiveness (*Evangelical Lutheran Worship*, pp. 243–244), the penitent can articulate the idea of our choice to live the godly life by using the following words: "I firmly intend to amend my life, and to seek help in mending what is broken."

Let the Children Come

Children will get more out of the readings they hear in church if they understand that the things we hear from week to week are connected. The gospels for the fourth through the seventh Sundays after Epiphany are good opportunities to point out this connectedness because they continue the Sermon on the Mount. Make the readings even more kid-friendly during these weeks by reading the gospel from the *Spark Story Bible* (pp. 264–275) on one or more Sundays.

Assembly Song
Gathering

Come down, O Love divine ELW 804

O Christ, our hope ELW 604

Holy Spirit, ever dwelling ELW 582, LBW 523

Psalmody

"Love the Lord Your God." *Psallite* A-112.

Mummert, Mark. "Psalm 119:1-8," Refrain 1, from PSCY.

Nelson, Ronald A. "Psalm 119:1-8" from PWA.

Hymn of the Day

Oh, that the Lord would guide my ways ELW 772, LBW 480 *EVAN*

Let us ever walk with Jesus ELW 802, LBW 487
   LASSET UNS MIT JESU ZIEHEN

I want to walk as a child of the light ELW 815, WOV 649 *HOUSTON*

Offering

O God, my faithful God   ELW 806, st. 2, LBW 504
Evening and morning   ELW 761

Communion

Thee we adore, O Savior   ELW 476, LBW 199
In all our grief   ELW 615, WOV 739
Come, gracious Spirit, heavenly dove   ELW 404

Sending

Christ is the king!   ELW 662
Praise the Lord, rise up rejoicing   ELW 544, LBW 196

Additional Assembly Songs

Jesus, the Light of the World   TFF 59
God himself is present   LBW 249

◐ Sosa, Pablo. Argentina. "Allí Está Jesús" from *Éste es el Día*. U. GIA G-7021.

◐ Swahili, trad. "Bwana awabariki/May God Bless Us and Keep Us." SATB. TFF 162.

✧ Cash, Ed/Chris Tomlin/Stephan Sharp. "Made to Worship" from WT.

✧ Cochran, Gordan/Jon Neufeld/Tim Neufeld. "Great in All the Earth" from CCLI.

✧ Getty, Keith/Stuart Townend. "In Christ Alone" from WT.

✧ Ingram, Jason/Matt Hammitt. "Let It Bring You Praise" from WT.

✧ Ligertwood, Brooke/David Strasser/Rich Mulling. "Like Incense/Sometimes by Step" from CCLI.

✧ Mcclarney, Chris/Anthony Skinner. "Your Love Never Fails" from WT.

Music for the Day
Choral

Hopp, Roy, arr. Bret Heim. "Fruitful Trees, the Spirit's Sowing." SATB, org. CPH 98-3181.

Lawson, Philip. "If Ye Love Me." SATB. Pavane P1241.

Livingston, Donald/William Mathis. "Come Down, O Love Divine." AFP 9780800675356.

Miller, Aaron David. "Eternal Light" from *The New Gloria Deo: Music for Small Choirs*. SAB, pno. AFP 9780806698403.

Scott, K. Lee. "Servants of Peace." SATB, org, opt br and assembly. SEL 425-822.

Wilby, Philip. "If Ye Love Me." SSATB, org. Banks Music (UK) ECS 191.

Children's Choir

● Anderson, Shari. "I Want to Walk as a Child of the Light" in *ChildrenSing in Worship, Vol. 2*. U, kybd, fl. AFP 9781451424126.

Cherwien, David M. "Filled with the Spirit's Power." U, org, fl. CPH 98-3469.

Proulx, Richard. "Happy Are Those." 2 pt trbl, org, fl, ob. GIA G-5336.

Keyboard / Instrumental

● Burkhardt, Michael. "I Want to Walk as a Child of the Light" from *Eight Improvisations on 20th Century Hymn Tunes*. Org. MSM 10-707.

● Kosche, Kenneth T. "Let Us Ever Walk with Jesus" from *For Manuals Only, Set 1*. Org or pno. CPH 97-7452.

● Manz, Paul. "Lasset uns mit Jesu ziehen" from *Ten Chorale Improvisations, Set 9*. Org. MSM 10-359.

Organ, Anne Krentz. "Lasst uns erfreuen" from *Be Thou My Vision: Piano Reflections*. Pno. AFP 9780800678524.

Handbell

● Afdahl, Lee. "The Lord's My Shepherd." 3 or 5 oct hb, opt 2 oct hc, L3. AFP 9780800659905.

● Behnke, John. "Let Us Ever Walk With Jesus." 3 oct, L2. CPH 97-7106.

Stitt, Julie. "I Want Jesus to Walk With Me." 3-6 oct, L4. AGEHR AG36031.

Tuesday, February 18
Martin Luther, renewer of the church, died 1546

On this day in 1546, Martin Luther died at the age of sixty-two. For a time, he was an Augustinian monk, but it is his work as a biblical scholar, translator of the Bible, public confessor of the faith, reformer of the liturgy, theologian, educator, and father of German vernacular literature that holds him in our remembrance. In Luther's own judgment, the greatest of all of his works was his catechism, written to instruct people in the basics of faith. And it was his baptism that sustained him in his trials as a reformer.

February 23, 2014
Seventh Sunday after Epiphany
Lectionary 7

In today's first reading we hear, "You shall be holy, for I the Lord *your God am holy." Yet we know we cannot achieve perfection. Our attempts to love neighbors and even our enemies fall short of what God desires for us. Yet in Jesus we see one who loved even those who persecuted and killed him. We are made holy in baptism, and forgiven at the table of God's mercy. As a people made holy by God, we go in peace to love as we have been loved.*

Prayer of the Day

Holy God of compassion, you invite us into your way of forgiveness and peace. Lead us to love our enemies, and transform our words and deeds to be like his through whom we pray, Jesus Christ, our Savior and Lord.

Gospel Acclamation

Alleluia. In those who obey the ¹ word of Christ,* the love of God has ¹ reached perfection. *Alleluia.* (1 John 2:5)

Readings and Psalm
Leviticus 19:1-2, 9-18

The Holiness Code in Leviticus urges people to be holy since God is holy. Holiness is lived out in partiality for and consideration of the poor and the weak. We are to love our neighbors as ourselves.

Psalm 119:33-40

Teach me, O Lord, the way of your statutes. (Ps. 119:33)

1 Corinthians 3:10-11, 16-23

Jesus Christ is the foundation of the church and its ministry. We are God's temple because God's Spirit dwells in us, and we belong to Christ. Hence we are called to build wisely upon this sure foundation not for our own benefit but for others to experience Christ's benefits.

Matthew 5:38-48

In the Sermon on the Mount, Jesus declares an end to the law of vengeance. God's people will respond to evil with love and forgiveness.

Preface   Sundays

Color   Green

Prayers of Intercession

The prayers are prepared locally for each occasion. The following examples may be adapted or used as appropriate.

Guided by the light of Christ, who has been made known to the nations, we offer our prayers for the church, the world, and all people in need.

A brief silence.

Holy and perfect God, you call us to share your word of love even when it seems like foolishness to the world. Make your church bold to proclaim our hope in Christ. Lord, in your mercy,

hear our prayer.

You make the sun to rise and the rain to fall on all. Feed rich and poor, land and animals, with your abundance. Lord, in your mercy,

hear our prayer.

You call us to the ways of justice. Lead all who govern in the path of justice, so that those in need will not be forgotten. Lord, in your mercy,

hear our prayer.

All in need belong to you through Christ. Strengthen weary caregivers. Comfort those who are sick and in pain (*especially*). Lord, in your mercy,

hear our prayer.

Help this congregation trust that your Spirit dwells in us. Show us the way to be your holy people. Lord, in your mercy,

hear our prayer.

Here other intercessions may be offered.

Sustain us, O God, until we gather with all your saints from every time and place (*especially Polycarp, Bishop of Smyrna and martyr*) in your eternal protection. Lord, in your mercy,

hear our prayer.

Radiant God, hear the prayers of your people, spoken or silent, for the sake of the one who has made his dwelling among us, your Son, Jesus Christ our Savior.

Amen.

Images in the Readings

The **enemy** is a metaphoric category throughout the Bible. Psychologists tell us that most humans care for only a small "sympathy group," and those further away receive less concern. In extending the Israelite call to love the neighbor, the Matthew reading includes several examples of the outsider—the evildoer, the enemy, the persecutor, the unrighteous, the tax collector—whom we are called to love. Too complete an overlap between the church and the nation makes such love of the enemy nearly impossible, and we need to resist such an overlap.

Leviticus ordered the farmers to leave some produce in the field for the poor to **glean**. The tale of Ruth and Boaz is set in the situation of the poor widows gleaning what the rich man leaves—a sort of ancient rummage sale. Yet Matthew calls us to far more care than this.

Most biblical societies had **temples**, understood as houses of the deities whose protection the people desired. Many were like the Lincoln Memorial: open porticoes with a central statue of the god or goddess. To honor the deity, devotees visited the temple, with gifts that supported its staff. Assuming an imminent eschaton, Paul sees no need for any such Christian buildings. Rather, the community is the temple within which God dwells.

Ideas for the Day

◆ Because of the way the calendar works, we do not often get to celebrate a seventh Sunday after Epiphany. However, this gospel text from the Sermon on the Mount is crucial to some portions of the Christian community, especially the historic peace churches: the Mennonites, Church of the Brethren, and the Amish. It is a good time to lift up in prayer our brothers and sisters in those communions for their witness to peace. Stories of radical love of the enemy and refusal to do violence can be found throughout Christian history, but perhaps most notably in recent times in the story of the West Nickel Mines School tragedy in Pennsylvania and the ensuing witness of the Amish community to forgiveness, detailed in *Amish Grace: How Forgiveness Transcended Tragedy,* by Donald Kraybill, Steven Nolt, and David Weaver-Zercher (San Francisco: Jossey-Bass, 2007). Another powerful resource on forgiveness is Helen Whitney's 180-minute documentary *Forgiveness: A Time to Love and a Time to Hate* (PBS, 2011), which examines hatred, violence, loss, and forgiveness in the context of the Pennsylvania school shootings and other high-profile events.

◆ The parable of the good Samaritan asks, Who is my neighbor? But today's gospel, about retaliation and enemies, might ask us to answer, honestly, Who is my enemy? Perhaps this morning's rite of confession and forgiveness can focus less on our desire for God's forgiveness and more on our need to forgive. What would it mean to pray, very intentionally, for those who have wronged us, those who oppose our attempts to fulfill God's mission in our lives, those who have expressed directly their opposition to our goals? The more honest we are in identifying those troubled relationships in our lives, the more we might discover as well our own need for forgiveness.

◆ "Do not even the Gentiles do the same?" (Matt. 5:47). For those of us without Jewish heritage, this gospel is a reminder that Jesus' "tribe" was not that of our ancestors—we become part of God's temple by grace. What lines of "tribal identity" inform our lives? How do we use our cars, our clothes, our jobs, our homes to proclaim our identity, and how often do we simply love those who love us? Invite worshipers, silently or in writing, to confess the unspoken ways we draw lines among peoples. Then share ways to speak welcome across those lines.

Connections with the Liturgy

In the prayers of intercession each Sunday, we are asked to pray for the whole world, the church universal, peace and justice in the world, the nations and those in authority, and the community. By attending to this list, we will regularly pray for those whom we might first think of as evildoers, enemies, persecutors, the unrighteous, and crooked political collaborators.

Let the Children Come

Children have probably noticed that colors in the church change from time to time. Today point out to them that green is in use and has been since Christmas. Where do they see this color in the worship space? Prepare children for the upcoming change of liturgical seasons by inviting them to watch for white next week (Transfiguration) and then purple during Lent. Some children may wish to wear the appropriate color on the appropriate day. Prepare a calendar or handout showing the church year colors. Children can refer to this calendar at home as they prepare for worship each week.

Assembly Song
Gathering

Built on a rock   ELW 652, LBW 365
Alleluia! Voices raise   ELW 828
Christ is made the sure foundation   ELW 645

Psalmody

"Change Your Heart and Mind." *Psallite* A-171.
Mummert, Mark. "Psalm 119: 33-40," Refrain 1, from PSCY.
Nelson, Ronald A. "Psalm 119:33-40" from PWA.

Hymn of the Day

Great God, your love has called us   ELW 358, WOV 666   *RYBURN*

You are holy   ELW 525   *DU ÄR HELIG*

Goodness is stronger than evil   ELW 721   *GOODNESS IS STRONGER*

Offering

Oh, praise the gracious power   ELW 651, WOV 750

O Jesus, joy of loving hearts   ELW 658, LBW 356

Communion

Thee we adore, O Savior   ELW 476, LBW 199

Bring peace to earth again   ELW 700

Eternal Spirit of the living Christ   ELW 402

You are holy   ELW 525

Sending

Awake, O sleeper, rise from death   ELW 452, WOV 745

Lord of glory, you have brought us   ELW 707

Additional Assembly Songs

❂ Jesus ose   TFF 144

When the storms of life are raging   TFF 198

❂ Kijugo, Joas. Tanzania. "The Love of God Almighty" from *Set Free: A Collection of African Hymns*. SATB and cantor. AFP 9780806600451.

✿ Cantelon, Ben/Jason Ingram/Mia Fieldes. "Be Exalted" from CCLI.

✿ Fellingham, Nathan. "Holy Holy" from WT.

✿ Foreman, Jonathan/Tim Foreman. "Meant to Live" from CCLI.

✿ Hughes, Tim. "Name Above all Names" from CCLI.

✿ Rend Collective Experiment. "Second Chance" from WT.

✿ Stanfill, Kristian. "Lord of All" from CCLI.

Music for the Day
Choral

Bell, John. "Love One Another." SAB. GIA G-5158.

Dengler, Lee. "Put On Love." SAB, pno. AFP 9781451420784.

Greene, J. William. "Oh, How I Love Your Law, O Lord." SATB. PAR MO207.

● Helgen, John. "You Are Holy." SATB, pno. AFP 9780800676452.

Sirett, Mark. "Immortal Love." SATB, pno. AFP 9781451401011.

Children's Choir

Eltringham, Susan. "Love Your Neighbor." U, pno/gtr. LS 140.

Johnston-Favreau, Cindy. "Jesu, Jesu, Fill Us with Your Love." 2 pt, kybd, fl. GIA G-3000.

Roff, Joseph. "Breathe in Me, O Holy Spirit." U/2 pt, kybd. CPH 98-2993POD.

Keyboard / Instrumental

Callahan, Charles. "O Day of Peace" from *Six Postludes on English Hymn Tunes*. Org. MSM 10-560.

❂ = global song
✿ = praise song
● = relates to hymn of the day

● Miller, Aaron David. "Ryburn" from *Improvisations for the Church Year for Organ, Vol 2*. Org. AFP 9780800676766.

● Raabe, Nancy M. "Du är helig" from *Grace and Peace, Vol. 3: Hymn Portraits for Piano*. Pno. AFP 9780806696959.

Sedio, Mark. "Jesu, Jesu, Fill Us with Your Love" from *Dancing in the Light of God: A Piano Collection*. Pno. AFP 9780800656546.

Handbell

Edwards, Dan. "Holy Is Our God." 3-5 oct, L2+. CG CGB699.

Page, Anna Laura. "Holy God We Praise Your Name." 3-5 oct, L2. CG CGB287.

Tucker, Sondra. "How Firm a Foundation." 3-5 oct hb, opt 1 oct hc, opt C inst, L2+. HOP 2435.

Sunday, February 23

Polycarp, Bishop of Smyrna, martyr, died 156

Polycarp was bishop of Smyrna (in present-day western Turkey) and a link between the apostolic age and the church at the end of the second century. He is said to have been known by John, the author of Revelation. In turn he was known by Iranaeus, bishop of Lyon in France, and Ignatius of Antioch. At the age of eighty-six he was martyred for his faith. When urged to save his life and renounce his faith, Polycarp replied, "Eighty-six years I have served him, and he never did me any wrong. How can I blaspheme my king who saved me?" The magistrate who made the offer was reluctant to kill a gentle old man, but he had no choice. Polycarp was burned at the stake, his death a testimony to the cost of renouncing temptation.

Tuesday, February 25

Elizabeth Fedde, deaconess, died 1921

Fedde was born in Norway and trained as a deaconess. In 1882, at the age of thirty-two, she was asked to come to New York to minister to the poor and to Norwegian seafarers. Her influence was wide-ranging, and she established the Deaconess House in Brooklyn and the Deaconess House and Hospital of the Lutheran Free Church in Minneapolis. She returned home to Norway in 1895 and died there.

Saturday, March 1

George Herbert, hymnwriter, died 1633

As a student at Trinity College, Cambridge, England, George Herbert excelled in languages and music. He went to college with the intention of becoming a priest, but his scholarship attracted the attention of King James I. Herbert served in parliament for two years. After the death of King James and at the urging of a friend, Herbert's interest in ordained ministry was renewed. He was ordained a priest in 1630 and served the little parish of St. Andrew Bremerton until his death. He was noted for unfailing care for his parishioners, bringing the sacraments to them when they were ill, and providing food and clothing for those in need. Herbert is best remembered, however, as a writer of poems and hymns such as "Come, My Way, My Truth, My Life" (ELW 816).

March 2, 2014
Transfiguration of Our Lord
Last Sunday after Epiphany

Today's festival is a bridge between the Advent-Christmas-Epiphany cycle that comes to a close today and the Lent-Easter cycle that begins in several days. On the mount of transfiguration Jesus is revealed as God's beloved Son, echoing the words at his baptism. This vision of glory sustains us as Jesus faces his impending death in Jerusalem.

We turn this week to Ash Wednesday and our yearly baptismal journey from Lent to Easter. Some churches put aside the alleluia at the conclusion of today's liturgy. This word of joy will be omitted during the penitential season of Lent and will be sung again at Easter.

Prayer of the Day

O God, in the transfiguration of your Son you confirmed the mysteries of the faith by the witness of Moses and Elijah, and in the voice from the bright cloud declaring Jesus your beloved Son, you foreshadowed our adoption as your children. Make us heirs with Christ of your glory, and bring us to enjoy its fullness, through Jesus Christ, our Savior and Lord, who lives and reigns with you and the Holy Spirit, one God, now and forever.

Gospel Acclamation

Alleluia. This is my | Son, my Chosen,* lis- | ten to him! *Alleluia.* (Luke 9:35)

Readings and Psalm
Exodus 24:12-18

At Mount Sinai, Moses experienced the presence of God for forty days and forty nights. The "glory of the Lord" settled on the mountain, and on the seventh day God called out to Moses. On the mountain God gave Moses the stone tablets inscribed with the ten commandments.

Psalm 2

You are my son; this day have I begotten you. (Ps. 2:7)

or Psalm 99

Proclaim the greatness of the LORD; worship upon God's holy hill. (Ps. 99:9)

2 Peter 1:16-21

At the transfiguration, God's voice was heard, declaring Jesus to be the beloved Son. By the activity of the Holy Spirit, God's voice continues to be heard through the word of scripture.

Matthew 17:1-9

Shortly before he enters Jerusalem, where he will be crucified, Jesus is revealed to his disciples in a mountaintop experience of divine glory called the transfiguration.

Preface   Transfiguration

Color   White

Prayers of Intercession

The prayers are prepared locally for each occasion. The following examples may be adapted or used as appropriate.

Guided by the light of Christ, who has been made known to the nations, we offer our prayers for the church, the world, and all people in need.

A brief silence.

God of glory and grace, you call us to wait upon your name. Give your church on earth the strength and patience to be the people you would have us be. Lord, in your mercy,

hear our prayer.

You created mountains and hills, caverns and valleys. Help us to be good stewards of the heights and depths of your creation. Lord, in your mercy,

hear our prayer.

Raise up leaders in this day with wisdom like Moses, so that all will know your peace and justice (*especially*). Lord, in your mercy,
hear our prayer.
You provide us with mercy and love through your beloved Son. Shine the light of his love to heal the sick, feed the hungry, and comfort the grieving. Be with all who suffer (*especially*). Lord, in your mercy,
hear our prayer.
You raise up your children and counsel us not to be afraid. Help this community of faith to be fearless in proclaiming the gospel. Lord, in your mercy,
hear our prayer.
Here other intercessions may be offered.
Holy Spirit, keep us in your care until you gather us with (*John and Charles Wesley and*) all the saints from every time and place in the company of our sovereign God. Lord, in your mercy,
hear our prayer.
Radiant God, hear the prayers of your people, spoken or silent, for the sake of the one who has made his dwelling among us, your Son, Jesus Christ our Savior.
Amen.

Images in the Readings

Once again the readings include the central biblical images of **light** and **mountain**.

Yet God is not only brilliant light: important for the readings is the image of the **cloud**. Although contemporary people tend to think of clouds as relating to weather conditions, in the Bible the cloud is a sign of the presence of God. It is as if God covers the earth, brings life, effecting much yet suddenly vanishing. Christians can add that from God as cloud rain down the waters of baptism.

We are so accustomed to the language of being children of a God who is like a father that we miss the astonishment of the early church, when this imagery was a religious surprise. Christ is to God as a **son** is to a father, and we are not pitiful creatures struggling to life in a hostile environment, but rather children cared for by a beneficent God. "Son of Man," on the other hand, is the biblical name for the apocalyptic judge, thus only paradoxically the beloved Son of God.

Ideas for the Day

◆ The gospel text not only transports us to a mountaintop—it takes us to an epiphany the likes of which few churchgoers ever expect this side of the grave. But as Jesus' "dazzling white" clothes are a precursor of the angels at his empty tomb, so is this Sunday a sneak preview of the resurrection. Many congregations bury the alleluia before Lent begins, but be sure that the alleluias you do speak and sing on this day are resurrection-flavored. Jesus transfigured before us is a sign of the transformation we all can anticipate when we see our savior face-to-face.

◆ It is said that when the poet Robert Frost was asked if he had hope for the future, he replied, "yes, and for the past also." The presence of Moses and Elijah with Jesus is a sign of the way God's salvation transcends our usual linear view of time, reaching back as well as forward with redemption and grace. What might it mean to stand on a mountaintop and look back on the regrets of our lives or the ravages of history and see the resurrection shining on those things already past? How would it change how we look forward, knowing that the past is redeemed already?

◆ "Get up and do not be afraid" (Matt. 17:7). Jesus' words echo those of the angels and of every epiphany of the gospels. Are the disciples afraid of what they have seen? Or afraid of returning to normal life now that they have seen this glory? Either way, Jesus commands that they go back down the mountain, following him to a scene that will be frightening beyond their imaginations: Jesus' arrest, humiliation, and death. Does this momentary vision of glory help them through this journey in the valley? How can our brief visions of God's love in worship strengthen us in the trials we have not yet foreseen? Teach your congregation the prayer for "ventures of which we cannot see the ending" (*Evangelical Lutheran Worship*, p. 304), and invite them to enter into each day this week with the words "get up and do not be afraid."

Connections with the Liturgy

At baptism, the candidate is signed with the cross, to which Jesus walks, and the minister calls each of the baptized "child of God." So each baptism recalls the transfiguration.

Let the Children Come

This Sunday concludes the Christmas cycle. Today's gospel is full of powerful images. If your church doesn't already do so, make crayons and paper available for children to use during the service today. Invite children (and adults) to listen carefully to the gospel and pick out an image that stands out to them, which they can draw and color during the sermon. Or, give copies of a detailed icon or picture of the transfiguration to the children that they can color.

Assembly Song
Gathering

Immortal, invisible, God only wise   ELW 834, LBW 526
Shine, Jesus, shine   ELW 671, TFF 64, W&P 123, WOV 651
O Morning Star, how fair and bright!   ELW 308, LBW 76

Psalmody and Acclamations

Mathis, William H. Refrain for "Psalm 99" from *After the Prelude: Year A*. U/cant, hb. CG CGB616 (digital version), CGB617 (printed version). Use with ELW psalm tone 6 or 10 (in C).

Roberts, Leon C. "Bow Down before the Holy Mountain of God (Psalm 99)." TFF 11.

Hopson, Hal H. "Psalm 2" from TP.

Ferguson, John. *Gospel Acclamations for Advent–Transfiguration.*

Hymn of the Day

Come, beloved of the Maker   ELW 306   JILL

Drawn to the Light   ELW 593   LA CROSSE

He comes to us as one unknown   ELW 737, WOV 768   REPTON

Offering

In thee is gladness   ELW 867

How good, Lord, to be here!   ELW 315, LBW 89

Communion

Alleluia, song of gladness   ELW 318

Jesus on the mountain peak   ELW 317

Now, Lord   ELW 202

Sending

We are marching in the light   ELW 866, W&P 148, WOV 650

Beautiful Savior   ELW 838, LBW 518

Additional Assembly Songs

How lovely on the mountains   TFF 99

Open our eyes, Lord   TFF 98, W&P 113

⊕ Halle, hallelujah   GS3 21

⊕ Scheer, Greg. Ghana traditional. "The Lord Is Ruler Over All" from *Global Songs for Worship*. SATB, gtr. Faith Alive/Calvin Institute of Christian Worship. 9781592554423.

✿ Beeching, Vicky. "Listening" from CCLI.

✿ Hellenbronth, Luke/Nikki Fletcher/Tim Hughes. "Wait for You" from CCLI.

✿ Houston, Joel/Matt Crocker/Scott Ligertwood. "Break Free" from CCLI.

✿ Redman, Matt. "Can I Ascend" from CCLI.

✿ Ruis, David. "Let Your Glory Fall" from CCLI.

✿ Wilson, Peter/Israel Houghton. "I Receive" from WT.

Music for the Day
Choral

Behnke, John. "This Is My Beloved Son." 2 pt, kybd or 3 oct hb/hc, opt wch. CPH 98-4106.

Ferguson, John. "Be Transformed." SATB, org. AFP 9780806698175.

Helgen, John. "Brighter Than the Sun." SATB, kybd. AFP 9780800659158.

Hofreiter, Paul W. "Anthem for Transfiguration." SATB, org. AFP 9780800664190.

Martinson, Joel. "Transfiguration." U, desc, org. PAR 9511.

Proulx, Richard. "Jesus, Lead the Way." SATB, org, br qrt, timp. GIA G-5370.

Children's Choir

Burkhardt, Michael. "Nimemwona Bwana" in *Part-Singing Global Style*. 3 pt, solo, shakers, claves, drm. MSM 50-9811.

Helgen, John. "Beautiful Savior." U, opt 2 pt, kybd. AFP 9780800638368.

Kohrs, Jonathan. "Down from the Mount of Glory." U, opt SATB, org. CPH 98-3222POD.

Keyboard / Instrumental

● Biery, James. "Repton" from *Contemplations on Four English Hymn Tunes*. Org. MSM 10-621.

Carter, John. "Beautiful Savior" from *Contemplative Folk Tunes for Piano*. Pno. AFP 9780800659776.

● Organ, Anne Krentz. "Repton" from *Come to Us, Creative Spirit: Piano Reflections*. Pno. AFP 9780800659042.

Phillips, Craig. "Deo gracias" from *O Love, How Deep: Three Hymn Settings for Organ*. Org. MSM 10-240.

Handbell

● Gramann, Fred. "Everlasting Light." 3-5 oct, L4. CG CGB361.

Keller, Michael. "Transfiguration." 5-7 oct, L6. AGEHR AG57002.

Tyrrell, Robyn. "Pandemonium (Psalm 2)." 4-6 oct, L4. AGEHR AG46024.

Sunday, March 2

John Wesley, died 1791; Charles Wesley, died 1788; renewers of the church

The Wesleys were leaders of a revival in the Church of England. Their spiritual discipline (or method) of frequent communion, fasting, and advocacy for the poor earned them the name "Methodists." The Wesleys were missionaries in the American colony of Georgia for a time, but returned to England discouraged. Following a conversion experience while reading Luther's *Preface to the Epistle to the Romans*, John was perhaps the greatest force in eighteenth-century revival. The brothers' desire was that the Methodist Societies would be a movement for renewal in the Church of England, but after their deaths the societies developed a separate status.

Charles wrote more than six hundred hymns, including "Hark! The Herald Angels Sing" (ELW 270), "Christ, Whose Glory Fills the Skies" (ELW 553), and "Love Divine, All Loves Excelling" (ELW 631).

⊕ = global song
✿ = praise song
● = relates to hymn of the day

LENT

PREPARING FOR LENT

Lent is a season when the church focuses on preparation of baptismal candidates and the continual process of conversion for everyone. It is a solemn and penitential period. Many churches even retire or bury their Alleluias for the duration of the season. Lent is grounded in and modeled after the forty days Jesus spent in the desert, tempted by the devil. As people of faith, we lay aside those practices and material goods that lead us into temptation, and we take up the full armor of God, especially scripture, prayer, almsgiving, and fasting. We do this not to enamor ourselves of our own sanctity, but rather to gather with the whole Christian community as it practices its participation in the death of Christ—that we might know the alleluia of the resurrection with Christ.

Lectionary

Of all the years to begin offering a catechumenal process in your congregation, lectionary year A is the most felicitous. In fact, many practitioners of the catechumenate recommend that the year A Lenten readings be used every year. These are the classic mystagogical texts in use since the early centuries of the church to guide catechumens into the way of Jesus. The recent *Go Make Disciples: An Invitation to Baptismal Living* (Augsburg Fortress, 2012), suggests:

> Especially for congregations having a significant group of baptismal candidates during the season of Lent, consider using the scripture readings from year A of the lectionary, regardless of the actual three-year lectionary cycle currently in use. The gospel readings about Nicodemus (John 3, the second Sunday in Lent of year A), the woman from Samaria (John 4, the third Sunday in Lent of year A), the healing of the man born blind (John 9, the fourth Sunday in Lent of year A), and the raising of Lazarus (John 11, the fifth Sunday in Lent of year A) are powerful stories about conversion and lend themselves particularly well to preparing for baptism. (116)

These four readings are some of the most vivid in all the gospels. Each one includes an encounter between a potential new convert and Jesus Christ. Each of the inquirers comes to Jesus out of, and is profoundly shaped by, their own station in life. Nicodemus, a religious leader, seeks clarification of his own religious tradition in relation to the teachings of Jesus. The woman from Samaria, though religious, comes from a tradition outside of Judaism, and so encounters Christ on the boundary, taking his message back to her own community. The man born blind meets Jesus in the process of making sense in his own life of his healing, and how to talk about that healing with those doubting around him. In the raising of Lazarus, we have the very conversion of death itself, Lazarus brought out of the bondage of death into life with his family, community, and Christ. Even the reading for the first Sunday in Lent fits in this structure, for it is the temptation of Jesus in the desert, although in this case the example is that of the devil who seeks to convert Jesus rather than live open to conversion by him.

Over the course of these weeks, what you have as a preacher and worship leader is a tremendous opportunity to illustrate how the encounters between Jesus and others in scripture are very much like how any of us, all of us, still encounter Jesus today. If Jesus can meet a foreign woman, a religious leader, a blind man, even a grieving community, and bring about transformation and faith, perhaps there is hope he can also do this among us.

Just so, all these readings offer a model for how to invite the assembly into an encounter with scripture during the Lenten season. What is the shape of the Lenten journey? It is nowhere better expressed than in Paul Hoffman's wonderful little book on The WAY at Phinney Ridge Lutheran in Seattle:

> A characteristic of The WAY . . . is that there is no curriculum. We have come to say that our curriculum is lectionary and life. What we mean by that is that every person—inquirer, new convert, or lifelong disciple—comes to the Scriptures with his or her own set of life experiences. *What does this mean?* The agonies and ecstasies of everyday living provide rich and abundant grist for discussion, enrichment, and interaction with the Word of God. This interaction allows for new and longtime Christians alike to listen for the voice of the Holy Spirit to lead and guide them. The WAY helps all

God's people to see the Spirit's breath blowing through their vocations, in marriage, in parenting, in sickness, in triumph, in every aspect of life, challenging or joyous.

The catechumenate . . . means a way of being with one another and with our God that is dialogical, relational, and drawn from the deep wells of the participants' real-life experiences and interactions with the Holy Scriptures. (*Faith Forming Faith: Bringing New Christians to Baptism and Beyond* [Cascade Books, 2012], 33)

Liturgical Arts

The season of Lent provides an opportunity to increase, revamp, or continue the liturgical arts that center around baptism. Although Lent is often a time of intense preparation of candidates for baptism, it also serves well as a focus point for the entire baptismal ministry of the congregation. Consider some of the following.

Enrollment of candidates for baptism. Near the conclusion of the time of study and reflection (the exploration stage of the catechumenate), those who desire to be baptized publicly may express that intention through the rite of enrollment, often held on the first Sunday in Lent. A form for the rite of enrollment is available on the *Go Make Disciples* Companion CD-ROM (Augsburg Fortress, 2012; ISBN 9781451426137) and in *Holy Baptism and Related Rites*, Renewing Worship, vol. 3 (Evangelical Lutheran Church in America, 2002). The book of enrollment (in which those preparing for baptism signed their names) could be prominently displayed somewhere in the worship space throughout the season, perhaps near the baptismal font if space allows.

Gather baptismal supplies from the community. Does someone in your congregation make candles for baptismal candidates? Or stitch baptism symbols on a napkin or towel? Have you recently considered where and how the water is prepared to fill the baptismal font? Do you have a potter who might make a pitcher to carry the water? Do you give a gift, such as a daily devotional resource?

If you are preparing for a full immersion baptism at the Easter Vigil, see "Constructing a Temporary Font" in *Go Make Disciples: An Invitation to Baptismal Living* (173). If possible, research locations to conduct the baptism in a local river or lake.

The daily prayer offices of the church are an important outgrowth of baptismal living and the ministry of the baptized.

The seasons of Lent and Advent invite prayerful reflection on the gift and hope of our relationship with God in Jesus Christ. Most congregations hold midweek Lenten services and some provide midweek Advent services.

These seasons provide excellent opportunities to use evening and/or morning prayer and put them deep into the memory bank of worshipers. With their emphasis on prayer, praise, and proclamation, these services offer solid grounding for a congregation's deepening of their life and mission. They also lend themselves well to the kind of contemplative mood that often seems appropriate during these seasons. (*Keeping Time: The Church's Years*, Using Evangelical Lutheran Worship, vol. 3 [Augsburg Fortress, 2009] 155)

In the tradition of the church, all midweek and non-communion liturgies were the responsibility of lay leaders. As you prepare midweek worship (a valued tradition in many congregations), consider how to ensure lay leadership is integral to these services. If you are planning midweek meals and learning opportunities (perhaps modeled after or even paired with the period of intense preparation for baptismal candidates), ask how these times of meditation and community might connect with baptismal living.

Music
Kyrie

Within the pattern of Sunday worship, specific portions of the liturgy are sung from week to week. These liturgical songs, functioning as a kind of infrastructure, are sometimes more relied upon than noticed. Take the Kyrie, for example. It is quite evocative of the Lenten season. The Roman church retained the Greek, making the Kyrie unique within the Latin rite—all the other liturgical songs being sung in Latin. The church in this period also often "troped" the Kyrie, adding petitions to the basic "Kyrie eleison. Christe eleison. Kyrie eleison." This practice influences the shape of the majority of the Kyries offered in the ten settings of Holy Communion in *Evangelical Lutheran Worship*. There are, however, some beautiful unembellished Kyries available in the Service Music section, including Dinah Reindorf's setting (ELW 151) and a selection from Franz Schubert's *Deutsche Messe* (ELW 152), among others. Select one of these simple settings for use during Lent, and include a brief history or comment on the Kyrie in the worship folder.

Expanded proclamation in song

What follows are suggestions for *two* hymns to pair with the gospel text for each of the Sundays in Lent. Consider singing one before and one after the gospel, or singing one before and one after the sermon. Comprehensive notes on all of these hymns are provided in *Hymnal Companion to Evangelical Lutheran Worship* (Augsburg Fortress, 2010).

Lent 1: Temptation of Jesus (Matthew 4)
ELW 320 The glory of these forty days
This anonymous Latin hymn "runs out the fasting and deliverance of Moses, Elijah, Daniel, and John in relation to Christ and then asks that we too may in fasting and prayer turn to God" (*Hymnal Companion*, 109).
ELW 319 O Lord, throughout these forty days
This hymn is, for many congregations, closely associated with the Lenten season. It was originally part of Claudia Hernaman's *Child's Book of Praise* (London, 1873).

Lent 2: Nicodemus (John 3)
ELW 456 Baptized in water
The text begins with an allusion to John 3:5 and then celebrates what God does in baptism—cleanses, offers an inheritance, makes promises, works death and life in Christ, sets free, offers forgiveness, and gifts the Spirit.
ELW 457 Waterlife
This introspective hymn "takes the marks of baptism—covenant, cleansing, love, and adoption in the trinitarian embrace—and reflects on their meaning and continuing resonance in the life of the Christian" (*Hymnal Companion*, 283).

Lent 3: Samaritan woman (John 4)
ELW 334 Tree of Life and awesome mystery
Marty Haugen constructed this hymn to match the year A readings for Lent. It is designed so that "the congregation sings back the scripture they have heard in the sermon" (*Hymnal Companion*, 128).

ELW 611 I heard the voice of Jesus say
"Each stanza is Jesus' call in the first two lines and our response in the last two, expressing the shalom that Jesus brings" (*Hymnal Companion*, 125).

Lent 4: Man born blind (John 9)
ELW 793 Be thou my vision
This is a prayer for the indwelling of Christ with his attributes, including vision.
ELW 724 All who love and serve your city
The product of a hymn-writing revival led by Ian Fraser and Erik Routley, this hymn was designed to be useful within a Christian Aid context. "It proclaims the mercy and judgment of God, along with our responsive responsibility to work while it is day in the cities where riots were raging across the United States in the 1960s" (*Hymnal Companion*, 581).

Lent 5: Raising of Lazarus (John 11)
ELW 495 We who once were dead
This hymn poses light and life in Christ against death and night, then offers eucharistic images in that context.
ELW 333 Jesus is a rock in weary land
This African American spiritual begins with Lazarus, but then "in typical African American fashion . . . one incident leads to others in a narrative of Christ as both servant and victor: from Lazarus to washing the disciples' feet to palms and victory over death and hell" (*Hymnal Companion*, 128). It is a hymn that expressly leads to Holy Week.

Worship Texts for Lent

Confession and Forgiveness

All may make the sign of the cross, the sign marked at baptism,
as the presiding minister begins.
Blessed be the holy Trinity, ✛ one God,
the fountain of living water,
the rock who gave us birth,
our light and our salvation.
Amen.

Come, let us acknowledge our sin and seek God's face,
that we may live.

Silence is kept for reflection.

Holy God,
we confess that we have turned away
from you and from our neighbors,
and in toward ourselves.
We have sought security in possessions
and the place of power in relationships.
We have trusted ourselves most of all.
Turn us back to you, O God.
In your mercy, forgive our sinfulness
and cleanse us from guilt and shame.
Guide us on the path of freedom
that is your gift to us in Christ our Lord.
Amen.

Hear for yourselves:
There is no condemnation for those who are in Christ Jesus.
In the waters of baptism
grace abounds for you and for all.
God turns to you in love
and puts away every sin, every wrong turn,
for the sake of ✛ Jesus,
the one God sent to save the world.
Amen.

Offering Prayer

God our provider,
you have not fed us with bread alone,
but with words of grace and life.
Bless us and these your gifts,
which we receive from your bounty,
through Jesus Christ our Lord.
Amen.

Invitation to Communion

Come to the table prepared for you.
Taste the overflowing grace of God.

Prayer after Communion

God of mercy,
we give you thanks for seating us at your table
and serving us with the food of eternal life.
We who once were dead
are now living members of your Son,
awakened by the breathing of your Spirit.
Send us out to awaken others to the mystery of your love,
which is revealed to all the world
in the one who came to give himself away,
Jesus Christ our Lord.
Amen.

Sending of Communion

Eternal God,
whose glory is revealed in the crucified and risen Lord,
bless those who go forth to share your word and sacrament
with our sisters and brothers
who are *sick/homebound/imprisoned.*
In your love and care, nourish and strengthen
those to whom we bring this communion
in the body and blood of your Son,
that we may all feast upon your abundant love
made known in Jesus Christ our Lord.
Amen.

Blessing

God the Father, + Son, and Holy Spirit
watch over your going out and your coming in,
from this time forth and forevermore.
Amen.

Dismissal

Go in peace. Remember the poor.
Thanks be to God.

SEASONAL RITES FOR LENT

Midweek Lenten Series: Making Change

Change is a constant in our lives. Some changes mark gradual transitions, as when daytime shifts toward twilight or winter turns to spring. Others happen in the blink of an eye, separating time into "before" and "after." We choose to undergo some changes after carefully considering our options, while others are forced upon us.

In the weeks, days, and hours before Jesus' crucifixion, the disciples also experienced change: a change of venue as the gates of Jerusalem approached; a change of plans as their long-awaited Messiah was arrested and tried; a change of circumstance as the crowds shouted "Crucify!"

Change is hard. We long for the expected and familiar, but all too often find ourselves in the midst of uncertainty and the unknown. We cannot predict how things will turn out. The hymnwriter Joachim Neander proclaimed God's steadfast love in the midst of life's inevitable changes: "All my hope on God is founded who will all my trust renew, who through change and chance will guide me, only good and only true. God unknown, God alone, call my heart to be thine own" (ELW 757).

Link to Sunday worship: The gospel readings for the Sundays in Lent for year A are filled with stories where Jesus creates the possibility of change and new life. He challenges Nicodemus to be born from above (Lent 2, John 3:1-17). He offers the Samaritan woman the living water that quenches all thirst (Lent 3, John 4:5-42). Jesus gives sight to the blind man (Lent 4, John 9:1-41) and raises Lazarus from the grave (Lent 5, John 11:1-45).

Overview

Week of Lent 1: Change of Season
"For everything there is a season." We hear those familiar words telling us that life is full of changes. Jesus' parables are also filled with images of life transformed. Just as the mustard seed grows into a tree or yeast turns flour into bread, we too are called to be agents of change in the kingdom of God. Christ did not come to earth to maintain the status quo, but rather to usher in a change of season.

Week of Lent 2: Change of Habit
Bad habits are hard to break. The letter to the Galatians urges us to replace them with the fruits of the Spirit. Love, patience, generosity, and self-control are just some of the good habits practiced by those whose foundation is built on Christ.

Week of Lent 3: Change of Circumstances
We move from elementary to middle school, or from our hometown to a new community. We lose a job, or gain a child, or accomplish a goal, or relinquish a dream. Through it all, we learn to give thanks to God in all circumstances.

Week of Lent 4: Change of Heart
Jesus' words to the Pharisees give us pause: "You honor me with your lips, but your hearts are far from me." Jesus invites us to experience a change of heart that will in fact change every part of our lives.

Week of Lent 5: Change of Plans
God's ways are not our own. We expect a conquering king and hero, but Jesus instead leads us down the road to Jerusalem and humbles himself on the cross. God changes our plans and replaces them with a love broader and deeper than anything we could imagine.

Opening Dialogue

Week 1 *(Based on ELW 757, "All my hope on God is founded")*
O God, you are the source of our hope.
Guide us through change and chance.
When we grow weary and faint,
call our hearts to be your own.
When our plans fall to dust,
be our temple and our tower.
When the world lacks joy and beauty,
reveal your splendor, light, and life.
O God, we praise you for the gift of your Son.
Strengthen us to follow the way of the cross.

Week 2 *(Isa. 2:3, 60:19)*
Come, let us go up to the mountain of the Lord,
to the house of the God of Jacob.
That he may teach us his ways;
that we may walk in his paths.
For out of Zion shall go forth instruction,
and the word of the Lord from Jerusalem.
The Lord will be our everlasting light,
and our God will be our glory.

Week 3 *(Ps. 62:2, 46:1-2)*
For all our blessings, we give thanks to the Lord.
God is our rock and salvation, a help in times of plenty.
With all our burdens, we pray to the Lord.
God is our rock and salvation, a help in times of need.
In all our celebrations, we sing praise to the Lord.
God is our rock and salvation, a help in times of joy.
With all our grief, we cry to the Lord.
God is our rock and salvation,
a help in times of sorrow.
We will not fear, though the earth should change.
God is our rock and salvation; thanks be to God!

Week 4 *(Song of Sol. 8:6, Ps. 139:23-24)*
Beloved, set me as a seal upon your heart,
as a seal upon your arm.
For love is strong as death;
passion fierce as the grave.
O God, search me and know my heart;
test me and know my thoughts.
See if there is any wicked way in me,
and lead me in the way everlasting.

Week 5 *(Mark 10:32-34, Luke 18:31-34, Matt. 16:22)*
We see Jesus walking ahead on the road.
He leads us toward Jerusalem.
We follow but are very afraid.
He says the Son of Man will be handed over.
We understand nothing about all these things.
He says the prophets' words will be fulfilled.
We hear him talk of suffering and death.
Forbid it, Lord! This must never happen to you!

Gathering Song

Week 1: All my hope on God is founded   ELW 757
Week 2: Here, O Lord, your servants gather   ELW 530
Week 3: Jesus is a rock in a weary land   ELW 333
Week 4: Spirit of God, descend upon my heart   ELW 800
Week 5: Holy God, holy and glorious   ELW 637

Greeting

The grace of our Lord Jesus Christ, the love of God,
and the communion of the Holy Spirit be with you all.
And also with you.

Prayer

Week 1 *(Gen. 8:22)*
O God of the ages, your creation revolves through seed-time and harvest, cold and heat, summer and winter, day and night. When the seasons come and go and uncertainty looms ahead, we long for the constancy of your love. Give us courage, wisdom, and patience to be your agents of change in the world. In Jesus' name we pray. **Amen.**

Week 2 *(Gal. 5:22-25)*
O God our strength, you are the foundation of our lives. Build up in us the habits of love, joy, peace, patience, kindness, generosity, faithfulness, gentleness, and self-control. Guide us by your Spirit and teach us your ways, that we embody your love to all the world. In Jesus' name we pray. **Amen.**

Week 3
O God our rock and salvation, you walk with us through all the ups and downs of life. Whatever our circumstances, bring us closer to you. Teach us to rejoice in the good times, find hope through the bad times, and always place our trust in you. In Jesus' name we pray. **Amen.**

Week 4 *(Eph. 3:14—4:1)*
O God of our longing, strengthen us and dwell in our hearts, that we be rooted and grounded in your love. Help us to comprehend the breadth and length and height and depth of your mercy shown to us on the cross. Fill our hearts with your grace, that we lead lives that radiate your love to all. In Jesus' name we pray. **Amen.**

Week 5

O God our surprise, you offer so much more than our own limited plans envision. You take our place, becoming our salvation through the cross. As we prepare for Holy Week, strengthen our hearts and minds to follow Jesus on the road to Jerusalem. When we betray like Judas, deny like Peter, and scatter like the disciples, forgive our frailties. Bring us the promise of resurrection and new life in you. In Jesus' name we pray. **Amen.**

Psalmody

Week 1: Psalm 90
Week 2: Psalm 1
Week 3: Psalm 103:1-5, 13-18
Week 4: Psalm 119:1-16
Week 5: Psalm 2

Reading

Week 1: Ecclesiastes 3:1-8
Week 2: Galatians 5:16-25
Week 3: 1 Thessalonians 5:12-24
Week 4: Ezekiel 36:22-28
Week 5: Isaiah 52:13-15

Response

How clear is our vocation, Lord   ELW 580, sts. 1, 4

Gospel Reading

Week 1: Luke 13:18-21
Week 2: Luke 6:46-49
Week 3: Luke 12:22-34
Week 4: Mark 7:1-8, 14-15, 21-23
Week 5: Mark 10:32-34

Reflection

Hymn of the Day

Week 1: As the sun with longer journey   ELW 329
Week 2: Build us up, Lord   ELW 670
Week 3: When we are living   ELW 639
Week 4: Change my heart, O God   ELW 801
Week 5: Lamb of God   ELW 336

Prayers

O God our help,
you walk with us through all of life's changes.
Grant us strength, patience, wisdom,
and understanding.
O God our hope,
you come to us in the life, death, and resurrection of Christ.
Show us your salvation,
and lead us in the way of the cross.
O God our shelter,
you enfold us like a mother hen gathering her chicks.
Watch over all who are sick, grieving, lonely,
and in need this day.
O God our home, you claim us as your beloved children.
Lord, remember us when you come into your kingdom.
Here other prayers may be offered.
All this we ask through the one who gave himself for us,
Jesus Christ, our Lord.
Amen.

Lord's Prayer

Let us pray together:
O triune God in heaven above,
your blessed name we hallow.
Your kingdom come,
your will be done
in this world as in heaven;
give bread for each new day begun;
our sins be all forgiven,
as we forgive what others do;
in every trial see us through;
from evil save us. Amen.

Offering

Offering Prayer (*Matt. 25:35*)

Steadfast God, you bless us amid all the changes and chances of life. Grant us servant hearts, that we may feed the hungry and welcome the stranger in the name of Jesus Christ, our Savior and Lord. **Amen.**

Blessing

Based on 2 Thessalonians 3:16

The Lord of peace give you peace at all times and in all ways. In the name of the Father, ✠ Son, and Holy Spirit. **Amen.**

Sending Song

Week 1: Great is thy faithfulness   ELW 733

Week 2: Let us ever walk with Jesus   ELW 802, LBW 487

Week 3: In the cross of Christ I glory   ELW 324, LBW 104

Week 4: Chief of sinners though I be   ELW 609, LBW 306

Week 5: That priceless grace   ELW 591

Dismissal

Go now in peace, for nothing can separate you from the love of God in Christ Jesus. **Thanks be to God.**

Some of the prayers are based on the text of "O God, our help in ages past" (ELW 632; text by Isaac Watts) and Luke 23:42.

Text of the Lord's Prayer from "Salvation unto us has come" (ELW 590). Text © 2006 Augsburg Fortress.

Accompanying Adults Preparing for Baptism

Lent is often used as the time to prepare candidates for baptism or for affirmation of baptism at the Vigil of Easter. Besides any public worship rites that occur during this pivotal time, how might congregations accompany candidates in their journey? How might the ministry of accompanying candidates for baptism and affirmation of baptism be in the forefront of Lenten and Easter celebrations?

Ideas for Lent

- When the rite of enrollment for those who will be baptized takes place on or near the first Sunday in Lent, the book of enrollment (in which those preparing for baptism signed their names) could be prominently displayed somewhere in the worship space throughout the entire season, perhaps near the baptismal font if space allows.
- Include candidates for baptism or affirmation of baptism in the prayers of intercession each week. Encourage the entire congregation to pray for the candidates each day during Lent.
- Speak about how practicing the disciplines of Lent (prayer, fasting, and works of love) is how the whole church accompanies baptismal candidates as they consciously enter more deeply into these Christian practices.

- Choose hymns and other music appropriate to the themes of conversion that are in the lectionary readings for Lent.
- For congregations holding midweek services of prayer, consider designing them around themes of conversion, discipleship, and rebirth.
- Choose a statement of faith as the focus of small group parish gatherings or classes. Consider using catechism materials from your own tradition, or perhaps even materials from another denominational tradition with which your congregation has a relationship (either a full communion agreement or a common support of service ministries in the wider community). Focus on the Apostles' Creed or the Lord's Prayer, since these elements of the liturgy are often handed over to candidates in the weeks prior to baptism.
- Incorporate the journey to baptism in preaching. Sermons that reflect upon the liturgical rite of enrollment for baptismal candidates, a call to renewal or to continuing conversion for (re)affirmers, or the various Lenten blessings serve to draw out the richness and meaning of these journeys for the entire worshiping assembly.

The Passion According to Matthew
Sunday of the Passion / Palm Sunday

Matthew 26:14—27:66

Preparation

You will need 2-10 groups of 4 readers each. Readers will need to be familiar with the script and should rehearse the entire passion at least twice. The reading should flow as if it were being proclaimed by one voice.

This is not the traditional dramatic reading of the passion. It is the people of God speaking to the people of God. Readers are not assigned to be heard as various characters. Instead, all of the readers are representatives of the assembly. This is accomplished best by having enough groups of four to surround the assembly. At least two groups of four, one facing each side of the assembly, would be minimum. If microphones are needed, one microphone for each group of four should be sufficient.

For convenience, each group of four might be assigned a letter or number, and that letter or number written into the space provided before each of the ten scenes.

Hymn stanzas may be sung by the assembly between some scenes. Singing between every scene might make this reading too long.

Script

All readers: The passion of our Lord Jesus Christ according to Matthew.

Group _____

I. The betrayal of Judas

1: One of the twelve, who was called Judas Iscariot, went to the chief priests and said,

2: What will you give me if I betray him to you?

3: They paid him thirty pieces of silver.

4: And from that moment he began to look for an opportunity to betray him.

Group _____

II. The last supper

1: On the first day of Unleavened Bread the disciples came to Jesus, saying,

2: Where do you want us to make the preparations for you to eat the Passover?

1: He said,

3: Go into the city to a certain man, and say to him, "The Teacher says, my time is near; I will keep the Passover at your house with my disciples."

4: So the disciples did as Jesus had directed them, and they prepared the Passover meal.

1: When it was evening, he took his place with the twelve; and while they were eating, he said,

3: Truly I tell you, one of you will betray me.

4: And they became greatly distressed and began to say to him one after another,

2: Surely not I, Lord?

3: The one who has dipped his hand into the bowl with me will betray me. The Son of Man goes as it is written of him, but woe to that one by whom the Son of Man is betrayed! It would have been better for that one not to have been born.

1: Judas, who betrayed him, said,

2: Surely not I, Rabbi?

3: You have said so.

4: While they were eating, Jesus took a loaf of bread, and after blessing it he broke it, gave it to the disciples, and said,

3: Take, eat; this is my body.

1: Then he took a cup, and after giving thanks he gave it to them, saying,

3: Drink from it, all of you; for this is my blood of the covenant, which is poured out for many for the forgiveness of sins. I tell you, I will never again drink of this fruit of the vine until that day when I drink it new with you in my Father's kingdom.

Group _____

III. The Mount of Olives

1: When they had sung the hymn, they went out to the Mount of Olives. Then Jesus said to them,

2: You will all become deserters because of me this night; for it is written, "I will strike the shepherd, and the sheep of the flock will be scattered. But after I am raised up, I will go ahead of you to Galilee."

1: Peter said to him,

3: Though all become deserters because of you, I will never desert you.

2: Truly I tell you, this very night, before the cock crows, you will deny me three times.

3: Even though I must die with you, I will not deny you.

4: And so said all the disciples.

Group _____

IV. Gethsemane

1: Then Jesus went with them to a place called Gethsemane; and he said to his disciples,

2: Sit here while I go over there and pray.

3: He took with him Peter and the two sons of Zebedee, and began to be grieved and agitated. Then he said to them,

2: I am deeply grieved, even to death; remain here, and stay awake with me.

1: And going a little farther, he threw himself on the ground and prayed,

2: My Father, if it is possible, let this cup pass from me; yet not what I want but what you want.

3: Then he came to the disciples and found them sleeping; and he said to Peter,

2: So, could you not stay awake with me one hour? Stay awake and pray that you may not come into the time of trial; the spirit indeed is willing, but the flesh is weak.

1: Again he went away for the second time and prayed,

2: My Father, if this cannot pass unless I drink it, your will be done.

3: Again he came and found them sleeping, for their eyes were heavy. So leaving them again, he went away and prayed for the third time, saying the same words. Then he came to the disciples and said to them,

2: Are you still sleeping and taking your rest? See, the hour is at hand, and the Son of Man is betrayed into the hands of sinners. Get up, let us be going. See, my betrayer is at hand.

1: While he was still speaking, Judas, one of the twelve, arrived; with him was a large crowd with swords and clubs, from the chief priests and the elders of the people. Now the betrayer had given them a sign, saying,

4: The one I will kiss is the man; arrest him.

3: At once he came up to Jesus and said,

4: Greetings, Rabbi!

3: and kissed him. Jesus said to him,

2: Friend, do what you are here to do.

3: Then they came and laid hands on Jesus and arrested him.

1: Suddenly, one of those with Jesus put his hand on his sword, drew it, and struck the slave of the high priest, cutting off his ear. Then Jesus said to him,

2: Put your sword back into its place; for all who take the sword will perish by the sword. Do you think that I cannot appeal to my Father, and he will at once send me more than twelve legions of angels? But how then would the scriptures be fulfilled, which say it must happen this way?

3: At that hour Jesus said to the crowds,

2: Have you come out with swords and clubs to arrest me as though I were a bandit? Day after day I sat in the temple teaching, and you did not arrest me. But all this has taken place, so that the scriptures of the prophets may be fulfilled.

1: Then all the disciples deserted him and fled.

Group _____

V. Trial before Caiaphas

1: Those who had arrested Jesus took him to Caiaphas the high priest, in whose house the scribes and the elders had gathered. But Peter was following at a distance, as far as the courtyard of the high priest; and going inside, he sat with the guards in order to see how this would end. Now the chief priests and the whole council were looking for false testimony against Jesus so that they might put him to death, but they found none, though many false witnesses came forward. At last two came forward and said,

2: This fellow said, "I am able to destroy the temple of God and to build it in three days."

1: The high priest stood up and said,

3: Have you no answer? What is it that they testify against you?

1: But Jesus was silent. Then the high priest said to him,

3: I put you under oath before the living God, tell us if you are the Messiah, the Son of God.

4: You have said so. But I tell you, from now on you will see the Son of Man seated at the right hand of Power and coming on the clouds of heaven.

1: Then the high priest tore his clothes and said,

3: He has blasphemed! Why do we still need witnesses? You have now heard his blasphemy. What is your verdict?

2: He deserves death!

1: Then they spat in his face and struck him; and some slapped him, saying,

2: Prophesy to us, you Messiah! Who is it that struck you?

Group _____

VI. Peter's denial; Judas's death

1: Now Peter was sitting outside in the courtyard. A servant-girl came and said to him,

2: You also were with Jesus the Galilean.

1: But he denied it before all of them, saying,

3: I do not know what you are talking about.

4: When he went out to the porch, another servant-girl saw him, and she said to the bystanders,

2: This man was with Jesus of Nazareth.

4: Again he denied it with an oath,

3: I do not know the man!

1: After a little while the bystanders came up and said to Peter,

2: Certainly you are also one of them, for your accent betrays you.

1: Then he began to curse, and he swore an oath,

3: I do not know the man!

1: At that moment the cock crowed.

4: Then Peter remembered what Jesus had said: "Before the cock crows, you will deny me three times." And he went out and wept bitterly.

1: When morning came, all the chief priests and the elders of the people conferred together against Jesus in order to bring about his death.

4: They bound him, led him away, and handed him over to Pilate the governor.

1: When Judas, his betrayer, saw that Jesus was condemned, he repented and brought back the thirty pieces of silver to the chief priests and the elders. He said,

3: I have sinned by betraying innocent blood.

2: What is that to us? See to it yourself.

1: Throwing down the pieces of silver in the temple, he departed; and he went and hanged himself.

4: But the chief priests, taking the pieces of silver, said,

2: It is not lawful to put them into the treasury, since they are blood money.

4: After conferring together, they used the money to buy the potter's field as a place to bury foreigners.

1: For this reason that field has been called the Field of Blood to this day. Then was fulfilled what had been spoken through the prophet Jeremiah, "And they took thirty pieces of silver, the price of the one on whom a price had been set, on whom some of the people of Israel had set a price, and they gave them for the potter's field, as the Lord commanded me."

Group _____

VII. Jesus before Pilate

1: Now Jesus stood before the governor; and the governor asked him,

2: Are you the King of the Jews?

3: You say so.

4: But when he was accused by the chief priests and elders, he did not answer. Then Pilate said to him,

2: Do you not hear how many accusations they make against you?

1: But he gave him no answer, not even to a single charge, so that the governor was greatly amazed.

4: Now at the festival the governor was accustomed to release a prisoner for the crowd, anyone whom they wanted. At that time they had a notorious prisoner, called Jesus Barabbas. So after they had gathered, Pilate said to them,

2: Whom do you want me to release for you, Jesus Barabbas or Jesus who is called the Messiah?

1: For he realized that it was out of jealousy that they had handed him over. While he was sitting on the judgment seat, his wife sent word to him saying, "Have nothing to do with this innocent man, for today I have suffered a great deal because of a dream about him."

4: Now the chief priests and the elders persuaded the crowds to ask for Barabbas and to have Jesus killed. The governor again said to them,

2: Which of the two do you want me to release for you?

1, 3, 4: Barabbas!

2: Then what should I do with Jesus who is called the Messiah?

1, 3, 4: Let him be crucified!

2: Why, what evil has he done?

1, 3, 4: Let him be crucified! Let him be crucified! Let him be crucified!

1: So when Pilate saw that he could do nothing, but rather that a riot was beginning, he took some water and washed his hands before the crowd, saying,

2: I am innocent of this man's blood; see to it yourselves.

1, 3, 4: His blood be on us and on our children.

4: So he released Barabbas for them; and after flogging Jesus, he handed him over to be crucified.

1: Then the soldiers of the governor took Jesus into the governor's headquarters, and they gathered the whole cohort around him. They stripped him and put a scarlet robe on him, and after twisting some thorns into a crown, they put it on his head. They put a reed in his right hand and knelt before him and mocked him, saying, "Hail, King of the Jews!" They spat on him, and took a reed and struck him on the head. And after mocking him, they stripped him of the robe and put his own clothes on him. Then they led him away to crucify him.

Group _____

VIII. Golgotha

1: As they went out, they came upon a man from Cyrene named Simon; they compelled this man to carry his cross. And when they came to a place called Golgotha (which means Place of a Skull), they offered him wine to drink, mixed with gall; but when he tasted it, he would not drink it.

2: And when they had crucified him, they divided his clothes among themselves by casting lots; then they sat down there and kept watch over him.

1: Over his head they put the charge against him which read,

1, 2: This is Jesus, the King of the Jews.

1: Then two bandits were crucified with him, one on his right and one on his left. Those who passed by derided him, shaking their heads and saying,

3: You who would destroy the temple and build it in three days, save yourself! If you are the Son of God, come down from the cross.

2: In the same way the chief priests also, along with the scribes and elders, were mocking him, saying,

4: He saved others; he cannot save himself. He is the King of Israel; let him come down from the cross now, and we will believe in him.

2: The bandits who were crucified with him also taunted him in the same way.

Group _____

IX. Jesus' death

1: From noon on, darkness came over the whole land until three in the afternoon.

2: And about three o'clock Jesus cried with a loud voice,

3: Eli, Eli, lema sabachthani?

2: that is, "My God, my God, why have you forsaken me?"

1: When some of the bystanders heard it, they said,

4: This man is calling for Elijah.

2: At once one of them ran and got a sponge, filled it with sour wine, put it on a stick, and gave it to him to drink. But the others said,

4: Wait, let us see whether Elijah will come to save him.

1: Then Jesus cried again with a loud voice and breathed his last.

(Pause for at least one minute.)

1: At that moment the curtain of the temple was torn in two, from top to bottom. The earth shook, and the rocks were split. The tombs also were opened, and many bodies of the saints who had fallen asleep were raised. After his resurrection they came out of the tombs and entered the holy city and appeared to many.

2: Now when the centurion and those with him, who were keeping watch over Jesus saw the earthquake and what took place, they were terrified and said,

4: Truly this man was God's Son!

2: Many women were also there, looking on from a distance; they had followed Jesus from Galilee and had provided for him. Among them were Mary Magdalene, and Mary the mother of James and Joseph, and the mother of the sons of Zebedee.

Group ———————

X. Burial

1: When it was evening, there came a rich man from Arimathea, named Joseph, who was also a disciple of Jesus. He went to Pilate and asked for the body of Jesus; then Pilate ordered it to be given to him. So Joseph took the body and wrapped it in a clean linen cloth and laid it in his own new tomb and went away. Mary Magdalene and the other Mary were there, sitting opposite the tomb.

2: The next day, that is, after the day of Preparation, the chief priests and the Pharisees gathered before Pilate and said,

3: Sir, we remember what that imposter said while he was still alive, "After three days I will rise again." Therefore command the tomb to be made secure until the third day; otherwise his disciples may go and steal him away, and tell the people, "He has been raised from the dead" and the last deception would be worse than the first.

1: Pilate said to them,

4: You have a guard of soldiers; go, make it as secure as you can.

2: So they went with the guard and made the tomb secure by sealing the stone.

All readers: The gospel of the Lord.

March 5, 2014
Ash Wednesday

Lent begins with a solemn call to fasting and repentance as we begin our journey to the baptismal waters of Easter. As we hear in today's readings, now is the acceptable time to return to the Lord. During Lent the people of God will reflect on the meaning of their baptism into Christ's death and resurrection. The sign of ashes suggests our human mortality and frailty. What seems like an ending is really an invitation to make each day a new beginning, in which we are washed in God's mercy and forgiveness. With the cross on our brow, we long for the spiritual renewal that flows from the springtime Easter feast to come.

Prayer of the Day

Almighty and ever-living God, you hate nothing you have made, and you forgive the sins of all who are penitent. Create in us new and honest hearts, so that, truly repenting of our sins, we may receive from you, the God of all mercy, full pardon and forgiveness through your Son, Jesus Christ, our Savior and Lord, who lives and reigns with you and the Holy Spirit, one God, now and forever.

or

Gracious God, out of your love and mercy you breathed into dust the breath of life, creating us to serve you and our neighbors. Call forth our prayers and acts of kindness, and strengthen us to face our mortality with confidence in the mercy of your Son, Jesus Christ, our Savior and Lord, who lives and reigns with you and the Holy Spirit, one God, now and forever.

Gospel Acclamation

Return to the ' Lord, your God,* who is gracious and merciful, slow to anger, and abounding in ' steadfast love. (Joel 2:13)

Readings and Psalm
Joel 2:1-2, 12-17

Because of the coming Day of the Lord, the prophet Joel calls the people to a community lament. The repentant community reminds God of his gracious character and asks God to spare the people, lest the nations doubt God's power to save.

or Isaiah 58:1-12

Shortly after the return of Israel from exile in Babylon, the people were troubled by the ineffectiveness of their fasts. God reminds them that outward observance is no substitute for genuine fasting that results in acts of justice, such as feeding the hungry, sheltering the homeless, and clothing the naked. Sincere repentance will lead to a dramatic improvement of their condition.

Psalm 51:1-17

Have mercy on me, O God, according to your steadfast love. (Ps. 51:1)

2 Corinthians 5:20b—6:10

The ministry of the gospel endures many challenges and hardships. Through this ministry, God's reconciling activity in the death of Christ reaches into the depths of our lives to bring us into a right relationship with God. In this way, God accepts us into the reality of divine salvation.

Matthew 6:1-6, 16-21

In the Sermon on the Mount, Jesus commends almsgiving, prayer, and fasting, but emphasizes that spiritual devotion must not be done for show.

Preface   Lent

Color   Purple

Prayers of Intercession

The prayers are prepared locally for each occasion. The following examples may be adapted or used as appropriate.
Returning to the Lord, our God, let us pray for the church, the world, and all of God's creation.
A brief silence.
Gracious and merciful God, empower your church to be an ambassador of reconciliation in the world. Lord, in your mercy,
hear our prayer.
Gracious and merciful God, restore creation to wholeness and strengthen our resolve to be good stewards of all that you have made. Lord, in your mercy,
hear our prayer.
Gracious and merciful God, make this the acceptable time for peace. Guide the leaders of all nations to put an end to war and violence (*especially*). Lord, in your mercy,
hear our prayer.

Gracious and merciful God, deliver those in need: the hungry, the afflicted, the imprisoned, and the ill (*especially*), that their joy be restored. Lord, in your mercy,
hear our prayer.
Gracious and merciful God, create a clean heart in all who worship here today and bless all who prepare during these forty days to be baptized at Easter. Lord, in your mercy,
hear our prayer.
Here other intercessions may be offered.
Gracious and merciful God, we give you thanks for all the saints who now partake in your heavenly treasure. Lord, in your mercy,
hear our prayer.
Into your hands, O God, we commend ourselves and all for whom we pray, trusting in your abundant mercy, through Jesus Christ, our Savior and Lord.
Amen.

Images in the Readings

Although cited only in the reading from Isaiah 58, **ashes** are the primary image for the day. Since the twelfth century, the ashes, made by burning last year's palms, cycle around from the triumphant celebration of Jesus' entry into Jerusalem to the humiliation of sinners covering their heads with ashes. Ashes also bring to mind the fire of the Easter Vigil. Honesty is always a good, if painful thing: this day we are honest about sin and death. The ash cross marks one's forehead as if it is the brand of one's owner. We journey forward wearing the sign of the cross.

The gospel reading is the source for the three **disciplines of Lent** that have proved useful for many of Christ's disciples. To increase one's giving to the poor, to increase one's attention to prayer, and to decrease one's focus on the self: the idea is that such disciplines open up the self to God and to the neighbor.

The acceptable time, the day of salvation, are ways Paul describes the here and now of the life of the baptized. Ash Wednesday calls us each day into life in Christ.

Several beloved hymns call Christ our **treasure**. The treasure described in both Matthew and Paul—"poor, yet making many rich"—is the countercultural value of the baptized life.

Ideas for the Day

◆ In Matthew, Jesus teaches about the spiritual practices of prayer, fasting, and almsgiving. Doing these with integrity, he says, means focusing on how they connect us to God and neighbor, not how they make us look impressive to others. These three practices are similar to three of the five "pillars" of Islam, core practices of Muslim life. Judaism also emphasizes prayer, fasting, and almsgiving, and all three traditions stress the confession of faith in one God. Ash Wednesday could be a time to repent of our focus on religious practices we use to divide us from others, including other religions, and focus on how we share similar ways of connecting to God and neighbor when we do so with integrity.

◆ Jesus urges his followers to keep their piety private, not a means of displaying one's righteousness to others. There is a strange irony in hearing this text and then marking foreheads with ashes, likely to be seen by others after they leave worship. How will preaching address this irony?

◆ In Joel, the horn used to call people to repentance is the *shofar*. This traditional Jewish instrument is usually made of a ram's horn. The blowing of the horn calls people to attentive worship and disciplined repentance. Consider blowing a shofar, or another type of horn, to call people to the solemn liturgy of Ash Wednesday. Or sound the horn at the beginning of the confession, followed by silence.

◆ Michael Coffey's poem "When My Time Comes for Ashes and Dust" connects Ash Wednesday's emphasis on the solemn reality of death with the call to full, exuberant living today. The poem's image of a funeral procession of drums awakens people to enjoy the rhythms of life "before your final walk down the aisle in a little ashy urn." The poem is online at www.mccoffey.blogspot.com. Search for the title.

Connections with the Liturgy

Ash Wednesday is an intensification of our regular rite of confession and forgiveness, a rare time in our culture during which we acknowledge our sin and beg for renewal. The Kyrie also recalls Ash Wednesday: Lord, have mercy, Lord, have mercy, over and over. At communion we sing, "Lamb of God, you take away the sin of the world, have mercy on us." There is always more and more need for mercy.

Let the Children Come

The imposition of ashes is a tactile and physical practice that children will be very curious about. Give children and parents a few minutes to discuss the following question, "Why do we say 'Remember you are dust and to dust you shall return' when we put the ashes on our foreheads?" Asking families to discuss this together will encourage parents to think about their own answer and will allow them to guide their children's understanding in a way that is developmentally appropriate to each child.

Assembly Song and Music for the Day

Because of the nature of this day, music suggestions are listed both by place in the service and categorized by type of leadership (in brackets): CC=Children's Choir; Ch=Choral; KI=Keyboard/Instrumental; HB=Handbell. Many suggestions require assembly participation.

Gathering

Psalm 51 (see Psalmody)

Kyrie   ELW 151–158 or from communion settings.

Daigle, Gary and Rory Cooney. "Hold Us in Your Mercy." *Music Sourcebook for Lent and the Three Days* S418. AFP 9780806670409.

Campbell, Jon Strommen. "Canticle of Joel." *Music Sourcebook* S404.

Haugen, Marty. "Now Is the Time of Grace." *Music Sourcebook* S403.

Jennings, Carolyn, "Litany for Lent." *Music Sourcebook* S417.

Your heart, O God, is grieved   ELW 602, LBW 96

◉ Colvin, Tom. Malawian song. "Humbly in Your Sight" from *Global Songs for Worship*. U, gtr. Faith Alive/Calvin Institute of Christian Worship. 9781592554423.

Psalmody and Acclamations

Haugen, Marty. "Be Merciful, O Lord." from TLP:S.

Gelineau, Joseph or Michel Guimont. "Ash Wednesday/ABC" LP:W4.

Mummert, Mark. "Psalm 103:8-14" from PSCY.

Patterson, Mark. "Psalm 51" in *ChildrenSing Psalms*. [CC]

Farlee, Robert Buckley. "Let Your Steadfast Love." *Music Sourcebook* S421.

Hymn of the Day

Lord Jesus, think on me   ELW 599, LBW 309   *SOUTHWELL*

Lord, whose love in humble service   ELW 712, LBW 423   *BEACH SPRING*

Be thou my vision   ELW 793   *SLANE*

Confession of Sin

Music Sourcebook for Lent and the Three Days includes four musical settings of texts for corporate confession of sin, one using the text in the Ash Wednesday service (S408), and others using the text from Corporate Confession and Forgiveness, Evangelical Lutheran Worship Leaders Edition, p. 603 (S409–S411).

Imposition of Ashes

Create in me a clean heart   ELW 185–188

Psalm 51 (if not used earlier in the service—see Psalmody)

Take, oh, take me as I am   ELW 814

Campbell, Jon Strommen "Canticle of Joel." *Music Sourcebook* S404.

◉ = global song
✿ = praise song
● = relates to hymn of the day

Haugen, Marty. "Now Is the Time of Grace." *Music Sourcebook* S403.

◉ Neto, Rodolfo Gaede. Brazil. "Pelas dores deste mundo/For the Troubles" from *Global Songs for Worship*. U, gtr. Faith Alive/Calvin Institute of Christian Worship. 9781592554423.

✿ Barnard, Shane/Kendall Combes. "Beauty for Ashes" from WT.

✿ Beeching, Vicky. "Undivided Heart" from CCLI.

Ferguson, John. "All Things of Dust to Dust Return." SATB, org. AFP 9780800677916. [Ch]

Scott, K. Lee. "Treasures in Heaven." 2 pt, kybd. AFP 9780800664282. [Ch]

Kosche, Kenneth. "Return to the Lord." 2 pt, kybd. CPH 98-3798. [CC]

Bach, J. S. "O Mensch, bewein' dein' Sünde gross" from *Das Orgelbüchlein*. Org. Various editions. [KI]

Setting the Table

Music Sourcebook for Lent and the Three Days includes an appendix with hymn stanzas appropriate for use during the setting of the table on this and other days. These stanzas are also included on the CD-ROM that accompanies the volume.

✿ Brown, Brenton. "Amazing God" from WT.

✿ Ellis, John. "I Stand for You" from WT.

Hurd, David. "Love Bade Me Welcome." SATB. SEL 418-610. [Ch]

Nelson, Ronald A. "Create in Me A Clean Heart." SATB a cappella. KJO 8808. [Ch]

Leavitt, John. "Create in Me." U, kybd. CPH 98-3711. [CC]

● Fedak, Alfred. "Variations on 'Beach Spring.'" Org. SEL 160-641. [KI]

● Leavitt, John. "Beach Spring" from *Wonder, Love, and Praise*. Pno. CPH 97-7021WEB. [KI]

● Glasgow, Michael. "Prayer for Guidance." 3-6 oct hb, opt 3 oct hc, L3+. JEF JHS9431. [HB]

Communion

Once we sang and danced   ELW 701

Softly and tenderly Jesus is calling   ELW 608, WOV 734

Just as I am, without one plea   ELW 592, LBW 296

✿ Crowder, David. "Fall on Your Knees" from WT.

Quintana, Ariel. "Here I Am." SATB, div, pno. Pavane P1344. [Ch]

Powell, Robert. "Cast Me Not Away." SATB, org. PAR 0708. [Ch]

● Carter, John. "Slane" from *Contemplative Folk Tunes for Piano*. Pno. AFP 9780800659776. [KI]

● Moats, William. "Lenten Contemplation." 3-5 oct hb, opt 3 oct hc, L2. CG CGB524. [HB]

Sending

Eternal Lord of love, behold your church   ELW 321

O Lord, throughout these forty days   ELW 319, LBW 99

✿ Ingram, Jason/Robbie Seay. "Kingdom and a King" from WT.

Friday, March 7

Perpetua and Felicity and companions, martyrs at Carthage, died 202

In the year 202 the emperor Septimius Severus forbade conversions to Christianity. Perpetua, a noblewoman, Felicity, a slave, and other companions were all catechumens at Carthage in North Africa. They were imprisoned and sentenced to death. Perpetua's father, who was not a Christian, visited her in prison and begged her to lay aside her Christian convictions in order to spare her life and spare the family from scorn. Perpetua responded and told her father, "We know that we are not placed in our own power but in that of God."

March 9, 2014

First Sunday in Lent

Today's gospel tells of Jesus' temptation in the desert. His forty-day fast becomes the basis of our Lenten pilgrimage. In the early church Lent was a time of intense preparation for those to be baptized at the Easter Vigil. This catechetical focus on the meaning of faith is at the heart of our Lenten journey to the baptismal waters of Easter. Hungry for God's mercy, we receive the bread of life to nourish us for the days ahead.

Prayer of the Day

Lord God, our strength, the struggle between good and evil rages within and around us, and the devil and all the forces that defy you tempt us with empty promises. Keep us steadfast in your word, and when we fall, raise us again and restore us through your Son, Jesus Christ, our Savior and Lord, who lives and reigns with you and the Holy Spirit, one God, now and forever.

Gospel Acclamation

One does not live by ' bread alone,* but by every word that comes from the ' mouth of God. (Matt. 4:4)

Readings and Psalm

Genesis 2:15-17; 3:1-7

Human beings were formed with great care, to be in relationship with the creator, creation, and one another. The serpent's promise to the first couple that their eyes would be opened led, ironically, to the discovery only that they were naked.

Psalm 32

Mercy embraces those who trust in the Lord. (Ps. 32:10)

Romans 5:12-19

Through Adam's disobedience, humanity came under bondage to sin and death, from which we cannot free ourselves. In Christ's obedient death, God graciously showers on us the free gift of liberation and life.

Matthew 4:1-11

Jesus experiences anew the temptations that Israel faced in the wilderness. As the Son of God, he endures the testing of the evil one.

Preface Lent

Color Purple

Prayers of Intercession

The prayers are prepared locally for each occasion. The following examples may be adapted or used as appropriate.

Returning to the Lord, our God, let us pray for the church, the world, and all of God's creation.

A brief silence.

Let us pray for the whole Christian church. (*Pause*) Instruct and teach your church in the way that it should go so that it worships and serves only you. Hear us, O God.

Your mercy is great.

Let us pray for the well-being of creation. (*Pause*) Renew all waters, lands, and skies to reflect your glory and guide us to be respectful in how we use all earthly resources. Hear us, O God.

Your mercy is great.

Let us pray for all nations and peoples. (*Pause*) Grant justice where there is inequity, peace where there is conflict, and wisdom for all who lead (*especially*). Hear us, O God.
Your mercy is great.

Let us pray for all in need. (*Pause*) Provide caring communities for all who are burdened by guilt, shame, addiction, and illness (*especially*). Preserve them from all trouble. Hear us, O God.
Your mercy is great.

Let us pray for this assembly. (*Pause*) Keep all who worship in this place steadfast in your word. Fill with your Spirit all who are preparing for baptism. Hear us, O God.
Your mercy is great.

Here other intercessions may be offered.

Let us give thanks for the faithful departed whose transgressions are forgiven and who now rejoice in heaven. (*Pause*) Lead us in their path. Hear us, O God.
Your mercy is great.

Into your hands, O God, we commend ourselves and all for whom we pray, trusting in your abundant mercy, through Jesus Christ, our Savior and Lord.
Amen.

Images in the Readings

Matthew writes that Jesus fasted for **forty days and forty nights**. In the Bible, forty is always the time between, the necessary span before the gracious conclusion. It is forty, days or years, that numbers the rain of Noah's flood, Moses on Mount Sinai, Israel in the wilderness, the spies scouting out Canaan, Israel in the hands of the Philistines, the taunting by Goliath, the reign of Saul, David, and Solomon, Ezekiel lying on his right side, Nineveh's repentance, and Jesus' appearance after Easter. For us, it is forty days until we celebrate the resurrection.

The **tree of knowledge of good and evil**—a stark contrast with the wondrous tree of life that appears again in Revelation 22—is a fascinating, ambiguous symbol, perhaps signifying the human tendency to replace God's way with one's own way, God's word with human knowledge. It is a mystery-tree that according to the story represents all that is wrong in human life.

Who initiated sin? In Genesis it is **the woman**, in Paul it is **Adam**—characters whom we recognize as being essentially ourselves.

The gospel describes the **devil** as the tempter, the power that seeks to lure us away from God. It is this devil that much Christian tradition has used to explain the talking serpent of Genesis 3. The tradition of art has not given us profound enough depictions of this primordial evil, but in the usual image of a creature part human, part monster, we can see another picture of ourselves.

Ideas for the Day

◆ In the baptismal liturgy we join the "no" of Jesus in the renunciations. "Do you renounce the devil and all the forces that defy God? Do you renounce the powers of this world that rebel against God? Do you renounce the ways of sin that draw you from God?" When we declare our profession of faith, we join the "yes" of Jesus and his singular commitment to the kingdom of God. Those preparing for baptism at Easter and those already baptized would do well to reflect on the renunciations in the light of today's gospel reading. Where do we recognize the powerful lure of evil, not only in personal choices but in systems and in the "principalities and powers"? What might a Lenten discipline look like that includes turning from those things that defy and rebel against God and draw us from God? What does turning to God's embrace look like?

◆ Luther commented that though the "old Adam" is drowned in baptism, that old Adam is a mighty good swimmer. Christian living involves a daily death to sin and rising to new life in Christ. *The Use of the Means of Grace* (1997) helps us see what daily dying and rising might look like: "confession and absolution, the readings of the Scriptures, preaching, the mutual comfort and consolation of the sisters and brothers, daily prayer and the sign of the cross, the remembrance of the catechism, and the profession of the creed" (Application 17B). Lent is a good time to lift up these spiritual practices. How might the preacher draw the assembly into faithful use of these things as ways to resist evil and seek first the kingdom of God?

◆ The popular television series *Mad Men* portrays the world of 1960s advertising executives intent on promoting products that promise fulfillment and meaning. The 2004 PBS documentary *The Persuaders* chronicles the evolution of that industry to the new century. Does the promise of some marketers resemble what the devil offers Jesus in the wilderness? What might it look like to resist such persuasive powers?

◆ Once Jesus shoos away the devil, angels came and waited upon him. Luther's evening prayer for households (*Evangelical Lutheran Worship*, p. 1167) is also found in the service of Evening Prayer (p. 318) and begs that we too might be waited upon: "Let your holy angels be with us, so that the wicked foe may have no power over us."

Connections with the Liturgy

Following Jesus, we respond to evil with the power of the word. Each Sunday we acknowledge the readings as "the word of the Lord," "Word of God, word of life." For the gospel, we stand, offering "Glory" to Christ, whom we laud in this word. In each baptismal liturgy, we recall this Sunday's gospel as we join with the candidates for baptism to renounce the devil, all the forces that defy God, and all the powers of this world that rebel against God. As God's Spirit enters us, we reject the spirit of evil that is both within and outside ourselves.

Let the Children Come

Help children listen actively by providing a question that will be answered during the readings for the day. Examples include, "Listen for what Jesus says about . . .", or "How many times do you hear the word _____ in today's readings?" As they listen to today's gospel reading, children can try to answer the following question: "What three temptations or challenges does the devil give to Jesus?"

Assembly Song
Gathering

The glory of these forty days   ELW 320, WOV 657
I want Jesus to walk with me   ELW 325, TFF 66, WOV 660
Great Litany   ELW 238

Psalmody and Acclamations

Bruxvoort-Colligan, Richard. "Unfailing Love (Psalm 32:3, 5)" from SR.
Helgen, John. "Psalm 32" from *ChildrenSing Psalms*. U, assembly, kybd.
Isele, David Clark/Hal H. Hopson. "Psalm 32" from TP.
Farlee, Robert Buckley. "Let Your Steadfast Love." *Music Sourcebook* S421.

Hymn of the Day

I want Jesus to walk with me   ELW 325, TFF 66, WOV 660
   SOJOURNER
Lord, keep us steadfast in your word   ELW 517, LBW 230
   ERHALT UNS, HERR
Lord Jesus, you shall be my song   ELW 808   *LES PETITES SOEURS*

Offering

Create in me a clean heart   ELW 187
Tree of Life and awesome mystery   ELW 334

Communion

If God my Lord be for me   ELW 788
Oh, love, how deep   ELW 322, LBW 88
Praise and thanks and adoration   ELW 783

Sending

Bless now, O God, the journey   ELW 326
Jesus, still lead on   ELW 624

Additional Assembly Songs

You are my hiding place   W&P 160
For God so loved the world   ASG 10

⊕ Bell, John. Scotland. "The Courage to Say No" from *The Courage To Say No: 23 Songs for Lent and Easter*. U. GIA G-4244.
⊕ Bell, John. Scotland. "The Temptations" from *Heaven Shall Not Wait*. U. GIA G-3646.
✿ Brown, Brenton. "Higher (Empires Fall)" from WT.
✿ Byrd, Marc/Daniel Doss/Sarah Hart. "Farther Than We Can Fall" from WT.
✿ Crowder, David. "Remedy" from CCLI.
✿ Keyes, Aaron/Jess Cates. "Dwell" from WT.
✿ Mote, Edward/Matt Redman/Robert Marvin/Tim Wanstall. "My Hope" from CCLI.
✿ Tomlin, Chris. "To the Only God" from CCLI.

Music for the Day
Choral

● Billingham, Richard. "I Want Jesus to Walk with Me." SATB, pno. AFP 9780800638719.
   Fedak, Alfred. "God First Made a Fruitful Garden." SATB, org. AFP 9780800676186.
● Haan, Raymond. "I Want Jesus to Walk with Me." SATB, pno. MSM 50-6058.
● Hogan, David. "Lord, Keep Us Steadfast." U, desc, kybd. ECS 4902.
   Keesecker, Thomas. "Oh, Love, How Deep." SATB, kybd. AFP 9781451420760.
   Marshall, Jane. "A Lenten Prayer." SAB. ECS 7085.

Children's Choir

   Bedford, Michael. "Forty Days and Nights" from *Seasonal Songs for Young Singers*. U, opt hb/hc, kybd. CG CGA1160.
● Miller, Aaron David. "I Want Jesus to Walk with Me." U, opt desc, kybd. AFP 9780800678418.
   Powell, Robert. "A Lenten Prayer." U, org, fl. CG CGA159.

Keyboard / Instrumental

● Bedford, Michael. "Sojourner" from *Rejoice, O Earth: Improvisations on World Songs*. Org. AFP 9781451424171.
   Cherwien, David. "Ein feste Burg" from *More Postludes on Well Known Hymns*. Org. AFP 9780800678425.
● Leavitt, John. "Lord, Keep Us Steadfast in Your Word" from *A Mighty Fortress: Sacred Reflections for Piano*. Pno. CPH 97-7254.
● Page, Anna Laura. "I Want Jesus to Walk with Me" from *Tell the Story: Ten Gospel Hymn Arrangements for Piano*. Pno. MSM 15-850.

Handbell

● Eithun, Sandra. "Lord, Keep Us Steadfast in Thy Word." 3-5 oct, L2+. CPH 97-7116.
   Haskell, Nancy. "Gethsemane." 3-5 oct hb, opt 2 oct hc, L3. RR BL5022.
● Sherman, Arnold. "The Journey." 3-6 oct, L3+. HOP 1897.

⊕ = global song
✿ = praise song
● = relates to hymn of the day

Monday, March 10

Harriet Tubman, died 1913; Sojourner Truth, died 1883; renewers of society

Harriet Tubman was born into slavery in Maryland and remained a slave until about age thirty when, fearing she would be sold and moved farther south, she escaped with the help of the Underground Railroad. After that, she helped about three hundred others to escape until slavery was abolished. After the Civil War, her home in Auburn, New York, became a center for women's rights and served the aged and poor.

Sojourner Truth, too, was born a slave, in New York state. Her birth name was Isabella. After slavery was abolished in New York in 1827, she was freed and, while working as a housekeeper, became deeply involved in Christianity. A number of years later, she discerned a call to become a preacher. Taking the name Sojourner Truth, she set out on an evangelistic journey, where people found her testimony to be deeply moving. In later life, she also became a popular speaker against slavery and for women's rights.

Wednesday, March 12

Gregory the Great, Bishop of Rome, died 604

Gregory was born into a politically influential family. At one time he held political office and at another time he lived as a monk, all before he was elected to the papacy. Gregory's work was extensive. He influenced public worship through the establishment of a lectionary and prayers to correlate with the readings. He established a school to train church musicians. Gregorian chant is named in his honor. He wrote a treatise underscoring what is required of a pastor serving a congregation. He sent missionaries to preach to the Anglo-Saxons who had invaded England. And at one time he organized distribution of grain during a shortage of food in Rome.

March 16, 2014
Second Sunday in Lent

During Lent we journey with all those around the world who will be baptized at the Easter Vigil. In today's gospel Jesus tells Nicodemus that he must be born of water and Spirit. At the font we are given a new birth as daughters and sons of God. As God made a covenant with Abraham, in baptism God promises to raise us up with Christ to new life. From worship we are sent forth to proclaim God's love for all the world.

Prayer of the Day

O God, our leader and guide, in the waters of baptism you bring us to new birth to live as your children. Strengthen our faith in your promises, that by your Spirit we may lift up your life to all the world through your Son, Jesus Christ, our Savior and Lord, who lives and reigns with you and the Holy Spirit, one God, now and forever.

Gospel Acclamation

The Son of Man must be ¹ lifted up,* that whoever believes in him may have e- ¹ ternal life. (John 3:14-15)

Readings and Psalm

Genesis 12:1-4a

God's call of Abram and Sarai has a clear purpose—that through them all the families of the earth would gain a blessing. As they set out on their journey they are accompanied by promises of land, nation, and a great reputation.

Psalm 121

I lift up my eyes to the hills; my help comes from the Lord. (Ps. 121:1, 2)

Romans 4:1-5, 13-17

In the person and example of Abraham we discover that a right relationship with God does not involve earning a reward from God but entails trusting God's promises. Abraham is the forebear and model for both Jews and Gentiles, because we too trust that ours is a God who gives life to the dead.

John 3:1-17

A curious Pharisee visits Jesus by night to learn from the teacher his friends reject. Jesus speaks to him about life in the Spirit and the kingdom of God.

Preface   Lent

Color   Purple

Prayers of Intercession

The prayers are prepared locally for each occasion. The following examples may be adapted or used as appropriate.

Returning to the Lord, our God, let us pray for the church, the world, and all of God's creation.

A brief silence.

We pray for the whole body of Christ. (*Pause*) That being born of the Spirit and blessed by God, your church may be a blessing to the world. Lord, in your mercy,

hear our prayer.

We pray for creation. (*Pause*) For water and wind in their many forms, that they nourish and renew the earth. Lord, in your mercy,

hear our prayer.

We pray for the world. (*Pause*) For all countries, tribes, races, and families, that they live in harmony and cooperation (*especially*). Lord, in your mercy,

hear our prayer.

We pray for all who are in need. (*Pause*) For the spiritually lost, the fearful, the confused, and the ill (*especially*), that the Lord will keep their going out and their coming in. Lord, in your mercy,

hear our prayer.

We pray for this assembly. (*Pause*) That having received all righteousness by faith, we boldly bear witness to a God who loves the whole world. Lord, in your mercy,

hear our prayer.

Here other intercessions may be offered.

We give thanks for the faithful departed. (*Pause*) For the example of faith by which they lived, that it sustain us until we all enter the reign of God in its fullness. Lord, in your mercy,

hear our prayer.

Into your hands, O God, we commend ourselves and all for whom we pray, trusting in your abundant mercy, through Jesus Christ, our Savior and Lord.

Amen.

Images in the Readings

John's language of "being born again" suggests the image of the **mother**. Historically, the church described itself as this mother and the font as the womb from which birth in God arises. Recently, also God is described as the mother who births a new creation. But birth is not easy, and Lent allows us forty days to reenvision that birth.

Abram's immigration to the land of promise offers the image of the **journey**. Lent provides forty days for the annual journey back to the mystery of the resurrection and the new life to which we are called.

Paul's language of justification assumes that God is a **judge** who requires of us a life of righteousness. That justification comes via faith does not eliminate the necessity for such a radical reorientation of the self before God. It is instructive to hold the image of judge next to that of the mother: each image nuances the other.

Ideas for the Day

◆ Instead of giving him answers, Jesus invites Nicodemus into an experience of the holy. Sometimes understanding God comes best through participation. Consider informal discussions in small groups during Lent, where people are given permission to reflect upon their experiences of prayer, worship, the Sunday readings, and faith in daily life. Honor their experiences, discuss them, and bring them to prayer before God.

◆ Lent is a pivotal time in the catechumenate process as adults engage in intense preparation for their baptism or affirmation of baptism at Easter. Consider this ancient/future process as a way of welcoming newcomers and forming disciples. *Go Make Disciples* (Augsburg Fortress, 2012) describes the process and includes ideas for Lent. Learn more from the North American Association for the Catechumenate (NAAC), at www.catechumenate.org.

◆ Phinney Ridge Lutheran Church, Seattle, has practiced the catechumenate for many years, and it has had a profound impact on the congregation's ministry. Learn about their story and the process in *Faith Forming Faith: Bringing New Christians to Baptism and Beyond*, by Phinney's lead pastor, Paul Hoffman (Eugene, OR: Cascade Books, 2012).

◆ Abram's journey and ours is summed up in these words from the Morning and Evening Prayer services (*Evangelical Lutheran Worship*, pp. 304 and 317): "O God, you have called your servants to ventures of which we cannot see the ending, by paths as yet untrodden, through perils unknown. Give us faith to go out with good courage, not knowing where we go, but only that your hand is leading us and your love supporting us; through Jesus Christ our Lord."

◆ "This life, therefore, is not godliness but the process of becoming godly, not health but getting well, not being but becoming, not rest but exercise. We are not now what we shall be, but we are on the way. The process is not yet finished, but it is actively going on. This is not the goal but it is the right road. At present, everything does not gleam or sparkle, but everything is being cleansed." —Martin Luther

Connections with the Liturgy

In the rite called Welcome to Baptism, we pray that the catechumen, whether an infant or an adult, be brought "in peace and joy to fullness of life in Christ" through the waters of baptism. In baptism we are, like Abram and Nicodemus, called to the fullness of new life.

Let the Children Come

Children may have heard the word "Lent" without knowing what it means. Share with them that Lent is a season and that it lasts 40 days. They may find it helpful to know that Ash Wednesday is the beginning of Lent and Holy Week is the end. Ask children: what is different at church during Lent? What is different in the world? Their answers may be practical rather than spiritual or theological, such as restaurants offering fish on Fridays, church services midweek, or Lenten suppers. Some may have family practices to share such as giving something up for Lent or doing special Lenten prayers and devotions.

Assembly Song
Gathering

This is the Spirit's entry now   ELW 448
We are baptized in Christ Jesus   ELW 451, WOV 698
Lift high the cross   ELW 660, LBW 377

Psalmody and Acclamations

Bruxvoort-Colligan, Richard. "God Is Holding Your Life (Psalm 121)" from SR.

Roberts, Leon C. "My Help Shall Come from the Lord (Psalm 121)." TFF 16.

Ogden, David. "I Lift Up My Eyes" from PCY, vol. 1.

Farlee, Robert Buckley. "Let Your Steadfast Love." *Music Sourcebook* S421.

Hymn of the Day

God loved the world   ELW 323   *ROCKINGHAM OLD*   LBW 292   *DIE HELLE SONN LEUCHT*
O living Breath of God   ELW 407, LCC 368   *VÅRVINDAR FRISKA*
Waterlife   ELW 457, W&P 145   *SPIRIT LIFE*

Offering

Create in me a clean heart   ELW 187

On my heart imprint your image   ELW 811, LBW 102

Communion

My faith looks up to thee   ELW 759, LBW 479

Tree of Life and awesome mystery   ELW 334

Loving Spirit   ELW 397

Sending

Restore in us, O God   ELW 328

How firm a foundation   ELW 796

Additional Assembly Songs

By the waters of Babylon   TFF 67

What can wash away my sin?   TFF 69

⊕ Guarani, trad. "Oré poriajú verekó/Lord, Have Mercy" from
   Worship and Rejoice. U, gtr. HOP 8020.

⊕ Li, Peo-chen. China. "May the Lord, Gracious God" from *Sound the
   Bamboo*. 2 pt. GIA G-6830.

✧ Dodson, Mike/Jeremy Bush/Patrick Dodd/David Crowder. "Can
   You Feel It?" from WT.

✧ Doerksen, Brian. "I Lift My Eyes Up" from CCLI.

✧ Gungor, Lisa/Michael Gungor/Michael Rossback. "I Will Never
   Stop" from CCLI.

✧ Houston, Joel/Matt Crocker. "Tear Down the Walls" from CCLI.

✧ Maher, Matt/Ike Ndolo/Tam Le. "Kyrie" from WT.

✧ Nockels, Nathan/Daniel Carson/Chris Tomlin/Christy Nockels. "All
   My Fountains" from WT.

Music for the Day
Choral

Garber, Aaron. "On My Heart Imprint Your Image." SATB, pno.
   AFP 9780800621513.

● Helgen, John. "O Living Breath of God." SAB, pno. AFP
   9780800621506.

Miller, Aaron David. "God So Loved the World." 2 pt, org, opt hb.
   AFP 9780800621445.

Moe, Daniel. "God So Loved the World." SATB. KJO 8808.

Pelz, Walter L. "Love and Mercy." SAB, org, ob. AFP
   9780800638696.

Weber, Paul D. "All Who Believe and Are Baptized." SATB, kybd, fl.
   CPH 98-4033.

Children's Choir

Bedford, Michael. "Psalm 121" in *ChildrenSing Psalms*. U, kybd, hb,
   opt assembly.

● Hanson, Handt. "Waterlife." ELW 457.

● Krentz, Michael E. "God Loved the World." U/2 pt, kybd. AFP
   9780800664084.

Keyboard / Instrumental

Albrecht, Mark. "St. Christopher/Rathbun" from *Easy Timeless
   Tunes for Solo Instrument and Piano, Volume 2*. Inst, kybd.
   AFP 9780800677879.

● Biery, James. "Rockingham" from *Wondrous Cross: Three Organ
   Pieces for Lent*. Org. MSM 10-429.

Carter, John. "The God of Abraham Praise" from *Folk Tunes for
   Piano*. Pno. AFP 9780800659776.

Perera, Ronald. "Five Meditations on Wondrous Love." Org. ECS
   4145.

Handbell

● Larson, Lloyd. "God So Loved the World." 3-5 oct, L2. LOR
   20/1521L.

Mazzatenta, Michael. "Breathe on Me, Breath of God." 3-5 oct, L2.
   AGEHR AG35308.

Moklebust, Cathy and David. "I Will Lift Mine Eyes Unto the Hills
   (Psalm 121)." 3-5 oct hb, L2. CG CGB529. Full score with opt
   org. CG CGB528.

Monday, March 17

Patrick, bishop, missionary to Ireland, died 461

At sixteen, Patrick was kidnapped by Irish pirates and sold
into slavery in Ireland. He himself admitted that up to this
point he cared little for God. He escaped after six years,
returned to his family in southwest Britain, and began to
prepare for ordained ministry. He later returned to Ireland,
this time to serve as a bishop and missionary. He made his
base in the north of Ireland and from there made many
missionary journeys, with much success. In his autobiography he denounced the slave trade, perhaps from his own
experience as a slave. Patrick's famous baptismal hymn to
the Trinity, "I Bind unto Myself Today" (ELW 450), can be
used as a meditation on Lent's call to return to our baptism.

Wednesday, March 19

Joseph, Guardian of Jesus

The gospels are silent about much of Joseph's life. We know
that he was a carpenter or builder by trade. The Gospel of
Luke shows him acting in accordance with both civil and
religious law by returning to Bethlehem for the census and
by presenting the child Jesus in the temple on the fortieth
day after his birth. The Gospel of Matthew tells of Joseph's
trust in God, who led him through visionary dreams.
Because Joseph is not mentioned after the story of a young
Jesus teaching in the temple, it is assumed that he died
before Jesus reached adulthood.

⊕ = global song
✧ = praise song
● = relates to hymn of the day

Friday, March 21

Thomas Cranmer, Bishop of Canterbury, martyr, died 1556

Cranmer was serving as bishop of Taunton in England when he was chosen by King Henry VIII to become archbishop of Canterbury, largely because Cranmer would agree to the king's divorce from Catherine of Aragon. Cranmer's lasting achievement is contributing to and overseeing the creation of the Book of Common Prayer, which in revised form remains the worship book of the Anglican Communion. He was burned at the stake under Queen Mary for his support of the Protestant Reformation.

Saturday, March 22

Jonathan Edwards, teacher, missionary to American Indians, died 1758

Edwards was a minister in Connecticut and described as the greatest of the New England Puritan preachers. One of Edwards's most notable sermons found its way into contemporary anthologies of literature. In this sermon, "Sinners in the Hands of an Angry God," he spoke at length about hell. However, throughout the rest of his works and his preaching he had more to say about God's love than God's wrath. His personal experience of conversion came when he felt overwhelmed with a sense of God's majesty and grandeur, rather than a fear of hell. Edwards served a Puritan congregation, where he believed that only those who had been fully converted ought to receive communion; his congregation thought otherwise. Edwards left that congregation and carried out mission work among the Housatonic Indians of Massachusetts. He became president of the College of New Jersey, later to be known as Princeton University.

March 23, 2014
Third Sunday in Lent

In today's gospel the Samaritan woman asks Jesus for water, an image of our thirst for God. Jesus offers living water, a sign of God's grace flowing from the waters of baptism. The early church used this gospel and those of the next two Sundays to deepen baptismal reflection during the final days of preparation before baptism at Easter. As we journey to the resurrection feast, Christ comes among us in word, bath, and meal—offering us the life-giving water of God's mercy and forgiveness.

Prayer of the Day

Merciful God, the fountain of living water, you quench our thirst and wash away our sin. Give us this water always. Bring us to drink from the well that flows with the beauty of your truth through Jesus Christ, our Savior and Lord, who lives and reigns with you and the Holy Spirit, one God, now and forever.

Gospel Acclamation

Lord, you are truly the Savior ¹ of the world;* give me this living water that I may never ¹ thirst again. (John 4:42, 15)

Readings and Psalm

Exodus 17:1-7

Because the thirsty Israelites quarreled with Moses and put the Lord to the test, Moses cried out in desperation to the Lord. The Lord commanded Moses to strike the rock to provide water for the people. The doubt-filled question— "Is the Lord among us or not?"—received a very positive answer.

Psalm 95

Let us shout for joy to the rock of our salvation. (Ps. 95:1)

Romans 5:1-11

Though we often hear that God helps those who help themselves, here Paul tells us that through Jesus' death God helps utterly helpless sinners. Since we who had been enemies are reconciled to God in the cross, we now live in hope for our final salvation.

John 4:5-42

Jesus defies convention to engage a Samaritan woman in conversation. Her testimony, in turn, leads many others to faith.

Preface   Lent

Color   Purple

Prayers of Intercession

The prayers are prepared locally for each occasion. The following examples may be adapted or used as appropriate.

Returning to the Lord, our God, let us pray for the church, the world, and all of God's creation.

A brief silence.

Lead your church, that justified by faith, it may bear testimony to your grace, your power, and your way of life. Hear us, O God.

Your mercy is great.

Bring the healing power of rain where there is drought and dry weather where there is flooding. Hear us, O God.

Your mercy is great.

Drench the earth with your peace, so that nations and their leaders ensure that all people have access to clean water for all their needs. Hear us, O God.

Your mercy is great.

Satisfy the thirst of all who long for you; the hungry, the poor, the fearful, and the ill (*especially*), that they draw deeply from your well of hope. Hear us, O God.

Your mercy is great.

Bless this congregation, that, showered with the promises of baptism, we welcome those who thirst for you. Hear us, O God.

Your mercy is great.

Here other intercessions may be offered.

We give you thanks for all the saints who endured in this world and have now entered your eternal rest. Hear us, O God.

Your mercy is great.

Into your hands, O God, we commend ourselves and all for whom we pray, trusting in your abundant mercy, through Jesus Christ, our Savior and Lord.

Amen.

Images in the Readings

The primary image for this Sunday is **water**. Water: that life as we know it on earth requires water is perhaps the reason that water figures in countless stories in all cultures, stories of rivers and seas, wells and rain. The Bible is overflowing with water stories, some of which we will hear at the Easter Vigil. In our time, daily showers, public fountains, swimming pools, and water parks provide society with the refreshment of water. Yet we are told that the next world wars will be over water, and current Christian ecologists urge care for the waters of the earth. In medieval Christian art, a picture of Moses striking the rock so that water can flow was set next to a depiction of Christ on the cross being pierced with the sword, as the water of life flowed from his side.

Another image for the day is the **rock**. In the Psalms, God is called rock 22 times. That water can flow from rock provides us with a double image for God.

Ideas for the Day

◆ Within the tradition of the catechumenate, this is the day to "hand over" the creed to those preparing for baptism. In *Welcome to Christ: Lutheran Rites for the Catechumenate* (Augsburg Fortress, 1997), these or similar words precede saying the creed: "As the woman of Samaria confessed her faith in Jesus Christ, the giver of the water of life, so the church confesses its need of Christ and its trust in God's mercy. We invite you whom God has chosen for baptism to join all the people of God in confessing the faith of the church" (p. 23). We stand alongside the woman at the well to confess our common belief. The preacher may want to reflect upon the creed, not as a statement of propositions but as a declaration of faith in the source of living water.

◆ Many people believed in Jesus because of the Samaritan woman's testimony. "He told me everything I have ever done" (John 4:39). Invite members of the faith community to share with others what Jesus means to them. During Lent, make a place for testimony. The point of such a faith practice isn't to impress people with our spirituality but to speak to the activity of God in our lives. We want others to receive the same gift that has been given to us. Two wonderful resources are *Tell It like It Is: Reclaiming the Power of Testimony,* by Lillian Daniel (Herndon, VA: Alban Institute, 2006); and *Testimony: Talking Ourselves into Being Christian,* by Tom Long (San Francisco: Jossey-Bass, 2004).

◆ Imagine the power of living water. Take the long view and begin to make plans for constructing a baptismal pool with flowing water. In the short term construct a temporary font for the Easter Vigil. See *Go Make Disciples* (Augsburg Fortress, 2012, p. 173) for suggestions about how to do this. One congregation purchased a galvanized steel trough to use as a baptismal font at their Vigil. It is filled for immersion baptism and is a place for people to gather and splash around in the water.

Connections with the Liturgy

In *Evangelical Lutheran Worship* Thanksgiving at the Font V (p. 71) are the words, "Praise to you for your saving waters. . . . The Israelites drink from your gushing rock, and the Samaritan woman will never be thirsty again." When using this Thanksgiving, names of specific local waters—rivers, lakes, the sea—can be inserted into the second paragraph: "Glory to you for oceans and lakes, for rivers and streams, for. . . ."

Let the Children Come

Make use of the baptismal font during worship. If possible, move it to a place worshipers will pass by when they enter and leave worship. Give children permission to touch the water, and guide their "water play" by demonstrating how to put the sign of the cross on the foreheads of their parents, selves, and siblings. The water in the font is so appealing to children, but parents may worry that the font is off limits and may try to steer their children away from it. Your verbal permission can serve as a reminder that baptism is for everyone to celebrate every day.

Assembly Song
Gathering

Glorious things of you are spoken ELW 647

Jesus, keep me near the cross ELW 335, TFF 73

I heard the voice of Jesus say ELW 332, 611; LBW 497

Psalmody and Acclamations

"Listen! Listen! Open Your Hearts!" *Psallite* A-36.

Haas, David. "If Today You Hear His Voice" from PCY, vol. 1.

Houge, Ben. "Oh, Come, Let Us Sing." W&P 107.

Farlee, Robert Buckley. "Let Your Steadfast Love." *Music Sourcebook* S421.

Hymn of the Day

As the deer runs to the river ELW 331 *JULION*

O blessed spring ELW 447, WOV 695 *BERGLUND*

Come, thou Fount of every blessing ELW 807, LBW 499, TFF 108 *NETTLETON*

Offering

Create in me a clean heart ELW 187

For all the faithful women ELW 419, sts. 1, 8

Communion

Rock of Ages, cleft for me ELW 623, LBW 327

Eat this bread ELW 472, TFF 125, WOV 709

Jesus, keep me near the cross ELW 335, TFF 73

Sending

As the sun with longer journey ELW 329, WOV 655

Guide me ever, great Redeemer ELW 618

Additional Assembly Songs

Down at the cross   TFF 72

Would you be free   TFF 76

- Lim, Swee Hong. Singapore. "Lord, Have Mercy" from *Sound the Bamboo*. U. GIA G-6830. ELW 158.
- Loh, I-to. Taiwan. Lord, Have Mercy/Ch'iu chu Lienmin Women" from *Sent by the Lord: Songs of the World Church, Vol 2*. U. GIA G-3740.
- Doss, Daniel. "Love like Rain" from CCLI.
- Houston, Joel. "You" from WT.
- Redman, Matt. "Light of the World" from WT.
- Redman, Matt/Chris Tomlin/Jason Ingram/Matt Maher. "White Flag" from WT.
- Rend Collective Experiment. "You Are My Vision" from WT.
- Stanfill, Kristian. "Spring of Life" from CCLI.

Music for the Day
Choral

- Cherwien, David. "O Blessed Spring." SATB, org, opt C inst. AFP 9781451420753.

  Davis, Taylor. "Hope of the World." SAB, kybd. AFP 9781451401004.

  Horn, Richard. "I Heard the Voice of Jesus Say." SAB, org/hp. MSM 50-6203.

  Keesecker, Thomas. "Jesus, Keep Me Near the Cross." AFP 9780800656027.

  Larter, Evelyn. "Come, You Sinners, Poor and Needy." SATB, kybd, vln. AFP 9781451400984.

  Simmons, Teri. "I Thirst for the Living Water." SATB, pno. GIA G-6335.

Children's Choir

Handel, G. F. "All Who Are Thirsty Come to the Spring." 2 pt, kybd. GIA G-5838.

Hassell, Michael. "Is There Anybody Here Who Loves My Jesus?" 2 pt, kybd. AFP 9780800674595.

White, David Ashley. "Come, Ye Sinners." 2 pt, kybd, oboe. AFP 9780800653248.

Wold, Wayne. "Song at the Well." U/2 pt, kybd. AFP 9780800674656.

Keyboard / Instrumental

- Callahan, Charles. "Come, Thou Fount of Every Blessing" from *American Folk Suite*. Pno. CPH 97-6972.

  Diemer, Emma Lou. "Psalm 95" from *Psalm Interpretations for Organ, Vol. 2*. Org. SMP 70/1319S.

- Leavitt, John. "Come, Thou Fount of Every Blessing" from *Wonder, Love, and Praise*. Pno. CPH 97-7021.

- Phillips, Craig. "Nettleton" from *Glad Praises We Sing: Four Preludes for Organ*. Org. SEL 160-814.

Handbell

Buckwalter, Karen. "Psalm 42." 4-6 oct, L5. BP HB251.

- Krug, Jason. "Come Thou Fount of Every Blessing." 3-5 oct hb, opt 3 oct hc, L3-. BP HB350.
- Moklebust, Cathy. "Come Thou Fount of Ev'ry Blessing." 3-5 oct hb, opt 2 oct hc, L3. CPH 97-6925.

Monday, March 24
Oscar Arnulfo Romero, Bishop of El Salvador, martyr, died 1980

Romero is remembered for his advocacy on behalf of the poor in El Salvador, though it was not a characteristic of his early priesthood. After being appointed as archbishop of San Salvador, he preached against the political repression in his country. He and other priests and church workers were considered traitors for their bold stand for justice, especially defending the rights of the poor. After several years of threats to his life, Romero was assassinated while presiding at the eucharist. During the 1980s thousands died in El Salvador during political unrest.

Tuesday, March 25
Annunciation of Our Lord

Nine months before Christmas the church celebrates the annunciation. In Luke the angel Gabriel announces to Mary that she will give birth to the Son of God, and she responds, "Here am I, the servant of the Lord." Ancient scholars believed that March 25 was also the day on which creation began and was the date of Jesus' death on the cross. Thus, from the sixth to eighth centuries, March 25 was observed as New Year's Day in much of Christian Europe.

Saturday, March 29
Hans Nielsen Hauge, renewer of the church, died 1824

Hans Nielsen Hauge was a layperson who began preaching about "the living faith" in Norway and Denmark after a mystical experience that he believed called him to share the assurance of salvation with others. At the time, itinerant preaching and religious gatherings held without the supervision of a pastor were illegal, and Hauge was arrested several times. He also faced great personal suffering: his first wife died, and three of his four children died in infancy.

🌐 = global song

✡ = praise song

● = relates to hymn of the day

March 30, 2014
Fourth Sunday in Lent

Baptism is sometimes called enlightenment. The gospel for this Sunday is the story of the man born blind healed by Christ. I was blind, but now I see, declares the man. In baptism God opens our eyes to see the truth of who we are: God's beloved sons and daughters. As David was anointed king of Israel, in baptism God anoints our head with oil, and calls us to bear witness to the light of Christ in our daily lives.

Prayer of the Day

Bend your ear to our prayers, Lord Christ, and come among us. By your gracious life and death for us, bring light into the darkness of our hearts, and anoint us with your Spirit, for you live and reign with the Father and the Holy Spirit, one God, now and forever.

Gospel Acclamation

Jesus says, I am the light ⁱ of the world;* whoever follows me will have the ⁱ light of life. (John 8:12)

Readings and Psalm

I Samuel 16:1-13

Samuel anointed David even though he was the eighth-oldest son of Jesse and did not match his brothers in height or other physical characteristics. With the anointing came endowment with the Spirit of the Lord, designating David as the Lord's chosen successor to Saul.

Psalm 23

You anoint my head with oil. (Ps. 23:5)

Ephesians 5:8-14

Because we now live in the divine light that is Jesus Christ, we conduct our lives in ways that reflect the light of Christ, so that our activity is truly pleasing to God.

John 9:1-41

Jesus heals a man born blind, provoking a hostile reaction that he regards as spiritual blindness to the things of God.

Preface   Lent

Color   Purple

Prayers of Intercession

The prayers are prepared locally for each occasion. The following examples may be adapted or used as appropriate.

Returning to the Lord, our God, let us pray for the church, the world, and all of God's creation.

A brief silence.

Anoint your church, O God, so that as children of light we shine brightly in a world that longs to know you. Lord, in your mercy,

hear our prayer.

Restore the green pastures and still waters of this earth and lead us to be responsible stewards of all that you have created. Lord, in your mercy,

hear our prayer.

Shepherd all peoples. Break the barriers of hatred and prejudice between those of different races, faiths, genders, age, ability, and sexual orientation, that we live peaceably together. Lord, in your mercy,

hear our prayer.

Bring goodness and mercy to all who suffer (*especially*), that they not want for anything. Lord, in your mercy,

hear our prayer.

Be present in this assembly and open our eyes so that we look, not on outward appearance, but upon one another's hearts. Lord, in your mercy,

hear our prayer.

Here other intercessions may be offered.

You have prepared a table for all who believe in you. We give you thanks for all our brothers and sisters in Christ who now dwell in your house forever. Lord, in your mercy,

hear our prayer.

Into your hands, O God, we commend ourselves and all for whom we pray, trusting in your abundant mercy, through Jesus Christ, our Savior and Lord.

Amen.

Images in the Readings

The primary image for the day is **light**. According to Genesis 1, light is the first creation of God. In John, Christ not only brings light: he is the very light of God. And so the synoptics describe the crucifixion as effecting an eclipse, and when Judas leaves the company for the betrayal, the author of John writes, "And it was night." The Ephesians reading emphasizes that the light that is Christ is now the light within each believer.

Another image for the day is the **anointing**. In ancient times, and still today in the British monarchy, consecrated oil is poured on the head of the one chosen to lead. In some Christian churches, an anointing is a necessary part of the baptismal ritual. What was dry and brittle is now limber with life.

David was a **shepherd**. According to Israelite memory, the people were nomadic herders before becoming urban dwellers. So David embodies the good old tradition, a more innocent time. Other ancient near eastern cultures also used the metaphor of the shepherd to describe their king. The sheep are the source of the people's life, and the shepherd ensures that livelihood.

Ideas for the Day

◆   The church has recovered the ancient understanding of baptism as "illumination" or "enlightenment." Lent was a time for catechumens to engage in the process of turning away from darkness and coming to the light of Christ. Those preparing for baptism or affirmation of baptism would do well to reflect on questions such as these: Where in my life can't I "see"? What will it take for me to be healed? How might Jesus restore my sight? How has faith in God changed my life? Do not reserve such questions for the candidates alone. Invite the entire faith community, including longtime Christians, to pray these questions and so live into the ongoing rhythm and mystery of dying and rising in Christ.

◆   In baptism we leave behind old commitments and turn toward new life in Christ. In *Leading through the Water* (Herndon, VA: Alban Institute, 2011), Paul Galbreath describes life in Christ as nothing less than a life of service to the neighbor and solidarity with those who suffer. Pay special attention to chapter 4, "Renunciations" (pp. 61–74). Through use of anecdote and story, the author thoughtfully discusses the illumination of baptism, not as an achievement but as a gift of God's grace, requiring the presence and support of the Christian community.

◆   The story of John Newton still inspires. He lived in darkness and, by God's grace, came to light. Newton's venerable hymn (ELW 779) bears witness to his conversion: "I once was lost, but now am found; was blind, but now I see." The film *Amazing Grace* (Samuel Goldwyn, 2006) chronicles the story of William Wilberforce, who was so influenced by Newton that he began to work toward abolition of the slave trade in England. In one poignant scene, he expresses his misgivings about entering into such a risky endeavor with friends. One of his friends offers advice: "You may praise God or change the world. We suggest you do both."

Connections with the Liturgy

Here are a few of the many connections between today's readings and worship throughout the year. (1) In the baptismal liturgy, the candidate is infused with the Spirit of God, as was David; the candidate may be anointed with oil, and so "sealed by the Holy Spirit"; and a lighted candle is presented as a symbol of the light who is Christ now enlightening the newly baptized. (2) In more churches now, the candidate is fully immersed in a pool. (3) At the Easter Vigil, we gather around the candle which symbolizes the risen Christ, who is dispelling the darkness of our heart and minds. This risen Christ "faithfully sheds light on all the human race." (4) For the blessing at the conclusion of the Sunday service, Luther preferred the Aaronic blessing. In the phrase "The Lord's face shine on you with grace and mercy," we hear again the call in Ephesians to rise into Christ's shining light. (5) And in evening prayer, the assembly gathers around a candle to praise Jesus Christ as the light of the world. It is as if each evening, we are the man born blind, acknowledging Christ as the light of our life.

Let the Children Come

"There remains yet the youngest." What a hopeful sentiment, not only for Samuel searching for God's chosen leader, but also for us. In our congregational life, God's blessing remains with us, searching, calling, and consecrating even our young ones. To share God's blessing upon the young, fill a small, clear pitcher or jar with olive oil and place it near the font. At the sending, invite children to be anointed, blessed. They may gather and hold out their palms so that a parent, mentor, or leader can make the sign of the cross over their hands in oil. Glass votive candleholders make perfect oil dishes for use in worship.

Assembly Song
Gathering

I want to walk as a child of the light   ELW 815, WOV 649

God, whose almighty word   ELW 673, LBW 400

Awake, O sleeper, rise from death   ELW 452, WOV 745

Psalmody and Acclamations

Haas, David. "You Are My Shepherd (Psalm 23)." Cant, SATB, assembly, pno, gtr, C inst, cello, hb. GIA G-4994.

Farlee, Robert Buckley. "Psalm 23," Refrain 3, from PSCY.

Haugen, Marty. "Shepherd Me, O God." ELW 780.

Farlee, Robert Buckley. "Let Your Steadfast Love." *Music Sourcebook* S421.

Hymn of the Day

Lead me, guide me   ELW 768, TFF 70   *LEAD ME, GUIDE ME*

Amazing grace, how sweet the sound   ELW 779, LBW 448
   NEW BRITAIN

You Are Mine   ELW 581, W&P 158   *YOU ARE MINE*

Offering

Create in me a clean heart   ELW 187

Christ, the life of all the living   ELW 339, LBW 97

Communion

You, dear Lord   ELW 702, LLC 429

O Christ, your heart, compassionate   ELW 722

Soul, adorn yourself with gladness   ELW 488/489, LBW 224

Sending

Be thou my vision   ELW 793

In the cross of Christ I glory   ELW 324, LBW 104

Additional Assembly Songs

I can hear my Savior calling   TFF 146

Guide my feet   TFF 153

⊕ Nzamuranza   GS3 6

⊕ Brazilian, trad. "Ouve, Senhor, eu estour clamando/Hear Me, O Lord" from *World Praise 2*. U, gtr. LifeWay Press. 9780633007010.

✿ Cantelon, Ben/Jason Ingram. "My Deliverer" from CCLI.

✿ Giglio, Louis/Chris Tomlin. "Amazing Grace (My Chains Are Gone)" from WT.

✿ Leonard, David/Kari Jobe/Leslie Jordan. "Here" from CCLI.

✿ Morgan, Reuben/Matt Crocker. "You Hold Me Now" from WT.

✿ Redman, Beth/Matt Redman. "You Never Let Go" from CCLI.

Music for the Day
Choral

• Carter, John. "Amazing Grace." SATB, kybd. AFP 9780800621377.

Dake, Kenneth. "I Will Arise." SATB. MSM 50-2850.

Ferguson, John. "The Lord's My Shepherd." SATB div, tamb. AFP 9781451401752.

• Haas, David/arr. Stan McDaniel. "You Are Mine." SATB, kybd. GIA G-7478.

Haugen, Marty. "Awake, O Sleeper." SATB, kybd, 2 C inst. GIA G-3290.

Schram, Ruth Elaine. "We Come to You for Healing, Lord." SAB, kybd, fl. AFP 9780800620202.

Children's Choir

• Eithun, Sandra. "Amazing Grace." U, pno. CG CGA1269.

Gifford, Nancy. "Light of Light." U, pno. CG CGA1162.

Hopson, Hal H. "Savior, Like a Shepherd Lead Us." U/2 pt, kybd, opt fl. CG CGA978.

Keyboard / Instrumental

• Caldwell, Charles. "Amazing Grace" from *Four American Hymns for Flute and Piano*. Fl, pno. CPH 97-7090.

Carlson, Bert J. "Near the Cross" from *Come Thou Fount: Piano Solos to Touch the Heart*. Pno. AFP 9780800676759.

Held, Wilbur. "What Wondrous Love Is This" from *Wondrous Love: Five Hymn Settings for Organ*. Org. MSM 10-573.

• Near, Gerald. "New Britain" from *Three Gospel Preludes for Organ*. Org. MSM 10-632.

Handbell

Lamb, Linda, "Psalm 23." 3-5 oct hb, opt 3 oct hc, L3. AGEHR AG35295.

• Tucker, Sondra. "You Are Mine." 3-5 oct hb, opt 2 oct hc, L3. GIA G-7063.

• Wagner, H. Dean. "Amazing Grace." 3-6 oct hb, opt 2-3 oct hc, L4. CG CGB392.

Monday, March 31
John Donne, poet, died 1631

This priest of the Church of England is commemorated for his poetry and spiritual writing. Most of his poetry was written before his ordination and is sacred and secular, intellectual and sensuous. He saw in his wife, Anne, glimpses of the glory of God and a human revelation of divine love. In 1615 he was ordained and seven years later he was named dean of St. Paul's Cathedral in London. By that time his reputation as a preacher was firmly in place. In his poem "Good Friday, 1613. Riding westward," he speaks of Jesus' death on the cross: "Who sees God's face, that is self life, must die; What a death were it then to see God die?"

Friday, April 4
Benedict the African, confessor, died 1589

Born a slave on the island of Sicily, Benedict first lived as a hermit and labored as a plowman after he was freed. When the bishop of Rome ordered all hermits to attach themselves to a religious community, Benedict joined the Franciscans, where he served as a cook. Although he was illiterate, his fame as a confessor brought many visitors to the humble and holy cook, and he was eventually named superior of the community. A patron saint of African Americans, Benedict is remembered for his patience and understanding when confronted with racial prejudice and taunts.

⊕ = global song
✿ = praise song
● = relates to hymn of the day

April 6, 2014
Fifth Sunday in Lent

In today's gospel Jesus reveals his power over death by raising Lazarus from the dead. The prophet Ezekiel prophesies God breathing new life into dry bones. To those in exile or living in the shadows of death, these stories proclaim God's promise of resurrection. In baptism we die with Christ that we might also be raised with him to new life. At the Easter Vigil we will welcome new sisters and brothers at the baptismal font, as we renew our baptismal promises.

Prayer of the Day

Almighty God, your Son came into the world to free us all from sin and death. Breathe upon us the power of your Spirit, that we may be raised to new life in Christ and serve you in righteousness all our days, through Jesus Christ, our Savior and Lord, who lives and reigns with you and the Holy Spirit, one God, now and forever.

Gospel Acclamation

I am the resurrection ǀ and the life;* whoever believes in me will ǀ never die. (John 11:25, 26)

Readings and Psalm

Ezekiel 37:1-14

Ezekiel's vision of the valley of dry bones is a promise that Israel as a nation, though dead in exile, will live again in their land through God's life-giving spirit. Three times Israel is assured that through this vision they will know that "I am the Lord."

Psalm 130

I wait for you, O Lord; in your word is my hope. (Ps. 130:5)

Romans 8:6-11

For Paul, Christian spirituality entails living in the reality of the Holy Spirit. The driving force behind our actions and values is not our sinful desire for self-satisfaction but the very Spirit by which God raised Jesus from the dead and will also raise us from the dead.

John 11:1-45

Jesus is moved to sorrow when his friend Lazarus falls ill and dies. Then, in a dramatic scene, he calls his friend out of the tomb and restores him to life.

Preface   Lent

Color   Purple

Prayers of Intercession

The prayers are prepared locally for each occasion. The following examples may be adapted or used as appropriate.

Returning to the Lord, our God, let us pray for the church, the world, and all of God's creation.

A brief silence.

Pour out your Spirit upon your church so that your people speak words of life to dry bones. Hear us, O God.

Your mercy is great.

Bring newness of life to all of creation: to animals, plants, lands, and sea, that they be refreshed. Hear us, O God.

Your mercy is great.

Unbind all nations, peoples, and tribes from violence and war. Breathe the breath of new life and reconciliation where there is conflict (*especially*). Hear us, O God.

Your mercy is great.

Stir up your healing power to redeem from illness all those who wait upon you (*especially*), that they know your stead-fast love. Hear us, O God.

Your mercy is great.

Inspire this congregation to honor and lift up the gifts of all artists, musicians, needle workers, painters, potters, and sculptors, that your glory be revealed. Hear us, O God.

Your mercy is great.

Here other intercessions may be offered.

We give you thanks for all the saints who have been lifted up to live with you in light eternal (*especially the artists Albrecht Dürer, Matthias Grünewald, and Lucas Cran-ach*). Hear us, O God.

Your mercy is great.

Into your hands, O God, we commend ourselves and all for whom we pray, trusting in your abundant mercy, through Jesus Christ, our Savior and Lord.

Amen.

Images in the Readings

Many medieval churches housed burials and contain even glass-cased skeletons, but most contemporary churches avoid picturing those bones that are left after the flesh has rotted away. Our culture avoids dealing directly and honestly with death: many people are even replacing the verb "died" with the term "passed," as if with everyone going off to heaven, there really is no death. In contrast, this Sunday presents us with the images of the **grave**, the **stink** of bodily decomposition, and the pile of **bones**. Furthermore, Paul's use of the term "**flesh**" as a metaphor for the misused human life intensifies this Sunday's honesty about human mortality. These texts represent the Bible's stark attention to the reality of death, both the "death" that is sin and the finality of death when our bodies die. For this Sunday, you might borrow a skeleton from a science classroom to hang prominently in the sanctuary. When we fully acknowledge the natural fact of death, we are ready to praise God's life as gift.

Ideas for the Day

◆ Ezekiel speaks the promise of God to dry bones. Jesus cries "Lazarus, come out!" God's Word summons life from death. Perhaps this takes place most reliably in worship, where we hear the declaration of forgiveness, good news in preaching, the greeting of peace, and the promise that Christ's gifts are "given and shed for you." The word is proclaimed in prayer, song, the visual arts, and more. God's word lifts us from sin, death, and despair, and we are given life. We are unbound and set free.

◆ Robert Farrar Capon likes to say that Jesus never met a corpse he didn't like. Along with Lazarus, examples include the widow of Nain's son and Jairus's daughter. According to Capon, these all rise, because Jesus "has that effect on the dead." Jesus says, "I am the resurrection and the life." The eternal mystery is *now*: "The mystery manifested in Jesus' death forgives us now because it is as present now as it was on the cross; the mystery manifested in his resurrection restores us now because it is as present now as it was when he left the tomb; and the mystery manifested in his judgment vindicates us now because it is as present now as it will be when he appears in glory" (*The Parables of Judgment*, Grand Rapids, MI: Eerdmans, 1989, pp. 70–71).

◆ A beautiful prayer for baptismal candidates invokes the power of the one who put sinew and flesh on dry bones and raised Lazarus from the tomb: "Merciful and most high God, creator and life-giver of all that is, you have called all people from darkness to light, from error into truth, from death into life. We ask you: grant grace to [names] and bless them. Raise them by your Spirit. Revive them by your word. Form them by your hand. Bring them to the water of life and to the bread and cup of blessing, that with all your people they may bear witness to your grace and praise you forever, through Jesus Christ our Lord. Amen." (*Evangelical Lutheran Worship*, p. 75)

Connections with the Liturgy

In the words of the baptismal liturgy, "By water and the Word God delivers us from sin and death and raises us to new life in Jesus Christ." Our creeds affirm not some immortality of the soul, but rather "the resurrection of the body, and the life everlasting," "the life of the world to come." Christians trust that God enlivens not only this natural existence, but also a life other than and beyond this world, a new creation after this entire created universe has come to its end. Our life in Christ begins at baptism and extends, by the mystery of God, beyond time and space.

Let the Children Come

"Suddenly there was a noise." In delightful ways and not, children make noise. On this Sunday late in Lent, God makes noise too. Rattling bones and a big voice announce that death has no hold on the beloved people of God. Jesus shouts through the tomb, "Lazarus, come out!" Even more than usual, welcome the noise of children this morning. Pass out rattles and ask the children to shake them each time they hear the word "bones" in the first reading. During the intercessions, invite the assembly to shout the name of a loved one, a parent, friend, or pet who has died. Use the shakers again in the sending hymn as the assembly leaves, bringing the message of life to the world.

Assembly Song
Gathering

Now the green blade rises   ELW 379, LBW 148
Christ, the life of all the living   ELW 339, LBW 97
We raise our hands to you, O Lord   ELW 690

Psalmody and Acclamations

Bruxvoort-Colligan, Richard. "We Wait in Hope for Your Word (Psalm 130)" from SR.
Farlee, Robert Buckley. "Psalm 130," Refrain 2, from PSCY.
Smith, Alan. "From the Depths I Call to You" from PS2.
Farlee, Robert Buckley. "Let Your Steadfast Love." *Music Sourcebook* S421.

Hymn of the Day

Restore in us, O God   ELW 328   BAYLOR
Awake, O sleeper, rise from death   ELW 452, WOV 745   AZMON
Lord, thee I love with all my heart   ELW 750, LBW 325   HERZLICH LIEB

Offering

Create in me a clean heart   ELW 187
As the grains of wheat   ELW 465, WOV 705

Communion

My faith looks up to thee   ELW 759, LBW 479

A lamb goes uncomplaining forth   ELW 340

As the sun with longer journey   ELW 329, WOV 655

Sending

O Christ the same   ELW 760, WOV 788

Eternal Lord of love, behold your church   ELW 321

Additional Assembly Songs

Weary of all trumpeting   WOV 785

🌐 Grains of wheat   LLC 392, WOV 708

🌐 Bell, John. Scotland. "Behold the Lamb of God 1" from *Come, All You People: Shorter Songs for Worship*. SAB. GIA G-4391.

🌐 Liberius, R. F. Pakistan. "Khudaya, rahem kar" from *Love and Anger*. U. GIA G-4947.

✧ Eaton, Chris/Gareth Robinson/John Hartley. "And Can It Be" from WT.

✧ Foote, Billy James. "You Are My King (Amazing Love)" from WT.

✧ Houston, Joel/Jill McCloghry. "Bones" from WT.

✧ Ingram, Jason/Matt Maher. "Alive Again" from CCLI.

✧ Myrin, Jonas/Matt Redman. "Fires" from CCLI.

✧ Sands, Aaron/Charlie Lowell/Dan Haseltine/Matt Odmark/Stephen Mason. "The Valley Song/Sing of Your Mercy" from CCLI.

Music for the Day
Choral

● Burkhardt, Michael. "Lord, Thee I Love with All My Heart." SATB, org, br qrt, assembly, opt fl, ob, timp. CPH 98-3985.

Farlee, Robert. "Rich in Promise." SAB, pno. AFP 9780800638856.

Larter, Evelyn. "What Wondrous Love Is This." SATB, org, vln. AFP 9780800621575.

Tanner, Robert. "Lazarus." SATB. GIA G-5851.

Young, Carlton. "Jesus Walked This Lonesome Valley." U, org. AFP 9781451401028.

Children's Choir

Haydn, Franz Joseph. "Out of the Depths" in *Canons for the Church Year*. 4 pt. MSM 50-9803.

Keesecker, Thomas. "Jesus Is a Rock in a Weary Land." U, kybd. AFP 9780800679187.

Pelz, Walter. "Psalm 130." U, opt assembly. CG CGA980.

Keyboard / Instrumental

● Behnke, John. "Lord, Thee I Love with All My Heart" from *Five Preludes of Praise, Set 6*. Org. CPH 97-7301.

● Bennett, Jeff. "Azmon" from *From the Cross to the Sky: Songs of Sacrifice and Salvation for the Piano*. Pno. LOR 70/1703L.

Drischner, Max. "Aus tiefer Not" from *Augsburg Organ Library: Lent*. Org. AFP 9780800658977.

Hassel, Michael. "St. Christopher" from *Jazz Lenten Journey for Piano*. Pno. AFP 9780800659493.

Handbell

Lichlyter, Mary. "Slow Waltz (Psalm 130)." 3-5 oct, L3+. BP HB151.

● Morris, Hart. "Caribbean Praise on 'Azmon.'" 3-5 oct hb, opt 3-4 oct hc, L3+. BP HB266.

● Parrish, Mary Kay. "Festival Prelude on 'Azmon.'" 3-5 oct hb, opt 3 oct hc, L3. MSM 30-842.

Sunday, April 6
Albrecht Dürer, died 1528; Matthias Grünewald, died 1529; Lucas Cranach, died 1553; artists

These great German artists revealed through their work the mystery of salvation and the wonder of creation. Dürer's work reflected the apocalyptic spirit of his time. Though he remained a Roman Catholic, he was sympathetic to Martin Luther's reforming work. Grünewald's paintings are known for their dramatic forms, vivid colors, and depiction of light. Cranach's work includes many fine religious examples and several portraits of Martin Luther. Cranach was also widely known for his woodcuts.

Wednesday, April 9
Dietrich Bonhoeffer, theologian, died 1945

Bonhoeffer (BON-heh-fer) was a German theologian who, at the age of twenty-five, became a lecturer in systematic theology at the University of Berlin. In 1933, and with Hitler's rise to power, Bonhoeffer became a leading spokesman for the Confessing Church, a resistance movement against the Nazis. He was arrested in 1943. He was linked to a failed attempt on Hitler's life and sent to Buchenwald, then to Schönberg prison. After leading a worship service on April 8, 1945, at Schönberg prison, he was taken away to be hanged the next day. His last words as he left were, "This is the end, but for me the beginning of life." *Evangelical Lutheran Worship* includes a hymn (626) by Bonhoeffer, "By Gracious Powers."

Thursday, April 10
Mikael Agricola, Bishop of Turku, died 1557

Agricola was consecrated as the bishop of Turku in 1554, without papal approval. As a result, he began a reform of the Finnish church along Lutheran lines. He translated the New Testament, the prayerbook, hymns, and the mass into Finnish, and through this work set the rules of orthography that are the basis of modern Finnish spelling. His thoroughgoing work is particularly remarkable in that he accomplished it in only three years. He died suddenly on a return trip from negotiating a peace treaty with the Russians.

🌐 = global song
✧ = praise song
● = relates to hymn of the day

April 13, 2014
Sunday of the Passion
Palm Sunday

Today's liturgy begins with a palm procession, commemorating Jesus' triumphal entry into Jerusalem. Quickly the tone of the service changes as we meditate upon Jesus' passion and death. Because this story is so central to our faith, we hear Matthew's account of the passion today and John's version on Good Friday. Though Jesus is obedient even unto death on the cross, he is exalted by God. We gather to remember his offering for the life of the world, and to be fed by his life-giving mercy. This holy week will culminate in the celebration of the Three Days of Jesus' suffering, death, and resurrection.

Prayer of the Day

Everlasting God, in your endless love for the human race you sent our Lord Jesus Christ to take on our nature and to suffer death on the cross. In your mercy enable us to share in his obedience to your will and in the glorious victory of his resurrection, who lives and reigns with you and the Holy Spirit, one God, now and forever.

or

Sovereign God, you have established your rule in the human heart through the servanthood of Jesus Christ. By your Spirit, keep us in the joyful procession of those who with their tongues confess Jesus as Lord and with their lives praise him as Savior, who lives and reigns with you and the Holy Spirit, one God, now and forever.

or

O God of mercy and might, in the mystery of the passion of your Son you offer your infinite life to the world. Gather us around the cross of Christ, and preserve us until the resurrection, through Jesus Christ, our Savior and Lord, who lives and reigns with you and the Holy Spirit, one God, now and forever.

Gospel Acclamation

Christ humbled himself and became obedient to the point of death—even death | on a cross.* Therefore God also highly exalted him and gave him the name that is above | every name. (Phil. 2:8-9)

Readings and Psalm

Procession with Palms: Matthew 21:1-11

Isaiah 50:4-9a

The servant of the Lord expresses absolute confidence in his final vindication, despite the fact that he has been struck and spit upon. This characteristic of the servant played an important role in the early church's understanding of the suffering, death, and resurrection of Jesus.

Psalm 31:9-16

Into your hands, O Lord, I commend my spirit. (Ps. 31:5)

Philippians 2:5-11

Paul uses an early Christian hymn to help us comprehend Jesus' obedient selflessness on the cross and how God has made Christ lord over all reality. The perspective of the cross becomes the way we rightly understand God, Christ, our own lives, and fellowship within the community of Christ.

Matthew 26:14—27:66 or Matthew 27:11-54

In fulfillment of scripture and obedience to God's will, Jesus goes to the cross so that a new covenant in his blood may bring forgiveness of sins. Even the soldiers who crucify him recognize him to be the Son of God.

Preface   Sunday of the Passion

Color   Scarlet *or* Purple

Prayers of Intercession

The prayers are prepared locally for each occasion. The following examples may be adapted or used as appropriate.

As we enter this holy week, together let us pray for the church, those in need, and all of God's creation.

A brief silence.

Let us pray for the church throughout the world, that our sisters and brothers in every land be renewed in the mystery of Christ's death and resurrection. Hear us, O God.

Your mercy is great.

Let us pray for the fragile gift of creation, that our world's many scars and sufferings find healing in God's mercy. Hear us, O God.

Your mercy is great.

Let us pray for the nations of the world, especially where betrayal and injustice reign and God's children perish by the sword of violence. Hear us, O God.

Your mercy is great.

Let us pray for those in need—for those who are grieved or distressed, lonely or despairing, ill or in pain (*especially*). Hear us, O God.

Your mercy is great.

Let us pray for those preparing for baptism and for all seeking renewal amid these holy days, that we might all be transformed in Christ's love poured out for the world. Hear us, O God.

Your mercy is great.

Here other intercessions may be offered.

Finally, let us give thanks for the saints, whose faithful witness, even unto death, has given to us the gift of the gospel. Hear us, O God.

Your mercy is great.

Into your hands, O God of love, we commend all for whom we pray, trusting in your mercy; through Jesus Christ, our Savior and Lord.

Amen.

Images in the Readings

Two opposite images of Christ come in the readings. First, Christ is **king**. In Matthew's passion narrative, he is acclaimed as the Son of David; he is the apocalyptic Son of Man, who will judge the world at the end of time; he is accused of falsely presenting himself as Messiah, yet affirmed by believers as the Christ; he is mocked as the "king of the Jews"; and ironically, even when dead, his body is attended by Roman guards. Much in American culture resists "king" as a positive image. Yet the hope that someone has ultimate power, absolute justice, and endless mercy persists in human imagination.

In an image that derives from the first and second readings, Christ is **servant**. God will vindicate the servant, even though he is now suffering. We are to adopt the mind of Christ Jesus, who became a servant, indeed a slave, for us. Once again, much in American culture resists "servant" as a positive image. Martin Luther's essay "The Freedom of the Christian" can help us here: through our baptism, we are both free, slaves to none, and simultaneously servants to all.

Ideas for the Day

◆ The reading of the Passion story is a vivid and moving experience, and can be enhanced and given new depth by showing artwork that illustrates the story while it is told. Use projected artwork from many Christian cultures and eras to give a broad Christian expression of the story and to stir the imaginations of the worshipers.

◆ Many hymns give beautiful expression to the Passion story. Consider breaking up the telling of the story with the assembly singing hymns that speak to each section. This can take the place of a sermon for the day, as the hymns allow for meditation and commentary on the text. Some hymns that work well include "By your hand you feed your people" (ELW 469), after the last supper (Matt. 26:29); "Stay with me" (ELW 348), after the garden of Gethsemane (Matt. 26:44); "You, dear Lord/Tú, Señor, que brillas" (ELW 702), after Peter's denial and weeping (Matt. 26:75); "O sacred head, now wounded" (ELW 351/352), after Jesus is mocked with the crown of thorns (Matt. 27:31); and "Were you there" (ELW 353), at the end of the reading (Matt. 27:66).

◆ The Passion reading from Matthew is the only gospel that includes the line: "His blood be on us and on our children" (Matt. 27:25). Historically, this misunderstood verse has been used to place collective guilt upon Jews of all generations for the death of Jesus, leading to prejudice and violence against Jews, especially during Holy Week. It may be wise, out of respect for this troubled history and the ongoing need to address historically why and how Jesus was executed by the Roman empire, to omit this verse from the passion reading with a note of explanation in the bulletin.

◆ The poem "Passiontide," by Michael Coffey, expresses the tension between wanting to hang on to Jesus and to our own lives (*we would rather hang on to you friend*), and the recognized need to let go and accept death, both Jesus' and our own, as the way to resurrection and transformation (*and so the time comes to let you go again*). The poem can be found at www.mccoffey.blogspot.com by searching for Passiontide.

Connections with the Liturgy

Each Sunday at the eucharistic table, we sing the Hosanna: just as Jesus processed before the people on the first Palm Sunday, so we acclaim Jesus before us in bread and wine. Hosanna: save us, Lord. As well, each Sunday's thanksgiving at the eucharistic table, like the song in Philippians, retells the Christian gospel. Jesus Christ is God for us, his death a living reality that gives us salvation.

Let the Children Come

Walking and shouting help make this special Sunday open to the propensities of children. We traipse around with leafy branches. We shout "Hosanna!" Perhaps we will cry "crucify" at the appropriate time during the passion reading. The texts for the day are difficult and vivid with violence. Equally vivid ritual actions help provide children a way through the day. In addition to leafy branches, let children wave red ribbons during the procession and gospel acclamation. You might invite the assembly, led by the children, to leave branches and ribbons near the font on their way to communion, just as the crowds placed branches on the road to welcome Jesus.

Assembly Song
Gathering

Ride on, ride on in majesty!   ELW 346, LBW 121

Prepare the royal highway   ELW 246

Lift high the cross   ELW 660, LBW 377

Psalmody and Acclamations

Haugen, Marty. "I Put My Life in Your Hands" from PCY, vol. 1.

Rossi, Richard Robert. "Father, I Put My Life in Your Hands." SATB, assembly. GIA G-5716.

Sedio, Mark. "Psalm 31," Refrain 1, from PSCY.

Farlee, Robert Buckley. "Let Your Steadfast Love." *Music Sourcebook* S421.

Hymn of the Day

My song is love unknown   ELW 343, WOV 661   *LOVE UNKNOWN* LBW 94   *RHOSYMEDRE*

Calvary   ELW 354, TFF 85   *CALVARY*

On my heart imprint your image   ELW 811, LBW 102 *DER AM KREUZ*

Offering

Jesus, I will ponder now   ELW 345, LBW 115

Jesus, remember me   ELW 616, W&P 78, WOV 740

Communion

Alas! And did my Savior bleed   ELW 337, LBW 98

Stay with me   ELW 348

Christ, the life of all the living   ELW 339, LBW 97

Sending

A lamb goes uncomplaining forth   ELW 340

Go to dark Gethsemane   ELW 347, LBW 109

Additional Assembly Songs

Ride on, King Jesus   TFF 182

King of my life   TFF 86

⊕ Chinula, Charles. Malawi. "Behold the Holy Lamb of God" from *The Courage to Say No: 23 Songs for Lent and Easter*. SATB and cantor. GIA G-4244.

⊕ Sato, Taihei. Japan. "Why Have You Forsaken Me?" from *Sound the Bamboo*. U. GIA G-6830.

✿ Brown, Brenton/Paul Baloche "Our God Saves" from WT.

✿ Crowder, David. "Here Is Our King" from WT.

✿ Ligertwod, Brooke. "Hosanna" from WT.

✿ Maher, Matt/Ike Ndolo/Tam Le. "Holy, Holy, Holy" from WT.

✿ Nifong, Alex. "Jesus Paid It All" from WT.

✿ Rodriguez, Freddy/Michael Gungor. "I Will Run" from CCLI.

Music for the Day
Choral

● Behnke, John. "Calvary." SATB, sop solo, pno. MSM 50-3056.

● Childs, Edwin. "My Song Is Love Unknown." SATB, org. MSM 50-3044.

● Cool, Jayne Southwick. "My Song Is Love Unknown." SATB, kybd. AFP 9781451401066.

Grundahl, Nancy. "Sing Hosanna! Sananina!" SATB, opt inst. AFP 9780800638726.

Hoiby, Lee. "Let This Mind Be in You." SATB, org. PRE 312407260.

Lindberg, Gerald N. "Blessed Is He." SATB, kybd. Pavane 1166.

Children's Choir

Ferguson, Michael. "Christus Factus Est." U, org. PAR 9323.

Patterson, Mark. "Sing Hosanna" in *Young ChildrenSing*. U, kybd. AFP 9780800676803.

Patterson, Mark. "The Triumphal Entry" in *ChildrenSing with Instruments*. U/2pt, pno, opt C inst. AFP 9780800620349.

Schulz, Tim. "Ride On, King Jesus." U/SATB, pno. CPH 98-3820.

Keyboard / Instrumental

Bach, J. S. "Valet will ich dir geben." Org. Various editions.

● Childs, Edwin T. "Calvary" from *Spirituals for Organ: For Manuals Only*. Kybd. AFP 9781451401141.

● Eithen, Sandra. "Rhosymedre" from *Love Is the Sunlight: Eight Hymn Preludes for Wedding or General Use*. Pno. CPH 97-7411WEB.

● Oliver, Curt. "Der am Kreuz" from *Built On a Rock: Keyboard Seasons*. Kybd. AFP 9780800654962.

Handbell

Gross, William. "Golgotha." 3-5 oct hb, opt 3 oct hc, L4. GIA G-7931.

● Moats, William. "Behold the Cross." 3-5 oct, L2-. Genesis Press GP2033.

● Moklebust, Cathy. "My Song Is Love Unknown." 3-5 oct, L3. CG CGB203.

⊕ = global song
✿ = praise song
● = relates to hymn of the day

April 14, 2014
Monday in Holy Week

During Holy Week some communities gather each day to meditate on Jesus' final days before his death on the cross. Today's gospel commemorates the anointing of Jesus by Mary, a foreshadowing of his death and burial. Isaiah speaks of the suffering servant who is a light for the nations and who faithfully brings forth justice. For Christians, Jesus' suffering is the path to resurrection and new life. We eagerly await the celebration of the great Three Days later this week.

Prayer of the Day

O God, your Son chose the path that led to pain before joy and to the cross before glory. Plant his cross in our hearts, so that in its power and love we may come at last to joy and glory, through Jesus Christ, our Savior and Lord, who lives and reigns with you and the Holy Spirit, one God, now and forever.

Gospel Acclamation

May I never boast of ׀ anything* except the cross of our Lord ׀ Jesus Christ. (Gal. 6:14)

Readings and Psalm
Isaiah 42:1-9

God's servant Israel is endowed with the Spirit in order to bring justice to the nations. The servant will not exercise authority boisterously or with violence, nor will weariness ever keep it from fulfilling its task. God's old promises have been fulfilled; the new assignment of the servant is to bring light to the nations.

Psalm 36:5-11

All people take refuge under the shadow of your wings. (Ps. 36:7)

Hebrews 9:11-15

Prior to Christ, forgiveness was mediated through animal sacrifice. Christ came as the great high priest to establish a new covenant. Through his blood we are liberated from our sins and promised eternal life.

John 12:1-11

A few days after raising Lazarus from the dead, Jesus visits the man's home. Lazarus's sister Mary is criticized when she anoints the feet of Jesus with costly perfume.

Preface   Sunday of the Passion

Color   Scarlet *or* Purple

April 15, 2014
Tuesday in Holy Week

As the great Three Days draw near, some communities gather each day of Holy Week for worship. Paul proclaims Christ crucified as the wisdom and power of God. Jesus speaks of the grain of wheat that falls into the earth and dies in order that it may bear fruit. We die with Christ in baptism that we may be raised with him to new life. We will celebrate this great mystery of death and resurrection at the Easter Vigil later this week.

Prayer of the Day

Lord Jesus, you have called us to follow you. Grant that our love may not grow cold in your service, and that we may not fail or deny you in the time of trial, for you live and reign with the Father and the Holy Spirit, one God, now and forever.

Gospel Acclamation

May I never boast of ׀ anything* except the cross of our Lord ׀ Jesus Christ. (Gal. 6:14)

Readings and Psalm
Isaiah 49:1-7

Here the servant Israel speaks for herself and acknowledges herself as God's secret weapon. Called like Jeremiah and John the Baptist before her birth, the servant is not only to restore Israel itself, but the servant's ultimate assignment is to bring news of God's victory to the ends of the earth. God in faithfulness has chosen Israel for this task.

Psalm 71:1-14

From my mother's womb you have been my strength. (Ps. 71:6)

I Corinthians 1:18-31

To the world, the word of the cross is silly, because it claims God's power is most fully revealed in complete, utter weakness. For those who are being saved, however, the word of the cross unveils God's true wisdom, power, and source of true life.

John 12:20-36

Knowing that his hour has come, Jesus announces that his death will be an exaltation. God's name will be glorified when his death draws people to new life.

Preface   Sunday of the Passion

Color   Scarlet *or* Purple

April 16, 2014
Wednesday in Holy Week

This day was formerly called "Spy Wednesday," an allusion to the gospel accounts in which Judas is identified as the betrayer of Jesus. As Jesus endured the suffering of the cross, we are called to run the race of life with perseverance, confident of the joy to come. In the Three Days, which begin tomorrow evening, we will journey with Christ from darkness to light, from captivity to freedom, from death to life.

Prayer of the Day

Almighty God, your Son our Savior suffered at human hands and endured the shame of the cross. Grant that we may walk in the way of his cross and find it the way of life and peace, through Jesus Christ, our Savior and Lord, who lives and reigns with you and the Holy Spirit, one God, now and forever.

Gospel Acclamation

May I never boast of | anything* except the cross of our Lord | Jesus Christ. (Gal. 6:14)

Readings and Psalm
Isaiah 50:4-9a

The servant of the Lord expresses absolute confidence in his final vindication, despite the fact that he has been struck and spit upon. This characteristic of the servant played an important role in the early church for understanding the suffering, death, and resurrection of Jesus.

Psalm 70

Be pleased, O God, to deliver me. (Ps. 70:1)

Hebrews 12:1-3

In the way of the cross, Jesus has blazed the trail for our salvation. With faithful perseverance, we follow in his footsteps.

John 13:21-32

At the last supper, Jesus identifies Judas Iscariot as the one who will betray him, and sends him on his way.

Preface   Sunday of the Passion

Color   Scarlet *or* Purple

THE THREE DAYS

PREPARING FOR THE THREE DAYS

Conform your life to the worship rhythms of the church this week. Cancel meetings, work longer days Monday through Wednesday. Do whatever you can to honor Holy Week and the Three Days of Maundy Thursday, Good Friday, Easter Vigil and Day. We gather with Christians around the world to celebrate and remember. On Maundy Thursday, we heed Christ's commandment to love one another—we wash each other's feet and share the meal he instituted. On Friday, we hear the passion of Christ according to John, the narrative of Jesus as a king crucified and reigning from the cross. This service does not "end," but instead continues to the Easter Vigil—the night, the very night, the passover of Christ from death to life. This is the high point of the church's year, the night the church welcomes new Christians by baptism, and lights the first of the resurrection candles.

Lectionary

Maundy Thursday, Good Friday, and the Vigil of Easter repeat the same lectionary texts every year rather than following a three-year cycle. There is kindness in this consistency. For preachers and worship planners shouldered with the responsibility of four consecutive (and widely varying) days of worship, the familiarity is helpful. In addition, some of the readings are so extensive in length that perhaps a very short sermon, or no sermon at all, may be warranted.

On the other hand, some preachers may approach these texts somewhat tired of the repetition. In spite of their arrival only once per year, fifteen or twenty years of preaching them may elicit some fatigue. So, what to do? First, consider reading the texts with people who have fresh eyes and ears. If, during Lent, a catechumenal group is in the stage of intense preparation for baptism at the Easter Vigil, bring them together for a special session to read and respond to these texts. Or bring together another specific group in the congregation—the quilting group, a men's breakfast, a small group—and invite them to break open the texts with you to prepare for preaching and reading them during the Three Days.

However, there is yet a larger and more important historical and theological issue. The truth is that we are not quite sure what Holy Week is or what it entails. The newest worship resources of our church emphasize the "Three Days." Some may consider that the map for the journey in *Evangelical Lutheran Worship* feels profoundly new. In reality, the map brought to expression in the current worship book is very old, representing some of the oldest worship practices of Christians known to us today. Indeed, the pattern of the Three Days was for many centuries "lost." During the centuries that the Three Days were no longer a vibrant congregational ritual,

several alternate Holy Week rituals came to be used, also by Lutherans. Protestant Holy Week rites have tended to accentuate the role of the preacher in telling the story of Christ's passion. Services based on the Franciscan devotion of the Stations of the Cross trace the way that Jesus walked. The Devotion of the Three Hours, created in 1687 by a Jesuit priest in Peru, combines the four gospels and presents sermons based on 'the seven last words' of Jesus. A Lenten devotion called Tenebrae developed out of the morning prayers of medieval monastic communities and includes psalms of lament, the reading of the passion, the extinguishing of candles, and a frightening crash. These rituals consider the death of Christ as an event separated from his resurrection. To balance these services of penitence and mourning at the cross, Easter Day came to focus attention on the moment of Christ's resurrection. Moravians developed the Easter sunrise service, and West Coast American Protestants popularized this ritual of celebrating the resurrection as they observed the sun rising. Many churches developed Easter Day into an extravagant celebration, with banks of flowers often obscuring the place for the meal and external musicians hired to provide extraordinary music for the largest worshiping assembly of the year (*Keeping Time: The Church's Years*, 95).

All of these patterns, and more, are in use in our churches. Careful worship planners will of necessity need to work through how to balance the call of the wider church (and even these denominational publishing house resources) to retrieve the ancient map of the Three Days. Some assemblies may replace older pieties with liturgical renewal; others may weave various pieties and liturgical practices into a new pattern. Whatever the local decision, contextualizing the assigned lectionary texts within this historical description and asking faithful questions about the relationship between the lectionary texts and the overall pattern for worship during these three days will necessarily shed fresh light on old texts.

Specifically, notice at least these. First, John's chronology is one day off from the synoptics and locates Jesus' last supper with the disciples one day earlier than the synoptics. Through this slight chronological shift, John makes a significant theological assertion: Christ becomes the Passover lamb.

Second, on Good Friday, we read from John (having heard the passion narrative from Matthew on Passion Sunday). Although there has been at times some discomfort with John's repeated use of the phrase "the Jews" (and this discomfort is warranted given the use of this text in subsequent generations), nevertheless, a careful study of John and other passion narratives during the Lenten season can invite congregations to reconsider their traditional understanding of the atonement. This year, for example, congregations may be invited to read the passion narrative as a conspiracy story. Just set John 18–19 in front of you and note all the ways, beginning with Judas, that the authorities or the Jews or the crowd conspire to kill Jesus, and a whole new sense of the "meaning" of Jesus presents itself. "Contemporary theologians are reexamining medieval theories of atonement and proposing new ones, and it is the preacher's responsibility to proclaim with gracious learning how Christ's death brings life to the baptized" (*Keeping Time*, 103).

Third, Easter Vigil has a lot of Word—four to twelve readings in addition to the regular New Testament reading and gospel. Because of this wealth of words, it is important to practice silence, long silence, between each reading. One of the worst mistakes readers and leaders make in public worship is to speed up the reading of long texts, as if that will make the worship experience more congenial. Just the opposite is the case. The longer a reading, the slower it needs to be read, the more silence needs to be kept. Because the Vigil is a complex and unique service, make sure to review the service in detail well in advance (*Evangelical Lutheran Worship*, 266–271; Leaders Edition, 643–653).

Some congregations hold a retreat and rehearsal for the Easter Vigil the Sunday prior, the evening of Passion Sunday. For a rich description of preparations for the Vigil and the importance of this preparation and rehearsal, see Paul Hoffman's chapters on "The Great Vigil of Easter" and "The Power of Passion Sunday Evening" in his *Faith Forming Faith: Bringing Christians to Baptism and Beyond* (Eugene, OR: Wipf and Stock, 2012, 54–65). He writes,

"One of the most significant acts of hospitality that a pastor can extend to lay participants in worship is acquainting them with the basic movements that will be required, the words that will be spoken and shared, the gestures that will be involved, and the meanings that these actions carry" (61). He continues, "Over the years, as the rehearsal has prepared all of us for the renewal of our baptismal life in the Vigil of Easter, one of the most profound insights that has occurred to us is this: we are not only rehearsing for the vigil. We are rehearsing for *new life in Christ*" (63–64).

Liturgical Arts

This section encourages you to celebrate the Three Days within the context of the larger practice of the catechumenate. Retrieval of this ancient pattern for the formation of new Christians and preparation for baptism and beyond is bringing new life in many places. If you have not yet reviewed them, purchase Paul Hoffman's *Faith Forming Faith: Bringing New Christians to Baptism and Beyond* and the comprehensive, ecumenical handbook to the catechumenate, Augsburg Fortress's *Go Make Disciples: An Invitation to Baptismal Living* and its companion CD-ROM. These resources provide an inexpensive and helpful way to begin to engage the catechumenate.

If you are already entertaining retrieving this ancient practice in your congregation, or if you are already engaged in it, check out online resources and conference opportunities at www.catechumenate.org.

Although the catechumenate includes art, music, texts, and liturgical resources, especially during this season think through the precise ways in which the "procedural rhetoric" of formation practices is itself an art. Ian Bogost, in his seminal *Persuasive Games: The Expressive Power of Videogames* (MIT Press, 2010) coins this term as a way of describing how games use their very processes to convert and transform. Procedural rhetoric is "the practice of using processes persuasively" (28). The catechumenate is perhaps one of the most ancient forms of procedural rhetoric; it persuades and invites and forms through a process. It does this very, very well. Although many of the components of the catechumenate are already aspects of church life many congregations implement (inquiry classes, Bible study, mentoring, worship, mystagogy), it is the way they are integrated together as a whole that has gravity and beauty.

If your congregation does not host a catechumenal process (many do not), consider initiating one; but more importantly, learn from it and adapt it and ask, "What is the procedural rhetoric active in our congregation that is forming new Christians in faith?" The Three Days are not simply days to offer far more than the normal number of worship services. They are a concentrated core around which all other ministries of the congregation can be organized, because they themselves are centered around the resurrection of Christ, which is the white hot core of everything we are about in the church.

As just one example of how hosting a catechumenal process might influence how other aspects of congregational life proceed, consider these questions: "Is the desire to welcome and receive new Christians listed among the prayer concerns of your parish? Do the weekly prayers of the people at worship include petitions for new men, women, and children to become a part of your community of faith? Is the receiving and welcoming of new Christians a part of the regular opening and closing prayers of the evangelism leadership team and the parish council?" (*Faith Forming Faith*, 97).

Music

If any one portion of the liturgy connects most to the Three Days, it is the Agnus Dei (Lamb of God). Take the opportunity through the Three Days to sing this often, and in various settings. See especially the settings available in the Service Music section of *Evangelical Lutheran Worship* (#194–199). Note the power of the repetition, three times singing "Lamb of God, you take away the sin of the world." Then, the doubled conclusion of the line, "have mercy on us," and the final "grant us peace." The first line summarizes the connection between Passover and Christ, Jesus Christ as the Lamb of God. In this way the hymn is an apt meditation on the readings especially for Maundy Thursday and Good Friday.

There is, additionally, beauty in petitioning the Lord twice to have mercy, to be who God is, merciful. But then, having trusted in God's mercy, to pray, "Grant us peace." For there is peace in having received mercy, and there is in the one who grants mercy, peace, for he is indeed our peace.

A wealth of musical resources is provided in *Music Sourcebook for Lent and the Three Days* (Augsburg Fortress, 2010). Assembly parts are provided on an accompanying CD-ROM. The core of this collection resulted from a gathering of composers in the summer of 2008. They were charged with writing music specifically for the liturgies as set out in *Evangelical Lutheran Worship*, using, in most cases, the texts that are there. The pieces were to have assembly involvement. The musical styles were left up to the composers (and range from chant to blues), but they needed to be accessible. Think of this *Music Sourcebook* as providing some traveling music. The acclamations and musical settings are not required to do the services, but they will greatly enrich those who use them, and they are composed by women and men who deeply know and love these services.

Practical Considerations

- Review the liturgies for Maundy Thursday, Good Friday, and the Vigil of Easter in *Evangelical Lutheran Worship* (Assembly Edition, pp. 258–270; Leaders Edition, pp. 628–653).
- See extensive backgrounds and practical helps for these days in *Worship Guidebook for Lent and the Three Days*, as well as additional music for the services in the companion *Music Sourcebook for Lent and the Three Days* (Augsburg Fortress).
- Arrange rehearsals for all the liturgies of the Three Days. These services are unique, so all worship leaders, even those who have been involved in previous years, need to prepare for their roles.
- Be sure that altar guild members are well equipped and informed about their tasks for these busy days.
- Order worship participation leaflets if used for the Good Friday service.
- Order bulletin covers for Holy Week services.
- It is helpful to prepare printed materials for worship leaders for the Three Days. Consider placing all the texts and musical resources needed into three-ring binders (ceremonial binders in liturgical colors are available from Augsburg Fortress). Highlight speaking parts and instructions for each worship leader in individual copies.
- Publicize Holy Week and Easter services in local newspapers, online (church website, Facebook, Twitter), and through other media. Consider designing and ordering an attractive banner to display curbside or on the church grounds.
- Arrange for a thorough cleaning of the worship space sometime between the Maundy Thursday liturgy and the Easter Vigil.
- Consider silencing bells or chimes from the beginning of the Maundy Thursday service until the hymn of praise at the Easter Vigil (or the first celebration of Easter).
- Determine whether additional handheld candles are needed for the Easter Vigil.
- Purchase a new paschal candle.
- Prepare extra communion elements and communionware needed for large numbers of communicants during Holy Week and Easter.
- If there will be baptisms of children and/or adults at the Easter Vigil (or on Easter Sunday), see the many helps and suggestions in *Washed and Welcome: A Baptism Sourcebook* and *Go Make Disciples: An Invitation to Baptismal Living* (Augsburg Fortress 2010, 2012).

WORSHIP TEXTS FOR THE THREE DAYS

MAUNDY THURSDAY

Confession and Forgiveness

Friends in Christ,
in this Lenten season we have heard our Lord's call
to struggle against sin, death, and the devil—
all that keeps us from loving God and each other.
This is the struggle to which we were called at baptism.
[We have shared this discipline of Lent with new brothers
and sisters in Christ who will be baptized at the Easter Vigil.]

Within the community of the church,
God never wearies of forgiving sin
and giving the peace of reconciliation.
On this night
let us confess our sin against God and our neighbor,
and enter the celebration of the great Three Days
reconciled with God and with one another.

Silence is kept for reflection.

Most merciful God,
**we confess that we are captive to sin
and cannot free ourselves.
We have sinned against you in thought, word, and deed,
by what we have done and by what we have left undone.
We have not loved you with our whole heart;
we have not loved our neighbors as ourselves.
For the sake of your Son, Jesus Christ,
have mercy on us.
Forgive us, renew us, and lead us,
so that we may delight in your will
and walk in your ways,
to the glory of your holy name. Amen.**

In the mercy of almighty God,
Jesus Christ was given to die for us,
and for his sake God forgives us all our sins.
As a called and ordained minister of the church of Christ
and by his authority, I therefore declare to you
the entire forgiveness of all your sins,
in the name of the Father, and of the ☩ Son,
and of the Holy Spirit.
Amen.

Greeting

The grace of our Lord Jesus Christ, the love of God,
and the communion of the Holy Spirit be with you all.
And also with you.

Offering Prayer

God of glory,
receive these gifts and the offering of our lives.
As Jesus was lifted up from the earth,
draw us to your heart in the midst of this world,
that all creation may be brought from bondage to freedom,
from darkness to light, and from death to life;
through Jesus Christ, our Savior and Lord.
Amen.

Invitation to Communion

Where charity and love abide, there is God.
Rejoice in this holy communion.

Prayer after Communion

Lord Jesus, in a wonderful sacrament
you strengthen us with the saving power
of your suffering, death, and resurrection.
May this sacrament of your body and blood
so work in us that the fruits of your redemption
will show forth in the way we live,
for you live and reign with the Father and the Holy Spirit,
one God, now and forever.
Amen.

VIGIL OF EASTER

Greeting

The grace of our Lord Jesus Christ, the love of God,
and the communion of the Holy Spirit be with you all.
And also with you.

Sisters and brothers in Christ, on this most holy night
when our Savior Jesus Christ passed from death to life,
we gather with the church throughout the world
in vigil and prayer. This is the passover of Jesus Christ.
Through light and the word,
through water and oil, bread and wine,
we proclaim Christ's death and resurrection,
share Christ's triumph over sin and death,
and await Christ's coming again in glory.

Offering Prayer

Blessed are you, O God, ruler of heaven and earth.
Day by day you shower us with blessings.
As you have raised us to new life in Christ,
give us glad and generous hearts,
ready to praise you and to respond to those in need,
through Jesus Christ, our Savior and Lord.
Amen.

Invitation to Communion

The disciples knew the Lord Jesus in the breaking of the bread.
Come to this table where you are known and loved.

Prayer after Communion

Loving God,
by your Spirit we are born anew,
and you nourish us like newborns with this holy food,
by which we grow into salvation.
Give us grace to live as your risen daughters and sons,
shining in the world with your marvelous light,
until you gather all creation to the heavenly table
where Christ reigns in glory forever.
Amen.

Blessing

The God of all grace,
who has called you to eternal glory in Christ,
restore, support, strengthen, and + bless you
by the power of the Holy Spirit,
now and forever.
Amen.

Dismissal

Go in peace. Share the good news.
Thanks be to God.

Worship texts for Easter Day and Easter Evening begin on page 184.

Seasonal Rites for the Three Days

Thanksgiving at the Table
Maundy Thursday

The presiding minister or a cantor may lead the acclamations using a simple tone.

Blessed are you, O living God,
sovereign of time and space.
You bring forth bread from the earth and fruit from the vine.
Your word leads us across the sea to freedom,
and you have carried us together to these holy Three Days.
Blessed be God forever!
Blessed be God forever!

Blessed are you, O living God,
for your glory revealed in Jesus Christ.
He is our Servant, who washes our feet with love.
He is our Lamb, whose blood takes away our sin.
He is our Host at this meal, offering us the cup of salvation.

In the night in which he was betrayed . . .
. . . Do this for the remembrance of me.
Blessed be God forever!
Blessed be God forever!

Blessed are you, O living God,
for the gift of your loving Spirit.
Fill this meal with the life of your Son.
Make us servants of one another and of everyone in need.
Bring us with all your people to the joy of the resurrection.
Blessed be God forever!
Blessed be God forever!
Amen, and amen.
Amen, and amen.

The Passion According to John
Good Friday

John 18:1—19:42

Preparation

*You will need three readers (**A**, **B**, and **C**). The presentation of this reading would be well served by a director. The director will need to take time to understand the script, the movement of the three readers, and the various positions within the worship space. Because each worship space is different, the director should decide where each position is best located in the space where this reading will be proclaimed. Position 1 needs to be in the center of the assembly. Position 7 may be the same as position 1. Position 6 (the crucifixion) is central and elevated if possible. Other positions are chosen to suit the worship space but should help reflect the movement in the script.*

The style used in this presentation of the Passion is that of ancient Greek drama. The readers may be understood as a chorus of three voices speaking as one. Movement by the readers is meant to indicate movement within the story. All movement takes place silently while another reader is speaking.

Script

[From position 1]
All readers: The passion of our Lord Jesus Christ according to John.

Reader A *[From position 1]*:
Jesus went out *[Reader B moves to position 2]*
with his disciples across the Kidron valley
to a place where there was a garden,
which he and his disciples entered.
Now Judas, who betrayed him, also knew the place,
because Jesus often met there with his disciples.
So Judas brought a detachment of soldiers
[Reader C moves to position 2]
together with police from the chief priests and the Pharisees,
and they came there with lanterns and torches and weapons.
Then Jesus, knowing all that was to happen to him,
came forward and asked them,
"Whom are you looking for?"
They answered, "Jesus of Nazareth."

Jesus replied, "I am he."
Judas, who betrayed him, was standing with them.
When Jesus said to them, "I am he,"
they stepped back and fell to the ground.
Again he asked them, "Whom are you looking for?"
And they said, "Jesus of Nazareth."
Jesus answered, "I told you that I am he.
So if you are looking for me, let these others go."
This was to fulfill the word that he had spoken,
"I did not lose a single one of those whom you gave me."
Then Simon Peter, who had a sword, drew it,
struck the high priest's slave, and cut off his right ear.
The slave's name was Malchus.
Jesus said to Peter, "Put your sword back into its sheath.
Am I not to drink the cup that the Father has given me?"

Reader B *[From position 2]:*
So the soldiers, their officer, and the Judean police
arrested Jesus and bound him.

[Reader C moves to position 3]
First they took him to Annas,
who was the father-in-law of Caiaphas,
the high priest that year.
Caiaphas was the one who had advised the Judeans
that it was better to have one person die for the people.

Simon Peter and another disciple followed Jesus.
[Reader A moves to position 3]
Since that disciple was known to the high priest,
he went with Jesus into the courtyard of the high priest,
but Peter was standing outside at the gate.
So the other disciple, who was known to the high priest,
went out, spoke to the woman who guarded the gate,
and brought Peter in.
The woman said to Peter,
"You are not also one of this man's disciples, are you?"
He said, "I am not."
Now the slaves and the police had made a charcoal fire
because it was cold,
and they were standing around it and warming themselves.
Peter also was standing with them and warming himself.

Then the high priest questioned Jesus about his disciples
and about his teaching.
Jesus answered, "I have spoken openly to the world;
I have always taught in synagogues and in the temple,
where all the Judeans come together.
I have said nothing in secret.
Why do you ask me?
Ask those who heard what I said to them;
they know what I said."
When he had said this,
one of the police standing nearby struck Jesus on the face,
saying, "Is that how you answer the high priest?"
Jesus answered, "If I have spoken wrongly, testify to the
wrong. But if I have spoken rightly, why do you strike me?"
Then Annas sent him bound to Caiaphas the high priest.

Now Simon Peter was standing and warming himself.
They asked him,
"You are not also one of his disciples, are you?"
He denied it and said, "I am not."
One of the slaves of the high priest,
a relative of the man whose ear Peter had cut off, asked,
"Did I not see you in the garden with him?"
Again Peter denied it, and at that moment the cock crowed.

Reader C *[from position 3]:*
Then they took Jesus from Caiaphas to Pilate's
headquarters.
[Reader A and Reader B move to position 4]
It was early in the morning.
They themselves did not enter the headquarters,
so as to avoid ritual defilement
and to be able to eat the Passover.
So Pilate went out to them and said,
"What accusation do you bring against this man?"
They answered, "If this man were not a criminal,
we would not have handed him over to you."
Pilate said to them,
"Take him yourselves and judge him according to your law."
The Judeans replied,
"We are not permitted to put anyone to death."
(This was to fulfill what Jesus had said
when he indicated the kind of death he was to die.)

Then Pilate entered the headquarters again,
summoned Jesus, and asked him,
"Are you the King of the Jews?"
Jesus answered, "Do you ask this on your own,
or did others tell you about me?"
Pilate replied, "I am not Jewish, am I?
Your own nation and the chief priests
have handed you over to me. What have you done?"
Jesus answered, "My kingdom is not from this world.
If my kingdom were from this world,
my followers would be fighting to keep me from being
handed over to the Judeans.
But as it is, my kingdom is not from here."
Pilate asked him, "So you are a king?"
Jesus answered, "You say that I am a king.
For this I was born, and for this I came into the world,
to testify to the truth.
Everyone who belongs to the truth listens to my voice."
Pilate asked him, "What is truth?"

After he had said this,
he went out to the Judeans again and told them,
"I find no case against him. But you have a custom
that I release someone for you at the Passover.
Do you want me to release for you the King of the Jews?"
They shouted in reply, "Not this man, but Barabbas!"
Now Barabbas was a bandit.

Reader A *[from position 4]*:
Then Pilate took Jesus and had him flogged.
[Reader B and Reader C move to position 5]
And the soldiers wove a crown of thorns and put it on his head,
and they dressed him in a purple robe.
They kept coming up to him, saying,
"Hail, King of the Jews!" and striking him on the face.
Pilate went out again and said to them,
"Look, I am bringing him out to you
to let you know that I find no case against him."
So Jesus came out, wearing the crown of thorns
and the purple robe.
Pilate said to them, "Here is the man!"
When the chief priests and the police saw him, they shouted,
"Crucify him! Crucify him!"

Pilate said to them,
"Take him yourselves and crucify him;
I find no case against him."
The Judeans answered him,
"We have a law, and according to that law
he ought to die because he has claimed to be the Son of God."

Now when Pilate heard this, he was more afraid than ever.
He entered his headquarters again and asked Jesus,
"Where are you from?"
But Jesus gave him no answer.
Pilate therefore said to him, "Do you refuse to speak to me?
Do you not know that I have power to release you,
and power to crucify you?"
Jesus answered him, "You would have no power over me
unless it had been given you from above; therefore the one
who handed me over to you is guilty of a greater sin."
From then on Pilate tried to release him,
but the Judeans cried out,
"If you release this man, you are no friend of the emperor.
Everyone who claims to be a king sets himself against the
emperor."

When Pilate heard these words, he brought Jesus outside
and sat on the judge's bench at a place called The Stone
Pavement, or in Hebrew Gabbatha.
Now it was the day of Preparation for the Passover;
and it was about noon.
He said to the Judeans, "Here is your king!"
They cried out, "Away with him! Away with him!
Crucify him!"
Pilate asked them, "Shall I crucify your king?"
The chief priests answered,
"We have no king but the emperor."
Then he handed him over to them to be crucified.
[Reader B moves to position 6]
Reader B *[from position 6], with a gesture, invites the
assembly to stand.*
So they took Jesus;
[Reader A and Reader C move to position 6]
and carrying the cross by himself,
he went out to what is called The Place of the Skull,
which in Hebrew is called Golgotha.

There they crucified him, and with him two others,
one on either side, with Jesus between them.
Pilate also had an inscription written and put on the cross.
It read, "Jesus of Nazareth, the King of the Jews."
Many of the Judeans read this inscription,
because the place where Jesus was crucified was near the city;
and it was written in Hebrew, in Latin, and in Greek.
Then the chief priests of the Jews said to Pilate,
"Do not write, 'The King of the Jews,' but,
'This man said, I am King of the Jews.'"
Pilate answered, "What I have written I have written."
When the soldiers had crucified Jesus,
they took his clothes and divided them into four parts,
one for each soldier.
They also took his tunic; now the tunic was seamless,
woven in one piece from the top.
So they said to one another,
"Let us not tear it, but cast lots for it to see who will get it."
This was to fulfill what the scripture says,
"They divided my clothes among themselves,
and for my clothing they cast lots."
And that is what the soldiers did.

Reader C [from position 6]:
Meanwhile,
[Reader A and Reader B move to position 7]
standing near the cross of Jesus were his mother,
and his mother's sister, Mary the wife of Clopas,
and Mary Magdalene.
When Jesus saw his mother
and the disciple whom he loved standing beside her,
he said to his mother, "Woman, here is your son."
Then he said to the disciple, "Here is your mother."
And from that hour the disciple took her into his own home.

After this, when Jesus knew that all was now finished,
he said (in order to fulfill the scripture), "I am thirsty."
A jar full of sour wine was standing there.
So they put a sponge full of the wine on a branch of hyssop
and held it to his mouth.
When Jesus had received the wine, he said,
"It is finished."
Then he bowed his head and gave up his spirit.

Pause in silence for at least 30 seconds.

Reader A [from position 7]:
Since it was the day of Preparation,
the Judeans did not want the bodies left on the cross
during the sabbath,
especially because that sabbath was a day of great solemnity.
So they asked Pilate to have the legs of the crucified men
broken and the bodies removed.
Then the soldiers came and broke the legs of the first
and of the other who had been crucified with him.
But when they came to Jesus
and saw that he was already dead, they did not break his legs.
Instead, one of the soldiers pierced his side with a spear,
and at once blood and water came out.
(He who saw this has testified so that you also may believe.
His testimony is true, and he knows that he tells the truth.)
These things occurred so that the scripture might be fulfilled,
"None of his bones shall be broken."
And again another passage of scripture says,
"They will look on the one whom they have pierced."

After these things, Joseph of Arimathea,
who was a disciple of Jesus,
though a secret one because of his fear of the Judeans,
asked Pilate to let him take away the body of Jesus.
Pilate gave him permission; so he came and removed his body.
[Reader C moves to position 7]
Nicodemus, who had at first come to Jesus by night, also came,
bringing a mixture of myrrh and aloes,
weighing about a hundred pounds.
They took the body of Jesus
and wrapped it with the spices in linen cloths,
according to the Jewish burial custom.
Now there was a garden in the place where he was crucified,
and in the garden there was a new tomb
in which no one had ever been laid.
And so, because it was the Jewish day of Preparation,
and the tomb was nearby, they laid Jesus there.

[From position 7]
All readers: The gospel of the Lord.

April 17, 2014
Maundy Thursday

With nightfall our Lenten observance comes to an end, and we gather with Christians around the world to celebrate the Three Days of Jesus' death and resurrection. At the heart of the Maundy Thursday liturgy is Jesus' commandment to love one another. As Jesus washed the feet of his disciples, we are called to follow his example as we humbly care for one another, especially the poor and the unloved. At the Lord's table we remember Jesus' sacrifice of his life, even as we are called to offer ourselves in love for the life of the world.

Prayer of the Day

Holy God, source of all love, on the night of his betrayal, Jesus gave us a new commandment, to love one another as he loves us. Write this commandment in our hearts, and give us the will to serve others as he was the servant of all, your Son, Jesus Christ, our Savior and Lord, who lives and reigns with you and the Holy Spirit, one God, now and forever.

or

Eternal God, in the sharing of a meal your Son established a new covenant for all people, and in the washing of feet he showed us the dignity of service. Grant that by the power of your Holy Spirit these signs of our life in faith may speak again to our hearts, feed our spirits, and refresh our bodies, through Jesus Christ, our Savior and Lord, who lives and reigns with you and the Holy Spirit, one God, now and forever.

Gospel Acclamation

I give you a ¹ new commandment,* that you love one another just as I ¹ have loved you. (John 13:34)

Readings and Psalm
Exodus 12:1-4 [5-10] 11-14

Israel remembered its deliverance from slavery in Egypt by celebrating the festival of Passover. This festival featured the Passover lamb, whose blood was used as a sign to protect God's people from the threat of death. The early church described the Lord's supper using imagery from the Passover, especially in portraying Jesus as the lamb who delivers God's people from sin and death.

Psalm 116:1-2, 12-19

I will lift the cup of salvation and call on the name of the Lord. (Ps. 116:13)

1 Corinthians 11:23-26

In the bread and cup of the Lord's supper, we experience intimate fellowship with Christ and with one another, because it involves his body given for us and the new covenant in his blood. Faithful participation in this meal is a living proclamation of Christ's death until he comes in the future.

John 13:1-17, 31b-35

The story of the last supper in John's gospel recalls a remarkable event not mentioned elsewhere: Jesus performs the duty of a slave, washing the feet of his disciples and urging them to do the same for one another.

Preface   Maundy Thursday

Color   Scarlet *or* White

Prayers of Intercession

The prayers are prepared locally for each occasion. The following examples may be adapted or used as appropriate.

As we enter these holy days, together let us pray for the church, those in need, and all of God's creation.

A brief silence.

O God, in great love you formed the church. Continue to fashion your people. Lead us into unity; teach us to wash each other's feet; gather us all at your one table of mercy. Hear us, O God.

Your mercy is great.

O God, with great delight you created the heavens and the earth. In the mystery of Christ's self-giving love, restore all things to health and unity in you. Hear us, O God.

Your mercy is great.

O God, you love every nation. Bring justice, hope, and peace to all the peoples of the earth (*especially*). Hear us, O God.

Your mercy is great.

O God, your compassion knows no bounds. Comfort those who grieve; console those in despair; make the sick whole in your unfailing love. (*We pray especially for…*) Hear us, O God.

Your mercy is great.

O God, your mercy endures forever and you love your people to the end. Wash us in your forgiveness and feed us with your love, making us your people, blessed and broken for the world. Hear us, O God.

Your mercy is great.

Here other intercessions may be offered.

O God, the saints sing the praises of your unending love. Keep us united with them always, until our faith is changed to sight and your love is all in all. Hear us, O God.

Your mercy is great.

Into your hands, O God of love, we commend all for whom we pray, trusting in your mercy; through Jesus Christ, our Savior and Lord.

Amen.

Images in the Readings

A primary image for Maundy Thursday is the **servant**. We recall from Passion Sunday's Servant Song that the image of servant is not a readily accessible symbol in today's society. Even waiters in many restaurants now present themselves not as servants but as personal friends. John's gospel suggests to us a lowly, even dirty, task as befitting what a true servant does.

The readings are filled with **body**: the body of the dead lamb, cooked and eaten; the body of Christ, shared in the bread; the body of the neighbor's literal feet. For people who like to keep their individual space, it is countercultural to share in one another's body in this public way.

The first reading says that it is the lamb's **blood** that reminds God not to punish the Israelites, and Paul says that the wine is a new covenant in Jesus' blood. In the ancient world, life was seen as residing in the blood. Thus pouring out of blood is giving up of life.

In all three readings, the people of God experience themselves as a **meal** community. Humans must eat to live, and humans eat together to become and maintain community. The Israelites are to keep the Passover meal "as a perpetual ordinance"; Paul assumes and corrects the meal practice of the Corinthians; John describes the last loving meal Jesus had with his disciples before his arrest. So it is over the centuries most Christian assemblies have shared a meal at their weekly meeting. The Three Days begins with this meal.

Ideas for the Day

◆ In his article in *Stricken by God?* (Hardin and Jersek, eds.; Grand Rapids, MI: Eerdmans, 2007, pp. 166–179), James Alison compares the eucharistic liturgy with the rites of the temple. In the temple liturgy, he argues, animal sacrifices and the bread of the presence were understood as offerings *of* the Lord, not offerings *for* the Lord. Alison imagines that the gathering around the Lord's table in holy communion is as if the holy of holies has been opened and God's forgiveness is graciously poured out *for us*. Atonement, therefore, is a liturgy, a drama that God enacts for us and with us.

◆ In *Tuesdays with Morrie* (New York: Doubleday, 1997), Mitch Albom discusses matters of life and death with his dying former college professor. In the last conversations the two discuss forgiveness (including self-forgiveness) and love; the latter, Albom says, follows no specific formula. "Love is when you are as concerned about someone else's situation as you are about your own" (p. 178). When Jesus realizes that his hour has come, he speaks about love as of ultimate importance. If you were giving your last lecture, what would you want to say? With whom would you share it?

◆ Take a moment to reflect how often we use expressions involving feet: head over heels, foot in the door, getting one's feet wet. For a list of expressions, visit www. foot-reflexologist.com/foot_metaphors.htm. Have fun with some of these sayings. What do some of them say when applied to our baptismal life of discipleship? How do our wet feet "walk the walk"?

◆ When Jesus set the example of footwashing, he wasn't only showing his skills as a teacher, but also his insight into human nature. The discovery of the brain's "mirror neurons" in the 1990s (as in *Mirroring People: The Science of Empathy and How We Connect with Others*, Marco Iacoboni, New York: Picador, 2009) made the same case as Aristotle (*Poetics* 4.1): humans are imitative by nature, and we pass on a great deal of information by example and imitation. The danger, however, is that imitation can cause conflict. Jesus' example is one of imitation that fosters community over rivalry.

Connections with the Liturgy

In *Evangelical Lutheran Worship*'s Thanksgiving at Table I, adapted from the 1958 *Service Book and Hymnal*'s compilation from ancient Christian sources, we cite this day's words of Paul: "For as often as we eat of this bread and drink from this cup, we proclaim the Lord's death until he comes."

Let the Children Come

Feet are just plain fun for some. For others, baring feet is vulnerable and scary. Let children lead the assembly in learning to serve each other by washing each other's feet. Let them carry and pour warm water, fold and set out towels and basins, and stand beside the footwashing stations to help out. A good mantra for teaching this potentially awkward ritual is: hold the heel, pour the water, wipe it dry. You might take a Sunday in Lent to practice this action with children during Sunday school and demonstrate it to worshipers at a midweek service.

Assembly Song and Music for the Day

Because of the nature of this day, music suggestions are listed both by place in the service and categorized by type of leadership (in brackets): CC=Children's Choir; Ch=Choral; KI=Keyboard/Instrumental; HB=Handbell. Many suggestions require assembly participation.

Laying On of Hands

Healer of our every ill ELW 612

Great God, your love has called us ELW 358, WOV 666

✿ Ingram, Jason/Kari Jobe. "One Desire" from CCLI.

Highben, Zebulon. "When We Are Tempted to Deny Your Son." SATB, org, opt vln. MSM 50-3073. [Ch]

Nelson, Ronald A. "If You Love One Another." U/2 pt, kybd. SEL 422-841. [CC]

● Biery, Marilyn. "Ubi caritas" from *Augsburg Organ Library: Lent.* Org. AFP 9780800658977. [KI]

● Near, Gerald. "Ubi caritas et amor" from *St. Augustine's Organbook: Ten Preludes on Gregorian Chant Melodies.* Org. AUR AE86. [KI]

Honoré, Jeffrey. "Where Charity and Love Prevail." 3 or 5 oct, L3. WLP 003417. [HB]

Psalmody and Acclamations

Haugen, Marty. "Our Blessing-Cup Is a Communion" from TLP:S.

McRae, Shirley W. "Psalm 116" from *ChildrenSing Psalms.* U, assembly, kybd, 5 hb.

Mummert, Mark. "Psalm 116," Refrain 1, from PSCY.

Sturm, Ike. "I Give You a New Commandment." *Music Sourcebook* S441.

Hymn of the Day

Where charity and love prevail ELW 359, LBW 126, TFF 84

TWENTY-FOURTH

Ubi caritas et amor ELW 642, WOV 665 *TAIZÉ UBI CARITAS*

Jesu, Jesu, fill us with your love ELW 708, TFF 83 *CHEREPONI*

Footwashing

Jesus is a rock in a weary land ELW 333

Love consecrates the humblest act ELW 360, LBW 122

✿ Assad, Audrey/Matt Maher/Michael Gungor/Paul Moak. "Love Comes Down" from CCLI.

❂ Sedio, Mark, arr. "Un mandamiento nuevo" from *Global Choral Sounds.* SATB. CPH 98-3610. [Ch]

Gjeilo, Ola. "Ubi Caritas." SATB. WAL WW1386. [Ch]

Setting the Table

Music Sourcebook for Lent and the Three Days includes an appendix with hymn stanzas appropriate for use during the setting of the table on this and other days. These stanzas are also included on the CD-ROM that accompanies the volume.

❂ Wild Goose Resource Group. Scotland. "I Heard the Voice of Jesus Calling" from *We Walk His Way: Shorter Songs for Worship.* U. GIA G-7403.

✿ Hall, Charlie. "All We Need" from WT.

Schack, David. "When You Woke That Thursday Morning." SATB, org, ob, opt assembly. MSM 50-3030. [Ch]

Anderson, Norma. "The Walk to Calvary." U, kybd. CG CGA739. [CC]

● Sedio, Mark. "Chereponi" from *Dancing in the Light of God: A Piano Collection.* Pno. AFP 9780800656546. [KI]

● Glasgow, Michael. "Jesus Loves Me." 2-6 oct hb, opt 2-6 oct antiphonal hc, L2+. RR BL5055. Full score. RR FS5055. Opt pno. RR BP5055. [HB]

Communion

Lamb of God, pure and sinless ELW 357, LBW 111

When twilight comes ELW 566, WOV 663

✿ Mooring, Leeland/Marc Byrd/Steve Hindalong. "Carried to the Table" from CCLI.

✿ Getty, Keith/Kristyn Getty/Stuart Townend. "Behold the Lamb" from CCLI.

Scheer, Greg. "Bread of the World in Mercy Broken." SATB, pno. AFP 9780800677930. [Ch]

Lowenberg, Kenneth. "Take and Eat." U/2 pt mxd, kybd. SEL 410-431. [CC]

● McMichael, Catherine. "Contemplation on 'Ubi Caritas.'" 3-5 oct hb, opt 3 oct hc, L3+. AGEHR AG36036. [HB]

● Mossing, Sally Drennan. "Ubi caritas" from *Christ, Be Our Light: Music for the Church Pianist.* Pno. AFP 9780800663858. [KI]

Stripping of the Altar

Highben, Zebulon M. "Lord, I Cry to You (Psalm 88)." *Music Sourcebook* S446.

Raabe, Nancy. "Psalm 88" from PSCY.

Farlee, Robert Buckley. "Psalm 22" from PWA.

St. Gregory of Nyssa Episcopal Church. "My God, My God (Psalm 22)." *Music Sourcebook* S447.

Harbor, Rawn. "My God, My God (Psalm 22)." TFF 2.

❂ = global song
✿ = praise song
● = relates to hymn of the day

April 18, 2014
Good Friday

At the heart of the Good Friday liturgy is the passion according to John, which proclaims Jesus as a triumphant king who reigns from the cross. The ancient title for this day—the triumph of the cross—reminds us that the church gathers not to mourn this day but to celebrate Christ's life-giving passion and to find strength and hope in the tree of life. In the ancient bidding prayer we offer petitions for all the world for whom Christ died. Today's liturgy culminates in the Easter Vigil tomorrow evening.

Prayer of the Day

Almighty God, look with loving mercy on your family, for whom our Lord Jesus Christ was willing to be betrayed, to be given over to the hands of sinners, and to suffer death on the cross; who now lives and reigns with you and the Holy Spirit, one God, forever and ever.

or

Merciful God, your Son was lifted up on the cross to draw all people to himself. Grant that we who have been born out of his wounded side may at all times find mercy in him, Jesus Christ, our Savior and Lord, who lives and reigns with you and the Holy Spirit, one God, now and forever.

Gospel Acclamation

Look to Jesus, who for the sake of the joy that was set before him endured the cross, disregard- ¹ ing its shame,* and has taken his seat at the right hand of the ¹ throne of God. (Heb. 12:2)

Readings and Psalm

Isaiah 52:13—53:12

The fourth servant poem promises ultimate vindication for the servant, who made his life an offering for sin. The early church saw in the servant's pouring himself out to death and being numbered with the transgressors important keys for understanding the death of Jesus.

Psalm 22

My God, my God, why have you forsaken me? (Ps. 22:1)

Hebrews 10:16-25

In the death of Jesus, forgiveness of sins is worked and access to God is established. Hence, when we gather together for worship and when we love others we experience anew the benefits of Jesus' death.

or Hebrews 4:14-16; 5:7-9

In his death Jesus functions as great high priest who experiences temptation and suffering in order that we would receive mercy and find grace, because he is the source of true salvation.

John 18:1—19:42

On Good Friday, the story of Jesus' passion—from his arrest to his burial—is read in its entirety from the Gospel of John.

Holy communion is normally not celebrated on Good Friday; accordingly, no preface is provided. The worship space having been stripped on the preceding evening, no paraments are used today.

Prayers of Intercession

On Good Friday, the church's ancient Bidding Prayer is said or sung. See Evangelical Lutheran Worship Leaders Edition, pp. 636–638.

Images in the Readings

The **cross** was the electric chair of the Roman Empire, the means of execution for the lowest criminals. Other cultures have seen in the shape of the cross a sign of the four corners of the earth itself. Christians mark the newly baptized with this sign, God coming through suffering and death, aligned with all who are rejected, and surprisingly in this way bringing life to the whole earth. In the suggested sixth-century hymn "Sing, my tongue," the cross is paradoxically likened to the archetypal tree of life.

In John's passion narrative, Jesus of Nazareth is called King of the Jews, the Son of God, and most significantly, I Aм, the very **name** of God. Christians see in the man dying on the cross the mystery of God's self-giving love. Along with the characters in John's passion, we can sing with the hymnwriter Caroline Noel, "At the name of Jesus every knee shall bow, every tongue confess him king of glory now."

In the Israelite sacrificial system, the **lamb** represented the life of the nomadic herders, and killing the lamb symbolized a plea that God would receive the animal's death as a gift to prompt divine mercy. The New Testament often uses the image of the lamb as one way to understand the meaning of Jesus' death. The book of Revelation recalls Good Friday in its vision of "a Lamb standing as if it had been slaughtered."

But any single image—such as the lamb—is not sufficient. Thus we are given the opposite image, Christ as the **high priest** who does the slaughtering. According to Israelite religion, the people needed an intermediary to approach God. Christ then is the mediator who prays to God for us. Yet for John, Christ is the God whom our prayers address. Good Friday lays each image next to another one, for no single metaphor can fully explain the mystery of Christ.

Ideas for the Day

◆ In the passion, the universality of the cross becomes clear: a universality of rejection. No one stands beside Jesus at his trial, and even the disciples who witness his crucifixion are rendered voiceless, mystified by the day's events. Dare we also allow ourselves to be silenced at the cross today? Can we honestly come to terms with our own rejection of what Jesus offers? Perhaps in the silence of our own "No!" to Jesus we can hear the resounding promise of God's "Yes!" to us in the cross.

◆ In myth, when we hear the word sacrifice, it usually means a sacrifice *to* something or someone, for example, an angry god. David Lose, in *Making Sense of the Cross* (Augsburg Fortress, 2011, p. 179), encourages us to think of Christ's self-giving as a sacrifice *for*, using the popular fictional example of Harry Potter's mother as she sacrifices her life *for* young Harry's. What other examples of sacrifices made *for*, instead of *to*, come to mind?

◆ In Shirley Jackson's story *The Lottery* (New York: Noonday Press, 1991, pp. 291–302), an annual lottery is held to select a victim, in the belief that human sacrifice will be rewarded with a plentiful harvest. The cries of victim Tessie Hutchison call the whole apparatus into question. Does not the passion of Jesus also call our systems into question? Andrew Marr, in *Tools for Peace: The Spiritual Craft of St. Benedict and Rený Girard* (New York: iUniverse, 2007, pp. 205–206), imagines a more positive ending to Jackson's story. Others join with Tessie, chanting, "It isn't fair! It isn't right!" until no stones are cast. May we not also say, "Not fair! Not right!" to the victim-making systems of our day?

◆ Martin Luther King Jr. understood the challenge of the cross: "The cross is something that you bear and ultimately that you die on. The cross may mean the death of your popularity. . . . It may cut your budget down a little, but take up your cross and just bear it" (*Autobiography*, New York: Time Warner, 1998, p. 343). The cross comes in different forms for each of us. What is the shape of your cross?

Connections with the Liturgy

The Sunday liturgy opens "in the name" of the triune God; we are baptized into this triune name of God. Christians say that it is because of the exaltation of Christ on the cross that we can call upon and be sheltered within the power of God's saving name. Each time Christians assemble, it is the mystery of the life-giving cross around which we gather. For Christians, no meeting can be so totally celebrative that it does not have at its core our faith in the salvific death of Christ.

Let the Children Come

A large, rough cross stands at the center of this liturgy. A congregation in Cleveland, Ohio, gives the confirmation class the honor of carving their names into the old wood every spring, and three teenagers are selected to carry it into the assembly on Good Friday. Once the cross is in the worship space, the assembly is invited to reverence it. Teach the children to bow, kneel, or embrace the cross. Save some of the palm branches or other greens from the previous Sunday. Perhaps the young ones have already woven them into cross shapes. Invite them to lay these and other special objects (the red ribbons from Passion Sunday) around the rough cross. Let the young lead the old in showing honor to our tree of life.

Assembly Song and Music for the Day

Because of the nature of this day, music suggestions are listed by place in the service and not categorized by type of leadership. Many suggestions require assembly participation.

Gathering

None

Psalmody and Acclamations

Harbor, Rawn. "My God, My God (Psalm 22)." TFF 2.

Mummert, Mark. "Psalm 22" from PSCY.

Witte, Marilyn. "My God, My God (Psalm 22)." *Music Sourcebook* S448.

Farlee, Robert Buckley. "Look to Jesus." *Music Sourcebook* S451.

Hymn of the Day

O sacred head, now wounded   ELW 351/352, LBW 116/117
   HERZLICH TUT MICH VERLANGEN

Calvary   ELW 354, TFF 85   *CALVARY*

On my heart imprint your image   ELW 811, LBW 102
   DER AM KREUZ

Procession of the Cross: Dialogue

Anderson, Kevin. "Behold, the Life-Giving Cross" and "We Adore You, O Christ." *Music Sourcebook* S457.

Plainsong. "Behold, the Life-Giving Cross" and "We Adore You, O Christ." *Music Sourcebook* S456.

Procession of the Cross: Solemn Reproaches

Fluellen, Jay. "Solemn Reproaches." *Music Sourcebook* S463.

Witte, Marilyn. "Solemn Reproaches." *Music Sourcebook* S461.

Farlee, Robert Buckley. "Solemn Reproaches of the Cross." SATB, solo, pno. AFP 9780800674724.

Procession of the Cross: We Glory in Your Cross

Haugen, Marty. "Adoramus te Christe/We adore you, O Christ." *Music Sourcebook* S469.

Weidler, Scott. "We Glory in Your Cross." *Music Sourcebook* S468.

Procession of the Cross: Other Choral Music

Benson, Robert. "Cross of Jesus" in *Augsburg Easy Choirbook, Volume 2: Music for the Church Year.* U, kybd. AFP 9780800677510.

Benson, Robert. "When I Survey the Wondrous Cross." SATB, org. AFP 9780800677992.

Haan, Raymond. "Were You There." SATB, org, cello. MSM 50-3502.

Hopson, Hal. "What Have We Done." SATB, pno. MSM 50-3505.

Simon, Julia. "Why the Cross?" U, kybd. AFP 9780800679163.

Hymn of Triumph

Sing, my tongue   ELW 355/356, LBW 118

There in God's garden   ELW 342, WOV 668

Tree of Life and awesome mystery   ELW 334

Additional Music Suggestions

The suggestions listed below may be appropriate for services other than the liturgy of Good Friday.

Assembly Songs

⊕ Jabusch, Willard. Russian folk melody. "From the Depths of Sin and Sadness" from *Global Songs for Worship*. SATB, gtr. Faith Alive/Calvin Institute of Christian Worship. 9781592554423.

⊕ Sagabi, Welile. South African traditional. "Woza nomthwalo/Come, Bring Your Burdens to God" from *We Walk His Way: Shorter Songs for Worship*. SATB. GIA G-7403.

✿ Rend Collective Experiment. "You Bled" from WT.

✿ Townend, Stuart. "How Deep the Father's Love for Us" from WT.

✿ Fieldes, Mia. "All for Love" from CCLI.

✿ Green, Melody. "There Is a Redeemer" from WT.

✿ Hughes, Tim. "When I Survey/Thank You for the Cross" from WT.

✿ Ligertwood, Brooke. "Lead Me to the Cross" from WT.

Choral

● Behnke, John. "Calvary." SATB, sop solo, pno. MSM 50-3056.

Benson, Robert. "When I Survey the Wondrous Cross." SATB, org. AFP 9780800677992.

Benson, Robert. "Were You There?" SATB. AFP 9781451420807.

Haan, Raymond. "Were You There." SATB, org, cello. MSM 50-3502.

Shute, Linda Cable. "Thirty Years Among Us." SATB, pno. AFP 9780800658649.

Children's Choir

Benson, Robert. "Cross of Jesus" in *Augsburg Easy Choirbook, Volume 2: Music for the Church Year.* U, kybd. AFP 9780800677510.

Simon, Julia. "Why the Cross?" U, kybd. AFP 9780800679163.

Willan, Healy. "O Savior of the World" in *We Praise Thee*. 3 pt trbl, opt org. CPH 98-1059pdf.

Keyboard / Instrumental

● Brahms, Johannes. "Herzlich tut mich verlangen" from *Eleven Chorale Preludes, Op. 122*. Org. Various editions.

● Carter, John. "Herzlich tut mich verlangen" from *Little Chorale Preludes for Piano*. Pno. AFP 9780800676728.

● Oliver, Curt. "On My Heart Imprint Your Image" from *Built On a Rock: Keyboard Seasons*. Pno. AFP 9780800654962.

Walcha, Helmut. "Herzliebster Jesu" from *A New Liturgical Year*. Org. AFP 9780800656713.

Handbell

Burroughs, Bob. "Road to Calvary." 3-5 oct, L4. MSM 30-302.

● Glasgow, Michael. "Dies Irae." 3-7 oct hb, opt 2 oct hc, L3-. CG CGB682. Full score with opt ob or C inst, opt cello. CG CGB681.

● Moats, William. "Behold the Cross." 3-5 oct, L2-. Genesis Press GP2033.

⊕ = global song
✿ = praise song
● = relates to hymn of the day

April 19, 2014
Resurrection of Our Lord
Vigil of Easter

This is the night! This is our Passover with Christ from darkness to light, from bondage to freedom, from death to life. Tonight is the heart of our celebration of the Three Days and the pinnacle of the church's year. The resurrection of Christ is proclaimed in word and sign, and we gather around a pillar of fire, hear ancient stories of our faith, welcome new sisters and brothers at the font, and share the food and drink of the promised land. Raised with Christ, we go forth into the world, aflame with the good news of the resurrection.

Prayer of the Day

Eternal giver of life and light, this holy night shines with the radiance of the risen Christ. Renew your church with the Spirit given us in baptism, that we may worship you in sincerity and truth and may shine as a light in the world, through your Son, Jesus Christ our Lord, who lives and reigns with you and the Holy Spirit, one God, now and forever.

or

O God, you are the creator of the world, the liberator of your people, and the wisdom of the earth. By the resurrection of your Son free us from our fears, restore us in your image, and ignite us with your light, through Jesus Christ, our Savior and Lord, who lives and reigns with you and the Holy Spirit, one God, now and forever.

Gospel Acclamation

Alleluia. Let us sing to the Lord, who has ˡ triumphed gloriously;* our strength and our might, who has become ˡ our salvation. *Alleluia.* (Exod. 15:1-2)

Vigil Readings and Responses

Readings marked with an asterisk are not omitted.

*1 Genesis 1:1—2:4a
Creation
Response: Psalm 136:1-9, 23-26
God's mercy endures forever. (Ps. 136:1)

2 Genesis 7:1-5, 11-18; 8:6-18; 9:8-13
Flood
Response: Psalm 46
The Lord of hosts is with us; the God of Jacob is our stronghold. (Ps. 46:7)

3 Genesis 22:1-18
Testing of Abraham
Response: Psalm 16
You will show me the path of life. (Ps. 16:11)

*4 Exodus 14:10-31; 15:20-21
Deliverance at the Red Sea
Response: Exodus 15:1b-13, 17-18
I will sing to the Lord, who has triumphed gloriously. (Exod. 15:1)

*5 Isaiah 55:1-11
Salvation freely offered to all
Response: Isaiah 12:2-6
With joy you will draw water from the wells of salvation. (Isa. 12:3)

6 Proverbs 8:1-8, 19-21; 9:4b-6
or Baruch 3:9-15, 32—4:4
The wisdom of God
Response: Psalm 19
The statutes of the Lord are just and rejoice the heart. (Ps. 19:8)

7 Ezekiel 36:24-28
A new heart and a new spirit
Response: Psalms 42 and 43
I thirst for God, for the living God. (Ps. 42:2)

8 Ezekiel 37:1-14
Valley of the dry bones
Response: Psalm 143
Revive me, O Lord, for your name's sake. (Ps. 143:11)

9 Zephaniah 3:14-20
The gathering of God's people
Response: Psalm 98
Lift up your voice, rejoice, and sing. (Ps. 98:4)

10 Jonah 1:1—2:1
The deliverance of Jonah
Response: Jonah 2:2-3 [4-6] 7-9
Deliverance belongs to the Lord. (Jonah 2:9)

11 Isaiah 61:1-4, 9-11

Clothed in the garments of salvation
Response: Deuteronomy 32:1-4, 7, 36a, 43a
Great is our God, the Rock, whose ways are just. (Deut. 32:3-4)

*12 Daniel 3:1-29

Deliverance from the fiery furnace
Response: Song of the Three 35–65
Praise and magnify the Lord forever. (Song of Thr. 35)

New Testament Reading and Gospel
Romans 6:3-11

We were incorporated into the death of Jesus Christ in baptism and so were liberated from the dominion of sin. We also anticipate that we will be incorporated into the resurrection of Christ and so will be liberated from the hold death has over our mortal bodies.

John 20:1-18

John's gospel describes the confusion and excitement of the first Easter: the stone is moved, disciples race back and forth, and angels speak to a weeping woman. Then, Jesus himself appears.

Preface   Easter

Color   White *or* Gold

Prayers of Intercession

The prayers are prepared locally for each occasion. The following examples may be adapted or used as appropriate.
Made alive to God in Christ Jesus, let us pray for the church, those in need, and all of God's creation.
A brief silence.
Holy God, renew your church throughout the world. Drown our fears. Rekindle our hope. Make us alive with the promise that death no longer has dominion. Hear us, O God.
Your mercy is great.
Ever-living God, as your Spirit swept over the waters of creation, so send your Spirit to renew the face of the earth. Even amid death and desolation, reveal your healing, hope, and new life. Hear us, O God.
Your mercy is great.
Liberating God, you break the chains of injustice and you lead your people into freedom. In every nation, hear the cries of those who yearn for freedom, justice, dignity, and peace (*especially*). Hear us, O God.
Your mercy is great.
God of new life, we cry out to you for those in need—for the hungry and despairing, for the sick and the dying (*especially*). Raise your people from the grave. Hear us, O God.
Your mercy is great.

God of the resurrection, bless those who are baptized this night. Bring all of us to die to sin and come alive to you. Recreate us in Christ's image, full of your compassion and love. Hear us, O God.
Your mercy is great.
Here other intercessions may be offered.
Eternal God, all the saints are singing "Alleluia," proclaiming the victory of your great love. Even now, gather us into the chorus of their praise, until we join them in glory and bless you forever. Hear us, O God.
Your mercy is great.
Into your hands, O God, we commend all for whom we pray, trusting in your mercy; through Jesus Christ, our crucified and risen Savior.
Amen.

Images in the Readings

At the beginning of the Vigil, Christ is symbolized by the candle that gives **light** to our darkness, and whose light remains bright even when we all share in its flame. The early church called baptism enlightenment. Sharing this light outdoors in darkness makes the image emotionally effective.

Each reading offers an image with which to picture salvation: the earth is God's perfect creation; we are saved in the ark during the flood; we are granted a reprieve from sacrifice; we escape the enemy army; we are enlivened by spring rains; we are instructed by Woman Wisdom; we are given a new heart; our bones are brought back to life; we enjoy a homeland; swallowed by the fish, we do not drown but are coughed up on dry ground; we wear party clothes; thrown into a furnace, we emerge untouched by the fire; we are risen with Christ; and although we do mistake Christ for the gardener, he appears to us and enlivens our faith.

Ideas for the Day

◆   Although there *may* be a sermon on this night, the real power of the word is expressed in image, in music, in the voices of the readers, in the space created for worship. For congregations that have been "doing" vigil for a number of years, consider what images might create the center of *this* year's vigil. Perhaps darkness and light will be a special focus, calling you to move from the most womb-like space of your building to a brightly lit communion table. Perhaps you want to draw every sense into the watery images of scripture, allowing sound, sight, touch, and even smell to remind believers of their own baptisms.

◆   Some worshipers may groan at the idea of five to twelve scripture readings. Though this is a night of great solemnity, consider how to add a bit of holy levity to the proceedings, particularly toward the end of the readings. The repetitions of Daniel 3 and the extremity of Nebuchadnezzar's hard-headed idolatry invite us to poke fun. Invite the lector (or a chorus of readers) to add a touch of Dr. Seuss rhythms to this text.

◆ In *A Watered Garden: Christian Worship and Earth's Ecology* (Augsburg Fortress, 2011), Benjamin Stewart invites us to consider our entire watershed as we celebrate baptism. Where does your community's water come from, before it reaches the tap? When we give thanks for the waters of baptism, consider naming those sources of life—Mississippi River, Columbia River, Lake Huron. Easter invites us into the alleluia of all creation—so consider ways to name those sources of life.

◆ In some traditions around the world, the first light of Easter Vigil is literally sent out into homes, divided but not diminished as families light their own candles and carry them home. Carrying home a lit candle isn't advisable in many or most circumstances. Consider this twist: Invite families to bring their own baptismal candles (or new ones if they no longer have a baptismal one) and light them from the Easter flame this night. Remind them that Christ's resurrection is also their own.

Connections with the Liturgy

Since the first century, the primary day for Christians to assemble around word and sacrament has been Sunday, because every Sunday is understood as the day of resurrection. The preface to the eucharistic prayer for standard Sundays says of Jesus Christ, "who on this day overcame death and the grave, and by his glorious resurrection opened to us the way of everlasting life."

Let the Children Come

Though it may keep them up past their bedtime, the Easter Vigil is one of the most child-friendly celebrations we share. Shining fire, living stories, splashing water, and rich bread and wine served on a colorful table invite everyone to receive the news of Christ's resurrection like little children. In the gathering, encourage people to freely tend to their needs and those of their children: lie down, run around, take a restroom break. Relieve the assembly from the assumption that they must stay put for the duration of this fulsome liturgy. Hopefully, staying put is not the plan anyway. Walking from the fire toward the reading space, getting up to dance with Miriam in the Exodus story, and following the huge candle to the holy bath and on to the table will allow all bodies young and old to remain engaged with the celebration.

Assembly Song and Music for the Day

Because of the nature of this day, music suggestions are listed both by place in the service and categorized by type of leadership (in brackets): CC=Children's Choir; Ch=Choral; KI=Keyboard/ Instrumental; HB=Handbell. Many suggestions require assembly participation.

Fire and Procession

Abbey of Gethsemani. "Song for the Lighting of the Fire." *Music Sourcebook* S470.

Haugen, Marty. "Light of Christ, Rising in Glory (Easter Vigil Procession)." *Music Sourcebook* S472.

Easter Proclamation

Haugen, Marty. "Easter Proclamation (Exsultet)." *Music Sourcebook* S474.

Lawton, Liam and John McCann. "Exsultet." SATB, AT soloists, assembly, opt 2 tpt. GIA G-5297.

Lundeen, Joel W., paraphrase of the Easter Proclamation. "Rejoice, Angelic Choirs, Rejoice!" *Music Sourcebook* S475.

Plainsong. "Easter Proclamation (Exsultet)." *Music Sourcebook* S473.

Vigil Readings and Responses

Responses to each reading are included in the Music Sourcebook for Lent and the Three Days. Related hymns are listed in Indexes to Evangelical Lutheran Worship. The responses listed below are from other resources.

1 Creation

Guimont, Michel. "Easter Vigil I" from PRCL.

🜨 Boyd, Mwalimu Glenn T. and J. Nathan Corbitt. East Africa. "Psalm 136/Kihaya melody" from *Four African Hymns*. SATB. CG CGA686.

Haugen, Marty. "Your Love Is Never Ending." SATB, C inst, gtr, kybd, assembly. GIA G-3479. [Ch]

🜨 Boyd, Mwalimu Glenn T. "Psalm 136, Wimbo Wa Shukrani (Hymn of Thanks)" from *Four African Hymns*. SATB, drm, shaker. CG CGA686. [Ch]

2 Flood

"A River Flows." *Psallite* A-238. Cant or SATB, assembly, kybd.

Guimont, Michel. "Easter Vigil II" from PRCL.

Patterson, Mark. "Psalm 46" from *ChildrenSing Psalms*. U/2 pt, kybd, fc, assembly. [CC]

Bruxvoort-Colligan, Richard. "God Is Our Shelter and Strength (Psalm 46)." SR.

3 Testing of Abraham

"My Portion and My Cup." *Psallite* A-54. Cant or SATB, assembly, kybd.

🜨 = global song

Alonso, Tony. "You Are My Inheritance" from TLP:S.

Guimont, Michel. "Easter Vigil III" from PRCL.

Gelineau, Joseph or Michel Guimont. "Easter Vigil II" from LP:W4.

4 Deliverance at the Red Sea

"Sing to the Lord." *Psallite* A-55. Cant or SATB, assembly, kybd.

Guimont, Michel. "Easter Vigil IV" from PRCL.

Haugen, Marty. "Let Us Sing to the Lord" from TLP:S.

Duncan, Norah IV. "Easter Vigil III" from LP:LG.

Schulz-Widmar, Russell. "Miriam Dances at the Red Sea." SATB, org. AFP 9780800621476. [Ch]

5 Salvation freely offered to all

"Joyfully You Will Draw Water." *Psallite* A-57.

Guimont, Michel. "Easter Vigil V" from PRCL.

Haugen, Marty. "You Will Draw Water Joyfully" from TLP:S.

✿ Redman, Matt/Jonas Myrin. "You Alone Can Rescue" from WT.

6 The wisdom of God

"Your Word Is Life, Lord." *Psallite* A-58.

Guimont, Michel. "Easter Vigil VI" from PRCL.

Alonso, Tony. "Lord, You Have the Words of Everlasting Life" from TLP:S.

❂ Canadian, source unknown. "Listen to the Word" from *We Walk His Way: Shorter Songs for Worship*. U. GIA G-7403.

7 A new heart and a new spirit

"Like a Deer That Longs for Running Streams." *Psallite* A-59.

Guimont, Michel. "Easter Vigil VII" from PRCL.

Haugen, Marty. "Like a Deer that Longs for Running Streams" from TLP:S.

Gelineau, Joseph or Michel Guimont. "Easter Vigil VII" from LP:W4.

✿ Gungor, Lisa. "We Will Run" from CCLI.

Adams, Jonathan. "Psalm 42: As Pants the Deer." SATB, pno. AFP 9781451420777. [Ch]

8 Valley of the dry bones

Makeever, Ray. "Show Me the Way (Psalm 143)." DH 45.

Guimont, Michel. "Easter Vigil VIII" from PRCL.

Daw, Carl P. Jr. "Hear My Prayer, O God" (*HYMN CHANT*) from PAS 143A.

9 The gathering of God's people

Guimont, Michel. "Easter Vigil IX" from PRCL.

Christopherson, Dorothy. "Psalm 98" from *ChildrenSing Psalms*. U, assembly, kybd, fc, tamb. [CC]

Bruxvoort-Colligan, Richard. "Shout for Joy (Psalm 98)" from SJ.

Bengtson, Bruce. "Psalm 98: O Sing to the Lord a New Song." SATB, org. AFP 9780800676278. [Ch]

Raabe, Nancy. "Sing to the Lord." U/2 pt, pno. CG CGA1241. [CC]

10 The deliverance of Jonah

Guimont, Michel. "Easter Vigil X" from PRCL.

Pavlechko, Thomas. "Jonah 2:2-3 [4-6] 7-9" from PSCY.

✿ Houston, Joel. "Beautiful Exchange" from CCLI.

11 Clothed in the garments of salvation

Guimont, Michel. "Easter Vigil XI" from PRCL.

Mummert, Mark. "Deuteronomy 32:1-4, 7, 36a, 43a" from PSCY.

Warren, George W., arr. May Schwarz. "Deuteronomy 32:1-4, 7, 36a, 43a" from PWA.

12 Deliverance from the fiery furnace

Gelineau, Joseph. "Canticle of the Three Children" from *Thirty Psalms and Two Canticles*. 3 cant, assembly, org. GIA G-1430.

Guimont, Michel. "Easter Vigil XII" from PRCL.

Procession to the Font

Highben, Zebulon M. "Processional Refrains." *Music Sourcebook* S471.

Springs of water, bless the Lord   ELW 214

All creatures, worship God most high   ELW 835, LBW 527

Litany of the saints   ELW 237

Biery, James. "Behold A New Creation." Cant, assembly, opt SAB. MSM 80-580. [Ch]

Setting the Table

Music Sourcebook for Lent and the Three Days includes an appendix with hymn stanzas appropriate for use during the setting of the table on this and other days. These stanzas are also included on the CD-ROM that accompanies the volume.

Signs and wonders   ELW 672

This is the feast   ELW 165, 166 or from one of the ten Holy Communion settings

We who once were dead   ELW 495, LBW 207

✿ Herbert, Nick/Tim Hughes. "Jesus Saves" from WT.

Cherwien, David. "At the Lamb's High Feast." SATB, org, tpt, timp, assembly. CPH 98-2864. [Ch]

Burkhardt, Michael. "Yonder Come Day." 2 pt/3 pt. MSM 50-5811. [CC]

Bach, J. S. "Christ lag in Todesbanden" from *Das Orgelbüchlein*. Org. Various editions. [KI]

Afdahl, Lee. "At the Lamb's High Feast." 3-5 oct hb, opt 2 oct hc, L2+. CPH 97-7309. [HB]

Communion

Pelz, Walter L. "Our Paschal Lamb, That Sets Us Free." *Music Sourcebook* S499.

At the Lamb's high feast we sing   ELW 362, LBW 210

Gospel Acclamation   ELW 173 (Hallelujah only; omit verse)

✿ Brown, Brenton/Don Williams. "Jesus, You Are Worthy" from CCLI.

✿ Fee, Steve. "All Because of Jesus" from WT.

❂ = global song
✿ = praise song

Miller, Aaron David. "Sonne der Gerechtigkeit" from *Eight Chorale Preludes for Manuals Only, Vol 2*. Org. AFP 9780800678470. [KI]

Organ, Anne Krentz. "Sonne der Gerechtigkeit" from *Reflections on Hymn Tunes for Holy Communion*. Pno. AFP 9780800654979. [KI]

Eithun, Sandra. "Tree of Life." 3-6 oct hb, opt 3 oct hc, L2+. CPH 97-7312. [HB]

Sending

We know that Christ is raised   ELW 449, LBW 189

Rise, O church, like Christ arisen   ELW 548

Come, you faithful, raise the strain   ELW 363, LBW 132

Ferguson, John. "Partita on At the Lamb's High Feast." Org. MSM 10-400. [KI]

McChesney, Kevin. "Comfort, Comfort Ye My People (Psalm 42)." 3-5 oct, L3. JEF JHS9401. [HB]

Saturday, April 19

Olavus Petri, priest, died 1552; Laurentius Petri, Bishop of Uppsala, died 1573; renewers of the church

These two brothers are commemorated for their introduction of the Lutheran movement to the Church of Sweden after studying at the University of Wittenberg. They returned home and, through the support of King Gustavus Vasa, began their work. Olavus published a catechism, hymnal, and a Swedish version of the mass. He resisted attempts by the king to gain royal control of the church. Laurentius was a professor at the university in Uppsala. When the king wanted to abolish the ministry of bishops, Laurentius persuaded him otherwise. The historic episcopate continues in Sweden to this day. Together the brothers published a complete Bible in Swedish and a revised liturgy in 1541.

April 20, 2014
Resurrection of Our Lord
Easter Day

On this day the Lord has acted! On the first day of the week God began creation, transforming darkness into light. On this, the "eighth day" of the week, Jesus Christ was raised from the dead. We celebrate this new creation in the waters of baptism and in the feast of victory. With great joy we celebrate this day of days, even as we begin the great fifty days of Easter. Filled with hope, we go forth to share the news that Christ is risen!

Prayer of the Day

O God, you gave your only Son to suffer death on the cross for our redemption, and by his glorious resurrection you delivered us from the power of death. Make us die every day to sin, that we may live with him forever in the joy of the resurrection, through your Son, Jesus Christ our Lord, who lives and reigns with you and the Holy Spirit, one God, now and forever.

or

God of mercy, we no longer look for Jesus among the dead, for he is alive and has become the Lord of life. Increase in our minds and hearts the risen life we share with Christ, and help us to grow as your people toward the fullness of eternal life with you, through Jesus Christ, our Savior and Lord, who lives and reigns with you and the Holy Spirit, one God, now and forever.

Gospel Acclamation

Alleluia. Christ, our paschal lamb, ¹ has been sacrificed.*
Therefore, let us ¹ keep the feast. *Alleluia.* (1 Cor. 5:7, 8)

Readings and Psalm
Acts 10:34-43

Peter's sermon, delivered at the home of Cornelius, a Roman army officer, is a summary of the essential message of Christianity: Everyone who believes in Jesus, whose life, death, and resurrection fulfilled the words of the prophets, "receives forgiveness of sins through his name."

or Jeremiah 31:1-6

This passage makes clear that God's final word is always "Yes." Because God's love is everlasting, God always remains faithful. Ancient Israel is assured that it will be rebuilt and have plentiful crops. The people of God too will ultimately be reunited.

Psalm 118:1-2, 14-24

This is the day that the LORD has made; let us rejoice and be glad in it. (Ps. 118:24)

Colossians 3:1-4

Easter means new life for us as it first meant new life for Christ. His resurrection reshapes the entire focus and motivation for our lives, since we are now hidden with the risen Christ in God.

or Acts 10:34-43

See above.

Matthew 28:1-10

Sorrow gives way to "fear and great joy" when two women are sent by an angel to proclaim the good news: Jesus is risen!

or John 20:1-18

John's gospel describes the confusion and excitement of the first Easter: the stone is moved, disciples race back and forth, and angels speak to a weeping woman. Then, Jesus himself appears.

Preface Easter

Color White or Gold

Prayers of Intercession

The prayers are prepared locally for each occasion. The following examples may be adapted or used as appropriate.

Made alive to God in Christ Jesus, let us pray for the church, those in need, and all of God's creation.

A brief silence.

O God, in Christ's death and resurrection your church is reborn. Bless your people in every nation: Orthodox, Catholic, Protestant, and Pentecostal. Raise us up to witness together to your undying love for the world. Hear us, O God.

Your mercy is great.

O God, your faithfulness extends to all the earth. On this Easter morn, we pray for creation. Make terror and destruction cease, and renew all things in the bright dawning of your love. Hear us, O God.

Your mercy is great.

O God, the resurrection of your Son means life for every nation. Show us that promise and hope. Heal nations scarred by injustice and greed; give hope to those ravaged by violence (*especially*). Hear us, O God.

Your mercy is great.

O God, your Son healed all who were oppressed. Bless those who heal and show compassion in Jesus' name, even as we pray for the many among us who are still in need (*especially*). Hear us, O God.

Your mercy is great.

O God, in the waters of baptism you call us by name and raise us to new life in you. Renew us with all faith, hope,

and love, that we might be Christ's risen body in the world. Hear us, O God.

Your mercy is great.

Here other intercessions may be offered.

O God, we give thanks for the saints whose lives proclaim the victory of your love. With them, give us courage to follow our crucified and risen Lord, until all things are gathered in his name. Hear us, O God.

Your mercy is great.

Into your hands, O God, we commend all for whom we pray, trusting in your mercy; through Jesus Christ, our crucified and risen Savior.

Amen.

Images in the Readings

Matthew's accounts of the crucifixion (27:51) and the resurrection (28:2) include **earthquakes**. The eastern Mediterranean area is prone to earthquakes. Although we explain earthquakes in geological terms, often at theophanies or in apocalyptic material in the Hebrew Scriptures, earthquakes are interpreted as manifestations of the power of God. Matthew means to say that the entire world was shaken by the actions of God at the tomb.

In biblical symbolism, **angels** are messengers of God, extensions of the power of God. The description of angels attending God suggest that heaven resembles an ancient royal court, in which the monarch has servants who carry out the sovereign's will. Like the Elohist source of the Old Testament, Matthew has people seeing an angel, rather than seeing the being of God. Luther's morning and evening prayers ask for God's presence in the form of "your holy angel."

The language of being **raised** from death relies on the commonplace human idea, evident in speech and story, that up is good and down is bad. The ancient three-tier universe placed divine powers on the top level, humans in the middle—between life and death—and the dead below the earth. In today's readings, God raised Jesus (Acts), we go up to Zion (Jeremiah), Christ is above at the right hand of God (Colossians), and the angel descends like lightning. Current scientific understandings of the universe teach us that there is no "up." Thus this language must function for us symbolically: up is life, down is death.

Ideas for the Day

◆ Wendell Berry's lovely poem "Manifesto: The Mad Farmer Liberation Front" (in his *New Collected Poems*, Berkeley, CA: 2012, and earlier collections) ends with the words "Practice resurrection." In the poem he also counsels: "Every day, do something that does not compute." Hear Berry reading the full text at www.youtube.com/watch?v=d7M6Qs01GGw. On Easter Sunday the numbers of visitors can tempt us into trying to "explain" the resurrection. Indeed, we must tell the biblical story, but the best witness on this day is the living community of the resurrected one. How might your worship tell the stories of how the resurrection can lead us to live in surprising and fearless ways? In what ways do Easter people live in ways that do not compute?

◆   The prefaces for the Easter season are the only ones that enjoin the "earth and sea and all their creatures" (*Evangelical Lutheran Worship Leaders Edition*, pp. 187–189) to join in the hymn of unending praise. We are reminded that resurrection is not a predictable natural event. It marks the beginning of the new creation, not just the redemption of human beings. Whether or not the signs of spring are around your community at Eastertide, look for ways to recognize that the whole creation is groaning for that redemption. If your congregation does not celebrate an Easter Vigil, perhaps there is a way to bring the great "Song of the Three" (see *Psalter for Worship*) into your Sunday morning worship.

◆   If you are preaching on Matthew's gospel, consider extending the reading to the end of chapter 28. The astonishing news of the resurrection is quickly followed by the bribe offered to the guards (Matt. 28:11-15) and the meeting at Galilee where the disciples "worshiped him; but some doubted" (v. 17). Indeed, our experience of the Easter news is always mixed in this way: we experience joy *and* fear, doubt *and* faith. And we often encounter those who wish the story would just go away. This dose of reality from Matthew can be a comfort to those who wonder why their faith in the resurrection is not stronger, and sometimes a surprise to those Easter worshipers who are on the fringes of the church.

Connections with the Liturgy

Every Sunday is a celebration of the resurrection. Thus each Sunday's worship includes references to today's readings. "On the third day he rose again," we affirm in the Nicene Creed. "He descended to the dead. On the third day he rose again," says the Apostles' Creed. "Christ has died, Christ is risen," we call out during the eucharistic prayer. When we receive the dismissal, it is as if we are the women seeing the risen Christ: "Go in peace. Share the good news."

Let the Children Come

Though this primary festival of our Christian faith is often observed with plastic grass and stuffed bunnies, we point to the risen Christ in real and living signs. Flowers will surely be in abundance this morning. Let the cross be adorned with flowers, too. Invite families to bring bunches of wildflowers or early blooms from their gardens to tie on to the tree "on which was hung the Savior of the whole world." As this Easter falls near Arbor Day, let the gospel message of new life speak to the renewal of our good green earth.

To poke a little fun at the commercialism of Easter in our culture, invite teenagers to tell a gospel story in shoebox diorama form using marshmallow Peeps! Gentle irreverence is good news when their creativity is welcomed this way.

Assembly Song

Gathering

Alleluia! Christ is arisen   ELW 375

Hail thee, festival day   ELW 394

The day of resurrection!   ELW 361

Psalmody and Acclamations

Barry, Martin. "This Is the Day." SATB, cant, assembly, kybd, gtr, opt ww qnt. GIA G-6395.

Proulx, Richard. "Psalm for Easter Day." SATB, cant, assembly, org, br qrt or sextet, opt hp. GIA G-5383.

Shute, Linda Cable. "This Is the Day." SATB, assembly, kybd, opt hb, C inst. AFP 9780800659745.

Pishner, Stephen. "This Is the Day: Psalm and Gospel Acclamation for Easter." SATB, cant, assembly, kybd, gtr, 11 hb. GIA G-6139.

Hymn of the Day

Awake, my heart, with gladness   ELW 378, LBW 129
    AUF, AUF, MEIN HERZ

Now the green blade rises   ELW 379, LBW 148   *NOËL NOUVELET*

Goodness is stronger than evil   ELW 721   *GOODNESS IS STRONGER*

Offering

Christians, to the paschal victim   ELW 371, LBW 137

At the Lamb's high feast we sing   ELW 362, LBW 210

Communion

Bread of life from heaven   ELW 474

We have seen the Lord   ELW 869

O sons and daughters, let us sing   ELW 387

Sending

Jesus Christ is risen today   ELW 365, LBW 151

Good Christian friends, rejoice and sing!   ELW 385

Additional Assembly Songs

The Lamb   TFF 89

They crucified my Savior   TFF 90

⊕ Sosa, Pablo. Argentina. "Éste es el Día/This Is the Day" from *Éste es el Día*. U. GIA G-7021.

⊕ Toppenberg, Edouard. Caribbean. "Hallelu, Let the People All Sing" from *Let the Peoples Sing: Volume One*. SATB. AFP 9780800675394.

⊕ = global song

✿ Byrd, Marc/Sarah Hart/Douglas Kaine Mckelvey. "Redemption Song" from WT.

✿ Cantelon, Ben. "Saviour of the World" from CCLI.

✿ Maher, Matt. "Resurrection Day" from CCLI.

✿ Rend Collective Experiment. "You Bled" from WT.

✿ Sampson, Marty/Jason Ingram/Brenton Brown. "Arise and Sing" from WT.

✿ Wesley, Charles. "Christ the Lord Is Risen Today" from CCLI.

Music for the Day
Choral

Bach, J. S. "Alleluia! For Christ the Lord Is Risen." SATB, org, inst. CPH 98-2101.

Farlee, Robert Buckley. "God's Paschal Lamb Is Sacrificed for Us." SATB, br qnt. AFP 9781451420708.

Fedak, Alfred. "Begin the Song of Glory Now." SATB, org, br. MSM 50-4014.

Helman, Michael. "This Is the Day." SAB, org. AFP 9780800638740.

Nagy, Russell. "Now, O Death Where Is Thy Sting?" SATB, br qrt, timp. BP JH519.

Near, Gerald. "An Easter Alleluia." SATB, org. MSM 50-4053.

Children's Choir

Albrecht, Mark. "Christ Is Alive, Alleluia." U, kybd. AFP 9780800677466.

Breedlove, Jennifer Kerr. "Early Easter Morning." 2 pt, kybd, opt hb. GIA G-5894.

Mudde, Willem. "At the Lamb's High Feast We Sing" in *A Second Morning Star Choir Book*. 2 pt, desc, org. CPH 97-4702.

Proulx, Richard. "Easter Carol." U, desc, org, fl. GIA G-4465.

Keyboard / Instrumental

● Larkin, Michael. "Now the Green Blade Rises" from *Rejoice! Ten Hymns for Christmas and Easter*. Pno. MSM 15-835.

● Miller, Aaron David. "Now the Green Blade Rises" from *Chorale Preludes for Piano in Traditional Styles*. Pno. AFP 9780800679033.

● Peeters, Flor. "Awake, My Heart, with Gladness" from *30 Chorale Preludes for Organ, Vol. 3 (Op. 70)*. Org. Edition Peters EP6025.

Powell, Robert J. "Easter Carillon." Br qrt, timp, org. MSM 20-449.

Handbell

● Behnke, John. "Awake, My Heart, With Gladness." 3-5 oct, L2+. CPH 97-7306.

Glasgow, Michael. "A Simple Dance." 2-3 oct hb, opt vln, L2+ (opt L4-). CG CGB637. 4-6 oct hb, opt vln, L2+ (opt L4-). CG CGB638.

● McChesney, Kevin. "Now the Green Blade Riseth." 3-6 oct hb, L3. HOP 1892. Opt orch. HOP 1892O. Opt band and orch. HOP 1892OB. Opt SATB choir and kybd. HOP C5161.

April 20, 2014
Resurrection of Our Lord
Easter Evening

Isaiah proclaims the great feast to come, when God will swallow up death forever. Paul invites us to celebrate the paschal feast with the unleavened bread of sincerity and truth. The Easter evening gospel tells of the risen Christ being made known to the disciples in the breaking of the bread. Our hearts burn within us as the hope of the resurrection is proclaimed in our midst, and as Jesus appears to us at the holy table.

Prayer of the Day

O God, whose blessed Son made himself known to his disciples in the breaking of bread, open the eyes of our faith, that we may behold him in all his redeeming work, Jesus Christ, our Savior and Lord, who lives and reigns with you and the Holy Spirit, one God, now and forever.

Gospel Acclamation

Alleluia. Our hearts ¹ burn within us* while you open to ¹ us the scriptures. *Alleluia.* (Luke 24:32)

Readings and Psalm
Isaiah 25:6-9

The prophet portrays a wonderful victory banquet at which death, which in ancient Canaan was depicted as a monster swallowing everyone up, will be swallowed up forever. The prophet urges celebration of this victory, which is salvation.

Psalm 114

Tremble, O earth, at the presence of the LORD. (Ps. 114:7)

1 Corinthians 5:6b-8

In preparation to celebrate Passover, God's people cleaned out all the old leaven from their homes. Paul draws on this practice to portray Christ as our Passover lamb whose sacrifice means that we now clean out the old leaven of malice and wickedness from our lives and replace it with sincerity and truth.

Luke 24:13-49

On the day of his resurrection, Jesus joins two disciples on the road to Emmaus and makes himself known to them in the breaking of bread.

Preface Easter

Color White *or* Gold

Monday, April 21

Anselm, Bishop of Canterbury, died 1109

This eleventh- and twelfth-century Benedictine monk stands out as one of the greatest theologians between Augustine and Thomas Aquinas. He is counted among the medieval mystics who emphasized the maternal aspects of God. Of Jesus Anselm says, "In sickness you nurse us and with pure milk you feed us." Anselm is perhaps best known for his "satisfaction" theory of atonement. He argued

that human rebellion against God demands a payment, but because humanity is fallen it is incapable of making that satisfaction. But God takes on human nature in Jesus Christ, Anselm proposed, in order to make the perfect payment for sin.

Wednesday, April 23

Toyohiko Kagawa, renewer of society, died 1960

Toyohiko Kagawa (toy-oh-hee-koh ka-ga-wah) was born in 1888 in Kobe, Japan. Orphaned early, he was disowned by his remaining extended family when he became a Christian. Kagawa wrote, spoke, and worked at length on ways to employ Christian principles in the ordering of society. His vocation to help the poor led him to live among them. He established schools, hospitals, and churches. He also worked for peace and established the Anti-War League. He was arrested for his efforts to reconcile Japan and China after the Japanese attack of 1940.

Friday, April 25

Mark, Evangelist

Though Mark himself was not an apostle, it is likely that he was a member of one of the early Christian communities. It is possible that he is the John Mark of Acts 12 whose mother owned the house where the apostles gathered. The gospel attributed to him is brief and direct. It is considered by many to be the earliest gospel. Tradition has it that Mark went to preach in Alexandria, Egypt, became the first bishop there, and was martyred.

EASTER

Preparing for Easter

What is Easter anyway? Christians consider Easter to be the "first day." From Easter comes the practice of worshiping Sunday morning. It is the first day of the week. It is also the "first day" of new creation, sometimes called the "eighth day" of the week, for on it Christ restored the image of God in the human and in so doing also brought restoration and renewal to all of creation (Ps. 118). The Easter season proceeds from and celebrates this "first day." In the resurrected Christ, there is time after the end, life after death, restoration of what was broken, the brightening of what had gone dark. In the fifty days of Easter, Christian communities around the world strive to worship God in a way that illustrates that the body of Christ lives now in the heavenly places and also in the gathered body in the world. Worship is where heaven and earth meet.

Lectionary

Some intriguing preaching options are available during the Easter season. Whatever choice is made, be sure to publicize the sermon topics for the Sundays of Easter in the Easter Sunday worship folder and through other channels. Because Easter is such a high attendance Sunday, it offers a great opportunity to proactively invite the assembly back for subsequent Sundays. A sermon series gives everyone a chance to anticipate what they might learn, how they might be challenged, what might inspire them, during the Sundays of Easter.

Don't schedule synod assemblies or vacation for the Sunday after Easter if you can help it. The second Sunday of Easter is an incredible mission moment to connect with inquirers. Think of this time as "new Christians time." Celebrate in your heart and in your prayers those newly baptized at the Easter Vigil. Write down the names of those you anticipate inviting to the next catechumenal inquiry season that will begin in the fall. Pray that the many who visited during Easter will be inspired to return and continue to worship and hear the gospel.

As to the lectionary—there is a First Peter series in here. Luther loved First Peter, as do many preachers, so that is one possibility. However, given our imaginative focus on how the catechumenate might proceed through the church year, Easter is typically the time for preachers to offer mystagogical sermons helping the newly baptized learn the mysteries of the faith, the sacraments, and the symbols of the church. For this reason, it is perhaps better to stick with the gospel readings.

Intriguingly, given that it is year A, the year of Matthew, no readings from the gospel of Matthew are heard during the Easter season other than the resurrection narrative read on Easter Day (Matt. 28:1-10). In fact, given that John 20:1-18 is also an option for Easter Day, some communities will leave Matthew behind for the entire fifty-day season. Why might this be? Well, first of all, although Matthew includes more detail about the resurrection of Christ than, say, Mark, it is still somewhat perfunctory. Luke and John both offer considerably more detail for the resurrection time. Jaroslav Pelikan has felicitously called this period, from the day of resurrection to the day of ascension, "the gospel of the forty days (*evangelium quadraginta dierum*)" (*Acts*, Brazos, 2005, 39), because during this time Luke and John both record ongoing teaching by Jesus.

Matthew, on the other hand, only hints at it. The lectionary bypasses the account of the priests and elders who pay off soldiers to give an alternative account of the empty tomb (Matt. 28:11-15). Matthew then concludes with the famous but also incomparably complex statement,

> Now the eleven disciples went to Galilee, to the mountain to which Jesus had directed them. When they saw him, they worshiped him; but some doubted. And Jesus came and said to them, "All authority in heaven and on earth has been given to me. Go therefore and make disciples of all nations, baptizing them in the name of the Father and of the Son and of the Holy Spirit, and teaching them to obey everything that I have commanded you. And remember, I am with you always, to the end of the age" (Matt. 28:16-20).

That last part, the great commission, gets all the press, but really the Easter season is more about the first part: "When they saw him, they worshiped him; but some doubted" (Matt. 28:17).

These texts will be the bookends for the Easter season. Matthew 28:1-10 is the reading for Easter. Matthew 28:16-20 is the reading for Trinity Sunday. In between, Matthew is silent, and space is given for a variety of readings from Luke and John. The readings on offer, although a transition from the Matthew thematic, are extraordinary and rich for mystagogical reflection with the assembly of believers, new and old alike. Selecting texts from these gospels is also appropriate, in the sense that they are (and especially John is) truly the resurrection gospels *par excellence*. Here is the basic structure, calling out the primary themes preachers might use to outline a sermon series.

Easter 2: John 20:19-31. Jesus appears: Peace be with you, receive the Holy Spirit, believe.

Easter 3: Luke 24:13-35. Jesus appears: Jesus walks, breaks bread, hearts burn.

Easter 4: John 10:1-10. Jesus is the gate; listen to his voice.

Easter 5: John 14:1-14. Jesus is the way, the truth, the life: so ask.

Easter 6: John 14:15-21. If you love me you will keep my commandments.

Easter 7: John 17:1-11. Jesus prays in unity and for unity.

Mystagogy is post-baptismal catechesis. There is a way to pair each of the gospel readings above with a portion of the catechism. It would look like this:

John 20:19-31: The Apostles' Creed
Luke 24:13-35: Holy Communion
John 10:1-10: Holy Baptism
John 14:1-14: The Lord's Prayer
John 14:15-21: The Ten Commandments
John 17:1-11: Reconciliation/Confession and Absolution

Consider weaving the catechism into your Easter season sermons. It is remarkable how readily they intersect. John 20 is all about belief and confession, which is the creed. Luke 24 illustrates how Christ is recognized in the breaking of the bread, thus the Lord's supper. Because baptism is the rite of entry into the life of the church, Jesus as the gate makes sense as a connecting reading (John 10). John 14 encourages the disciples and all Christians to ask for whatever they need, thus the Lord's Prayer. The next section of John 14 mentions the commandments, and thus the ten commandments. And finally, the unity prayer in John 17 is very much related to the content of the catechism training Christians how to confess and receive the absolution.

Liturgical Arts

"Space is dancingly experienced."

–Rudolf Schwarz, The Church Incarnate: The Sacred Function of Christian Architecture (Chicago: Henry Regnery, 1958), 27.

Consider worship as a "built environment." Often when we think about built environments, we focus on the architecture. And certainly architectural space is one aspect of built environments. But liturgical arts can and should encompass even more than simply the church building or the sanctuary, because in fact the whole world and everything that is built is part of human experience and thus a part of Christian experience. T. J. Gorringe, in the first book ever written on the theology of built environments, writes, "Christianity brings to all debates about the structures of the world through which we reproduce ourselves—economics, social and criminal justice, but also town planning and building—its understanding of God become flesh, 'whereby and according to which', as von Balthasar says, they build" (*A Theology of the Built Environment: Justice, Empowerment, Redemption* [Cambridge University Press, 2002], 2–3).

Because the Easter season is the time in which the church considers not only redemption in Christ through his resurrection, but also the restoration of all creation, it is an excellent time to consider all the ways that space as a whole can be "dancingly experienced." This would include the worship space, gathering space, and church building, obviously, but also the way communities move in the space, and also how communities move in daily life, on their way to and from church, and so much more. Ask: how do the church grounds exemplify a Christian theology of the built environment? How do our cars? Our bikes? What aspects or qualities of the built environment let new creation shine through in everything we do and build?

Furthermore, Gorringe argues that

a Trinitarian theology eliminates any fundamental distinction between sacred and secular. . . . We find in Scripture, classically in the Magnificat, a preference for the everyday, the modest, humble and ordinary, and we cannot but take account of that in reflecting on the built environment. . . . Christianity, I shall claim, is wedded to the little tradition . . . which for the most part comes to us only in scraps, in folk memories, songs, tales and ballads, in pamphlets crudely written." (Gorringe, 8–9)

Gorringe contrasts the "little tradition" with the "great tradition" of "the written and celebrated, the work of the philosophers, historians, theologians, the learned" (Gorringe, 8). His thesis offers the intriguing possibility that all the "little tradition" things congregations are engaged in from week to week—printing bulletins, cleaning the worn carpet, sharpening the pew pencils, making coffee—are, in fact, exemplary of Christian faith precisely in their mundanity.

Consider this insight. Then consider it again. Then consider it again. Repeatedly consider it and it might properly reconstruct everything you thought you knew about Christian worship and the built environment.

Music

If the "Lamb of God" is the liturgical song most connected to the Three Days, the most appropriate response to it during the Easter season is the Alleluia. The Alleluia, not sung or said during Lent in many churches, is brought back resoundingly in the church's hymns on Easter. One great hymn to sing throughout this season is "Hallelujah! We sing your praises" (ELW 535). Some churches may want to adopt this hymn as their sending hymn throughout the fifty days.

Note also how many Easter hymns include the word *Alleluia*. It may be worth drawing the assembly's attention to the place and value of this mellifluous, onomatopoetic word, never translated but simply borrowed from its sources in Hebrew and Greek, meaning "praise God." Worship during Easter is replete with the Alleluia. It finds its way into many hymns, is sung around the gospel, spoken in the liturgical greetings and dismissal. In addition to the through-composed gospel acclamations in each of the ten settings of Holy Communion in *Evangelical Lutheran Worship*, there are more Alleluia options in the Service Music section in a variety of styles (#168–175). If your community has never experimented with these, try the Celtic Alleluia (ELW 174). It is easy to sing with or without instrumentation.

Ascension

Very little in popular literature makes an attempt to explore the mystery of Jesus' ascension. One exception to this is the work of Marilynne Robinson, much of whose fiction takes seriously absence in presence and presence in absence. She writes:

> There was a moment in which Jesus, as a man, a physical presence, left that supper at Emmaus. His leave-taking was a profound event for which the supper itself was a precursor. Presence is a great mystery, and presence in absence, which Jesus promised and has epitomized, is, at a human scale, a great reality for all of us in the course of ordinary life.
>
> I am persuaded for the moment that this is in fact the basis of community. I would say, for the moment, that community, at least community larger than the immediate family, consists very largely of imaginative love for people we do not know or whom we know very slightly. . . . We live on a little island of the articulable, which we tend to mistake for reality itself. We can and do make small and tedious lives as we sail through the cosmos on our uncannily lovely little planet, and this is surely remarkable. But we do so much else besides. For example, we make language. . . . Democracy, in its essence and genius, is imaginative love for and identification with a community with which, much of the time and in many ways, one may be in profound disagreement ("Imagination and Community" in *When I Was A Child I Read Books* [Farrar, Straus, and Giroux, 2012], 20, 21, 28).

A compelling argument such as Robinson's should lead us to consider how and where to hold Ascension worship, not whether. It is a perfect worship context for ecumenical gatherings, outdoor worship, anything or any place that allows worship to be the place where absence in presence, difference in community, can find expression.

WORSHIP TEXTS FOR EASTER

Confession and Forgiveness

All may make the sign of the cross, the sign marked at baptism,
as the presiding minister begins.
Blessed be the holy Trinity, ✠ one God,
the life beyond all death,
the joy beyond all sorrow,
our everlasting home.
Amen.

or

Blessed be the God and Father of our Lord ✠ Jesus Christ,
by whose Spirit we have been reborn to a living hope
through the resurrection of Jesus Christ from the dead.
Amen.

Rejoicing in Christ's victory over sin and death,
let us come before God who calls us to repentance.

Silence is kept for reflection.

God of life,
by the resurrection of your Son
you make everything new.
Newness scares us,
and we confess to shutting our doors in fear.
We have not listened to voices that challenge us.
We have resisted the Holy Spirit
moving us in new directions.
Our hearts are slow to believe your promises.
Forgive us, O God,
and renew us to embrace without fear
the new life you have given us in Jesus Christ.
Amen.

People of God:
Christ is alive, and death has lost its power.
Through the waters of baptism
you have been born anew by the living word of God.
Know that your sins are forgiven in ✠ Jesus' name
and that the Spirit of the risen Christ is alive in you
both now and forever.
Amen.

Offering Prayer

Blessed are you, O God, ruler of heaven and earth.
Day by day you shower us with blessings.
As you have raised us to new life in Christ,
give us glad and generous hearts,
ready to praise you and to respond to those in need,
through Jesus Christ, our Savior and Lord.
Amen.

Invitation to Communion

The disciples knew the Lord Jesus in the breaking of the bread.
Come to this table where you are known and loved.

Prayer after Communion

Loving God,
by your Spirit we are born anew,
and you nourish us like newborns with this holy food,
by which we grow into salvation.
Give us grace to live as your risen daughters and sons,
shining in the world with your marvelous light,
until you gather all creation to the heavenly table
where Christ reigns in glory forever.
Amen.

Sending of Communion

Eternal God,
whose glory is revealed in the crucified and risen Lord,
bless those who go forth to share your word and sacrament
with our sisters and brothers
who are *sick/homebound/imprisoned.*
In your love and care, nourish and strengthen
those to whom we bring this communion
in the body and blood of your Son,
that we may all feast upon your abundant love
made known in Jesus Christ our Lord.
Amen.

Blessing

The God of all grace,
who has called you to eternal glory in Christ,
restore, support, strengthen, and + bless you
by the power of the Holy Spirit,
now and forever.
Amen.

Dismissal

Go in peace. Share the good news.
Thanks be to God.

SEASONAL RITES FOR EASTER

Accompanying Newly Baptized Adults

What happens beyond baptism or affirmation of baptism? If adults have been baptized at the Easter Vigil, during the Easter season they move into a stage in the catechumenate called baptismal living. The goal of this stage is for the newly baptized and those who have recently affirmed their baptism to live in response to God's sacramental grace and reflect on the mysteries of faith and the implications for daily living. The congregation's role is to get to know the newly baptized, affirm them in ministry, and invite them into ongoing mutual accountability for discipleship.

Ideas for the Easter Season

- During worship, the newly baptized could be set apart during the fifty days of Easter by wearing special symbols designed and given to them by the members of the congregation such as white robes or crosses.
- Include the newly baptized and those who have newly affirmed their baptism in the prayers of intercession.
- Invite congregational members to reflect on Christian vocation in classes or in workshops that explore various aspects of ministry in daily life.
- Consider establishing groups for people in specific industries, fields of work, or areas of personal responsibility (education, health care, legal affairs, government, business, parenting, etc.) so that they might receive support from one another in the practice of their baptismal vocation. Such groups could meet in an ongoing basis on weekdays (maybe even for breakfast or on a lunch hour) and in locations that are close to people's workplaces.

- Include an affirmation of Christian vocation as a public rite for all the baptized, particularly on the Day of Pentecost (see *Evangelical Lutheran Worship*, 84). Such a rite may include an option for the newly baptized or newly affirmed to give testimony about their gifts and calling to ministry. Consider extending this opportunity to moments throughout the fifty days (or indeed at other times) for people to provide public testimony arising from their stories of conversion as well as to witness to the ways in which they see God using their gifts for ministry in the world. A few minutes of public witness after communion may provide a powerful context for the congregation to be blessed and sent forth into the world to love and serve God.
- Begin each Sunday of Easter with a thanksgiving for baptism or include a congregational renewal of baptismal vows. Sprinkle the assembly with water from the font or invite worshipers to the font to remember baptism in their own ways.
- Since numerous lectionary readings throughout the season of Easter in each of the three lectionary years relate to baptism or communion, preach on the sacraments frequently during this time. Relate the sacraments to baptismal living and life that is sustained by holy communion.
- Let the sacramental symbols of Easter be treated powerfully in the worship environment, prayers, and songs of the season.
- In addition to sessions with the newly baptized and those who have recently affirmed baptism, provide opportunities for others in the congregation to reflect upon the Vigil of Easter and how the movements, actions, gestures, signs, and symbols in it inform and shape Christian identity and living.

Day of Pentecost
Acts 2:1-21

Preparation

You will need a minimum of 11 and a maximum of 21 readers. This reading will need at least two good rehearsals after the readers have received and prepared their scripts.

The **Narrator** *reads from the lectern, pulpit, or ambo.* **Peter** *and the* **Apostles** *(4-10 evenly divided between male and female readers) stand in front of the assembly, possibly on a raised level. The first paragraph read by the Narrator should be read slowly to help the assembly envision the setting of this narrative. As the Narrator begins, Peter and the Apostles go to their place in front of the assembly and the* **Readers** *stand in their places.*

Those identified as "Reader 1," "Reader 2," etc., represent the various nations of people gathered together. These numbered readers are scattered throughout the assembly. Odd-numbered readers are **Group 1.** *Even-numbered readers are* **Group 2.**

Sound effects

During the first paragraph, create a sound like the "rush of a violent wind" if possible. If your worship space has a pipe organ, pulling a stop out half way will allow wind to escape from the organ chamber. Other wind sounds could be created with a very large fan or a rain stick. For "divided tongues, as of fire," try wind chimes or a high-pitched cluster of notes on the organ. As the disciples are "filled with the Holy Spirit" they may quietly begin to mumble unintelligible words. At "amazed and astonished" all sounds stop abruptly.

Script

Narrator: A reading from Acts.

When the day of Pentecost had come,
the apostles were all together in one place.
Begin wind sounds.
And suddenly from heaven there came a sound
like the rush of a violent wind,
and it filled the entire house where they were sitting.
Begin tongues of fire sounds.

Divided tongues, as of fire, appeared among them,
and a tongue rested on each of them.
All of them were filled with the Holy Spirit
(apostles begin mumbling)
and began to speak in other languages,
as the Spirit gave them ability.
A brief pause.

Now there were devout Jews from every nation under heaven
living in Jerusalem.
And at this sound the crowd gathered and was bewildered,
because each one heard them speaking
in the native language of each.
All sound stops abruptly.
Amazed and astonished, they asked,

Group 1: Are not all these who are speaking Galileans?

Group 2: How is it that we hear, each of us, in our own native language?

Reader 1: Parthians!

Reader 2: Medes!

Reader 3: Elamites!

Reader 4: Residents of Mesopotamia!

Reader 5: Judea!

Reader 6: Cappadocia!

Reader 7: Pontus and Asia!

Reader 8: Phrygia and Pamphylia!

Reader 9: Egypt and the parts of Libya belonging to Cyrene!

Group 1: Visitors from Rome, both Jews and proselytes!

Group 2: Cretans and Arabs!

Groups 1 and 2: In our own languages we hear them speaking about God's deeds of power!

Narrator: All were amazed and perplexed, saying to one another, "What does this mean?"

Group 2: *(Each person in the group speaks as if talking to one another within the crowd, echoing the narrator.)* What does this mean? What does this mean? What does this mean?

Narrator: But others sneered and said,

Group 1: *(in unison)* They are filled with new wine!

Narrator: But Peter, standing with the eleven, raised his voice and addressed them,

Peter: Men of Judea and all who live in Jerusalem, let this be known to you, and listen to what I say. Indeed, these are not drunk, as you suppose, for it is only nine o'clock in the morning. No, this is what was spoken through the prophet Joel:

Peter and 1 female Apostle:
In the last days it will be, God declares, that I will pour out my Spirit upon all flesh,

Peter and 2 female Apostles:
and your sons and your daughters shall prophesy,*

Peter and all Apostles:
and your young men shall see visions, and your old men shall dream dreams.

Peter and 2 male Apostles:
Even upon my slaves, both men and women, in those days I will pour out my Spirit; and they shall prophesy.*

Peter and 2 female Apostles:
And I will show portents in the heaven above and signs on the earth below, blood, and fire, and smoky mist.

Peter and all Apostles:
The sun shall be turned to darkness and the moon to blood, before the coming of the Lord's great and glorious day.

All Readers: Then everyone who calls on the name of the Lord shall be saved!

Narrator: The word of the Lord.

Pronunciation guide
Mesopotamia = mes-oh-poh-TAY-mee-uh
Cappadocia = kap-uh-DOH-shee-uh
Phrygia = FRIJ-yuh
Pamphylia = pam-FIL-yuh
Cyrene = sy-REE-nuh
*The word *prophesy* is a verb and pronounced PROF-uh-sigh.

Rogation Days

Stewardship of creation is an ongoing ministry in the church. The creation that God declared good is entrusted to the care of humankind. Exercising that care is one dimension of daily Christian discipleship. Rogation Days are a way for the church to honor God for the gift of creation and to pray for the land, the gift of labor, and the needs of all people.

Rogation Days were traditionally celebrated during the fifty days of Easter on the Monday, Tuesday, and Wednesday before Ascension Day. The word Rogation has its roots in the Latin word that means to ask or petition, and it comes from the ancient introit for the Sunday preceding the Ascension. In some places the celebrations of Rogation Days were quite elaborate and included processions from the church to and around fields while asking for God's blessing.

Churches that have maintained the practice of celebrating Rogation Days no longer mark these days specifically before Ascension. Instead, Rogation Days are celebrated at times and places that meet local needs. With an increased awareness of the need for the stewardship of creation both within the church and within contemporary culture, the themes of thanksgiving for the land and petitions for a fruitful earth may be adapted around broader cultural celebrations of Earth Day (April 22).

Although Rogation Days are agricultural celebrations, they are not solely for rural congregations. These days underscore the dependence of all people, urban and rural, on the fruitfulness of the earth and human labor. The themes of Rogation Days may be highlighted in a special worship service or in prayers of intercession in the Sunday assembly during the spring.

A set of propers appropriate to the Stewardship of Creation from Evangelical Lutheran Worship (p. 63) is provided below. These propers include prayers traditionally used for Rogation Days: a prayer for fruitful seasons and a prayer for the stewardship of creation. If a service is scheduled in a rural area at a representative farm or field, the "General Order of Blessing" from Evangelical Lutheran Worship Occasional Services for the Assembly may be used or adapted.

Hymns to mark Rogation Days might include any of the hymns under the topics of Creation, Preservation, or Stewardship listed in various hymn indexes. "We plow the fields and scatter" (ELW 680/681) or an adaptation of St Francis's Canticle of the Sun such as "All creatures, worship God most high!" (ELW 835) would be particularly appropriate to highlight our dependence on, and our stewardship of, God's gift of creation.

Stewardship of Creation

Preface of the season, or Sundays

Color of the season

Prayer of the Day

Almighty God, Lord of heaven and earth,
we humbly pray that your gracious providence
may give and preserve to our use
the fruitfulness of the land and the seas;
and may prosper all who labor therein,
that we, who are constantly receiving good things
from your hand, may always give you thanks,
through Jesus Christ, our Savior and Lord. **Amen.**

or

Merciful Creator, your hand is open wide
to satisfy the needs of every living creature.
Make us always thankful for your loving providence;
and grant that we,
remembering the account that we must one day give,
may be faithful stewards of your good gifts,
through Jesus Christ, our Savior and Lord. **Amen.**

Gospel Acclamation

Alleluia. Let the sea roar, and all that fills it; let the rivers [|] clap their hands;* let the hills ring out with joy be- [|] fore the Lord. *Alleluia.* (Ps. 98:7, 8)

Readings and Psalm

Job 38:1-11, 16-18
Psalm 104:1, 13-23 *or* Psalm 104:24-35
O Lord, how manifold are your works! (Ps. 104:24)
1 Timothy 6:6-10, 17-19
Luke 12:13-21

April 27, 2014
Second Sunday of Easter

In today's gospel the risen Christ appears to the disciples and offers them the gift of peace. Even amid doubts and questions, we experience the resurrection in our Sunday gathering around word and meal, and in our everyday lives. Throughout the coming Sundays of Easter the first two readings will be from the Acts of the Apostles and the first letter of Peter. Even as the early Christians proclaimed the resurrection, we rejoice in the new birth and living hope we receive in baptism.

Prayer of the Day

Almighty and eternal God, the strength of those who believe and the hope of those who doubt, may we, who have not seen, have faith in you and receive the fullness of Christ's blessing, who lives and reigns with you and the Holy Spirit, one God, now and forever.

Gospel Acclamation

Alleluia. Blessed are those who ¦ have not seen* and yet have come ¦ to believe. *Alleluia.* (John 20:29)

Readings and Psalm

Acts 2:14a, 22-32

After the Holy Spirit came to the apostles on Pentecost, Peter preaches the gospel to the gathered crowd. He tells them that Jesus, who obediently went to his death according to God's plan, was raised from the dead by God. Finally, he appeals to scripture, quoting Psalm 16:8-11, to show that Jesus is the Messiah: though crucified, the risen Jesus is now enthroned.

Psalm 16

In your presence there is fullness of joy. (Ps. 16:11)

I Peter 1:3-9

This epistle was written to encourage Christians experiencing hardships and suffering because of their faith in Christ. The letter opens by blessing God for the living hope we have through Christ's resurrection even in the midst of difficult circumstances and surroundings.

John 20:19-31

The risen Jesus appears to his disciples, offering them a benediction, a commission, and the gift of the Holy Spirit. But one of their number is missing, and his unbelief prompts another visit from the Lord.

Preface   Easter

Color   White

Prayers of Intercession

The prayers are prepared locally for each occasion. The following examples may be adapted or used as appropriate.

Made alive in Christ and filled with his Spirit, let us pray for the church, the world, and all of God's creation.
A brief silence.

Ever-living God, you awaken faith amidst our doubts and fears. Reveal your presence so that we recognize your power at work in your church and throughout the world. ~~Hear us,~~ O God. *Lord.*
Your mercy is great.

Holy Creator, the earth receives your promise of new life: seeds die to bear fruit and plants decay to nourish the soil. Restore all living things as you intend. Hear us, O God.
Your mercy is great.

Giver of peace, when you make your presence known, you do so by offering peace. Bring such peace to peoples and nations ravaged by war, violence, and natural disaster. Hear us, O God.
Your mercy is great.

Healing God, you breathe hope into rooms of despair. Be with the sick, the lonely, the grieving, and those in any need (*especially*). Hear us, O God.
Your mercy is great.

God of welcome, you are with this assembly as we worship. Bless all those who God draws to this community and be with those who cannot be present this day. Hear us, O God.
Your mercy is great.

Here other intercessions may be offered.

God of life, with you all things are possible. With the saints (*especially*) make us live in hope, trusting that though we do not see, we believe. Hear us, O God.
Your mercy is great.

Receive our prayers, merciful God, and dwell in us richly, through Jesus Christ, our life and our redeemer.
Amen.

Images in the Readings

Usually depictions of the crucified Christ include the marks on his **hands and side**. Our archeological knowledge that for crucifixions nails were driven through the wrist ought not negate the symbolism of the palm, which is central to a person's hand. Neither need we get fascinated by the accounts of the stigmata, for we all carry the mark of the crucified and risen Christ on our palm each time we receive the body of Christ at communion. In John 19:34, blood and water flow from the wound on Jesus' side, and church tradition has seen in this detail not an erroneous description of human anatomy, but rather the proclamation that baptism and eucharist flow from the death of Christ.

Each year on the second Sunday of Easter we meet **doubting Thomas**. He is all of us, and we doubters are glad to share with all other doubters the peace of the risen Christ.

That Christ is **king** is an image behind the reading from Acts: King David testifies to this power; Jesus is now on David's throne; Christ is the anointed one, the messiah.

God is the Father of our Lord Jesus Christ, and in baptism we have been given a new **birth**, to live as children of this heavenly father. The imagery continues: only children receive the full inheritance.

Ideas for the Day

◆ Fear and anxiety are two feelings that come through in the reading from 1 Peter as well as the reading from John's gospel. In the context of church leadership, fear and anxiety can be fed by things both real and imagined; yet through it all, there is calm and grounding that must be maintained by leaders if the goals of congregational health and progress are to be achieved. An excellent and well-reviewed resource is *Congregational Leadership in Anxious Times: Being Calm and Courageous No Matter What*, by Peter L. Steinke (Herndon, VA: Alban Institute, 2006). Steinke's research and writing has addressed much that is of value concerning congregations as emotional systems, and the benefit of leaders being a nonanxious presence in the midst of those systems. The peace that Jesus shared with his disciples in the upper room gave them a new perspective on their fear and anxiety. And with that new perspective they began to evangelize the world.

◆ Consider the real dilemma of Thomas: did he need any more proof of the resurrection of Jesus than the other disciples, or was he just absent from the assembly when Jesus showed himself the first time? What did Thomas really miss by his absence from the assembled gathering of disciples on that first resurrection evening? Consider what is missed by any member of the congregation when they are absent from the gathered assembly, including the peace and presence of the risen Lord that is gifted and shared, and the many ways

that happens. Consider also what is missed by the congregation when any member is absent from the gathered assembly, including the gifts, spirit, and personality that do not get shared in that member's absence.

◆ How clear and strong is the proclamation of the crucifixion and resurrection of Jesus in your regular Sunday preaching? Examine whether it is something that your preaching assumes, or something that is clearly and regularly proclaimed. Ask one or more members who are good listeners to offer you periodic critiques of your sermons from that perspective.

Connections with the Liturgy

Each Sunday Christians exchange with one another the peace of the risen Christ. In some assemblies, the Peace has become a kind of seventh-inning stretch during which everyone chats with everyone else about the week's news. It is important to remember the liturgical intention of this greeting: we are enacting John 20, receiving from one another the Peace that Christ gave to the disciples. We fill the room with the life of the Holy Spirit, breathing to one another the meaning of Christ's death and resurrection.

Let the Children Come

Peace be with you. When we repeat the words of Jesus on Sunday morning, we announce the Lord's forgiveness on our neighbor. Take a moment to mention the power in this seemingly simple part of worship. If worshipers in your assembly usually stick to their seats, invite the children to move around and find a new face and hand to bless with the peace of Christ. Or urge children to shake as many hands as possible, spreading widely the presence of Jesus.

Assembly Song
Gathering

The risen Christ   ELW 390
Come, you faithful, raise the strain   ELW 363
Rise, O church, like Christ arisen   ELW 548

Psalmody

Hopson, Hal H. "Psalm 16" from TP.
Inwood, Paul. "Centre of My Life" from PS2.
Miller, Aaron David. "Psalm 16," Refrain 3, from PSCY.

Hymn of the Day

We walk by faith   ELW 635   *SHANTI*   WOV 675   *DUNLAP'S CREEK*
Be not afraid   ELW 388   *BE NOT AFRAID*
The peace of the Lord   ELW 646, LLC 471   *LA PAZ DEL SEÑOR*

Offering

Now the green blade rises   ELW 379, LBW 148

Let the vineyards   ELW 183

Communion

Peace, to soothe our bitter woes   ELW 381, LBW 338

Now We Remain   ELW 500, W&P 106

Behold, how pleasant   ELW 649, LLC 468

Sending

That Easter day with joy was bright   ELW 384

Thine is the glory   ELW 376, LBW 145

Additional Assembly Songs

Low in the grave he lay   TFF 94

Open our eyes, Lord   TFF 98

- ⊕ John Bell. Scotland. "Goodness Is Stronger Than Evil" from *Global Songs for Worship*. SATB, gtr. Faith Alive/Calvin Institute of Christian Worship. 9781592554423. ELW 721.

- ⊕ Yoruba, trad. "Aleluya Y'in Louwa/Alleluia, Praise the Lord" from from *Global Praise 3*. U. GBGMusik, General Board of Global Ministries, United Methodist Church.

- ✿ Brown, Brenton/Jason Ingram. "Joyful (The One Who Saves)" from CCLI.

- ✿ Edwards, Mark/Stuart Townend. "There Is a Hope" from CCLI.

- ✿ Elliott, Charlotte/Daniel Doss/William Batchelder Bradbury. "Just as I Am" from CCLI.

- ✿ Ligertwood, Brooke. "You'll Come" from WT.

- ✿ Rend Collective Experiment. "Faithful" from CCLI.

- ✿ Zschech, Darlene/Marty Sampson. "His Glory Appears" from CCLI.

Music for the Day
Choral

- ● Burkhardt, Michael. "We Walk by Faith." SATB, org, opt hb, br qrt. CPH 98-3953.

  Clemens, James. "Although the Doors Were Closed." SATB, kybd. CPH 98-3394.

  Ellingboe, Bradley. "Let Us Talents and Tongues Employ." SATB, org, fl, perc. KJO 8833.

  Farlee, Robert Buckley. "Christ Is Living: Cristo Vive." SATB, perc. AFP 9780800658830.

  Ferguson, John. "Come, You Faithful, Raise the Strain." SATB, org. AFP 9780800677961.

  Schwoebel, David. "Christ Is Risen! Alleluia!" SATB, org, br. AFP 9780800638733.

Children's Choir

Bender, Jan. "Come, Ye Faithful, Raise the Strain" in *The Morning Star Choir Book*. CPH 97-6287.

Nelson, Ronald A. "He Rose." U, opt desc, kybd. SEL 422-401.

⊕ = global song
✿ = praise song
● = relates to hymn of the day

Taylor, Jim. "Christ the Lord Is Risen." 2 pt trbl, kybd, fl. CG CGA710.

Keyboard / Instrumental

Farnam, Lynnwood. "Toccata on O filii et filiae." Org. PRE 113-25819.

- ● Mossing, Sally Drennan. "Be Not Afraid" from *In Heaven Above: Piano Music for Funerals and Memorials*. Pno. AFP 9781451401912.

- ● Mann, Adrian. "Shanti" from *Blest Are They: Preludes for Low Instrument and Keyboard*. Inst, kybd. AFP 9780800679422.

  Pattterson, Mark. "Resurrection Suite" from *Rejoice, the Lord Is King! Arrangements for Piano*. Pno. MSM 15-799.

Handbell

Dobrinski, Cynthia. "Canticle of Faith." 3-5 oct, L3. HOP 1932.

Krug, Jason. "Christ Is Alive!" 3-6 oct, L3-. BP HB366.

Waldrop, Tammy. "Give to the Winds Thy Fears." 3 or 5 oct hb, opt 3 oct hc, opt wch, L2. ALF 36514.

Tuesday, April 29

Catherine of Siena, theologian, died 1380

Catherine of Siena was a member of the Order of Preachers (Dominicans), and among Roman Catholics she was the first woman to receive the title Doctor of the Church. She was a contemplative and is known for her mystical visions of Jesus. This gift of mysticism apparently extended back into her childhood, much to the dismay of her parents, who wanted her to be like other children. Catherine was a humanitarian who worked to alleviate the suffering of the poor and imprisoned. She was also a renewer of church and society and advised both popes and any persons who told her their problems. Catherine's contemplative life was linked to her concern for the poor and suffering. She is a reminder that prayer and activism belong together.

Thursday, May 1

Philip and James, Apostles

Philip was one of the first disciples of Jesus, who after following Jesus invited Nathanael to "come and see." According to tradition, Philip preached in Asia Minor and died as a martyr in Phrygia. James, the son of Alphaeus, is called "the Less" (meaning "short" or "younger") to distinguish him from another apostle named James who is commemorated July 25. Philip and James are commemorated together because the remains of these two saints were placed in the Church of the Apostles in Rome on this day in 561.

Friday, May 2

Athanasius, Bishop of Alexandria, died 373

Athanasius (ath-an-AY-shus) attended the Council of Nicaea in 325 as a deacon and secretary to the bishop of Alexandria. At the council, and when he himself served as bishop of Alexandria, he defended the full divinity of Christ against the Arian position held by emperors, magistrates, and theologians. Because of his defense of the divinity of Christ, he was considered a troublemaker and was banished from Alexandria on five occasions. As bishop, one of his paschal letters to surrounding bishops gives a list for books that should be considered canonical scripture. He lists the twenty-seven New Testament books that are recognized today.

May 4, 2014
Third Sunday of Easter

Today's gospel begins with two disciples walking to Emmaus, overcome with sadness, loss, and disappointment. They had hoped Jesus, who was crucified, would be the one to redeem Israel! Yet the risen Christ walks with them, and then opens their eyes in the breaking of the bread. Each Sunday our hearts burn within us as the scriptures are proclaimed and Christ appears to us as bread is broken and wine is poured. The story of Emmaus becomes the pattern of our worship each Lord's day.

Prayer of the Day

O God, your Son makes himself known to all his disciples in the breaking of bread. Open the eyes of our faith, that we may see him in his redeeming work, who lives and reigns with you and the Holy Spirit, one God, now and forever.

Gospel Acclamation

Alleluia. Our hearts ' burn within us* while you open to ' us the scriptures. *Alleluia.* (Luke 24:32)

Readings and Psalm

Acts 2:14a, 36-41

Today's reading is the conclusion of Peter's sermon preached following the giving of the Holy Spirit to the apostles on the day of Pentecost. The center of his preaching is the bold declaration that God has made the crucified Jesus both Lord and Christ.

Psalm 116:1-4, 12-19

I will call on the name of the Lord. (Ps. 116:13)

1 Peter 1:17-23

The imagery of exile is used to help the readers of this letter understand that they are strangers in a strange land. Christians no longer belong to this age. Through the death of Christ we belong to God, so that our focus, faith, and hope are no longer on such things as silver or gold.

Luke 24:13-35

The colorful story of Jesus' appearance to two disciples on the road to Emmaus answers the question of how Jesus is to be recognized among us. Here, he is revealed through the scriptures and in the breaking of bread.

Preface Easter

Color White

Prayers of Intercession

The prayers are prepared locally for each occasion. The following examples may be adapted or used as appropriate.

Made alive in Christ and filled with his Spirit, let us pray for the church, the world, and all of God's creation.

A brief silence.

We pray for the church, that reborn as children of God, we recognize Christ's presence moving within and among us. Hear us, O God.

Your mercy is great.

We pray for creation, that being astounded at the earth's goodness, we live and work in a wise and sustainable manner. Hear us, O God.

Your mercy is great.

We pray for the world and those who govern, that when blinded by fear and mistrust, eyes are opened to ways of freedom and reconciliation. Hear us, O God.

Your mercy is great,

We pray for those in need: those who are homeless, lost, bereaved, orphaned, or sick (*especially*). Make known to them the wholeness you alone can bring. Hear us, O God. **Your mercy is great.**

We pray for the newly baptized, that they daily discover Christ walking before, beside, and behind them wherever their paths may lead. Hear us, O God. **Your mercy is great.**

Here other intercessions may be offered.

We give thanks for the saints (*especially Monica, mother of Augustine*). Though we see dimly in this life, we look for Christ's promised glory yet to be revealed. Hear us, O God. **Your mercy is great.**

Receive our prayers, merciful God, and dwell in us richly, through Jesus Christ, our life and our redeemer. **Amen.**

Images in the Readings

The **meal** of Emmaus is one of the many Lucan accounts of eating with Jesus, and Luke's accounts follow the biblical theme that God feeds the people. To be true to the biblical image of the life shared with Christ, the bread that we break, the wine that we share, and our methods of distribution ought to make clear that holy communion is a meal. A loaf of bread or a large circular flat bread, home baked or purchased from a local store and broken for all to see, presents a quite different image of salvation than do medieval quarter-sized tasteless hosts bought from an ecclesiastical supply company. Think about the image presented by your eating and drinking.

The **preaching** of Peter and the teaching of Christ along the road are images of our receiving the "living and enduring" saving word.

The passage from 1 Peter presents an array of images, one rushing along after another. A significant image for the book of 1 Peter is **exile**: the baptized are living in an alien land. When Christians become too comfortable in what Acts calls "this corrupt generation," we are called to be ransomed out of it and purified by obedience to the truth.

Ideas for the Day

◆　How do you react in the midst of a crisis? How do you act after a crisis? Each scripture passage before us today gives insight into that part of our human nature. Whether the crisis is persecution, moral decision, grief, or any number of other things, our human nature acts and reacts on many different levels. Stephen Paul Bouman, former bishop of the Metro New York Synod (ELCA), in his book *Grace All Around Us: Embracing God's Promise in Tragedy and Loss* (Augsburg Fortress, 2007), talks of many of the human actions and reactions of the people of God in New York City surrounding the events of September 11, 2001. In chapter 4,

"Repairers of the Breach," he uses the Emmaus Road story in some ways that speak to being able to use the tools of faith in the midst of crisis.

◆　The response to the preaching of Peter in Acts 2 was immediate. As a result of hearing the preached word, decisions were made, lives were changed, and many were added to the numbers of the community of believers in what God had done through the life and ministry of Jesus. In many communities of faith—for example, the communities of the historic African American denominations—an invitation to discipleship is made immediately after the sermon for any hearers who have been moved by the preached word to enter into a process of study and growth that would lead to discipleship, baptism, and membership in the faith community. Consider the differences in expectations of the preached word that are prevalent in mainline Protestant denominations.

◆　There's a story of an abused, homeless dog that is found and cared for by a compassionate dog-lover. After being nursed back to health, the dog disappears, much to the sadness and annoyance of the caretaker. Soon, however, the dog returns with another dog that is in even worse shape than the first dog had been. Consider how and why the good news gets shared with others who are on a road-to-Emmaus journey.

Connections with the Liturgy

Every eucharistic service repeats the story of Emmaus: we are walking together, we welcome a stranger, we hear the word, we share the meal, we recognize at our table the risen Christ, and we go to tell others. The frontispiece for the Holy Communion section of *Evangelical Lutheran Worship* (p. 89) depicts the couple of Emmaus at table with the risen Christ. The art was drawn by the contemporary Chinese artist He Qi.

The gospel acclamation for Setting Ten of Holy Communion (*Evangelical Lutheran Worship*, p. 205) specifically quotes the Emmaus account when we sing, "Open now your saving word. Let it burn like fire within us." It is as if hearing the gospel reading, we are the disciples running back to Jerusalem, telling the others about meeting Jesus on the road.

Let the Children Come

Saint Augustine said, "It is solved by walking." Faith is a journey, sometimes smooth, sometimes bumpy. This morning we meet two journeying friends who are sad. After walking, talking, and eating with the risen Christ, they are made glad again. Ask children to think about walking to a friend's house, or walks they take with animals or family members. Invite them to remember surprises along the way, people they met, something new they noticed on their path.

Assembly Song
Gathering

This joyful Eastertide   ELW 391, WOV 676

Alleluia! Jesus is risen!   ELW 377, TFF 91, WOV 674

Christ Jesus lay in death's strong bands   ELW 370

Psalmody

McRae, Shirley W. "Psalm 116" from *ChildrenSing Psalms*. U, assembly, kybd, 5 hb.

Mummert, Mark. "Psalm 116," Refrain 1, from PSCY.

Roberts, Leon C. "I Will Call Upon the Name of the Lord (Psalm 116)." TFF 14.

Hymn of the Day

Day of arising   ELW 374   *RAABE*

We who once were dead   ELW 495, LBW 207   *MIDDEN IN DE DOOD*

Come, let us eat   ELW 491, TFF 119   *A VA DE*

Offering

As we gather at your table   ELW 522

Let us talents and tongues employ   ELW 674, TFF 232, WOV 754

Communion

Abide, O dearest Jesus   ELW 539

At the Lamb's high feast we sing   ELW 362, LBW 210

Bread of life, our host and meal   ELW 464

Sending

With high delight let us unite   ELW 368, LBW 140

Hallelujah! We sing your praises   ELW 535, WOV 722

Additional Assembly Songs

He is Lord   TFF 95

Open our eyes, Lord   TFF 98, W&P 113

⊕ Hamba nathi/Come, walk with us   GS2 6

✪ Ingram, Jason/Sean Curran. "Taste of Eternity" from CCLI.

✪ Lowell, Charlie/Dan Haseltine/Matt Odmark/Stephen Mason. "This Road" from CCLI.

✪ MacIntosh, Jonathan/Sarah MacIntosh/Vicky Beeching. "Salvation Day" from CCLI.

✪ Maher, Matt. "Great Things" from CCLI.

✪ Sampson, Marty/Mia Fieldes. "Savior King" from WT.

✪ Tomlin, Chris/Jesse Reeves/J.D. Walt. "The Wonderful Cross" from WT.

Music for the Day
Choral

● Cherwien, David. "Day of Arising." SATB, C inst, org. MSM 50-5020.

✪ Farlee, Robert, arr. Argentina. "Cristo vive/Christ Is Risen." SATB, perc. AFP 9780800658830.

Frahm, Frederick. "Now Christ Is Risen from the Dead." 2 pt, pno. AFP 9780800678920.

Praetorius, Michael. "Stay with Us, Lord" from *Chantry Choirbook*. SATB. AFP 9780800657772.

Scott, K. Lee. "O Risen Lord." SAB or SATB, org, ob. MSM 50-4405/ MSM 4004.

Children's Choir

Helgen, John. "Come, Let Us Eat." U, pno, opt Orff insts. AFP 9780800679354.

Hildebrand, Kevin. "For You, O Lord, Have Delivered My Soul from Death." U, org. CPH 98-3866.

Liebergen, Patrick M. "Dona Nobis Pacem." SSA, kybd, opt fl. HIN HMC1965.

Keyboard / Instrumental

Bach, J. S. "Christ ist erstanden" from *Das Orgelbüchlein*. Org. Various editions.

● Ferko, Frank. "A va de" from *Augsburg Organ Library: Baptism and Holy Communion*. Org. AFP 9780800623555.

Maynard, Lynette. "I Am the Bread of Life" from *In Heaven Above: Piano Music for Funerals and Memorials*. Pno. AFP 9781451401912.

● Miller, Aaron David. "Raabe" from *Chorale Preludes for Piano in Traditional Styles*. Pno. AFP 9780800679033.

Handbell

Gramann, Fred. "Alleluia! The Strife Is O'er." 3-6 oct hb, L2+. LOR 20/1377L. Full score with opt org. LOR 20/1378L.

● Moklebust, Cathy. "Come, Let Us Eat." 3-5 oct hb, opt perc, L3. CG CGB152.

Tucker, Sondra. "I Will Arise." 2-3 oct, L2+. CG CGB525.

Sunday, May 4
Monica, mother of Augustine, died 387

Monica was married to a pagan husband who was ill-tempered and unfaithful. She rejoiced greatly when both her husband and his mother became Christian. But it is because she is the mother of Augustine that she is best known. Monica had been a disciple of Ambrose, and eventually Augustine came under his influence. Almost everything we know about Monica comes from Augustine's *Confessions*, his autobiography. She died far from her home but said to her son, "Do not fret because I am buried far from our home in Africa. Nothing is far from God, and I have no fear that God will not know where to find me, when Christ comes to raise me to life at the end of the world." Her dying wish was that her son remember her at the altar of the Lord, wherever he was.

⊕ = global song
✪ = praise song
● = relates to hymn of the day

Thursday, May 8

Julian of Norwich, renewer of the church, died around 1416

Julian (or Juliana) was most likely a Benedictine nun living in an isolated cell attached to the Carrow Priory in Norwich (NOR-rich), England. Definite facts about her life are sparse. However, when she was about thirty years old, she reported visions that she later compiled into a book, *Sixteen Revelations of Divine Love*, a classic of medieval mysticism. The visions declared that love was the meaning of religious experience, provided by Christ who is love, for the purpose of love. A prayer and a hymn attributed to Julian are included in *Evangelical Lutheran Worship* (p. 87, #735).

Friday, May 9

Nicolaus Ludwig von Zinzendorf, renewer of the church, hymnwriter, died 1760

Count Zinzendorf was born into an aristocratic family and after the death of his father was raised by his Pietistic grandmother. This influence was a lasting one, and he moved away from what he felt was an overly intellectual Lutheranism. When he was twenty-two, a group of Moravians asked permission to live on his lands. He agreed, and they established a settlement they called Herrnhut, or "the Lord's watch." Eventually worldwide Moravian missions emanated from this community. Zinzendorf participated in these missions and is also remembered for writing hymns characteristic of his Pietistic faith, including "Jesus, Still Lead On" (ELW 624).

May 11, 2014
Fourth Sunday of Easter

Today is sometimes called "Good Shepherd Sunday." Jesus is called the "gate" of the sheep in today's gospel. The risen Christ opens the way to abundant life. He anoints our heads with oil and guides us beside the still waters of our baptism. Each Sunday he spreads a feast before us in the midst of the world's violence and war. We go forth to be signs of the resurrection and extend God's tender care to all creation.

Prayer of the Day

O God our shepherd, you know your sheep by name and lead us to safety through the valleys of death. Guide us by your voice, that we may walk in certainty and security to the joyous feast prepared in your house, through Jesus Christ, our Savior and Lord, who lives and reigns with you and the Holy Spirit, one God, now and forever.

Gospel Acclamation

Alleluia. Jesus says, I am | the good shepherd.* I know my own and my | own know me. *Alleluia.* (John 10:14)

Readings and Psalm
Acts 2:42-47

Today's reading is a description of life in the community following Peter's sermon on the day of Pentecost, when the Spirit was outpoured on God's people. This new community is founded on the teachings of the apostles and sustained in the breaking of the bread.

Psalm 23

The LORD is my shepherd; I shall not be in want. (Ps. 23:1)

1 Peter 2:19-25

Doing the right things does not guarantee that one will not experience difficulties, hardships, rejection, or even suffering. Here Christ is presented as the model for our path of endurance and loyalty to God, particularly in the midst of adversity.

John 10:1-10

Jesus uses an image familiar to the people of his day to make a point about spiritual leadership. Good shepherds bring people to life through Jesus, but those who avoid Jesus are dangerous to the flock.

Preface   Easter

Color   White

Prayers of Intercession

The prayers are prepared locally for each occasion. The following examples may be adapted or used as appropriate.
Made alive in Christ and filled with his Spirit, let us pray for the church, the world, and all of God's creation.
A brief silence.

Gracious God: Your voice sings in the church. Bless our worship, that sharing bread in communion, we also share abundantly with people in every place. Lord, in your mercy, **hear our prayer.**

Your voice sings in creation. Preserve pastures and city parks, oceans and local water sources, so that nature provides life and protection for all creatures. Lord, in your mercy, **hear our prayer.**

Your voice sings among the nations. Curb the desire for vengeance; turn us from dishonest speech and deceitful living; lead us in your truth. Lord, in your mercy, **hear our prayer.**

Your voice sings among those in need: the poor, the homeless, the suffering, the afflicted, the ill and hospitalized (*especially*); for those who will die this day. Lord, in your mercy, **hear our prayer.**

Your voice sings in our homes. Open the hearts of those who provide mothering care, that Christ's love would be revealed in the generosity shown to all our children. Lord, in your mercy, **hear our prayer.**

Here other intercessions may be offered.

We offer thanks for the saints (*especially*) who, having followed your voice in this life, now dwell with you forever, joining their voices in endless praise. Lord, in your mercy, **hear our prayer.**

Receive our prayers, merciful God, and dwell in us richly, through Jesus Christ, our life and our redeemer. **Amen.**

Images in the Readings

To deepen our contemplation of the metaphor of Christ as **shepherd**, it is good to review the positive use that the Bible makes of the image of **sheep**. The Jewish Scriptures remembered their people as having been sheep and goat herders. Sheep signified the communal life of the people, constituted a source of food and clothing, and functioned as the primary sacrificial gifts to God. The single wandering lamb from the parable of the lost sheep is not the image in John 10. Nor is a bare-footed white-robed man a realistic depiction of the shepherd, who by the first century was thought of as lower-class and religiously unclean. In Genesis 29, Rachel is a shepherd.

Still today some herders in Iran, after gathering the sheep into an enclosure at night, lay themselves down to sleep at the opening of the pen. The wolf cannot enter through the opening, because the body of the herder has become the **gate**. In some medieval churches, the main doorway was elaborately decorated with biblical scenes, sometimes also surrounded with the signs of the zodiac, as if the door was a symbol of Christ, proclaimed in the Bible and encompassing the universe. The body of our Lord, taken in holy communion, is a gate to eternal life.

The image in Acts 2 of the Christian **commune** connects with the church's actual history and present situation, in that the baptized, living with generous hearts, contribute to all who have need. It is appropriate that at every meeting of Christians for worship there be a collection of money, goods, or services for the needy.

Ideas for the Day

◆ Jesus says in John 10 that he came so that those who believe may have life, "and have it abundantly" (v. 10). What images come to mind when you hear the term *abundant life*? Acts 2:42-47 seems to describe a Jesus community that on many levels was living an abundant life. Based on how you hear the Acts text, place adjectives before each of the following aspects of community that are described: worship, teaching, stewardship, small groups, outreach. Consider a sermon series on this text that can cast visions of present and potential abundance in these areas of ministry in your context. Or consider a Bible study on this text that is shared with leaders and members of the groups responsible for those different aspects of ministry. Incorporate the adjectives and images you hear in the text, and invite more from others.

◆ Shepherds are rare in our twenty-first-century North American context. However, in the first-century Palestinian context, shepherds were seen by most as lower class and religiously unclean, despite their important function in society. Yet Jesus had no trouble comparing himself to such a generally despised figure. Was Jesus having an identity crisis? What are some inclusiveness issues that his comparison brings to mind? How can reminders of who Jesus identifies with speak to inclusiveness issues in your local context?

◆ First Peter speaks of keeping faith, loyalty, and hope in the midst of unjust persecution. *The Hunger Games*, by Suzanne Collins (New York: Scholastic, 2008), is a popular trilogy that has opened many eyes and spoken to many hearts about the same issues. In the story the people who lived in the districts of Panem were suffering unjustly at the hands of those in power. Katniss, the sixteen-year-old main character of the story, kept faith, loyalty, and hope that are in many ways comparable to the faith, loyalty, and hope that Christians have had to keep through the ages. Young people in particular have been able to make many important connections with present-day issues of power, poverty, and oppression as a result of reading and discussing this popular book series.

Connections with the Liturgy

The commendation spoken at the close of Christian burial (*Evangelical Lutheran Worship*, p. 283) asks the Savior to receive "a sheep of your own fold, a lamb of your own flock," and the final blessing (p. 285) refers to our Lord Jesus as "the great shepherd of the sheep."

Let the Children Come

May 9 is the commemoration of Julian of Norwich, a fellow sheep of God's flock who wrote beautifully about the tenderness and kindness of God. On this morning when we read of God's shepherding presence toward us and the secular world honors mothers, read or sing "Mothering God, you gave me birth" (ELW 735), based on the words of Julian of Norwich. Ask the assembly or the children to share what images or words in the hymn stand out. Or, simply point back to baptism, in which we, like sheep, are carried away from sin, death, and danger.

Assembly Song
Gathering

All people that on earth do dwell   ELW 883, LBW 245
Good Christian friends, rejoice and sing!   ELW 385
I know that my Redeemer lives!   ELW 619, LBW 352

Psalmody and Acclamations

Haugen, Marty. "The Lord Is My Shepherd" from TLP:S.
Ollis, Peter. "The Lord Is My Shepherd" from PS2.
Bruxvoort-Colligan, Richard. "My Love Is My Shepherd (Psalm 23)" from SR.
Pishner, Stephen. "This Is the Day: Psalm and Gospel Acclamation for Easter." SATB, cant, assembly, kybd, gtr, 11 hb. GIA G-6139.

Hymn of the Day

What feast of love   ELW 487, WOV 701   GREENSLEEVES
Have no fear, little flock   ELW 764, LBW 476   LITTLE FLOCK
Shepherd me, O God   ELW 780   SHEPHERD ME

Offering

You satisfy the hungry heart   ELW 484, WOV 711
God extends an invitation   ELW 486, LLC 397

Communion

The King of love my shepherd is   ELW 502, LBW 456
At the Lamb's high feast we sing   ELW 362, LBW 210
Lord, who the night you were betrayed   ELW 463, LBW 206

Sending

Praise the Lord, rise up rejoicing   ELW 544, LBW 196
God be with you till we meet again   ELW 536, TFF 157

Additional Assembly Songs

God sent his Son   TFF 93
◑ Aquí del pan partido tomaré   LLC 384
◑ Dexter, Noel. Caribbean. "The Lord Is My Shepherd" from *Let the Peoples Sing: Volume One*. SATB. AFP 9780800675394.
✪ Brown, Brenton/Doug Bacon. "Wonderful" from WT.
✪ Craig, Shawn/Dave Koch/Dave Clark. "This Is How It Feels to Be Free" from WT.
✪ Crowder, David. "You're Everything" from CCLI.
✪ Freeman, Ronnie/Daniel Doss. "Blessed Is the One" from WT.
✪ Redman, Matt/Steven Curtis Chapman. "With One Voice" from WT.
✪ Webster, Miriam. "Angel of the Lord" from CCLI.

Music for the Day
Choral

Biery, James. "The Lord Is My Shepherd." Children/S solo, SATB. MSM 50-6057.
Frahm, Frederick. "My Shepherd Will Supply My Need." SAB, kybd. AFP 9780800675530.
Hildebrand, Kevin. "You, Jesus, Are My Shepherd True." SATB, kybd, 1 or 2 C inst. CPH 98-3891.
● Keesecker, Thomas. "What Feast of Love." SA(T)B, opt 2 hb. MSM 50-7510.
Leavitt, Paul. "The Lord Is My Shepherd." SATB. AFP 9780806697178.
● Shields, Valerie. "Have No Fear, Little Flock." SATB, tpts, timp, org. KJO 8853.

Children's Choir

Arnn, John. "I Am the Good Shepherd." U, kybd. SEL 422-810.
Kemp, Helen. "The Good Shepherd." 2 pt, pno. CG CGA1079.
Payne, John R. "I Am Jesus' Little Lamb." U/2 pt, kybd, opt hb, opt hc. CPH 98-4055.
Stearns, Peter Pindar. "Savior, Like a Shepherd Lead Us" in *Two Youth Anthems*. SA, pno/org. PAR 0500.

Keyboard / Instrumental

● Burkhardt, Michael. "Have No Fear, Little Flock" from *Voluntaries for Worship*. Org. MSM 10-557.
● Organ, Anne Krentz. "Have No Fear, Little Flock" from *In Heaven Above: Piano Music for Funerals and Memorials*. Pno. AFP 9781451401912.
Patterson, Mark. "My Shepherd Will Supply My Need" from *Rejoice, the Lord Is King! Arrangements for Piano*. Pno. MSM 15-799.
Wright, Searle. "Prelude on Brother James' Air." Org. OXF 9780193850781.

◑ = global song
✪ = praise song
● = relates to hymn of the day

Handbell

- McFadden, Jane. "Have No Fear, Little Flock." 3-5 oct hb, opt 3 oct hc, L2. CPH 97-6922.
- Roberts, Philip. "Shepherd Me, O God." 3-6 oct hb, opt 3-6 oct hc, L3. GIA G-7255.

  Wissinger, Kathleen. "Broken for You." 3-5 oct, L3. AGEHR AG35179.

Wednesday, May 14

Matthias, Apostle

After Christ's ascension, the apostles met in Jerusalem to choose a replacement for Judas. Matthias was chosen over Joseph Justus by the casting of lots. Little is known about Matthias, and little is reported about him in the account of his election in Acts 1:15-26. Matthias traveled among the disciples from the beginning of Jesus' ministry until his ascension. His task, after he was enrolled among the eleven remaining disciples, was to bear witness to the resurrection.

May 18, 2014
Fifth Sunday of Easter

As we continue to celebrate the fifty days of Easter, today's gospel includes Jesus' promise that he goes to prepare a place for his followers in his Father's house. Our baptism commissions us to share Jesus' mission in the world. As First Peter reminds us, we are a holy people, called to proclaim the one who called us out of darkness into light. In words and deeds we bear witness to the risen Christ—our way, our truth, our life.

Prayer of the Day

Almighty God, your Son Jesus Christ is the way, the truth, and the life. Give us grace to love one another, to follow in the way of his commandments, and to share his risen life with all the world, for he lives and reigns with you and the Holy Spirit, one God, now and forever.

Gospel Acclamation

Alleluia. I am the way, the truth, | and the life.* No one comes to the Father ex- | cept through me. *Alleluia.* (John 14:6)

Readings and Psalm

Acts 7:55-60

Stephen was one of the seven men chosen by the apostles to serve tables so that the apostles could be free to serve the word (Acts 6:1-6). Stephen does more than distribute food, however. For his preaching of God's word, he becomes the first martyr of the faith.

Psalm 31:1-5, 15-16

Into your hands, O LORD, I commend my spirit. (Ps. 31:5)

I Peter 2:2-10

Christ is the cornerstone of God's saving work and the foundation of our lives. We are God's chosen, holy people who continuously celebrate and declare the mercy of God we experience through Jesus Christ.

John 14:1-14

On the night that he is to be arrested, Jesus shares final words with his disciples. As the one through whom God is known, he promises to go before them and act on their behalf.

Preface   Easter

Color   White

Prayers of Intercession

The prayers are prepared locally for each occasion. The following examples may be adapted or used as appropriate.

Made alive in Christ and filled with his Spirit, let us pray for the church, the world, and all of God's creation.

A brief silence.

God our salvation: you have made us your living stones in the waters of baptism. We pray for the church and its leaders; for the newly baptized; for missionaries around the world. (*Pause*) Lord, in your mercy,

hear our prayer.

God our home: your Spirit dwells with creation. We pray for the earth; for clean water and air; for the earth's

foundation; for the lands all creatures inhabit. (*Pause*)
Lord, in your mercy,
hear our prayer.
God our way: you call us to paths of justice. We pray for
nations and leaders; for courts and legislatures; for strife-
torn communities; for our enemies. (*Pause*) Lord, in your
mercy,
hear our prayer.
God our refuge: you deliver us in times of trouble. We pray
for the rejected and persecuted; for neglected infants and
children; for the sick (*especially*); for all in need. (*Pause*)
Lord, in your mercy,
hear our prayer.
God our shelter: you draw all people to yourself. We pray
for those who are homeless and those with inadequate hous-
ing; for all who come to this building seeking a safe haven.
(*Pause*) Lord, in your mercy,
hear our prayer.
Here other intercessions may be offered.
God our life: you prepare a place for us. We give thanks for
the witness of your saints (*especially Erik, King of Sweden*).
(*Pause*) Lead us also in Christ's way and truth. Lord, in
your mercy,
hear our prayer.
Receive our prayers, merciful God, and dwell in us richly,
through Jesus Christ, our life and our redeemer.
Amen.

Images in the Readings

For some Christians and pieties, the image of Christ as the
way has been used to condemn most other people. John's
community did indeed think of itself as enjoying the greatest **truth** and **life** eternal. However, we are called to recognize the Way as the good news that God loves the whole
world, as the wideness of God's mercy.

John's metaphor of the Father's **house** and its many
dwelling places has been literalized for many Christians, as
if heaven were a king's mansion with outbuildings provided
for the lesser inhabitants. In a different application of this
image, the house is the room in which we weekly gather:
here God dwells. Here God serves up our meals. 1 Peter
uses the image of house to be a metaphor for the believing
community.

1 Peter is filled with images. Several medieval mystics
used the image of the eucharist being **milk**. The central
image of this passage is Christ as the **cornerstone**, the
living stone, of the house that is the church. Many cor-
nerstones are engraved with the date of construction. For
Christians, this date is the year of our baptism. Perhaps
those congregations that publish members' birthdays could
replace these dates with their baptismal anniversary.

Ideas for the Day

◆ Late in the Easter season, the focus of both the lectionary and our common liturgical life has shifted from trumpets and butterflies to the deeper implications of new life
in Christ. By now, the Easter banners and the white cloth
draped on the cross might to some look tired. Consider let-
ting artists in your congregation design a seven-week instal-
lation using the worship space as a canvas and the weekly
lections as a palette. How might they illustrate the progress
of the Easter season visually and emphasize Easter as the
"queen of seasons," with a fresh visual component each
Sunday? For something simple but effective, invite garden-
ers to bring in flowers or greens each week to adorn the
altar and nave.

◆ The Easter life means we lose our lives for Christ's sake
and the sake of the world. This is powerfully illustrated in
the 2010 film *Of Gods and Men*, the story of eight Trappist
monks in Algeria who chose to stay with the Muslim community they served, despite the threat of civil war, then are
murdered by terrorists. The film is a remarkable testimony
to lives poured out in service to others, even others who are
"enemies," even at the cost of one's own life. Today, pray
for the persecuted church throughout the world, that God
would use the example of martyrs like Stephen (and modern-day martyrs too) to plant courage and self-sacrificial
love in the entire church.

◆ It is deeply symbolic, even ironic, that Stephen is killed
with stones for building his life and work on the chief
cornerstone, Jesus Christ. Stones might be used to visually illustrate today's readings. Small, smooth stones with
engraved words are popular both as decoration and as devotional items. Is it possible to give each worshiper something
similar? A good source for custom-engraved stones is www.
stonewords.com. Or consider a simple, unpolished stone or
rock, or perhaps use larger stones to form a cairn or other
artistic display to draw the eye and mind to Christ, the sure
foundation.

Connections with the Liturgy

As we are dismissed from worship, we go in peace, because
Christ is with us. Christ is with us on the way: Christ is our
Way.

Cited from *Daily Prayer*, a 1941 publication by Eric
Milner-White and George Wallace Briggs, in both Morning
Prayer (p. 304) and Evening Prayer (p. 317) in *Evangelical
Lutheran Worship*, is a beloved prayer that asks God to be
with us as we journey on the way. "You have called your servants to ventures of which we cannot see the ending . . .
knowing that your hand is leading us and your love supporting us." We can think of Thomas's question to Jesus as
we pray this prayer.

Let the Children Come

Jesus promises, "I go to prepare a place for you." Ask children to tell or think about their favorite corner of their house, apartment, or yard. What makes it special? Talk about the special corners and places within the church building and sanctuary. What makes this place special? Invite them to gather in an unusual spot, like underneath the altar or behind the organ. Every place has something blessed and special about it, just as every child is blessed and loved by God.

Assembly Song
Gathering

Here, O Lord, your servants gather   ELW 530
Christ is alive! Let Christians sing   ELW 389
Alleluia! Jesus is risen!   ELW 377, TFF 91, WOV 674

Psalmody and Acclamations

Guimont, Michel. "Psalm 31" from PRCL.
Haugen, Marty. "I Put My Life in Your Hands" from PCY, vol. l.
Sedio, Mark. "Psalm 31," Refrain 1, from PSCY.
Pishner, Stephen. "This Is the Day: Psalm and Gospel Acclamation for Easter." SATB, cant, assembly, kybd, gtr, 11 hb. GIA G-6139.

Hymn of the Day

We all are one in mission   ELW 576, WOV 755   *KUORTANE*
Come, my way, my truth, my life   ELW 816, LBW 513   *THE CALL*
You are the way   ELW 758, LBW 464   *DUNDEE*

Offering

Awake, my heart, with gladness   ELW 378
Lord God, we praise you   ELW 558

Communion

I received the living God   ELW 477, WOV 700
I know that my Redeemer lives!   ELW 619, LBW 352
Now all the vault of heaven resounds   ELW 367

Sending

Blessing, Honor, and Glory   ELW 433, W&P 21
We know that Christ is raised   ELW 449, LBW 189

Additional Assembly Songs

I heard an old, old story   TFF 97
To go to heaven   TFF 181
☉ Bell, John. Scotland. "Who Am I?" from *Heaven Shall Not Wait.* U. GIA G-3646.
☉ Hehe tune, arr. Austin Lovelace. Tanzania. "Christ Is the Way" from *Set Free: A Collection of African Hymns.* SATB and cantor. AFP 9780806600451.
☆ Barnard, Shane. "Hearts of Servants" from WT.

☆ Giglio, Louie/Kristian Stanfill/Brett Younker. "Alive and Running" from WT.
☆ Green, Keith/Melody Sievright-Green. "You Are the One" from CCLI.
☆ Houston, Joel/Jonathon Douglass. "One Way" from CCLI.
☆ Mullins, Rich. "That Where I Am" from CCLI.
☆ Redman, Matt/Jonas Myrin. "All That Really Matters" from WT.

Music for the Day
Choral

Costello, Michael. "Sing with All the Saints in Glory." SATB, org, fl, opt assembly. AFP 9780806698311.
DeLong, Richard. "Come, My Way, My Truth, My Life." SATB. ECS 4525.
Heim, Bret. "God, Who Built This Wondrous Planet." SATB, org, br qrt, timp, assembly. CPH 98-3307.
Leavitt, John. "The Call." 2 pt mxd, kybd. GIA G-3081.
Schalk, Carl. "Christ Goes Before." SATB, opt assembly, org, br qrt, timp. MSM 50-9049A.
Schelat, David. "I Received the Living God." 2 pt mxd, org. AFP 9780806697109.

Children's Choir

Bedford, Michael. "Christ Be My Leader." U/2 pt, org. AFP 9780800677435.
Cool, Jayne Southwick. "The Life, the Truth, the Way." U/2 pt, pno. AFP 9780800674670.
Culli, Benjamin M. "In Thee, O Lord, Do I Put My Trust." 2 pt trbl, kybd. CPH 98-4029.

Keyboard / Instrumental

● Cherwien, David. "Kuortane" from *Organ Plus One: Hymn Preludes for Organ and a Solo Instrument.* Org, inst. AFP 9780800656188.
Larkin, Michael. "This Joyful Eastertide" from *Rejoice! Ten Hymns for Christmas and Easter.* Pno. MSM 15-835.
● Trapp, Lynn. "Come, My Way, My Truth, My Life" from *In the Mystery of Christ.* Pno. CPH 97-6884.
Willan, Healey. "Gelobt sei Gott" from *A New Liturgical Year.* Org. AFP 9780800656713.

Handbell

● McChesney, Kevin. "Come My Way, My Truth, My Life." 2-3 oct, L2. LOR 20/1554L.
● McChesney, Kevin. "O Lord, Now Let Your Servant (We All Are One in Mission)" from *All Things Bright and Beautiful/O Lord, Now Let Your Servant.* 3-5 oct, L2+. AFP 11-10687. Out of print.
Sewell, Gregg. "Bound to Go Where Jesus Is." 3-5 oct, L3-. GIA G-8038.

☉ = global song
☆ = praise song
● = relates to hymn of the day

Sunday, May 18

Erik, King of Sweden, martyr, died 1160

Erik, long considered the patron saint of Sweden, ruled from 1150 to 1160. He is honored for efforts to bring peace to the nearby pagan kingdoms and for his crusades to spread the Christian faith in Nordic lands. He established a protected Christian mission in Finland that was led by Henry of Uppsala. As king, Erik was noted for his desire to establish fair laws and courts and for his concern for the poor and sick. Erik was killed by a Danish army that approached him at worship on the day after the Ascension. He is reported to have said, "Let us at least finish the sacrifice. The rest of the feast I shall keep elsewhere." As he left worship he was killed.

Wednesday, May 21

Helena, mother of Constantine, died around 330

Wife of the co-regent of the West, Helena (or Helen) was mother of Constantine, who later became Roman emperor. After he was converted to Christianity, he influenced her also to become Christian. From that point she lived an exemplary life of faith, particularly through acts of generosity toward the poor. She is also remembered for traveling through Palestine and building churches on the sites she believed to be where Jesus was born, where he was buried, and from which he ascended.

Saturday, May 24

Nicolaus Copernicus, died 1543; Leonhard Euler, died 1783; scientists

Remembering scientists such as Copernicus and Euler offers an opportunity to ponder the mysteries of the universe and the grandeur of God's creation. Copernicus is an example of a renaissance person. He formally studied astronomy, mathematics, Greek, Plato, law, medicine, and canon law. He also had interests in theology, poetry, and the natural and social sciences. Copernicus is chiefly remembered for his work as an astronomer and his idea that the sun, not the earth, is the center of the solar system.

Euler (oy-ler) is regarded as one of the founders of the science of pure mathematics and made important contributions to mechanics, hydrodynamics, astronomy, optics, and acoustics.

May 25, 2014
Sixth Sunday of Easter

Jesus does not leave his followers orphaned. Through the Holy Spirit Jesus comes to abide with his disciples of every generation. As Pentecost draws near, we are reminded that the risen Christ dwells in us as the Spirit of truth. We receive this Spirit in baptism and pray that in our gathering around the Lord's table the Spirit will transform us to be the body of the risen Christ in the world.

Prayer of the Day

Almighty and ever-living God, you hold together all things in heaven and on earth. In your great mercy receive the prayers of all your children, and give to all the world the Spirit of your truth and peace, through Jesus Christ, our Savior and Lord, who lives and reigns with you and the Holy Spirit, one God, now and forever.

Gospel Acclamation

Alleluia. Those who love me will keep my word, and my Fa- ¹ ther will love them,* and we will come to them and make our ¹ home with them. *Alleluia.* (John 14:23)

Readings and Psalm

Acts 17:22-31

In Athens, Paul faces the challenge of proclaiming the gospel to Greeks who know nothing of either Jewish or Christian tradition. He proclaims that the "unknown god" whom they worship is the true Lord of heaven and earth who will judge the world with justice through Jesus, whom God has raised from the dead.

Psalm 66:8-20

Bless our God, you peoples; let the sound of praise be heard. (Ps. 66:8)

1 Peter 3:13-22

Christians have a zeal for doing what is right in God's eyes no matter what the circumstances because in baptism we are saved and made alive. Thus our Christian beliefs and behavior are to be a matter of public record just as our baptism is.

John 14:15-21

In final words to his disciples on the night of his arrest, Jesus encourages obedience to his commandments and speaks of the Spirit, who will be with them forever.

Preface   Easter

Color   White

Prayers of Intercession

The prayers are prepared locally for each occasion. The following examples may be adapted or used as appropriate.

Made alive in Christ and filled with his Spirit, let us pray for the church, the world, and all of God's creation.
A brief silence.

You abide with your church, O God. Empower us with your Spirit, so that your people speak and live the love revealed in Jesus. Hear us, O God.
Your mercy is great.

You abide with your creation, O God. Breathe on fields and forests, lakes and oceans, and all living things so that they thrive as you intend. Hear us, O God.
Your mercy is great.

You abide with the nations, O God. Reveal your truth, so that nations and peoples govern in peace and advocate for justice. Hear us, O God.
Your mercy is great.

You abide with the needy, O God. Cheer the sorrowful, protect the orphan, support the grieving, and heal the sick (*especially*). Hear us, O God.
Your mercy is great.

You abide with the fearful, O God. Transform fear into freedom for the life Christ has promised. Hear us, O God.
Your mercy is great.

Here other intercessions may be offered.

We remember, O God, those who have died in the faith. Assure us of your life-giving Spirit until that day when we will abide with you forever. Hear us, O God.
Your mercy is great.

Receive our prayers, merciful God, and dwell in us richly, through Jesus Christ, our life and our redeemer.
Amen.

Images in the Readings

John calls the Spirit of truth our **Advocate**. This image implies a trial and the probability of judgment. Standing before God, we need someone to speak on our behalf. The reading from 1 Peter also includes the image of a trial in which we must defend our stance.

In John 14, Jesus uses adoption imagery for those who receive the Spirit of truth. Yet Paul's sermon at the Areopagus calls all his pagan hearers God's **offspring**. For centuries, Jewish and Christian theologians have discussed how humans are both like and unlike God, how we enact our relationship to the Divine. A dominant teaching has been that, just as God cares for creation, so as God's offspring we are to be dedicated to that care.

The church is the **ark**, floating above the chaos of the seas, brought in safety to the harbor. One early Christian bishop directed his clergy to hold the baptismal candidates down under the water three times until they rose up gasping for air. The water of baptism not only gently washes the infant; it also joins the candidate to the death and resurrection of Christ. The eighteenth-century Welsh Methodist poet Ann Griffiths wrote, "We'll yet escape the drowning / Because God is our ark."

Ideas for the Day

◆ Festivals like Ascension and Epiphany are rich occasions deserving of observance on their proper days, helping complete the ritual narrative told during the rest of the season. Christ's exhortation to keep his commandments out of love, and his promise of the Holy Spirit, which will not leave us orphaned after Jesus' ascension, is directly connected to the commission he gives his followers to make disciples of all nations.

◆ In some churches, the practice of *asperges*, or sprinkling the congregation with water by using an evergreen branch or other tool, has been embraced as a sense-engaging physical reminder of baptism. In other congregations such a thing is regarded as "too Catholic." While an ideal time to introduce the asperges is at the Easter Vigil, or at the beginning of worship with a remembrance of baptism, the reading from 1 Peter today also provides a backdrop for the rite.

◆ In many Danish Lutheran churches and churches of Danish heritage, a model ship is suspended over the pews or font, illustrating that the church is a ship that sails toward God, the new ark in which God places people through baptism, rescuing them from sin and death. The place in the church building where the worshipers sit is properly called the nave, which comes from the Latin word *navis*, which means ship. Teach people this word. While many might still call it the sanctuary, there is something wonderful about knowing we are sitting in God's vessel. Depending on the shape of your building, have people look up: often, the ceiling of the nave will resemble an overturned boat—a further reminder that God shelters us, keeping us safe in this baptismal ark.

◆ Jesus names the Holy Spirit the Advocate, a title derived from the Latin word meaning "to call to one's help." God calls the Spirit alongside us for comfort and aid; we also are called to stand with those in need, giving counsel and intercession. Today, consider recognizing the law-related professions and honoring those in your congregation who assist others with matters of the law.

Connections with the Liturgy

In the liturgy for Holy Baptism (*Evangelical Lutheran Worship*, p. 230), the thanksgiving over the font likens the water in the font to the waters of the flood, through which God delivered Noah and his family. The additional thanksgivings at the font, II, IV, and V (pp. 70–71), also use Noah's flood as a metaphor for baptism.

Let the Children Come

During the joyful Easter season, we sing and say many alleluias: in a canticle of praise, in hymns and songs, in the gospel acclamation, in worship texts. Highlight this abundance of Alleluias by inviting the children to raise their hands high whenever they hear, say, or sing this word.

Assembly Song
Gathering

Dear Christians, one and all, rejoice ELW 594
Now thank we all our God ELW 839/840, LBW 533/534
Christ is alive! Let Christians sing ELW 389

Psalmody and Acclamations

Smith, Alan. "Shout with Joy" from PS2.
Farlee, Robert Buckley. "Psalm 66," Refrain 3, from PSCY.
Organ, Anne Krentz. "Psalm 66:8-20" from PWA.
Pishner, Stephen. "This Is the Day: Psalm and Gospel Acclamation for Easter." SATB, cant, assembly, kybd, gtr, 11 hb. GIA G-6139.

Hymn of the Day

Thy holy wings ELW 613, WOV 741 *BRED DINA VIDA VINGAR*
Abide with me ELW 629, LBW 272 *EVENTIDE*
Children of the heavenly Father ELW 781, LBW 474
    TRYGGARE KAN INGEN VARA

Offering

Come down, O Love divine ELW 804
My God, how wonderful thou art ELW 863, LBW 524

Communion

Waterlife ELW 457, W&P 145

Beautiful Savior   ELW 838, LBW 518

Holy God, holy and glorious   ELW 637

Sending

Go, my children, with my blessing   ELW 543

Praise God, from whom all blessings flow   ELW 884, LBW 564

Additional Assembly Songs

We praise thee, O God   TFF 100

Our Paschal Lamb, that sets us free   WOV 679

☸ Haya tune, arr. Joas Kijugo. Tanzania. "The Love of God Almighty" from *Set Free: A Collection of African Hymns*. SATB and cantor. AFP 9780806600451.

✿ Assad, Audrey/Phillip LaRue. "Known" from CCLI.

✿ Hamilton, Dan/Robbie Seay/Ryan Owens/Taylor Johnson. "Hallelujah, God Is Near" from CCLI.

✿ Houston, Joel. "Father" from CCLI.

✿ Jamieson, Kevin/Stuart Townend. "The King Has Come" from CCLI.

✿ Morgan, Reuben/Scott Ligertwood. "Freedom Is Here" from CCLI.

✿ Redman, Matt/Tofer Brown/Bryan Brown/Chris Tomlin. "Not Ashamed" from WT.

Music for the Day

Choral

● Diemer, Emma Lou. "Thy Holy Wings." SATB, pno, fl, cello. MSM 50-6523.

Livingston, Donald/William Mathis. "Come Down, O Love Divine." AFP 9780800675356.

Rosewall, Michael. "Now Thank We All Our God." 2 pt mxd, pno. AFP 9780800623852.

Young, Carlton. "I Will Not Leave You Comfortless." SATB, pno. HOP CY3354.

Children's Choir

● Burkhardt, Michael. "Thy Holy Wings." U/2 pt/3 pt, pno, opt ob, opt cl, opt cello. MSM 50-5552.

Patterson, Mark. "Shout with Joy!" U, pno. CG CGA1251.

Ziegenhals, Harriet. "We All Are God's Children." U/2 pt, kybd, fl. CG CGA971.

Keyboard / Instrumental

Bach, J. S. "Von Gott will ich nicht lassen" from *Leipzig Chorales*. Org. Various editions.

● Ferguson, John. "Tryggare kan ingen vara" from *Thy Holy Wings: Three Swedish Folk Hymn Preludes*. Org. AFP 9780800647957.

● Oines, Sylvia. "Abide with Me" from *In Heaven Above: Piano Music for Funerals and Memorials*. Pno. AFP 9781451401912.

● Organ, Anne Krentz. "Children of the Heavenly Father" from *In Heaven Above: Piano Music for Funerals and Memorials*. Pno. AFP 9781451401912.

Handbell

● Mazzatenta, Michael. "Thy Holy Wings." 3-6 oct hb, opt 3 oct hc, L2. GIA G-8175.

● Geisler, Herbert. "Safely in the Shepherd's Arms." 3-5 oct, L2+. MSM 30-816.

● Stephenson, Valerie. "Abide with Me." 3-5 oct, L1+. CG CGB547.

Tuesday, May 27

John Calvin, renewer of the church, died 1564

John Calvin began his studies in theology at the University of Paris when he was fourteen. In his mid-twenties he experienced a conversion that led him to embrace the views of the Reformation. His theological ideas are systematically laid out in his *Institutes of the Christian Religion*. He is also well known for his commentaries on scripture. He was a preacher in Geneva, was banished once, and then later returned to reform the city under a theocratic constitution.

☸ = global song
✿ = praise song
● = relates to hymn of the day

May 29, 2014
Ascension of Our Lord

In today's gospel the risen Christ ascends into heaven and his followers are assured that the Spirit will empower them to be witnesses throughout the earth. The disciples were told to not gaze up into heaven to look for Jesus; we find his presence among us as we proclaim the word and share the Easter feast. We too long for the Spirit to enliven our faith and invigorate our mission.

Prayer of the Day

Almighty God, your only Son was taken into the heavens and in your presence intercedes for us. Receive us and our prayers for all the world, and in the end bring everything into your glory, through Jesus Christ, our Sovereign and Lord, who lives and reigns with you and the Holy Spirit, one God, now and forever.

or

Almighty God, your blessed Son, our Savior Jesus Christ, ascended far above all heavens that he might fill all things. Mercifully give us faith to trust that, as he promised, he abides with us on earth to the end of time, who lives and reigns with you and the Holy Spirit, one God, now and forever.

Gospel Acclamation

Alleluia. Go and make disciples of all nations, | says the Lord;* I am with you always, to the end | of the age. *Alleluia.* (Matt. 28:19, 20)

Readings and Psalm

Acts 1:1-11

Before he is lifted into heaven, Jesus promises that the missionary work of the disciples will spread out from Jerusalem to all the world. His words provide an outline of the book of Acts.

Psalm 47

God has gone up with a shout. (Ps. 47:5)

or Psalm 93

Ever since the world began, your throne has been established. (Ps. 93:2)

Ephesians 1:15-23

The risen and exalted Christ reigns over the entire universe. The author of Ephesians prays that we would be given the wisdom to comprehend this and display it through love toward others.

Luke 24:44-53

On the day of his ascension, Jesus leaves his disciples with a commission, a blessing, and a promise of the Holy Spirit.

Preface Ascension

Color White

Prayers of Intercession

The prayers are prepared locally for each occasion. The following examples may be adapted or used as appropriate.

Made alive in Christ and filled with his Spirit, let us pray for the church, the world, and all of God's creation.

A brief silence.

Eternal God, your life and love know no bounds. Send forth the church to be your witnesses in every time and place. Hear us, O God.

Your mercy is great.

Mighty God, the creation resounds with your glory. Fill the universe with your wisdom, so that planets, stars, and space sing your praises. Hear us, O God.

Your mercy is great.

Sovereign God, you rule in justice and mercy. Direct all in power and authority so that they lead wisely and humbly. Hear us, O God.

Your mercy is great.

Steadfast God, your mercy is never-ending. We pray for those who are abandoned, hopeless, grieving, and hurting (*especially*). Hear us, O God.

Your mercy is great.

Gracious God, your ways are not our ways. We pray for Sunday school teachers and Christian educators, that they guide us as we seek Christ's wisdom. Hear us, O God.

Your mercy is great.

Here other intercessions may be offered.

Holy God, we remember with thanksgiving the saints (*especially Jiří Tranovský, hymn writer*). With the saints and angels, make us sing boldly of your boundless love. Hear us, O God.

Your mercy is great.

Receive our prayers, merciful God, and dwell in us richly, through Jesus Christ, our life and our redeemer. **Amen.**

Images in the Readings

Ascension Day plays with the ancient cosmological picture of the three-tier universe, the highest level of which is **heaven**, or "the heavens." Over the centuries, Christians have speculated in quite different ways about what this heaven is. By the nineteenth century, heaven came to be described as a kind of summer camp, perfection in populist human terms. In the Bible, "heaven" is a synonym for God, a way to speak about divine majesty and mercy. In Acts, the ascending Jesus is covered with a cloud, which in the Hebrew Scriptures usually refers to the elusive presence yet cosmic power of God. It is important that today's references to heaven not suggest that it is a place that is far away.

Luke has two men in **white robes** speaking with the disciples. The Christian church has regularized the wearing of white robes as the sign of baptism. We now can all speak of the power of the ascended Christ.

In Ephesians, the **body of Christ** is the church imagined like Atlas, a giant standing on earth holding up the skies, the head being Christ, and the body being the church that fills the world. Today we blend this understanding of "body of Christ" with the bread we eat and the assembly gathered to worship.

Ideas for the Day

◆　On Ascension Day, the psalmist cries in Psalm 47 that "God has gone up with a shout." Almost instinctively, we assume that the shouting part of this reference is assigned to us, a sort of acclamation to a "job well done!" for God. But what if that shouting comes not from us, but *from God*? What if—in fact—it is God who is "shouting" into the world words like resurrection, and grace, and ascension? This "reassignment" of the shout can be powerful and grace-filled, a reminder that God is the actor on Ascension Day, and we are the recipients of grace. The source of the shout can be also a reminder to us of other biblical Christological themes: that Jesus himself is the Word of God (the shout!), that the Word (the shout!) continues to be heard and echo long after it is first uttered, and that the Word (the shout!) speaks life into places of death. Who is doing the shouting here that accompanies Jesus' ascension?

◆　The days between Ascension and Pentecost are "in between," a transition from Easter to the missional urging of the Spirit. While still part of the Great Fifty Days, the whole of the Christian life might find echo in this space: "all things are passing," as St. Theresa said, "God alone is changeless." The promise of Ascension is a reminder that God is present with us through transitions of all kinds, carrying us safely (as was done on Easter) from what *was* to what is *becoming*.

◆　Location, location, location! Planners of liturgy and preaching need to be careful how we speak of the physical location of Jesus on Ascension Day. He "is seated at the right hand of the Father," but is as much present in bread and wine among us now, and Ascension affords us an opportunity to have serious discussion and real inquiry into what a "real presence" means, now in a new way. The custom of extinguishing the paschal candle on this day should thus be avoided; Jesus is still with us, and Easter is still at work. Indeed, can it ever be finished?

Connections with the Liturgy

"He ascended into heaven and is seated at the right hand of the Father," says the Nicene Creed. "He ascended into heaven, he is seated at the right hand of the Father," says the Apostles' Creed.

Let the Children Come

Some children who are full of daydreams are living signs of wonder among us. They remind us to look up in awe. Other children, whose lives are so difficult that daydreaming is a form of survival, call us to look around at the needs and hurts of the world and to respond. After the liturgy, invite everyone outside to look up and find pictures in the clouds and to look around at the needs of the neighborhood.

Assembly Song
Gathering

Lord, you give the great commission   ELW 579, WOV 756

Crown him with many crowns   ELW 855

Rejoice, for Christ is king!   ELW 430

Psalmody and Acclamations

Haugen, Marty. "God Mounts His Throne" from TLP:S.

Inwood, Paul. "A Blare of Trumpets" from PS2.

Anderson, Mark. "Psalm 93" from PSCY.

Schalk, Carl. "Psalm 93" from PWA.

Pishner, Stephen. "This Is the Day: Psalm and Gospel Acclamation for Easter." SATB, cant, assembly, kybd, gtr, 11 hb. GIA G-6139.

Hymn of the Day

Blessing, Honor, and Glory   ELW 433, W&P 21
　　　BLESSING, HONOR, AND GLORY

O Christ, our hope   ELW 604   *LOBT GOTT, IHR CHRISTEN*

Beautiful Savior   ELW 838, LBW 518   *SCHÖNSTER HERR JESU*

Offering

My Lord of light   ELW 832, WOV 796

The peace of the Lord   ELW 646, LLC 471

Communion

Now we join in celebration   ELW 462, LBW 203
Lord, enthroned in heavenly splendor   ELW 475, LBW 172
Let all mortal flesh keep silence   ELW 490, LBW 198

Sending

Christ is alive! Let Christians sing   ELW 389
Lord, enthroned in heavenly splendor   ELW 475, LBW 172

Additional Assembly Songs

O God of God, O Light of light   LBW 536

⊕ Jesus, we want to meet   TFF 145

⊕ Chua, Daniel K.L. "Jesus Is Lord" from *Global Songs for Worship*. U, kybd, gtr. Faith Alive/Calvin Institute of Christian Worship. 9781592554423.

⊕ Ghanian tune, arr. John Bell. "When Our Master Jesus Went Away" from *The Courage To Say No: 23 Songs for Lent and Easter*. SATB with cantor. GIA G-4244.

✿ Brown, Brenton. "We Will Worship Him" from CCLI.

✿ Houston, Joel/Marty Sampson. "Shout Unto God" from WT.

✿ Maher, Matt/Kari Jobe. "We Exalt Your Name" from WT.

✿ Mckelvey, Douglas Kaine/Ed Cash/Tim Neufeld. "Great Is the Lord" from WT.

✿ Mooring, Leeland/Jack Mooring/Matt Bronleewe. "Yes You Have" from WT.

✿ Norman, Bebo/Jason Ingram. "I Will Lift My Eyes" from CCLI.

Music for the Day
Choral

Cherwien, David. "Up Through Endless Ranks of Angels." SAB, org, opt tpt. AFP 9780800658816.

Farlee, Robert Buckley. "Light's Glittering Morn." 2 pt, org. MSM 50-4048.

Hakes, Derek. "Fairest Lord Jesus." SATB, pno. BP 1657.

Landes, Rob. "Peace I Leave with You." SATB, org. MSM 50-5000.

Scott, K. Lee. "Jesus, My All, to Heaven Is Gone" from *Rejoice Now My Spirit: For Medium High Voice*. Sop solo. AFP 9780800651084.

Weidner, Raymond. "God Has Gone Up with a Shout." SSATBB/solo, org, br qrt, timp. PAR 0315.

Children's Choir

Vaughan Williams, Ralph. "Hail Thee, Festival Day!" ELW 394.

Lowenberg, Kenneth. "Come, All Children, Join to Sing." U, opt desc, kybd, opt glock, xyl. HIN HMC 1892.

Wagner, Douglas E. "Clap Your Hands, Sing for Joy!" U, pno. Triune Music Inc. LOR 10/2583K.

Keyboard / Instrumental

• Buxtehude, Dietrich. "Chorale Prelude on 'Lobt Gott, ihr Christen allzugleich'." Org. Various editions.

• Carter, John. "Schönster Herr Jesu" from *Contemplative Folk Tunes for Piano*. Pno. AFP 9780800659776.

Cook, John. "Fanfare for Organ." Org. NOV 590228.

• Stevens, Wendy. "Beautiful Savior" from *Rejoice! Engaging Hymn Settings for Piano*. Pno. CPH 97-7171.

Handbell

McChesney, Kevin. "Ascension." 3-5 oct hb, L3. RW 8188. Full score with pno. RW 8188FS.

• Smith, Vicki. "Beautiful Savior (Fairest Lord Jesus)." 3-5 oct, L2. CPH 97-6873.

Stephenson, Valerie. "Hail Thee, Festival Day (Christians, Lift Up Your Hearts)." 3-6 oct hb, opt 3-5 oct hc, opt org, opt tpt, opt assembly, L3. CG CGB488.

Thursday, May 29
Jiří Tranovský, hymnwriter, died 1637

Jiří Tranovský (YEAR-zhee truh-NOF-skee) is considered the "Luther of the Slavs" and the father of Slovak hymnody. Trained at the University of Wittenberg in the early seventeenth century, Tranovský was ordained in 1616 and spent his life preaching and teaching in Prague, Silesia, and finally Slovakia. He produced a translation of the Augsburg Confession and published his hymn collection *Cithara Sanctorum* (Lyre of the Saints), the foundation of Slovak Lutheran hymnody.

Saturday, May 31
Visit of Mary to Elizabeth

Sometime after the Annunciation, Mary visited her cousin Elizabeth. This occasion is sometimes referred to simply as "The Visitation." Elizabeth greeted Mary with the words "Blessed are you among women," and Mary responded with her famous song, the Magnificat. Luke's gospel tells that even John the Baptist rejoiced and leapt in his mother's womb when Elizabeth heard Mary's greeting. On this festival two women are seen: one, seemingly too old to have a child, bears the last prophet of the old covenant, and the other, quite young, bears the incarnate Word and the new covenant.

⊕ = global song
✿ = praise song
● = relates to hymn of the day

June 1, 2014
Seventh Sunday of Easter

In these days between Ascension and Pentecost, we gather with the disciples in the upper room, waiting for the Spirit to transform the church around the world. In today's gospel Jesus prays for his followers and for their mission in his name. Amid religious, social, and economic divisions, we seek the unity that Jesus had with his Father. Made one in baptism, we go forth to live our faith in the world, eager for the unity that God intends for the whole human family.

Prayer of the Day

O God of glory, your Son Jesus Christ suffered for us and ascended to your right hand. Unite us with Christ and each other in suffering and in joy, that all the world may be drawn into your bountiful presence, through Jesus Christ, our Savior and Lord, who lives and reigns with you and the Holy Spirit, one God, now and forever.

Gospel Acclamation

Alleluia. I will not leave you orphaned, ¹ says the Lord.*
I am com- ¹ ing to you. *Alleluia.* (John 14:18)

Readings and Psalm

Acts 1:6-14

Today's reading is part of the introduction to the narrative of the outpouring of the Spirit on Pentecost. These verses tell of the risen Lord's conversation with his disciples on the eve of his ascension.

Psalm 68:1-10, 32-35

Sing to God, who rides upon the clouds. (Ps. 68:4)

1 Peter 4:12-14; 5:6-11

Our faith in Christ does not make us immune from the scorn of others. Nevertheless, we are to resist the designs of evil when we experience disparagement from others, because we trust God's grace will strengthen and guide us.

John 17:1-11

On the night before his crucifixion, Jesus prays to his heavenly Father, asking that those who continue his work in this world will live in unity.

Preface Ascension

Color White

Prayers of Intercession

The prayers are prepared locally for each occasion. The following examples may be adapted or used as appropriate.

Made alive in Christ and filled with his Spirit, let us pray for the church, the world, and all of God's creation.
A brief silence.

For the body of Christ, made one yet suffering divisions; for strength to proclaim the gospel; for those who do not believe. Lord, in your mercy,
hear our prayer.

For farmers planting the seeds that grow our food; for sun and rain in right proportion; for lands suffering flood or drought. Lord, in your mercy,
hear our prayer.

For those who hold authority over others; for presidents, governors, and mayors; for generals and officers; for executives and managers; for parents and teachers. Lord, in your mercy,
hear our prayer.

For those suffering or in want; for victims of abuse; for those who are depressed or anxious; for estranged families; for the ill or hospitalized (*especially*). Lord, in your mercy,
hear our prayer.

For this assembly; for its leaders, council, and committees, that difference and division not obscure the oneness we share in Christ. Lord, in your mercy,
hear our prayer.
Here other intercessions may be offered.

We give thanks for (*Justin, martyr, and*) all who lived and died in faith. Make us one with them, trusting the one hope to which we are called. Lord, in your mercy,
hear our prayer.

Receive our prayers, merciful God, and dwell in us richly, through Jesus Christ, our life and our redeemer.
Amen.

Images in the Readings

John writes about the **name** of God. When we say, "Stop in the name of the law," we mean that our very invoking of "the law" brings with it the powerful authority behind the law. So the name of God conveys divine mercy and might. Jews still today, careful not to misuse God's name, invoke Hashem, "the Name," as a circumlocution for God. Christians can call upon the name of the Lord by invoking Jesus Christ.

Eternal life, John writes in this chapter, is knowing God now.

As did the gospel of the First Sunday of Lent, 1 Peter speaks in a literal way about the **devil**. One of the primary questions raised by the world's religions is why there is evil in the world and within the human heart. Borrowed from dualistic religions, the image of the devil personifies the power of evil into a kind of perpetually troublesome anti-God. Christians trust in the mighty hand of God to protect them against this adversary.

Ideas for the Day

◆   From the pastor's perspective, "in between times" can be particularly daunting to some people, and this Sunday (between Ascension and Pentecost) is a good time to address that directly. Though physically gone, Jesus does not stop speaking to us or caring about us, and in fact is quite talkative, especially for someone who has ascended. In each community, there are those between certainty and despair, between hope and fear, between a Jesus who seems gone and words of eternal life from a talkative Jesus. His speaking confirms what we know but sometimes have difficulty feeling: God's people are not left alone, a fact that needs to be preached, sung, tasted, and felt again and again. It is powerful grace—grace that can be powerfully realized in the gathered liturgical assembly.

◆   Jesus' "high priestly prayer" is an intercessory prayer on behalf of those he loves. If Christians are called to this task of intercession, how does the paschal mystery inform *how* we ask on behalf of others and *how* we make our prayers to God? Prayer can be a slippery fish, as we do not know how "intercessions" work, or if they are capable of redirecting (through God's grace!) the future. Wise worship planners will take this seriously, as much of current discourse about prayer sees it as a simple vending-machine formula devoid of grace. Prayer is complicated, and intercessory prayer even more so. Jesus' prayer today (in typical Johannine high-speak) is complex. Perhaps prayer is better regarded as something *done* than as something *thought about* too much (like bodies being raised up: better done than figured out).

◆   The image of fire in the second reading is a curious anticipation of Pentecost, but not at all inappropriate. Yes, something strange is about to happen, but do not be surprised. Remember how John the Baptist said *this* baptism would be with fire. Did we think it would be simple? Or painless? It was not for Jesus. Would we expect it to be different for us—we who are his body?

Connections with the Liturgy

In the profession of faith in the rite of Baptism (*Evangelical Lutheran Worship*, p. 229), the candidates are asked to "renounce the devil and all the forces that defy God." Christians are asked to take seriously the power of that "roaring lion" about which 1 Peter warns us.

Let the Children Come

The fifty days of Easter are coming to an end. What a temptation it is to treat this day as if it were an ordinary Sunday in summer. Ring the bells. Sing a song of resurrection. Carry fragrant spring flowers into the nave. If the season of Easter dwindles to a whimper, the eyes and ears and noses of the children will pick up no clues that the season is about to change.

Assembly Song
Gathering
Lord, enthroned in heavenly splendor   ELW 475, LBW 172
Rise, O Sun of righteousness   ELW 657
A hymn of glory let us sing   ELW 393

Psalmody and Acclamations
Guimont, Michel. "Psalm 68" from PRCL.
Kelly/Weber. "Psalm 68" from TP.
Messner, Sally. "Psalm 68:1-10, 32-35" from PWA.
Pishner, Stephen. "This Is the Day: Psalm and Gospel Acclamation for Easter." SATB, cant, assembly, kybd, gtr, 11 hb. GIA G-6139.

Hymn of the Day
Loving Spirit   ELW 397, WOV 683   *RESTORATION*
I come with joy   ELW 482   *DOVE OF PEACE*
Christ is the king!   ELW 662   *BEVERLY*

Offering
I come with joy   ELW 482
Like the murmur of the dove's song   ELW 403, WOV 685

Communion
You satisfy the hungry heart   ELW 484, WOV 711
As the grains of wheat   ELW 465, WOV 705
One bread, one body   ELW 496, TFF 122, W&P 111, WOV 710
Heaven is singing for joy   ELW 664

Sending
Alleluia! Sing to Jesus   ELW 392, LBW 158
Thine the amen   ELW 826, WOV 801

Additional Assembly Songs

This is my body   TFF 121

Open our eyes, Lord   TFF 98, W&P 113

⊕ Iona Community. "Behold, I Make All Things New" from *Come All You People: Shorter Songs for Worship.* SATB. GIA G-4391.

⊕ Dexter, Noel, arr. Caribbean. "Peace and Love" from *Let the Peoples Sing: Volume One.* SATB. AFP 9780800675394.

✿ Fieldes, Mia/Raymond Badham. "Adonai" from CCLI.

✿ Ingram, Jason/Jonas Myrin/Matt Redman. "We Could Change the World" from CCLI.

✿ Ingram, Jason/Kristian Stanfill. "Always" from WT.

✿ Rend Collective Experiment. "Build Your Kingdom Here" from WT.

✿ Tomlin, Chris/J.D. Walt. "Uncreated One" from CCLI.

✿ Townend, Stuart/Keith Getty. "O Church Arise" from WT.

Music for the Day
Choral

● Anders, Charles/arr. Paul Bouman. "Christ Is the King." SATB, br qrt. GIA G-3016.

Keesecker, Thomas. "Oh, Love, How Deep." SATB, org. AFP 9781451420760.

Schalk, Carl. "Catch the Vision! Share the Glory!" SATB, org. MSM 50-6006.

Schalk, Carl. "Lord, It Belongs Not to My Care." SATB, org. AFP 9780800645908.

Scott, K. Lee. "Angels Visit When We Sing." SATB, pno, opt str. MSM 50-9220.

Children's Choir

Berthier, Jacques. "There Is One Lord" in *Music from Taizé.* GIA G-2778.

Handel, G. F. "Lord, Hear Our Thanks" in *G. F. Handel: A Collection of Anthems for Children, Youth and Adults.* U, org/pno. CG CGC10.

Sleeth, Natalie. "Praise the Lord." U/2 pt, kybd. HIN HMC 207.

Keyboard / Instrumental

● Burkhardt, Michael. "Dove of Peace" from *Easy Hymn Settings: General (Communion).* Org. MSM 10-515.

● Held, Wilbur. "Restoration" from *Wondrous Love: Five Hymn Settings for Organ.* Org. MSM 10-573.

● Mossing, Sally Drennan. "Dove of Peace" from *Christ, Be Our Light: Music for the Church Pianist.* Pno. AFP 9780800663858.

● Pinkston, Daniel S. "Restoration" from *Three Hymns for Clarinet and Piano.* Cl, pno. MSM 20-761.

Handbell

● Philips, Judy. "Dove of Peace." 3-6 oct, L3+. GIA G-7292.

● Tucker, Sondra. "I Will Arise." 2-3 oct, L2+. CG CGB525.

Ward, Robert. "King of Kings." 3-6 oct, L3. AGEHR AG36046.

Sunday, June I
Justin, martyr at Rome, died around 165

Justin was born of pagan parents. At Ephesus he was moved by stories of early Christian martyrs and came under the influence of an elderly Christian man he met there. Justin described his conversion by saying, "Straightway a flame was kindled in my soul and a love of the prophets and those who are friends of Christ possessed me." Justin was a teacher of philosophy and engaged in debates about the truth of Christian faith. He was arrested and jailed for practicing an unauthorized religion. He refused to renounce his faith, and he and six of his students, one a woman, were beheaded.

Justin's description of early Christian worship around the year 150 is one of the foundations of the church's pattern of worship, East and West.

Tuesday, June 3
John XXIII, Bishop of Rome, died 1963

In his ministry as a bishop of Venice, John (then Archbishop Roncalli) was loved by his people. He visited parishes and established new ones. He had warm affection for the working class—he himself was the child of Italian peasants—and he worked at developing social-action ministries. At age seventy-seven he was elected bishop of Rome. Despite the expectation that he would be a transitional pope, he had great energy and spirit. He convened the Second Vatican Council to open the windows of the church and "let in the fresh air of the modern world." The council brought about great changes in Roman Catholic worship, changes that have influenced Lutherans and many other Protestant churches as well.

The Martyrs of Uganda, died 1886

Christianity had been introduced to Uganda after 1877, but was made available primarily to those in the court of King Mutesa. His successor, King Mwanga, was angered by these Christian members of the court whose first allegiance was not to him but to Christ. On June 3, 1886, thirty-two young men were burned to death for refusing to renounce Christianity. Other martyrs followed. But many were impressed by the confident manner in which these Christians went to their deaths, and the persecution led to a much stronger Christian presence in the country.

⊕ = global song
✿ = praise song
● = relates to hymn of the day

Thursday, June 5

Boniface, Bishop of Mainz, missionary to Germany, martyr, died 754

Boniface (his name means "good deeds") was born Wynfrith in Devonshire, England. He was a Benedictine monk who at the age of thirty was called to missionary work among the Vandal tribes in Germany. His first missionary attempt was unsuccessful, but he returned two years later and was able to plant the gospel in an area filled with superstitious and violent practices. He led large numbers of Benedictine monks and nuns in establishing churches, schools, and seminaries. Boniface was also a reformer. He persuaded two rulers to call synods to put an end to the practice of selling church offices to the highest bidder. Boniface was preparing a group for confirmation on the eve of Pentecost when he and they were killed by a band of pagans.

June 7, 2014
Vigil of Pentecost

At this liturgy we gather in vigilant prayer as the disciples did in the days preceding Pentecost. Our world waits for an end to war and violence. The whole creation waits for an end to suffering. With undying hope we pray for the crowning gift of Easter—the Spirit of the risen Christ among us.

Prayer of the Day

Almighty and ever-living God, you fulfilled the promise of Easter by sending the gift of your Holy Spirit. Look upon your people gathered in prayer, open to receive the Spirit's flame. May it come to rest in our hearts and heal the divisions of word and tongue, that with one voice and one song we may praise your name in joy and thanksgiving; through Jesus Christ, our Savior and Lord, who lives and reigns with you and the Holy Spirit, one God, now and forever.

Gospel Acclamation

Alleluia. Come, Holy Spirit, fill the hearts [|] of your faithful,* and kindle in us the fire [|] of your love. *Alleluia.*

Readings and Psalm
Exodus 19:1-9

At Sinai God assured Israel that they were God's prized possession and commissioned them to serve as mediating priests for the nations. God's word spoken to Moses is the basis of the people's trust.

or Acts 2:1-11

Believers are filled with the Spirit to tell God's deeds.

Psalm 33:12-22

The Lord is our helper and our shield. (Ps. 33:20)

or Psalm 130

There is forgiveness with you. (Ps. 130:4)

Romans 8:14-17, 22-27

The Holy Spirit has made us God's children who eagerly await the glorious future God has prepared for all of creation. While we cannot fully see what God has in store for us and creation, we eagerly anticipate it in hope. Even when we are unable to pray, the same Spirit prays for us.

John 7:37-39

Jesus describes the Holy Spirit as living water, quenching the thirst of all who come to him and filling the hearts of believers till they overflow.

Preface   Vigil and Day of Pentecost

Color   Red

Saturday, June 7

Seattle, chief of the Duwamish Confederacy, died 1866

Noah Seattle was chief of the Suquamish tribe and later became chief of the Duwamish Confederacy, a tribal alliance. When the tribes were faced with an increasing number of white settlers, Seattle chose to live and work peacefully with them rather than engage in wars. After Seattle became a Roman Catholic, he began the practice of morning and evening prayer in the tribe, a practice that continued after his death. On the centennial of his birth, the city of Seattle—named for him against his wishes—erected a monument over his grave.

June 8, 2014
Day of Pentecost

Today's festival derives its name from the Jewish festival of Pentecost, observed fifty days after Passover. On the fiftieth day of Easter we celebrate the Holy Spirit as the power of God among us that heals, forgives, inspires, and unites. In the reading from Acts, images of wind and fire describe the Spirit poured out on disciples of all nations. In John's gospel the risen Christ breathes the Spirit on his followers on Easter evening. In the one Spirit we are baptized into one body, and at the Lord's table the Spirit unites us for witness in the world.

Prayer of the Day

O God, on this day you open the hearts of your faithful people by sending into us your Holy Spirit. Direct us by the light of that Spirit, that we may have a right judgment in all things and rejoice at all times in your peace, through Jesus Christ, your Son and our Lord, who lives and reigns with you and the Holy Spirit, one God, now and forever.

Gospel Acclamation

Alleluia. Come, Holy Spirit, fill the hearts ⌐ of your faithful,* and kindle in us the fire ⌐ of your love. *Alleluia.*

Readings and Psalm

Acts 2:1-21

Pentecost was a Jewish harvest festival that marked the fiftieth day after Passover. Luke portrays the Holy Spirit being poured out upon the disciples before the gathered and astonished people assembled in Jerusalem for the festival. Filled with the Spirit, the disciples were able to witness to the power of Christ's resurrection.

or Numbers 11:24-30

The Spirit of God rested upon seventy elders in Israel who had been chosen to share the burden of leadership with Moses. When some became jealous that two others also had the spirit and could prophesy, Moses said that he hoped that all of God's people would be prophets.

Psalm 104:24-34, 35b

Send forth your Spirit and renew the face of the earth. (Ps. 104:30)

1 Corinthians 12:3b-13

Paul is helping the Corinthians understand the relationship between our God-given unity and Spirit-created diversity. The Spirit creates the unity of faith and gives all Christians diverse gifts for the common benefit of all. We need one another's diverse spiritual gifts, because the same Spirit has given them to each person for the common good.

or Acts 2:1-21

See above.

John 20:19-23

The risen Jesus appears to his disciples, offering them a benediction, a commission, and the gift of the Holy Spirit.

or John 7:37-39

Jesus describes the Holy Spirit as living water, quenching the thirst of all who come to him and filling the hearts of believers till they overflow.

Preface   Vigil and Day of Pentecost

Color   Red

Prayers of Intercession

The prayers are prepared locally for each occasion. The following examples may be adapted or used as appropriate.

Made alive in Christ and filled with his Spirit, let us pray for the church, the world, and all of God's creation.

A brief silence.

Your Spirit gathers the church. With your grace, enliven bishops, pastors, teachers, and artists, that they proclaim the gospel of peace in their own languages. Hear us, O God.

Your mercy is great.

Your Spirit animates the creation. By your power, renew the earth. Fill us with wonder for your handiwork, that we be partners with you in restoring land, skies, and seas. Hear us, O God.

Your mercy is great.

Your Spirit enlightens the nations. By your wisdom, direct governments and international organizations, that your peace free those held captive by misunderstanding and violence. Hear us, O God.

Your mercy is great.

Your Spirit revives body and soul. In your mercy, soothe the afflicted, uplift the sorrowful, comfort the grieving, and heal the sick (*especially*). Hear us, O God.

Your mercy is great.
Your Spirit energizes this faith community. Spur on young and old alike to use their creative talents for building up the body of Christ. Hear us, O God.
Your mercy is great.
Here other intercessions may be offered.
Your Spirit raised Jesus from the dead. Baptized in his name, help us trust the Spirit's power now and in the life to come with all the saints. Hear us, O God.
Your mercy is great.
Receive our prayers, merciful God, and dwell in us richly, through Jesus Christ, our life and our redeemer.
Amen.

Images in the Readings

Anthropologists describe **fire** as one of the markers of the human species. For tens of thousands of years, humans gathered around fire for light, warmth, protection, community, and better food. Many passages in the Bible liken God to fire. The Holy Spirit of God appeared on Sinai in flames of fire, which on Pentecost appeared on the forehead of each believer. Moses experienced God in fire; through fire the Israelites presented offerings to God; God led the people through the wilderness with a pillar of fire. Seraphim are fire-spirits, extensions of the divine. Yet fire is also a sign of divine judgment: the angel in Eden hides the tree of life from humanity with a sword of fire, and John the Baptist predicts that fire will consume the chaff. Fire both occasions human life and has the power to destroy. Think fire, think God.

The Hebrew noun *ruach* can be translated into English as **spirit**, breath, or wind. *Spirit* is the most amorphous of these words. In Christian theology, the Spirit that we experience is the Spirit of the risen Christ, a spirit of service, a spirit of love, a spirit of resurrection beyond death.

In the narrative in Numbers, **seventy** elders receive the Spirit. In the Bible, seventy is a number that connotes totality, seven times ten. In Genesis 10, there are seventy nations in Israel's world; Jacob moves to Egypt with seventy family members; and there are many more seventies. Luke says that seventy were sent out to preach the word.

Ideas for the Day

◆ One of the ancient understandings of confirmation was that the Holy Spirit arrived in one's life in stages: a little at baptism, and the rest at confirmation. Regardless of the truth of this understanding (which has theological problems), the idea that the Holy Spirit comes to God's people in different ways at different times is something worth thinking about on Pentecost. How has the Holy Spirit provided special graces in the past? How might the Spirit be "stirred up" (to use the language of Affirmation of Baptism) for special purposes, at a time that is "ripe" in the eyes of God for a "new thing" to happen?

◆ The Holy Spirit is the Paraclete (comforter), but is also dangerous, and it is in this second manifestation that the "good news" is—in fact—*not* good news for people or systems (or the church) that would try to block its work. The Spirit is unpredictable, and some discussion today is warranted about the degree to which we are comfortable (or exceptionally *uncomfortable*) with the unpredictability of what the Spirit is doing. How do we develop a spirituality of *pneuma* that is content with not knowing what will happen next, or how? Might such a spirituality open *us* to being the ones moved out of the way by the Spirit when it is determined to accomplish the work of God?

◆ Some biblical scholars believe that the references to time (for example, it was nine o'clock in the morning) may have to do with the liturgical cycle of prayer. If this is true, then what might the Acts reading have to say about the times and seasons we gather to pray as fertile ground for the Spirit's activity? Far from the wild and free movement of the Spirit, this might add yet another aspect: how is the Spirit *both* free and unpredictable *and* operable within structure? To confine it to one (or the other) is to confine the Spirit, a dangerous undertaking in which one will be burned.

Connections with the Liturgy

In Thanksgiving at the Table X (*Evangelical Lutheran Worship*, p. 69), we praise God with these words: "O God, you are Breath: send your Spirit on this meal. O God, you are Fire: transform us with hope."

In the Presentation for Holy Baptism (*Evangelical Lutheran Worship*, p. 227), the baptized community is described in phrases recalling this Sunday's readings in 1 Corinthians and Acts: "We are united with all the baptized in the one body of Christ, anointed with the gift of the Holy Spirit, and joined in God's mission for the life of the world."

If John 20 is chosen for this day, see the second Sunday of Easter for a discussion of the greeting of peace.

Let the Children Come

Kids love color (don't we all). In addition to having banners and decorations in the worship space, give children red streamers or pieces of red cloth to wave during worship songs. In addition to the streamers, during the weeks before Pentecost invite the congregation to bring in rhythm instruments that you can pass out for everyone to play, especially during the first and last hymns. You could also have kids make instruments to use in worship. It is fun for kids to see adults playing and having fun alongside of them.

Assembly Song
Gathering

O day full of grace   ELW 627, LBW 161
O Holy Spirit, enter in   ELW 786, LBW 459
Hail thee, festival day!   ELW 394

Psalmody and Acclamations

"Alleluia, Send Out Your Spirit." *Psallite* A-93.
Alonzo, Tony. "Lord, Send Out Your Spirit/Señor, Envía Tu
   Espíritu." SAB, cant, assembly, pno, gtr. GIA G-7241.
Joncas, Michael. "Lord, Send Out Your Spirit (Psalm 104)." SATB,
   cant, assembly, org or str qrt, hp. GIA G-7141.
Pishner, Stephen. "This Is the Day: Psalm and Gospel Acclamation
   for Easter." SATB, cant, assembly, kybd, gtr, 11 hb. GIA G-6139.

Hymn of the Day

God of tempest, God of whirlwind   ELW 400   *CWM RHONDDA*
O living Breath of God   ELW 407, LLC 368   *VÅRVINDAR FRISKA*
Come down, O Love divine   ELW 804   *DOWN AMPNEY*

Offering

Spirit of Gentleness   ELW 396, WOV 684
Lord, you give the great commission   ELW 579, sts. 1, 2; WOV 756

Communion

Loving Spirit   ELW 397
Veni Sancte Spiritus   ELW 406, WOV 686
Gracious Spirit, heed our pleading   ELW 401, TFF 103, WOV 687

Sending

Remember and rejoice   ELW 454
God of tempest, God of whirlwind   ELW 400

Additional Assembly Songs

Spirit of the living God   TFF 101
Holy Spirit, descend   TFF 107
⊕ Lim, Swee Hong. China. "Wei yuan Shen di ai/May the Love of the
   Lord" from *Global Songs for Worship*. U, gtr. Faith Alive/
   Calvin Institute of Christian Worship. 9781592554423.
⊕ Simeone, Inés and Horacio Vivares. "Sopla fuerte/Blow Wild and
   Blow Freely" from *Global Songs for Worship*. U, gtr. Faith
   Alive/Calvin Institute of Christian Worship. 9781592554423.
✿ Beeching, Vicky. "Breath of God" from CCLI.
✿ Carson, Daniel/Jason Ingram/Kristian Stanfill/Louie Giglio. "Spirit
   Fall" from CCLI.
✿ Hughes, Tim. "Consuming Fire" from WT.
✿ Nockels, Christy/Nathan Nockels. "A Mighty Fortress" from WT.
✿ Powell, Aaron/Elias Dummer/Eric Fusilier/Josh Vanderlaan.
   "Spark" from CCLI.
✿ Reeves, Jesse/Daniel Carson/Chris Tomlin/Travis Nunn/Matt
   Gilder. "Sing, Sing, Sing" from WT.

Music for the Day
Choral

Benson, Robert. "Fresh Fire." SATB, org. AFP 9780800678913.
Hillert, Richard. "Called and Gathered by the Spirit." SA(T)B,
   children, desc, br qrt, timp. GIA G-5350.
Hopson, Hal. "With a Mighty Wind and Tongues of Fire." SATB,
   org. AFP 9781451420814.
Miller, Aaron David. "Creator Spirit, Who Gave Us Life." SATB,
   pno. AFP 9781451420678.
von Kampen, David. "Breath of the Living God." 2 pt mxd, pno, opt
   C inst, tamb. CPH 98-4099.
Williams, Ralph Vaughn, arr. John Eggert. "Holy Spirit, Gift of
   God." SATB div, org, opt desc/assembly/ob, C/B-flat inst.
   MSM 50-5415.

Children's Choir

Bedford, Michael. "Veni Sancte Spiritus" in *Singing the Seasons*. U,
   kybd, hb. CG CGA854.
Blersch, Jeffrey. "Holy Spirit, Light Divine" in *Children Rejoice and
   Sing*. U, C inst. CPH 97-7074.
Owen, Harold. "Breathe on Me, Breath of God." U, kybd. GIA
   G-5113.
Patterson, Mark. "Spirit, Come Down" in *ChildrenSing with
   Instruments*. U/2 pt, pno, opt C inst. AFP 9780800620349.

Keyboard / Instrumental

● Biery, Marilyn. "Come Down, O Love Divine" from *The Lord Is
   Risen: Easter and Pentecost Music for Organ or Piano*. Kybd.
   MSM 10-428.
Hayes, Mark. "Spirit of God, Descend Upon My Heart" from
   Mark Hayes: Hymns for the Intermediate Pianist. Pno. LOR
   70/1554L.
Near, Gerald. "Veni creator" from *Chantworks, Set 3: Organ Music
   for the Church Year based upon Gregorian Chant Melodies*.
   Org. AUR AE44.
● Powell, Robert J. "Come Down, O Love Divine" from *Hail Thee,
   Festival Day: Five Hymn Settings for Organ*. Org. MSM
   10-585.

Handbell

● Dobrinski, Cynthia. "God of Grace and God of Glory (Guide Me, O
   Thou Great Jehovah)." 3-6 oct hb, opt tpt, L3. HOP 2531.
Glasgow, Michael. "The Spirit Within." 3-7 oct hb, opt 3, 4 or 7 oct
   hc, opt cl, L3. CG CGB760.
● Wissinger, Kathleen. "Sketches on 'Down Ampney.'" 3-6 oct hb, opt
   3-5 oct hc, L3+. LOR 20/1428L.

⊕ = global song
✿ = praise song
● = relates to hymn of the day

Monday, June 9

Columba, died 597; Aidan, died 651; Bede, died 735; renewers of the church

These three monks from the British Isles were pillars among those who kept alive the light of learning and devotion during the Middle Ages. Columba founded three monasteries, including one on the island of Iona, off the coast of Scotland. That monastery was left in ruins after the Reformation but today is home to an ecumenical religious community. Aidan, who helped bring Christianity to the Northumbria area of England, was known for his pastoral style and ability to stir people to charity and good works. Bede was a Bible translator and scripture scholar. He wrote a history of the English church and was the first historian to date events *anno Domini* (A.D.), "year of our Lord." Bede is also known for his hymns, including "A Hymn of Glory Let Us Sing!" (ELW 393).

Wednesday, June 11

Barnabas, Apostle

The Eastern church commemorates Barnabas as one of the Seventy commissioned by Jesus. Though he was not among the Twelve mentioned in the gospels, the book of Acts gives him the title of apostle. His name means "son of encouragement." When Paul came to Jerusalem after his conversion, Barnabas took him in over the fears of the other apostles, who doubted Paul's discipleship. Later, Paul and Barnabas traveled together on missions. At the Council of Jerusalem, Barnabas defended the claims of Gentile Christians in relation to the Mosaic law.

Saturday, June 14

Basil the Great, Bishop of Caesarea, died 379; Gregory, Bishop of Nyssa, died around 385; Gregory of Nazianzus, Bishop of Constantinople, died around 389; Macrina, teacher, died around 379

The three men in this group are known as the Cappadocian fathers; all three explored the mystery of the Holy Trinity. Basil was influenced by his sister Macrina to live a monastic life, and he settled near the family estate in Caesarea. Basil's Longer Rule and Shorter Rule for monastic life are the basis for Eastern monasticism to this day, and express a preference for communal monastic life over that of hermits. Gregory of Nazianzus (nah-zee-AN-zus) was sent to preach on behalf of the Orthodox faith against the Arians in Constantinople, though the Orthodox did not have a church there at the time. He defended Orthodox trinitarian and Christological doctrine, and his preaching won over the city. Gregory of Nyssa (NISS-uh) was the younger brother of Basil the Great. He is remembered as a writer on spiritual life and the contemplation of God in worship and sacraments.

Macrina (muh-CREE-nuh) was the older sister of Basil and Gregory of Nyssa. She received an excellent education centered on the Bible, and when her fiancé died she devoted herself to the pursuit of Christian perfection. She was a leader of a community, based at the family estate, dedicated to asceticism, meditation, and prayer. Macrina's teaching was influential within the early church.

TIME AFTER PENTECOST
SUMMER

SUMMER

AUTUMN

NOVEMBER

PREPARING FOR SUMMER

Summer is not a liturgical season per se, but it does coincide with the beginning of a long period in the church calendar often called Ordinary Time or the Time after Pentecost. This is the time in the church year between Trinity Sunday and the beginning of Advent. Because one insight of Christian faith is that the ordinary and mundane, the earthly, the baby born in Bethlehem and small portions of bread at communion, are in fact extraordinary, we are invited in this ordinary time to consider the beauty of the plain, the everyday, the simple. They are, in the words of Gerard Manley Hopkins, "charged with the grandeur of God." So summer, flowing out of the celebrations of Pentecost and Trinity, is the beginning of the time in which we find the "extra" in the "ordinary." If labels are required for this season, perhaps we ought to call it "Extraordinary Time."

Trinity

The Spirit is being-as-possibility. Precisely in this way is the Father freed to be the Father, the Son to be the Son, and all three themselves in their mutually coinhering life perichoretically circulating around the neighborhood. This is at least one way to start to get a fresh view of how to talk about the Trinity on Trinity Sunday, and beyond. A danger on Trinity Sunday is either to turn the Trinity into a math game, or to avoid it and simply call it a mystery. The Trinity is not a math puzzle, and it is a mystery, but not mystery as something about which one cannot speak, but rather mystery as something about which one is compelled to speak to explore and develop it.

Typically in Western theology, the Spirit ends up being the shared love of the Father and the Son (especially in Augustine). So the Father and the Son are "subsistent" beings, clearly identifiable as persons because of their antecedent narratives, whereas the Spirit is the love between them. This explanation is helpful as far as it goes, but it risks leaving little "there" there for who the Spirit actually is as a full person in the life of the Trinity.

The question is, "Where does the Spirit 'stand' to be him- or herself over against the Father and the Son?" One of the best, but still insufficient, responses is that the Spirit is God's own liberating future (see, for example, Robert Jenson's first volume of his *Systematic Theology*).

In Eastern Orthodoxy, on the other hand, the Spirit is really more independent as a person (no *filioque*, for example), but then all the processional and monarchical language of that tradition ends up making all three members of the Trinity more static even than in the West, since the Spirit is in a sense less free to set the other two members of the Trinity free in their particularity because the ontology in the East is more being-as-persistence rather than being-as-possibility. Theologians wrestling with this concept have thus tried to find a way to speak of the Spirit as God's divine future, thus grounding the Spirit not in a developmental past but an anticipated future. Thus being is not grounded in persistence from some previous past, but rather is given to us out of the future. This theological perspective changes the meaning of that little word, "Is."

Everything written here is offered simply as a springboard for the preacher's own reflections as you begin to think through how to preach on Trinity Sunday. How do you in your own reflections wrestle with this?

Lectionary

Although the remainder of this season is not Trinity-themed, Trinity Sunday is the perfect way to kick off the summer season. Trinitarian theology equips us for the life of summer. How so? By helping us reflect on the relationship between God and the world, something that happens as we head out for summer camps, spend more time in the outdoors, and generally speaking spend a bit more time engaged with God's creation. "Nicholas Lash has argued that it is the task of the doctrine of the Trinity to obviate the danger of eliding God and the world, and therefore falling into idolatry, by insisting on *both* God's presence to the world, *and* God's difference. The doctrine gives us a grammar by which to speak of God. Thus, in the doctrine of the Spirit 'we learn to find God in all life, all freedom, all creativity and vitality . . . each unexpected attainment of relationship and community'" (T. J. Gorringe, *A Theology of the Built Environment: Justice, Empowerment, Redemption* [Cambridge University Press, 2002], 16–17).

Let this way of thinking deeply inhabit how you read and interpret the lectionary texts throughout the summer. Trinitarian theology is not a puzzle to work through, but gives us a grammar by which to speak of God, especially as we spend time with biblical texts, act as good hermeneuts, and interpret the texts for the assembly.

The summer series of readings presents some especially intriguing possibilities. As is typical for "extraordinary time," lots of time is given over to the middle section of the gospel for the year—in this case, Matthew. After the great commission text (Matt. 28:16-20) for Trinity Sunday, the summer months are devoted almost exclusively to the middle of Matthew:

Date	Gospel (Matthew)	Complementary first reading
June 22	10:24-39	Jeremiah 20:7-13
June 29	10:40-42	Jeremiah 28:5-9
July 6	11:16-19, 25-30	Zechariah 9:9-12
July 13	13:1-9, 18-23	Isaiah 55:10-13
July 20	13:24-30, 36-43	Isaiah 44:6-8
July 27	13:31-33, 44-52	1 Kings 3:5-12
August 3	14:13-21	Isaiah 55:1-5
August 10	14:22-33	1 Kings 19:9-18
August 17	15:[10-20] 21-28	Isaiah 56:1, 6-8
August 24	16:13-20	Isaiah 51:1-6
August 31	16:21-28	Jeremiah 15:15-21

You can see from this list that to be prepared to preach on Matthew through the summer months, preachers and worship leaders should at the very least sit down and read Matthew 10–16 as a whole to get a sense of the overall flow of this section. It would also be helpful to reread the whole Gospel of Matthew in one sitting, if time allows (assuming here that preachers and worship leaders took one time through the gospel at the very beginning of the church year).

A couple of notes. A Romans series runs straight through the summer and part of the fall. Although it is not the focus of our notes here, it is an excellent alternative preaching series to consider. The Old Testament readings that accompany the Matthew gospel readings are "complementary," selected to resonate with the gospel in some way. In the preceding chart, you can see how frequently the gospel pairs with prophetic texts, especially from Isaiah and Jeremiah. Even 1 Kings 19:9-18, though itself not a prophetic book, is a pericope from the life of Israel's "first" prophet.

It might be said that Matthew, of the gospels, is a particularly prophetic gospel. Although prophetic themes are not unique or exclusive to Matthew, they are especially emphasized. Think, for example, of the Sermon on the Mount, or Matthew 25. The kingdom of God theology implicit in much of Matthew, together with the strong emphasis on Jesus as the expected Messiah, ensures that the pairing of Matthew with readings from the Old Testament

prophets is appropriate and consonant. In addition to reading a good commentary on Matthew, preachers would do well to read a commentary on at least one of the prophets (such as Isaiah), or a general work on the voice of the prophets such as Abraham Joshua Heschel's *The Prophets,* or *Fortress Introduction to the Prophets* by Rodney Hutton (Fortress Press, 2004).

Especially fruitful for this summer season is to think about the literary genre of the Old Testament reading in comparison to the gospel. Many of the gospel readings are parables. How do parables compare to the voice of the prophets? Despite their differences in terms of literary genres, how do they complement and inform each other?

Liturgical Arts

Augsburg Fortress has been developing a new series: *Compass: Christian Explorations of Daily Living.* The series editor, David H. Jensen, describes it this way,

Everyday practices matter for Christian faith. Our ordinary routines—eating, cooking, working, walking, shopping, playing, and parenting—are responses to the life God gives to the world. Bodies, baths, meals, and households matter to Christian faith because God takes these everyday practices and materials as God's own: blessing, redeeming, and transforming them. This series considers everyday practices as sites for theological reflection. When we pay close attention to everyday practices, we can glimpse classical Christian themes— redemption, creation, and incarnation—in new light. The series does not attempt to apply classical doctrines to particular practices but to offer narratives of ordinary routines, explore how immersion in them affects Christian life in a global world, and imagine how practice might re-form theology and theology reform practice.

Titles thus far in the series include (paired with readings they might inform):

Listening to Popular Music	Jeremiah 20:7-13
Working	Matthew 11:25-30
Shopping	Matthew 13:44-52
Eating and Drinking	Isaiah 55:1-5
Dreaming	1 Kings 19:9-18
Parenting	Matthew 15:10-28
Traveling	Isaiah 56:1, 6-8
Clothing	Isaiah 51:1-6
Playing	Matthew 16:21-28

Reading the list of titles is itself an evocative exercise. It can enliven the imagination of worship planners as to the full extent to which everyday practices can indeed be the site for theological reflection. Worship leaders do well, especially in this long, extraordinary season, to weave these aspects of daily life into the worship practices of the church. They present an opportunity to explore how immersion in these practices affects worship life in a global world, and how the practices might re-form worship and worship reform practice.

Music

If the Alleluia is the portion of the liturgy appropriate to the season of Easter, the creed is a portion appropriate to extraordinary time. Pentecost and Trinity Sunday set the tone, and encourage continuing and ongoing reflection on the Trinity, or, better, trinitarian reflection on the life of worship and the life of the world. The confession of a creed encourages this practice.

The creed is typically spoken, but it can be sung. Danish Lutherans, for example, sing the creed weekly in worship. You can hear versions at www.dr.dk/radio/play-erseneste/radiogudstjenesten. Here are some other examples of sung creeds.

- Rich Mullin's contemporary setting "Creed" (www.youtube.com/watch?v=9LR2hFP1yb4).
- John Ylvisaker's "I Believe, I Do Believe" (www.ylvisaker.com).
- Gale Kramer's "Nicene Creed" (www.worship.ca/docs/ww_138_Sung_Nicene_Creed.pdf).
- Martin Luther's adaptation of the creed, "We all believe in one true God" (ELW 411).

- A chorale version of the Apostles' Creed that congregations can sing, based on the familiar tune BEACH SPRING (www.sheetmusicplus.com/title/Lord-I-Believe-The-Apostles-Creed/5903476).

Finally, some emerging churches set the speaking of the creed to various kinds of ambient background music, including didgeridoo, guitar, or even techno beats. Although these settings for the creed may not be appropriate for all settings, enough diversity has been listed here for most congregations to consider at least one of them.

Summer is a long season in the church calendar. It is an excellent time to vary the approach to music in worship. Consider at least some of these possibilities. First, go back through the musical selections for Advent, Christmas, Epiphany, Lent, and Easter, and ask what styles of music (or what types of listeners/singers) have been left out thus far that might receive better representation during the summer months. Has your community focused on international hymnody to the exclusion of favorite tunes written on North American soil? Have you sung only hymns and contemporary music from the twentieth century and nothing from the early church? Review where you have been, and then plan a strategy to celebrate an additional style of music during the summer months.

Holy Communion Setting Ten in *Evangelical Lutheran Worship* is particularly well suited to expanding hymn selections, because it is a hymn setting of the liturgy. Consider this option.

WORSHIP TEXTS FOR SUMMER

Confession and Forgiveness

All may make the sign of the cross, the sign marked at baptism, as the presiding minister begins.

Blessed be the holy Trinity, ✛ one God,
who forgives all our sin,
whose mercy endures forever.
Amen.

In the presence of God, who sees our hearts and our minds,
let us confess our sin.

Silence is kept for reflection.

God our strength,
we confess that we are captive to the power of sin
that dwells within us.
We put ourselves first and others last.
What we think will make us happy
leaves us longing for more.
Even when we want to do what is good,
we find ourselves doing the opposite.
Rescue us from death's grip on our lives,
and raise us up day by day,
that we may be alive to God in Christ Jesus.
Amen.

Sisters and brothers,
all have fallen short of the glory of God;
therefore we are justified by God's grace as a gift.
Nothing can separate us
from the love of God in ✛ Christ Jesus,
in whom we have forgiveness of sin, life, and salvation.
Amen.

Offering Prayer

God of mercy and grace,
the eyes of all wait upon you,
and you open your hand in blessing.
Fill us with good things at your table,
that we may come to the help of all in need,
through Jesus Christ, our redeemer and Lord.
Amen.

Invitation to Communion

Everyone who hungers, come to the table.
Eat what is good, that you may live.

Prayer after Communion

We thank you, Lord of heaven and earth,
that you have fed us in a way our hearts can understand,
with the saving body and blood of Jesus Christ.
Enliven us by your presence in this meal,
that we may be your presence in the world,
through Jesus Christ, our Savior and Lord.
Amen.

Sending of Communion

Gracious God,
loving all your family with a mother's tender care:
As you sent the angel to feed Elijah with heavenly bread,
assist those who set forth to share your word and sacrament
with those who are *sick, homebound, and imprisoned.*
In your love and care, nourish and strengthen
those who will receive this sacrament,
and give us all the comfort of your abiding presence
through the body and blood of your Son,
Jesus Christ, our Lord.
Amen.

Blessing

May God the sower
make you good and fertile soil.
May Christ the seed
bloom and grow in your words and actions.
May the fruitful Spirit
bring forth a bountiful yield in your lives.
God the Father, ☩ Son, and Holy Spirit
bless you now and forever.
Amen.

Dismissal

Go in peace. Serve the Lord.
Thanks be to God.

SEASONAL RITES FOR SUMMER

Travels, Trips, and Journeys
A Service of Word and Song for Summer

Summer often brings vacations, travels, and opportunities to step out of the busyness of our daily lives. We visit with family and friends, encounter new places and experiences, and enjoy rest and relaxation.

Scripture tells us of many travelers and journeys. Abraham set off with a promise and little else. The Israelites began their forty-year trek with excitement but soon complained and grumbled when the way became difficult. Mary and Joseph had little control over their destination or departure date. The magi rerouted their trip after visiting Herod. Jesus and his disciples wandered through towns and countryside. Paul ventured out with zeal and purpose, finding welcome in some places and hostility in others.

This service progresses through the stages of many journeys: Plans and Preparations, Setting Out, On the Road, When the Way Becomes Hard, and Joyful Homecomings. Whatever our travels of life, God remains our steadfast guide and companion.

This service could be used as a Service of the Word on a Sunday or weekday when members of the congregation are traveling to a synod or churchwide assembly, youth gathering, camp, retreat, or mission trip. Consider asking worshipers to bring a drawing, photograph, or memento from their own favorite trip to display in a gathering space. To extend the theme, worshipers could contribute a short writing to a newsletter or blog about a journey or travel experience that deepened their faith.

Gathering Song

Guide me ever, great Redeemer   ELW 618

Greeting

The God who created space and time,
journeyed with us in human form,
and travels with us still,
be with you all.
And also with you.

Prayer

Let us pray.
O God, our beginning and our end, you kept Abraham and Sarah in safety throughout the days of their pilgrimage, you led the children of Israel through the midst of the sea, and by a star you led the magi to the infant Jesus. Protect and guide us when we travel. Make our ways safe and our homecomings joyful, and bring us at last to our heavenly home, where you dwell in glory with our Lord Jesus Christ and the life-giving Holy Spirit, one God, now and forever.
Amen.

Psalmody: Psalm 139:1-12

PLANS AND PREPARATIONS

Reading: Ephesians 6:10-17 *Put on the armor of God*

A brief silence for prayer and meditation.

Dialogue and Prayer

What should we pack as we begin our journey?
What should we bring along?
The word of God to illumine our path.
The light of Christ to show us the way.
The gifts of the Spirit to share with those we meet.
The love of God to be our compass and guide.

Let us pray. God of our salvation,
you are the source of all our beginnings.
As we plan for our journeys,
strengthen us through your word.
Orient our lives toward Christ,
the bright Morning Star.
Send your Holy Spirit as our companion along the way.
In Jesus' name we pray. Amen.

Hymn: O Word of God incarnate   ELW 514

SETTING OUT

Reading: Genesis 12:1-9 *God calls Abraham and sends him out*

A brief silence for prayer and meditation.

Dialogue and Prayer

God called to Abraham:
"Go! Set out! And I will bless you."
God calls to us:
"Come! Feel the water on your head!
Hear the promise of new life.
Spread my word through all the world."

Let us pray. God of beginnings,
you called Abraham and Sarah,
leading them to unknown places.
In the waters of baptism, you claim us
and send us out as your children.
Wash us with your grace
and shower us with your Spirit,
so that we journey into the world
overflowing with your love.
In Jesus' name we pray. Amen.

Hymn: I'm going on a journey   ELW 446

ON THE ROAD

Reading: Mark 1:35-39 *Jesus travels and preaches throughout Galilee*

A brief silence for prayer and meditation.

Dialogue and Prayer

On the Galilean road, Jesus stopped to reflect and pray.
We, too, long for rest and a balm for our souls.
Seeing those in need, Jesus healed, taught, and fed.
We are called to live as servants,
loving our neighbors as ourselves.
Holding the children close, Jesus blessed them;
for to such as these the kingdom of heaven belongs.
On the road to Bethlehem,
the true light came into the world.
And the Word became flesh and lived among us,
and we have seen his glory.

Let us pray. God of incarnation,
you entered our world as a tiny baby
and you journey with us
through each stage of our lives.
Be with our children and youth
who are growing in your love.
Guide us all as the years and decades pass.
Send us in the light of your grace and truth.
In Jesus' name we pray. Amen.

Hymn: How small our span of life   ELW 636

WHEN THE WAY BECOMES HARD

Reading: 1 Kings 19:1-8 *Elijah in the wilderness*

A brief silence for prayer and meditation.

Dialogue and Prayer

We sit like Elijah alone in the wilderness.
"It is enough, O Lord."
The troubles of life overwhelm our spirits.
"It is enough, O Lord."
The way seems too dark; the valleys, too deep.
"It is enough, O Lord."
God rescues us from despair and grants us strength.
"You are beloved, my precious child."

Let us pray. God of our sorrows,
when we grieve a loved one, face an illness, or lose a job,
the road seems long, lonely, and treacherous.
Comfort us in our despair,
guide us through the wilderness,
and enfold us in your loving embrace.
Grant your mercy and peace
to all those in need this day.
In Jesus' name we pray. Amen.

Hymn: Jesus, still lead on   ELW 624

JOYFUL HOMECOMINGS

Reading: Philippians 3:12—4:1 *Pressing toward the heavenly goal*

A brief silence for prayer and meditation.

Dialogue and Prayer *(based on John 14–15)*

"Do not let your hearts be troubled."
We believe in God, we believe in Christ.
"I go to prepare a dwelling place for you."
You are the way, the truth, and the life.
"As the Father has loved me, so I have loved you."
Lord, we abide in your love.
"You know the way to the place where I am going."
Jesus, lead us in the path of your peace.

Let us pray. God of resurrection,
neither death nor life will separate us from your love.
Walk with us when our journeys lead toward home.
Strengthen us to follow the way of the cross
and bring us at last
into the joy of your heavenly kingdom.
In Jesus' name we pray. Amen.

Hymn: Just a closer walk with thee   ELW 697

Reflection

The reflection may include a brief commentary, teaching, or personal witness; non-biblical readings; interpretation through music or other art forms; or guided conversation among those present.

The reflection may conclude:
God's word is a lamp to our feet
and a light to our path.

Hymn

Lord Jesus, you shall be my song   ELW 808
I want to walk as a child of the light   ELW 815, WOV 649
God be with you   W&P 50

Creed

Prayers of Intercession

With the whole people of God in Christ Jesus, let us pray for the church, those in need, and all of God's creation.
A brief silence.
O God, we give you thanks for those who have traveled the path of faith: for Abraham and Sarah, who trusted in your promise; for Mary and Joseph, who acted according to your word; for Paul, who spread the good news of Christ. Lead us also in your way, your truth, and your life. God of the journey,
hear our prayer.
Watch over all who travel. Grant rest and joy for their spirits. Be with bus drivers, flight attendants, pilots, road crews, and all who strive to make our travels safe and our homecomings joyful. God of the journey,
hear our prayer.
You sent your Son into the messiness of our world. Smooth the pathways between people and nations, that together we will move toward your justice and peace. God of the journey,
hear our prayer.
You walk with us on all the paths of life. Be with those facing hardship this day: the grieving, the poor, the lost, the sick (*especially*). Hold them in the palm of your hand. God of the journey,
hear our prayer.
Here other intercessions may be offered.
Into your hands, gracious God, we commend all for whom we pray, trusting in your mercy; through Jesus Christ, our Savior.
Amen.

Peace

Offering

Offering Song

O Trinity of love and pow'r,
all trav'lers guard in danger's hour
from rock and tempest, fire and foe,
protect them wheresoe'er they go;
thus evermore shall rise to thee
glad hymns and praise from land and sea.
(ELW 756, st. 4)

Thanksgiving for the Word

Let us pray.
O God of justice and love, we give thanks to you that you
illumine our way through life with the words of your Son.
Give us the light we need, awaken us to the needs of others,
and at the end bring all the world to your feast; through
Jesus Christ, our Savior and Lord, to whom, with you and
the Holy Spirit, be honor and glory forever.
Amen.

Lord's Prayer

Blessing

The Lord watch over your going out and your coming in,
from this time forth forevermore.
In the name of the Father, + Son, and Holy Spirit.
Amen.

Sending Song

Lord, dismiss us with your blessing   ELW 545

Dismissal

Go in peace. Christ goes with you.
Thanks be to God.

June 15, 2014
The Holy Trinity
First Sunday after Pentecost

Though the word trinity *is not found in the scriptures, today's second reading includes the apostolic greeting that begins the liturgy: The grace of our Lord Jesus Christ, the love of God, and the communion of the Holy Spirit be with you all. In the gospel Jesus sends his disciples forth to baptize in the name of the Father, and the Son, and the Holy Spirit. More than a doctrine, the Trinity expresses the heart of our faith: we have experienced the God of creation made known in Jesus Christ and with us always through the Holy Spirit. We celebrate the mystery of the Holy Trinity in word and sacrament, as we profess the creed, and as we are sent into the world to bear witness to our faith.*

Prayer of the Day

Almighty Creator and ever-living God: we worship your glory, eternal Three-in-One, and we praise your power, majestic One-in-Three. Keep us steadfast in this faith, defend us in all adversity, and bring us at last into your presence, where you live in endless joy and love, Father, Son, and Holy Spirit, one God, now and forever.

or

God of heaven and earth, before the foundation of the universe and the beginning of time you are the triune God: Author of creation, eternal Word of salvation, life-giving Spirit of wisdom. Guide us to all truth by your Spirit, that we may proclaim all that Christ has revealed and rejoice in the glory he shares with us. Glory and praise to you, Father, Son, and Holy Spirit, now and forever.

Gospel Acclamation

Alleluia. Holy, holy, holy is the ׀ LORD of hosts;* God's glory fills ׀ the whole earth. *Alleluia.* (Isa. 6:3)

Readings and Psalm
Genesis 1:1—2:4a

This first creation story reached its current form during the crisis of the Babylonian exile of the people of Israel. God, not their captors' god Marduk, was responsible for their existence. God created women and men as rulers over creation, to preserve and protect it. God also rested on the seventh day, hallowing that day forever as the sabbath.

Psalm 8

How majestic is your name in all the earth! (Ps. 8:1)

2 Corinthians 13:11-13

Paul closes a challenging letter to the Corinthians with an appeal to Christian fellowship grounded in the triune harmony of Christ's grace, God's love, the Spirit's partnership.

Matthew 28:16-20

After his resurrection, Jesus summons his remaining disciples and commissions them to baptize and teach all nations in the name of Father, Son, and Holy Spirit.

Preface Holy Trinity

Color White

Prayers of Intercession

The prayers are prepared locally for each occasion. The following examples may be adapted or used as appropriate.

Strengthened by the Spirit who gives us words to speak and hearts that care, let us bring our hopes and needs to God who listens.

A brief silence.

Almighty God, you send your people into the world as beacons of light and hope. Bless the ministry of churches everywhere, that they take strength from your promise to be with us always. Let us pray.

Have mercy, O God.

With a word, you brought forth the majesty of creation: rolling hills, fragrant meadows, thundering seas. Inspire us to cherish and preserve them as stewards of your good land. Let us pray.

Have mercy, O God.

Be with those in the path of violence and war. Guard them against harm and give them a future with hope. Send your peace to the places that need it the most (*especially*). Let us pray.

Have mercy, O God.

Give strength to those bearing heavy burdens: addiction, mental illness, loneliness, and grief. Heal those whose bodies and souls are hurting (*especially*). Let us pray.

Have mercy, O God.

Enable this congregation to support all families. Strengthen fathers and all who nurture, so that they guide with wisdom, gentleness, and grace. Let us pray.

Have mercy, O God.

Here other intercessions may be offered.
We give thanks for all the saints who rest eternally in your loving care. Enliven our witness by their example. Let us pray.
Have mercy, O God.
We lift our prayers to you, God of mercy, confident that all things are in your hands. In Jesus' name we pray.
Amen.

Images in the Readings

If by Matthew's language of **Father, Son, and Holy Spirit** we imagine two males and a mist, the biblical imagery is failing us. God is beyond all things, dead and alive in Jesus Christ, and experienced in the assembly. Many contemporary hymns add to the doctrinal language other imagery in hopes of opening up the mystery of God. In Genesis 1, God is creator, word, and breath. In Paul, God is love, grace, and communion.

The rhetorically magnificent story of **creation** in Genesis 1 poetically describes the entire universe as originally perfect and formed by God to focus on human need. According to biblical scholars, Genesis 1 was written as praise of the God of Israel, rather than as revealed science, and according to Christian theology, God's creating continues throughout time, rather than being a single prehistoric event. Creation by God through the Word in the Spirit happens today. The post-exilic authors sought also to ground the Jewish Sabbath in God's resting on the seventh day. Christians have moved their holy day from Saturday rest to Sunday assembly so as to meet the Risen Christ on the day of the resurrection.

Ideas for the Day

◆ The gospel and second reading evoke themes of gathering and sending in the name of the triune God: the disciples gather with Jesus on the mountain and are sent to make disciples, and Paul's closing benediction to the Corinthians has become a standard liturgical greeting. The weekly rhythm of gathering and sending in Lutheran worship evokes images of inhaling and exhaling—each a different movement, but both equally necessary. Visualize the church "breathing" people in and out. For inspiration, search the Internet for time-lapse video of people breathing. Inhaling and exhaling could also connect with the image of God's "wind" or "spirit" as breath (Gen. 1:2).

◆ Around this time of year, many schools in North America hold graduation ceremonies called "commencement," which is both a sending and a new beginning. Consider how Jesus' words to his disciples are a kind of commencement and how Jesus' sending-out in the name of the triune God is different from a secular new beginning. Popular and timely commencement speeches are often posted on the Internet and could provide inspiration; check out those by Anne Lamott (at the University of California at Berkeley, 2003), Steve Jobs (Stanford University, 2005), and David McCullough Jr. (Wellesley High School, 2012).

◆ For some congregations summer means changes in the rhythm of gathering and sending. More leisure or travel means smaller Sunday gatherings, sometimes significant numbers of seasonal visitors, or camps or other special events where people gather in refreshing ways and are sent out newly equipped for mission. In the liturgy, consider adding a special greeting for visitors or a sending for travelers, highlighting the creative, redeeming, and sustaining work of God.

◆ The Greek word for the "communion" of the Holy Spirit also means "sharing in." As the Trinity highlights the inclusivity of God, this is a good day to highlight your community's efforts to share in word and sacrament ministry with all, including those who cannot gather for worship because of illness, caretaking responsibilities, or work. See Dietrich Bonhoeffer's book on Christian community, *Life Together*, for some powerful language about the privilege of gathering in community and the purposes for being sent from the community (Fortress Press, 2005).

Connections with the Liturgy

The standard greeting with which to begin the Sunday liturgy (*Evangelical Lutheran Worship*, p. 98) quotes 2 Corinthians: "The grace of our Lord Jesus Christ, the love of God, and the communion of the Holy Spirit be with you all." Christian worship begins not with the usual social hello of "Good morning." To some grieving and troubled worshipers and in times of great communal sorrow, it is not a "good morning." Rather, we are privileged to use the uniquely Christian greeting: we give to one another the grace, love, and communion of the triune God.

The "holy kiss" that Paul speaks of is the earliest version in the worshiping assembly of our greeting of peace.

Let the Children Come

The sign of the cross not only marks us as Christians, it also invokes the Trinity. A baptismal hymn begins, "I bind unto myself today the strong name of the Trinity by invocation of the same, the Three in One and One in Three" (ELW 450). Martin Luther encouraged each Christian to make the sign of the cross upon rising each morning. Have the children been taught to make this baptismal gesture across their bodies?

Assembly Song

Gathering

Rise, shine, you people! ELW 665, LBW 493

Holy, holy, holy, Lord God Almighty! ELW 413, LBW 165

Come, all you people ELW 819, TFF 138, WOV 717

Psalmody

Valentine, Timothy, SJ. "How Majestic Your Name." SAB, cant, assembly, gtr, kybd, opt inst. GIA G-4833.

Hopson, Hal H. "Psalm 8" from TP.

Bruxvoort-Colligan, Richard. "How Great Is Your Name (Psalm 8)" from SJ.

Hymn of the Day

Father most holy ELW 415, LBW 169 *CHRISTE SANCTORUM*

Mothering God, you gave me birth ELW 735, WOV 769 *NORWICH*

When long before time ELW 861, WOV 799
THE SINGER AND THE SONG

Offering

Come, join the dance of Trinity ELW 412

Thy strong word ELW 511, sts. 1, 6; LBW 233

Communion

O living Breath of God ELW 407, LLC 368

O God in heaven ELW 748

God loved the world ELW 323, LBW 292

Sending

Listen, God is calling ELW 513, TFF 130, WOV 712

Holy God, we praise your name ELW 414, LBW 535

Additional Assembly Songs

Oh, let the Son of God enfold you TFF 105

In the name of the Father TFF 142

⊕ Imakoma Yasushige. Japan. "Mikotoba o kudasai" from *Global Songs for Worship*. SATB, gtr. Faith Alive/Calvin Institute of Christian Worship. 9781592554423.

⊕ Loh, I-to, arr. Chinese melody. "For the Beauty of the Earth" from *Sound the Bamboo*. U. GIA G-6830.

✿ Brown, Brenton/Paul Baloche. "Our God Saves" from WT.

✿ Crowder, David/Matt Maher. "O Great God, Give Us Rest" from WT.

✿ Getty, Keith/Stuart Townend. "Benediction" from CCLI.

✿ Le, Tam/Matt Maher. "Gloria" from CCLI.

✿ Tomlin, Chris/David Crowder/John Henry Gower/Louie Giglio. "Joyous Light" from CCLI.

✿ Tomlin, Chris/Jesse Reeves/Ed Cash. "How Great Is Our God" from WT.

Music for the Day

Choral

Cherwien, David. "Blest God, All Glorious." SATB, bar, org, tpt, assembly. CPH 98-3146.

● Erickson, Richard. "When Long before Time." SATB, org. AFP 9780800656768.

Heim, Bret. "All Glory Be to God Alone." U, kybd, opt 2 vlns. CPH 98-3619.

Johnson, Ralph. "Creating God, Your Fingers Trace." 2 pt, pno. KJO 6366.

Children's Choir

Burkhardt, Michael. "Come, Let's Dance" from *Three Canonic Folksongs for Young Singers*. 2 pt/3 pt/4 pt, kybd. CG CGA863.

Carter, John. "How Excellent Is Your Name." 2 pt, pno. AFP 9780800674557.

Helgen, John. "Psalm 8" in *ChildrenSing Psalms*. U, kybd, hb, fc.

Petersen, Lynn. "We All Believe in One True God." U, desc, kybd, vln/C inst. GIA G-4926.

Keyboard / Instrumental

● Hobby, Robert A. "Christe Sanctorum" from *Six Preludes for the Church Year*. Org. MSM 10-716.

● Linneweber, Edie. "Norwich" from *Christ Is Near: Hymn Settings for the Church Pianist*. Pno. AFP 9781451401158.

Miller, Aaron David. "Holy, Holy, Holy, Lord God Almighty" from *Chorale Preludes for Piano in Traditional Styles*. Pno. AFP 9780800679033.

Post, Piet. "Fantasy on 'Holy, Holy, Holy.'" Org. PRE 163-00033.

Handbell

Mazzatenta, Michael. "Ancient Tribes" from *Southwestern Spirit Suite*. 3-5 oct, L2+. FTT 20127.

Page, Anna Laura. "Children of the Heavenly Father." 3-5 oct hb, opt 2 oct hc, L2+. BP HB264.

Thompson, Martha Lynn. "I Was There to Hear Your Borning Cry." 3-5 oct hb, opt 3-6 oct hc, opt vocal solo or narr, L2. CG CGB503.

Saturday, June 21

Onesimos Nesib, translator, evangelist, died 1931

Onesimos (oh-NESS-ee-mus neh-SEEB) was born into the Oromo people of Ethiopia. He was captured by slave traders and taken from his homeland to Eritrea, where he was bought, freed, and educated by Swedish missionaries. He translated the Bible into Oromo and returned to his homeland to preach the gospel. His tombstone includes a verse from Jeremiah 22:29, "O land, land, land, hear the word of the Lord!"

⊕ = global song
✿ = praise song
● = relates to hymn of the day

June 22, 2014
Time after Pentecost — Lectionary 12

Jeremiah knew the frustration of having his words rejected. Jesus declares that his words may not bring peace, but division. In baptism we are buried with Christ that we may walk in newness of life. As we take stands for the sake of justice and lose our lives for the sake of others, we need not be afraid. The hairs of our head are counted. In baptism we are marked with the cross of Christ forever.

Prayer of the Day

Teach us, good Lord God, to serve you as you deserve, to give and not to count the cost, to fight and not to heed the wounds, to toil and not to seek for rest, to labor and not to ask for reward, except that of knowing that we do your will, through Jesus Christ, our Savior and Lord.

Gospel Acclamation

Alleluia. Jesus says, The Spirit of the Lord will testify on ˡ my behalf,* and you also ˡ are to testify. *Alleluia.* (John 15:26, 27)

Readings and Psalm
Jeremiah 20:7-13

Jeremiah accuses God of forcing him into a ministry that brings him only contempt and persecution. Yet Jeremiah is confident that God will be a strong protector against his enemies and commits his life into God's hands.

Psalm 69:7-10 [11-15] 16-18

Answer me, O Lord, for your love is kind. (Ps. 69:16)

Romans 6:1b-11

In baptism we were incorporated into the reality of Christ's death. Our lives in the present are marked and shaped by his crucifixion, just as our lives in the future will be marked and shaped by his resurrection.

Matthew 10:24-39

Jesus warns his disciples that their ministry in his name will meet with opposition, requiring absolute trust in God and an unswerving commitment to their Lord.

Semicontinuous reading and psalm
Genesis 21:8-21

Unable to conceive a child, Sarah selected Hagar, her Egyptian maid, to be a surrogate mother. Though Hagar gave birth to Ishmael, Sarah subsequently gave birth to a son named Isaac, which led to Sarah's sending away of Hagar and Ishmael. God, however, heard Ishmael's cry and promised to make of him a great nation.

Psalm 86:1-10, 16-17

Have mercy on me; give your strength to your servant. (Ps. 86:16)

Preface   Sundays

Color   Green

Prayers of Intercession

The prayers are prepared locally for each occasion. The following examples may be adapted or used as appropriate.

Strengthened by the Spirit who gives us words to speak and hearts that care, let us bring our hopes and needs to God who listens.

A brief silence.

We pray for healing worship, that your love will fill our hearts through our songs and prayers and give us strength to spread your word. Lord, in your mercy,
hear our prayer.

We pray for healing growth, that this land you have made will continue to sustain life of all kinds—plants, animals, and people. Lord, in your mercy,
hear our prayer.

We pray for healing words among peoples and places where violence, mistrust, anger, and division reign. Send your Spirit to bring much-needed peace to our relationships and our world. Lord, in your mercy,
hear our prayer.

We pray for healing rest for those whose bodies and spirits are weary and in pain (*especially*). Surround them with your care and love. Lord, in your mercy,
hear our prayer.

We pray for healing time, when we can focus on you and your renewing love. Amidst our busy lives, help us to stop, focus, and rest in you. Lord, in your mercy,
hear our prayer.

Here other intercessions may be offered.

We pray for healing hope for those whose loved ones have died, and give thanks for the lives of those who have gone before us in faith. Lord, in your mercy,
hear our prayer.
We lift our prayers to you, God of mercy, confident that all things are in your hands. In Jesus' name we pray.
Amen.

Images in the Readings

God's care for **sparrows** calls us to trust in God, since Matthew states here and in chapter 7 (see Lectionary 8) that humans have more value than birds. Sparrows were among the cheapest birds sold in the markets of Matthew's time. Unfortunately, such biblical passages have been used to devalue God's creation, as if humans are the only creatures to receive divine blessing. Here Matthew states that God does indeed care for the sparrow.

Of course Matthew's description of the natural and married **family** experiencing hatred is disturbing. Matthew even assumes that discipleship will bring about such dissension. Pacifist Christians assert that Matthew's word about the **sword** is only metaphoric, but even as metaphor, it is a harsh word about the difficulties of the Christian life. In Paul's imagery, the Christian life requires our old self to be crucified, as if baptism aims the sword at oneself.

Matthew's words about a reversal of **slave and master** may sound benign to Americans who believe in equality, but such words would have sounded bizarre—like losing one's life to live—to citizens of a slave culture. Matthew is saying that cultural patterns may be totally inappropriate for those who follow Christ.

Ideas for the Day

◆   Today's gospel raises questions about how and why Christianity attracts new followers even when Christians are honest about the costs of discipleship. With visitors or new members, how does your community put into words both the costs and joys of discipleship? Gregg Levoy shares this perspective in his book *Callings: Finding and Following an Authentic Life*: "Jesus promised those who would follow him only three things, says writer Marty Babcock: 'That they would be absurdly happy, entirely fearless, and always in trouble'" (New York: Three Rivers Press, 1997). Read a longer excerpt, on "The Dignity of Daring," at www.gregglevoy.com/dignity_of_daring.html.

◆   Some Christians need help acknowledging Christ to others, especially if they don't come from an evangelistic background or if they are uncomfortable expressing their beliefs. *A Story Worth Sharing: Engaging Evangelism*, edited by Kelly A. Fryer, could start a fruitful conversation, especially the chapter "Sharing the Story Every Day," by Kirk Livingston (Augsburg Fortress, 2004).

◆   Martin Luther emphasized a daily dying to sin and rising to eternal life in personal practice. In addition to a corporate thanksgiving for baptism in worship, demonstrate one or more ways to observe a daily baptismal remembrance individually. A printed reminder of prayers, postures, or other suggestions could facilitate bringing the practice home. To complement many excellent Lutheran baptismal resources, Joan Huyser-Honig's article "Remembering Baptism: Living Wet" offers ideas for baptismal remembrance in worship and daily life. Find it at worship.calvin.edu/resources/ (click on Resource Library and search for Living Wet).

◆   In Christian tradition, the summer solstice is associated with John the Baptist, whose feast day is June 24. Not only does it fall six months before Christ's birth, but the now-decreasing daylight also reminded people of John's words about Jesus: "He must increase, but I must decrease" (John 3:30). The same image of decreasing daylight could reflect metaphorically on the decrease of ego in dying to sin and losing one's life for Jesus' sake.

Connections with the Liturgy

In the confession and forgiveness of the Sunday liturgy (*Evangelical Lutheran Worship*, pp. 94–96), one of the texts by which the presiding minister announces God's forgiveness cites today's second reading: "God, who is rich in mercy, loved us even when we were dead in sin, and made us alive together with Christ."

Many of the psalms that we sing resemble the reading from Jeremiah: we lament our situation before God, and then we praise God, even if our terrible situation remains. God is praised because God is God, not because we were relieved of our troubles.

Let the Children Come

During the time after Pentecost we hear stories about God's Word and Spirit moving through the work of the first disciples and beyond. As you enter into this season give kids a chance to tell their story. You may be surprised how they see God in the world around them. Ask questions like "What do you think makes God happy?" or "What makes God sad?" or "How does God care for us?" Create a journal, a scrapbook, a poster, or a video for the congregation to see the responses.

Assembly Song
Gathering

How firm a foundation   ELW 796, LBW 507
Give to our God immortal praise!   ELW 848, LBW 520
We are baptized in Christ Jesus   ELW 451, WOV 698

Psalmody

Bankson, Jeremy. "Psalm 69:7-10 [11-15], 16-18" from PCY, vol. 1.

Gelineau, Joseph or Michel Guimont. "Twelfth Sunday in Ordinary Time/A" from LP:W4.

Pavlechko, Thomas. "Psalm 86:1-10, 16-17" from SMP.

Hymn of the Day

Will you come and follow me   ELW 798, W&P 137   *KELVINGROVE*

Let us ever walk with Jesus   ELW 802, LBW 487
   LASSET UNS MIT JESU ZIEHEN

O God, my faithful God   ELW 806, LBW 504
   WAS FRAG ICH NACH DER WELT

Offering

O Jesus, I have promised   ELW 810, LBW 503

Take up your cross, the Savior said   ELW 667, LBW 398

Communion

Borning Cry   ELW 732, W&P 69, WOV 770

Have no fear, little flock   ELW 764, LBW 476

O Christ, your heart, compassionate   ELW 722

Sending

Let all things now living   ELW 881, LBW 557

Will you come and follow me   ELW 798, W&P 137

Additional Assembly Songs

Joys are flowing like a river   TFF 110

I'm going on a journey   ELW 446, TFF 115

⊕ Nyberg, Anders, arr. South African traditional. "Ewe, Thina/We Walk His Way" from *Two Songs of Hope and Healing from South Africa*. SATB. GIA G-7627.

⊕ Perera, Homero R. Argentina. "Tenemos esperanza" from *Tenemos esperanza: We Have Hope*. U, pno, gtr, perc. GBGMusik, General Board of Global Ministries, United Methodist Church.

✿ Brown, Brenton/Paul Baloche. "Hosanna (Praise Is Rising)" from WT.

✿ Cash, Ed/Matt Maher. "As It Is in Heaven" from WT.

✿ Crayenord, Case/Chris McClarney/Henk Pool/John Hartley/Michael Tyler/Miriam Webster. "Defender" from CCLI.

✿ Mooring, Jack/Leeland Mooring/Steve Wilson. "Sound of Melodies" from CCLI.

✿ Redman, Matt. "Mission's Flame" from WT.

✿ Smith, Martin/Nick Herbert/Tim Hughes. "Keep the Faith" from CCLI.

Music for the Day
Choral

Coleman, Gerald Patrick. "Christ Is with Me." 2 pt, kybd, C inst. CPH 98-3120.

Farlee, Robert Buckley. "To Christ Belong." SATB, org, fl, assembly. AFP 9781451420791.

Giamanco, Anthony. "Take Up Your Cross." 2 pt, pno. AFP 9780800678968.

Hopson, Hal. "His Eye Is on the Sparrow" from *He's Got the Whole World in His Hands: Three Sacred Solos for High Voice*. Sop solo, pno. MSM 40-500.

Roth, John. "Just a Drop of Living Water." Sop/Tenor solo, U/2 pt. CPH 98-3264.

Children's Choir

"Baptized in Water." ELW 456.

Coleman, Gerald Patrick. "Christ Is with Me." 2 pt, opt SATB, C inst, pno. CPH 98-3051.

Sleeth, Natalie. "Everywhere I Go." U/2 pt, kybd. CG CGA171.

Keyboard / Instrumental

• Cherwien, David. "Lasset uns mit Jesu ziehen" from *Organ Plus, Volume 2: Hymn Preludes for Organ and Instruments*. Org, inst. AFP 9780800678548.

Leavitt, John. "Go, My Children, with My Blessing" from *A Mighty Fortress: Sacred Reflections for Piano*. Pno. CPH 97-7254.

• Miller, Aaron David. "Kelvingrove" from *Organ Preludes on Folk Songs*. Org. AFP 9780800677572.

• Raabe, Nancy. "Lasset uns mit Jesu ziehen" from *Grace and Peace, Vol. 3: Hymn Portraits for Piano*. Pno. AFP 9780806696959.

Handbell

• Behnke, John. "Let Us Ever Walk With Jesus." 3 oct, L2. CPH 97-7106.

• Nelson, Susan. "Will You Come and Follow Me (The Summons)." 3-5 oct hb, opt C inst, L3. AGEHR AG35289.

Thompson, Martha Lynn. "O God, Our Faithful God (O God, Thou Faithful God)." 3-5 oct hb, opt 2 oct hc, opt C inst, opt vocal solo, L3. MSM 30-827.

Tuesday, June 24
John the Baptist

The birth and life of John the Baptist is celebrated exactly six months before Christmas Eve. For Christians in the Northern Hemisphere, these two dates are deeply symbolic. John said that he must decrease as Jesus increased. According to tradition, John was born as the days are longest and then steadily decrease, while Jesus was born as the days are shortest and then steadily increase. In many countries this day is celebrated with customs associated with the summer solstice.

⊕ = global song
✿ = praise song
● = relates to hymn of the day

Wednesday, June 25

Philipp Melanchthon, renewer of the church, died 1560

Though he died on April 19, Philipp Melanchthon (meh-LAHNK-ton) is commemorated today because of his connection with the Augsburg Confession. Colleague and co-reformer with Martin Luther, Melanchthon was a brilliant scholar, known as "the teacher of Germany." The University of Wittenberg hired him as its first professor of Greek, and there he became a friend of Luther. Melanchthon was a popular professor—even his classes at six in the morning had as many as six hundred students. As a reformer he was known for his conciliatory spirit and for finding areas of agreement with fellow Christians. He was never ordained.

Presentation of the Augsburg Confession, 1530

On this day in 1530 the German and Latin editions of the Augsburg Confession were presented to Emperor Charles of the Holy Roman Empire. The Augsburg Confession was written by Philipp Melanchthon and endorsed by Martin Luther and consists of a brief summary of points in which the reformers saw their teaching as either agreeing with or differing from that of the Roman Catholic Church of the time. In 1580 when the *Book of Concord* was drawn up, the unaltered Augsburg Confession was included as the principal Lutheran confession.

Friday, June 27

Cyril, Bishop of Alexandria, died 444

Remembered as an outstanding theologian as well as a contentious personality, Cyril defended the orthodox teachings about the person of Christ against Nestorius, bishop of Constantinople. Nestorius taught that the divine and human natures of Christ were entirely distinct, and therefore Mary could not be referred to as the *theotokos*, or bearer of God. This conflict, which also had roots in a rivalry for preeminence between Alexandria and Constantinople, involved all of the major Christian leaders of the time, including the patriarchs of Rome, Antioch, and Jerusalem, and finally also the emperor. In the end it was decided that Cyril's interpretation, that Christ's person included both divine and human natures, was correct.

Saturday, June 28

Irenaeus, Bishop of Lyons, died around 202

Irenaeus (ee-ren-AY-us) believed that the way to remain steadfast to the truth was to hold fast to the faith handed down from the apostles. He believed that only Matthew, Mark, Luke, and John were trustworthy gospels. Irenaeus was an opponent of gnosticism and its emphasis on dualism. As a result of his battles with the gnostics, he was one of the first to speak of the church as "catholic." By catholic he meant that local congregations did not exist by themselves but were linked to one another in the whole church. He also maintained that this church was not contained within any national boundaries. He argued that the church's message was for all people, in contrast to the gnostics and their emphasis on "secret knowledge."

June 29, 2014
Peter and Paul, Apostles

Today we celebrate two great figures of the early church, Peter and Paul, who represent the spread of the gospel to both Jews and Gentiles and, according to tradition, were martyred on this date. The witness of Peter and Paul inspires us as we seek ways to faithfully proclaim the gospel in our contemporary context.

Prayer of the Day

Almighty God, we praise you that your blessed apostles Peter and Paul glorified you by their martyrdoms. Grant that your church throughout the world may always be instructed by their teaching and example, be knit together in unity by your Spirit, and ever stand firm upon the one foundation who is Jesus Christ our Lord, for he lives and reigns with you and the Holy Spirit, one God, now and forever.

Gospel Acclamation

Alleluia. This Jesus | God raised up,* and of that all of | us are witnesses. *Alleluia.* (Acts 2:32)

Readings and Psalm

Acts 12:1-11

King Herod had James killed and had Peter put in prison, under heavy guard. In what Peter first believes is only a vision, an angel leads him past unseeing guards, out of the prison, and to freedom.

Psalm 87:1-3, 5-7

Glorious things are spoken of you, O city of our God. (Ps. 87:3)

2 Timothy 4:6-8, 17-18

Paul has faithfully persevered in the mission the Lord had given to him. Near life's end he rests in the promise of eternal life, confident that the Lord who has rescued him in the past will bring him into the heavenly kingdom.

John 21:15-19

Jesus invites Simon Peter to declare his love for him three times, in a manner reminiscent of the three times that Peter earlier denied Christ. Jesus commissions him to feed his sheep and predicts that he will die as a martyr for God.

Preface   Apostles

Color   Scarlet *or* Red

Prayers of Intercession

The prayers are prepared locally for each occasion. The following examples may be adapted or used as appropriate.

Strengthened by the Spirit who gives us words to speak and hearts that care, let us bring our hopes and needs to God who listens.

A brief silence.

For those who endure suffering and hardship for the sake of the gospel, that they be strengthened for their courageous witness. Let us pray.

Have mercy, O God.

For the marvel of all living things that inhabit our planet, that we will preserve and protect the common life we share with all creation. Let us pray.

Have mercy, O God.

For the nations of the world, that despite differences of color, creed, and custom, we live in peace; and for wisdom for all world leaders. Let us pray.

Have mercy, O God.

For those who struggle with doubt, despair, and the search for meaning, that they bring their questions and find their answers in you. Let us pray.

Have mercy, O God.

For all who long for Christian community, and for the people in this congregation who with their hospitality and caring provide it. Let us pray.

Have mercy, O God.

Here other intercessions may be offered.

With thanksgiving for the saints who have kept the faith and now rest in you (*especially the apostles Peter and Paul*), and for courage to run the race set before us. Let us pray.

Have mercy, O God.

We lift our prayers to you, God of mercy, confident that all things are in your hands. In Jesus' name we pray.

Amen.

Images in the Readings

The image of believers as **lambs** and **sheep** fits with the biblical imagery of God and of Christ as shepherd. The word "pastor" means shepherd. Counter to much in current Christian mentality, here as in many places in the Scriptures the faith is a communal experience. Even the single lost sheep of Luke is brought back to the fold.

Luke's account of this escape of Peter from prison involves an **angel**. An angel is a messenger of the will and word of God; in the Old Testament, angels are understood as extensions of God, as the way that humans can experience God. The tradition of art has not helped in our mental pictures of these perfect beings that in ways mysterious connect us with God. In this story, the angel enacts the will of God: to free Peter from death at this time.

The passage about Paul's death uses one metaphor after another: the good fight, the race, the crown, the judge, the lion's mouth, the heavenly kingdom. A metaphor that is less accessible to many worshipers comes from pagan religious language: a **libation** was wine or oil poured out on the ground in offering to a deity at a temple or shrine or during a formal dinner. Christians can imagine their entire lives as libations, goodness poured out for others in praise of God.

Ideas for the Day

◆ Learning to follow God in Christ Jesus so deeply transformed both Peter and Paul that even their names were changed. In powerfully sparse language, the African American spiritual "Changed Mah Name" tells the story of call and sacrifice threaded throughout this day's texts: "I tol' Jesus it would be alright if He changed mah name / Jesus tol' me I would have to live humble if He changed mah name / Jesus tol' me that the world would be 'gainst me if He changed mah name / But I tol' Jesus it would be alright if He changed mah name." For a new choral setting of this spiritual see "Changed Mah Name" by Larry Christensen (MorningStar Music, 2010).

◆ In the final scene of the epic Harry Potter novels and movies, Harry tells his son, Albus Severus Potter: ". . . you were named after two headmasters of Hogwarts. One of them was a Slytherin and he was probably the bravest man I ever knew." Like Peter and Paul (who, respectively, denied Jesus on the night of his death and persecuted the early church), Albus Dumbledore and Severus Snape made morally questionable choices, yet died in service of the common good. These popular, iconic characters provide an entry point for talking with children about how God calls flawed and wounded people to lead the church for the sake of the world.

◆ Remembered as leaders of the early church, Peter and Paul's true brilliance lay in knowing who to follow. For a pithy, yet profound, lesson on the significance of being the first followers of a visionary leader, check out the YouTube video "First Follower: Leadership Lessons from Dancing Guy," which has been viewed almost two million times. In just three minutes the video illustrates how a movement happens, reminding us that "the best way to make a

movement, if you really care, is to courageously follow and show others how to follow."

Connections with the Liturgy

The conclusion of the Lord's Prayer echoes the last verse of the second reading: To God be the glory forever and ever. For Christians, *glory* is a double word, denoting both the divine splendor of the Almighty and the "pouring out" of the blood of Jesus on the cross.

Let the Children Come

An apostle is one who is sent out by Jesus to bring messages to the world. Invite kids to share in worship a song they have learned in Sunday school or VBS. Could the singing be recorded or videotaped to share with homebound members later?

Assembly Song

Gathering

Lift high the cross   ELW 660, LBW 377
For all the saints   ELW 422, LBW 174
Holy God, we praise your name   ELW 414, LBW 535

Psalmody

Farlee, Robert Buckley. "Psalm 87:1-3, 5-7" from PWC.
Goss, John. "Psalm 87" from *Anglican Chant Psalter*. Church Publishing Corp.
"Glorious Things of You Are Spoken." ELW 647.

Hymn of the Day

By all your saints   ELW 420, LBW 177   KING'S LYNN
Faith of our fathers   ELW 812, LBW 500   ST. CATHERINE
Glorious things of you are spoken   ELW 647   BLAENWERN
   LBW 358   AUSTRIA

Offering

Come, we that love the Lord   ELW 625, TFF 135, WOV 742
Lord Jesus, you shall be my song   ELW 808

Communion

Where cross the crowded ways of life   ELW 719, LBW 429
There is a balm in Gilead   ELW 614, TFF 185, WOV 737
O God in heaven   ELW 748

Sending

Ye watchers and ye holy ones   ELW 424, LBW 175
Bless now, O God, the journey   ELW 326

Additional Assembly Songs

I shall not be moved   TFF 147
Keep the faith   DH 98

⊕ Entre el vaivén de la ciudad/Where cross the crowded ways of life
   LLC 513

⊕ Bambelela SP 1

✿ Houston, Joel/Matt Crocker. "Search My Heart" from WT.

✿ Lang, Braden/Joel Davies. "More than Anything" from CCLI.

✿ Powell, Mac/Trevor Morgan. "How Great" from CCLI.

✿ Rea, Jonathan/Keith Getty. "God of Grace" from CCLI.

✿ Redman, Matt/Beth Redman. "Let My Words Be Few" from WT.

✿ Townend, Stuart/Simon Brading. "Christ Be in My Waking" from WT.

Music for the Day
Choral

Cherwien, David. "Give Me Jesus" from *To God Will I Sing: A Collection of Solos for the Church Year.* MH solo, kybd. AFP 9780800674335.

Giamanco, Anthony. "Take Up Your Cross." 2 pt, pno. AFP 9780800678968.

Johnson, David. "Souls of the Righteous" from *To God Will I Sing: A Collection of Solos for the Church Year.* MH solo, kybd. AFP 9780800674335.

Keesecker, Thomas. "In Our Day of Thanksgiving" from *The New Gloria Deo, Vol. 2.* SAB, pno. AFP 9781451424133.

Martinson, Joel. "By All Your Saints." 2 pt mxd, org. AFP 9780800651602.

Schack, David. "The Lord Is My Shepherd" from *To God Will I Sing: A Collection of Solos for the Church Year.* MH solo, kybd. AFP 9780800674335.

Children's Choir

Liebergen, Patrick. "Come Follow Me Forever." 2 pt, kybd. GIA G-5387.

Organ, Anne Krentz. "Follow Jesus." 2 pt, kybd. AFP 9780800677428.

Sleeth, Natalie. "If You Love Me." U, opt hb, opt glock/xyl. LS 147.

Keyboard / Instrumental

● Callahan, Charles. "Faith of Our Fathers" from *Six Meditations on English Hymn Tunes.* Org. CPH 97-6189.

Miller, Aaron David. "The Church of Christ, in Every Age" from *Chorale Preludes for Piano in Traditional Styles.* Pno. AFP 9780800679033.

● Powell, Robert. "Glorious Things of You Are Spoken" from *Rejoice, Give Thanks, and Sing: Hymn Preludes for Organ.* Org. AFP 9780806698151.

● Sullivan, Christine. "By All Your Saints" from *In Heaven Above: Piano Music for Funerals and Memorials.* Pno. AFP 9781451401912.

Handbell

● Eithun, Sandra. "Glorious Things of Thee Are Spoken." 3-6 oct hb, opt 3-5 oct hc, L2. SF 286583.

● Glasgow, Michael. "Faith of the Saints." 3-7 oct hb, opt tpt, L2+. LOR 20/1614L.

● McKechnie, D. Linda. "Resounding Alleluias." 3-5 oct hb, L3. CG CGB559. Full score with opt C inst, opt B-flat inst, opt org/kybd. CG CGB558. Opt SATB choir. CG CGA1141.

⊕ = global song
✿ = praise song
● = relates to hymn of the day

June 29, 2014
Time after Pentecost — Lectionary 13

The welcome of baptism is for all God's children. This baptismal gift sets us free from the power of sin and death. In today's gospel, Christ promises that the disciple who gives a cup of cold water to the little ones serves Christ himself. From worship we are sent on our baptismal mission: to serve the little ones of this world and to be a sign of God's merciful welcome.

Prayer of the Day

O God, you direct our lives by your grace, and your words of justice and mercy reshape the world. Mold us into a people who welcome your word and serve one another, through Jesus Christ, our Savior and Lord.

Gospel Acclamation

Alleluia. You are a chosen race, a royal priesthood, a ˈ holy nation,* in order that you may proclaim the mighty acts of the one who called you out of darkness into his ˈ marvelous light. *Alleluia.* (1 Peter 2:9)

Readings and Psalm
Jeremiah 28:5-9

Through a symbolic action, Jeremiah insisted that Judah and all the surrounding nations should submit to the king of Babylon. Hananiah contradicted Jeremiah, who in reply insisted that Hananiah's rosy prediction should not be believed until it came true. God confirmed the word of Jeremiah and sentenced the false prophet Hananiah to death (vv. 16-17).

Psalm 89:1-4, 15-18

Your love, O LORD, forever will I sing. (Ps. 89:1)

Romans 6:12-23

Sin is an enslaving power that motivates us to live self-serving, disobedient lives. Sin's final payoff is death. We, however, have been set free from sin's slavery to live obediently under God's grace, whose end is the free gift of eternal life.

Matthew 10:40-42

When Jesus sends his disciples out as missionaries, he warns them of persecution and hardships they will face. He also promises to reward any who aid his followers and support their ministry.

Semicontinuous reading and psalm
Genesis 22:1-14

Abraham was prepared to obey God's command in the midst of extreme contradiction: the child to be sacrificed is the very child through whom Abraham is to receive descendants. God acknowledged Abraham's obedient faith, and Abraham offered a ram in the place of his son Isaac.

Psalm 13

I trust in your unfailing love, O LORD. (Ps. 13:5)

Preface   Sundays

Color   Green

Prayers of Intercession

The prayers are prepared locally for each occasion. The following examples may be adapted or used as appropriate.

Strengthened by the Spirit who gives us words to speak and hearts that care, let us bring our hopes and needs to God who listens.

A brief silence.

Fill your church with bold witnesses who will work for justice, serve with compassion, share your love, and spread the gospel. Lord, in your mercy,

hear our prayer.

Pour out your Spirit on those without access to fresh water, and on those who dig wells to provide it for them, that they may be refreshed. Lord, in your mercy,

hear our prayer.

Stir in the hearts of those who thirst for justice, that they bring peace, speak out against oppression, and preserve human dignity across the globe. Lord, in your mercy,

hear our prayer.

Make families everywhere be places of safety, encouragement, and love. Protect and uphold healthy relationships between husbands and wives, parents and children, friends and neighbors, and all your people. Lord, in your mercy,

hear our prayer.

Wherever there is brokenness, bring healing. Bind up our wounds, teach us compassion, and dry our tears. Be especially with those we name now. (*Pause*) Give them comfort, reconciliation, and hope. Lord, in your mercy,
hear our prayer.
Here other intercessions may be offered.
Thank you for those who through their words and deeds have passed on the faith from one generation to the next (*especially the apostles Peter and Paul*). Lord, in your mercy,
hear our prayer.
We lift our prayers to you, God of mercy, confident that all things are in your hands. In Jesus' name we pray.
Amen.

Images in the Readings

Both of the two primary images in today's readings are somewhat alien to us. In the Bible, a true **prophet** is not a fortune teller or a court appointee, but rather the mouthpiece of God, proclaiming not what will be, but what is. For Christians, the preeminent prophet is Christ, whose words of God are spoken through the scriptures and in the bread and wine. The words are always double-sided, attending to both human sin and divine mercy—what Lutherans have called "law and gospel."

The idea in a **slave** economy is that everyone is born into a lifelong place in a hierarchy in which each obeys those who are above and cares for those who are below. Persons could not choose or alter their place in the hierarchy, and many Christians taught that God was responsible for who was placed where in this ordering of obedience. Despite our resistance to this idea, Paul writes that we are all born slaves of sin. The freedom of our will comes only through baptism, administered in many denominations even to infants, transferring our allegiance over to God and the neighbor. We are enslaved to God—in our culture, not an attractive suggestion.

Ideas for the Day

◆ Both Jeremiah and Matthew recognize that a prophet's words are not always well received. The American poet Walt Whitman sets that awareness with artful words in the fifth stanza of his poem "Song of the Open Road," which closes with the lines: "I will scatter myself among men and women as I go, / I will toss a new gladness and roughness among them, / Whoever denies me it shall not trouble me, / Whoever accepts me he or she shall be blessed and shall bless me."

◆ The worldview from which Paul writes to the Romans, in which a significant percentage of the population were slaves to someone, is jarring and repugnant to most modern listeners. In a society in which personal freedom is assumed, invite the assembly to reflect on their national identity. As

with slavery in Paul's time, today it is taken as normal that a person is automatically a citizen of the nation within whose boundaries he or she is born. Read through this interpretive lens, Paul is challenging us to renounce the manner of living common in the many "nations" we inhabit that lead to death, and to claim our citizenship in the "nation" of God, which promises eternal life to all its citizens.

◆ "One of the most remarkable stories I've heard of Christian hospitality to those who move around in search of survival and a better life is one telling of the 'water ministry' that groups of mostly Latina women carry out at the borders," writes the Rev. Dr. Nelson Rivera, in "On Immigration and the Immigrant Other" (*Journal of Lutheran Ethics*, Nov. 2008). The call to hospitality in Matthew's gospel speaks to acceptance not only of the message but also the messenger. In the world of the early church, public accommodations were not only expensive but unsafe. In a hot, dry climate a cup of cold water was truly a welcome source of relief. The same remains true today for those attempting the dangerous crossing at the southern border of the United States.

Connections with the Liturgy

Each Sunday, after the first and second readings, the lector calls out, "The word of the Lord" or "Word of God, word of life." We all respond, "Thanks be to God," even when the word has been a hard one to hear. Jeremiah and Matthew invite us to welcome the true words proclaimed by a prophet sent by God, and in the liturgy the church acclaims that the Bible is this true word and the lector has indeed been sent by God to proclaim the word of life.

Let the Children Come

It is the practice in some congregations to invite noncommuning children to receive a blessing while older siblings or parents receive communion. What is the motivation for such a practice? How does the child perceive the invitation to come to the table where he or she will *not* receive the bread and cup? Are noncommuning older children and adults also invited to receive a blessing at the altar? And, what is the purpose of the blessing extended to all at the end of the liturgy?

Assembly Song
Gathering

To be your presence ELW 546
The church of Christ, in every age ELW 729, LBW 433
God is here! ELW 526, WOV 719

Psalmody

Guimont, Michel. "Psalm 89" from PRCL.
Ogden, David. "I Will Sing" from PS1.

Duncan, Norah IV. "Thirteenth Sunday in Ordinary Time/A" from LP:LG.

Haugen, Marty. "Psalm 13" from PSCY.

Hymn of the Day

By all your saints   ELW 420, LBW 177   *KING'S LYNN*

In Christ called to baptize   ELW 575   *ST. DENIO*

All Are Welcome   ELW 641   *TWO OAKS*

Offering

Where cross the crowded ways of life   ELW 719, LBW 429

Just as I am, without one plea   ELW 592, LBW 296

Communion

As we gather at your table   ELW 522

Behold, how pleasant   ELW 649, LLC 468

O God in heaven   ELW 748

Sending

Let us ever walk with Jesus   ELW 802, LBW 487

Lord of glory, you have bought us   ELW 707, LBW 424

Additional Assembly Songs

Glory, glory, hallelujah!   TFF 148

⊕ Mirad cuán bueno/Behold, how good and delightful   LLC 475

⊕ Bell, John. "The Love of God Comes Close" from *Love and Anger: Songs of Lively Faith and Social Justice*. U. GIA G-4947.

⊕ Martinez, Salvador T. Philippines. "Let Heaven Your Wonders Proclaim" from *Sent by the Lord: Songs of the World Church, Vol 2*. U. GIA G-3740.

✤ Assad, Audrey/Chris Tomlin/Matt Maher. "You Revive Me" from CCLI.

✤ Fellingham, Lou/Mike Busbee/Nathan Fellingham. "Build This House" from CCLI.

✤ Ingram, Jason/Robby Seay. "Kingdom and a King" from WT.

✤ Lavik, Jadon/Marc Byrd/Steve Hindalong. "Hear Our Song" from CCLI.

✤ McCloghry, Jill. "We the Redeemed" from WT.

✤ Tomlin, Chris/Jason Ingram/Rueben Morgan. "I Will Follow" from WT.

Music for the Day

Choral

Burkhardt, Michael. "The Lord Now Sends Us Forth." 2 pt mxd, pno, perc, opt assembly. MSM 50-5412.

Dake, Kenneth. "God Is Here." SATB, org. MSM 50-8960.

Haugen, Marty. "All Are Welcome." SATB, kybd, 2 ww/br qrt, timp. GIA G-4166.

Martinson, Joel. "By All Your Saints." 2 pt mxd, org. AFP 9780800651602.

Scott, K. Lee. "As We Gather at Your Table." SAB, org. AFP 9780800678081.

Children's Choir

Beall, Mary Kay, John Carter. "We Are Called to Be His Servants." U/2 pt, pno. AFP 9780800675455.

Dvořák, Antonin. "I Will Sing New Songs of Gladness" in *A Third Morning Star Choir Book*. U, kybd. CPH 97-4972.

Glover, Rob. "Embrace My Way and Cross." U, kybd/gtr. GIA G-4594.

Keyboard / Instrumental

● Callahan, Charles. "Postlude on 'St. Denio'" from *The Rejoicing: A Postlude Collection for Organ*. Org. MSM 10-505.

● Schmoltze, Ron. "Two Oaks" from *A Song in the Journey: New and Old Tunes for Organ*. Org. AFP 9780800679026.

● Shaw, Timothy. "St. Denio" from *Great Hymns of Faith for the Church Pianist*. AFP 9780800621674.

● Sullivan, Christine. "By All Your Saints" from *In Heaven Above: Piano Music for Funerals and Memorials*. Pno. AFP 9781451401912.

Handbell

● Mallory, Ron. "Immortal, Invisible, God Only Wise." 3-5 oct, L2+. MSM 30-720.

● McAninch, Diane. "Prelude on 'All Are Welcome.'" 3-5 oct hb, opt 3 oct hc, opt fl, L3. GIA G-7083.

Waugh, Timothy. "For All the Saints." 3 or 5 oct hb, opt 2 oct hc, L2. CPH 97-7317.

Tuesday, July 1

Catherine Winkworth, died 1878; John Mason Neale, died 1866; hymn translators

Neale was an English priest associated with the movement for church renewal at Cambridge. Winkworth lived most of her life in Manchester, where she was involved in promoting women's rights. These two hymnwriters translated many hymn texts into English. Catherine Winkworth devoted herself to the translation of German hymns, nineteen of which are included in *Evangelical Lutheran Worship*; the fourteen hymn translations of John Mason Neale in the collection represent his specialization in ancient Latin and Greek hymns.

⊕ = global song
✤ = praise song
● = relates to hymn of the day

sundays and seasons

Order Now
for 2015—Year B

Sundays and Seasons 2015—Year B

978-1-4514-2569-7 ....$39.00
(2 or more $32.00 ea.)

Worship Planning Calendar 2015—Year B

The perfect complement to *Sundays and Seasons*. Spiral-bound, this is both an appointment calendar and a workbook for preparing worship. Contains daily lectionary reading citations.

978-1-4514-2570-3 ....$22.00

SAVE 15%—2015 Combo Pack
Sundays and Seasons & Worship Planning Calendar

Sundays and Seasons and the Worship Planning Calendar work together to save you time and provide all you need to prepare engaging worship.

ED024247 ....$51.00
($61.00 if purchased separately)

SundaysandSeasons.com

SundaysandSeasons.com saves you time and effort by providing content and tools to plan worship flexibly and easily for your weekly bulletin or projection. Includes content from all ELCA worship volumes, clip-art, NRSV Bible, children's bulletins, and more!

Visit **sundaysandseasons.com** for more information.

Words for Worship 2015—Year B

This CD-ROM contains texts and graphical files with content from *Evangelical Lutheran Worship*. Also includes week-to-week elements from *Lectionary for Worship, Year B; Sundays and Seasons 2015*; and *Psalter for Worship Year B,* Evangelical Lutheran Worship edition.

978-1-4514-2574-1 ....$199.00

Worship Planning Resources 2015 Year B Order Form

To order by mail, detach, fold, and seal your completed card. Please be sure to attach postage. You can also order by calling 1-800-328-4648, faxing 1-800-722-7766, or visiting our online store at augsburgfortress.org.

SHIP TO _____

Address _____

City _____

State_____ Zip _____

Phone _____

E-mail _____

BILL TO _____

Address _____

City _____

State_____ Zip _____

Phone _____

METHOD OF PAYMENT *(select one)*

AF Account #_____

Credit Card #_____

Exp. Date_____ *Card must be valid through Sept. 2013. Products ship Aug. 2013.*

Signature_____
Signature required on all credit card orders.

Sundays and Seasons 2015
QTY: _____ 978-1-4514-2569-7 ....$39.00*
QTY: _____ SUNSEASONS ....Standing Order

Worship Planning Calendar 2015
QTY: _____ 978-1-4514-2570-3 ....$22.00*
QTY: _____ WRSHPPLNCL ....Standing Order

Combo Pack 2015
QTY: _____ ED024247 ....$51.00*
QTY: _____ SUNSEAWPC ....Standing Order

Words for Worship 2015
QTY: _____ 978-1-4514-2574-1 ....$199.00*

Calendar of Word and Season 2015
QTY: _____ 978-1-4514-2576-5 ....$10.95*
QTY: _____ CALWRDSESN ....Standing Order

Church Year Calendar 2015
QTY: _____ 978-1-4514-2571-0 ....$1.95*

Church Year Calendar 2015 PDF
ONLINE 978-1-4514-2572-7 ....$9.96

Bread for the Day 2015
QTY: _____ 978-1-4514-2573-4 ....$8.95*

Ritual Lectionary, Year B
QTY: _____ 978-0-8066-5611-3 ....$115.00*

Study Edition Lectionary, Year B
QTY: _____ 978-0-8066-5612-0 ....$27.50*

The RCL: 20th Anniversary Annotated Edition
QTY: _____ 978-1-4514-3603-7 ....$30.00*

AUGSBURG FORTRESS   PRJ024624

Prices do not include shipping. Prices valid through April 1, 2014.

Detach this card, fold it in half here, and seal the edges.

sundays and seasons

Order Now
for 2015—Year B

Great gifts and useful resources for living the church's year!

Bread for the Day 2015

Bible readings and prayers for the full year. Follows the daily lectionary. Quantity discounts available.

978-1-4514-2573-4

Quantity	1–9	10–99	100–299	300–499	500-999	1,000+
Price	$8.95	$7.16	$6.71	$6.27	$5.37	$4.48

Calendar of Word and Season 2015—Year B

Full-color wall calendar with room for adding family and church activities. Features beautiful art each month and identifies church festivals, national holidays, the color of the day, and Revised Common Lectionary citations. 8³/₈" x 10⁷/₈". Spiral-bound and punched for hanging.

978-1-4514-2576-5

Quantity	1–11	12–49	50–99	100–499	500+
Price	$10.95	$4.50	$3.50	$3.00	$2.50

Church Year Calendar 2015—Year B

Provides dates, lectionary readings, hymn of the day, and the liturgical color for each Sunday and festival. The ideal time-saver for all who live by the liturgical year. Two-sided. 11" x 8½".

978-1-4514-2571-0

Quantity	1–11	12–99	100+
Price	$1.95	$0.83	$0.75

Lectionary for Worship, Ritual Edition—Year B
978-0-8066-5611-3 .... *$115.00*

Lectionary for Worship, Study Edition—Year B
978-0-8066-5612-0 .... *$27.50*

The Revised Common Lectionary: 20th Anniversary Annotated Edition
978-1-4514-3603-7 .... *$30.00*

Shipping and Handling

Prices and Product Availability are subject to change without notice.

Sales Tax: Exempt customers must provide Augsburg Fortress with a copy of their state-issued exemption certificate prior to purchase. Customers without tax-exempt status must add applicable state/province and local sales tax for their area. Canadian customers will be charged GST.

Shipping Charges are additional on all orders. U.S. and Canadian orders (except U.S. cash orders) are assessed actual shipping charges based on standard group rates. Additional shipping charges are assessed for expedited service requests and international shipments.

Return Policy: With proof of purchase, non-dated, in print product in saleable condition may be returned for credit. Please call customer service at 1-800-328-4648 (U.S.) or 1-800-265-6397 (Canada) for assistance if you receive items that are damaged, defective, or were shipped in error. Specific return restrictions apply to some product lines. Please contact us prior to returning a special order item or item shipped directly from the manufacturer. Send U.S. order returns by a secure, prepaid, traceable method to the Augsburg Fortress Distribution Center, 4001 Gantz Road, Suite E., Grove City, Ohio 43123-1891. Canadian orders may be returned to Augsburg Fortress Canadian Distribution Center, 500 Trillium Drive, Box 9940, Kitchener, Ontario N2G 4Y4.

Thursday, July 3

Thomas, Apostle

Thomas is perhaps best remembered as "Doubting Thomas." But alongside this doubt, the Gospel of John shows Thomas as fiercely loyal: "Let us also go, that we may die with him" (John 11:16). And John's gospel shows

Thomas moving from doubt to deep faith. Thomas makes one of the strongest confessions of faith in the New Testament, "My Lord and my God!" (John 20:28). From this confession of faith, ancient stories tell of Thomas's missionary work to India, where Christian communities were flourishing a thousand years before the arrival of sixteenth-century missionaries.

July 6, 2014

Time after Pentecost — Lectionary 14

The mystery of God's ways is sometimes hidden from the wise and intelligent. Jesus associates with the lowly and outcast. Like Paul, we struggle with our own selfish desires and seek God's mercy and forgiveness. We gather to be refreshed by Christ's invitation: "Come to me, all you that are weary." Gathered around word, water, and meal, we find rest for our souls.

Prayer of the Day

You are great, O God, and greatly to be praised. You have made us for yourself, and our hearts are restless until they rest in you. Grant that we may believe in you, call upon you, know you, and serve you, through your Son, Jesus Christ, our Savior and Lord.

Gospel Acclamation

Alleluia. Blessed are you, Lord of ¹ heav'n and earth;* you have revealed these ¹ things to infants. *Alleluia.* (Matt. 11:25)

Readings and Psalm

Zechariah 9:9-12

The coming messianic king will inaugurate an era of disarmament and prosperity. Because of God's covenant with Israel, they are designated as "prisoners of hope."

Psalm 145:8-14

The Lord is gracious and full of compassion. (Ps. 145:8)

Romans 7:15-25a

Life enslaved under sin is a catch-22 existence in which we know good but do not do it and do things we know to be bad. Through Jesus Christ, God has set us free from such a futile existence.

Matthew 11:16-19, 25-30

Jesus chides people who find fault with both his ministry and that of John the Baptist. He thanks God that wisdom

and intelligence are not needed to receive what God has to offer.

Semicontinuous reading and psalm

Genesis 24:34-38, 42-49, 58-67

The marriage of Isaac and Rebekah helped to fulfill God's promise that Abraham and Sarah would become the ancestors of many nations. While her family urged delay, Rebekah eagerly set out to meet Isaac.

Psalm 45:10-17

God has anointed you with the oil of gladness. (Ps. 45:7)

or Song of Solomon 2:8-13

Arise, my love, my fair one, and come away. (Song of Sol. 2:10)

Preface   Sundays

Color   Green

Prayers of Intercession

The prayers are prepared locally for each occasion. The following examples may be adapted or used as appropriate.

Strengthened by the Spirit who gives us words to speak and hearts that care, let us bring our hopes and needs to God who listens.

A brief silence.

O God, strengthen and empower your church. Where it is weak or timid, raise up leaders. Support it with your gift of inner strength and peace. Let us pray.
Have mercy, O God.

Creator God, the earth groans when we do not regard it with loving care. Forgive us for polluting the water and the air, for stripping the land of its natural resources, and for caring more about our own comfort than the long-term health of the planet. Let us pray.
Have mercy, O God.

How beautiful it is when people dwell together in unity. Help us appreciate the differences among us, to seek to understand one another, and to work together for harmony. Let us pray.
Have mercy, O God.

Holy source of hope, so many people are in pain today. Give us hearts of compassion, hands that heal, and lips that speak words of comfort and encouragement. Surround with your love all those in need (*especially*). Let us pray.
Have mercy, O God.

As you walked with Abraham and Sarah, the magi, and all who follow your call, be with those who travel this day: pilots and truckers, cab drivers and train engineers, those on vacation and those on the road for work. Let us pray.
Have mercy, O God.

Here other intercessions may be offered.

Alpha and Omega, you are with us from our first breath to our last. We give thanks for the faithful departed who now rest in your loving arms (*especially the martyr Jan Hus*). May the promise of the resurrection sustain those who trust in you. Let us pray.
Have mercy, O God.

We lift our prayers to you, God of mercy, confident that all things are in your hands. In Jesus' name we pray.
Amen.

Images in the Readings

The **yoke** ties together two beasts of burden. According to this image, Christians do not walk alone, but are tied to Christ and to one another.

In the several centuries before Christ, Jewish poetry developed the image of **wisdom**. Borrowing from neighboring polytheistic religions the picture of the divine consort, the great goddess who personified wisdom, Jews adapted this divine female figure into a way to speak of God's law, a beautiful and powerful aspect of the Almighty, who guided the people into truth. Christians altered the image once again, seeing Christ as this wisdom, whose words sound like foolishness to the world. In the eighth-century "O" antiphons preceding Christmas and versified in the hymn "O come, O come, Emmanuel," Christ is our Wisdom, coming in strength and beauty.

Ideas for the Day

◆ The rest Jesus promises in the gospel is echoed in the prayer of the day, which quotes Augustine's *Confessions*: "You have made us for yourself, and our hearts are restless until they rest in you" (Book 1, Chapter 1). So many people today are seeking a connection to God, self-identifying as "spiritual but not religious." They wander between faith practices and prayer methods as if searching for a strong cell phone signal. What will help your people find a "full bars" connection to God?

◆ We think of a yoke as the device that tied a beast to its work. But it was also used to hook two oxen together to share the plow. Christ uses the metaphor to emphasize our connectedness to others who have taken on his yoke, sharing the burden of service—thereby making it lighter for everyone. This could be humorously illustrated with a three-legged race. Another reference is St. Benedict, whose *Rule for Monks* is the foremost guide for monastic community living (his commemoration day falls on July 11). How does your congregation intentionally live and serve together?

◆ In the film *Babette's Feast* (Orion, 1987), a master chef prepares a five-star meal for a group of people who are, at first, sulky and suspicious. Even though the meal takes days and a small fortune to prepare, Babette doesn't mind the work, because it flows out of her naturally. In the end her effort transforms those to whom she offers it. This is an excellent metaphor for the easy yoke of Christ: his grace in our lives, expressed through service and worship, is not burdensome drudgery but rather flows out of us when we are in touch with the Father, as Jesus was—and it has the power to change all who come into contact with it.

Connections with the Liturgy

The oracle from Zechariah provides the background for the palm procession at the outset of Holy Week, since Christians have seen the figure of a triumphant king, paradoxically riding a donkey, to be Jesus Christ.

The prayer of Catherine of Siena (*Evangelical Lutheran Worship*, p. 87) uses Matthew's image of wisdom as her address to Christ.

Let the Children Come

A few weeks ago (June 22) children may have been invited to tell about where they see God in the world. This week help them ask parents and grandparents the same questions—or ask them what their parents think. Provide questions to take home for conversation during a family mealtime.

Assembly Song
Gathering

Light dawns on a weary world   ELW 726

Rejoice, ye pure in heart!   ELW 873/874

Come to me, all pilgrims thirsty   ELW 777

Psalmody

Guimont, Michel. "Psalm 145" from PRCL.

Whitney, Rae E. "O My God and King and Savior" (HOLY MANNA) from PAS 145F.

Brugh, Lorraine. "Psalm 45," Refrain 2, from PSCY.

Pelz, Walter E. "Psalm 45:10-17" or "Song of Solomon 2:8-13" from PWA.

Sedio, Mark. "Song of Solomon 2:8-13" from PSCY.

Pavlechko, Thomas. "Song of Solomon 2:8-13" from SMP.

Hymn of the Day

We've come this far by faith   ELW 633, TFF 197   THIS FAR BY FAITH

Great is thy faithfulness   ELW 733, WOV 771   FAITHFULNESS

Lord of all hopefulness   ELW 765, LBW 469   SLANE

Offering

Day by day   ELW 790, WOV 746

Come, gracious Spirit, heavenly dove   ELW 404, LBW 475

Communion

God loved the world   ELW 323

Jesus, keep me near the cross   ELW 335, TFF 73

We walk by faith   ELW 635, WOV 675

Your will be done   ELW 741, TFF 243

Sending

How sweet the name of Jesus sounds   ELW 620, LBW 345

Just a closer walk with thee   ELW 697, TFF 253

Additional Assembly Songs

Come unto me   DH 27

Rich in promise   OBS 75

⊕ Pantou, Rudolf R. Indonesia. "Soft the Master's Love Song" from *Sound the Bamboo*. U. GIA G-6830.

✧ Brown, Brenton/Ken Riley. "Everlasting God" from WT.

✧ Gungor, Michael. "Be Praised" from WT.

✧ Hamilton, Dan/ Robbie Seay/ Ryan Owens/Taylor Johnson. "Come Ye Sinners" from CCLI.

✧ Houston, Joel. "From the Inside Out" from WT.

✧ Hughes, Tim. "Giver of Life" from CCLI.

✧ Sumrall, Jon Micah. "Ready for You" from WT.

Music for the Day
Choral

Fleming, Larry L. "Come unto Me" from *Augsburg Motet Book*. SATB. AFP 9781451423709.

⊕ = global song
✧ = praise song
● = relates to hymn of the day

● Helgen, John. "The All-Day Hymn (Lord of All Hopefulness)." KJO 8822.

Horn, Richard. "I Heard the Voice of Jesus Say." SAB, org/hp. MSM 50-6203.

Husberg, Amanda. "I Heard the Voice of Jesus Say." SAB, pno, opt fl. CPH 98-4092.

● Schrader, Jack. "Great Is Thy Faithfulness." SAB, pno. HOP CH672.

Scott, K. Lee. "Jesus Calls Us" from *Treasures in Heaven*. 2 pt, org. AFP 9780800679477.

Children's Choir

Hopson, Hal. "God of Mercy, We Implore Thee." 2 pt, kybd. HOP AG7213.

Marcello, Benedetto. "Oh, Hold Thou Me Up" in *The Morning Star Choir Book*. 2 pt, kybd. CPH 97-6287.

White, David Ashley. "Come, Ye Sinners." 2 pt, kybd, ob. AFP 9780800653248.

Keyboard / Instrumental

● Carter, John. "Slane" from *Contemplative Folk Tunes for Piano*. Pno. AFP 9780800659776.

Near, Gerald. "Solemn Prelude on a Theme of Thomas Tallis." Org. MSM 10-168.

● Phillips, Craig. "Slane" from *O Love, How Deep: Three Hymn Settings for Organ*. Org. MSM 10-240.

● Wagner, Douglas E. "Great Is Thy Faithfulness" from *Seek Ye First: For Piano*. Pno. HOP 8118.

Handbell

McKlveen, Paul. "Faith." 3-5 oct, L2+. JEF JHS9396.

● Thompson, Martha Lynn. "Great Is Thy Faithfulness." 3-5 oct hb, opt 3 oct hc, L2+. HOP 2268.

● Wagner, Douglas. "Lord of All Hopefulness." 3-5 oct hb, opt fl or vln, L2+. LOR 20/1387L.

Sunday, July 6

Jan Hus, martyr, died 1415

Jan Hus was a Bohemian priest who spoke against abuses in the church of his day in many of the same ways Luther would a century later. He spoke against the withholding of the cup at the eucharist and because of this stance was excommunicated, not for heresy but for insubordination toward his archbishop. He preached against the selling of indulgences and was particularly mortified by the indulgence trade of two rival claimants to the papacy who were raising money for war against each other. He was found guilty of heresy by the Council of Constance and burned at the stake. The followers of Jan Hus became known as the Czech Brethren and eventually continued as the Moravian Church.

Friday, July 11
Benedict of Nursia, Abbot of Monte Cassino, died around 540

Benedict is known as the father of Western monasticism. He was educated in Rome but was appalled by the decline of life around him. He went to live as a hermit, and a community of monks came to gather around him. In the prologue of his rule for monasteries he wrote that his intent in drawing up his regulations was "to set down nothing harsh, nothing burdensome." It is that moderate spirit that characterizes his rule and the monastic communities that are formed by it. Benedict encourages a generous spirit of hospitality, saying that visitors to Benedictine communities are to be welcomed as Christ himself.

Saturday, July 12
Nathan Söderblom, Bishop of Uppsala, died 1931

In 1930, this Swedish theologian, ecumenist, and social activist received the Nobel Prize for peace. Söderblom (ZAY-der-blom) saw the value of the ancient worship of the church catholic and encouraged the liturgical movement. He also valued the work of liberal Protestant scholars and believed social action was a first step on the path toward a united Christianity. He organized the Universal Christian Council on Life and Work, one of the organizations that in 1948 came together to form the World Council of Churches.

July 13, 2014
Time after Pentecost — Lectionary 15

God's word is like the rain that waters the earth and brings forth vegetation. It is also like the sower who scatters seed indiscriminately. Our lives are like seeds sown in the earth. Even from what appears to be little, dormant, or dead, God promises a harvest. At the Lord's table we are fed with the bread of life, that we may bear fruit in the world.

Prayer of the Day

Almighty God, we thank you for planting in us the seed of your word. By your Holy Spirit help us to receive it with joy, live according to it, and grow in faith and hope and love, through Jesus Christ, our Savior and Lord.

Gospel Acclamation

Alleluia. The word is very ¹ near to you;* it is in your mouth and ¹ in your heart. *Alleluia.* (Deut. 30:14)

Readings and Psalm
Isaiah 55:10-13

God's word to Israel's exiles is as sure and effective as never-failing precipitation. Their return to the Holy Land in a new exodus is cheered on by singing mountains and by trees that clap their hands.

Psalm 65:[1-8] 9-13

Your paths overflow with plenty. (Ps. 65:11)

Romans 8:1-11

There is no condemnation for those who live in Christ. God sent Christ to accomplish what the law was unable to do: condemn sin and free us from its slavery. The Spirit now empowers proper actions and values in our lives and gives us the promise of resurrected life.

Matthew 13:1-9, 18-23

In Matthew's gospel, both Jesus and his disciples "sow the seed" of God's word by proclaiming the good news that "the kingdom of heaven is near." Now, in a memorable parable, Jesus explains why this good news produces different results in those who hear.

Semicontinuous reading and psalm
Genesis 25:19-34

Although Jacob was younger than his twin, Esau, he eventually gets the birthright away from his brother. Jacob is portrayed in the Bible as deceptive, gripping his brother when he came out of the womb and driving a hard bargain by buying the birthright for a bowl of lentils.

Psalm 119:105-112

Your word is a lamp to my feet and a light upon my path. (Ps. 119:105)

Preface Sundays

Color Green

Prayers of Intercession

The prayers are prepared locally for each occasion. The following examples may be adapted or used as appropriate.

Strengthened by the Spirit who gives us words to speak and hearts that care, let us bring our hopes and needs to God who listens.

A brief silence.

Merciful God, you give your word to guide, correct, teach, and inspire. Draw us into your story, and give us wisdom, understanding, and obedient hearts as we follow your Son Jesus. Lord, in your mercy,

hear our prayer.

The amazing cycle of birth, growth, and death sustains your creation. Bring forth an abundant harvest, keep farmers safe, and teach us to cherish life in all its forms and stages. Lord, in your mercy,

hear our prayer.

In places of war, bring peace, and in places of hatred, sow love. Help world leaders set aside their prejudices, put down their weapons, and work together for the good of all people. Lord, in your mercy,

hear our prayer.

We live in a land of plenty, and still there are those without enough to eat. Give us generous hearts to those who are hungry. Bless the hands of those who work so that others might eat. Lord, in your mercy,

hear our prayer.

Raise up leaders for your church who will tend to your harvest. We lift up seminaries and church colleges, bishops and synod staffs, Lutheran World Relief and the Lutheran World Federation, as they live out their callings to serve. Lord, in your mercy,

hear our prayer.

Here other intercessions may be offered.

Bless the memory of those who now worship at your eternal throne (*especially*) and bless those who worship in hopeful expectation of your eternal kingdom. Lord, in your mercy,

hear our prayer.

We lift our prayers to you, God of mercy, confident that all things are in your hands. In Jesus' name we pray.

Amen.

Images in the Readings

Although seed was valuable, the **sower** strewed the seed widely. In Christian imagination, the sower is Christ, and also the preacher, and also every Christian spreading the good news to others.

Those who live in the Spirit bear good **fruit**, says Matthew. The imagery of plentiful growth recurs throughout the Bible and can alert us to the beauteous variety of plants and trees we humans can enjoy. In the vision of the heavenly city in the book of Revelation the tree of life can by itself produce twelve different fruits.

The **trees** are clapping their hands. The troublesome thorn is replaced by the medicinally useful evergreen cypress, identified as a tree used in the building of the temple. The briar has been replaced with myrtle, an aromatic evergreen used in the rituals of Sukkoth.

Ideas for the Day

◆ The artist Vincent Van Gogh did several paintings entitled *The Sower*, paying homage to the painting of the same subject by his contemporary, Jean-François Millet. Millet's work is dominated by a man, fulfilling the mandate to "fill the earth and subdue it" (Gen. 1:28). Van Gogh's final painting is quite different. The human is balanced equally by a tree (a reference to Christ or the cross, perhaps) and a sun forming what looks like a halo around the sower's head (many images are online, for example, www.lifeofvangogh.com/theSower.html). Van Gogh's painting emphasizes our role in spreading the gospel (the sower's face is obscured, anonymous), and how we must work in cooperation with the creation to complete our mandate. At www.artway.eu (search for "Sowing the Seeds of Faith"), James Romaine offers a "painterly" analysis that many preachers would find helpful.

◆ The agrarian motif of today's gospel is a kind of foreign language to many of us. We do not live close to the land, and most of us have never grown our food from seed. To better understand the process you could speak to a farmer or gardener, or even have one participate in the worship service. These persons have unique insight into plant production and can freshen this well-known story. Questions you might ask: Why would the sower throw seed indiscriminately? How does root structure figure into the health of the plant, and do different plants need different soil depths? How do thorns choke a plant—are they quick and violent, or slow and insidious? What is in "good" soil?

◆ One chore of summer is to tend the garden and yank the weeds competing with the crops. Attention might be given to our receptivity to the greatest seed of all—the mighty word of God. What pathways in our hearts are trampled hard because of other traffic? What precious words get picked off because of flighty thoughts and ravenous temptations? What seeds from God get wasted because we are petrified by worldly concerns and have never taken the time to let our hearts be plowed in readiness for the word to enter in? What initial germinations of God's word get scorched as soon as our life runs into a burning problem?

Connections with the Liturgy

In each Thanksgiving at the Table, we pray with Paul that the Spirit of God come to dwell among us: with your Word and Holy Spirit to bless us; Holy God, we long for your Spirit; Come, Holy Spirit; pour out upon us the Spirit of your love; send now, we pray, your Holy Spirit, whose breath revives us for life; Come, Spirit of freedom!; we pray for the gift of your Spirit, in our gathering, within this meal, among your people; the life of the Spirit of our risen Savior, to establish our faith in truth; Come, Holy Spirit.

Let the Children Come

On July 11 (just two days ago) the church calendar commemorates Benedict of Nursia, Abbot of Monte Cassino. Benedictine men and women who follow Benedict's Rule for monasteries find life in the practice of hospitality. They welcome strangers as if they were welcoming Christ himself. How does your congregation welcome children in worship? Are they seen as interruptions? Are they shown ways they can be welcoming to others?

Assembly Song
Gathering

What is this place   ELW 524
God, who stretched the spangled heavens   ELW 771, LBW 463
Joyous light of heavenly glory   ELW 561

Psalmody

Hopson, Hal H. "Psalm 65" from TP.
Long, Larry J. "Psalm 65," Refrain 1, from PSCY.
Makeever, Ray. "Psalm 65:[1-8] 9-13" from PWA.
Shepperd, Mark. "Psalm 119:105-112" from PWA.

Hymn of the Day

Lord, let my heart be good soil   ELW 512, W&P 52   GOOD SOIL
Have you thanked the Lord?   ELW 829, TFF 270   LAMOTTA
God, whose farm is all creation   ELW 734   HARVEST GIFTS

Offering

Accept, O Lord, the gifts we bring   ELW 691, WOV 759
For the fruit of all creation   ELW 679, WOV 760
Lord, your hands have formed   ELW 554, WOV 727

Communion

This is my Father's world   ELW 824, LBW 554
Many and great, O God   ELW 837, WOV 794
On what has now been sown   ELW 550, LBW 261

Sending

Sent forth by God's blessing   ELW 547, LBW 221
We plow the fields and scatter   ELW 680/681, LLC 492

Additional Assembly Songs

The trees of the field   W&P 138
The thirsty fields drink in the rain   WOV 714
☻ Young-Soo, Nah. Korea. "Look and Learn" from *Sent by the Lord: Songs of the World Church, Vol 2*. U. GIA G-3740.
✿ Crowder, David. "I Need Words" from CCLI.
✿ Fielding, Ben. "Kingdom Come" from CCLI.
✿ Ligertwood, Brooke. "Desert Song" from WT.
✿ McDonald, Shawn. "Rise" from CCLI.
✿ Morgan, Reuben. "This Is How We Overcome" from CCLI.
✿ Smith, Martin/Stuart Garrard. "Rain Down" from CCLI.

Music for the Day
Choral

Fedak, Alfred. "This Touch of Love." MH solo, org. MSM 40-830.
Haydn, Franz Joseph. "How Marvelous Is the Power of God." High voice solo, kybd. ECS 1.1914.
Helgen, John. "Spirit of God, Descend." SATB, kybd, cello. AFP 9780800676377.
Schalk, Carl. "Thy Word Is like a Garden, Lord." U, org, fl. CG CGA1089.
Scott, K. Lee. "Gracious Spirit, Dwell with Me." 2 pt, org. AFP 9780800646134.

Children's Choir

Dauermann, Stuart. "The Trees of the Field." LS 109.
Roff, Joseph. "Breathe in Me, O Holy Spirit." U, 2 pt, kybd. CPH 98-2993.
Schalk, Carl. "Thy Word Is like a Garden." U, org, fl. CG CGA1089.

Keyboard / Instrumental

● Albrecht, Mark. "Good Soil" from *Timeless Tunes for Piano and Solo Instrument, Volume 3*. Inst, kybd. AFP 9780800675035.
Ferguson, John. "For the Beauty of the Earth" from *A Thanksgiving Triptych*. Org. MSM 10-603.
Leavitt, John. "Lord, Keep Us Steadfast in Your Word" from *A Mighty Fortress: Sacred Reflections for Piano*. Pno. CPH 97-7254.
Wold, Wayne. "Liebster Jesu" from *Augsburg Organ Library: Baptism and Holy Communion*. Org. AFP 9780800623555.

☻ = global song
✿ = praise song
● = relates to hymn of the day

Handbell

Cota, Patricia. "Change My Heart, O God." 3-5 oct hb, opt 2 oct hc, L3. HOP 2136.

Helman, Michael. "We Plow the Fields and Scatter." 3-6 oct hb, opt 3-5 oct hc, opt U vcs. ALF 29956.

McChesney, Kevin. "Give Thanks." 3-5 oct, L2. FB FBBGH1006.

Thursday, July 17

Bartolomé de Las Casas, missionary to the Indies, died 1566

Bartolomé de Las Casas was a Spanish priest and a missionary in the Western Hemisphere. He first came to the West while serving in the military, and he was granted a large estate that included a number of indigenous slaves. When he was ordained in 1513, he granted freedom to his servants. This act characterized much of the rest of Las Casas's ministry. Throughout the Caribbean and Central America, he worked to stop the enslavement of native people, to halt the brutal treatment of women by military forces, and to promote laws that humanized the process of colonization.

July 20, 2014
Time after Pentecost — Lectionary 16

It is an age-old question: why is there evil in the world? In the parable of the wheat and the weeds Jesus suggests that both grow together until the harvest. With Paul, we long for the day that all creation will be set free from bondage and suffering. Having both weeds and wheat within us, we humbly place our hope in the promises of God, and from the Lord's table we go forth to bear the fruit of justice and mercy.

Prayer of the Day

Faithful God, most merciful judge, you care for your children with firmness and compassion. By your Spirit nurture us who live in your kingdom, that we may be rooted in the way of your Son, Jesus Christ, our Savior and Lord.

Gospel Acclamation

Alleluia. My word shall accomplish that | which I purpose,* and succeed in the thing for | which I sent it. *Alleluia.* (Isa. 55:11)

Readings and Psalm
Isaiah 44:6-8

God claims the right to sole rule, because God announces things that actually do happen, while supposed divine opponents remain silent. God is Israel's redeemer, that is, the best brother or sister they ever had.

or Wisdom 12:13, 16-19

God's deeds of forgiveness and gift of hope indicate that God's faithful people must also show kindness. No other god cares for all people.

Psalm 86:11-17

Teach me your way, O Lord, and I will walk in your truth. (Ps. 86:11)

Romans 8:12-25

For Paul, true spirituality means that we experience the reality of the Spirit, which enables us to pray as God's children, keeps us in solidarity with creation, and gives us unseen hope that God will liberate us and creation from bondage to death and decay.

Matthew 13:24-30, 36-43

Jesus tells a parable about the co-existence of good and evil in this world. God's judgment will remove all evildoers and causes of sin, but not until the end of human history.

Semicontinuous reading and psalm
Genesis 28:10-19a

God's graciousness to Jacob is shown in God's revelation of the divine self to the patriarch, who is running for his life after cheating his brother Esau out of the family inheritance. Jacob promises that if God brings him back to the land, he will be loyal to God and give God a tenth of everything.

Psalm 139:1-12, 23-24

You have searched me out and known me. (Ps. 139:1)

Preface Sundays

Color Green

Prayers of Intercession

The prayers are prepared locally for each occasion. The following examples may be adapted or used as appropriate.

Filled by the Spirit, let us join the whole people of God in Christ Jesus in praying for the church, those in need, and all of God's creation.

A brief silence.

Lord of the harvest, sow the seeds of your word throughout the world, that all your children grow into your kingdom. Use our hands to tend your garden, wherever it may be. Lord, in your mercy,

hear our prayer.

Send the summer winds to bring much-needed rain and blow the hope of what is unseen through your creation, that it be set free from decay to bear good fruit. Lord, in your mercy,

hear our prayer.

Lord of all nations, guide our leaders with your strength and wisdom as they search for common ground (*especially*). Through your mercy show them the way to justice and peace. Lord, in your mercy,

hear our prayer.

Listen to the cries of your people waiting patiently for your healing hand and comforting Spirit (*especially*). Ease the sufferings of this present time and fill us with hope. Lord, in your mercy,

hear our prayer.

Teach your way, O Lord, to our congregation. Help us walk in your truth, grow together in your word, mirror your patience, treat one another with kindness, and sing your praises with undivided hearts. Lord, in your mercy,

hear our prayer.

Here other intercessions may be offered.

Lord of hosts, you are the first and the last, gathering all those who have gone before us into one. Thank you for your steadfast love and for their faithful witness. Lord, in your mercy,

hear our prayer.

Into your loving hands, gracious God, we commend all for whom we pray, trusting in your abundant mercy; through Jesus Christ, our Savior.

Amen.

Images in the Readings

Contemporary English-language Bibles cleverly translate this parable with nouns that sound nearly identical: wheat and **weeds**. It is easy to think of the other as a weed. Christian theology reminds us that each one of us is both wheat and weed. In Martin Luther's language, we are always both saint and sinner.

Once again this Sunday's readings give us the images of the seed and the harvest. In explicating the allegory, Matthew writes about the furnace of **fire**, where there will be weeping and gnashing of teeth. Scholars suggest that the image of eternal separation from God as fire, Gehenna, recalled the perpetually burning refuse dump that was outside the city walls. Thus God's judgmental fire was about expulsion from the community and destruction of what is worthless. That this fire is an image is made clear in that people are gnashing their teeth; thus they still have bodies, which are however not being burned up.

We are **children** of God: not natural offspring, but instead adopted; beloved; dependent; obedient.

That the entire universe is **in labor** is a striking image of God's creation that rejects a commonplace Christian notion that God cares only for human beings. According to biblical theology, all God's creation is good; all creation has fallen; all is groaning in pain until God brings about new birth. As in the natural world, so in the human part of it: countless mothers die in childbirth, for new birth is a painful, even dangerous event. The image of all the earth in labor fits well with our scientific knowledge of the earth and its creatures, all of which must continually struggle for life. The natural world is not a benign zoo, but rather billions of life forms created by God that all are headed toward decay.

God is **the first and the last**. The book of Revelation casts this as Alpha and Omega, A and Z. So Christian theology has taught that God was before all things, and when all things come to their end, what will remain is God.

Ideas for the Day

◆ One way to unpack this gospel is to ask the people to look within, discerning what is good wheat but also what weeds remain. Martin Luther coined the phrase *simul justus et peccator* (simultaneously saint and sinner); in other words, there is always good and bad in each of us. Despite having "the first fruits of the Spirit," we continue to "groan inwardly while we wait for . . . the redemption of our bodies" (Rom. 8:23). But there is hope: God will one day burn away the impurities within us, "all causes of sin" (Matt. 13:41). While we wait, we can ask the Holy Spirit to be our own personal weed-killer.

◆ Jane Austin's novel *Pride and Prejudice* (available in several film adaptations) is an excellent, well-known story about mistakenly judging a book by its cover. The protagonist, Elizabeth Bennet, dislikes her counterpart, Mr. Darcy, almost from the moment she meets him. Until she gets a fuller picture of his motives and history, she does not understand who he truly is. The reader knows before she does how mistaken she is in her judgment. This illustrates why we cannot determine who in our midst might be a "weed," for we are within the story, not writing it. Only God, as author of the universe, knows the full narrative—the history, motivations, and heart of each human being—and so only God can determine who (if anyone) will be counted among the weeds.

◆   Paul encourages us to pray to God as "Abba! Father!" It's a cry of relief and respect from the child who holds a place of honor in the family. Our adoption by God rescues us from futility, setting us free to live into our potential. How might you challenge your congregation to "pay forward" this remarkable redemption?

Connections with the Liturgy

Already in the mid 50s, Paul indicates that Christians address God as their loving Father. For Paul, God being "Abba" to human "children" is no natural situation, but results only because of the sufferings of Jesus Christ. The most common Christian prayer throughout the centuries opens by calling God our Father.

Let the Children Come

Prayer helps to keep us rooted in Christ and have a better understanding of who we are as God's people. Show children ways they can pray with their whole body. To show praise, stand with legs further than hip distance apart and arms raised (making the letter "X" with your body). To ask for help tap both hands on the top of your chest. During the prayers of intercession and the thanksgiving at the table, invite children and adults to mirror the posture of the intercessor and presider with their arms and hands.

Assembly Song
Gathering

Come, ye thankful people, come   ELW 693, LBW 407
We raise our hands to you, O Lord   ELW 690
O Holy Spirit, root of life   ELW 399, WOV 688

Psalmody

Dean, Stephen. "Lord, You Are Good and Forgiving" from PS3.
Guimont, Michel. "Psalm 86" from PRCL.
Haugen, Marty. "Psalm 139" from PSCY.

Hymn of the Day

As the grains of wheat   ELW 465, WOV 705   *AS THE GRAINS*
Almighty God, your word is cast   ELW 516, LBW 234   *ST. FLAVIAN*

We plow the fields and scatter   ELW 680, LLC 492
SAN FERNANDO

Offering

Spread, oh, spread, almighty Word   ELW 663, LBW 379
Will you let me be your servant   ELW 659

Communion

Neither death nor life   ELW 622
Blessed assurance   ELW 638, TFF 118, WOV 699
All earth is hopeful   ELW 266, TFF 47, WOV 629

Sending

Now thank we all our God   ELW 839/840, LBW 533/534
Sing to the Lord of harvest   ELW 694, LBW 412

Additional Assembly Songs

Thy word   TFF 132, W&P 144
☻ Tú diste a Israel   LLC 476
☻ Olson, A. Louise Anderson. Tanzania. "Praised Be the Rock" from *Set Free: A Collection of African Hymns.* SATB. AFP 9780806600451.
✿ Brown, Brenton. "All for You" from WT.
✿ Carman/Steve Camp. "Revive Us O Lord" from CCLI.
✿ Hall, Charlie. "Give Us Clean Hands" from WT.
✿ Minter, Kelly/Matt Maher/Stuart Townend. "Glory Be to God" from CCLI.
✿ Stanfill, Kristian. "Kingdom" from CCLI.
✿ Tomlin, Chris/Ed Cash. "God Almighty" from CCLI.

Music for the Day
Choral

Handel, George F. "Lord, You Have Searched Me." 2 pt mxd, kybd. MSM 50-5118.
Hendrickson, John. "Lord, You Have Searched Me Out." SAB, pno. AFP 9780800677022.
Holstein, Jane. "For the Fruit of All Creation." SAB, pno. HOP C5424.
● Johnson, Roy. "Almighty God, Your Word Is Cast." SATB, org. GIA G-2968.

Children's Choir

Handel, G. F. "Praise the King." 2 pt, kybd. ALF PROCH02971.
Hopson, Hal H. "O Lord, You Know Me Completely (*O Dios tú me conoces*)." CG CGA833.
Shaw, Timothy. "Teach Me Your Way." U/2 pt, kybd, opt C inst. CG CGA1081.

Keyboard / Instrumental

● Hamilton, Gregory. "As the Grains" from *As the Grains of Wheat: Piano Settings for Worship.* Pno. AFP 9780800675776.

☻ = global song
✿ = praise song
● = relates to hymn of the day

- Martin, Gilbert. "St. Flavian" from *The Lord's Supper: Communion Meditations for Organ and Piano.* Org, pno. LOR 70/1673L.
  Nelson, Ronald A. "St. George's Windsor" from *Easy Hymn Settings for Organ.* Org. AFP 9780806698045.
- Schmoltze, Ron. "As the Grains" from *A Song in the Journey: New and Old Tunes for Organ.* Org. AFP 9780800679026.

Handbell

Geschke, Susan. "Thy Word." 2-3 oct, L2. HOP 2250.
Sherman, Arnold. "Thanksgiving (Simple Gifts)." 3-5 oct hb, L2+. BP HB203. Opt SATB choir and kybd. BP BP1237.
Stephenson, Valerie. "If I Take the Wings of the Morning" (based on Psalm 139:9-10). 2-3 oct hb, opt 2-3 oct hc, L2. RW 8171. 3-5 oct hb, opt 2-3 oct hc, L2. RW 8172.

Tuesday, July 22

Mary Magdalene, Apostle

The gospels report Mary Magdalene was one of the women of Galilee who followed Jesus. She was present at Jesus' crucifixion and his burial. When she went to the tomb on the first day of the week to anoint Jesus' body, she was the first person to whom the risen Lord appeared. She returned to the disciples with the news and has been called "the apostle to the apostles" for her proclamation of the resurrection. Because John's gospel describes Mary as weeping at the tomb, she is often portrayed in art with red eyes. Icons depict her standing by the tomb and holding a bright red egg, symbol of the resurrection.

Wednesday, July 23

Birgitta of Sweden, renewer of the church, died 1373

Birgitta (beer-GEE-tuh) was married at age thirteen and had four daughters with her husband. She was a woman of some standing who, in her early thirties, served as the chief lady-in-waiting to the queen of Sweden. She was widowed at the age of thirty-eight, shortly after she and her husband had made a religious pilgrimage. Following the death of her husband the religious dreams and visions that had begun in her youth occurred more regularly. Her devotional commitments led her to give to the poor and needy all that she owned, and she began to live a more ascetic life. She founded an order of monks and nuns, the Order of the Holy Savior (Brigittines), whose superior was a woman. Today the Society of St. Birgitta is a laypersons' society that continues her work of prayer and charity.

Friday, July 25

James, Apostle

James is one of the sons of Zebedee and is counted as one of the twelve disciples. Together with his brother John they had the nickname "sons of thunder." One of the stories in the New Testament tells of their request for Jesus to grant them places of honor in the kingdom. They are also reported to have asked Jesus for permission to send down fire on a Samaritan village that had not welcomed them. James was the first of the Twelve to suffer martyrdom and is the only apostle whose martyrdom is recorded in scripture. He is sometimes called James the Elder to distinguish him from James the Less, commemorated with Philip on May 1, and James of Jerusalem, commemorated on October 23.

July 27, 2014
Time after Pentecost — Lectionary 17

As Solomon prays for wisdom, we seek to more deeply know the treasures of faith. In today's gospel Jesus offers everyday images that reveal to us the reign of God: a tree that becomes a sheltering home, yeast that penetrates and expands, a treasured pearl, a net that gains a great catch. Even as we seek the riches of God's reign, the great surprise is that God's grace finds us first!

Prayer of the Day

Beloved and sovereign God, through the death and resurrection of your Son you bring us into your kingdom of justice and mercy. By your Spirit, give us your wisdom, that we may treasure the life that comes from Jesus Christ, our Savior and Lord.

Gospel Acclamation

Alleluia. Many will come from | east and west* and will eat in the king- | dom of heaven. *Alleluia.* (Matt. 8:11)

Readings and Psalm

1 Kings 3:5-12

Because Solomon did not ask for long life, riches, or the defeat of his enemies, God gave him what he asked for: wisdom to govern the people well. In verse 13 God gives him additional honor and riches beyond compare.

Psalm 119:129-136

When your word is opened, it gives light and understanding. (Ps. 119:130)

Romans 8:26-39

These words celebrate the depth of God's actions for us. Through Christ's death for us and the activity of the Spirit praying for us, we are fused to God's love poured out in Jesus Christ. Nothing, not even death itself, is able to separate us from such incredible divine love.

Matthew 13:31-33, 44-52

Throughout Matthew's gospel, Jesus and his disciples proclaim the good news that "the kingdom of heaven is near!" Here, Jesus offers several brief parables that explore the implications of this announcement for people's lives.

Semicontinuous reading and psalm

Genesis 29:15-28

The young shepherd Jacob met his match in the old shepherd, Laban, his father-in-law. Laban gave Jacob his older daughter, Leah, when he had promised to give him Rachel. Jacob worked fourteen years to earn his favorite wife, Rachel, but the years seemed like a few days because of his love for her.

Psalm 105:1-11, 45b

Make known the deeds of the LORD among the peoples. Hallelujah! (Ps. 105:1, 45)

or Psalm 128

Happy are they who follow in the ways of God. (Ps. 128:1)

Preface   Sundays

Color   Green

Prayers of Intercession

The prayers are prepared locally for each occasion. The following examples may be adapted or used as appropriate.

Filled by the Spirit, let us join the whole people of God in Christ Jesus in praying for the church, those in need, and all of God's creation.

A brief silence.

Gracious Lord, the unfolding of your words gives light to those who love your name throughout the world. Fill the hearts of all preachers and teachers with your wisdom. Lord, in your mercy,

hear our prayer.

Your earth is filled with abundant life: fish, animals, and plants of all shapes and sizes, from the smallest shrub to the greatest tree. Teach us to conserve these gifts for the benefit of all. Lord, in your mercy,

hear our prayer.

Righteous God, people of all nations clamor for justice. Give their leaders understanding minds to discern between good and evil, govern wisely, and listen to their suffering people. Lord, in your mercy,

hear our prayer.

Faithful One, we trust that all things work together for good. Bring hope to those who have no job, who have no place to call home, or who are in any need (*especially*). Lord, in your mercy,
hear our prayer.
Search our hearts and minds and open the doors of this congregation to those who seek refuge or need a place to belong, that all who come to us find shelter in our life together. Lord, in your mercy,
hear our prayer.
Here other intercessions may be offered.
Your face shines upon those faithful servants who now rest with you in your heavenly kingdom. Remind us that neither death nor life can separate us from your love in Christ Jesus. Lord, in your mercy,
hear our prayer.
Into your loving hands, gracious God, we commend all for whom we pray, trusting in your abundant mercy; through Jesus Christ, our Savior.
Amen.

Images in the Readings

The parables are full of images that raise many questions. The **mustard seed** actually grows into a straggly annual bush, not the monumental tree of life (see for example Ezekiel 31:2-9) that is paradoxically evoked in the opening parable. In Jewish religious symbolism, the preferred sex is the man, the holy minister is a priest, and the holy bread is unleavened; yet in the parable the woman adds **leaven** to three measures of flour. The man sells "all that he has" to gain a **treasure**, and we think of Solomon's dream, for whom the preferred treasure was wisdom that comes only from God. The **net** that catches all kinds of fish is a commonplace symbol for the church. Yet by "the kingdom of heaven" Matthew does not mean merely "the church."

The first reading in the complementary series is one of the several biblical tales about the **wisdom of Solomon**, a phrase come into our language to signify immense and deep understanding. According to the monarchical myths of the ancient Near East, the king was anointed by God, next in power to God, God's servant, even God's son. Yet the later stories in 2 Kings describe Solomon as having been as prone to foolishness and error as any other king, as having given in to many temptations that separated him from the love of God. For Christians, Christ himself is wisdom.

Ideas for the Day

◆ The mustard seed and yeast metaphors lend themselves to comic interpretations of the gospel. Small things having a much larger impact than expected is a theme in many classic comic tales. In the television series *I Love Lucy*, the "Pioneer Women" episode includes the famous scene of Lucy

baking bread. After putting thirteen cakes of yeast—instead of the called-for three—into the dough, the bread explodes out of the oven in an eighteen-foot-long loaf. How might we look for the humorous ways that God's small seeds and tiny amounts of yeast have a large impact in our lives?

◆ The image of the mustard shrub growing large enough to allow birds to nest in it helps us understand the welcome and hospitality that grows from a life of grace and mercy. The church can be a place that, even though it may be relatively small and insignificant in its own setting, has grace and love large enough to welcome, feed, and house others, both physically and spiritually. Explore ways that some small things that form the core of the church—welcome, word, baptism, eucharist, healing, service—create a place where many can find rest and call their home.

◆ The ending of the Matthew reading emphasizes that both the old and the new are treasures of great worth for God's kingdom. Many congregations experience tension between old and new. Here is an opportunity to celebrate how old and new work together. It could be an important time to affirm a congregation's traditions and long-term members and ministries, and to welcome the new that adds to and enhances what already is. Individual persons in particular may need to hear appreciation for their place in the life of the church and the work of God's kingdom, whether they are newcomers and full of creativity and energy or have been faithful and hardworking church members for many years.

Connections with the Liturgy

At each Holy Communion, we read from the ancient scriptures, and the sermon explicates a meaning of these texts for contemporary life: thus we are the householder who brings out of the treasury what is new and what is old.

Both the first and second reading speak about prayer. Whenever the church gathers for worship, the assembly prays for the church, the world of nature, the human community, all who are sick or suffering, and the specific needs of that congregation. Our intercessions, recalling Romans 8:26, are always "not as we ought, but as we are able" (*Evangelical Lutheran Worship*, p. 109). We pray along with the risen Christ, who Paul writes is interceding for us.

Let the Children Come

Children could lead the congregation in singing "O day of peace" (ELW 711) today. This song highlights images of the reign of God unfolding among us and is a prayer for God's ongoing work. Younger children could learn one stanza in advance of the service. Older children or teenagers could prepare in advance to join in. As demonstrated beautifully in the 2012 Olympic opening ceremonies, children and youth leading this song can be the assembly's prayer today and become a continuing refrain through worshipers' minds through the week.

Assembly Song
Gathering

All my hope on God is founded   ELW 757, WOV 782
Open your ears, O faithful people   ELW 519, TFF 715
Gather Us In   ELW 532, WOV 718

Psalmody

Kallman, Daniel. "Psalm 119:129-136" from PWA.
Walker, Christopher. "Teach Me O God" from PS3.
Hughes, Howard. "Walk in His Ways (Psalm 128)." Cant, opt SATB, assembly, org. GIA G-5624.

Hymn of the Day

Be thou my vision   ELW 793, WOV 776   SLANE
Soul, adorn yourself with gladness   ELW 488, LBW 224   SCHMÜCKE DICH   ELW 489, LLC 388   CANTO AL BORINQUEN
We eat the bread of teaching   ELW 518   WISDOM'S FEAST

Offering

Let us go now to the banquet   ELW 523, LLC 410
Accept, O Lord, the gifts we bring   ELW 691, WOV 759

Communion

Jesus, priceless treasure   ELW 775, LBW 457/458
Soul, adorn yourself with gladness   ELW 488/489, LBW 224
Neither death nor life   ELW 622

Sending

God, who stretched the spangled heavens   ELW 771, LBW 463
The God of Abraham praise   ELW 831, LBW 544
Blessed be the name/Heri ni jina   ELW 797

Additional Assembly Songs

Bring forth the kingdom   W&P 22
From God can nothing move me   LBW 468
- Harling, Per. Sweden. "Holy, Holy, Holy: Sanctus from a Groaning Creation" from *Global Praise 2*. SATB, kybd, gtr. GBGMusik, General Board of Global Ministries, United Methodist Church.
- Sosa, Pablo. Argentina. "Tuyo es el Reino/Yours Is the Kingdom" from *Éste es el Día*. U. GIA G-7021.
- Assad, Audrey/Matt Maher/Michael Gungor/Paul Moak. "Love Comes Down" from CCLI.
- Crocker, Matt. "To Know Your Name" from CCLI.
- Hughes, Rachel/Tim Hughes. "Living for Your Glory" from CCLI.
- Nockels, Nathan/Christy Nockels. "Choose" from CCLI.
- Rend Collective Experiment. "Build Your Kingdom Here" from WT.
- Rend Collective Experiment. "You Are My Vision" from WT.

Music for the Day
Choral

Beck, John Ness. "Who Shall Separate Us?" SATB, org. SMP AM261.
Chepponis, James. "If God Is for Us." Cant/SATB, kybd, C inst, opt br qrt, timp, hb, gtr. GIA G-5948.
Lovelace, Austin. "The Kingdom of God." SB/2 pt mxd. GIA G-3250.
- Perkins, Scott. "Soul, Adorn Yourself with Gladness." SATB, org. AFP 9781451424041.
- Sherman, Arnold. "Be Thou My Vision." SATB, org. MSM 50-6023.

Children's Choir

Barta, Daniel. "Lead Me in Your Truth." 2 pt, pno. CG CGA880.
Newbury, Kent A. "Wisdom and Understanding." SSA, opt acc. HOP SP692.
Wilson, Terry D. "As a Child I Give Thanks." 2 pt trbl, pno. AFP 9780800620332.

Keyboard / Instrumental

- Bach, J. S. "Schmücke dich, O liebe Seele" from *The Leipzig Chorales*. Org. Various editions.
- Carter, John. "Slane" from *Contemplative Folk Tunes for Piano*. Pno. AFP 9780800659776.
- Phillips, Craig. "Prelude on Slane" from *O Love How Deep: Three Hymn Settings for Organ*. Org. MSM 10-240.
- Pinkston, Daniel. "Be Thou My Vision" from *Three Hymns for Clarinet and Piano*. Cl, pno. MSM 20-761.

Handbell

- Eithun, Sandra. "Soul, Adorn Yourself with Gladness." 3-5 oct hb, opt fl, L2+. CPH 97-7385.
Lamb, Linda. "Let Us Break Bread Together." 3-5 oct, L2. HOP 2347.
- Page, Anna Laura. "Be Thou My Vision." 3-5 oct hb, opt 3 oct hc, opt fl, L3. CG CGB670.

Monday, July 28

Johann Sebastian Bach, died 1750; Heinrich Schütz, died 1672; George Frederick Handel, died 1759; musicians

These three composers have done much to enrich the worship life of the church. Johann Sebastian Bach drew on the Lutheran tradition of hymnody and wrote about two hundred cantatas, including at least two for each Sunday and festival day in the Lutheran calendar of his day. He has been called "the fifth evangelist" for the ways he proclaimed the gospel through his music. George Frederick Handel was not primarily a church musician, but his great work *Messiah* is a musical proclamation of the scriptures. Heinrich Schütz wrote choral settings of biblical texts and paid special attention to ways his composition would underscore the meaning of the words.

- = global song
- = praise song
- = relates to hymn of the day

Tuesday, July 29
Mary, Martha, and Lazarus of Bethany

Mary and Martha are remembered for the hospitality and refreshment they offered Jesus in their home. Following the characterization drawn by Luke, Martha represents the active life, Mary the contemplative. Mary is identified in the fourth gospel as the one who anointed Jesus before his passion and who was criticized for her act of devotion. Lazarus, Mary's and Martha's brother, was raised from the dead by Jesus as a sign of the eternal life offered to all believers. It was over Lazarus's tomb that Jesus wept for love of his friend.

Olaf, King of Norway, martyr, died 1030

Olaf is considered the patron saint of Norway. In his early career he engaged in war and piracy in the Baltic and in Normandy. In Rouen, though, he was baptized and became a Christian. He returned to Norway, succeeded his father as king, and from then on Christianity was the dominant religion of the realm. He revised the laws of the nation and enforced them with strict impartiality, eliminating the possibility of bribes. He thereby alienated much of the aristocracy. The harshness that he sometimes resorted to in order to establish Christianity and his own law led to a rebellion. After being driven from the country and into exile, he enlisted support from Sweden to try to regain his kingdom, but he died in battle.

August 3, 2014
Time after Pentecost — Lectionary 18

In today's first reading God invites all who are hungry or thirsty to receive food and drink without cost. Jesus feeds the hungry multitude and reveals the abundance of God. At the eucharistic table we remember all who are hungry or poor in our world today. As we share the bread of life, we are sent forth to give ourselves away as bread for the hungry.

Prayer of the Day

Glorious God, your generosity waters the world with goodness, and you cover creation with abundance. Awaken in us a hunger for the food that satisfies both body and spirit, and with this food fill all the starving world; through your Son, Jesus Christ, our Savior and Lord.

Gospel Acclamation

Alleluia. One does not live by ¹ bread alone,* but by every word that comes from the ¹ mouth of God. *Alleluia.* (Matt. 4:4)

Readings and Psalm
Isaiah 55:1-5

God invites Israel to a great feast at which both food and drink are free. God also promises to make an everlasting covenant with all the people, with promises that previously had been limited to the line of kings. As David was a witness to the nations, these nations shall now acknowledge the ways in which God has glorified Israel.

Psalm 145:8-9, 14-21

You open wide your hand and satisfy the desire of every living thing. (Ps. 145:16)

Romans 9:1-5

This begins a new section in Paul's letter in which he will deal with the place of Israel in God's saving plan. He opens by highlighting how Israel's heritage and legacy include being God's children, having God's covenants, being given God's law, participating in worship of God, and receiving divine promises.

Matthew 14:13-21

After John the Baptist is murdered, Jesus desires a time of solitude. Still, his compassion for others will not allow him to dismiss those who need him, and he is moved to perform one of his greatest miracles.

Semicontinuous reading and psalm
Genesis 32:22-31

Jacob wrestled all night with God, and when God wanted to get away as dawn was breaking, Jacob would not let God go until God had blessed him. Jacob's name is changed to Israel to mark his new relationship with God as he enters the land. Jacob is astonished that he remains alive after seeing God face to face.

Psalm 17:1-7, 15

I shall see your face; when I awake, I shall be satisfied. (Ps. 17:15)

Preface   Sundays

Color   Green

Prayers of Intercession

The prayers are prepared locally for each occasion. The following examples may be adapted or used as appropriate.

Filled by the Spirit, let us join the whole people of God in Christ Jesus in praying for the church, those in need, and all of God's creation.

A brief silence.

Incline your ear and come to us, gracious and merciful God. Raise up among our congregations strong leaders to guide mission work (*especially Bread for the World*), so that everyone who hungers is fed. Lord, in your mercy,
hear our prayer.

The earth flourishes in your steadfast love and care. Open your hand to satisfy the desire of every living thing, and have compassion over all that you have made. Lord, in your mercy,
hear our prayer.

In this war-torn world, the thirst for justice and peace is never quenched. We pray for those who live under tyranny (*especially*). Watch over them and be near to all who call upon your name. Lord, in your mercy,
hear our prayer.

When we are falling, hold us up; when we are bowed down with grief or loneliness, raise us up; when we are hungry, fill us; when we are sick, heal us. We remember (*especially*). Lord, in your mercy,
hear our prayer.

Accompany all those experiencing life transitions: those pursuing new studies; those who are retiring; and those moving to new communities. Give them the courage to embrace change and flourish in their new roles. Lord, in your mercy,
hear our prayer.

Here other intercessions may be offered.

With gratitude for their loving witness and faith-filled lives, we remember those who have died. Receive the praise of all those who call upon your name. Lord, in your mercy,
hear our prayer.

Into your loving hands, gracious God, we commend all for whom we pray, trusting in your abundant mercy; through Jesus Christ, our Savior.
Amen.

Images in the Readings

The most common biblical image for divine mercy is **food**. In Genesis 1, the plants and trees that God created are given to humans as food. Ancient narratives told of God providing food during famine. The Israelites' memories of their nomadic years recalled a miraculous food, manna, which God sent to keep them alive in the wilderness. Religious rules commanded the faithful to share their food with the hungry and to abstain from eating with the wicked. Disobedience was met with the punishment of deprivation of food. The people of Israel themselves were likened to food that God has planted. Food or no food was central to all the primary religious festivals of the Old Testament. Poems described the law of God as if it is nourishing food. Christ was born in Bethlehem, which means "house of bread." In John's metaphoric theology, Christ says, "I am the bread of life." We need food to live, and Christians have each week served out the word and the sacrament as the food that Christ continues to distribute to those of us who are hungry.

The oracle from Isaiah includes **wine** as one of the foodstuffs that God gives away freely. Wine was not only the safest drink in the ancient world, but it signifies communal celebration, as if the alcohol symbolizes the Spirit that alters the human body into unity with others around the table. However the church has often been stingy with its wine: only the smallest sip is granted, or none at all, and since at least 1869, when Thomas Welch invented pasteurized grape juice, wine has sometimes been replaced with a tamer drink. Each congregation may want to think through how the image of wine is conveyed in its communion practice.

Ideas for the Day

◆   When the disciples see the large crowd and the small quantity of food, they ask Jesus to send the people away, because they don't think they are able to handle it, even with his help. But Jesus says to them: *You do it.* Jesus could have gone along with the disciples' self-limiting expectations and said, "You're right. Nothing good can be done here. And you're incapable of doing much anyway." But in calling them to do it themselves, with Jesus' help, he is affirming that more good can happen in the world than they ever imagined—when God is at work *through them.* The church is often a place with self-limiting expectations. Explore how Jesus is saying "You do it" to the church today, and hear how this can be a challenging but affirming word to God's people.

◆ The word *companion* literally means "one you break bread with." In breaking bread with the crowd, Jesus is expressing the abundance of his companionship with people. In a culture that has become increasingly isolated and lonely for many people, the offer of companionship can be a great gift. The church as the body of Christ in the world is a community that breaks bread with everyone, without limitations based on race, class, or past deeds. The sermon could recall ways your congregation, perhaps in cooperation with others, shares meals with people and groups in the community as an expression of God's kingdom and as a loving offer of companionship to all the lonely and hungry.

◆ Consider using the poem, "The Bread That Satisfies," by Michael Coffey, as a prayer or meditation on the text. The poem is online at www.mccoffey.blogspot.com. Search for the title.

Connections with the Liturgy

The description of Jesus feeding the multitude says that "taking the loaves, he blessed and broke the loaves and gave them to his disciples." These words are echoed in the synoptic gospels' accounts of Jesus' meal on the night when he was betrayed and so are included in every great thanksgiving (for example, *Evangelical Lutheran Worship*, p. 109). What Jesus did during his ministry—thanking God for bread and distributing it to those around him—he continues to do through us in holy communion.

Let the Children Come

If you don't typically have homemade communion bread for worship, consider asking someone to bake bread this weekend. In the early part of the service, invite children to meet the baker. Ask them to use all their senses (look, listen, smell, touch, taste) to find bread in the worship. They will hear about bread in the readings. "I wonder," you might ask, "Will it be a lot or a little? Will it be enough?" Prepare a family with young children to bring forward the bread and wine for communion at the offering.

Assembly Song
Gathering

Praise and thanksgiving   ELW 689, LBW 409
Come, thou Fount of every blessing   ELW 807, LBW 499, TFF 108
God extends an invitation   ELW 486, LLC 397

Psalmody

Alonso, Tony or Marty Haugen. "The Hand of the Lord" from TLP:A.
Hopson, Hal H. "Psalm 145" from TP.

Makeever, Ray. "Psalm 145:8-9, 14-21" from PWA.
Marshall, Jane. "Psalm 17." U, kybd. CG CGA891.

Hymn of the Day

All earth is hopeful   ELW 266, TFF 47, WOV 629   *TODA LA TIERRA*
All who hunger, gather gladly   ELW 461   *HOLY MANNA*
United at the table   ELW 498, LLC 408   *UNIDOS EN LA FIESTA*

Offering

Let us talents and tongues employ   ELW 674, TFF 232, WOV 754
O Jesus, joy of loving hearts   ELW 658, LBW 356
God extends an invitation/Nuestro Padre nos invita   ELW 486

Communion

O living Bread from heaven   ELW 542, LBW 197
Lord, whose love in humble service   ELW 712, LBW 423
Break now the bread of life   ELW 515, LBW 235

Sending

Praise the One who breaks the darkness   ELW 843
Praise and thanks and adoration   ELW 783, LBW 470

Additional Assembly Songs

Lord, I hear of showers of blessings   TFF 120
Song over the Waters   W&P 127
🌐 Ocean of love   GS3 8
🌐 Prescod, Patrick. Caribbean. "Communion Hymn" from *Let the Peoples Sing*. SATB. AFP 9780800675394.
✿ Brown, Brenton/Glen Robertson. "All Who Are Thirsty" from CCLI.
✿ Crowder, David/Jeremy Bush/Mike Dodson/Patrick Dodd. "Can You Feel It?" from CCLI.
✿ Gustafson, Katie/John Hartley/Chris Eaton. "Be Still My Soul" from WT.
✿ Nockels, Christy/Nathan Nockels. "Life Light Up" from CCLI.
✿ Staines, Bill/Matt Maher. "Look like a Fool" from CCLI.
✿ Tomlin, Chris/Fanny Jane Crosby/Matt Redman/Robert S. Lowry. "All the Way My Savior Leads Me" from CCLI.

Music for the Day
Choral

Berger, Jean. "The Eyes of All Wait upon Thee" from *Augsburg Motet Book*. SATB. AFP 9781451423709.
Frahm, Frederick. "Christ Is the Bread of Life." SAB, org. AFP 9780800676575.
James, Gary. "Break Now the Bread of Life." U, kybd. MSM 50-8306.
Lovelace, Austin. "Bread of the World in Mercy Broken." SATB. PAR PPM 0227.
Mathews, Peter. "Bread of Heaven." 2 pt, org. MSM 50-8340.
Shaw, Timothy. "For the Bread Which You Have Broken." SATB, pno. MSM 50-9760.

🌐 = global song
✿ = praise song
● = relates to hymn of the day

Children's Choir

Bach, J. S. "O, My Savior." U, kybd. GIA G-2354.

Hopson, Hal. "Jesus Fed the Hungry Thousands." U, kybd. HOP JR221.

Vivaldi, A. "Esurientes Implevit Bonis (He Fills the Hungry with Truly Good Things)." SA, kybd, opt cello. MSM 50-9920.

Keyboard / Instrumental

Biery, Marilyn. "Bread of Life" from *An American Perspective: Settings of Old and New Tunes for Organ.* Org. AFP 9781451401820.

- Cherwien, David. "Toda la tierra" from *O God beyond All Praising: Hymn Settings for Organ.* Org. AFP 9780800657246.

- Larkin, Michael. "Holy Manna" from *Simple Gifts: Piano Meditations on American Hymn Tunes and Spirituals.* Pno. MSM 15-836.

- Miller, Aaron David. "All Who Hunger, Gather Gladly" from *Chorale Preludes for Piano in Traditional Styles.* Pno. AFP 9780800679033.

Handbell

- Eithun, Sandra. "Reflection on 'Holy Manna' (Brethren, We Have Met to Worship)." 3-6 oct hb, opt 3 or 5 oct hc, opt fl, opt dulcimer, L2+. LOR 20/1637L.

- Rogers, Sharon. "God Who Stretched the Spangled Heavens." 3-5 oct hb, opt 2 oct hc, L2. AFP 1110873. Out of print.

- Thompson, Karen. "Holy Manna." 2-3 oct hb, opt 3 oct hc, L2. CG CGB736.

Friday, August 8

Dominic, founder of the Order of Preachers (Dominicans), died 1221

Dominic was a Spanish priest who preached against the Albigensians, a heretical sect that held gnostic and dualistic beliefs. Dominic believed that a stumbling block to restoring heretics to the church was the wealth of clergy, so he formed an itinerant religious order, the Order of Preachers (Dominicans), who lived in poverty, studied philosophy and theology, and preached against heresy. The method of this order was to use kindness and gentle argument, rather than harsh judgment, to bring unorthodox Christians back to the fold. Dominic was opposed to burning Christians at the stake. Three times Dominic was offered the office of bishop, which he refused so that he could continue in his work of preaching.

● = relates to hymn of the day

August 10, 2014
Time after Pentecost — Lectionary 19

Elijah finds the presence of God not in earthquake, wind, or fire, but in the sound of sheer silence. When the disciples face a great storm on the sea, they cry out with fear. Jesus says: "Take heart, it is I; do not be afraid." Amid the storms of life, we gather to seek the calm presence of Christ that soothes our fears. In comforting words of scripture and in the refreshing bread and cup of the eucharist, God grants us peace and sends us forth to be a sign of God's presence to others.

Prayer of the Day

O God our defender, storms rage around and within us and cause us to be afraid. Rescue your people from despair, deliver your sons and daughters from fear, and preserve us in the faith of your Son, Jesus Christ, our Savior and Lord.

Gospel Acclamation

Alleluia. I wait for ˈ you, O Lᴏʀᴅ;* in your word ˈ is my hope. *Alleluia.* (Ps. 130:5)

Readings and Psalm
1 Kings 19:9-18

On Mount Horeb, where God had appeared to Moses with typical signs of God's presence—earthquake, wind, and fire—Elijah now experienced God in "sheer silence." God assured Elijah that he is not the only faithful believer. Seven thousand Israelites are still loyal. God instructed Elijah to anoint two men as kings and to anoint Elisha as his own successor.

Psalm 85:8-13

I will listen to what the Lᴏʀᴅ God is saying. (Ps. 85:8)

Romans 10:5-15

A right relationship with God is not something we achieve by heroic efforts. It is a gift received in the proclamation whose content is Jesus Christ. This proclaimed word creates our faith in the Lord Jesus Christ. Hence Christian proclamation is an indispensable component of God's saving actions.

Matthew 14:22-33

Matthew's gospel typically portrays Jesus' disciples as people of "little faith" who fail despite their best intentions. In this story, Matthew shows how Jesus comes to the disciples when they are in trouble and sustains them in their time of fear and doubt.

Semicontinuous reading and psalm
Genesis 37:1-4, 12-28

Though Joseph was Jacob's favorite son, his jealous brothers sold him into slavery. Judah, who protected Joseph's life, later gives a moving speech before Joseph in Egypt, indicating that the brothers had changed their ways (44:18-34).

Psalm 105:1-6, 16-22, 45b

Make known the deeds of the Lᴏʀᴅ among the peoples. Hallelujah! (Ps. 105:1, 45)

Preface   Sundays

Color   Green

Prayers of Intercession

The prayers are prepared locally for each occasion. The following examples may be adapted or used as appropriate.

Filled by the Spirit, let us join the whole people of God in Christ Jesus in praying for the church, those in need, and all of God's creation.

A brief silence.

Lord of all, how beautiful are the feet of those who bring good news. We pray for missionaries across the world. Keep them safe and bless the work they do in your name. Lord, in your mercy,

hear our prayer.

You have given us vast seas, great lands, and abundant natural resources to feed a hungry planet. Give us also grateful hearts and willing hands to care for these good gifts. Lord, in your mercy,

hear our prayer.

Be present with those across this earth who are hiding from their enemies, and who are afraid they are all alone (*especially*). Wrap them securely in the mantle of your loving presence. Lord, in your mercy,

hear our prayer.

Calm the storms that sweep across families dealing with the death of a loved one, and the grief of those who mourn

(*especially*). Fill their aching hearts with your peace and hope for the future. Lord, in your mercy,
hear our prayer.
Guide pastors, teachers, volunteers, and worship planners as they prepare educational opportunities for all ages, and creative ways to worship you. Place your word on their lips and in their hearts. Lord, in your mercy,
hear our prayer.
Here other intercessions may be offered.
Faithful One, thank you for all the saints who have gone before us (*especially Lawrence, deacon and martyr*). We take heart in your saving grace, which reaches out to us across all eternity. Lord, in your mercy,
hear our prayer.
Into your loving hands, gracious God, we commend all for whom we pray, trusting in your abundant mercy; through Jesus Christ, our Savior.
Amen.

Images in the Readings

The disciples are nearly drowned by the storm of **wind and waves**. Many poetic passages in the Bible speak of wind and waves as though they are harbingers of death and of a sea monster as embodying chaos. In the tale of Jonah, God both sends the storm and calms it. The theophany in Job 38 credits God with having control over the sea, and the authors of Genesis 1, in praising God's creative power, report that God created the sea monsters.

Mount Horeb, where Elijah meets God, is Mount Sinai. According to Exodus, God had appeared in earthquake, wind, and fire, but Elijah encounters only **silence**. This story comforts many of the faithful, for whom there seems to be more sheer silence than powerful wind from the Spirit.

Much Christian iconography has drawn the church as the **boat** from which Jesus, the I AM who is God, brings calm to the waters experienced by the faithful. We assemble weekly in the nave—think "navy"—to receive the peace of Christ.

Ideas for the Day

◆ Much sermonic attention is given to Peter's attempted stroll out on the turbid waters. We try to analyze or psychologize why Peter sank. Lack of faith in God? Did he take his eyes off Jesus? Insufficient trust? Or did he succumb to his fear of the windstorm? We know one thing for certain: Peter sank because he left the boat! If he had stayed in the boat—among the community of believers—he would not have sunk. When we, like Peter, leave the community of the faithful (as represented by the boat), our odds of sinking increase exponentially. Perhaps our message for this Sunday is: stay in boat, remain in community, rely on one another, and worship together, strengthened by the presence of Christ.

◆ In her book *The Worshiping Body: The Art of Leading Worship*, Kimberly Bracken Long stresses the necessity of the community as we live and worship together in Christ. She writes: "The transcendent God who is so far beyond our comprehension is also God incarnate, the Word who is made flesh and speaks that Word to, and through, our own beautifully imperfect frames, surprising us with divine graces and binding us to one another in ways that would be otherwise impossible" (Louisville, KY: Westminster John Knox, 2009, p. 23).

◆ If the ancient church understood the boat to symbolize the community of believers, how might we reclaim or reemphasize this symbol? What would a boat-blessing ritual look like in your community? Fishing boats, canoes, kayaks, sailboats, yachts, and other watercraft owners may be present in your worshiping community. Invite people to bring to worship photos, keys, paddles, lifejackets, or other such items to represent their boat. Pray over them this week. Include in your prayers all those serving in the navy, people who live out their vocation on the water, and folks living in areas susceptible to hurricanes and tropical storms. For communities near a body of water, perhaps worship could happen near the water's edge.

Connections with the Liturgy

Paul wrote to the Romans that if you confess with your lips that Jesus is Lord and believe in your heart that God raised him from the dead, you will be saved, and in today's gospel story, the disciples confess Jesus as the Son of God. So whenever we confess the creed, on each Sunday, at every baptism, we join with Paul and with the disciples in the boat to call Jesus Christ the Son of God, our Lord, and we believe that he rose again on the third day.

Paul's citation of Isaiah 52:7, "how beautiful are the feet of the messenger," applies not only to called ministers: at the dismissal of holy communion, one option is, "Go in peace. Share the good news." We are all to spread the gospel.

Let the Children Come

Ask children "What are you most afraid of?" Use their thoughts and concerns to develop one or two petitions for the prayers of intercession today. Prayers developed on the spot or in advance from conversations with children might include things very similar to content within the readings today (storms, fire, scary people). Ask children how they know God is with them through those times. If they're not sure, imagine together with them how God is present in silence and in story, with a hand outstretched to save us. Each petition could end with the words: Save us, Jesus.

Assembly Song
Gathering

Lord, take my hand and lead me   ELW 767, LBW 333

Eternal Father, strong to save   ELW 756, LBW 467

Oh, sing to the Lord   ELW 822, WOV 795, TFF 274

Psalmody

Balhoff, Mike, Gary Daigle and Darryl Ducote. "Lord, Let Us See Your Kindness." SATB, cant, assembly, kybd, gtr. GIA G-5397.

Haugen, Marty. "Let Us See Your Kindness" from PCY, vol. l.

Harbor, Rawn. "O Lord, Let Us See Your Kindness (Psalm 85)." TFF 8.

Makeever, Ray. "Tell What God Has Done for Us (Psalm 105)" from DH.

Hymn of the Day

All my hope on God is founded   ELW 757, WOV 782   MICHAEL

My faith looks up to thee   ELW 759, LBW 479   OLIVET

Praise, praise! You are my rock   ELW 862   ZACHARY WOODS ROCK

Offering

Evening and morning   ELW 761, st. 3

What a fellowship, what a joy divine   ELW 774, TFF 220, WOV 780

Communion

Precious Lord, take my hand   ELW 773, TFF 193, WOV 731

When peace like a river   ELW 785

We've come this far by faith   ELW 633, TFF 197

Sending

My life flows on in endless song   ELW 736, TFF 222, WOV 781

Jesus, Savior, pilot me   ELW 755, LBW 334

Additional Assembly Songs

Walk across the water   DH 69

⊕ Si tú puedes, cántalo/Everybody, sing it out   LLC 596

⊕ Lee, Dong Hoon. Korea. "Dark Is the Night" from *Sound the Bamboo*. U. GIA G-6830.

✿ Assad, Audrey. "Slow" from CCLI.

✿ Brown, Brenton. "Like the Angels" from CCLI.

✿ Fieldes, Mia. "Here in My Life" from WT.

✿ Fieldes, Mia. "I Believe in Jesus" from WT.

✿ Rend Collective Experiment. "Second Chance" from CCLI.

✿ Tomlin, Chris/Daniel Carson/Jesse Reeves/Matt Maher. "My Deliverer" from CCLI.

Music for the Day
Choral

Farlee, Robert Buckley. "My Faith Looks Up to Thee." U, pno. AFP 9780800621483.

Kelly, Ryan. "Unto the Lord Lift Thankful Voices" from *Augsburg Motet Book*. SATB. AFP 9781451423709.

Meyer, Edward. "Lord, Take My Hand" from *Seven Hymn Settings for Small Choirs*. SAB, kybd. CPH 97-6965.

Nelson, Eric. "How Can I Keep from Singing?" SATB, a capella. AFP 9780800675172.

Wonacott, Glenn, "The Joy of the Lord Is My Song." 2 pt mxd, pno. Pavane 1363.

Children's Choir

Bedford, Michael. "Be Still and Know That I Am God" in *Two Psalms for Young Singers*. U, kybd, opt hb/hc. CG CGA1140.

Proulx, Richard. "In Te Speravi Domine (In You Have I Hoped O Lord)." 2 pt trbl. PAR 9521.

Simon, Julia. "God Be in My Head." U/2 pt, pno. AFP 9780800664039.

Keyboard / Instrumental

● Burkhardt, Michael. "Voluntary on 'All My Hope on God Is Founded.'" Org. MSM 10-734.

Leavitt, John. "If Thou But Trust in God to Guide You" from *A Mighty Fortress: Sacred Reflections for Piano*. Pno. CPH 97-7254.

Phillips, Craig. "Wer nur den lieben Gott" from *O Love, How Deep: Three Hymn Settings for Organ*. Org. MSM 10-240.

● Raabe, Nancy M. "My Faith Looks Up to Thee" from *In Heaven Above: Piano Music for Funerals and Memorials*. Pno. AFP 9781451401912.

Handbell

● Helman, Michael. "My Faith Looks Up to Thee." 3-5 oct hb, opt 3-5 oct hc, L2. CPH 97-7240.

Krug, Jason. "Faith, Hope, and Love." 3-6 oct hb, opt 2 oct hc, L2. LOR 20/1570L.

Lamb, Linda. "The Solid Rock." 3-5 oct, L2. ALF 25336.

Sunday, August 10

Lawrence, deacon, martyr, died 258

Lawrence was one of seven deacons of the congregation at Rome and, like the deacons appointed in Acts, was responsible for financial matters in the church and for the care of the poor. Lawrence lived during a time of persecution under the emperor Valerian. The emperor demanded that Lawrence surrender the treasures of the church. Lawrence gathered lepers, orphans, the blind and lame. He brought them to the emperor and said, "Here is the treasure of the church." This act enraged the emperor, and Lawrence was sentenced to death. Lawrence's martyrdom was one of the first to be observed by the church.

⊕ = global song
✿ = praise song
● = relates to hymn of the day

Monday, August 11

Clare, Abbess of San Damiano, died 1253

At age eighteen, Clare of Assisi heard Francis preach a sermon in a church in town. From that time, she determined to follow in his example of Christian living. With Francis's help (and against the wishes of her father) she and a growing number of companions established a women's Franciscan community, called the Order of Poor Ladies, or Poor Clares. She became a confidante and advisor to Francis, and in standing up against the wishes of popes for the sake of maintaining complete poverty, she helped inspire other women to pursue spiritual goals.

Wednesday, August 13

Florence Nightingale, died 1910;
Clara Maass, died 1901; renewers of society

When Florence Nightingale decided she would be a nurse, her family was horrified. In the early 1800s nursing was done by people with no training and no other way to earn a living. Florence trained at Kaiserswerth, Germany, with a Lutheran order of deaconesses. She returned home and worked to reform hospitals in England. Nightingale led a group of thirty-eight nurses to serve in the Crimean War, where they worked in appalling conditions. She returned to London as a hero and resumed her work there for hospital reform.

Clara Maass was born in New Jersey and served as a nurse in the Spanish-American War, where she encountered the horrors of yellow fever. She later responded to a call for subjects in research on yellow fever. During the experiments, which included receiving bites from mosquitoes, she contracted the disease and died. The commemoration of these women invites the church to give thanks for all who practice the arts of healing.

Thursday, August 14

Maximilian Kolbe, died 1941;
Kaj Munk, died 1944; martyrs

Father Kolbe was a Franciscan priest, born Raymond Kolbe. After spending some time working in Asia, he returned in 1936 to his native Poland, where he supervised a friary that came to house thousands of Polish war refugees, mostly Jews. The Nazis were watching, however, and he was arrested. Confined in Auschwitz, Kolbe gave generously of his meager resources and finally volunteered to be starved to death in place of another man who was a husband and father. After two weeks, he was executed by a lethal injection.

Kaj (pronounced KYE) Munk, a Danish Lutheran pastor and playwright, was an outspoken critic of the Nazis, who occupied Denmark during the Second World War. His plays frequently highlighted the eventual victory of the Christian faith despite the church's weak and ineffective witness. The Nazis feared Munk because his sermons and articles helped to strengthen the Danish resistance movement. He was executed by the Gestapo on January 5, 1944.

Friday, August 15

Mary, Mother of Our Lord

The church honors Mary with the Greek title *theotokos*, meaning God-bearer. Origen first used this title in the early church, and the councils of Ephesus and Chalcedon upheld it. Luther upheld this same title in his writings. The honor paid to Mary as *theotokos* and mother of our Lord goes back to biblical times, when Mary herself sang, "from now on all generations will call me blessed" (Luke 1:48). Mary's life revealed the presence of God incarnate, and it revealed God's presence among the humble and poor. Mary's song, the Magnificat, speaks of reversals in the reign of God: the mighty are cast down, the lowly are lifted up, the hungry are fed, and the rich are sent away empty-handed.

August 17, 2014
Time after Pentecost — Lectionary 20

In Isaiah we hear that God's house shall be a house of prayer for all people and that God will gather the outcasts of Israel. The Canaanite woman in today's gospel is a Gentile, an outsider, who is unflinching in her request that Jesus heal her daughter. As Jesus commends her bold faith, how might our church extend its mission to those on the margins of society? In our gathering around word and meal we receive strength to be signs of comfort, healing, and justice for those in need.

Prayer of the Day

God of all peoples, your arms reach out to embrace all those who call upon you. Teach us as disciples of your Son to love the world with compassion and constancy, that your name may be known throughout the earth, through Jesus Christ, our Savior and Lord.

Gospel Acclamation

Alleluia. Jesus preached the good news | of the kingdom*
and cured every sickness a- | mong the people. *Alleluia.*
(Matt. 4:23)

Readings and Psalm
Isaiah 56:1, 6-8

The prophet calls upon Israel to do justice in view of God's imminent intervention to save. Righteousness and obedience define who belongs to the Israelite community—not race, nationality, or any other category.

Psalm 67

Let all the peoples praise you, O God. (Ps. 67:3)

Romans 11:1-2a, 29-32

God has not rejected Israel. Rather, the call and gifts of God are irrevocable, so that while all have been disobedient, God has mercy upon all.

Matthew 15:[10-20] 21-28

Jesus teaches his disciples that true purity is a matter of the heart rather than outward religious observances. Almost immediately, this teaching is tested when a woman considered to be pagan and unclean approaches him for help.

Semicontinuous reading and psalm
Genesis 45:1-15

Moved to tears by Judah's plea on behalf of Benjamin, Joseph declares, "I am Joseph!" and asks, "Is my father still alive?" The evil intent of the brothers had been trumped by God's using Joseph to preserve many lives at a time of famine.

Psalm 133

How good and pleasant it is to live together in unity.
(Ps. 133:1)

Preface Sundays

Color Green

Prayers of Intercession

The prayers are prepared locally for each occasion. The following examples may be adapted or used as appropriate.

Filled by the Spirit, let us join the whole people of God in Christ Jesus in praying for the church, those in need, and all of God's creation.

A brief silence.

Lord, your house is a house of prayer for all peoples, all outcasts, and all who love your name. Reach into our hearts and focus our attention on this central mission of your gospel. Lord, in your mercy,
hear our prayer.

Embrace all of creation in your loving arms and show us a better way to care for your earth. Increase our understanding of the atmosphere and oceans, and help us protect endangered species. Lord, in your mercy,
hear our prayer.

You ask us to maintain justice and do what is right, that all nations know peace. Uphold those international organizations striving to work together for the good of all. Lord, in your mercy,
hear our prayer.

Shine your face upon those in need of healing for bodies, minds, and spirits (*especially*). Strengthen our faith and fill us with hope as we humbly kneel before you. Lord, in your mercy,
hear our prayer.

Open our hearts to the visitors among us, and to their gifts and questions. Fill them with your welcoming presence. Watch over those who are absent and bring them safely home. Lord, in your mercy,

hear our prayer.
Here other intercessions may be offered.
As you gather the faithful who have died into your eternal home, remind us of everything they have taught us in your name. Thank you for their presence among us (*especially*).
Lord, in your mercy,
hear our prayer.
Into your loving hands, gracious God, we commend all for whom we pray, trusting in your abundant mercy; through Jesus Christ, our Savior.
Amen.

Images in the Readings

That Jesus obliquely refers to the Canaanite woman as a **dog** has inspired much creative interpretation over the centuries. Traditionally the sentence was explained away as the technique Jesus employed to test the woman's faith. Some contemporary exegesis reads the exchange seriously and thus credits the woman with instructing Jesus about the breadth of God's mercy. Both of these explanations assume that the story is accurate historical reporting. The story also suggests that if our faith is strong enough, our wishes will be granted. Like the Jesus of Matthew's narrative, we too think of the other as a dog. Like the storyteller, we hope that our faith will bring us instant healing. It is a difficult story to proclaim and expound.

Despite our knowledge of anatomy, the **heart** continues over the millennia to be an image for the source and center of human intention.

Ancient temples were understood to be **houses of the deity.** Architecturally similar to the Lincoln Memorial, an open structure housed a statue of the god or goddess, and sacrifices were offered before the image of the divine. After the exile, strict traditionalists urged hierarchical regulations about how close to the presence of God each type of person could come. But Third Isaiah rejects this understanding of worship, saying the house of God will welcome all peoples. Christians have thought about their churches as in some way houses of God for all peoples. Yet for Christians, God dwells in the community and in word and sacrament, not in a house, and church buildings are less like temples and more like meeting places for the communal prayer of all peoples.

Ideas for the Day

◆   Posture is an important interpretive lens for the gospel text today. We are told that the Canaanite woman "came and knelt" before Jesus. If the woman is on all fours prostrating herself before Jesus, then maybe Jesus' comparison to a dog is not as jarring as it first seems. Her posture is indeed canine-like; she is like a hungry dog, begging Jesus for mercy for her demon-possessed daughter. Are we not the same? At times, aren't we all desperate for mercy for

ourselves or for a loved one? Pain, emptiness, suffering, addiction, heartache, disease, death: the weight of our humanity is at times too much to bear. It is enough to send us to our knees—on all fours—panting, begging, barking for mercy from the one who is able to do something about it. Jesus' response is the same for us as it is for the Canaanite woman: "Let it be done for you as you wish." Mercy!

◆   Where in the liturgy might the assembly be invited to consider a kneeling posture? Kneeling during the confession or at communion may be natural for a worshiping community, but what about during the Kyrie? How might this strengthen our connection to the Canaanite woman's plea, "Have mercy on me, Lord"? What if the assembly was instructed to read the woman's words while on their knees? How might the practice of standing for the gospel proclamation be experienced anew if the assembly were instructed to kneel instead? But let's remember that it is important for worship leaders to be sensitive to those with mobility issues when providing posture instructions.

◆   The Matthew text is a healing story. In verse 28, we are told that the Canaanite's daughter was instantly healed. But what does it mean to be healed? Each person has a concept of what healing means for her or him. At the outset of worship, consider passing out note cards with this statement on it: "For me, healing looks like. . . ." Create space in the worship for people to fill in the blank. Then, during the sermon, invite individuals who feel comfortable to share what they have written.

Connections with the Liturgy

Each Sunday that we sing Kyrie, we join with the Canaanite woman pleading for the Lord's mercy. In the Bible "Lord" is a complex title. In its most common usage it is an address to a distinguished male; in early Christian confession it affirmed the resurrection of Jesus the Messiah; and in Jewish theological language it substituted for pronouncing the Hebrew name of God. Christian invocation of the Lord is a Trinitarian title: God as Lord, Christ as Lord, the Spirit as "the Lord and giver of life."

Let the Children Come

What is fair? This is a major life question even when we're little. Have you ever whined because someone else got something good and you didn't? The woman Jesus meets today shows faith even when Jesus seems unfair. Jesus is so impressed by her faith, his healing word goes beyond his own community. God is better than fair. This week, point out how when we sing or pray the *Kyrie*, "Lord, have mercy," we are remembering how God is better than fair. This prayer helps us to let go of our arguing about who deserves what and to be still with God.

Assembly Song
Gathering

All Are Welcome   ELW 641

Gather Us In   ELW 532, WOV 718

When morning gilds the skies   ELW 853, LBW 546

Psalmody

Chepponis, James. "Let Nations Sing Your Praise." Cant, assembly, opt SATB, kybd, gtr, 17 hb, B-flat or C inst. GIA G-4226.

Brown, Teresa. "O God, Be Gracious" from PS1.

Bruxvoort-Colligan, Richard. "Sharing the Road (Psalm 133)" from SR.

Hymn of the Day

Let us go now to the banquet   ELW 523, LLC 410
  VAMOS TODOS AL BANQUETE

O Christ the healer, we have come   ELW 610, LBW 360   *DISTRESS*

In Christ there is no east or west   ELW 650, TFF 214   *MCKEE*

Offering

There's a wideness in God's mercy   ELW 587/588, LBW 290

Soli Deo Gloria   ELW 878

Communion

One bread, one body   ELW 496, TFF 122, W&P 111, WOV 710

Healer of our every ill   ELW 612, WOV 738

Creating God, your fingers trace   ELW 684, WOV 757

Sending

Oh, sing to the Lord   ELW 822, LLC 598, TFF 274, WOV 795

Baptized and Set Free   ELW 453, W&P 14

Additional Assembly Songs

Heal me, O Lord   TFF 189

Song over the Waters   W&P 127

⊕ Prescod, Patrick. Caribbean. "Let All the Peoples Praise You/Todos los pueblos canten" from *Let the Peoples Sing*. SATB. AFP 9780800675394.

⊕ Trad. Greek melody. "Kyrie Eleison" from *Sent by the Lord: Songs of the World Church, Vol 2*. U. GIA G-3740.

✿ Brown, Brenton. "Adoration" from WT.

✿ Fielding, Ben/Reuben Morgan. "God Is Able" from WT.

✿ Hall, Charlie. "Constant" from CCLI.

✿ Powell, Mac/Trevor Morgan. "How Great" from CCLI.

✿ Redman, Matt/Paul Baloche. "Rising" from CCLI.

✿ Zschech, Darlene/Reuben Morgan. "Blessed" from CCLI.

Music for the Day
Choral

Gibbons, Orlando. "Oh Lord, Increase My Faith." SATB. GIA G-2900.

Gieseke, Richard. "O Christ, the Healer, We Have Come." SAB, kybd. CPH 98-2815.

Hampton, Calvin/arr. Rick McNeely. "There's a Wideness in God's Mercy." SATB, pno. GIA G-7378.

Schram, Ruth Elaine. "We Come to You for Healing, Lord." SAB, pno, fl. AFP 9780800620202.

Children's Choir

Hobby, Robert A. "Song of Hope." U/2 pt/4 pt, kybd, perc. MSM 50-8112A.

Gieseke, Richard W. "May the Peoples Praise You, O God." U, kybd. CPH 98-2929.

Pergolesi, G. B. "Fidelia Omni Mandata Ejus." U, pno, vln. HIN HMC2236.

Keyboard / Instrumental

Bach, J. S. "Schmücke dich, o liebe Seele" from *Leipzig Chorales*. Org. Various editions.

● Childs, Edwin T. "Distress" from *Communion Hymns for Organ, Vol 1*. Org. AFP 9781451420821.

● Mackie, Dave. "Let Us Go Now to the Banquet" from *By Day and By Night: Piano Settings*. Pno. AFP 9781451420890.

● Page, Anna Laura. "In Christ There Is No East or West" from *Blest Be the Tie: Ten Hymn Arrangements for Piano*. Pno. MSM 15-838.

Handbell

Edwards, Dan. "I Will Arise and Go to Jesus." 3 or 5 oct, L2+. CG CGB264.

McAninch, Diane. "Healer of Our Every Ill." 2-3 oct hb, opt 2 oct hc, L2. GIA G-7286.

Morris, Hart. "Faithful Promises." 3-5 oct, L4-. BP HB267.

Wednesday, August 20

Bernard, Abbot of Clairvaux, died 1153

Bernard was a Cistercian monk who became an abbot of great spiritual depth. He was a mystical writer deeply devoted to the humanity of Christ who emphasized the inner human experience of prayer and contemplation. He was critical of one of the foremost theologians of the day, Peter Abelard, because he believed Abelard's approach to faith was too rational and did not provide sufficient room for mystery. Bernard's devotional writings are still read today. His sermon on the Song of Solomon treats that Old Testament book as an allegory of Christ's love for humanity. Bernard wrote several hymns that are still sung today in translation, including "Jesus, the Very Thought of You" (ELW 754).

⊕ = global song

✿ = praise song

● = relates to hymn of the day

August 24, 2014
Time after Pentecost — Lectionary 21

In Isaiah the people are bid to look to their spiritual ancestors as the rock from which they were hewn. Jesus declares that the church will be built on the rock of Peter's bold confession of faith. God's word of reconciliation and mercy are keys to the church's mission. Paul urges us to not be conformed to this world, but to offer our bodies as a living sacrifice, using our individual gifts to build up the body of Christ. From the table we go forth to offer our spiritual worship through word and deed.

Prayer of the Day

O God, with all your faithful followers of every age, we praise you, the rock of our life. Be our strong foundation and form us into the body of your Son, that we may gladly minister to all the world, through Jesus Christ, our Savior and Lord.

Gospel Acclamation

Alleluia. You are | the Messiah,* the Son of the | living God. *Alleluia.* (Matt. 16:16)

Readings and Psalm
Isaiah 51:1-6

Just as God had called Abraham and Sarah and given them many descendants, so now God offers comfort to Zion. God's deliverance will come soon and will never end.

Psalm 138

O Lord, your steadfast love endures forever. (Ps. 138:8)

Romans 12:1-8

In response to God's merciful activity, we are to worship by living holistic, God-pleasing lives. Our values and viewpoints are not molded by this age, but are transformed by the Spirit's renewing work. God's grace empowers different forms of service among Christians, but all forms of ministry function to build up the body of Christ.

Matthew 16:13-20

At a climactic point in Jesus' ministry, God reveals to Peter that Jesus is "the Messiah, the Son of the living God," and Jesus responds with the promise of a church that will overcome the very gates of Hades.

Semicontinuous reading and psalm
Exodus 1:8—2:10

The brave Hebrew midwives defied Pharaoh to save many infants from death. When the mother of Moses placed him in a basket in the Nile, the daughter of Pharaoh found him, adopted him, and brought him up. But the sister of Moses and his mother played crucial roles in this drama.

Psalm 124

We have escaped like a bird from the snare of the fowler. (Ps. 124:7)

Preface   Sundays

Color   Green

Prayers of Intercession

The prayers are prepared locally for each occasion. The following examples may be adapted or used as appropriate.

Filled by the Spirit, let us join the whole people of God in Christ Jesus in praying for the church, those in need, and all of God's creation.

A brief silence.

Lord of the church, remind us that though we are many, we are one body in Christ. Teach us to use our grace-given gifts with generosity, compassion, and humility. Lord, in your mercy,

hear our prayer.

Your Spirit blows over all the wild places of this earth, reminding us who is in control. Preserve the wilderness areas and coastlands, and help us minimize our impact upon the land. Lord, in your mercy,

hear our prayer.

Transform all nations by renewing the minds of their people. Provide adequate educational facilities and well-trained teachers for students of every age so that they learn, grow, and fulfill your purpose for their lives. Lord, in your mercy,

hear our prayer.

Stretch out your hand to preserve us from trouble and deliver us from poverty. We pray for peace and reconciliation among all people. Lord, in your mercy,

hear our prayer.

Give a discerning spirit to our congregation as we prepare for outreach ministries, programming for families and youth, and meaningful worship. Assign each member a measure of faith to make your vision a reality. Lord, in your mercy,

hear our prayer.

Here other intercessions may be offered.

We give you heartfelt thanks for the diligent leadership and faithful service of those who have died and now rest in you (*especially the apostle Bartholomew*). Continue to build your church upon that strong and enduring foundation. Lord, in your mercy,

hear our prayer.

Into your loving hands, gracious God, we commend all for whom we pray, trusting in your abundant mercy; through Jesus Christ, our Savior.

Amen.

Images in the Readings

As with the readings of Lectionary 9, **rock** is an image for the day. The psalms speak of the safety accorded by the rock; the prophet likens his religious heritage to a rock; Simon gets the name Peter, "Rocky." The Sermon on the Mount speaks of Jesus' teaching as a rock on which we are to build, and Paul writes in 1 Corinthians 4 that the rock from which water flowed was Christ. According to Jewish legend, the miraculous rock followed the Israelites throughout their nomadic decades, perpetually providing water. For Christians, the water of baptism follows the body of Christ, watering us throughout our journey.

According to the worldview of the New Testament, **Hades**, the lowest of the three levels of the universe, housed the dead. Matthew uses the category Hades to indicate the challenge that confronts the Christian community: to fight against the power of death. Especially Eastern Orthodox Christians recall this worldview in their beloved icon of the resurrection, in which Christ is standing on the broken doors of Hades and is raising from death into his arms both Adam and Eve.

The Isaiah reading includes the image of the **arm of the LORD**. In the Old Testament, God is described in terms humans know: God has ears, eyes, a mouth, fingers, hands, and strong arms. In the story of Noah's flood, God even smells the pleasant odor of the animal sacrifices. Our task is to ensure that these bodily images do not demote the divine into merely a superman. Christians can apply these very images to **the body** of Christ.

Ideas for the Day

◆ Today is a rock-solid day. In our gospel reading, Jesus proclaims to Peter (Rocky), "You are Peter, and on this rock I will build my church" (Matt. 16:18). This metaphor for Peter and church is also applied to God as well as Jesus' other teachings. The metaphoric language of rock abounds in scripture. The challenge for this day, then, is to reinvigorate or revive this sometimes overused metaphor so that it speaks anew in our context. In their book *Worship Words: Discipling Language for Faithful Ministry*, Debra and Ron Rienstra name the problem when they write: "God is a rock and a fortress, we say, and the words convey a vague impression of strength, but our minds remain blank. No pictures appear, our senses feel nothing, our emotions often remain steady. One of our tasks as worship leaders, then, is to make the old metaphors come alive again—and to find new ones, too, that fit with the old ones but also keep them new and refreshed" (Grand Rapids, MI: Baker Academic, 2009, p. 120). So here is our task, and following are some ideas to consider in pursuit of it.

◆ In the worship folder or on an overhead screen, try highlighting in bold some of the rocky metaphoric language and its associations (stronghold, foundation, refuge, strength, for example) printed throughout the liturgy. This simple alteration will give the metaphor added emphasis.

◆ Consider passing out a small rock to everyone as they enter the worship space. With a rock in hand, the sense of touch will reinforce the metaphorical words spoken and sung. At a set time—perhaps at the conclusion of the sermon—allow people to come forward and place their rock near the baptismal font. For it is from this rock, the rock of our salvation, where the water of life unites us as one.

◆ Is there anyone who plays electric guitar in your community? Ask them to accompany the congregation as they sing a rock-and-roll version (think Jimmy Hendrix style) of "Rock of Ages, cleft for me" or "A mighty fortress is our God."

◆ What happens when the physical rocks upon which we live give way? On January 12, 2010, an earthquake shook the already-suffering nation of Haiti, causing untold devastation. In worship, highlight that disaster and the ELCA's and ELCIC's ongoing efforts to help. Take up a special offering as recovery work continues for Haiti.

Connections with the Liturgy

In the creed the church joins Peter to name Jesus "Christ," God's only Son, and in pronouncing the forgiveness of sin, the minister takes up the authority to "loose on earth" what we trust will be loosed "in heaven," that is, with God.

Let the Children Come

Jesus says to Peter today that he is the rock that the church will be built on. Jesus picks a person, a great reminder that the people are the church. How are we as a congregation remembering the good gifts that children bring as part of the congregation? How do we honor the people they are and the ways God works through them during the week? As children return to school, how do we send them from worship into their weeks? This week, try a sending like this: "As you go to school and work, go in peace. Learn and grow."

Assembly Song

Gathering

O Holy Spirit, enter in   ELW 786, LBW 459

Alleluia! Voices raise   ELW 828

Lord Jesus Christ, be present now   ELW 527, LBW 253

Jesus is a rock in a weary land   ELW 333

Psalmody

Cooney, Rory. "Psalm 138: On the Day I Called." Cant, SAB, assembly, kybd, gtr, fl. OCP 10474.

Joncas, Michael. "In the Sight of the Angels (Psalm 138)." SATB, cant, assembly, hp or kybd, opt fl, ob, cello. GIA G-7139.

Inwood, Paul. "In the Presence of the Angels" from PS3.

Pavlechko, Thomas. "Psalm 124" from PWA.

Hymn of the Day

Take my life, that I may be   ELW 583   *TOMA MI VOLUNTAD*
        ELW 685, LBW 406   *PATMOS*

My hope is built on nothing less   ELW 596/597, LBW 293/294
        THE SOLID ROCK/MELITA

Faith of our fathers   ELW 812/813, LBW 500   *ST. CATHERINE*

Offering

We Are an Offering   ELW 692, W&P 146

O Jesus, joy of loving hearts   ELW 658, LBW 356

Communion

O Savior, precious Savior   ELW 820, LBW 514

We all are one in mission   ELW 576, WOV 755

How small our span of life   ELW 636

Sending

The church's one foundation   ELW 654, LBW 369

Built on a rock   ELW 652, LBW 365

Additional Assembly Songs

When upon life's billows   TFF 173

🌐 Trad. Nyanga, Zambia. "Chimwemwe mwa Yesu/Rejoice in Jesus" from Lutheran World Federation website. U, gtr.

✧ Brown, Brenton. "Good News" from WT.

✧ Houston, Joel. "The Stand" from WT.

✧ Jobe, Kari/Lincoln Brewster/Mia Fieldes. "What Love Is This" from CCLI.

✧ Neufeld, Jon/Tim Neufeld/Ben Glover. "Reign in Us" from WT.

✧ Sampson, Marty/Mia Fieldes. "Savior King" from WT.

✧ Tomlin, Chris/Daniel Carson/Ed Cash/Jesse Reeves. "Jesus Messiah" from CCLI.

Music for the Day

Choral

● Martinson, Joel. "We All Are One in Mission" from *Augsburg Easy Choirbook, Vol. 1.* 2 pt mxd, org. AFP 9780800676025.

Miller, Aaron David. "Praise the Rock of Our Salvation." SAB, kybd. AFP 9780800676506.

● Nelson, Daniel. "Take My Life, That I May Be." SATB, pno. KJO C9314.

● Sedio, Mark. "Take My Life, That I May Be: Toma, oh Dios, mi voluntad." SATB, pno. AFP 9780800658298.

Children's Choir

Burkhardt, Michael. "Ososo" in *Part-Singing Global Style.* U/2 pt, kybd. MSM 50-9811.

de LaLande, Michel-Richard. "My Soul Has Trusted in God (Sustinuit Anima Mea)." U, kybd, C inst, opt cello or bsn. AFP 9780800679132.

Meyer, Daniel C. "With My Whole Heart." U, pno. GIA G-5116.

Keyboard / Instrumental

● Callahan, Charles. "Faith of Our Fathers" from *Six Meditations on English Hymn Tunes.* Org. CPH 97-6189.

● Maynard, Lynette. "Toma mi voluntad" from *Let It Shine: Worship Music for Solo Piano.* Pno. AFP 9780800677640.

● Wilson, John. "The Solid Rock" from *Familiar Hymns for the Piano.* Pno. HOP 236.

● Wold, Wayne. "Melita" from *Augsburg Organ Library: Summer.* Org. AFP 9780800676872.

Handbell

● Longhin, Daniel. "Faith of Our Fathers." 3-5 oct, L2+. JEF JHS9202.

McKlveen, Paul. "Take My Life and Let It Be." 3-5 oct hb, opt 3 oct hc, L3. CG CGB539.

● Morris, Hart. "The Solid Rock." 3-6 oct, L4. AGEHR AG35148.

Monday, August 25

Bartholomew, Apostle (transferred)

Bartholomew is mentioned as one of Jesus' disciples in Matthew, Mark, and Luke. The list in John does not include him but rather Nathanael. These two are therefore often assumed to be the same person. Except for his name on these lists of the Twelve, little is known. Some traditions say Bartholomew preached in India or Armenia following the resurrection. In art, Bartholomew is pictured holding a flaying knife to indicate the manner in which he was killed.

🌐 = global song
✧ = praise song
● = relates to hymn of the day

Thursday, August 28

Augustine, Bishop of Hippo, died 430

Augustine was one of the greatest theologians of the Western church. Born in North Africa, he was a philosophy student in Carthage, where he later became a teacher of rhetoric. Much of his young life was a debauched one. As an adult he came under the influence of Ambrose, the bishop of Milan, and through him came to see Christianity as a religion appropriate for a philosopher. Augustine was baptized by Ambrose at the Easter Vigil in 387. He was ordained four years later and made bishop of Hippo in 396. Augustine was a defender of the Christian faith and argued, against the Donatists, that the holiness of the church did not depend on the holiness of its members, particularly the clergy, but that holiness comes from Christ, the head of the church. Augustine's autobiography, *Confessions*, tells of his slow movement toward faith and includes the line "Late have I loved thee."

Moses the Black, monk, martyr, died around 400

A man of great strength and rough character, Moses the Black was converted to Christian faith toward the close of the fourth century. Prior to his conversion he had been a thief and a leader of a gang of robbers. The story of his conversion is unknown, but eventually he became a desert monk at Skete. The change in his heart and life had a profound impact on his native Ethiopia. He was murdered when Berber bandits attacked his monastery.

August 31, 2014
Time after Pentecost — Lectionary 22

The prophet Jeremiah speaks of the incurable wound of his suffering, yet finds in God's words the delight of his heart. When Peter doesn't grasp Jesus' words about suffering, Jesus tells the disciples they will find their lives in losing them. Such sacrificial love is described by Paul when he urges us to associate with the lowly and not repay evil with evil. In worship we gather as a community that we might offer ourselves for the sake of our suffering world.

Prayer of the Day

O God, we thank you for your Son, who chose the path of suffering for the sake of the world. Humble us by his example, point us to the path of obedience, and give us strength to follow your commands, through Jesus Christ, our Savior and Lord.

Gospel Acclamation

Alleluia. May the God of our Lord Jesus Christ enlighten the eyes | of our hearts,* so that we may know the hope to which | God has called us. *Alleluia.* (Eph. 1:17, 18)

Readings and Psalm

Jeremiah 15:15-21

Jeremiah's delight in the word of the Lord is contradicted by the heaviness of God's hand upon him and God's seeming unfaithfulness. God's tough love to Jeremiah says that if he repents, he will be allowed to continue in his strenuous ministry. Jeremiah is strengthened by the simple words: "I am with you."

Psalm 26:1-8

Your love is before my eyes; I have walked faithfully with you. (Ps. 26:3)

Romans 12:9-21

Paul presents benchmarks for faithful relationships with Christians and non-Christians. Love is the unflagging standard of our behavior. When we encounter evil, we do not resort to its tactics but seek to overcome it with good. While Christians cannot control the actions and attitudes of others, we seek to live at peace with all people.

Matthew 16:21-28

After Peter confesses that Jesus is "the Messiah, the Son of the living God" (16:16), Jesus reveals the ultimate purpose of his ministry. These words prove hard to accept, even for a disciple whom Jesus has called a "rock."

Semicontinuous reading and psalm
Exodus 3:1-15

Moses experienced the call of God when God appeared to him in a bush that burned but was not consumed. When Moses expressed his unworthiness, God promised to be with him. When Moses objected that people would demand to know God's name, God revealed the personal name, Yahweh (I AM WHO I AM), or the LORD. Israel discovered God's true identity when God took them out of Egypt.

Psalm 105:1-6, 23-26, 45b

Make known the deeds of the LORD among the peoples. Hallelujah! (Ps. 105:1, 45)

Preface   Sundays

Color   Green

Prayers of Intercession

The prayers are prepared locally for each occasion. The following examples may be adapted or used as appropriate.

Filled by the Spirit, let us join the whole people of God in Christ Jesus in praying for the church, those in need, and all of God's creation.

A brief silence.

O Lord, you know and see all that your baptized accomplish across the church universal. Prove us and try us; test our hearts and minds as we walk in faithfulness with you. Lord, in your mercy,
hear our prayer.

As the summer breezes wane, and forests and foliage begin their colorful journey into fall, make us ever mindful of these earthly blessings and renew our zeal to care for your creation. Lord, in your mercy,
hear our prayer.

Teach us to live peaceably with all nations, our enemies, and those who seek to do us harm. Bring light into the dark corners of the world and give courage to organizations that seek to overcome evil with good (*especially*). Lord, in your mercy,
hear our prayer.

When our pain is unceasing, give us patience in suffering. When our wounds refuse to be healed, remember us with your mercy. When hope seems lost, remind us that you are with us always. (*Especially we remember. . .*) Lord, in your mercy,
hear our prayer.

As we rally our congregation's time, talents, and resources, remove the stumbling blocks that hinder our desire to put you first. Give us the courage to deny ourselves, take up our cross, and follow you. Lord, in your mercy,
hear our prayer.

Here other intercessions may be offered.

We remember with gratitude those who have recently died (*especially*). Through the lives of your saints, show us how to hold fast to what is good. Lord, in your mercy,
hear our prayer.

Into your loving hands, gracious God, we commend all for whom we pray, trusting in your abundant mercy; through Jesus Christ, our Savior.
Amen.

Images in the Readings

That believers are to deny themselves, take up their **cross** and follow Jesus has been a commonplace message throughout Christian centuries. Care must be taken that more privileged persons do not mouth these words to the less privileged, to those with minimal power to affect their own situation, as if what Jesus meant was to suffer in silence. All the baptized have been marked by the cross, and in the mystery of the resurrection, this cross is the way to life. Perhaps the cross we are called to carry is someone else's, that we willingly help to carry. One possibility is that Matthew was referring to the Tau, the sign of the end time for those who await the return of Christ.

Jesus calls Peter **Satan**, the one who opposes God. Ancient Israel knew no supernatural power of evil. In the book of Job, the Satan is in God's throne room, goading God and accusing the righteous. By the time of Jesus, largely through influence of their Zoroastrian neighbors, Jews had come to believe in a supernatural being who personified evil and who, like the medieval devil, tempted persons to immoral behavior. Yet Christian theology has always resisted the popular dualist idea that there is a good god and a bad god and that human life is the battlefield between God and the devil. According to the New Testament, evil, although still present, has already been conquered in Christ's resurrection. Satan is behind us.

The **burning coals** is an image for the shame that evildoers will experience when they encounter Christian forgiveness and generosity. In Romans 12:20, Paul is quoting Proverbs 25:21-22, an example of the degree to which Christian ethics repeats the teachings of the Hebrew scriptures.

Ideas for the Day

◆   "If any want to become my followers, let them deny themselves and take up their cross and follow me" (Matt. 16:24). Imagine replacing your community's mission statement with these words of Jesus from today's gospel text. How would this look at the top of your church's website or on the signboard out in front of your worship space? It is not the most inviting or attractive mission statement—quite the contrary. It could repel people from the church. Yet here it stands as Jesus' call to those who follow him. Reflecting on the theology of the cross, Douglas John Hall writes: "It is paramount for all serious Christians today to ask whether expansionism of any kind, whether territorial or as a bid for ever-greater numbers of converts, really belongs to the mission of the Christian church" (*The Cross in Our Context: Jesus and the Suffering World*, Fortress Press, 2003, pp. 188–189). How might Jesus' words (and Hall's) challenge our understanding of mission in our community?

◆ Many Christian households have crosses mounted on their walls or adorning their mantles. Prior to this Sunday, invite people to bring crosses from their home to the church. Encourage each household to write up the history or significance of the cross on a half-sheet of paper. In the narthex or gathering space, create a display of these crosses. Consider beginning worship this day amid these crosses, offering a blessing upon them before processing in to the sanctuary.

◆ Today may be an excellent day for an extended gospel processional. During the gospel acclamation, have the assembly sing "Lift high the cross" (ELW 660) or another cross-centered song. As the hymn is sung, the crucifer, book bearer, and torch bearers could circle the assembly a few times before ending in the center of the people. The gospeler then proclaims this "cross-bearing" text from Matthew amid the assembled. As a response to the reading, the congregation could be encouraged to make the sign of the cross, to punctuate the words with ritual action. At the conclusion, allow silence to accompany the gospel procession's return, while all eyes remain fixed on the cross.

Connections with the Liturgy

The authors of the New Testament maintained a strong belief in the eschaton, the end of the world coming sooner or later and the judgment to which today's gospel refers. In the language of the creeds, "he will come to judge the living and the dead" and "he will come again in glory to judge the living and the dead." Paul's words, "Bless those who persecute you," are a reminder to Christians to include prayer for their enemies in the weekly intercessions.

Recalling Paul's message to the Romans, one option in *Evangelical Lutheran Worship* for the final blessing calls on God to grant us "to live in harmony with one another" and to fill us "with all joy and peace in believing."

Let the Children Come

God cares about what you do with your money. Maybe you have a little money now, but as you get older, you likely have more money. How you use that money is important to God because it shows what's most important to you. In a reverse offering, give three quarters to each child at worship this weekend with the invitation to use one each to 1) share, 2) save, and 3) spend (www.sharesavespend.com/). This is a

model, a practice, for sharing significantly—a way to show how we can give our life away and overcome evil with good.

Assembly Song
Gathering

For the beauty of the earth   ELW 879, LBW 561
Son of God, eternal Savior   ELW 655, LBW 364
Lord our God, with praise we come   ELW 730, LBW 244

Psalmody

Lawton, Liam. "Evermore I'll Sing Your Praise." Cant, assembly, kybd, gtr. GIA G-5294.
Guimont, Michel. "Psalm 26" from PRCL.
Warner, Steven C. "Harbor of My Heart" from PAS 16B.
Makeever, Ray. "Tell What God Has Done for Us (Psalm 105)" from DH.

Hymn of the Day

Healer of our every ill   ELW 612, WOV 738
    HEALER OF OUR EVERY ILL
Take up your cross, the Savior said   ELW 667   *BOURBON*
    LBW 398   *NUN LASST UNS DEN LEIB BEGRABEN*
Lord Jesus, you shall be my song   ELW 808   *LES PETITES SOEURS*

Offering

Blest be the tie that binds   ELW 656, LBW 370
Will you come and follow me   ELW 798, W&P 137

Communion

Day by day   ELW 790, WOV 746
Just a closer walk with thee   ELW 697, TFF 253
Strengthen for service, Lord   ELW 497

Sending

Jesus, still lead on   ELW 624, LBW 341
Rise, O church, like Christ arisen   ELW 548

Additional Assembly Songs

We will glorify   TFF 281, W&P 154
Christ, burning Wisdom   OBS 51
◉ Dexter, Noel. Caribbean. "I Come to the Cross" from *Let the Peoples Sing*. SATB. AFP 9780800675394.
◉ Loh, I-to. Taiwan. "Christ Is Our Peace" from *Sound the Bamboo*. U. GIA G-6830.
✿ Busbee, Mike. "Make Me like You" from WT.
✿ Fusilier, Eric/Joshua Vanderlaan/Elias Dummer/Aaron Powell. "My God" from WT.
✿ Hall, Charlie. "Marvelous Light" from WT.
✿ Hughes, Rachel/Tim Hughes. "Living for Your Glory" from CCLI.
✿ Redman, Matt/Stuart Townend. "You Rescued Us" from CCLI.
✿ Rend Collective Experiment "The Cost" from WT.

◉ = global song
✿ = praise song

Music for the Day
Choral

Busarow, Donald. "Day by Day." SATB. MSM 50-6004.

Cherwien, David. "Prayer for Peace." 2 pt mxd, org. MSM 50-9209.

Farlee, Robert Buckley. "To Christ Belong." SATB, org, fl, assembly. AFP 9781451420791.

● Haugen, Marty. "Healer of Our Every Ill." 2 pt mxd, kybd, C inst. GIA G-3478.

Leavitt, John. "Come, Follow Me." SAB, org, C inst. GIA G-3028.

Young, Jeremy. "God Has Spoken, Bread Is Broken." SAB, pno. AFP 9780800655877.

Children's Choir

Manz, Paul. "Let Us Ever Walk with Jesus." U, org. MSM 50-9405.

Patterson, Mark. "I Will Give My Heart to the Lord" in *Young ChildrenSing*. U, kybd, opt Orff inst/hc. AFP 9780800676803.

Scott, K. Lee. "My Great Reward." 2 pt, kybd. CPH 98-2715.

Tucker, Margaret. "Christ's Own Body." U/2 pt, kybd, opt assembly, opt hb. CG CGA801.

Keyboard / Instrumental

● Hamilton, Gregory. "Healer of Our Every Ill" from *Piano Blessings*. Pno. AFP 9781451420906.

● Honoré, Jeffrey. "Healer of Our Every Ill" from *Contemporary Hymn Settings for Organ*. Org. AFP 9780800674786.

Near, Gerald. "Ubi caritas et amor" from *St. Augustine's Organbook*. Org. AUR AE86.

● Stevens, Wendy Lynn. "Bourbon" from *How Sweet the Sound: Piano Arrangements for Worship*. Pno. AFP 9780806696966.

Handbell

Glasgow, Michael. "Healing Spirit." 3-7 oct hb, opt 3 oct hc, fl, opt perc, L3-. CG CGB754.

● McAninch, Diane. "Healer of Our Every Ill." 2-3 oct hb, opt 2 oct hc, L2. GIA G-7286.

Moklebust, Cathy. "Rejoice! He Is Risen! (Rejoice in the Spirit)." 2-3 oct hb, opt 3-6 oct hc, L2+. CG CGB720. 3-6 oct hb, opt 3-6 oct hc, L2+. CG CGB721.

Tuesday, September 2
Nikolai Frederik Severin Grundtvig, bishop, renewer of the church, died 1872

Grundtvig was one of two principal Danish theologians of the nineteenth century; the other was Søren Kierkegaard. Grundtvig's ministry as a parish pastor had a difficult start. He was officially censured after his first sermon, though he did receive approval a year later to be ordained. He served with his father for two years but was unable to receive a call for seven years after that. In 1826 he was forced to resign after he attacked the notion that Christianity was merely a philosophical idea rather than God's revelation made known to us in Christ and through word and sacrament. This belief would be a hallmark of Grundtvig's writing. He spent his last thirty-three years as a chaplain at a home for elderly women. From his university days he was convinced that poetry spoke to the human spirit better than prose. He wrote more than a thousand hymns, including "God's Word Is Our Great Heritage" (ELW 509).

TIME AFTER PENTECOST
AUTUMN

SUMMER

AUTUMN

NOVEMBER

PREPARING FOR AUTUMN

Autumn in the church calendar is a non-liturgical season that follows a non-liturgical season. The lectionary texts for the fall continue the pattern already set during the summer: consecutive readings from the gospel of Matthew with complementary readings from the Old Testament, and continuous readings from some of the lesser but still great Pauline epistles. However, for almost all congregations, autumn is a new season because of the academic calendar and the beginning of another school year. It is often also the beginning of Sunday school and other church programs after a summer of difference or rest. It is completely appropriate, then, to practice this season as a time for fresh starts, new beginnings, and reinvigoration.

Holy Cross Day and Reformation Sunday?

Autumn includes options for celebrating two festival days, Holy Cross Day on September 14 and Reformation Sunday on October 26. Unless these festival days are deeply ingrained in the piety of your local community, consider skipping these days and continuing with the assigned lectionary texts for "extraordinary time." Both Sundays include crucial readings from the Gospel of Matthew that otherwise are lost.

Lectionary

By now we have come at the Gospel of Matthew from any number of directions. We have read the texts that form the basis for festival days such as Christmas and Easter. We have examined the "conspiracy" narrative leading up to Christ's crucifixion. Through the summer months special attention has been given to the narrative arc of Jesus' life, especially his parabolic teaching and the deepening understanding of Jesus as the promised Messiah bringing about the kingdom of God.

Autumn is likely the time best suited for returning to a good introduction in a commentary to the gospel itself. Preachers may have exhausted certain insights in their summer preaching, and need fresh insight. It is also a time for consolidating insights, perhaps even reviewing key themes from the gospel, so that the assembly ends year A with such a deep sense of Matthew as a gospel that they will retain the insights and be prepared to compare them, in year B, to the way Mark crafts the gospel message.

Here are a couple of examples of big-picture insights that can reinvigorate preaching on the gospel texts through autumn. First, here are the gospels and their complementary Old Testament readings. Notice that the lectionary continues to link Matthew strongly with Isaiah, but does weave in a couple of historical readings from the five books of Moses, plus two significant readings from Ezekiel:

Date	Gospel (Matthew)	Complementary first reading
September 7	18:15-20 (community)	Ezekiel 33:7-11
September 14	18:21-35 (community)	Genesis 50:15-21
September 21	20:1-16 (leadership)	Jonah 3:10—4:11
September 28	21:23-32 (true people)	Ezekiel 18:1-4, 25-32
October 5	21:33-46 (true people)	Isaiah 5:1-7
October 12	22:1-14 (wise people)	Isaiah 25:1-9
October 19	22:15-22 (wise people)	Isaiah 45:1-7
October 26	22:34-46 (wise people)	Leviticus 19:1-2, 15-18

Second, Frederick Dale Bruner, in his *Matthew: A Commentary* (Eerdmans, two volumes), considers Matthew as being two different "books." Matthew 1–12 he labels the Christbook, covering Christ's coming (chapters 1–4), words (5–7), work (8–9), mission (10), and person (11–12). The second half of Matthew, the majority of which we read in year A during summer and autumn, he labels the Churchbook. The structure is as follows:

The Church's faith (also called the sermon of parables)
- Kingdom (13)
- Responsibility (14)
- Catholic evangelicalism (15)
- Church (16)
- Authority (17)

The Church's love (also called the little sermon on the mount)
- Community (18)
- Home (19)
- Leadership (20)

The Church's history
- True people of God (21)
- Wise people of God (22)
- False people of God (23)

If we look at just this overall structure, if offers some compelling and powerful ways to come at the Matthew texts for this long series of Sundays from Holy Trinity through the fall. In fact, these can almost be lined out as a sermon series itself. Given that Matthew is the most systematic and didactic of all the gospels, preachers and worship leaders could make use of the overall structure lined out in Frederick Dale Bruner's commentary to teach catechetically chapter by chapter through the entire gospel (for a full outline of Matthew chapter by chapter, see Bruner's commentary, p. xxvii).

Liturgical Arts

Pastors and liturgical arts leaders often wonder what to do about seasonal environment and the desires of wedding parties and families at funerals. How much is the church willing to change or remove to make room for the artistic sensibilities of families planning a funeral or wedding? In these situations, how might seasonal planning teams and worship leaders experiment with some level of mutuality?

Here's one example. At a wedding in one congregation, the family brought Mason jars filled with water and live green and white flowers. These jars were then tied with a ribbon, attached to bailing twine, and the twine was used to hang the jars from the pews. This was a natural and organic way to spruce up the worship space for the wedding. The family left the flower jars in the worship space as a gift to the congregation's Sunday morning worship. It just so happened that the next week the congregation was hosting a canning party with a local hunger advocacy organization, canning leftover produce from the farmer's market for food pantries and shelters. So the wedding art not only beautified the worship space and celebrated the occasion, it also helped point out the door in mission. Strict rules against families contributing to the worship space environment would have foreclosed this movement of the Spirit.

In addition, although a couple will rarely pick accent colors based on the color of the season, they may be interested in knowing whether the stole of the pastor matches or clashes with their selections. A creative conversation between clergy and couple early on in the wedding planning can end up benefiting everyone. And remember, a wedding is often the first time young adults have ever been given the opportunity to think about liturgical planning. They are newbies. Smacking down on their ideas simply because they do not match our own current liturgical sensibilities dishonors their creativity and will ensure their never wishing to serve on an altar guild or worship planning team in the future. We can learn from families in their funeral and wedding preparations. Take notes. Write ideas down, and adapt them for Sunday worship. For more on this, see "Funeral" and "Marriage" in *The Christian Life* (Augsburg Fortress, 2008, pp. 149–208).

Music

A lot of innovation is happening in liturgical rock. One center for the commissioning and premiering of folk, pop, rock, and indie settings of the liturgy is Mercy Seat in Minneapolis, Minnesota. Mercy Seat archives each new liturgy on its website, www.nemercy.org/category/liturgy/. These settings are solidly in the indie/emo genre, so will appeal to communities already trying to offer liturgical settings arising from, but moving beyond, the contemporary Christian music scene.

For communities that are into more mainstream CCM, fall is a good time to go check the charts and see what is new and popular. CCLI maintains a variety of lists of popular songs, one of the most useful of which is its top 25, www.ccli.com/licenseholder/Top25Lists.aspx. One of the most difficult tasks for congregations trying to do contemporary music that fits the lectionary is that of trying to match themes and concepts. Few comprehensive indexes exist pairing the lectionary texts to specific contemporary worship songs. *Sundays and Seasons* provides some weekly suggestions. Furthermore, the range of contemporary worship songs is different from the range of classical hymnody, at least in part because these songs were and are composed for different purposes. Where some ancient hymns were written to reinforce and express the theology of the church, or even perform a catechetical function, contemporary songs are more often songs of praise, designed to express the heartfelt faith of the community as it praises the Lord. When possible, match songs to the lectionary texts, but also consider the possibility that the gathering music or other musical sets sung during a contemporary service are perfectly fine without needing to match the themes in the readings. You have permission to go rogue and just sing songs the Spirit moves you to sing.

Finally, consider Nate Houge's "Stumbling Service" as a resource to center your band-led worship solidly in the folk-punk liturgical tradition (natehouge.com/music/stumbling-service/). "The 'Stumbling Service' is a band-driven communion liturgy drawing heavily from the Gospel of Mark lectionary readings. It can be led with the provided stand-alone bulletin, augmented with additional scripture and song inserts, or broken apart as individual songs in other worship environs. You can punk it up or folk it down.

The boot on the front is a call to follow, an acknowledgment of our stumbling, a symbol of change, a tool for work, and an allusion to our faith journeys—stumbling and all—with the hope of one more step toward the cross." If you launch this liturgy in the fall of 2014, perhaps introducing one or two songs, you will be set to sing it regularly during year B, 2015, with the Gospel of Mark.

One other alternative: commission a new liturgy for the fall for use in your context. Identify a local musician, give them the texts of the liturgy, and set them to work (and pay them well).

Worship Texts for Autumn

Confession and Forgiveness

All may make the sign of the cross, the sign marked at baptism,
as the presiding minister begins.

Blessed be the holy Trinity, ☩ one God,
the Sovereign over all the earth,
the Wisdom from on high,
our merciful Judge and Savior.
Amen.

Let us boldly approach the throne of grace,
trusting in God's mercy and love.

Silence is kept for reflection.

Generous and faithful God,
we confess to you all the ways,
known and unknown,
that we reject and undermine your steadfast love.
Though you made us your people,
we treat strangers with suspicion.
Though you forgave our debts,
we collect without mercy.
Yet we are quick to pass judgment on others.
Have mercy on us, O God,
and remember your promise to us,
for the sake of Jesus Christ, our Lord.
Amen.

The grass withers, the flower fades,
but the word of our God will stand forever.
Through the living Word, ☩ Jesus Christ,
God forgives your every debt, your every sin,
and gives you a new heart and a new spirit.
Amen.

Offering Prayer

Merciful God, as grains of wheat scattered upon the hills
were gathered together to become one bread,
so let your church be gathered together
from the ends of the earth into your kingdom,
for yours is the glory through Jesus Christ, now and forever.
Amen.

Invitation to Communion

The reign of God is at hand.
Come, taste the joy prepared for you.

Prayer after Communion

O God, the host at every meal,
at this table you spread out a feast for all peoples,
the bread of life and the cup of salvation.
Send us from this banquet
to invite others into these good things,
to let justice roll down like waters,
and to care for the least of our sisters and brothers;
through Jesus Christ, our Sovereign and our Savior.
Amen.

Sending of Communion

Gracious God, you took the form of a servant,
offering yourself as food, comfort, and strength
to a sick and hurting world.
Anoint with a servant heart
those who take your word and sacrament
to our sisters and brothers
in their homes/in prisons/in hospitals.
Grant grace, mercy, healing, and hope
to those who feast on your body and blood
and receive your words of new life.
May we all recognize that we have a place and a home
in the body of our Lord Jesus Christ.
Amen.

Blessing

The blessing of almighty God,
the Father of glory,
☩ Jesus Christ our peace,
and the Spirit of truth,
be upon you and remain with you always.
Amen.

Dismissal

Go in peace. Christ is with you.
Thanks be to God.

SEASONAL RITES FOR AUTUMN

Blessing of Lectors

These prayers for illumination may be used to bless those who serve as readers of scripture and to prepare the assembly for the hearing of God's word. This action underscores the importance of the ministry of lectors and of the public reading of the scriptures as an event that brings Christ, the Word, into the midst of the people.

After the prayer of the day and just before the readings, the lector/s may come forward for the blessing and stand before the presider. These prayers may be used as presented or as models for presiders who choose to pray freely over the readers. They may be adapted for use with more than one reader.

Let us pray.
Gracious God, we do not live by bread alone,
but by every word that comes from you.
Bless *name*, who will read to us the scriptures.
Make us hunger for the Word of life,
Jesus Christ our Lord.
Amen.

or
Let us pray.
Bless *name*, O Lord, as *he/she* reads to us the scriptures.
As rain and snow come down from heaven
and do not return until the earth is watered,
let your word not return empty,
but accomplish your purpose
and succeed in that for which it was sent;
through Jesus Christ our Lord.
Amen.

or
Let us pray.
God Almighty, we ask your blessing upon *name*
as *he/she* reads to us the scriptures.
May the words of *his/her* mouth
and the meditations of our hearts
be acceptable in your sight, O Lord,
our rock and our redeemer.
Amen.

Blessings for Teachers and Students

For the marvels of your creation,
we praise you, O God.
For the opportunity to explore and study,
we praise you, O God.
For those who guide us, teachers and mentors,
we praise you, O God.
Teach us your ways and guide us in your path,
for you are the creator of all that is seen and unseen.
Amen.

or
Let us pray for all who are beginning a new school year,
that both students and teachers
will be blessed in their academic endeavors.

Almighty God, you give wisdom and knowledge.
Grant teachers the gift of joy and insight,
and students the gift of diligence and openness,
that all may grow in what is good and honest and true.
Support all who teach and all who learn,
that together we may know and follow your ways;
through Jesus Christ our Lord.
Amen.

Presentation of the Bible

A representative of the congregation may present a Bible to each person. These or similar words may be spoken:
Receive this Bible.
Hear God's word with us.
Learn and tell its stories.
Discover its mysteries.
Honor its commandments.
Rejoice in its good news.
May God's life-giving word
inspire you and make you wise.

Blessing of Animals

This service may be used entirely on its own, perhaps for an observance on or near the commemoration of Francis of Assisi, renewer of the church, 1226 (October 4). Various elements of this order may also be incorporated into another worship service, though this material is not intended to replace the customary Sunday worship of the congregation. For practical reasons this service may be conducted outdoors or in a facility other than a congregation's primary worship space.

Greeting and Prayer

The grace of our Lord Jesus Christ, the love of God, and the communion of the Holy Spirit be with you all.
And also with you.

Let us pray.
Sovereign of the universe, your first covenant of mercy was with every living creature. When your beloved Son came among us, the waters of the river welcomed him, the heavens opened to greet his arrival, the animals of the wilderness drew near as his companions. With all the world's people, may we who are washed into new life through baptism seek the way of your new creation, the way of justice and care, mercy and peace; through Jesus Christ, our Savior and Lord.
Amen.

or
Source and sustainer of life, we cherish the myriad works of your hands. Water, earth, and sky are yours, as are all their inhabitants, wild and tame. We thank you for creatures that nourish and serve us, befriend, enrich, entertain, and protect us. May we, who are made in your image, care for them well. And may your groaning yet wondrous creation rally and thrive, revealing to all who come after us your wise, redemptive, transfiguring love; through Jesus Christ, our Savior and Lord.
Amen.

Readings

Genesis 1:1, 20-28
Genesis 6:17-22
Psalm 8
Psalm 84:1-4
Psalm 148

The reading of scripture is followed by silence for reflection. Other forms of reflection may also follow, such as brief commentary, teaching, or personal witness; non-biblical readings; interpretation through music or other art forms; or guided conversation among those present.

Song

God of the sparrow   ELW 740
Oh, that I had a thousand voices   ELW 833
All creatures, worship God most high!   ELW 835
All things bright and beautiful   WOV 767
This is my Father's world   ELW 824

Blessing of Animals

The leader may ask all who have brought pets or animals to the celebration to come forward for the following prayer.

The Lord be with you.
And also with you.

Let us pray.
Gracious God, in your love you created us in your image and made us stewards of the animals that live in the skies, the earth, and the sea. Bless us in our care for our pets and animals (*names of pets may be added here*). Help us recognize your power and wisdom in the variety of creatures that live in our world, and hear our prayer for all that suffer overwork, hunger, and ill treatment. Protect your creatures, and guard them from all evil, now and forever.
Amen.

The Lord's Prayer

Blessing

Almighty God bless us,
and direct our days and our deeds in peace.
Amen.

September 7, 2014
Time after Pentecost — Lectionary 23

Conflict is a part of relationships and life in community. Jesus' words in today's gospel are often used in situations having to do with church discipline. The prophet Ezekiel tells of warning the wicked to turn from their ways, and Paul reminds us that love is the fulfilling of the law. We gather in the name of Christ, assured that he is present among us with gifts of peace and reconciliation.

Prayer of the Day

O Lord God, enliven and preserve your church with your perpetual mercy. Without your help, we mortals will fail; remove far from us everything that is harmful, and lead us toward all that gives life and salvation, through Jesus Christ, our Savior and Lord.

Gospel Acclamation

Alleluia. In Christ God was reconciling the world to himself,* entrusting the message of reconcilia- tion to us. *Alleluia.* (2 Cor. 5:19)

Readings and Psalm

Ezekiel 33:7-11

God appointed Ezekiel as a sentinel for the house of Israel. Ezekiel must faithfully convey God's warnings to the people. Remarkably, God—who is about to attack Jerusalem—gives a warning with the hope that repentance will make the attack unnecessary.

Psalm 119:33-40

I desire the path of your commandments. (Ps. 119:35)

Romans 13:8-14

The obligation of Christians is to love one another and so fulfill the heart and goal of the law. Clothes make the person as we "put on the Lord Jesus Christ" and live today in light of the future God has in store for us.

Matthew 18:15-20

Jesus offers practical advice to his disciples on how individuals—and the church as a whole—should show wrongdoers their need for repentance.

Semicontinuous reading and psalm

Exodus 12:1-14

Israel remembered its deliverance from slavery in Egypt by celebrating the festival of Passover. This festival featured the Passover lamb, whose blood was used as a sign to protect God's people from the threat of death. The early church described the Lord's supper using imagery from the Passover, especially in portraying Jesus as the lamb who delivers God's people from sin and death.

Psalm 149

Sing the Lord's praise in the assembly of the faithful. (Ps. 149:1)

Preface Sundays

Color Green

Prayers of Intercession

The prayers are prepared locally for each occasion. The following examples may be adapted or used as appropriate.

With the whole people of God in Christ Jesus, let us pray for the church, those in need, and all of God's creation.
A brief silence.

God of love, your church is a place of relationship. Give us understanding to care for you and each other with our whole hearts. Hear us, O God.
Your mercy is great.

God of love, your creation is a precious gift. Turn our hearts to share its resources wisely rather than in selfish gain. Hear us, O God.
Your mercy is great.

God of love, your desire for us is peace. Lead us along paths of justice and give us delight in living with honor and loving our neighbor. Hear us, O God.
Your mercy is great.

God of love, your ways are goodness and life. Free us from those things that create fear and dread, loneliness and heartache, pain and disgrace (*especially*). Hear us, O God.
Your mercy is great.

God of love, you gather us around your word, your font, and your table. Teach us to be a community of grace and witness. Hear us, O God.
Your mercy is great.

Here other intercessions may be offered.

God of love, your promise to us is resurrection. Confirm in us that promise as we remember those who have died trusting in you. Hear us, O God.
Your mercy is great.
Trusting in your mercy and goodness, we bring before you these prayers and whatever else you see that we need, in the name of the one who sets us free, Jesus Christ, our Savior.
Amen.

Images in the Readings

We are **bound**, we are **loosed**: these are strong images describing the powers that hold us captive and the gift of God's Spirit that frees us for a life of love. The responsibility for correction, discipline, and forgiveness belongs to the community.

Tax collectors were despised collaborators who were infamous for cheating. Mercifully, Jesus is described as eating with tax collectors. This is good news for all of us.

Ezekiel calls us to be **sentinels**, those assigned to watch from the city walls for both any approaching dangers and any welcome visitors. The life of the Christian is an active life, watching in the world for the bad and the good and reporting to the community what we see.

Paul calls us to wake up; the **day** has come; get dressed, wearing Christ; for today there might be a battle.

In his mixing of metaphors, Paul blends the robe of baptism with the **armor** of a warrior. It's a dangerous world out there, everywhere affected by human sin.

Ideas for the Day

◆ Mutual accountability is something many people have trouble with, especially in a society shaped by overwhelming ideas of self-determination. Each of today's readings speaks of accountability of some kind, and preachers and liturgists will do well to consider the ways that *accountability* as a concept is framed as a gift rather than a burden. How is accountability freeing rather than limiting? How does our responsibility for one another within the body of Christ free us to serve? The proclamation of mutual accountability is in many ways countercultural, a theme that is enacted in the liturgy, which by definition is a communally accountable exercise.

◆ Themes of *reconciliation* are also prominent in the texts, and thought might be given to the difference between confession and reconciliation, terms that are not mutually exclusive but can—in an intentional way—enrich one another. In the Protestant mindset, confession all too often seems to be between the believer and God alone, while reconciliation implies a restoration of relationship between the individual and God, *and* between the individual and the community—a triangle of sorts. How do these terms play off one another and deepen our understanding of what it means to "return to the LORD, your God"? (Joel 2:13).

◆ In the Matthew text Jesus says that a church member who sins and refuses efforts of correction and reconciliation is to be regarded as a "Gentile and a tax collector"—that is, as an outsider who remains welcome and in need of the gospel. Jesus treated both Gentiles and tax collectors as welcome guests in the kingdom of God. Such inclusion would seem to indicate that God's efforts to restore relationship never end, but rather welcome with even greater hospitality those who have estranged themselves from the community. How might such hospitality extend (and be increased) even to those who have cut themselves off from God's kingdom?

Connections with the Liturgy

It is almost as if the gospel reading provides an outline for much Sunday worship: we confess our sins, we are loosed from sin's bonds, we intercede for all the world, and we gather around the table to meet the risen Christ. As well, Paul alludes to baptism, our putting on Jesus Christ. This is what it means to be the church of Christ.

Let the Children Come

Sometimes we can't solve problems all by ourselves. We need helpers. Although no one wants to be a "tattle-tale," it's good to ask for help. Sometimes, we feel like we're supposed to know how to handle hard things all on our own, even as children. Sometimes we think church is about showing our "best selves." But that's not true. We are called into community to serve one another in our brokenness and help each other in times of trial.

Assembly Song
Gathering

Earth and all stars! ELW 731, LBW 558
Lord of all nations, grant me grace ELW 716, LBW 419
Praise, my soul, the King of heaven ELW 865, LBW 549

Psalmody

"Change Your Heart and Mind." *Psallite* A-171.
Walker, Christopher. "Teach Me O God" from PS3.
Becker, John W. "Psalm 119:33-40" from PWA.
Pavlechko, Thomas. "Psalm 149" from SMP.

Hymn of the Day

Forgive our sins as we forgive ELW 605, LBW 307 *DETROIT*
God, when human bonds are broken ELW 603, WOV 735 *MERTON*
In all our grief ELW 615, WOV 739 *FREDERICKTOWN*

Offering

Where charity and love prevail ELW 359, LBW 126
When we are living ELW 639, LLC 462

Communion

As we gather at your table   ELW 522

At the Lamb's high feast we sing   ELW 362, LBW 210

Draw us in the Spirit's tether   ELW 470, WOV 703

Sending

Joyful, joyful we adore thee   ELW 836, LBW 551

Blessed be the name   ELW 797

Additional Assembly Songs

Lord, this day we've come to worship   TFF 137

Hope of the world   LBW 493

Let us put on the clothes of Christ   GS2 32

◉ Mxdana, George. South Africa. "Alleluia" from *Sent by the Lord: Songs of the World Church, Vol 2*. U. GIA G-3740.

✿ Gillies, Brandon/Israel Houghton/Michael Gungor. "People of God" from CCLI.

✿ Hall, Charlie/Matt Redman. "Center" from WT.

✿ Houston, Joel/Jonathon Douglass. "One Way" from CCLI.

✿ Hughes, Tim/Martin Smith. "Holding Nothing Back" from WT.

✿ Maher, Matt/Steve Wilson. "Hold Us Together" from WT.

✿ Redman, Matt. "Praise Awaits You" from CCLI.

Music for the Day

Choral

Atwood, Thomas. "Teach Me, O Lord" from *Augsburg Motet Book*. SATB. AFP 9781451423709.

Dengler, Lee. "Put On Love." SAB, kybd. AFP 9781451420784.

● Keesecker, Thomas. "In All Our Grief." 2 pt mxd, kybd. AFP 9780806697352.

Lawton, Liam/Paul A. Tate. "Where Two or Three Are Gathered." SATB, C inst, assembly. GIA G-7566.

Rosebrock, Stephen. "Evening and Morning." 2 pt mxd, kybd, fl. CPH 98-3988.

Stopford, Philip. "Teach Me, O Lord." SATB, org. MSM 50-8865.

● White, David Ashley. "Forgive Our Sins As We Forgive." 2 pt mxd, kybd. SEL 410-611.

Children's Choir

Berg, Ken. "Search Me, O God." U, pno. CG CGA1245.

Chepponis, James J. "God Is a God of Love." U, org, opt tpt, opt hb. GIA G-2542.

Van Oss, Richard L. "Jesus, Jesus, Let Us Tell You." U, opt glock, opt xyl. LS 144.

Keyboard / Instrumental

● Callahan, Charles. "Improvisation on 'Merton'" from *Advent Music for Manuals, Set 2*. Org. MSM 10-011.

● Cherwien, David. "Fredericktown" from *O God beyond All Praising: Hymn Settings for Organ*. Org. AFP 9780800657246.

● Organ, Anne Krentz. "Fredericktown" from *Woven Together: Reflections for Piano and Solo Instrument*. Inst, pno. AFP 9780800658168.

Sedio, Mark. "Chereponi" from *Dancing in the Light of God: A Piano Collection*. Pno. AFP 9780800656546.

Handbell

Roberts, Philip. "Gather Us In." 3-5 oct hb, opt C inst, L4. GIA G-6704.

Sherman, Arnold. "Prayer." 3-5 oct, L3. LOR 20/1147L.

Waldrop, Tammy. "How Deep the Father's Love for Us." 3 or 5 oct hb, opt 2 oct hc, opt narr, L2+. ALF 31749.

Tuesday, September 9

Peter Claver, priest, missionary to Colombia, died 1654

Peter Claver was born into Spanish nobility and was persuaded to become a Jesuit missionary. He served in Cartagena (in what is now Colombia) by teaching and caring for the slaves. The slaves arrived in ships, where they had been confined in dehumanizing conditions. Claver met and supplied them with medicine, food, clothing, and brandy. He learned their dialects and taught them Christianity. He called himself "the slave of the slaves forever." Claver also ministered to the locals of Cartagena who were in prison and facing death.

Saturday, September 13

John Chrysostom, Bishop of Constantinople, died 407

John was a priest in Antioch and an outstanding preacher. His eloquence earned him the nickname "Chrysostom" ("golden mouth"), but it also got him into trouble. As bishop of Constantinople he preached against corruption among the royal court. The empress, who had been his supporter, sent him into exile. His preaching style emphasized the literal meaning of scripture and its practical application. This interpretation stood in contrast to the common style at the time, which emphasized the allegorical meaning of the text.

September 14, 2014
Holy Cross Day

This festival, which originated in the fourth century, celebrates the triumph of the cross. Paul reminds us that Christ crucified is the power and wisdom of God. As Moses put a serpent on a pole to be a source of healing for the Israelites, we lift high the cross as the sign of our health and salvation. Each time we make the sign of the cross we remember our baptism into the death and resurrection of Christ.

Prayer of the Day

Almighty God, your Son Jesus Christ was lifted high upon the cross so that he might draw the whole world to himself. To those who look upon the cross, grant your wisdom, healing, and eternal life, through Jesus Christ, our Savior and Lord, who lives and reigns with you and the Holy Spirit, one God, now and forever.

Gospel Acclamation

Alleluia. May I never boast of | anything* except the cross of our Lord | Jesus Christ. *Alleluia.* (Gal. 6:14)

Readings and Psalm

Numbers 21:4b-9

When the people spoke against God and Moses, the Lord sent poisonous snakes against them. Moses interceded for the people, and the Lord ordered him to erect a serpent of bronze on a pole. All who looked at it after having been bitten by a serpent would live.

Psalm 98:1-4

The LORD has done marvelous things. (Ps. 98:1)

or Psalm 78:1-2, 34-38

God was their rock and the Most High God their redeemer. (Ps. 78:35)

1 Corinthians 1:18-24

At the heart of the Christian message is the word of the cross. This proclamation seems foolish to many because it reveals true divine power in the absolute weakness of Christ's crucifixion. True wisdom understands how ours is a God who suffers for and with humankind in the cross.

John 3:13-17

After explaining to Nicodemus that one must be born of water and Spirit, Jesus speaks of being lifted up on the cross, with reference to the bronze serpent lifted up by Moses in the desert. Here the Son of God is revealed as the source of healing.

Preface   Sunday of the Passion

Color   Scarlet *or* Red

Prayers of Intercession

The prayers are prepared locally for each occasion. The following examples may be adapted or used as appropriate.

With the whole people of God in Christ Jesus, let us pray for the church, those in need, and all of God's creation.

A brief silence.

For the whole church of God: its leaders, missionaries, youth workers, chaplains, pastors, bishops, and all the baptized. Help us proclaim Christ crucified. Hear us, O God.
Your mercy is great.

For all creation: seeds that are sown, fields that are harvested, winds that blow, rains that fall, animals that roam, and the fruits of the earth. Fill us with thanksgiving for these gifts. Hear us, O God.
Your mercy is great.

For the leaders of this world: presidents, prime ministers, monarchs, parliaments, elected representatives, and heads of corporations. Inspire them to do what is right and just even if it looks foolish. Hear us, O God.
Your mercy is great.

For all who suffer in mind and body: the bullied and the shamed, the brokenhearted and the beaten-down, the sick and the dying (*especially*). Heal them with the encouragement of the gospel. Hear us, O God.
Your mercy is great.

For the mission of this congregation, its ministries, stewardship, fellowship, outreach, homebound, children, volunteers, staff, and council. Make us a beacon of your love. Hear us, O God.
Your mercy is great.

Here other intercessions may be offered.

In thanksgiving for the blessed dead: those martyred and those who gave themselves in love, those who died alone and those who died tragically, that they, together with all your saints, be lifted up in your glory. Hear us, O God.
Your mercy is great.

Trusting in your mercy and goodness, we bring before you these prayers and whatever else you see that we need, in the name of the one who sets us free, Jesus Christ, our Savior. **Amen.**

Images in the Readings

We are so accustomed to the **cross** as the primary symbol of the Christian faith that we forget that it was not until the time of the Emperor Constantine, who outlawed crucifixions, that Christians used it to signify the faith. John's interpretation of the story from Numbers illustrates how religious imagery gains one layer of meaning on top of another. From a Canaanite goddess symbol, through an Israelite story of God's saving power, into the Roman Empire's practice of the execution of the lowliest criminals, into our churches and onto our bodies, the cross is for Christians the symbol that in God, death is transformed into the entry into new life. In medieval church art, it was common to depict the two scenes side-by-side: the serpent on the pole and Christ on the cross. It is common in Hindu art to depict the god Krishna with a blue face: the story is told that humans were dying of poison, and Krishna drank the poison to save the people, but it turned his face blue. So in John's use of the Numbers story, it is as if Christ saves us from poison.

John's Gospel speaks of God saving, not the church, but the **world**. Most contemporary Christians understand that it is not our job to escape the world that God so loved. Rather, in the Sending of our service (*Evangelical Lutheran Worship*, p. 93), we are sent out into the world, embodying Christ and witnessing to God's Spirit.

Among the books in the Old Testament is **Wisdom** literature, much of which conveys logical advice for succeeding in life: "do this, and you will live well." However, Paul uses "wisdom" as a way to describe salvation through the cross, which is the opposite of logical and successful. That the cross is God's wisdom turns a historic religious category on its head.

Ideas for the Day

◆ The cross has become so commonplace to us that we no longer grasp its scandal. If you asked people—for example—to wear a small silver electric chair around their neck instead of a cross, they might look at you with offense. Has the cross lost something when it is, to many, a symbol of quaint religiosity rather than a sign of offense? Might this instead speak to us of our comfort level with religion rather than the ways it should call us to radical life reorientation? Preachers and worship planners will do well to consider how the cross has become a sign that baptizes the status quo rather than challenges it, a dangerous proposition for the Christian life and for the world into which such crosses are carried.

◆ It is worth considering on this day the extent to which Christianity has given "aid and comfort" to systems in conflict with the base understandings of the gospel. Holy Cross has its origins in the miraculous finding of the true cross by Helena while she was tromping about the Holy Land. Her "discovery" further merged religion and empire into a seamless whole that could be used (and was) by powerful people to retain power. In this way, how might Holy Cross Day stand as a warning to us to be wary of the ways empires use religion, and vice versa, for their own glorious goals?

◆ If your parish has a processional cross but does not use it regularly, you may wish to consider using it today (and perhaps each Sunday) as a sign of the crucified Christ we follow. Some discussion in a parish about the difference between a plain cross and a crucifix may be in order here, because—and it bears reminding—we do not worship the cross per se, but rather the one *on* the cross. For those who object "yes, but he is risen!" a gentle reminder might be that Jesus rose from a tomb, not a cross. Luther himself declared that a crucifix should be hung by every pulpit, a reminder that we "preach Christ crucified." We do, and we preach him risen too. The cross is all that and more.

Connections with the Liturgy

Thanksgiving at the Table I (*Evangelical Lutheran Worship*, pp. 108–109) was crafted from historic eucharistic prayers by Luther Reed, an early twentieth-century liturgical scholar who worked to revive such thanksgivings at holy communion. The prayer cites John 3:16, the gospel for this day.

Let the Children Come

We make the sign of the cross on each other in baptism; we do the same thing as we commend a body to its grave. At the beginning and end of life and all along the way, we remember that the God we know in Jesus is with us through that gesture. Invite families to imagine how to make the sign of the cross in worship today and in daily life: when we take a bath, go on a journey, head into a challenging day, sleep, and wake up. The cross is the promise of God that through life and death, God is there.

Assembly Song
Gathering

O God, my faithful God   ELW 806, LBW 504
Christ is made the sure foundation   ELW 645
Lord our God, with praise we come   ELW 730

Psalmody

Christopherson, Dorothy. "Psalm 98" from *ChildrenSing Psalms*. U, kybd, fc, tamb.
Organ, Anne Krentz. "Psalm 98:1-4" from PWC.

Hesla, Bret. "Shout unto God (Psalm 98)" from *Justice, Like a Base of Stone.* AFP 9780800623562.

Farlee, Robert Buckley. "Psalm 78:1-2, 34-38" from PWC.

Hymn of the Day

Jesus, keep me near the cross   ELW 335, TFF 73   *NEAR THE CROSS*

Sing, my tongue   ELW 355/356   *PANGE LINGUA/FORTUNATUS NEW*

Take up your cross, the Savior said   ELW 667   *BOURBON*

Offering

Let us ever walk with Jesus   ELW 802, LBW 487

Oh, praise the gracious power   ELW 651, WOV 750

Communion

Now We Remain   ELW 500, W&P 106

Tree of Life and awesome mystery   ELW 334

When I survey the wondrous cross   ELW 803, TFF 79

Sending

Lift high the cross   ELW 660, LBW 377

On our way rejoicing   ELW 537, LBW 260

Additional Assembly Songs

On a hill far away   TFF 77

O Lord, open my eyes   TFF 134

⊕ Berthier, Jacques. France. "Salvator Mundi" from *Music from Taizé, Volume 1.* U, kybd, instr. GIA G-2433S.

⊕ Cuéllar, Guillermo. El Salvador. "Cordero de Dios" from *El Salvador: Misa Popular Salvadoreña.* U, kybd, gtr. GIA G-4159.

✿ Assad, Audrey/Chris Tomlin/Matt Maher. "No Greater Love" from CCLI.

✿ Hughes, Tim. "Beautiful One" from WT.

✿ Maher, Matt/Mia Fieldes. "Christ Is Risen" from WT.

✿ Morgan, Reuben/Ben Fielding. "Stronger" from WT.

✿ Redman, Matt/Paul Baloche. "I Cling to the Cross" from CCLI.

✿ Smith, Martin. "Message of the Cross" from CCLI.

Music for the Day

Choral

Bengtson, Bruce. "Psalm 98: O Sing to the Lord a New Song." SATB, org. AFP 9780800676278.

● Bouman, Paul. "Take Up Your Cross." SATB. SEL 420-617.

● Courtney, Craig. "Near the Cross." SATB, pno. BP 1746.

Grier, Gene. "Sing, My Tongue, the Glorious Battle." 2 pt mxd, pno. GIA G-5773.

Goss, John. "God So Loved the World" from *Augsburg Motet Book.* SATB. AFP 9781451423709.

● Harris, Ed. "Jesus, Keep Me Near the Cross." SATB, pno. HIN 1165.

Wold, Wayne. "God So Loved the World." SAB, org. AFP 9781451420692.

Children's Choir

Bach, J. S. "Jesu, Joy of Man's Desiring." U/2 pt, hb, vln, kybd. HOP F989.

Haugen, Marty. "Tree of Life and Awesome Mystery." ELW 334.

Rutter, John. "Lord of the Dance." U, kybd. HOP C5102.

Simon, Julia. "Why the Cross?" U, kybd. AFP 9780800679163.

Keyboard / Instrumental

● Carlson, Bert J. "Near the Cross" from *Come Thou Fount: Piano Solos to Touch the Heart.* Pno. AFP 9780800676759.

Cherwien, David. "Lift High the Cross: Prelude and Postlude." Org. MSM 10-726.

● Powell, Robert J. "Bourbon" from *Sent Forth: Short Postludes for the Day.* Org. AFP 9780800654887.

● Trapp, Lynn. "Pange lingua" from *In the Mystery of Christ.* Pno. CPH 97-6884.

Handbell

● Glasgow, Michael. "Rest at the Cross." 3-7 oct hb, opt 3-6 oct hc, opt vln, L3. LOR 20/1657L.

● Krug, Jason. "Beneath the Cross of Jesus." 3-6 oct hb, opt 3 oct hc, L3. BP HB384.

● Sylvester, Susan. "A Plainchant Meditation: Morning Suite." 3 oct, L3. AFP 9780800655464.

September 14, 2014
Time after Pentecost — Lectionary 24

In today's second reading Paul questions why we judge one another, since we all stand before the judgment of God. Yet we do sin against one another, and Jesus' challenge that we forgive seventy-seven times reveals God's boundless mercy. When we hear the words of forgiveness in worship and sign ourselves with the cross, we are renewed in baptism to be signs of reconciliation in the world.

Prayer of the Day

O Lord God, merciful judge, you are the inexhaustible fountain of forgiveness. Replace our hearts of stone with hearts that love and adore you, that we may delight in doing your will, through Jesus Christ, our Savior and Lord.

Gospel Acclamation

Alleluia. We have an advocate, Jesus | Christ the righteous;*
your sins are forgiven on account | of his name. *Alleluia.*
(1 John 2:1, 12)

Readings and Psalm
Genesis 50:15-21

After Jacob's death, the brothers of Joseph begged for forgiveness for the crime they had done against him. You intended to do me harm, Joseph said, but God used this as an opportunity to do good and save many lives.

Psalm 103:[1-7] 8-13

Lord, you are full of compassion and mercy. (Ps. 103:8)

Romans 14:1-12

This Christian community has significant struggles with diversity. Here Paul helps us understand that despite different practices in worship and personal piety, we do not judge one another. All Christians belong to the Lord Jesus Christ who died for all of us and will judge each of us.

Matthew 18:21-35

When Peter asks about the limits of forgiveness, Jesus responds with a parable that suggests human forgiveness should mirror the unlimited mercy of God.

Semicontinuous reading and psalm
Exodus 14:19-31

Having decided to let the Israelites go from Egypt, Pharaoh had second thoughts and sent his army after them (14:5-8). Though the passage through the Red Sea became a sign of salvation for the people of Israel, Pharaoh's forces drowned in the waters. As a result the Israelites believed in the Lord and in the Lord's servant Moses.

Psalm 114

Tremble, O earth, at the presence of the Lord. (Ps. 114:7)

or Exodus 15:1b-11, 20-21

I will sing to the Lord, who has triumphed gloriously. (Exod. 15:1)

Preface   Sundays

Color   Green

Prayers of Intercession

The prayers are prepared locally for each occasion. The following examples may be adapted or used as appropriate.

With the whole people of God in Christ Jesus, let us pray for the church, those in need, and all of God's creation.
A brief silence.
Speak kindly to your whole church, O God. Give us tongues that speak words of welcome and acceptance. Hear us, O God.
Your mercy is great.
Shower us with your gifts, O God. Give us hands that share the wealth of your creation and that tend to its keeping. Hear us, O God.
Your mercy is great.
Silence our quarreling, O God. Hold us accountable to one another as brothers and sisters and make us eager to reconcile and quick to forgive. Hear us, O God.
Your mercy is great.
Satisfy us with good things, O God. Give healing to those who suffer in mind, body, and soul, give respite to those who care for them, and hope for all those who worry (*especially*). Hear us, O God.
Your mercy is great.
Make your ways known to us, O God. Hold us upright as we work for justice in our neighborhoods, communities, our nation, and the world. Hear us, O God.
Your mercy is great.

Here other intercessions may be offered.

You, O God, are the Lord of the dead and the living. Hold us, together with all the saints, in your redeeming and steadfast love today and all days. Hear us, O God.
Your mercy is great.
Trusting in your mercy and goodness, we bring before you these prayers and whatever else you see that we need, in the name of the one who sets us free, Jesus Christ, our Savior.
Amen.

Images in the Readings

Seventy-seven plays with the ancient idea that seven is the number of fullness and perfection, because seven combines three, a number that suggests divinity, and four, recalling the corners of the flat earth. So with seventy-seven, Jesus multiplies the number of total perfection.

Matthew's allegory utilizes imagery from the economic system of the first century: a **lord** was the owner of land and of all those who work the land, and a **slave** was one perpetually in the service of another. In our English-language Bibles, "Lord" translates the Hebrew and the Greek words that denote such a masculine societal authority figure. Christian faith in Christ's resurrection occasions the claim that "Jesus is Lord." "Lord" is the usual circumlocution used in our Bibles to render YHWH, God's first name. That we are slaves of God is New Testament imagery, albeit not a currently popular metaphor.

By the mysterious design of God, **Joseph** brought life to his people. Early Christian preachers saw in the Joseph story a parallel to Jesus, who was first brought low but was then raised to power and authority so as to forgive everyone and to feed the world.

Ideas for the Day

◆　The powerful emotions in this gospel story could be highlighted by pantomiming or acting out the story—the slave's fear, the lord's pity, the fellow slaves' sense of injustice, the lord's fury. In particular, *pity* provides an interesting image; the word literally means "moved in the bowels," which the ancients understood to be the seat of compassion. That Greek word also describes the good Samaritan encountering the injured man, and often Jesus when he encounters the sick, hungry, or confused. What does it look like when someone is "moved in the guts" to act with compassion and mercy?

◆　Romans 14:1-12 calls Christians to forbear with others and avoid judging them, complementing the forgiveness commanded in Matthew. In Lutheran tradition, the concept of *adiaphora* can help people avoid judgment on things "neither commanded nor forbidden by God," also referred to as "matters of indifference" (Article X of *The Solid*

Declaration of the Formula of Concord (online at bookofconcord.org/sd-adiaphora.php). While interpretations differ on what qualifies as adiaphora, the concept could help explore the texts for today in light of past or present disagreements within your community.

◆　As difficult as it can be to forgive and forbear, it can also be difficult to respond to the mercy and forgiveness one receives, including the feeling that one is in another's debt. Suzanne Collins's popular teen novel *The Hunger Games* tells the story of Katniss and Peeta, two teens from the same town who are struggling to survive in an arena where twenty-four teenagers are fighting to the death (New York: Scholastic, 2008). Katniss is often confused by and sometimes angry about Peeta's kind and merciful actions toward her, beginning with his sharing a loaf of bread when they were children.

◆　In worship, confession and absolution and the sharing of peace are signs of reconciliation and forgiveness. You could emphasize the communal aspect by inviting people to use the confession and forgiveness in Night Prayer (*Evangelical Lutheran Worship*, p. 320). Some Christian traditions place the confession immediately before the greeting of peace, as the liturgy moves toward communion.

Connections with the Liturgy

The Lord's Prayer includes a petition that summarizes today's allegory: "Forgive us our sins, as we forgive those who sin against us." Matthew's version of this prayer uses the word "debt," and Luke's both "debt" and "sin." The 1988 international English translation of the prayer uses "sin," since "debt" now usually connotes finances, and "trespass," begun in the third century, now usually refers to walking on another's private property.

"First be reconciled with your brother or sister," says Matthew 5:24. One of the meanings of the liturgy's greeting of peace enacts Joseph's forgiveness of his brothers: we are reconciled with one another before we join together at the table of the risen Christ. Not merely a morning greeting, the passing of the peace is a sign of forgiveness within the community.

Let the Children Come

Everybody makes mistakes. There are times when all of us hurt another person. How can our bodies, words, and actions all show that we want to make it right? The person in the gospel falls on his knees and asks for mercy, but when he receives that he seems to forget right away and doesn't pass it on to others. In worship and at home, we can model simple practices of confession and forgiveness. Our challenge is to teach kids to show with their words, bodies, and actions this learned behavior. "I'm sorry. I forgive you." It's practicing our way into new ways of being.

Assembly Song
Gathering

All creatures, worship God most high!   ELW 835

My Lord, what a morning   ELW 438, TFF 40, WOV 627

Father, most holy   ELW 415, LBW 169

Psalmody

Alonso, Tony or Marty Haugen. "The Lord Is Kind and Merciful" from TLP:A.

Makeever, Ray. "Bless the Lord (Psalm 103)" from DH.

Schwandt, Daniel E. "Psalm 114" from PSCY.

Raabe, Nancy. "Exodus 15" from PSCY.

Hymn of the Day

I come with joy   ELW 482   *DOVE OF PEACE*

Forgive our sins as we forgive   ELW 605, LBW 307   *DETROIT*

When we are living   ELW 639, LLC 462   *SOMOS DEL SEÑOR*

Offering

As we gather at your table   ELW 522

Come to the table   ELW 481, W&P 33

Communion

Wade in the water   ELW 459, TFF 114

We eat the bread of teaching   ELW 518

Seed that in earth is dying   ELW 330

Sending

Praise the Lord, rise up rejoicing   ELW 544, LBW 196

In peace and joy I now depart   ELW 440

Additional Assembly Songs

Take me to the water   TFF 117

We have come into his house   TFF 136

⊕ Sanna, sannanina   GS2 13

⊕ Shaha, Bart. Bangladesh. "Lord, We Did Not Live Up to Your Teachings" from *Sound the Bamboo*. U. GIA G-6830.

✧ Brown, Brenton. "All I Want" from WT.

✧ Eskelin, Ian/Jon Neufeld/Tim Neufeld. "Absolutely" from CCLI.

✧ Garrard, Stuart/Martin Smith. "Majesty (Here I Am)" from WT.

✧ Heaslip, Eoghan. "Blessing, Honor" from WT.

✧ Keyes, Aaron/Andy Lehman. "Not Guilty Anymore" from WT.

✧ Small, Andrew/Stuart Townend. "Salvation's Song" from CCLI.

Music for the Day
Choral

Cherwien, David. "In Thee Is Gladness." SATB, org, opt rec, perc. CG CGA873.

Costello, Michael. "In Thee Is Gladness." U, assembly, org, C inst. MSM 50-4300.

⊕ = global song
✧ = praise song
● = relates to hymn of the day

● Hobby, Robert. "Forgive Our Sins As We Forgive." SAB, org. CPH 98-2870.

● Hopson, Hal. "When We Are Living: Pues si vivimos." SATB, kybd. AFP 9780800658304.

● Schalk, Carl. "I Come with Joy to Meet My Lord." SATB, org. HOP AG7923.

Scott, K. Lee. "As We Gather at Your Table." SAB, kybd. AFP 9780800678081.

Children's Choir

Holden-Holloway, Deborah. "I Will at All Times Bless the Lord." U, kybd. SEL 422-901.

Kosche, Kenneth. "Bless God's Holy Name." 2 pt, kybd, opt hb. CG CGA766.

White, David Ashley. "Forgive Our Sins as We Forgive." 2 pt, kybd. SEL 410-611.

Keyboard / Instrumental

● Adams, Robert Train. "Dove of Peace" from *I Come with Joy*. Pno. AFP 9780800678494.

● Burkhardt, Michael. "Dove of Peace" from *Easy Hymn Settings: General (Communion)*. Org. MSM 10-515.

● Held, Wilbur. "Forgive Our Sins As We Forgive" from *Seven Settings of American Folk Hymns*. Org. CPH 97-5829.

● Raabe, Nancy. "Detroit" from *Day of Arising: A Tapestry of Musical Traditions*. Pno. AFP 9780800637460.

Handbell

● Roberts, Philip. "Sacred Harp Suite." 5 oct, L2+. GIA G-6448.

● Tucker, Sondra. "I Come with Joy." 3-5 oct hb, opt 3 oct hc, L3-. ALF 27059.

● Tucker, Sondra. "Somos del Señor." 3-5 oct hb, opt 3 oct hc, opt bng, L3+. AGEHR AG35256.

Tuesday, September 16

Cyprian, Bishop of Carthage, martyr, died around 258

Cyprian worked for the unity of the church and cared for his flock in North Africa during a time of great persecution. During Cyprian's time as bishop many people had denied the faith under duress. In contrast to some who held the belief that the church should not receive these people back, Cyprian believed they should be welcomed into full communion after a period of penance. He insisted on the need for compassion in order to preserve the unity of the church. His essay *On the Unity of the Catholic Church* stressed the role of bishops in guaranteeing the visible, concrete unity of the church. Cyprian was also concerned for the physical well-being of the people under his care. He organized a program of medical care for the sick during a severe epidemic in Carthage.

Wednesday, September 17

Hildegard, Abbess of Bingen, died 1179

Hildegard lived virtually her entire life in convents, yet was widely influential within the church. After an uneventful time as a nun, she was chosen as abbess of her community. She reformed her community as well as other convents. Around the same time, she began having visions and compiled them, as instructed, in a book she called *Scivias*. Hildegard's importance went beyond mysticism. She advised and reproved kings and popes, wrote poems and hymns, and produced treatises in medicine, theology, and natural history. She was also a musician and an artist.

Thursday, September 18

Dag Hammarskjöld, renewer of society, died 1961

Dag Hammarskjöld (HAH-mar-sheld) was a Swedish diplomat and humanitarian who served as secretary general of the United Nations. He was killed in a plane crash on this day in 1961, in what is now Zambia, while he was on his way to negotiate a cease-fire between the United Nations and the Katanga forces. For years Hammarskjöld had kept a private journal, and it was not until that journal was published as *Markings* that the depth of his Christian faith was known. The book revealed that his life was a combination of diplomatic service and personal spirituality, and of contemplation on the meaning of Christ in his life and action in the world.

September 21, 2014
Time after Pentecost — Lectionary 25

Matthew narrates one of Jesus' controversial parables, in which Jesus says the reign of God is like workers who get paid the same no matter when they start. When God changes his mind about punishing Nineveh for their evil ways, Jonah is angry. Yet God is gracious and merciful, abounding in steadfast love. In baptism we receive the grace of God that is freely given to all. As Luther wrote, in the presence of God's mercy we are all beggars.

Prayer of the Day

Almighty and eternal God, you show perpetual lovingkindness to us your servants. Because we cannot rely on our own abilities, grant us your merciful judgment, and train us to embody the generosity of your Son, Jesus Christ, our Savior and Lord.

Gospel Acclamation

Alleluia. Open our ¹ hearts, O Lord,* to give heed to what is said ¹ by your Son. *Alleluia.*

Readings and Psalm

Jonah 3:10—4:11

After Jonah's short sermon in 3:4, the Ninevites all repented and God decided to spare the city. Jonah objected to this and became even more angry when God ordered a worm to destroy a plant that was providing shade. The book ends with a question that challenges any who are not ready to forgive: You, Jonah, are all worked up about a bush, but should not I be concerned about a hundred and twenty thousand Ninevites who do not know the difference between their right and left hands?

Psalm 145:1-8

The Lord is slow to anger and abounding in steadfast love. (Ps. 145:8)

Philippians 1:21-30

Paul writes to the Philippians from prison. Though he is uncertain about the outcome of his imprisonment, he is committed to the ministry of the gospel and calls on the Philippians to live lives that reflect and enhance the gospel mission.

Matthew 20:1-16

Jesus tells a parable about God's generosity, challenging the common assumption that God rewards people according to what they have earned or deserve.

Semicontinuous reading and psalm

Exodus 16:2-15

Faced with hunger in the wilderness, the Israelites longed for life back in Egypt and said they wished the exodus had never happened. Then God miraculously and graciously gave them quails and manna to eat.

Psalm 105:1-6, 37-45

Make known the deeds of the Lord among the peoples. Hallelujah! (Ps. 105:1, 45)

Preface   Sundays

Color   Green

Prayers of Intercession

The prayers are prepared locally for each occasion. The following examples may be adapted or used as appropriate.

With the whole people of God in Christ Jesus, let us pray for the church, those in need, and all of God's creation.
A brief silence.

Generous God, you claim us as your own and your church declares your greatness. Make all who serve you, especially our bishops, pastors, missionaries, diaconal ministers, and chaplains serving institutions and the military, firm in one spirit. Hear us, O God.
Your mercy is great.

The goodness of your creation is a celebration of your mighty acts. Enable us to appreciate the smallest to the largest of wonders and to be worthy stewards of all your gifts. Hear us, O God.
Your mercy is great.

People of all nations sing aloud of your righteousness. Incite us to commit acts of peace, break down barriers, crush complacency, and stand up to intolerance. Hear us, O God.
Your mercy is great.

Strengthen those who suffer (*especially*). Transform pain into purpose, sorrow into courage, fear into generosity, and loneliness into compassion. Hear us, O God.
Your mercy is great.
Form the desire of our congregation to live as the body of Christ in the world. Place among us overflowing fonts and tables set as a feast for all people. Hear us, O God.
Your mercy is great.
Here other intercessions may be offered.
The lives of your saints (*especially Matthew, apostle and evangelist*) are evidence of your salvation. Give meaning to all our days, then grant us peaceful deaths and unite us with those we love in praising your name. Hear us, O God.
Your mercy is great.
Trusting in your mercy and goodness, we bring before you these prayers and whatever else you see that we need, in the name of the one who sets us free, Jesus Christ, our Savior.
Amen.

Images in the Readings

The **vineyard** is a common biblical metaphor that designates the religious community. In biblical times wine was not only usually safer to drink than water, but it also symbolized the shared joy of the community. Its production relies on both the blessing of the Creator and the long-term joint efforts of growers and vintners, and its alcohol transforms our very bodies. Yet many congregations are quite stingy with the cup.

The Jonah story provides many allegorical images: **Nineveh** is the powerful enemy; **Tarshish** is for Jonah the farthest destination in the opposite direction away from Nineveh, across the Mediterranean Sea; the **bush** suggests personal comfort; the **worm** suggests God's correction to our selfishness; the **wind** is the breath of God; **Jonah** himself is a comic depiction of our very selves and of the church when we live out of typical human emotions. We too often do not know our right from our left hand. It is a great story.

The **spirit** of the risen Christ will bring us into the unity expressive of a mutually forgiving community.

Ideas for the Day

◆   How one hears today's gospel depends on the character one relates to most: an early worker, who feels cheated; a late worker, who feels fortunate; or the owner, who is generous. With different voices or people acting out each role, let each of the three characters speak directly to listeners. Some scholars think the parable spoke of different generations of Matthew's community, in which contemporary leaders, the latecomers, supposedly did not compare to earlier ones. To underline that context, invite a longtime member and

a newer disciple to speak about their experiences of God's generous grace.

◆   The desire to receive credit and be rewarded for one's work or behavior is part of human nature. This can make God's unearned grace seem unnatural and even offensive. Emphasize the communion meal as the unearned generosity of God poured out to all, no matter who one is or from where one has come. You might craft a special invitation to communion or use one like the Iona Community's liturgy, which includes the line "Come to this table, you who have much faith and you who would like to have more" (*Iona Community Worship Book*, Glasgow, Scotland: Wild Goose Publications, 1991).

◆   Scientists differ on the age children begin to understand the concept of fairness. Some say it happens around four years old, but other studies show that even babies can recognize unequal treatment. Many stories for young readers treat this topic, often in the context of sibling rivalry. Perhaps use this story about fairness to explore reactions to this gospel: *It's Not Fair!* by Amy Krouse Rosenthal and Tom Lichtenheld (New York: HarperCollins, 2008).

◆   While the subject of this parable is God's grace, not economics, many worshipers wrestle with the story from that perspective. It's an opportunity to point out that God seems not to follow or support any particular human attempt to systematize fairness—neither capitalism's emphasis on receiving what one has earned, nor socialism's efforts to achieve equity, as in the slogan popularized by Karl Marx: "From each according to his ability, to each according to his need" (Critique of the Gotha Program, 1875). Neither accounts for God's inexplicable generosity.

Connections with the Liturgy

The last sentence of the book of Jonah indicates that God cares also for the animals. Following the outline of the intercessions in *Evangelical Lutheran Worship*, we pray every Sunday for the well-being of creation. Much of that well-being is our responsibility, but we pray also for God's continuing creative power over the earth, for divine mercy granted to "many animals."

Let the Children Come

How are the last first in your community? Do you have parking spots reserved for visitors? Do worship leaders commune last as a sign of serving guests first? Do you expect and welcome newcomers publicly? Are children treated with full membership in the community, which their baptism gives them?

Assembly Song
Gathering
When morning gilds the skies   ELW 853

Rise up, O saints of God!   ELW 669

Lord of light   ELW 688, LBW 405

Psalmody
Haas, David. "I Will Praise Your Name" from PCY, vol. 1.

Hopson, Hal H. "Psalm 145" from TP.

Whitney, Rae E. "O My God and King and Savior" (HOLY MANNA) from PAS 145F.

Makeever, Ray. "Tell What God Has Done for Us (Psalm 105)" from DH.

Hymn of the Day
All who love and serve your city   ELW 724   NEW ORLEANS
LBW 436   BIRABUS

Will you let me be your servant   ELW 659   THE SERVANT SONG

Give Me Jesus   ELW 770, TFF 165   GIVE ME JESUS

Offering
Take my life, that I may be   ELW 583, 685; LBW 406

We give thee but thine own   ELW 686, LBW 410

Communion
O Christ, what can it mean for us   ELW 431

There's a wideness in God's mercy   ELW 587/588

Salvation unto has come   ELW 590

Sending
Voices raised to you   ELW 845

Signs and wonders   ELW 672

Additional Assembly Songs
Come to Jesus   TFF 156

God has smiled on me   TFF 190

⊕ Hamba nathi/Come, walk with us   GS2 6

⊕ Gibson, Colin A. New Zealand. "For the Man and for the Woman" from *Sound the Bamboo*. U. GIA G-6830.

☼ Brown, Brenton/Matt Maher. "Come Let Us Return (Gloria)" from CCLI.

☼ Crowder, David. "Alleluia Sing" from CCLI.

☼ Maher, Matt. "Your Grace Is Enough" from WT.

☼ Mcclarney, Chris/Chris Eaton/John Hartley. "Immortal Invisible" from WT.

☼ Nockels, Christy. "By Our Love" from CCLI.

☼ Redman, Matt. "Here Is Love" from WT.

Music for the Day
Choral
Blersch, Jeffrey. "Voices Raised to You We Offer." SATB, br qrt, timp. CPH 98-4105.

Haan, Raymond. "Every Day I Will Bless You (Psalm 145:1-4)." SATB, kybd. MSM 50-7066.

Hampton, Calvin. "There's a Wideness in God's Mercy." SATB, pno. GIA G-7378.

Helgen, John. "Give Me Jesus." SSA/2 pt/U, vc. KJO 6310.

Sedio, Mark. "Take My Life, That I May Be: Toma, oh Dios, mi voluntad." SATB, pno. AFP 9780800658298.

Children's Choir
Mendelssohn, Felix. "I Will Sing of Thy Great Mercies." 2 pt, kybd. HOP AG7228.

Page, Anna Laura and Jean Anne Shafferman. "Jonah (Quit Your Belly-Achin'!)." U/2 pt, kybd, opt narr. ALF 00-26429.

Rathmann, Dawn. "Go Forth." U, kybd, opt gtr. CPH 98-3332.

Keyboard / Instrumental
Burkhardt, Michael. "Come, Labor On" from *At the Name of Jesus: Four Hymns of Devotion*. Org. MSM 10-747.

● Childs, Edwin T. "Give Me Jesus" from *Spirituals for Organ: Manuals Only*. Org. AFP 9781451401141.

Miller, Aaron David. "There's a Wideness in God's Mercy" from *Chorale Preludes for Piano in Traditional Styles*. Pno. AFP 9780800679033.

● Porter, Rachel Trelstad. "Give Me Jesus" from *Praise, My Soul: Hymn Arrangements for Piano*. Pno. AFP 9780800659516.

Handbell
● Behnke, John. "Give Me Jesus." 4-6 oct hb, opt 3-5 oct hc, L4. AGEHR AG46025.

● Page, Anna Laura. "Give Me Jesus." 3-5 oct hb, opt 2 oct hc, L3. CG CGB727.

Wagner, Douglas. "Great Is the Lord" (based on Psalm 25). 3-5 oct, L2. LOR 20/1356L.

Monday, September 22

Matthew, Apostle and Evangelist (transferred)
Matthew ("Levi" in the gospels of Mark and Luke) was a tax collector for the Roman government in Capernaum. Tax collectors were distrusted because they were dishonest and worked as agents for a foreign ruler, the occupying Romans. In the gospels, tax collectors are mentioned as sinful and despised outcasts, but it was these outcasts to whom Jesus showed his love. Matthew's name means "gift of the Lord." Since the second century, tradition has attributed the first gospel to him.

⊕ = global song
☼ = praise song
● = relates to hymn of the day

September 28, 2014
Time after Pentecost — Lectionary 26

Jesus' parable about two sons who don't do what they say reveals surprises in the reign of God, such as prostitutes and tax collectors going before others into God's kingdom. In the reading from Ezekiel the people question whether the ways of the Lord are unfair; instead they are to repent and turn to the Lord. Paul urges us to look to Christ as a model of humility, looking to the interests of others above our own. Nourished by the broken bread and shared cup, we offer our lives for the sake of our needy world.

Prayer of the Day

God of love, giver of life, you know our frailties and failings. Give us your grace to overcome them, keep us from those things that harm us, and guide us in the way of salvation, through Jesus Christ, our Savior and Lord.

Gospel Acclamation

Alleluia. My sheep hear my voice, ¹ says the Lord;* I know them and they ¹ follow me. *Alleluia.* (John 10:27)

Readings and Psalm
Ezekiel 18:1-4, 25-32

Ezekiel challenges those who think they cannot change because of what their parents were and did, or who think they cannot turn from their wicked ways. God insistently invites people to turn and live.

Psalm 25:1-9

Remember, O Lord, your compassion and love. (Ps. 25:6)

Philippians 2:1-13

As part of a call for harmony rather than self-seeking, Paul uses a very early Christian hymn that extols the selflessness of Christ in his obedient death on the cross. Christ's selfless perspective is to be the essential perspective we share as the foundation for Christian accord.

Matthew 21:23-32

After driving the moneychangers out of the temple (21:12), Jesus begins teaching there. His authority is questioned by the religious leaders, who are supposed to be in charge of the temple.

Semicontinuous reading and psalm
Exodus 17:1-7

Because the thirsty Israelites quarreled with Moses and put the Lord to the test, Moses cried out in desperation to the Lord. Nevertheless, the Lord commanded Moses to strike the rock to provide water for the people. The doubt-filled question—"Is the Lord among us or not?"—received a dramatic and positive answer.

Psalm 78:1-4, 12-16

We will recount to generations to come the power of the Lord. (Ps. 78:4)

Preface   Sundays

Color   Green

Prayers of Intercession

The prayers are prepared locally for each occasion. The following examples may be adapted or used as appropriate.

With the whole people of God in Christ Jesus, let us pray for the church, those in need, and all of God's creation.

A brief silence.

Fill your church throughout the world with the spirit to work for your pleasure. Hear us, O God.

Your mercy is great.

Teach us how to value and enjoy the beauty of your creation with humility and to set aside selfish ambitions in how we share its resources. Hear us, O God.

Your mercy is great.

Refresh the people of all nations with your compassion and love and give us the same mind in Christ, living in peace with loving hearts. Hear us, O God.

Your mercy is great.

Rush to the aid of those who wait for you (*especially*). Heal their pain, mend their brokenness, take away their sorrow, lift them out of their troubles, and relieve their burdens. Hear us, O God.

Your mercy is great.

Encourage us in our lives together. Lead us in your path and teach us to care for the needs of the poor, the exploited, and the outcast. Hear us, O God.

Your mercy is great.

Here other intercessions may be offered.

Make our joy complete in the knowledge of the good news of the resurrection. Console those who mourn and give us the assurance of your presence in this life and the next. Hear us, O God.

Your mercy is great.

Trusting in your mercy and goodness, we bring before you these prayers and whatever else you see that we need, in the name of the one who sets us free, Jesus Christ, our Savior.

Amen.

Images in the Readings

The parable speaks of a good and a bad **son**. Christianity lauds yet another son, the "only Son," who both answers yes and does the will of God. In the biblical worldview, a son is not understood as an independent agent, but is an extension of the father, owing the father everything. Even according to the biological understanding of the time, it was the sperm that conveyed full humanity to the fetus. This sense of the child's connection with the parent is evident also in the reading from Ezekiel. Our culture values children more as independent entities, however much they still need their parents' care.

We are very distant from the first-century's horror at the image of the **cross**. The Roman government reserved this method of death by torture for the lowest criminals, and in Deuteronomy 21, even God is said to curse anyone executed by hanging on a tree. In the fourth century, the emperor Constantine outlawed crucifixion as a mode of execution, and since then jewels and gold, art and design have made of the cross an often-beauteous sign of veneration. Some scholars suggest that "even death on a cross" is a Pauline interpolation into the hymn. The Good Friday liturgy invites persons to come forward to a full-sized rough-hewn cross and bend the knee before it in praise of Jesus.

Ideas for the Day

◆ Jesus disrupts the usual order of things—and this includes authority. The Pharisees throw the rulebook at Jesus when they ask him about the source, the origin of his authority. "By what authority. . . ?" Obviously not by the one the Pharisees have established. Jesus' authority is not found in religious law. The Pharisees hide behind their self-invented authority. They observe the commandments to make themselves look good, rather than hearing the call to serve the neighbor.

◆ The surprising piece here is that true authority finds itself on the outside. Jesus is the outsider par excellence in this story. He is outside the boundaries the Pharisees want to establish. And he is the defender of the outsider (the tax collector and the prostitute). He places himself with the marginalized (even unto death, on the cross, outside the walls). Some religious communities, like the Little Sisters of Jesus, live this identity with the outsider not simply in service to the marginalized but living, completely assimilating with the poorest. We can sing their song, "Lord Jesus, you shall be my song" (ELW 808) with them.

◆ As someone beyond convention, Jesus looks to the heart, not to mere words. Things are so easy to promise and so arduous to fulfill. Parents can experience this on an almost daily basis—and not only from the kids' broken promises, but their own as well. Sure, I'll take you swimming; just let me finish these e-mails! And then, a long time later, the reminder comes unabashedly from the kids of the unfulfilled promise. "Yes" is easy to say. The action, the gesture, the deed, however, reveals the heart. God the judge sees the heart and does not function as a human judge pondering "the scales of justice." God's fairness seems terribly unfair—giving the sinner the same chance as the righteous, rewarding the eleventh-hour worker the same as the one who worked all day. God's fairness rejoices in the one who turns and lives (Ezekiel). God's fairness works in the midst of death bringing life. Confession and forgiveness could pick up on these themes: confessing the "yes" turned "no" and rejoicing in God's continual "yes" spoken to us in baptism.

Connections with the Liturgy

Today's second reading includes the central Christian affirmation that Jesus is Lord. That is, we grant to Jesus the same title that originally referred to God. In greeting one another with the peace of "the Lord" and in the opening dialogue of holy communion—"The Lord be with you"—"the Lord" is the risen Christ, the one who suffered death on a cross and has been exalted in the resurrection. The classic hymn of praise, "Glory to God in the highest," concludes by referring to the Trinity, "Jesus Christ, with the Holy Spirit, in the glory of God the Father," as Lord.

Let the Children Come

"I have no pleasure in the death of anyone" (Ezek. 18:32). In worship, we practice praising God, not judging people. Judging is not our job. That's God's job and even God doesn't want to do it. How can we show families with small children that as we worship, we are not judging extra noise or movement? After all, as a drama teacher once pointed out, children are not made to be still or silent. If we're going to ask them to do that, we better have a really good reason why. How can we show "a new heart and a new spirit"?

Assembly Song
Gathering

At the name of Jesus   ELW 416, LBW 179

God is here!   ELW 526, WOV 719

Awake, my soul, and with the sun   ELW 557

Psalmody

Mathis, William H. Refrain for "Psalm 25" from *After the Prelude: Year A*. U/cant, hb. CG CGB616 (digital version). CGB617 (printed version). Use with ELW psalm tone 6 or 7 (in C).

Parker, Val. "Psalm 25: To You, O Lord, I Lift My Soul." SATB, assembly, kybd, gtr. OCP 21060.

Pavlechko, Thomas. "Psalm 78:1-4, 12-16" from SMP.

Hymn of the Day

Our Father, we have wandered   ELW 606, WOV 733
   HERZLICH TUT MICH VERLANGEN

What God ordains is good indeed   ELW 776   *WAS GOTT TUT*

O Master, let me walk with you   ELW 818, LBW 492   *MARYTON*

Offering

Strengthen for service, Lord   ELW 497

Take, oh, take me as I am   ELW 814

Communion

Come down, O Love divine   ELW 804

As the deer runs to the river   ELW 231

You are holy   ELW 525

Sending

The Lord now sends us forth   ELW 538, LLC 415

Amen, we praise your name   ELW 846, TFF 279, WOV 786

Additional Assembly Songs

Yield not to temptation   TFF 195

Spirit Friend   LS 69

Guide My Feet   TFF 153, GS3 29

⊕ Sizohamba naye/We will go with God   GS2 10

⊕ Loh, I-to. Taiwan. "Jesus Christ Sets Free to Serve" from *Sound the Bamboo*. U, perc. GIA G-6830.

✡ Gungor, Lisa/Michael Gungor. "Giving It All to You" from CCLI.

✡ Hall, Charlie/Kendall Combes/Trent Austin. "The Solid Rock" from WT.

✡ Houston, Joel/Reuben Morgan. "The First and the Last" from CCLI.

✡ Hughes, Tim. "Everything" from WT.

✡ Ingram, Jason/Jon Neufeld/Matt Bronleewe/Tim Neufeld. "The Hand That Holds the World" from CCLI.

✡ Townend, Stuart. "O My Soul" from CCLI.

Music for the Day
Choral

Anerio, Giovanni Francesco. "Christ Humbled Himself" from *Augsburg Motet Book*. SATB. AFP 9781451423709.

Dake, Kenneth. "God Is Here." SATB, org. MSM 50-8960.

Farlee, Robert Buckley. "O Blessed Spring." SATB, org, ob, opt assembly. AFP 9780800654245.

Hobby, Robert. "Strengthen for Service." 2 pt, org, opt assembly. AFP 9780800678265.

Larter, Evelyn. "What Wondrous Love Is This." SATB, org, vln. AFP 9780800621575.

Nelson, Ronald A. "Christ Humbled Himself." U, org, fl. SEL 422-902.

Children's Choir

Burkhardt, Michael. "I Lift My Soul." U/2 pt/3 pt, pno, opt ob, opt cl, opt cello. MSM 50-5552.

Cool, Jayne Southwick. "Psalm 25" in *ChildrenSing Psalms*. U, kybd.

Haugen, Marty. "In the Cross of Christ." *Gather* 515.

Keyboard / Instrumental

Burkhardt, Michael. "At the Name of Jesus" from *At the Name of Jesus: Four Hymns of Devotion*. Org. MSM 10-747.

● Decker, Pamela. "Herzlich tut mich verlangen" from *Augsburg Organ Library: Lent*. Org. AFP 9780800658977.

● Hassell, Michael. "Maryton" from *Traveling Tunes: Hymn Arrangements for Solo Instrument and Piano*. Inst, pno. AFP 9780800656195.

Organ, Anne Krentz. "Aurelia" from *Piano Reflections for the Church Year*. Pno. AFP 9780800674748.

Handbell

Childers, Brian. "I Want Jesus to Walk with Me." 3-5 oct hb, L3+. HOP 2463. Opt fl or vln, opt perc. HOP 2463P.

● McChesney, Kevin. "O Master, Let Me Walk with Thee." 3-5 oct, L1. JEF JHS9419.

Morris, Hart. "Children, Go Where I Send Thee." 3-5 oct, L4. Ring Out! Press RO3205.

Monday, September 29
Michael and All Angels

On this festival day the church ponders the richness and variety of God's created order and the limits of human knowledge of it. The scriptures speak of angels (the word means "messengers") who worship God in heaven, and in both testaments angels speak for God on earth. They are remembered most vividly as they appear to the shepherds and announce the birth of the Savior. Michael is an angel

⊕ = global song

✡ = praise song

● = relates to hymn of the day

whose name appears in Daniel as the heavenly being who leads the faithful dead to God's throne on the day of resurrection. In Revelation, Michael fights in a cosmic battle against Satan.

Tuesday, September 30

Jerome, translator, teacher, died 420

Jerome is remembered as a biblical scholar and translator. Rather than choosing classical Latin as the basis of his work, he translated the scriptures into the Latin that was spoken and written by the majority of the persons in his day. His translation is known as the Vulgate, from the Latin word for *common*. While Jerome is remembered as a saint, he could be anything but saintly. He was well known for his short temper and his arrogance, although he was also quick to admit to his personal faults. Thanks to the work of Jerome, many people received the word in their own language and lived lives of faith and service to those in need.

Saturday, October 4

Francis of Assisi, renewer of the church, died 1226

Francis was the son of a wealthy cloth merchant. In a public confrontation with his father, he renounced his wealth and future inheritance and devoted himself to serving the poor. Francis described this act as being "wedded to Lady Poverty." Under his leadership the Order of Friars Minor (Franciscans) was formed, and they took literally Jesus' words to his disciples that they should take nothing on their journey and receive no payment for their work. Their task in preaching was to "use words if necessary." Francis had a spirit of gladness and gratitude for all of God's creation. This commemoration has been a traditional time to bless pets and animals, creatures Francis called his brothers and sisters. A prayer and a hymn attributed to St. Francis are included in *Evangelical Lutheran Worship* (p. 87, #835).

Theodor Fliedner, renewer of society, died 1864

Fliedner's (FLEED-ner) work was instrumental in the revival of the ministry of deaconesses among Lutherans. While a pastor in Kaiserswerth, Germany, he also ministered to prisoners in Düsseldorf. Through his ministry to prisoners, he came in contact with Moravian deaconesses, and it was through this Moravian influence that he was convinced that the ministry of deaconesses had a place among Lutherans. His work and writing encouraged women to care for those who were sick, poor, or imprisoned. Fliedner's deaconess motherhouse in Kaiserswerth inspired Lutherans all over the world to commission deaconesses to serve in parishes, schools, prisons, and hospitals.

October 5, 2014
Time after Pentecost — Lectionary 27

In today's gospel reading, Jesus tells a parable of the vineyard, an image of Israel, the prophets' mission, and Christ's death. For Christians, the vineyard also speaks of God's love poured out in the blood of Christ, given to us for the forgiveness of sin. Grafted onto Christ the vine at baptism, we are nourished with wine and bread, that we may share Christ's sufferings and know the power of his resurrection.

Prayer of the Day

Beloved God, from you come all things that are good. Lead us by the inspiration of your Spirit to know those things that are right, and by your merciful guidance, help us to do them, through Jesus Christ, our Savior and Lord.

Gospel Acclamation

Alleluia. Jesus says, I chose you and ap- | pointed you* to go and bear fruit | that will last. *Alleluia.* (John 15:16)

Readings and Psalm
Isaiah 5:1-7

The prophet sings a sad, parable-like love song about the relationship between God and Israel. In this song Israel is compared to a promising vineyard. Despite God's loving care, the vineyard that is Israel has brought forth "wild grapes" of injustice and distress, when fine grapes of justice and righteousness were expected.

Psalm 80:7-15

Look down from heaven, O God; behold and tend this vine. (Ps. 80:14, 15)

Philippians 3:4b-14

Paul reviews some of his supposed credentials, which no longer have any bearing in comparison to the right relationship he has been given through the death of Christ. The power of Christ's resurrection motivates him to press on toward the ultimate goal, eternal life with Christ.

Matthew 21:33-46

Jesus tells a parable to the religious leaders who are plotting his death, revealing that their plans will, ironically, bring about the fulfillment of scripture.

Semicontinuous reading and psalm
Exodus 20:1-4, 7-9, 12-20

The God of the Exodus graciously gave Israel the Ten Commandments. Primarily stated as negative imperatives, the Ten Commandments forbid gross sins such as murder, adultery, theft, and perjury. In most of life they grant Israel freedom to live righteously, with maximum love for God and neighbor.

Psalm 19

The statutes of the LORD are just and rejoice the heart. (Ps. 19:8)

Preface   Sundays

Color   Green

Prayers of Intercession

The prayers are prepared locally for each occasion. The following examples may be adapted or used as appropriate.

With the whole people of God in Christ Jesus, let us pray for the church, those in need, and all of God's creation.
A brief silence.

Sing a love song to us, O God, with verses that rouse us to be the church in a world where faith is met with cynicism. Hear us, O God.
Your mercy is great.

Sing a love song to us, O God, with verses that motivate us to rebuild where storms have torn down, droughts have sucked dry, and waters have flooded. Hear us, O God.
Your mercy is great.

Sing a love song to us, O God, with verses that provoke us to create change where there is injustice, freedom where there is captivity, and harmony where there is violence. Hear us, O God.
Your mercy is great.

Sing a love song to us, O God, with verses that compel us to provide relief to those who suffer, comfort to those who mourn, protection to those who are vulnerable, and compassion to those who are scorned. Hear us, O God.
Your mercy is great.

Sing a love song to us, O God, with verses that lift us out of complacency and into our communities to share the priceless gift of knowing Christ Jesus as Lord. Hear us, O God.
Your mercy is great.

Here other intercessions may be offered.

Sing a love song to us, O God, with verses that assure us of eternal life, where, together with all your saints, we will join you in a song that has no end. Hear us, O God.
Your mercy is great.

Trusting in your mercy and goodness, we bring before you these prayers and whatever else you see that we need, in the name of the one who sets us free, Jesus Christ, our Savior.
Amen.

Images in the Readings

The importance of wine in the diet of biblical societies is evident in the Bible's continual use of the **vineyard** as an image of the people. Wine, suggesting the goodness of communal participation, serves as a corrective to more recent individualist interpretations of Christian faith. Vineyards grow from age-old roots and require dedicated tending. God owns the vineyard: we are only renters; we need to collaborate with one another to produce good wine.

The passage in the Psalms about the rejected stone becoming the **cornerstone** caught on in Christianity. In Ephesians 2:20 Paul calls Christ Jesus the cornerstone of the household of God; in Acts 4:11 Luke uses cornerstone as a metaphor for Christ, as does the author of 1 Peter in 2:7. It is yet another biblical image about the reversal of values that God intends. The idea is that a huge stone at the foundation is not merely a decorative marker but actually supports the weight of the building above.

Ideas for the Day

◆ The people are the vineyard. The community of faith is the precious harvest, tended carefully and with much effort and love. The metaphor is more astounding than we realize. Life in Israel was focused around harvest time (barley, wheat, fruits, olives). Its major festivals were also (Passover, Booths). A plentiful harvest was due solely to God's goodness. And here the people (the community) are compared to the vineyard—the diamond among the jewels (see Gail Ramshaw, "Harvest," *Treasures Old and New*, Fortress Press, 2002). The people are the prized possession, but they only produce sour, wild grapes. Both Isaiah and Jesus in the parable describe this sourness as bloodshed. The people have turned against their neighbor, have murdered and plundered. A cry is heard. Injustice abounds. The wine of celebration has been reserved for just a few, rather than opening to a table of communion. The prayer of offering becomes all the more pertinent: "Let the vineyards be fruitful, Lord, and fill to the brim our cup of blessing."

◆ The readings work closely together this week. Pride in many forms is a major connecting theme. There is the disappointed pride in the reading from Isaiah. God's pride in God's vineyard turns sour. In Philippians, Paul boasts in his earthly identity, but only to point out that this is a displaced pride. In Jesus' parable, the selfish pride of the tenants leads to their destruction. Pride can be turned in on itself. It can also be turned toward the other, toward Jesus and a flourishing life in which the fruits of the vineyard are for all to share.

◆ God places a cornerstone in the foundation. The cornerstone in buildings, the first stone laid, was traditionally the stone upon which the entire structure was constructed. Today, despite steel and glass buildings, we still understand the concept. The hopes and dreams of a people are cemented into a building by means of a symbolic cornerstone, engraved with a date and perhaps holding a time capsule. But in the reading from Matthew, the "cornerstone" of the vineyard is rejected. The foretaste of the feast becomes simply a relishing in one's own accomplishments. Communion becomes exclusionary, an insider rite.

Connections with the Liturgy

The poetic litany of Good Friday, called the Solemn Reproaches, newly adapted for our century, includes the refrain "what more could I have done for you," echoing Isaiah 5:4, and in its fourth stanza, we refer to the church as the vineyard that brings forth bitter fruit.

Let the Children Come

In today's gospel, when the messengers checked on the grape harvest, their expectations were harshly trampled. Thankfully, children's expectations aren't trampled when they attend worship. Sunday after Sunday, young children begin to repeat and trust the elements of worship: music, ritual, prayers, and quiet time. Children begin to figure out what happens in worship, and where they fit in the process. You can help children remember what to count on every Sunday by teaching them a simple rhyme about worship: We sing, we pray, we're at God's house today.

Assembly Song
Gathering

Jesus loves me! ELW 595
Lord Christ, when first you came to earth ELW 727
Open your ears, O faithful people ELW 519, TFF 715

Psalmody

Furlong, Sue. "God of Hosts, Bring Us Back" from PS1.
Becker, John W. "Psalm 80:7-15" from PWA.
Wold, Wayne L. "Psalm 80," Refrain 2, from PSCY.
Cool, Jayne Southwick. "Psalm 19" from *ChildrenSing Psalms*. U, kybd.

Hymn of the Day

God the sculptor of the mountains ELW 736, TFF 222
There in God's garden ELW 342, WOV 668 *SHADES MOUNTAIN*

My song is love unknown   ELW 343, WOV 661   *LOVE UNKNOWN*
LBW 94   *RHOSYMEDRE*

Offering

Let the vineyards be fruitful   ELW 181, 182, 183, 184
Accept, O Lord, the gifts we bring   ELW 691, WOV 759

Communion

If you but trust in God to guide you   ELW 769
My Lord of light   ELW 832, WOV 796
When I survey the wondrous cross   ELW 803, TFF 79

Sending

Thine the amen   ELW 826, WOV 801
The church of Christ, in every age   ELW 729, LBW 433

Additional Assembly Songs

Pass me not, O gentle Savior   TFF 150
Behold and tend this vine   DH 39
* Cambodian folk tune. "Cambodian Lord's Prayer" from *Global Choral Sounds*. SATB, cant, perc. CPH 98-3610.
* East African tune. "I Truly Am the Vine" from *Set Free: A Collection of African Hymns*. SATB. AFP 9780806600451.
* Ellis, John. "I Stand for You" from WT.
* Keyes, Aaron/Matt Boswell/Tony Fisher. "Sinless Savior" from CCLI.
* Morgan, Reuben/Robert Fergusson. "We Will See Him" from CCLI.
* Redman, Beth/Matt Redman. "For the Cross" from CCLI.
* Rend Collective Experiment. "You Bled" from WT.
* Staines, Bill/Matt Maher. "Look like a Fool" from CCLI.

Music for the Day
Choral

Farlee, Robert Buckley. "How Precious Is Your Steadfast Love." SATB. AFP 9780800678241.
Hildebrand, Kevin. "How Clear Is Our Vocation, Lord." SATB, org. CPH 98-3671.
Hopson, Hal. "How Clear Is Our Vocation, Lord." SATB, org. MSM 50-8824.
Scott, K. Lee. "A Vineyard Grows." SATB, org, opt fl/ob. MSM 50-9010.

Children's Choir

DeLong, Richard. "Saviour, Teach Me Day by Day." U trbl, kybd. ECS 4796.
Miller, Aaron David. "I Know the Lord's Laid His Hands on Me." U, pno. AFP 978080067834.
Sebesta, Donald. "Day by Day." U, opt desc, pno, opt cello. AFP 9780800638382.
Shippey, Jonathan. "I Will Comfort You." SA, pno, cello. HIN HMC 1931.

Keyboard / Instrumental

* Adams, Robert Train. "Love Unknown" from *I Come with Joy*. Pno. AFP 9780800678494.
  Carter, John. "The God of Abraham Praise" from *Contemplative Folk Tunes for Piano*. Pno. AFP 9780800659776.
  Sanders, Bernard Wayne. "Ornament of Grace." Inst, org. CPH 97-7288.
* Scott, K. Lee. "Voluntary on Shades Mountain." Org. MSM 10-592.

Handbell

* Brandon, Gregg. "My Song Is Love Unknown." 4-5 oct hb, opt 3-4 oct hc, L3. SHW HP5458. Full score with opt vln, opt cello. SHW HP5459.
  Dobrinski, Cynthia. "In the Garden." 3-5 oct, L2. HOP 1313.
* Kerr, J. Wayne. "There in God's Garden." 3-5 oct hb, opt fl, L2. MSM 30-820.

Monday, October 6
William Tyndale, translator, martyr, died 1536

William Tyndale was ordained in 1521, and his life's desire was to translate the scriptures into English. When his plan met opposition from King Henry VIII, Tyndale fled to Germany, where he traveled from city to city, living in poverty and constant danger. He was able to produce a New Testament in 1525. Nine years later he revised it and began work on the Old Testament, which he was unable to complete. He was captured, tried for heresy, and burned at the stake. Miles Coverdale completed Tyndale's work, and the Tyndale-Coverdale version was published as the "Matthew Bible" in 1537. For nearly four centuries the style of this translation has influenced English versions of the Bible such as the King James (Authorized Version) and the New Revised Standard Version.

Tuesday, October 7
Henry Melchior Muhlenberg, pastor in North America, died 1787

Muhlenberg (MYOO-len-berg) was prominent in setting the course for Lutheranism in North America. He helped Lutheran churches make the transition from the state churches of Europe to a new identity on American soil. Among other things, he established the first Lutheran synod in America and developed an American Lutheran liturgy. His liturgical principles became the basis for the Common Service of 1888, used in many North American service books for a majority of the past century. That Muhlenberg and his work are remembered today was anticipated at his death. The inscription on his grave reads, in Latin, "Who and what he was, future ages will know without a stone."

* = global song
* = praise song
* = relates to hymn of the day

October 12, 2014
Time after Pentecost — Lectionary 28

In Isaiah we are given a vision of the great feast to come, when God will wipe away death forever. In Jesus' parable about a great banquet, those invited do not come, so the invitation is extended to others. In our liturgy God spreads a table before us. Even amid anxiety and hardship we rejoice in the peace of God which surpasses all understanding. With great joy we feast at the table of the Lord, and we go forth to share the wonderful invitation with others hungering and thirsting for the abundant life of God.

Prayer of the Day

Lord of the feast, you have prepared a table before all peoples and poured out your life with abundance. Call us again to your banquet. Strengthen us by what is honorable, just, and pure, and transform us into a people of righteousness and peace, through Jesus Christ, our Savior and Lord.

Gospel Acclamation

Alleluia. This is the Lord for whom ˈ we have waited;* let us be glad and rejoice in ˈ God's salvation. *Alleluia.* (Isa. 25:9)

Readings and Psalm

Isaiah 25:1-9

After a hymn of praise acknowledging God as a shelter for the poor, the prophet portrays a wonderful victory banquet at which death—which in ancient Canaan was depicted as a monster swallowing everyone up—will be swallowed up forever. The prophet urges celebration of this victory of salvation.

Psalm 23

You prepare a table before me, and my cup is running over. (Ps. 23:5)

Philippians 4:1-9

Though writing from prison and facing an uncertain future, Paul calls on the Philippians to rejoice and give thanks to God no matter what the circumstance. God's peace is with us and binds together our hearts and minds in Jesus Christ, especially when things around us do not seem peaceful.

Matthew 22:1-14

Jesus tells a parable indicating that the blessings of God's kingdom are available to all, but the invitation is not to be taken lightly.

Semicontinuous reading and psalm

Exodus 32:1-14

After Israel sinned by worshipping the golden calf, Moses interceded with God to spare Israel, lest the Egyptians conclude that God had evil intents in the Exodus. Moses reminds God of the promises God made to Israel's matriarchs and patriarchs.

Psalm 106:1-6, 19-23

Remember, O Lord, the favor you have for your people. (Ps. 106:4)

Preface Sundays

Color Green

Prayers of Intercession

The prayers are prepared locally for each occasion. The following examples may be adapted or used as appropriate.

With the whole people of God in Christ Jesus, let us pray for the church, those in need, and all of God's creation.
A brief silence.

Come near us, Lord God. Let your church rejoice at your banquet where all are invited and welcomed, washed and fed, forgiven and chosen. Hear us, O God.
Your mercy is great.

Come near us, Lord God. Let your creation rejoice in green pastures, beside still waters, on mountaintops, in harvested fields, along city streets, down country roads, and throughout the valleys. Hear us, O God.
Your mercy is great.

Come near us, Lord God. Let your world rejoice in peace which surpasses understanding, at tables overflowing with good food and drink, and where shrouds of sorrow are lifted. Hear us, O God.
Your mercy is great.

Come near us, Lord God. Let your people rejoice with faces wiped free of tears, minds unbound from disgrace, bodies freed from suffering, and souls restored. (*Especially we pray for . . .*) Hear us, O God.

Your mercy is great.

Come near us, Lord God. Let your faithful rejoice in every assembly, in praise and singing, word and deed, unrestrained from worry and unchained from fear. Hear us, O God.

Your mercy is great.

Come near us, Lord God. Let those who wait for you rejoice with all the saints, whose names are in the book of life and who now sit at the great feast with you. Hear us, O God.

Your mercy is great.

Trusting in your mercy and goodness, we bring before you these prayers and whatever else you see that we need, in the name of the one who sets us free, Jesus Christ, our Savior.

Amen.

Images in the Readings

Here is a listing of only some of this Sunday's images. Matthew's parable merges several biblical images that describe our life with God. The **wedding** suggests lifelong love, commitment to the other, and communal joy in the union as a description of God's choosing and caring for us. Especially in a culture in which food was not plentiful and cheap, the **feast** connotes communal participation and extraordinary fullness. God is likened to a **king**, to whom is due honor and service. We are **guests**: that is, the meal is God's, not ours. The **wedding robe** suggests the white garment of baptism. Since the Bible often describes God as light, **outer darkness** suggests life totally distant and apart from God. Paul calls the somewhat problematic Philippian assembly his **crown**. Another ten images fill the poem from Isaiah. God not only throws out the unprepared guest: God also **shelters** us from storm, removes the **shroud** that finally covers all humans, like some kind of monster **eats up death**, and like a lover or a parent **wipes away our tears**.

Ideas for the Day

◆   The stories of festivals and banquets are rich in these readings. We all know the joy of gathering, celebrating, eating, and drinking. It is a common and essentially human form of communication, bonding, remembering, hoping, living. Yet human feasts are usually exclusionary. A small circle of family and friends are invited. The coming celebration of Thanksgiving is an example. In Isaiah and in Matthew the feast is extravagant. All people are invited. No membership cards are required to gain access. The prayer of the day picks up on this theme: "you have prepared a table before all peoples." This feast is so extraordinary that all tears, even death itself, are wiped away. The table of communion invites us into a radical vision of peace and justice in the world—for all people.

◆   God shares a treasure with all the people. The treasure is life itself, and it is shared with us in celebration—in food and drink, in bread and wine. But the question is also posed: what do we treasure? Some don't hear the invitation because they are too focused on their own earthly treasures. They turn away. Others, enjoying the feast, ignore what it means, what is being offered. "Taste and see that the LORD is good." Our food, our treasure, is God. *This* meal continually forms us anew into people for the world. Thanksgiving at the Table I (*Evangelical Lutheran Worship*, p. 109) captures this when it pleads, "that we and all who share in the body and blood of Christ . . . may be formed to live as your holy people."

◆   Jesus expects there to be unbelievers in our midst. Jesus' parable in the gospel today has some similarities with the parables of Matthew 13. Like the fisherman (Matt. 13:47-50) and the householder with weed and wheat growing together (Matt. 13:24-30), the king's servants gather everyone in sight. No questions are asked. There is no doctrinal quiz. No one judges whether they are sufficiently schooled in social graces. That sweeping invitation no doubt resulted in there being some odd company at the wedding banquet for the king's son. Keep odd company, Jesus advises in his parable. It's not up to us to make judgments about those who answer the gospel invitation to faith.

Connections with the Liturgy

Again in *Evangelical Lutheran Worship*, one possible invitation to the table is "Come to the banquet." The eucharistic prayers IV, VI, and VII refer to the feast. In prayer X, recalling Isaiah 25:6, we praise God as wine, who will "warm our hearts and make us one."

Let the Children Come

This Sunday's scripture texts about a great feast and hearty banquet remind us that God's table, the altar, stands at the center of our weekly eucharist. Underline the faith/home connection by asking children how many people eat at their table at home and where they sit. Walk with children to the altar, God's table. Notice with them that there's plenty of space at God's table—always room for one more. And no matter where we stand or kneel each Sunday at God's table, God says, "Welcome!" and feeds us.

Assembly Song
Gathering

Arise, my soul, arise!   ELW 827

God extends an invitation   ELW 486, LLC 397

Give to our God immortal praise!   ELW 848

Psalmody

Alonso, Tony or Marty Haugen. "I Shall Live in the House of the Lord" from TLP:A. Cant, assembly, C inst.

Glynn, John. "My Shepherd Is the Lord" from PS2.

Hughes, Howard. "Psalm 23" from TP.

Bruxvoort-Colligan, Richard. "My Love Is My Shepherd (Psalm 23)" from SR.

Pavlechko, Thomas. "Psalm 106:1-6, 19-23" from SMP.

Hymn of the Day

As we gather at your table   ELW 522   *IN BABILONE*

Let us go now to the banquet   ELW 523, LLC 410
   VAMOS TODOS AL BANQUETE

Thine the amen   ELW 826, WOV 801   *THINE*

Offering

All depends on our possessing   ELW 589

The numberless gifts of God's mercies   ELW 683

Communion

United at the table   ELW 498, LLC 408

Oh, sing to the Lord   ELW 822

Take my life, that I may be   ELW 583, 685; LBW 406

Sending

Sent forth by God's blessing   ELW 547, LBW 221

At the Lamb's high feast we sing   ELW 362, LBW 210

Additional Assembly Songs

Give thanks   TFF 292, W&P 41

Glory to God, we give you thanks   WOV 787

◑ Come, the banquet hall is ready   GS2 14

◑ Feliciano, Francisco F. Philippines. "The Lord Is My Shepherd" from *Sound the Bamboo*. SATB. GIA G-6830.

✧ Hall, Charlie/Todd Cromwell. "My Drink" from CCLI.

✧ Ingram, Jason/Robbie Seay. "Kingdom and a King" from WT.

✧ Maher, Matt. "I Rejoice in You" from CCLI.

✧ Oakley, Paul. "Because of You There's a Place" from WT.

✧ Tomlin, Chris/Louie Giglio/Jesse Reeves/Daniel Carson. "Chosen Generation" from WT.

✧ Townend, Stuart. "Psalm 23" from CCLI.

Music for the Day
Choral

Burroughs, Bob. "Think About These Things." U/2 pt, kybd, C inst. AFP 9780806698373.

Clarke, Jeremiah. "My Shepherd Is the Living Lord" from *Augsburg Motet Book*. SATB. AFP 9781451423709.

Frahm, Frederick. "My Shepherd Will Supply My Need." SAB, kybd. AFP 9780800675530.

◑ = global song
✧ = praise song
● = relates to hymn of the day

Trotta, John Michael. "And Peace Shall Guard You." SATB. MSM 50-9213.

Children's Choir

Carter, John. "The Shepherd Psalm." 2 pt, kybd. HOP A555.

Vivaldi, A. "Et Exultavit." U, pno. HAL 884088241797.

Wienhorst, Richard. "Let the Peace of Christ Rule in Your Hearts." U trbl, kybd. ECS 5711.

Keyboard / Instrumental

Manz, Paul. "Toccata on At the Lamb's High Feast." Org. MSM 10-423.

● Miller, Aaron David. "Thine" from *Augsburg Organ Library: Autumn*. Org. AFP 9780800675790.

● Organ, Anne Krentz. "Thine" from *Reflections on Hymn Tunes for Holy Communion*. Pno. AFP 9780800654979.

● Rodriguez, Penny. "In Babilone" from *He Leadeth Me: Ten Hymn Arrangements for Piano*. Pno. MSM 15-840.

Handbell

● Griffin, Jackie. "Festive Celebration." 5 oct hb, L3. FTT 201885HB. Br qnt. FTT 201885B. Org. FTT 201885O. Timp. FTT 201885P. Full score. FTT 201885M. Complete set (8 hb pts, 1 of all other pts). FTT 201885.

Larson, Lloyd. "At the Table of the Lord." 3-4 oct, L2+. LOR 20/1294L.

Taranto, A. Steven. "Bell Prayer." 3-5 oct, L2. CG CGB627.

Monday, October 13, 2014
Day of Thanksgiving (Canada)

See Day of Thanksgiving (U.S.A.), pp. 341–343.

Wednesday, October 15
Teresa of Ávila (Teresa de Jesús), teacher, renewer of the church, died 1582

Teresa of Ávila (AH-vee-la) is also known as Teresa de Jesús. She chose the life of a Carmelite nun after reading the letters of Jerome. Frequently sick during her early years as a nun, she found that when she was sick her prayer life flowered, but when she was well it withered. Steadily her life of faith and prayer deepened, and she grew to have a lively sense of God's presence with her. She worked to reform her monastic community in Ávila, which she believed had strayed from its original purpose. Her reforms asked nuns to maintain life in the monastic enclosure without leaving it and to identify with those who are poor by not wearing shoes. Teresa's writings on devotional life have enjoyed a wide readership.

Friday, October 17

Ignatius, Bishop of Antioch, martyr, died around 115

Ignatius was the second bishop of Antioch, in Syria. It was there that the name "Christian" was first used to describe the followers of Jesus. Ignatius is known to us through his letters. In them he encouraged Christians to live in unity sustained with love while standing firm on sound doctrine. Ignatius believed Christian martyrdom was a privilege. When his own martyrdom approached, he wrote in one of his letters, "I prefer death in Christ Jesus to power over the farthest limits of the earth. . . . Do not stand in the way of my birth to real life." Ignatius and all martyrs are a reminder that even today Christians face death because of their faith in Jesus.

Saturday, October 18

Luke, Evangelist

St. Luke is identified by tradition as the author of both Luke and Acts. Luke is careful to place the events of Jesus' life in both their social and religious contexts. Some of the most loved parables, including the good Samaritan and the prodigal son, are found only in this gospel. Luke's gospel has also given the church some of its most beautiful songs: the Benedictus sung at morning prayer, the Magnificat sung at evening prayer, and the Nunc dimittis sung at the close of the day. These songs are powerful witnesses to the message of Jesus Christ.

October 19, 2014
Time after Pentecost — Lectionary 29

In today's first reading God uses the Gentile ruler Cyrus to accomplish divine purposes. When the Pharisees try to trap Jesus, he tells them to give the emperor what belongs to him and to God what belongs to God. To gather for worship reminds us that our ultimate allegiance is to God rather than to any earthly authority. Created in the image of God, we offer our entire selves in the service of God and for the sake of the world.

Prayer of the Day

Sovereign God, raise your throne in our hearts. Created by you, let us live in your image; created for you, let us act for your glory; redeemed by you, let us give you what is yours, through Jesus Christ, our Savior and Lord.

Gospel Acclamation

Alleluia. Shine like stars | in the world;* holding fast to the | word of life. *Alleluia.* (Phil. 2:15, 16)

Readings and Psalm
Isaiah 45:1-7

The prophet announces that Cyrus the Persian emperor is the one the Lord has anointed to end Israel's exile. The Lord makes this choice so that the whole world will recognize this Lord as the only God. Persia had a god of light and a god of darkness; the Lord claims sovereignty over both light and darkness.

Psalm 96:1-9 [10-13]

Ascribe to the LORD honor and power. (Ps. 96:7)

1 Thessalonians 1:1-10

Most likely this letter is the first written by Paul. Paul is giving pastoral encouragement and reassurances to new Christians living in an antagonistic pagan environment. Their commitment of faith, love, and hope makes them a model for other new Christian communities.

Matthew 22:15-22

After Jesus begins teaching in the temple, religious leaders try to trap him with questions. First they ask if God's people should pay taxes to an earthly tyrant like Caesar.

Semicontinuous reading and psalm
Exodus 33:12-23

Moses successfully interceded with God to accompany Israel to the holy land after their sin with the golden calf.

In response to a request to display his glory, God recites a sentence that appears frequently in the Old Testament: "I will be gracious to whom I will be gracious." Moses is not allowed to see God's face, but only God's back.

Psalm 99

Proclaim the greatness of the LORD our God. (Ps. 99:5)

Preface   Sundays

Color   Green

Prayers of Intercession

The prayers are prepared locally for each occasion. The following examples may be adapted or used as appropriate.

With the whole people of God in Christ Jesus, let us pray for the church, those in need, and all of God's creation.

A brief silence.

Lord of the church, help us to give to you what is yours. Make us faithful stewards of our time, talents, and treasures. Hear us, O God.

Your mercy is great.

Lord of creation, help us to share our bounties. Plant in us a willing and able desire to utilize the world's resources wisely and without bias. Hear us, O God.

Your mercy is great.

Lord of the nations, help us to put aside malice. Teach us to fight for justice, to liberate the oppressed, and to advocate for those who have no voice. Hear us, O God.

Your mercy is great.

Lord of life, help us in our need. Restore the minds, bodies, and spirits of those who are sick and soothe those who despair (*especially*). Hear us, O God.

Your mercy is great.

Lord of all, help us to support one another. Bless our communities, sustain local businesses, and remove enmity between neighbors. Hear us, O God.

Your mercy is great.

Lord of the resurrection, help us to rejoice in your promises. Gladden the hearts of those who grieve. Greet those who die with your reviving grace. Hear us, O God.

Your mercy is great.

Trusting in your mercy and goodness, we bring before you these prayers and whatever else you see that we need, in the name of the one who sets us free, Jesus Christ, our Savior.

Amen.

Images in the Readings

Typically, a **coin** is impressed with an image of the authority upon which the coin relies. In the USA, coins and bills bear the picture of presidents who function as model representatives of the sovereign people. In baptism, it is the cross of Christ that has been impressed on our bodies: he is the authority to whom we owe allegiance. As to taxes: Christians in different countries have widely ranging views about how much of our days' wages is rightly owed to the government.

The Isaiah reading plays with the idea of one's **name**. God calls Cyrus by name; God's personal name is YHWH, represented in most English-language Bibles as "the LORD." In his encouragement to the Thessalonians, Paul writes of God the Father, the Lord Jesus Christ, and the Holy Spirit. In baptism, the candidates are first called by their secular name, after which this triune name of God is placed on them. Yet in the second century, Justin Martyr wrote that to imagine that we can know and speak the very name of the almighty God is madness. Perhaps the name of God that we are given in the Bible is like a potholder, a way to hold on to something that is far too hot for bare human hands.

Ideas for the Day

◆   Standing before Pontius Pilate, Jesus proclaims that his kingdom is not of this world. In divisive times, it is vital to remember that the reign of God will not be ushered in by earthly means: one cannot vote the kingdom in or out. Yet we are also called to participate in the affairs of the world, serving as light, salt, and yeast. The exhortation to "render therefore unto Caesar" what is his and give to God the things that are God's, if not carefully parsed, can lead either to a wholehearted engagement in political machinations— to where the gospel becomes inseparable from a party platform—or it can lead to quietism and dualism, in which the events of the church and of the state have little to do with one another.

◆   The Lutheran doctrine of the two kingdoms explains that God rules the world in two ways: in the earthly realm, through temporal means such as civil government, and in the spiritual realm, through the gospel of trust in Christ alone. In his book *Martin Luther's Understanding of God's Two Kingdoms* (Grand Rapids, MI: Eerdmans, 2010), William J. Wright challenges the prevailing assumption that this dialectic is primarily political. He argues that a misreading of this doctrine, and even of political concepts like separation of church and state or the premise of a so-called "naked" public square, leads to compartmentalization in the daily life of Christians and stunts the full, mature growth of faith that informs action.

◆   1 Timothy 2:1-2 commands us to pray specifically for those in authority. Often, our prayers for politicians and world leaders are directive—enumerating what we think they should do—rather than simply commending them to God, knowing that God reigns through these earthly "left-hand" vessels and knows best what they need and how to use them. Try assigning the names of local, state, and national politicians and officials to prayer teams, or give each worshiper today a leader's name to take home, with the direction to pray for blessings for this person, as they would for a friend, regardless of political affiliation or affinity.

Connections with the Liturgy

That Paul writes of "remembering you in our prayers" models for us the Sunday intercessions. The prayer of the day and the eucharistic prayer offer occasions for the assembly to pray for itself, while the primary purpose of the intercessions is to pray for everything and everybody else in the world. The petition for "the church universal" can focus each week on some community of believers other than our own, especially those experiencing persecution.

Let the Children Come

When children hear Jesus talking about coins in the gospel, they may remember seeing money in church. Each week at worship children watch the ushers circulating offering plates (maybe older children serve as ushers, too), and learn that at church we share our money. At church we put our money together and create a larger pile. But after we collect the offerings, then what? What happens to the money we collect at worship? Children probably wonder (and adults do too!). Share three pictures of projects that your church offerings support.

Assembly Song
Gathering

God of grace and God of glory   ELW 705, LBW 415
O God beyond all praising   ELW 880, WOV 797
You servants of God   ELW 825, LBW 252

Psalmody

Alonso, Tony or Marty Haugen. "Give the Lord Glory" from TLP:A.
Hopson, Hal H. "Psalm 96" from TP.
Becker, John W. "Psalm 96:1-9 [10-13]" from PWA.
Shute, Linda Cable. "Psalm 96," Refrain 2, from PSCY.
Messner, Sally. "Psalm 99" from PWA.

Hymn of the Day

We give thee but thine own   ELW 686, LBW 410   HEATH
All my hope on God is founded   ELW 757, WOV 782   MICHAEL
Sing praise to God, the highest good   ELW 871, LBW 542
    LOBT GOTT DEN HERREN, IHR

Offering

We give thee but thine own   ELW 686, LBW 410
We raise our hands to you, O Lord   ELW 690

Communion

When our song says peace   ELW 709
Lord, Be Glorified   ELW 744, TFF 248, W&P 89
Lift every voice and sing   ELW 841, LBW 526, TFF 296

Sending

Earth and all stars!   ELW 731
Holy, holy, holy, Lord God Almighty!   ELW 413

Additional Assembly Songs

Have thine own way, Lord   TFF 152
Give thanks   TFF 292, W&P 41
Everything that we have   GS2 34
⊕ Pangosban, Ben. Philippines. "Sing a Song to the Lord" from *Sound the Bamboo*. U. GIA G-6830.
✿ Crist, Ben. "Hear Our Prayers" from CCLI.
✿ Eaton, Chris/John Hartley. "Praise the Lord Who Reigns Above" from WT.
✿ Ellis, John. "King" from WT.
✿ Fieldes, Mia/Lincoln Brewster. "God, You Reign" from WT.
✿ Gillies, Jadwin/Joel Houston/Reuben Morgan. "For Your Name" from CCLI.
✿ Sampson, Marty. "All Day" from CCLI.

Music for the Day
Choral

Cherwien, David. "God of Grace and God of Glory." SATB, org, assembly, opt hb, br qrt. MSM 60-7021.
Hildebrand, Kevin. "Sing Praise to God the Highest Good." SATB, org, br qnt, timp. CPH 98-3983.
Schalk, Carl. "All Things Are Yours, My God." SATB, org, opt assembly. MSM 50-9032.
Schütz, Heinrich. "Sing to the Lord a New Song" from *Augsburg Motet Book*. SATB. AFP 9781451423709.
Spurlock, William. "Earth and All Stars." SATB, kybd. AFP 9780800638818.

Children's Choir

Bedford, Michael. "God Has Come to Every Nation." U/2 pt, pno, tamb. CG CGA882.
Heim, Brett. "All Glory Be to God Alone." U, 2 vln, cont. CPH 97-6896.
Sleeth, Natalie. "With Music I Will Praise Thee." SA, kybd, opt hb. HIN HMC2069.

Keyboard / Instrumental

● Burkhardt, Michael. "Voluntary on All My Hope on God Is Founded." Org. MSM 10-734.
● Manz, Paul. "Lobt Gott den Herren, ihr" from *Improvisations on Hymns of Praise*. Org. MSM 10-750.

⊕ = global song
✿ = praise song
● = relates to hymn of the day

Maynard, Lynette, L. "Take My Life, That I May Be" from *Let It Shine: Worship Music for Solo Piano*. Pno. AFP 9780800677640.

Powell, Robert J. "Bunessan" from *Three Pieces for Treble Instrument and Keyboard*. C inst, kybd. MSM 20-821.

Handbell

McChesney, Kevin. "Offertory." 3-5 oct, L3. BP HB326.

Sherman, Arnold. "Canticle of Praise." 3-5 oct, L4-. AGEHR AG35288.

Tucker, Sondra. "Melody of Hope." 3-5 oct hb, opt 3-5 oct hc, L2+. CG CGB725.

Thursday, October 23

James of Jerusalem, martyr, died around 62

James became an early leader of the church in Jerusalem. He is described in the New Testament as the brother of Jesus, and secular historian Josephus calls James the brother of Jesus, "the so-called Christ." Little is known about James, but Josephus reported that the Pharisees respected James for his piety and observance of the law. His enemies had him put to death.

October 26, 2014

Reformation Sunday

On this day we celebrate the heart of our faith: the gospel of Christ—the good news—that makes us free! We pray that the Holy Spirit would continue to unite the church today in its proclamation and witness to the world. In the waters of baptism we are made one body; we pray for the day that all Christians will also be one at the Lord's table.

Prayer of the Day

Almighty God, gracious Lord, we thank you that your Holy Spirit renews the church in every age. Pour out your Holy Spirit on your faithful people. Keep them steadfast in your word, protect and comfort them in times of trial, defend them against all enemies of the gospel, and bestow on the church your saving peace, through Jesus Christ, our Savior and Lord, who lives and reigns with you and the Holy Spirit, one God, now and forever.

or

Gracious Father, we pray for your holy catholic church. Fill it with all truth and peace. Where it is corrupt, purify it; where it is in error, direct it; where in anything it is amiss, reform it; where it is right, strengthen it; where it is in need, provide for it; where it is divided, reunite it; for the sake of your Son, Jesus Christ, our Savior, who lives and reigns with you and the Holy Spirit, one God, now and forever.

Gospel Acclamation

Alleluia. If you continue in my word, you are truly ¹ my disciples,* and you will know the truth, and the truth will ¹ make you free. *Alleluia.* (John 8:31-32)

Readings and Psalm

Jeremiah 31:31-34

The renewed covenant will not be breakable, but like the old covenant it will expect the people to live upright lives. To know the Lord means that one will defend the cause of the poor and needy (Jer. 22:16). The renewed covenant is possible only because the Lord will forgive iniquity and not remember sin. Our hope lies in a God who forgets.

Psalm 46

The Lord of hosts is with us; the God of Jacob is our stronghold. (Ps. 46:7)

Romans 3:19-28

Paul's words stand at the heart of the preaching of Martin Luther and the other Reformation leaders. No human beings make themselves right with God through works of the law. We are brought into a right relationship with God through the divine activity centered in Christ's death. This act is a gift of grace that liberates us from sin and empowers our faith in Jesus Christ.

John 8:31-36

Jesus speaks of truth and freedom as spiritual realities known through his word. He reveals the truth that sets people free from sin.

Preface Sundays

Color Red

Prayers of Intercession

The prayers are prepared locally for each occasion. The following examples may be adapted or used as appropriate.

With the whole people of God in Christ Jesus, let us pray for the church, those in need, and all of God's creation.
A brief silence.

Make us free to be the church in the world, God of grace. Form our mission and ministry in ways that truly and tangibly give new life, hope, and grace in abundance. Hear us, O God.

Your mercy is great.

Make us free to be one with your creation, God of grace. Fill us with your Spirit and lead us to find better ways to honor what you have given us. Help us to abandon wasteful habits. Hear us, O God.

Your mercy is great.

Make us free to be brothers and sisters, God of grace. Shatter the distinctions that create hatred and fear. Open our eyes to see one another as people who bear the image and likeness of Christ. Hear us, O God.

Your mercy is great.

Make us free to be whole and healthy persons, God of grace. Give respite to caregivers, infuse medical workers with skill, inspire scientists to find cures, and make us well in mind, body, and soul (*especially*). Hear us, O God.

Your mercy is great.

Make us free to be people of purpose, God of grace. Reform apathy into action, bless us with a determination to let go of those things that keep us stagnant, and drive us to witness to the gospel. Hear us, O God.

Your mercy is great.

Make us free to be still and know you, God of grace. Join our voices with the saints (*especially Philipp Nicolai, Johann Heermann, Paul Gerhardt, and the men and women of the Reformation*) who now sing in one heavenly choir. Hear us, O God.

Your mercy is great.

Trusting in your mercy and goodness, we bring before you these prayers and whatever else you see that we need, in the name of the one who sets us free, Jesus Christ, our Savior.

Amen.

Images in the Readings

The gospel's image of **freedom** presents a challenge to contemporary Americans, and perhaps to other Western societies as well, since popularly "freedom" is understood as the right of the individual to live out personal choices. John's gospel suggests instead that the freedom granted in Christ is the freedom of the son, who remains in the father's house and does the will of that father. Sixteenth-century Christians used this proclamation of freedom to leave behind church regulations of the medieval church, but even Martin Luther wrote detailed interpretations of the Ten Commandments, understood as "law" for Christian use. We are free to be obedient children.

A **covenant** was a legal agreement in which the master promised protection because the participants met certain requirements. Ancient Israelites adopted this cultural category for their understanding of the relationship that God had offered the chosen people. Christians continued to use this language in articulating the renewed relationship with God that was affected through Christ. Particularly Methodists have kept this language alive in referring to the Baptismal Covenant and in their annual Covenant Renewal ceremonies. Lutherans understand the covenant as God's continuing mercy given in word and sacrament.

Ideas for the Day

◆ Reformation Day observances can, at the extremes, either become pep rallies for Martin Luther (complete with a triumphal whiff of anti-Catholicism) or are downplayed as embarrassingly dated, at odds with modern ecumenical sensibilities. To seek a middle way, it helps to pay attention to the Lutheran reform movement as both protestant *and* catholic. Host a Reformation hymn sing this afternoon, but ask a local Roman Catholic priest to write and deliver reflections on the hymns. Invite a Catholic clergyman or layperson to discuss with your congregation the "Joint Declaration on the Doctrine of Justification," the historic 1999 agreement between Catholics and Lutherans. Or hold an old-fashioned Reformation festival, inviting neighboring churches of various denominations to take part, choosing hymns and readings from each tradition's reformers.

◆ The Reformation has been provocatively described as a way for more people to eat ice cream if there are more flavors than vanilla. The Lutheran "flavor of ice cream" is one of our great gifts to the whole church. Try teaching your congregation a distinctively Lutheran hymn, such as "All depends on our possessing" (ELW 589) or Paul Gerhardt's beautiful bedtime prayer "Now rest beneath night's shadow" (ELW 568). In our fine tradition of sung theology sinking deep into the soul, why not spend the month of October memorizing a hymn together as a parish?

◆ In the Large Catechism, Luther calls individual confession and forgiveness a "splendid gift and inexpressible treasure." While the rite is included in our worship books and even detailed in the Small Catechism, most people do not know this "wonderful, precious and comforting thing" (*Book of Concord*, Robert Kolb and Timothy J. Wengert, eds., Augsburg Fortress, 2000, p. 479). For the sake of that comfort, it is worth the patient teaching and effort involved in reintroducing individual confession to modern parishes, perhaps offering it once a month, or during Lent or Holy Week. This is a concrete, deeply moving way in which Christ makes us know the truth—of our sin, and of his boundless mercy—and that truth makes us free!

Connections with the Liturgy

In the opening confession and forgiveness in *Evangelical Lutheran Worship*'s Holy Communion (p. 95), we confess that "we are captive to sin." This language recalls Jesus' words in today's gospel that we are slaves to sin.

The rite of Baptism within *Evangelical Lutheran Worship* (p. 231) announces that the newly baptized are now daughters and sons of God. We now have a place in God's house forever.

Baptismal sponsors promise to help the newly baptized live "in the covenant of baptism," recalling the imagery from Jeremiah. The new covenant is sealed by Christ's blood, poured out for us in the weekly meal of grace (*Evangelical Lutheran Worship*, pp. 108, 109).

Let the Children Come

A young acolyte stares at the flame on her acolyte stick as she slowly walks down the aisle. She's intently focused on her ministry—safely delivering her light to the candles on the altar. Worship comes alive for children like this young acolyte as they become participants and offer their gifts and abilities to the worshiping community. Today is Reformation Sunday, and our readings focus us on the truth of our faith—as surely as a flame focuses a young acolyte. God's truth sets us free—young and old together.

Assembly Song
Gathering

The church of Christ, in every age   ELW 729, LBW 433
A mighty fortress is our God   ELW 503–505
Christ is made the sure foundation   ELW 645

Psalmody

Hopson, Hal H. "Psalm 46" from TP.
Bruxvoort-Colligan, Richard. "God Is Our Shelter and Strength (Psalm 46)" from SR.
Harbor, Rawn. "The Lord of Hosts Is with Us (Psalm 46)." TFF 6.

Hymn of the Day

Listen, God is calling   ELW 513, TFF, 130, WOV 712
      NENO LAKE MUNGU
That priceless grace   ELW 591, TFF 68   *THAT PRICELESS GRACE*
Rise, O Sun of righteousness   ELW 657   *SONNE DER GERECHTIGKEIT*

Offering

We give thee but thine own   ELW 686, LBW 410
Oh, praise the gracious power   ELW 651, WOV 750

Communion

Jesus, priceless treasure   ELW 775, LBW 457/458
Kyrie! God, Father   ELW 409, LBW 168
Come with us, O blessed Jesus   ELW 501

Sending

Salvation unto us has come   ELW 590
O day full of grace   ELW 627, LBW 161

Additional Assembly Songs

Wonderful grace of Jesus   TFF 184
Only by grace   W&P 112
⊕ Now I know   GS3 7
⊕ Gibson, Colin A. New Zealand. "He Came Singing Love" from *Sound the Bamboo*. SATB. GIA G-6830.
✿ Brown, Brenton/Paul Baloche. "Because of Your Love" from WT.
✿ Fee, Steve. "All Because of Jesus" from WT.
✿ Hall, Charlie. "Freedom Song" from CCLI.
✿ Houston, Joel/Matt Crocker/Scott Ligertwood. "Break Free" from CCLI.
✿ Ligertwood, Brooke/Scott Ligertwood. "Beneath the Waters (I Will Rise)" from WT.
✿ Nockels, Christy/Nathan Nockels. "My Master" from CCLI.

Music for the Day
Choral

Behnke, John. "By Grace and Word and Faith." SATB, hb. Sacred Music Press AM781.
Bender, Jan. "O God, O Lord, of Heaven and Earth." SATB, org, opt tpts and assembly. AFP 9780800652500.
Chepponis, James. "If God Is for Us." SATB or cant, desc, C inst, br qrt, timp. GIA G-5948.
● Helgen, John. "That Priceless Grace." SATB, kybd. AFP 9780800658595.
Mozart, W. A. "God Is Our Refuge" from *Augsburg Motet Book*. SATB. AFP 9781451423709.
Weber, Paul. "A Mighty Fortress." SATB, children, org, br, timp, perc, opt assembly. MSM 60-8005.

Children's Choir

Bach, J. S. "God Is Ever Sun and Shield" from *A Third Morning Star Choir Book*. U, ob/fl, cont. CPH 97-4972.
Bertalot, John. "God Is Our Hope." 2 pt trbl, kybd. CG CGA444.
Bristol, Lee Hastings. "Lord, Keep Us Steadfast in Your Word." U, org. ECS 4902.
Costello, Michael. "God of Grace and God of Glory." U/2 pt mxd, org, br qnt, opt timp, opt cym, opt assembly. MSM 60-6004.

⊕ = global song
✿ = praise song
● = relates to hymn of the day

Keyboard / Instrumental

- Miller, Aaron David. "Sonne der Gerechtigkeit" from *Eight Chorale Preludes for Manuals Only, Vol 2*. Org. AFP 9780800678470.
  Oliver, Curt. "Variations on Built on a Rock the Church Shall Stand" from *Built on a Rock: Keyboard Seasons*. Pno. AFP 9780800654962.
- Organ, Anne Krentz. "Sonne der Gerechtigkeit" from *Reflections on Hymn Tunes for Holy Communion*. Pno. AFP 9780800654979.
  Walcha, Helmut. "Ein feste Burg" from *A New Liturgical Year*. Org. AFP 9780800656713.

Handbell

- Afdahl, Lee. "At the Lamb's High Feast." 3-5 oct hb, opt 2 oct hc, L2+. CPH 97-7309.
  Eithun, Sandra. "Amazing Grace." 3-6 oct hb, opt 3 oct hc, L2. RR BL5056.
  Tucker, Sondra. "Morning Canticle." 2-3 oct hb, opt 2-3 oct hc, L2+. CG CGB233.

October 26, 2014
Time after Pentecost — Lectionary 30

Jesus' summary of the law in today's gospel echoes our first reading from Leviticus. We are called not only to love God with heart, soul, and mind, but also to love our neighbor as ourselves. It is out of such deep care that Paul shares the gospel with the Thessalonian community. In the confession of sins, we acknowledge that we have not loved God, neighbor, and self; yet we gather to hear the word of forgiveness and to be strengthened by word and meal to be signs of God's love and mercy in the world.

Prayer of the Day

O Lord God, you are the holy lawgiver, you are the salvation of your people. By your Spirit renew us in your covenant of love, and train us to care tenderly for all our neighbors, through Jesus Christ, our Savior and Lord.

Gospel Acclamation

Alleluia. Beloved, since God loved [1] us so much,* we also ought to love [1] one another. *Alleluia.* (1 John 4:11)

Readings and Psalm
Leviticus 19:1-2, 15-18

The holiness code in Leviticus urges people to be holy because God is holy. Holiness is lived out in partiality for and consideration of the poor and the weak. We are to love our neighbors as ourselves. God's people exercise justice and love in their dealings with one another.

Psalm 1

Their delight is in the law of the LORD. (Ps. 1:2)

1 Thessalonians 2:1-8

Paul uses maternal imagery to depict the caring and nurturing relationship he shares with the Thessalonian Christians. When he first came to their city it was not to benefit himself but to share the gospel with them, which was his responsibility as an apostle of Christ.

Matthew 22:34-46

Put on the spot by the Pharisees, Jesus displays wisdom by summarizing the law of God in just two commandments and by demonstrating the Messiah must be more than the son of David.

Semicontinuous reading and psalm
Deuteronomy 34:1-12

Before his death, Moses, who was not allowed to enter the holy land, was granted the right to see the land from Mount Nebo. The statement that no prophet has arisen in Israel like Moses (34:10) stands in tension with Deuteronomy 18:15 (God will "raise up for you a prophet like me") and led to the expectation that another Moses would still come. In several New Testament passages Jesus is identified as that prophet.

Psalm 90:1-6, 13-17

Show your servants your works, and your splendor to their children. (Ps. 90:16)

Preface   Sundays

Color   Green

Prayers of Intercession

The prayers are prepared locally for each occasion. The following examples may be adapted or used as appropriate.

With the whole people of God in Christ Jesus, let us pray for the church, those in need, and all of God's creation.

A brief silence.

As the whole church, focus us to love you and our neighbors in the ways we create policy, define our mission, determine budgets, and vision for the future. Hear us, O God.

Your mercy is great.

As stewards of creation, instruct us to love you and our neighbors in the ways we use the gifts of this planet. Keep us mindful of the needs of the generations to come. Hear us, O God.

Your mercy is great.

As people of the world, teach us to love you and our neighbors in the ways we judge one another, work for peace, set aside prejudice, and work for justice. Hear us, O God.

Your mercy is great.

As ministers of your word, teach us to love you and our neighbors in the ways we care for those who suffer (*especially*). Give us compassionate hearts, gentle hands, and minds that craft healing. Hear us, O God.

Your mercy is great.

As a community, guide us to love you and our neighbors in the ways we share ourselves with others. Support us in building relationships, having open minds, and being confident in the gospel. Hear us, O God.

Your mercy is great.

Here other intercessions may be offered.

As your children, lead us to love you and our neighbors in the ways we remember those who have died, but still guide our faith (*especially Philipp Nicolai, Johann Heermann, Paul Gerhardt, and the men and women of the Reformation*). Hear us, O God.

Your mercy is great.

Trusting in your mercy and goodness, we bring before you these prayers and whatever else you see that we need, in the name of the one who sets us free, Jesus Christ, our Savior.

Amen.

Images in the Readings

The term **law** is tricky for us. According to the covenant in the Old Testament, the law was graciously given by God to delineate the way toward communal happiness. However, Paul uses the term critically, teaching that keeping these 613 commands will not bring us to God. Luther uses the term far more broadly to refer to everything in the Bible that preaches our sin and announces our death. For many contemporary hearers, the term means governmental regulations. Our task is to make sure that the meaning of any particular use of the term is clear. Psychologists suggest,

in accord with Luther, that confronting the truth of the human condition is, although sad, finally welcomed; but then as Christians we gladly take refuge in the gospel of God's love in Christ Jesus.

Probably in 1 Thessalonians 2:7 Paul is suggesting that evangelists are like a **nursing mother**, since the children are her own. So Paul offers a balance to Matthew's image of the late-first-century church leader as an exegetical authority. Both are helpful images.

Psalm 110 pictures the messiah sitting at the **right hand** of God. In ancient Near Eastern courts, the prince or a kind of prime minister sat on the right side of the monarch. From the psalm the phrase made it all the way into our creeds. In the fifteenth century, the mystic Julian reminds us that the phrase is a metaphor: "But it is not meant that the Son sits on the right hand as one man sits by another in this life, for there is no such sitting, as to my sight, in the Trinity." She suggests that the metaphor means that Son is "right in the highest nobility of the Father's joy."

Ideas for the Day

◆ Martin Luther struggled with the idea of God as an implacable lawgiver, ready to punish the unworthy. Such was Luther's distress that he was often sunk in despair, afraid that he was cut off from the mercy of God. His confessor once urged him simply to love God. Luther's reaction was swift and violent: "Love God? I hated him!" (Roland Bainton, *Here I Stand*, Peabody, MA: Hendrickson, 1950, p. 41). People are still longing for release from the torment of sin, so we should pay special attention to how we speak words of absolution. In corporate confession, try not to rush through the confession; allow plenty of silence. Look at worshipers, use a direct form of absolution, and have the words of pardon memorized as much as you can, saying them deliberately. Don't be afraid to use "I forgive you," because it's not about the worship leader, it's claiming the authority of Christ to speak his word of forgiveness to people who are dying for it.

◆ Intellectually, we know that love is, as the band Boston sang, "more than a feeling." But too often the command to love God and neighbor is reduced to inoffensive, vaguely positive emotions, instead of the gritty exertion that results first in our death, then in our rebirth as people with new eyes to see Christ in those around us. Loving God means willing and working for what God wills and names as good, especially with regard to our neighbor. With the late-October focus on the Reformation, today is an excellent time to explore with your congregation what Christian love looks like. Try an open forum or conversation in which adults and older youth wrestle with questions: Is there anything we think of as "loving" that really isn't? How does right belief and theology contribute to or detract from the love of neighbor? Lutherans have been accused of neglecting the love of neighbor in favor of the love of God, but can the two be separated? What are the special gifts of the churches of the Reformation in leading others to love God with heart, mind, and strength?

Connections with the Liturgy

Each time we use *Evangelical Lutheran Worship*'s first option for an opening prayer of confession, we cite today's gospel: "we have not loved our neighbors as ourselves."

Let the Children Come

The Bible we use in worship may appear to children as a big, heavy tome. They may be overwhelmed by all the words in a Bible, especially if they are just learning to read. Children are surprised to learn that in Jesus' time, most people did not know how to read. In our time, it may look like you need to read in order to worship God. But children can worship—by praying, by bringing their openness, by listening, by tasting. Jesus helped the people who couldn't read by giving them some simple words to remember: love, God, neighbor.

Assembly Song
Gathering

Love divine, all loves excelling   ELW 631
O God, our help in ages past   ELW 632, LBW 320
To be your presence   ELW 546

Psalmody

Horman, John D. "Psalm 1" from *ChildrenSing Psalms*. U, kybd.
Hopson, Hal H. "Psalm 1" from TP.
Harbor, Rawn. "Happy Are They (Psalm 1)" TFF 1.
True, Lori. "You Have Been Our Dwelling Place." Cant, SATB, assembly, kybd, gtr, C inst. GIA G-6067.

Hymn of the Day

Great God, your love has called us   ELW 358, WOV 666   *RYBURN*
Forgive our sins as we forgive   ELW 605, LBW 307   *DETROIT*
Come, my way, my truth, my life   ELW 816   *THE CALL*

Offering

Jesu, Jesu, fill us with your love   ELW 708, TFF 83
When the poor ones   ELW 725, LLC 508

Communion

Lord of all nations, grant me grace   ELW 716, LBW 419
Bring Peace to Earth Again   ELW 700
When Jesus came to Jordan   ELW 305, WOV 647

Sending

Goodness is stronger than evil   ELW 721
O Zion, haste   ELW 668, LBW 397

Additional Assembly Songs

Fill my cup, let it overflow   TFF 127
Great day!   TFF 164

🌐 Cuban, anon. "Enviado soy de Dios/Sent Out in Jesus' Name" from *Tenemos esperanza: We Have Hope*. 2 pt, pno, gtr, perc. GBGMusik, General Board of Global Ministries, United Methodist Church. ELW 538.

🌐 Trad. Thai melody. "Happy Is He Who Walks in God's Wise Way" from *Sound the Bamboo*. U. GIA G-6830.

✿ Barnard, Shane/Kendall Combes. "Beauty for Ashes" from WT.

✿ Crowder, David/Mike Dodson/Jason Solley/Mike Hogan/Jeremy Bush/Jack Parker. "No One like You" from WT.

✿ Ellis, John. "I Stand for You" from WT.

✿ Maher, Matt/Sarah Reeves. "Shout of the King" from CCLI.

✿ Rend Collective Experiment "The Cost" from WT.

✿ Tomlin, Chris/Daniel Carson/Jason Ingram. "Jesus My Redeemer" from CCLI.

Music for the Day
Choral

Cherwien, David. "When the Poor Ones." SATB, pno/gtr. MSM 50-5425.

● Hobby, Robert. "Forgive Our Sins As We Forgive." SAB, org. CPH 98-2870.

Scott, K. Lee. "The Call" from *Treasures in Heaven*. 2 pt, org. AFP 9780800679477.

Williams, Ralph Vaughan. "The Call." SATB, kybd. ECS 1.5245.

Children's Choir

Bedford, Michael. "I Will Love the Lord." U/2 pt, kybd. CG CGA419.
Hillert, Richard. "Happy Are Those Who Delight." U, org, fl, opt str. GIA G-4259.
Hopson, Hal. "Fill Us with Your Love." U/2 pt/2 pt mxd. HOP HH3923.

Keyboard / Instrumental

● Held, Wilbur. "Forgive Our Sins As We Forgive" from *Seven Settings of American Folk Hymns*. Org. CPH 97-5829.

● Miller, Aaron David. "Ryburn" from *Organ Improvisations for the Church Year: For Organ, Vol 2*. Org. AFP 9780800676766.

● Raabe, Nancy. "Detroit" from *Day of Arising: A Tapestry of Musical Traditions*. Pno. AFP 9780800637460.

● Trapp, Lynn. "Come, My Way, My Truth, My Life" from *In the Mystery of Christ*. Pno. CPH 97-6884.

🌐 = global song
✿ = praise song
● = relates to hymn of the day

Handbell

Helman, Michael. "Rondo of Praise." 3-6 oct hb, opt 3-4 oct hc, L3+. CG CGB310.

● McChesney, Kevin. "Come My Way, My Truth, My Life." 2-3 oct, L2. LOR 20/1554L.

● Roberts, Philip. "Sacred Harp Suite." 5 oct, L2+. GIA G-6448.

Sunday, October 26

Philipp Nicolai, died 1608; Johann Heermann, died 1647; Paul Gerhardt, died 1676; hymnwriters

These three outstanding hymnwriters all worked in Germany during times of war and plague. When Philipp Nicolai was a pastor in Westphalia, the plague killed thirteen hundred of his parishioners. One hundred seventy people died in one week. His hymns "Wake, Awake, for Night Is Flying" (ELW 436) and "O Morning Star, How Fair and Bright!" (ELW 308) were included in a series of meditations he wrote to comfort his parishioners during the plague. The style of Johann Heermann's hymns moved away from the more objective style of Reformation hymnody toward expressing the emotions of faith. Among his hymns is the plaintive text "Ah, Holy Jesus" (ELW 349). Paul Gerhardt lost a preaching position at St. Nicholas Church in Berlin because he refused to sign a document stating he would not make theological arguments in his sermons. The author of beloved hymns such as "O Sacred Head, Now Wounded" (ELW 351), some have called Gerhardt the greatest of Lutheran hymnwriters.

Tuesday, October 28

Simon and Jude, Apostles

Little is known about Simon and Jude. In New Testament lists of the apostles, Simon the "zealot" or Cananaean is mentioned, but he is never mentioned apart from these lists. Jude, sometimes called Thaddeus, is also mentioned in lists of the Twelve. At the last supper Jude asked Jesus why he had chosen to reveal himself to the disciples but not to the world. A traditional story about Simon and Jude says that they traveled together on a missionary journey to Persia and were both martyred there.

Friday, October 31

Reformation Day

By the end of the seventeenth century, many Lutheran churches celebrated a festival commemorating Martin Luther's posting of the Ninety-five Theses, a summary of the abuses in the church of his time. At the heart of the reform movement was the gospel, the good news that it is by grace through faith that we are justified and set free.

Saturday, November 1

All Saints Day

The custom of commemorating all of the saints of the church on a single day goes back at least to the third century. All Saints celebrates the baptized people of God, living and dead, who make up the body of Christ. We remember all who have died in the faith and now serve God around the heavenly throne.

TIME AFTER PENTECOST

NOVEMBER

PREPARING FOR NOVEMBER

The medium really is the message this month. November marks the end of the church year, the end of a year of reading from the Gospel of Matthew, and in many places in North America, the end of green leaves, gardens, and grass. In this season, the lectionary texts are also all about endings. On November 2 we observe All Saints Sunday, remembering those who have completed their baptismal journey and now rest in God. We celebrate being knit together with them in Christ who has conquered death and united those who were separated. And for the remainder of the month, we read from that great chapter of Matthew, Matthew 25, Jesus Christ's final great sermon before his arrest and crucifixion. It is itself a sermon on "last things," the last judgment and the end of the world. And because the last judgment and the end of the world are themselves "in Christ," even Christ's own sermon is itself about himself.

Lectionary

Many if not most congregations will observe All Saints Sunday, so these lectionary comments skip straight to the Sunday after All Saints, reserving commentary for All Saints for the special section at the end of this essay.

November 9	Matthew 25:1-13
November 16	Matthew 25:14-30
November 23	Matthew 25:31-46

This series of readings is appropriate for the end of a church year because they come from the chapter in Matthew that deals with the last judgment and the end of the world. It is serendipitous to be able to address apocalyptic texts at the same moment when the church year is coming to an end, and in another way, when summer life and vitality is coming to an end in the turn to fall and winter, as November heralds the dying of the landscape in many northern regions. Since All Saints Sunday is also the day we commemorate those whose earthly life has passed, really the whole month is a month of endings.

The month is spent almost completely with Matthew 25. Of this chapter, Frederick Dale Bruner writes,

The purpose of these four stories [in this chapter] is to teach the *practical* ways "to keep alert for the any-day coming of Christ" that was taught so powerfully in the preceding chapter. Chap. 24 taught us *that* Christ is coming back; chap. 25 teaches us *how to wait* for that coming. At the center of all three parables [Bruner includes the parable of the faithful or unfaithful servant, Matthew 24:45-51 as part of chapter 25] is an "Absent One" who comes back again for judgment; and in all four stories, individual destiny depends on how one lives for—or perhaps more deeply: whether one believes in—this Absent-but-Coming One" (*Matthew: A Commentary*, vol. 2, p. 535).

The thematic of Matthew 25 indicated by Bruner thus becomes not only excellent content for the conclusion of the church year, but also excellent *anticipation* of the themes for Advent and the beginning of the next church year.

The *how to wait* has ethical content. Many readers of Matthew 25 have picked up on this. Some ministry networks or even PACs are named after the chapter. Invite worshipers to explore this chapter and its ethical implications. Invite them to reflect with a neighbor, or via some journaling on a blank page of the bulletin, on what they typically do while they are waiting. How do they make use of their time? Have them discuss with each other or jot notes about these questions: What does living with anticipation feel like? How does it shape your emotional landscape? Finally, let the assembly exegete itself: Did you recently feed, water, clothe, visit, or host someone? How did this recent action of yours compare with Matthew 25?

Liturgical Arts

Much of the doctrinal and ethical content of Matthew 25 can be illuminated if worship planners utilize props, decorations, or art that illustrate some of the items mentioned in the parables and narrative of the chapter. Here are a few ideas.

Matthew 25:1-13. Place ten oil lamps or tea lights, all lit, where they can be seen easily. Five of the lamps or tea lights should be rigged so that they go out within the first ten minutes (or so) of worship. The other five continue burning throughout the service. Or, a bold choir or worship ensemble might come to worship dressed like a wedding party.

Matthew 25:14-30. Mock up a model of a talent or an equivalent weight (http://en.wikipedia.org/wiki/Talent_(measurement)). During worship let children or the entire community take turns picking it up. Or, invite a banker or financial advisor to talk about their faith in relationship to their investment and financial planning decisions.

Matthew 25:31-46. Display an icon of the Son of Man coming in glory attended by angels. Icons depicting this are often titled "Last Judgment" or "Awesome Judgment." One such image can be found here: http://saintsilouan.org/calendar/pre-lenten-sundays/sunday-of-the-last-judgment/. Or, images of separating sheep and goats might be depicted via well-selected photographs or digital images displayed on a screen.

Finally, because the saints care for their neighbors (who collectively are, as it were, Christ) through simple things—food, drink, welcome, clothing, care for the sick, visits to prison—consider illustrating these caregiving activities through actual physical objects, like pitchers and water glasses, tables set for a meal, wardrobes full of clothing, or through panels or posters depicting the classic works of mercy congregations engage in as part of their mission, such as prison ministry, food pantries, well-digging projects, deaconess ministries, and more. The traditional enumeration of the corporal works of mercy is: to feed the hungry; to give drink to the thirsty; to clothe the naked; to harbor the harborless; to visit the sick; to ransom the captive; to bury the dead.

Music

To continue a seasonal focus on one portion of the liturgy, the obvious choice for November is the *Nunc dimittis*, the song of Simeon. At the end of the church year, the end of the liturgy: "Now, Lord, you let your servant go in peace." *Evangelical Lutheran Worship* includes a number of musical settings of this song: pages 113 and 135, and #200–203, 313, 440. The song of Simeon is also the gospel canticle for night prayer (compline). The plainsong chant version of it available in *Evangelical Lutheran Worship* (p. 324) is particularly well suited to be sung at the bedside of those who are dying, or to children or others at bedtime. The song

itself is based on Luke 2:29-32, sung at the time the elderly Simeon, having waited patiently into his old age for the coming of the Messiah, meets the infant Jesus presented in the temple, and sings that he is now prepared, he can go in peace, for God's word has been fulfilled.

Also helpful during this month are the hymns organized in *Evangelical Lutheran Worship* under the category End Time (#433–441). Perhaps the most fitting from this set is "Wake, awake, for night is flying" (#436). Also consider "Sing with all the saints in glory" (#426) as a theme hymn the entire month.

All Saints, Thanksgiving, and Christ the King

All Saints and Christ the King Sundays allow year A to go out with a bang, offering in public worship the reading of two of the high points in the Gospel of Matthew. All Saints Sunday includes the Sermon on the Mount, especially the beatitudes (Matt. 5:1-12). Christ the King offers the "Sermon on the End of the World," a description of the last judgment and that famous phrase, "As you did it to one of the least of these who are members of my family, you did it to me" (25:40). There are many direct parallels between the ethic of the Sermon on the Mount and the ethic of the Sermon on the End of the World. Both are also sermons spoken immediately prior to major events in the life of Christ. The first is his major sermon before he goes about the countryside teaching and healing. The second is proclaimed immediately before his path to Jerusalem and crucifixion.

Both sermons are best understood if everything said in them applies first of all to Jesus himself. He is both the source and content of his own sermon. It is in this way that Christ is indeed the King, a king who gathers all saints. A robust doctrinal approach to preaching and teaching on these two Sundays will not separate the concept of the communion of saints from the concept of Jesus Christ as King, but rather will illustrate how the two are integrally tied together. One excellent recent book that helps readers understand the relationship between Christ as King and the body of Christ (the church) in its life for the world is N. T. Wright's *How God Became King* (HarperCollins, 2011). A study of this book during November, in anticipation of the upcoming season of Advent, would be most appropriate.

WORSHIP TEXTS FOR NOVEMBER

Confession and Forgiveness

All may make the sign of the cross, the sign marked at baptism,
as the presiding minister begins.
Blessed be the holy Trinity, + one God,
the Sovereign over all the earth,
the Wisdom from on high,
our merciful Judge and Savior.
Amen.

Let us boldly approach the throne of grace,
trusting in God's mercy and love.

Silence is kept for reflection.

Generous and faithful God,
we confess to you all the ways,
known and unknown,
that we reject and undermine your steadfast love.
Though you made us your people,
we treat strangers with suspicion.
Though you forgave our debts,
we collect without mercy.
Yet we are quick to pass judgment on others.
Have mercy on us, O God,
and remember your promise to us,
for the sake of Jesus Christ, our Lord.
Amen.

The grass withers, the flower fades,
but the word of our God will stand forever.
Through the living Word, + Jesus Christ,
God forgives your every debt, your every sin,
and gives you a new heart and a new spirit.
Amen.

Offering Prayer

Merciful God, as grains of wheat scattered upon the hills
were gathered together to become one bread,
so let your church be gathered together
from the ends of the earth into your kingdom,
for yours is the glory through Jesus Christ, now and forever.
Amen.

Invitation to Communion

The reign of God is at hand.
Come, taste the joy prepared for you.

Prayer after Communion

O God, the host at every meal,
at this table you spread out a feast for all peoples,
the bread of life and the cup of salvation.
Send us from this banquet
to invite others into these good things,
to let justice roll down like waters,
and to care for the least of our sisters and brothers;
through Jesus Christ, our Sovereign and our Savior.
Amen.

Sending of Communion

Gracious God, you took the form of a servant,
offering yourself as food, comfort, and strength
to a sick and hurting world.
Anoint with a servant heart
those who take your word and sacrament
to our sisters and brothers
in their homes/in prisons/in hospitals.
Grant grace, mercy, healing, and hope
to those who feast on your body and blood
and receive your words of new life.
May we all recognize that we have a place and a home
in the body of our Lord Jesus Christ.
Amen.

Blessing

The blessing of almighty God,
the Father of glory,
✝ Jesus Christ our peace,
and the Spirit of truth,
be upon you and remain with you always.
Amen.

Dismissal

Go in peace. Christ is with you.
Thanks be to God.

Seasonal Rites for November

Remembering Those Who Have Died

Remembering Those Who Have Died may be used at any time of the year. It is especially appropriate on a significant anniversary of a loved one's death, such as one month following death or on the date of death in a succeeding year. It is also useful during the month of November, when the church remembers all the saints.

Gathering

The leader begins with one or both of the following, or in similar words.

Blessed be the God and Father of our Lord Jesus Christ,
the source of all mercy and the God of all consolation,
who comforts us in all our sorrows
so that we can comfort others in their sorrows
with the consolation we ourselves have received from God.

or

When we were baptized in Christ Jesus,
we were baptized into his death.
We were buried therefore with him by baptism into death,
so that as Christ was raised from the dead
by the glory of the Father,
we too might live a new life.
For if we have been united with him in a death like his,
we shall certainly be united with him
in a resurrection like his.

Word

The following or another appropriate psalm may be sung or spoken.
Psalm 121

One or more of the following or other appropriate scripture passages may be read.
Isaiah 49:15-16
John 11:25-26
1 Thessalonians 4:13-14
2 Timothy 2:8, 11
Hebrews 12:1-2

Reflection on the readings may follow. Informal conversation among those present may be appropriate.

Prayer

The leader continues with one or more of the following or other appropriate prayers.

O God, we remember with thanksgiving
those who have loved and served you on earth,
who now rest from their labors, especially *name/s*.
Keep us in union with all your saints,
and bring us with them to the joyous feast of heaven;
through Jesus Christ, our Savior and Lord.
Amen.

O God, our help in ages past
and our hope for years to come:
We give you thanks for all your faithful people
who have followed the light of your word
throughout the centuries into our time and place.
Here individual names may be spoken.
As we remember these people,
strengthen us to follow Christ through this world
until we are carried into the harvest of eternal life,
where suffering and death will be no more.
Hear our prayer in the name
of the good and gracious shepherd,
Jesus Christ, our Savior and Lord.
Amen.

Lord Jesus, by your death you took away the sting of death.
Strengthen us to follow in faith where you have led the way,
that we may at length fall asleep in you
and wake in your likeness;
to you, the author and giver of life, be all honor and glory,
now and forever.
Amen.

O Lord, support us all the day long of this troubled life,
until the shadows lengthen and the evening comes
and the busy world is hushed, the fever of life is over,
and our work is done.
Then, in your mercy, grant us a safe lodging,
and a holy rest, and peace at the last,
through Jesus Christ our Lord.
Amen.

The Lord's Prayer is prayed by all. The leader may introduce the prayer with these or similar words.

Gathered into one by the Holy Spirit, let us pray as Jesus taught us.

Our Father . . .

Sending

A hymn or acclamation may be sung.

The leader concludes with a blessing.

Almighty God bless us,
defend us from all evil,
and bring us to everlasting life.
Amen.

The greeting of peace may be shared by all.

NOTES ON THE SERVICE

This order is informal and flexible in nature, and may be adapted to the context and circumstances. The service may take place in the home or at the place where the person's body has been interred. Family members, friends, or the pastor may lead the service or share its leadership as desired.

Before or after the sentences at the Gathering, the leader may note the occasion for the service. Following the reading/s, those present may share in reflection and conversation.

Service music and hymns may include the following.

223	All of Us Go Down to the Dust
423	Shall We Gather at the River
426	Sing with All the Saints in Glory
619	I Know That My Redeemer Lives, sts. 1-2, 7-8
632	O God, Our Help in Ages Past, sts. 1-2, 5

Additional psalms, readings, and hymns are listed in the propers for the funeral service (Occasional Services for the Assembly, p. 336).

Elements of this service may also be included in the worship of the assembly on All Saints Day. Before the service or after the hymn of the day, the presiding minister may say these or similar words:

In joyful expectation of the resurrection to eternal life, we remember this day those who have gone before us in faith and who now rest from their labors, especially those family members and friends who are dear to us [and who have died since last All Saints Day].

Either the first or the second prayer from this service or a similar prayer is then prayed. The names of those who are being remembered may be read as indicated. A bell may be tolled following the reading of each name.

November 2, 2014
All Saints Sunday

All Saints celebrates the baptized people of God, living and dead, who are the body of Christ. As November heralds the dying of the landscape in many northern regions, the readings and liturgy call us to remember all who have died in Christ and whose baptism is complete. At the Lord's table we gather with the faithful of every time and place, trusting that the promises of God will be fulfilled and that all tears will be wiped away in the new Jerusalem.

Prayer of the Day

Almighty God, you have knit your people together in one communion in the mystical body of your Son, Jesus Christ our Lord. Grant us grace to follow your blessed saints in lives of faith and commitment, and to know the inexpressible joys you have prepared for those who love you, through Jesus Christ, our Savior and Lord, who lives and reigns with you and the Holy Spirit, one God, now and forever.

Gospel Acclamation

Alleluia. They are before the ⁣ᴵ throne of God,* and the one who is seated on the throne will ᴵ shelter them. *Alleluia.* (Rev. 7:15)

Readings and Psalm
Revelation 7:9-17

The book of Revelation is written to seven churches in western Asia Minor during a time of great oppression. Today's reading is a response to the question asked in 6:17: "Who is able to stand?" The writer gives the faithful the assurance of God's protection and a vision of victory.

Psalm 34:1-10, 22

Fear the LORD, you saints of the LORD; for those who fear the LORD lack nothing. (Ps. 34:9)

1 John 3:1-3

A saint is one who has been set apart by God for God's purposes. God, out of divine love, set us apart to be the children of God. Our holy hope is that we shall see God as God really is.

Matthew 5:1-12

In the beatitudes, Jesus provides a unique description of those who are blessed with God's favor. His teaching is surprising and shocking to those who seek wealth, fame, and control over others.

Preface   All Saints

Color   White

Prayers of Intercession

The prayers are prepared locally for each occasion. The following examples may be adapted or used as appropriate.

Remembering the saints who have gone before us and giving thanks for God's blessings, we pray for the church, all in need, and God's good creation.

A brief silence.

We pray for the whole church, gathered in word and sacrament, in prayer, praise, and thanksgiving, to continue to bring care and blessing to all. Lord, in your mercy,

hear our prayer.

We pray for wisdom, courage, and commitment to help restore your good creation, that clean water, air, and the fruits of the earth are available for future generations. Lord, in your mercy,

hear our prayer.

We pray for nations suffering from oppression, war, and economic uncertainty. Raise up leaders who will work for peace. Lord, in your mercy,

hear our prayer.

We pray for our sisters and brothers who are hungry and thirsty, who need peace, who are persecuted, and all who need your healing touch through our hands (*especially*). Lord, in your mercy,

hear our prayer.

We pray for our congregation's ministries (*new or continuing ministries may be named here*), that we continue reaching out to our neighborhood and community to share the goodness you offer through Christ. Lord, in your mercy,

hear our prayer.

Here other intercession may be offered.

We give thanks for all our faithful departed (*those who have died during the past year may be named*) and the witness we see in their faithful lives. Lord, in your mercy,

hear our prayer.

Receive our prayers and hopes, Good Shepherd, and bring us safely into all joy and peace, through Christ our Lord.

Amen.

Images in the Readings

The main image in the gospel reading is **the kingdom of heaven**. The image of kingdom stresses a communal and social reality, not an individual psychic experience. This image has been so narrowed by especially nineteenth-century artists into a kind of summer camp in the skies that it is not easy to see in the image God's transforming rule of righteousness. In Revelation, the kingdom is imagined with all the angels and saints gathered around God's throne, a depiction common in medieval art but itself distant from our understanding of the universe.

The reading from Revelation resembles a concordance of biblical imagery, each of which connects with numerous biblical passages: **every nation, throne, Lamb, palm branches, angels, the four living creatures, washed, blood, hunger, thirst, the sun's heat, shepherd, springs of the water of life.** That the saints are **robed in white** suggests early Christian baptismal garb, and the word "alb" refers to these white robes that clothe the baptized. In true metaphoric fashion, in which words assert the opposite of a literal meaning, the robes are made white by being washed in blood.

Ideas for the Day

◆ In a scene from her Pulitzer Prize winning novel, *Beloved* (New York: Knopf, 1987), Toni Morrison casts a vision of the saints who have "come out of the great ordeal," reminiscent of today's reading from Revelation, which challenges us to remember the lived experience of those Jesus names in the beatitudes: "She did not tell them to clean up their lives or go and sin no more. She did not tell them they were the blessed of the earth, its inheriting meek or its glorybound pure. She told them that the only grace they could have was the grace they could imagine. That if they could not see it, they would not have it. 'Here,' she said, 'in this place, we flesh; flesh that weeps, laughs; flesh that dances on bare feet in grass. Love it. Love it hard.'"

◆ Reminding us that "these are not impossible hero stories; these are simply people of commitment and conviction and courage who invite us to join them in their daily practice," Anne Sutherland Howard, Episcopal priest and executive director of the Beatitudes Society, shares the stories of nine young pastors and seminarians striving to put the beatitudes into practice, in her book *Claiming the Beatitudes: Nine Stories from a New Generation* (Herndon, VA: Alban Institute, 2009).

◆ A common practice in many congregations on All Saints Day is to read the names of those in the community who have died in the past year, as a way of demonstrating our belief that all the baptized are saints of God. This practice embodies the reading from Revelation, in which the martyrs are envisioned as gathered around the throne of God, in a state of perpetual worship. That same reading describes those gathered as "robed in white," a reference to baptismal garments, and the passage from 1 John reminds us that "we are God's children now" by virtue of our baptism. In recognition of this, consider reading not only the names of those who have died this past year—but those who have been baptized in your community as well.

Connections with the Liturgy

"This is the feast," an optional canticle of praise in *Evangelical Lutheran Worship* (p. 101), quotes today's reading from Revelation: "blessing and honor, glory and might. . . ," and an optional call to the table (p. 112) cites today's psalm: "Taste and see that the Lord is good."

Let the Children Come

On All Saints Sunday, we often speak of "giants of the faith." From a child's perspective in the pew, everyone may look like a giant! Be sensitive to children's point of view in church. Sit down at eye level with children whenever they are invited to gather at the front of the worship space. On All Saints Sunday, invite a couple senior "saints" to sit with the children during Children's Time, and read their favorite childhood Bible stories.

Assembly Song
Gathering

For all the saints   ELW 422, LBW 174
Ye watchers and ye holy ones   ELW 424, LBW 175
Holy God, we praise your name   ELW 414, LBW 535
Wade in the water   ELW 457

Psalmody

Joncas, Michael. "I Will Bless the Lord (Psalm 34)." Cant, SAB, assembly, kybd, opt fl. GIA G-7282.
Makeever, Ray. "I Will Bless You, O God" from DH.
Harbor, Rawn. "Taste and See the Goodness of the Lord (Psalm 34)." TFF 5.

Hymn of the Day

Each winter as the year grows older   ELW 252, WOV 628
   CAROL OF HOPE
Jerusalem, my happy home   ELW 628   LAND OF REST
Blest are they   ELW 728, WOV 764   BLEST ARE THEY

Offering

By all your saints   ELW 420, st. 2
Give Thanks for Saints   ELW 428

Communion

Behold the host arrayed in white   ELW 425, LBW 314
Thee we adore, O Savior   ELW 476, LBW 199

Let all mortal flesh keep silence   ELW 490, LBW 198

Sending

For all your saints, O Lord   ELW 427

Rejoice in God's saints   ELW 418, WOV 689

Additional Assembly Songs

Some glad morning when this life is o'er   TFF 176

Swing low, sweet chariot   TFF 171

☾ Bell, John. Scotland. "The Love of God Comes Close" from *Love and Anger: Songs of Lively Faith and Social Justice*. U. GIA G-4947.

☾ Chen-Chang, Yang. China. "In All the Seasons Seeking God" from *Sound the Bamboo*. U. GIA G-6830.

✿ Cash, Ed/Matt Redman/Chris Tomlin. "How Can I Keep from Singing" from WT.

✿ Parker, Jack/David Crowder. "O, for a Thousand Tongues to Sing" from WT.

✿ Powell, Aaron/Elias Dummer/Eric Fusilier/Josh Vanderlaan. "Yours" from CCLI.

✿ Redman, Matt/Jonas Myrin. "How Great Is Your Faithfulness" from CCLI.

✿ Seay, Robbie/Ryan Owens/Taylor Johnson/Ted A. Tjornhorn. "Let Our Faith Be Not Alone" from CCLI.

✿ Stanfill, Kristian. "Kingdom" from CCLI.

Music for the Day
Choral

● Cherwien, David. "Jerusalem, My Happy Home." SATB, kybd/hp, ob. MSM 50-8113.

Ellingboe, Bradley. "Behold a Host, Arrayed in White." SAB, pno. AFP 9780806698212.

Hillert, Richard. "Called and Gathered by the Spirit." SA(T)B, children, desc, br qrt, timp. GIA G-5350.

Martinson, Joel. "By All Your Saints." 2 pt mxd, org. AFP 9780800651602.

Schulz-Widmar, Russell. "Jerusalem, Jerusalem." 2 pt, pno. AFP 9780800655211.

Thompson, James Michael. "A Canticle for Communion: O Taste and See (Psalm 34)." SATB, kybd. OCP 30100641.

Williams, Ralph Vaughan. "O Taste and See" from *Augsburg Motet Book*. SATB, org. AFP 9781451423709.

Children's Choir

● Burkhardt, Michael. "Jerusalem, My Happy Home." U/2 pt, org, assembly, hb. MSM 60-8102.

Burnam, Jack Warren. "An Endless Alleluia." 2 pt, kybd/org. SEL 420-285.

Lowenberg, Kenneth. "Blessed Are the Poor in Spirit." U/2 pt, kybd. SEL 410-557.

Miller, Aaron David. "I've Got a Robe." 2 pt trbl, pno. AFP 9780800638061.

Keyboard / Instrumental

Callahan, Charles. "A Memorial Prelude" from *Preludes for Flute and Organ*. Fl, org. MSM 20-606.

● Mayo, Becky Slagle. "All Saints Day Medley" from *In Heaven Above: Piano Music for Funerals and Memorials*. Pno. AFP 9781451401912.

Neswick, Bruce. "Prelude and Fugue on Sine Nomine" from *Augsburg Organ Library: November*. Org. AFP 9780800658960.

● Organ, Anne Krentz. "Blest Are They" from *In Heaven Above: Piano Music for Funerals and Memorials*. Pno. AFP 9781451401912.

Handbell

● Glasgow, Michael. "Faith of the Saints." 3-7 oct hb, opt tpt, L2+. LOR 20/1614L.

● Helman, Michael. "Blest Are They." 3-6 oct hb, opt 3-5 oct hc, opt fl, L3-. GIA G-7043.

● Moklebust, Cathy. "Jerusalem, My Happy Home (I Come with Joy to Meet My Lord)." 3-5 oct hb, opt 3 oct hc, L3. CG CGB632. Full score with opt perc, opt fl, opt cello. CG CGB631.

☾ = global song
✿ = praise song
● = relates to hymn of the day

November 2, 2014
Time after Pentecost — Lectionary 31

Micah declares God's condemnation of those who abhor justice. Jesus warns against hypocrisy. Paul urges the Thessalonians to lead a life worthy of God. Called to be humble servants, we gather for worship, seeking justice and welcoming all people to share the banquet of life.

Prayer of the Day

O God, generous and supreme, your loving Son lived among us, instructing us in the ways of humility and justice. Continue to ease our burdens, and lead us to serve alongside of him, Jesus Christ, our Savior and Lord.

Gospel Acclamation

Alleluia. You have one instructor, | the Messiah;* the greatest among you will | be your servant. *Alleluia.* (Matt. 23:10, 11)

Readings and Psalm

Micah 3:5-12

The Lord announces judgment against prophets who can be bribed to give favorable oracles. Because rulers too can be bribed to practice injustice, Micah announces the coming destruction of Jerusalem. Later, Jeremiah escaped execution because of Micah's daring precedent (Jer. 26:18-19).

Psalm 43

Send out your light and truth, that they may lead me. (Ps. 43:3)

I Thessalonians 2:9-13

Paul uses paternal imagery to depict the guidance and encouragement he provided to the Thessalonians. They received from Paul the word of God, which energizes their faith.

Matthew 23:1-12

Jesus encourages his disciples to obey the words of Moses they hear from their teachers, but to shun the hypocrisy and pretension of those who do not practice what they teach.

Semicontinuous reading and psalm

Joshua 3:7-17

The Lord promises to be with Joshua as the Lord was with Moses. The entry into the promised land was a liturgical procession in which the priests carried the ark of the covenant, the sign of the Lord's presence.

Psalm 107:1-7, 33-37

We give thanks to you, LORD, for your wonderful works. (Ps. 107:8)

Preface Sundays

Color Green

Prayers of Intercession

The prayers are prepared locally for each occasion. The following examples may be adapted or used as appropriate.

Remembering the saints who have gone before us and giving thanks for God's blessings, we pray for the church, all in need, and God's good creation.

A brief silence.

We pray for your church throughout the world. Make your people always humble and willing to bring your word of life into every place. Lord, in your mercy,

hear our prayer.

We give thanks for your creation's amazing blessings. Guide us to work diligently so those blessings are available to future generations. Lord, in your mercy,

hear our prayer.

We pray for peace among nations, for cooperation and mutual respect to become the way that leaders and people build renewed communities. Lord, in your mercy,

hear our prayer.

We pray for the hungry, those who see no end to their search for meaningful labor, all who struggle to provide for their children, and any in need (*especially*). Lord, in your mercy,

hear our prayer.

We pray for our congregation, that you strengthen us as we bring your good news into our neighbors' daily lives. Lord, in your mercy,

hear our prayer.

Here other intercessions may be offered.

We give thanks for all our faithful departed (*those who have died during the past year may be named*) and the witness we see in their faithful lives. Lord, in your mercy,

hear our prayer.

Receive our prayers and hopes, Good Shepherd, and bring us safely into all joy and peace, through Christ our Lord. **Amen.**

Images in the Readings

In the second reading and the gospel, God is likened to a **father.** First-century Jews did not address YHWH as father, but in Greco-Roman paganism, Jupiter was indeed "Father of fathers." The New Testament adopts this cultural title for God, yet distinguishes the one who is father of Jesus from the father Jupiter who blasts humankind with lightning, alienates men from each other, and rapes women at will. Especially fourth-century theologians wrote about what Christians mean by calling God Father, explicitly denying that any male sexuality is intended. The psalm for the day illumines "father" by praising God who gives strength, light, truth, joy, gladness, help. Our address "Father" tries to contain these ideas, and far more.

Throughout scripture, God talks. God's **word** is heard from the beginning of time, it is spoken through the mouths of prophets and preachers, and it is embodied in Jesus Christ himself. The power and authority vested in this Word challenges our culture's post-modern preference for relativism. The churches that take ordination with high seriousness hope that the authority of proclaiming the word is merged with a vocation to servanthood.

Yet again on this Sunday we are called to be **servants.** The extent to which this call is countercultural cannot be exaggerated.

Ideas for the Day

◆　Jesus decries the culture of hypocritical leadership that was entrenched in the religious establishment of his day. In a lecture titled "Michelin: An Example of Humility in Leadership" (online at YouTube), Alexandre Havard tells the story of Édouard Michelin, CEO of Michelin Tires, and Marios Miniol, the self-taught engineer who invented the radial tire. Their collaboration changed an entire industry, highlighting the importance of cultivating cultures that respect people's talents over their titles.

◆　Jesus' words are hard for preachers to address precisely because they describe the difficulty clergy have practicing what they preach. Pastors, like all people, struggle to live up to their own best intentions. Sometimes, though, it is their very position as leaders and teachers that leads to the pride and arrogance Jesus condemns. In his book *Humble Leadership: Being Radically Open to God's Guidance and Grace* (Herndon, VA: Alban Institute, 2007), N. Graham Standish describes the vulnerable work of remaining humble as a leader. This Sunday in particular, preachers will want to look inward before delivering the sermon.

◆　Clergy and laity alike may struggle to translate the concept of humble leadership into observable behavior. Social scientists bring some clarity to the subject in a study (lengthily!) titled "Modeling How to Grow: An Inductive Examination of Humble Leader Behaviors, Contingencies, and Outcomes" (*Academy of Management Journal*, Aug. 2012), as reported in *The Atlantic* magazine online (Jan. 13, 2012). After interviewing a number of leaders across a variety of industries, a common definition of humble leadership emerged. Humble bosses "lead by example, admit their mistakes, and recognize their followers' strengths." The study found that humble leadership is associated with "more learning-oriented teams, more engaged employees, and lower voluntary employee turnover."

◆　Because these texts fall on the Sunday on which All Saints Sunday is traditionally observed, worship planners are encouraged to attend to the radically egalitarian nature of the community Jesus calls for in their remembrance of the saints this day. Be careful that the naming of those who have died does not become an occasion for the exaltation of some over others due to their station in life or visibility within the church.

Connections with the Liturgy

"Our Father in heaven" remains the primary Christian address to God. It is good to attend to what Christian theology has meant by that title, as well as what meanings it has denied.

The "peace" that we call out to each other on Sunday is not a pleasant morning greeting, because like the prophets Micah decries, we "have something to eat." Rather, the peace is the radically altered existence that comes from the Spirit of the risen Christ.

Let the Children Come

Jesus reminds us that good leaders are humble leaders. We learn to be humble leaders by trying to be followers—followers of Jesus' ways of love, healing, and forgiveness. Worship gives us a chance to practice our following skills. We follow a liturgy, a lectionary, a cross, and a way of worship practiced by God's people over centuries. Children follow along by making the sign of the cross, finding the hymn in the hymnal, standing up and sitting down, making music, and following the procession of fellow worshipers to the baptismal font and the communion table.

Assembly Song
Gathering
Praise to the Lord   ELW 844

On Jordan's stormy bank I stand   ELW 437, TFF 49

Praise to you, O God of mercy   ELW 208

Psalmody
Guimont, Michel. "Psalm 43" from PRCL.

Hobby, Robert A. "Psalm 43" from PWA.

Woehr, Roland. "Psalm 43," Refrain 1, from PSCY.

Pavlechko, Thomas. "Psalm 107:1-7, 33-37" from SMP.

Hymn of the Day
Will you let me be your servant   ELW 659   *THE SERVANT SONG*

Lord, whose love in humble service   ELW 712, LBW 423
   BEACH SPRING

Canticle of the Turning   ELW 723, W&P 26
   STAR OF COUNTY DOWN

Offering
My soul does magnify the Lord   ELW 882, TFF 168

Gather Us In   ELW 532, WOV 718

To God our thanks we give   ELW 682

Communion
Come to us, creative Spirit   ELW 687, WOV 758

Be thou my vision   ELW 793

Come to the table   ELW 481, W&P 33

Sending
Soli Deo Gloria   ELW 878

Let the whole creation cry   ELW 876

Additional Assembly Songs
What a blessing   TFF 139

If when you give the best of your service   TFF 172

⊕ Szokolay, Sándor. Hungary. "Jesus Christ Our Living Lord" from *Global Songs for Worship*. SATB, gtr. Faith Alive/Calvin Institute of Christian Worship. 9781592554423.

✧ Galanti, Gio/Jay Cook. "Follow the Son" from CCLI.

✧ Hall, Charlie. "One Thing" from CCLI.

✧ Hill, Rob/Tim Hughes. "May the Words of My Mouth" from CCLI.

✧ Morgan, Reuben. "Your Unfailing Love" from WT.

✧ Sampson, Marty/Matt Crocker/Scott Ligertwood. "Take It All" from CCLI.

✧ Wesley, Charles/Chris Eaton/Gareth Robinson/John Hartley. "And Can It Be" from CCLI.

Music for the Day
Choral
Carter, John, "Come to the Table Where Bread Is Broken." SAB, kybd. HOP C5242.

● Costello, Michael. "Canticle of the Turning." SATTBB, org, tbn, opt assembly. AFP 9781451401615.

● Schwoebel, David. "The Servant Song." SATB, pno, opt ob. MSM 50-5202.

Scott, K. Lee. "Tell Out, My Soul." SATB, fl, hb, org. CPH 89-3096.

Children's Choir
Scott, K. Lee. "As We Gather at Your Table" from *Augsburg Easy Choirbook,* vol. 2. SAB, org. AFP 9780800677510.

Weber, Paul. "When You Pass Through the Waters." U or 2 pt, pno. MSM 50-0501.

Wold, Wayne L. "To the Banquet, Come" from *LifeSongs*. U, kybd. AFP 9780806642710.

Keyboard / Instrumental
Albrecht, Mark. "Thaxted" from *Timeless Tunes for Flute and Piano*. Fl, pno. AFP 9780800659073.

● Fedak, Alfred. "Variations on 'Beach Spring.'" Org. SEL 160-641.

● Leavitt, John. "Beach Spring" from *Wonder, Love, and Praise*. Pno. CPH 97-7021.

● Miller, Aaron David. "Star of County Down" from *Organ Preludes on Folk Songs*. Org. AFP 9780800677572.

Handbell
● Helman, Michael. "Lord, Whose Love through Humble Service (God, Whose Giving Knows No Ending)." 3-5 oct hb, opt 3 oct hc, L3. CG CGB586.

Wagner, Douglas. "Forever." 3-5 oct hb, L3. LOR 20/1462L. Full score. LOR 302415L.

Ziemelis, Miervaldis. "Joshua Fit the Battle of Jericho." 3-5 oct, L3. AGEHR AG35270.

Monday, November 3

Martín de Porres, renewer of society, died 1639
Martín was the son of a Spanish knight and Ana Velázquez, a freed black slave from Panama. Martín apprenticed himself to a barber-surgeon in Lima, Peru, and was known for his work as a healer. Martín was a lay brother in the Order of Preachers (Dominicans) and engaged in many charitable works. He was a gardener as well as a counselor to those who sought him out. He was noted for his care of all the poor, regardless of race. His own religious community described him as the "father of charity." His work included the founding of an orphanage, a hospital, and a clinic for dogs and cats. He is recognized as an advocate for Christian charity and interracial justice.

⊕ = global song

✧ = praise song

● = relates to hymn of the day

Friday, November 7

John Christian Frederick Heyer, died 1873; Bartholomaeus Ziegenbalg, died 1719; Ludwig Nommensen, died 1918; missionaries

Three missionaries are commemorated on this date. Heyer was the first missionary sent out by American Lutherans. Ordained in 1820, he established Sunday schools and taught at Gettysburg College and Seminary. Heyer became a missionary in the Andhra region of India. During a break in his mission work he received the M.D. degree from what would later be Johns Hopkins University.

Bartholomaeus Ziegenbalg (ZEEG-en-balg) was a missionary to the Tamils of Tranquebar on the southeast coast of India. The first convert to Christianity was baptized about ten months after Ziegenbalg began preaching. His missionary work was opposed by the local Hindus and also by Danish authorities in that area. Ziegenbalg was imprisoned for his work on a charge of converting the natives. Today, the Tamil Evangelical Lutheran Church carries on his work.

Ludwig Ingwer Nommensen was born in Schleswig-Holstein, Germany. In the early 1860s he went to Sumatra to serve as a Lutheran missionary. His work was among the Batak people, who had previously not seen Christian missionaries. Though he encountered some initial difficulties, the missions began to succeed following the conversion of several tribal chiefs. Nommensen translated the scriptures into Batak while honoring much of the native culture.

November 9, 2014

Time after Pentecost — Lectionary 32

Today the prophet Amos calls for justice to roll down like waters. Paul urges us to encourage one another with the promised coming of the Lord. Jesus tells the parable of the wise and foolish bridesmaids. Surrounded by the faithful of every time and place, we celebrate Christ's coming in our midst in the word of life and the feast of victory—the marriage feast of the lamb.

Prayer of the Day

O God of justice and love, you illumine our way through life with the words of your Son. Give us the light we need, and awaken us to the needs of others, through Jesus Christ, our Savior and Lord.

Gospel Acclamation

Alleluia. Keep awake[1] and be ready,* for you do not know on what day your[1] Lord is coming. *Alleluia.* (Matt. 24:42, 44)

Readings and Psalm
Amos 5:18-24

In the days of Amos people thought that the day of the Lord would be a time of great victory, but Amos announced that it would be a day of darkness, not light. He said liturgy is no substitute for obedience. The Lord demands justice and righteousness in the community.

or Wisdom 6:12-16

Wisdom is part of the structure of the universe and is easily accessible to those who want to find her. Wisdom actually seeks people out. People who are wise are free from care.

Psalm 70

You are my helper and my deliverer; O Lord, do not tarry. (Ps. 70:5)

or Wisdom 6:17-20

The beginning of wisdom is the most sincere desire for instruction. (Wis. 6:17)

1 Thessalonians 4:13-18

Some of the Thessalonians are worried that dead Christians will be excluded from the resurrection to eternal life when Christ comes again. Paul reassures them with the word of hope that all Christians, living or dead, will be raised into everlasting life with Christ.

Matthew 25:1-13

Jesus tells a parable about his own second coming, emphasizing the need for readiness at all times.

Semicontinuous reading and psalm

Joshua 24:1-3a, 14-25

In this farewell speech, Joshua exhorts the people to serve only the Lord. Joshua erected a stone monument to serve as a witness to the solemn promise the people had made to serve the Lord.

Psalm 78:1-7

We will recount to generations to come the power of the LORD. (Ps. 78:4)

Preface   Sundays

Color   Green

Prayers of Intercession

The prayers are prepared locally for each occasion. The following examples may be adapted or used as appropriate.

Remembering the saints who have gone before us and giving thanks for God's blessings, we pray for the church, all in need, and God's good creation.

A brief silence.

Holy God, we desire your wisdom and instruction. Fill our gatherings with your spirit of joy, that the church's daily work be life-giving. Lord, in your mercy,

hear our prayer.

Word of life, as you spoke this good creation into being, guide our actions and help us renew and protect the earth's resources. Lord, in your mercy,

hear our prayer.

Judge of the nations, guide us to bring down barriers so peace will flow over all nations like an ever-flowing stream. Lord, in your mercy,

hear our prayer.

Healer of our every ill, teach us to be watchful for people who need healing, especially for people whose needs are easily overlooked. (*Especially we pray for . . .*) Lord, in your mercy,

hear our prayer.

Righteous Teacher, guide our congregation that we will, in all circumstances, encourage one another with words of peace, forgiveness, and mercy. Lord, in your mercy,

hear our prayer.

Here other intercessions may be offered.

Eternal One, we give you thanks for all the saints who lived and died in faith. Grant us one day to know also the full measure of your eternal life. Lord, in your mercy,

hear our prayer.

Receive our prayers and hopes, Good Shepherd, and bring us safely into all joy and peace, through Christ our Lord.

Amen.

Images in the Readings

The **wedding feast** is a biblical image for our life with God, and Christians have used the image as one way to describe holy communion. Philipp Nicolai's hymn "Wake, awake, for night is flying" (ELW 436), honored by some Christians with the title the Queen of Chorales, is a fine example of the use of marriage imagery. In biblical times, a wedding was not about personal choice and lavish expense, but about the communal celebration of the promise of new life and commitment.

Christians have used the **lamp** as an image for the word of God, with which we see God's way. Many Christians use oil as part of the ritual of baptism.

When Amos writes of the **waters** and "ever-flowing stream," Christians think of the water of baptism, which means to carry us, in the ship of the church, into a life of justice and righteousness.

Many Christians have literalized Paul's eschatological imagery of Christ's **appearance** in the skies, an **archangel**, a **trumpet**, and **clouds**. Recall that for Paul, this picture fit scientifically with his understanding of the universe. For us it does not, and to be Christian does not mean to hide in archaic thinking. Thus we need use care when citing this first-century picture of the end of all things. We repeat Martin Luther: "What is this? What does this mean?"

Ideas for the Day

◆   Like Paul, the church over the centuries has developed poetic ways for describing the reality of death while still expressing the hope of the resurrection. Some would say "he's gone home" or, in a more Southern style, "she's gone home to glory." In medieval times we might have said "he's been raised to the church triumphant," indicating that one is still in the church but now lives outside of time in the fullness of God's victory over death and reconciliation of the world. A simple phrase used in some churches is "The resurrection of . . . ," reminding us of our belief that death is the place where new life begins.

◆   The words of the prophet Amos are jarring, intentionally. Complacency afflicts communities of every age and every era, and congregations must always keep awake to the possibility that they have come to worship seeking only consolation, not expecting confrontation. Julie Richardson Brown and Courtney Richards shine a light on the stories of young adults heeding Amos's call to pursue justice, in *It's Not All About You: Young Adults Seeking Justice* (St. Louis: Chalice Press, 2012). While some of these young adults are churched and others are not, all share a conviction that the life of discipleship cannot divorce worship of God from justice for those God loves.

◆   Commentaries on the parable of the bridesmaids vary widely in their theological interpretation of this text.

Some suggest that Christians are called to emulate the wise virgins, who are prepared to wait as long as it takes for the bridegroom to arrive, while others caution against the easy allegory and encourage us to enter the parable through the experience of those shut out of the wedding banquet. What these commentaries share is the centrality of hope. For a contemporary illustration of the life-giving power of hope for those who wait in darkness, review the story of the thirty-three Chilean miners trapped for sixty-nine days in the 2010 Copiapó mining accident. Like the bridesmaids in Jesus' parable, the miners awaited their rescue together, avoiding predictions of when that day would come.

Connections with the Liturgy

As part of the thanksgiving at the table prayers I, III, IV, VI, VII, VIII, and IX in *Evangelical Lutheran Worship*, the assembly calls out the ecumenically popular credo "Christ has died. Christ is risen. Christ will come again." With Paul we place our faith in the death and resurrection of Christ, and we stand with Amos, Paul, and Matthew to anticipate the coming of God our Savior. Christians believe that Christ comes, not only at the end of time, but here this Sunday in word, bread, and wine.

Let the Children Come

"Get ready!" advises today's parable. Sunday worship requires lots of people every week to help get ready. For example, altar guild members or sacristans prepare the worship space, and lectors prepare to read. Someone prepares the prayers of intercession, and others prepare the worship folder. Liturgy is "the work of the people," and a host of people get the work of liturgy done each week. Invite some behind-the-scenes helpers to tell children about how they "get ready" for Sunday, and how families can participate.

Assembly Song
Gathering

Wake, awake, for night is flying ELW 436, LBW 31
Arise, my soul, arise! ELW 827
O God beyond all praising ELW 880

Psalmody

Mathis, William H. Refrain for "Psalm 70" from *After the Prelude: Year A*. U/cant, hb. CG CGB616 (digital version). CGB617 (printed version). Use with ELW psalm tone 9 (in Dm).
Hallock, Peter. "Psalm 70" from TP.
Weidler, Scott C. "Wisdom 6:17-20" from PSCY.
Messner, Sally. "Psalm 78:1-7" from PWA.

Hymn of the Day

Wait for the Lord ELW 262 *WAIT FOR THE LORD*
When long before time ELW 861, WOV 799
     THE SINGER AND THE SONG
Soon and very soon ELW 439, W&P 128, WOV 744, TFF 38
     VERY SOON

Offering

Wait for the Lord ELW 262
Come, we that love the Lord ELW 625, TFF 135, WOV 742

Communion

When peace like a river ELW 785, TFF 194
For the bread which you have broken ELW 494, LBW 200
When long before time ELW 861, WOV 799

Sending

Rejoice, rejoice, believers ELW 244, LBW 25
Soon and very soon ELW 439, TFF 38, W&P 128, WOV 744

Additional Assembly Songs

Jesus, we are gathered TFF 140
May God bless us TFF 162
⊕ Sizohamba naye/We will go with God GS2 10
⊕ Bell, John. Scotland. "Send Out Your Light" from *Come, All You People: Shorter Songs for Worship*. SAB. GIA G-4391.
✿ McCracken, Sandra. "Justice Will Roll Down" from CCLI.
✿ Neufeld, Jon/Tim Neufeld. "Filled with Your Glory" from CCLI.
✿ Rend Collective Experiment. "Build Your Kingdom Here" from WT.
✿ Sampson, Marty/Jason Ingram/Brenton Brown. "Arise and Sing" from WT.
✿ Smith, Martin/Tim Hughes. "Love Shine Through" from CCLI.
✿ Tomlin, Chris/Reuben Morgan. "Awakening" from WT.

Music for the Day
Choral

● Cherwien, David. "When Long before Time." SATB, org, assembly. CPH 98-3481.
● Erickson, Richard. "When Long before Time." SATB, org. AFP 9780800656768.
● Helgen, John. "Soon and Very Soon." SATB, pno. KJO 8889.
Nelson, Eric. "It Is Well with My Soul." SATB, pno. AFP 9780800677343.
● Schrader, Jack. "Soon and Very Soon." SAB, pno. HOP GC984.
Scott, K. Lee. "Keep Your Lamps Trimmed and Burning" from *Treasures in Heaven*. 2 pt, org. AFP 9780800679477.

⊕ = global song
✿ = praise song
● = relates to hymn of the day

Children's Choir

Carter, John. "My Heart Is in Your Keeping." 2 pt/kybd. HOP JC298.

Helgen, John. "Keep Your Lamps Trimmed and Burning." U, opt desc, pno. AFP 9780800677497.

Schalk, Carl. "Where Charity and Love Prevail." 2 pt trbl, ob, org. CPH 98-2701POD.

Keyboard / Instrumental

Burkhardt, Michael. "On Jordan's Stormy Banks I Stand" from *Hymns for the Saints*. Org. MSM 10-742.

Hopson, Hal H. "Steal Away." Inst, pno. MSM 20-550.

● Manz, Paul. "When Long before Time" from *Three Hymn Settings for Organ, Set 1*. Org. MSM 10-522.

● Schrader, Jack. "Soon and Very Soon" from *Amazing Grace*. Pno. HOP 8138.

Handbell

● Honoré, Jeffrey. "Soon and Very Soon." 3-5 oct hb, opt 3-5 oct hc, opt cym or hi-hat, L3. CPH 97-7248.

Thompson, Martha Lynn. "I Waited for the Lord" (based on Psalm 40). 3-5 oct hb, opt C inst, opt vcs. GIA G-7364.

Tucker, Sondra. "Awesome God." 3-5 oct, L3+. HOP 2246.

Tuesday, November 11

Martin, Bishop of Tours, died 397

Martin's pagan father enlisted him in the army at age fifteen. One winter day, a beggar approached Martin for aid, and he cut his cloak in half and gave a portion to the beggar. Later, Martin understood that he had seen the presence of Christ in that beggar, and this ended his uncertainty about Christianity. He soon asked for his release from his military duties, but he was imprisoned instead. After his release from prison he began preaching, particularly against the Arians. In 371 he was elected bishop of Tours. As bishop he developed a reputation for intervening on behalf of prisoners and heretics who had been sentenced to death.

Søren Aabye Kierkegaard, teacher, died 1855

Kierkegaard (KEER-keh-gore), a nineteenth-century Danish theologian whose writings reflect his Lutheran heritage, was the founder of modern existentialism. Though he was engaged to a woman he deeply loved, he ended the relationship because he believed he was called to search the hidden side of life. Many of his works were published under a variety of names, so that he could reply to arguments from his own previous works. Kierkegaard's work attacked the established church of his day—its complacency, its tendency to intellectualize faith, and its desire to be accepted by polite society.

● = relates to hymn of the day

November 16, 2014
Time after Pentecost — Lectionary 33

Our readings during November speak of the end times. Zephaniah proclaims that the coming day of the Lord will be filled with wrath and distress. Paul says it will come like a thief in the night and urges us to be awake and sober. Jesus tells the parable of the talents, calling us to use our gifts, while we still have time, for the greater and common good. In a world filled with violence and despair, we gather around signs of hope—word, water, bread and wine—eager to welcome the good news of Christ's coming among us.

Prayer of the Day

Righteous God, our merciful master, you own the earth and all its peoples, and you give us all that we have. Inspire us to serve you with justice and wisdom, and prepare us for the joy of the day of your coming, through Jesus Christ, our Savior and Lord.

Gospel Acclamation

Alleluia. Abide in me as I a- ¹ bide in you;* those who abide in me ¹ bear much fruit. *Alleluia.* (John 15:4, 5)

Readings and Psalm
Zephaniah 1:7, 12-18

Zephaniah (like the prophet Amos in last week's first reading) presents the day of the Lord as one of judgment and wrath. Descriptions of the last day in the New Testament include details taken from Old Testament accounts of the day of the Lord.

Psalm 90:1-8 [9-11] 12

So teach us to number our days that we may apply our hearts to wisdom. (Ps. 90:12)

1 Thessalonians 5:1-11

Though we do not know and cannot calculate the day of Christ's return, we live faithfully in the here and now as we anticipate the day when we will be given eternal salvation through our Lord Jesus Christ.

Matthew 25:14-30

Jesus tells a parable about his second coming, indicating that it is not sufficient merely to maintain things as they are. Those who await his return should make good use of the gifts that God has provided them.

Semicontinuous reading and psalm
Judges 4:1-7

Deborah was a prophetess and judge, who, with her general, Barak, led a victorious holy war against a stronger Canaanite force from the north.

Psalm 123

Our eyes look to you, O God, until you show us your mercy. (Ps. 123:2)

Preface   Sundays

Color   Green

Prayers of Intercession

The prayers are prepared locally for each occasion. The following examples may be adapted or used as appropriate.

Remembering the saints who have gone before us and giving thanks for God's blessings, we pray for the church, all in need, and God's good creation.

A brief silence.

We pray for the church, that it continues to sow seeds of mercy, love, forgiveness, and joy, even as it anticipates your coming again to bring restoration to the new heaven and earth. Lord, in your mercy,

hear our prayer.

We pray for all creation, for the wonder of climate and tide, of mountains, valleys, rivers, and oceans, that we become better stewards of this bounty. Lord, in your mercy,

hear our prayer.

We pray for all nations, their leaders and governments, that they replace power, pride, greed, and enmity with justice, mercy, reconciliation, and peacemaking. Lord, in your mercy,

hear our prayer.

We pray for the lonely, the disheartened, those who suffer from debilitating illness, those who cannot speak for themselves, and those in any need (*especially*). Lord, in your mercy,

hear our prayer.

We pray for our congregation's leaders, that they continue to encourage us and send us out in peace and love to follow your call. Lord, in your mercy,

hear our prayer.

Here other intercessions may be offered.

We give thanks for all the saints, for their faithfulness and perseverance in following you, whose examples will bring us closer to you. Lord, in your mercy,
hear our prayer.
Receive our prayers and hopes, Good Shepherd, and bring us safely into all joy and peace, through Christ our Lord.
Amen.

Images in the Readings

It is interesting that our English word **talent** meaning ability comes from interpretations of this parable. Christians believe that God's creation is ongoing, that every human capability is a gift from the Creator, and that we are called to use all of God's creation wisely.

Zephaniah's litany describing **a day of wrath** continues in our time, especially in popular disaster movies. Humans continue to be fearful of an unknown future. When Christians gather on Sunday before an image of the crucified Christ, we acknowledge our fears, and protecting ourselves with the breastplate and helmet of the faith, we join together hoping for God's mercy.

Paul likens the coming of the end to **labor pains**. With the pregnant woman, we hope that the pains will lead to life. The infant will come into the light.

Ideas for the Day

◆ The traditional folktale "The Tortoise and the Hare" tells the story of a speedy rabbit so complacent and sure of winning the race that he is beaten by the slow-but-steady tortoise. What parallels do you see between the moral of this story and the readings for today? How would the folktale end differently if it were more like the passage from 1 Thessalonians: "so that whether we are awake or asleep we may live with him" (5:10)?

◆ In *Healing the Heart of Democracy* (San Francisco: Jossey-Bass, 2011), Parker Palmer writes that we are called to stand, with Jesus, in a tragic gap—the gap between the world we live in, with all its injustices, and the world we know is possible. The key to standing in the gap, Palmer writes, is not going to the extremes of cynicism or idealism. Like the readings assigned for this day, particularly the reading from Zephaniah, Palmer warns against complacency and urges readers to live in the tension of the here-and-not-yet. "Standing in the Tragic Gap," a short video of Palmer explaining this concept, is available for purchase at www.theworkofthepeople.com.

◆ Through the parable of the talents, Jesus urges us to take the risk of investing the gifts God has given us—investing ourselves—in our communities. The spring 2012 issue of *LifeLines,* the ELCA's World Hunger newsletter (www.elca.org/hunger) focused on microfinance and microloans, one way for people and communities of faith to invest in the well-being of neighbors near and far.

◆ To get into the mindset of the servant who buries his talent, literally or creatively dig a hole and imagine what you would want to keep safe there. What are you afraid of losing? What do you have trouble risking or trusting to the care of others? If you chose to actually dig a hole, what did you learn about the servant and his experience from your experience?

Connections with the Liturgy

Paul's description of us as "children of light" is found in the rite of Holy Baptism: a candle, lighted from the paschal candle of Easter, is presented to the newly baptized. Jesus, the light of life, gives light to the baptized, and we are to live so that others may see us shining with Christ.

Let the Children Come

How do we empower more children to use their talents in worship? It's easy to encourage the children who have already developed many talents, like good readers or steady acolytes. But there are lots of other children whom we may neglect to foster because their leadership skills are still "buried." These children may seem too loud or animated to serve as book bearers or too quiet or withdrawn to participate in the ministry of ushers. But their energy or quiet reserve often means they'll be great leaders someday! They're just waiting for church leaders to glimpse their hidden potential and patiently help them grow via small opportunities.

Assembly Song
Gathering

Lord of light   ELW 688, LBW 405
Lord of glory, you have bought us   ELW 707
Lord of our life   ELW 766, LBW 366

Psalmody

Mathis, William H. Refrain for "Psalm 90" from *After the Prelude: Year A.* U/cant, hb. CG CGB616 (digital version). CGB617 (printed version). Use with ELW psalm tone 1 or 6 (in C).
Guimont, Michel. "Psalm 90" from PRCL.
Walker, Christopher. "Fill Us, Lord, with Your Love" from PS3.
Jennings, Carolyn. "Psalm 123" from PSCY.

Hymn of the Day

Joyous light of heavenly glory   ELW 561   *JOYOUS LIGHT*
Christ, Be Our Light   ELW 715   *CHRIST, BE OUR LIGHT*
Through the night of doubt and sorrow   ELW 327, LBW 355
   EBENEZER

Offering

Let us talents and tongues employ   ELW 674, TFF 232, WOV 754

For the fruit of all creation   ELW 679, WOV 760

Communion

Light dawns on a weary world   ELW 726

I want to walk as a child of the light   ELW 815, WOV 649

You Are Mine   ELW 581, W&P 158

Sending

O Christ the same   ELW 760, WOV 788

Oh, happy day when we shall stand   ELW 441

The right hand of God   ELW 889

Additional Assembly Songs

Come and go with me   TFF 141

God be with you   TFF 160

⦿ Chen-Chang, Yang. China. "In All the Seasons Seeking God" from *Sound the Bamboo*. U. GIA G-6830.

✿ Camp, Jeremy/Jon Egan. "Not Ashamed" from WT.

✿ Doerksen, Brian. "The Jesus Way" from briandoerksen.com.

✿ Hughes, Tim/Martin Smith. "Holding Nothing Back" from WT.

✿ Jordan, Leslie. "I Am Set Free" from CCLI.

✿ Rend Collective Experiment. "Faithful" from CCLI.

✿ Robinson, Gareth. "We See Love" from garethrobinson.net.

Music for the Day

Choral

Haydn, Franz Josef. "Through Every Age, Eternal God" from *Augsburg Motet Book*. SATB. AFP 9781451423709.

Langlois, Kris. "I Want to Walk as a Child of the Light." SAB, org. AFP 9780800678197.

Rentz, Earlene. "On Jordan's Stormy Banks I Stand (*LAND OF REST*)." SATB, pno. MSM 50-8117.

Rowan, William. "Christ Is the World's Light." SATB, org, opt assembly. GIA G-7775.

● Schalk, Carl. "Joyous Light of Glory." SATB, pno. CPH 98-3354.

Scott, K. Lee. "Send Out Your Light." SATB, org, opt vln, harp. AFP 9781451424003.

White, David Ashley. "Promised Land (On Jordan's Stormy Banks I Stand)" SAB, kybd, fl, perc, opt assembly. SEL 520-425.

Children's Choir

DeLong, Richard. "A Prayer of St. Patrick." 2 pt trbl, kybd. ECS 4798.

Horman, John. "The Gift." U/2 pt, kybd. AFP 9780800664060.

Miller, Aaron David. "I Want Jesus to Walk with Me." U, opt desc, kybd. AFP 9780800678418.

Keyboard / Instrumental

Ashdown, Franklin D. "St. Anne Variations" from *Eight Festive Postludes*. Org. CPH 97-7329.

● Miller, Aaron David. "Ebenezer" from *Augsburg Organ Library: Epiphany*. Org. AFP 9780800659349.

● Mossing, Sally Drennan. "Christ, Be Our Light" from *Christ, Be Our Light: Music for the Church Pianist*. Pno. AFP 9780800663858.

● Shaw, Timothy. "Ebenezer" from *Great Hymns of Faith for the Church Pianist*. Pno. AFP 9780800621674.

Handbell

● Behnke, John. "Thy Strong Word." 3-5 oct, L2. CPH 97-7113.

● Tucker, Sondra. "Fantasy on 'Ebenezer.'" 3-5 oct, L4-. BP HB269.

Wissinger, Kathleen. "Light and Shine." 3-5 oct hb, opt 3 oct hc, L3. HOP 2467.

Monday, November 17

Elizabeth of Hungary, renewer of society, died 1231

This Hungarian princess lived her entire life in east-central Germany, and is often called Elizabeth of Thuringia. Married to a duke, she gave large sums of money, including her dowry, for relief of the poor and sick. She founded hospitals, cared for orphans, and used the royal food supplies to feed the hungry. Though she had the support of her husband, her generosity and charity did not earn her friends within the royal court. At the death of her husband, she was driven out. She joined a Franciscan order and continued her charitable work, though she suffered abuse at the hands of her confessor and spiritual guide. Her lifetime of charity is particularly remarkable when one remembers that she died at the age of twenty-four. She founded two hospitals, and many more are named for her.

⦿ = global song

✿ = praise song

● = relates to hymn of the day

November 23, 2014
Christ the King
Last Sunday after Pentecost — Lectionary 34

On this final Sunday of the church year our gospel is Jesus' great story of judgment. In the end, the faithful are those who served Christ by ministering to those who are poor, hungry, naked, sick, or estranged. In the first reading God is the shepherd who seeks the lost, weak, and injured and feeds them with justice. We gather this day to celebrate the reign of Christ and his victory over death, yet awaiting the consummation of all things yet to come. Acknowledging Christ as our merciful ruler, we go forth that his reign may be known in our loving words and deeds.

Prayer of the Day

O God of power and might, your Son shows us the way of service, and in him we inherit the riches of your grace. Give us the wisdom to know what is right and the strength to serve the world you have made, through Jesus Christ, our Savior and Lord, who lives and reigns with you and the Holy Spirit, one God, now and forever.

Gospel Acclamation

Alleluia. Blessed is the one who comes in the name | of the Lord.* Blessed is the coming kingdom of our an- | cestor David. *Alleluia.* (Mark 11:9)

Readings and Psalm
Ezekiel 34:11-16, 20-24

Since Israel's kings proved to be bad shepherds, Ezekiel declares that the Lord will assume the role of shepherd in Israel. The Lord will also set over them a shepherd-messiah, "my servant David," who will feed and care for the people.

Psalm 95:1-7a

We are the people of God's pasture and the sheep of God's hand. (Ps. 95:7)

Ephesians 1:15-23

In this passage, God is praised for revealing ultimate divine power in raising Jesus from the dead. The resurrected, exalted Christ is Lord both of the church and the entire universe, now and in the age to come.

Matthew 25:31-46

Jesus compares himself to a king who moves among his subjects to see how he is treated: what is done for the least of those who belong to his family is truly done for him.

Semicontinuous reading and psalm
Ezekiel 34:11-16, 20-24

See above.

Psalm 100

We are God's people and the sheep of God's pasture. (Ps. 100:3)

Preface   Ascension *or* Sundays

Color   White *or* Green

Prayers of Intercession

The prayers are prepared locally for each occasion. The following examples may be adapted or used as appropriate.

Remembering the saints who have gone before us and giving thanks for God's blessings, we pray for the church, all in need, and God's good creation.

A brief silence.

For your whole church, that it will continue to joyfully proclaim your love to the world, let us pray.

Have mercy, O God.

For our care of creation, that we resist the temptations to use it wastefully and seek more opportunities for restoration and wise use, let us pray.

Have mercy, O God.

For all nations of the world, that they will come to the knowledge that your peace brings plenty and your wisdom brings justice, let us pray.

Have mercy, O God.

For our brothers and sisters in any need, that we tend to their wounds and hurts, bringing healing, hope, and comfort in your name (*especially*), let us pray.

Have mercy, O God.

For our congregation, that we do everything possible to bring joy and peace into our neighborhoods and communities, let us pray.

Have mercy, O God.

Here other intercessions may be offered.

For the blessed gifts of saintly lives (*especially Clement, Bishop of Rome and Miguel Agustín Pro, martyr*), that they inspire the witness of all believers who live in your promises, let us pray.

Have mercy, O God.

Receive our prayers and hopes, Good Shepherd, and bring us safely into all joy and peace, through Christ our Lord. **Amen.**

Images in the Readings

Calling this Sunday Christ the **King** may elevate that image above all others. Currently on the world scene some nations have rejected monarchies, some maintain figurehead monarchs, and some, while often not using the term "king," maintain heads of state with absolute, even ruthless, power over the people. The Bible promises that God's power and majesty differ radically from the reign of most human monarchs. Thus we need to use the image of king as correcting the image of king. Several hymns do a splendid job of playing the image against itself. As an example of how God's reign differs from that of human monarchs, the baptized saints receive riches and power from God. Some churches prefer the phrase "the reign of Christ" as stressing the activity, rather than the status: unfortunately English has the problem of the homonym "rain."

In the Bible, written within a culture that treasured its pastoral past, **sheep and goats** are images of the life God gives to the people. Like sheep and goats, we are created by God to live together and offer ourselves for others. It is an urban prejudice to defame sheep as dirty and stupid.

Matthew's parable was depicted in sculptures over the main doorway and in wall paintings over the chancel of countless Christian churches, and one can imagine the fun that artists had in shaping the monsters on the left side of Christ the **judge**. As this imagery becomes less important for some Christians, it is important not to lose the biblical call that we saints are to live out the justice that God intends, serving each needy person who is Christ-for-us.

As the first-century decades progressed, **saints** became an increasingly common term for the baptized people of God. The usual English translation of "being personally holy," the word saint is used differently by the several Christian branches. In Ephesians, everyone who is enlightened is called saint, the meaning most Protestants have retained.

Ideas for the Day

◆ When we meet people who are hungry, thirsty, strangers, naked, sick, or imprisoned we are meeting Christ the King. When meeting earthly kings and queens, there are rules to follow (when to speak, what gestures to use, how close you can get). "Why are there rules for meeting the Queen?"—a BBC article (www.bbc.co.uk/news/magazine-13558270) about President Obama's 2011 visit with the royal family—gives examples of royal protocol. Compare the protocol we might follow when meeting Christ the King

through our neighbors in need with the protocol recommended when visiting with British royalty.

◆ The reading from Ezekiel presents the image of judging "between sheep and sheep" (34:22). The prophet uses some unexpected criteria for judging these metaphorical sheep: preferring sheep that are lean, injured, lost, and weak to sheep that are fat and strong. Search online for 4-H sheep judging criteria, borrow local judging guidelines from someone in your congregation, or interview someone with firsthand experience judging sheep to highlight the difference between actual sheep-judging and God's expectation-shattering preference for the poor.

◆ In Matthew, Christ the King is described as a shepherd. Some modern shepherds are using technology to keep track of their sheep: a collar with a heart monitor senses when sheep are in distress and sends a text message to the shepherd, along with the sheep's location. If you could send a text to Christ the Shepherd, what would it say?

◆ Judgment texts suggest questions about how human judgment is different from God's judgment. For a light-hearted exercise in human judgment, play a game of *Apples to Apples* or another game where players rotate acting as judge. What can you learn about your friends from the different ways they act and choices they make as judges, and how does this compare to what we learn in these readings about Christ the King as judge?

◆ Tell the story of one of the least pleasant people you've ever met—and how you also met Christ in that person.

Connections with the Liturgy

Annually on Good Friday, in the revised Solemn Reproaches, we conclude our litany of confession with a paragraph in which we repeat the words of today's Matthean parable: we gave Christ no food, no drink, we did not welcome him, we gave him no clothes. Remembering his parable, we beg for God's mercy, and we worship Christ who reigned from the cross.

Each Sunday that we sing the classic canticle of praise "Glory to God in the highest," we repeat Ephesians' language of the risen Christ "seated at the right hand" of Power in the heavenly places.

Psalm 95, which in our lectionary marks the close of Year A, was appointed by Benedict in the sixth century as the psalm with which all monks and nuns were to begin their praise each day. *Evangelical Lutheran Worship* continues this practice in Morning Prayer, in which Psalm 95 is the first option for the opening of our daily praise (p. 299).

Let the Children Come

We culminate our church year with Christ the King Sunday, a festival celebration. The concept of a church year ending may be too abstract for children, especially since neither the calendar year nor the school year is ending. But children truly understand and enjoy a celebration, and they love to find one in church! Create streamers using the colors of the church year: blue, white, red, purple, and green. Include children in a special processional and recessional, instructing them to wave their streamers as a sign of thanks and praise for Christ's continuing love every day, all year long.

Assembly Song
Gathering
All hail the power of Jesus' name! ELW 634
Rejoice, for Christ is king! ELW 430
Praise, my soul, the King of heaven ELW 865, LBW 549

Psalmody
"Come, Let Us Sing to the Lord" from ELW Morning Prayer, pp. 300–301.
Geary, Patrick. "Listen to the Voice of the Lord" from PS2.
"All People That on Earth Do Dwell." ELW 883.
Houge, Ben. "Oh, Come, Let Us Sing." W&P 107.
Makeever, Ray. "Come with Joy (Psalm 100)" from DH.

Hymn of the Day
Lord of glory, you have bought us ELW 707, LBW 424 HYFRYDOL
The trumpets sound, the angels sing ELW 531, W&P 139
   THE FEAST IS READY
O Christ the same ELW 760 RED HILL ROAD WOV 778
   LONDONDERRY AIR

Offering
As we gather at your table ELW 522
O Christ, what can it mean for us ELW 431

Communion
Lo! He comes with clouds descending ELW 435
Blessing and honor ELW 854
O Savior, precious Savior ELW 820

Sending
Thine the amen ELW 826, WOV 801
Jesus shall reign ELW 434, LBW 530

Additional Assembly Songs
The King of glory W&P 136
King of kings W&P 80
⊕ Amen. Alleluia! GS2 11
● Bell, John. Scotland. "The Love of God Comes Close" from *Love and Anger: Songs of Lively Faith and Social Justice.* U. GIA G-4947.

☼ Crowder, David. "O Praise Him" from WT.
☼ Crowder, David/Louie Giglio. "All This Glory" from CCLI.
☼ Dunlop, James/Matt Crocker. "You Deserve" from CCLI.
☼ Eaton, Chris/John Hartley. "Praise the Lord Who Reigns Above" from WT.
☼ Kirkland, Eddie/Steve Fee. "We Crown You" from CCLI.
☼ Maher, Matt/Sarah Reeves. "Shout of the King" from CCLI.

Music for the Day
Choral
Eicker, Edward. "What You Have Done." SATB, cant, kybd, C inst, assembly. GIA G-7699.
Fredel, Andrew Paul. "Spirit of Wisdom" SATB. GIA G-7351.
Le Jeune, Claude. "All You That Dwell upon the Earth" from *Augsburg Motet Book.* SA/T/B. AFP 9781451423709.
● Schalk, Carl. "O Christ the Same." SATB, org. AFP 9780800678272.
Sebesta, Donald. "The Lamb Will Be a Shepherd Now." SATB, kybd, ob or fl. AFP 9780800677060.
Walker, David Charles/Robert Brewer. "King of Glory, King of Peace." 2 pt mxd, org. SEL 418-609.

Children's Choir
DeLong, Richard. "Loving Shepherd of the Sheep." U trbl, kybd. ECS 4795.
Lawson, Philip. "King of Glory, King of Peace." U/2 pt, pno. MSM 50-7061.
Paradowski, John R. "Tunaomba Mungu Atawale (We Pray God to Reign)." U, pno, opt SATB, tri, guiro, small shekere (or egg shaker), claves, and African drm. CG CGA1171.
Weber, Jacob B. "Once He Came in Blessing." SA, opt B, pno, opt C instr. CPH 98-4086.

Keyboard / Instrumental
● Phillips, Craig. "Toccata on Hyfrydol." Org. SEL 160-675.
● Raabe, Nancy. "Red Hill Road" from *How Good It Is: Piano Settings of Carl Schalk Hymn Tunes.* Pno. AFP 9781451401165.
Vaughan Williams, Ralph. "Bryn Calfaria" from *Three Preludes on Welsh Hymn Tunes.* Org. Various editions.
Wolff, S. Drummond. "Crown Him with Many Crowns." Br qrt, org. MSM 20-430.

Handbell
● Peery, Charles. "Londonderry Gardens." 3-5 oct hb, opt 2 oct hc, L3. MSM 30-922.
Thompson, Martha Lynn. "King of Kings and Lord of Lords." 3-6 oct hb, opt tamb, L2. HOP 2549.
● Wissinger, Kathleen. "Hyfrydol." 2-3 oct, L1+. LOR 20/1434L.

⊕ = global song
☼ = praise song
● = relates to hymn of the day

Sunday, November 23

Clement, Bishop of Rome, died around 100

Clement was the third bishop of Rome and served at the end of the first century. He is best remembered for a letter he wrote to the Corinthian congregation, still having difficulty with divisions in spite of Paul's canonical letters. Clement's writing echoes Paul's. "Love . . . has no limits to its endurance, bears everything patiently. Love is neither servile nor arrogant. It does not provoke schisms or form cliques, but always acts in harmony with others." Clement's letter is also a witness to early understandings of church government and the way each office in the church works for the good of the whole.

Miguel Agustín Pro, martyr, died 1927

Miguel Agustín Pro grew up among oppression in Mexico, where revolutionaries accused the church of siding with the rich. He was a Jesuit priest who served during a time of intense anticlericalism, and therefore he carried out much of his ministry in private settings. He worked on behalf of the poor and homeless. Miguel and his two brothers were arrested, falsely accused of throwing a bomb at the car of a government official, and executed by a firing squad. Just before the guns fired, he yelled, "¡Viva Cristo Rey!" which means "Long live Christ the king!"

Monday, November 24

Justus Falckner, died 1723; Jehu Jones, died 1852; William Passavant, died 1894; pastors in North America

A native of Saxony, Falckner was the son of a Lutheran pastor and, seeing the stresses his father endured, did not plan on becoming a pastor himself, though he studied theology in Halle. Instead, he joined with his brother in the real estate business in Pennsylvania. Through this business he became acquainted with a Swedish pastor in America, and finally he decided to become ordained. He served congregations in New York and New Jersey. Not only was he the first Lutheran ordained in North America, but he published a catechism that was the first Lutheran book published on the continent.

Jones was a native of Charleston, South Carolina. Ordained by the New York Ministerium in 1832, he became the Lutheran church's first African American pastor. Upon returning to South Carolina he was arrested under a law prohibiting free blacks from reentering the state, so he was unable to join the group of Charlestonians he had been commissioned to accompany to Liberia. For nearly twenty years Jones carried out missionary work in Philadelphia in the face of many difficulties. There he led in the formation of the first African American Lutheran congregation, St. Paul's, and the construction of its church building.

William Passavant created and nurtured a new level of organized social ministry in western Pennsylvania. It was the seed of the system of social services that is now known as Lutheran Services in America. Passavant and his legacy sought to serve the poorest of the poor, providing shelter, medical, and living assistance.

Tuesday, November 25

Isaac Watts, hymnwriter, died 1748

Isaac Watts was born in England to a family of nonconformists, people who thought the Church of England had not carried its reforms far enough. As a youth, Watts complained to his father about the quality of hymnody in the metrical psalter of his day. That was the start of his hymnwriting career. He wrote about six hundred hymns, many in a two-year period beginning when he was twenty years old. Some of Watts's hymns are based on psalms, a nonconformist tradition. When criticized for writing hymns not taken from scripture, he responded that if we can pray prayers that are not from scripture but written by us, then surely we can sing hymns that we have made up ourselves. Ten of Watts's hymn texts are in *Evangelical Lutheran Worship*, including "O God, Our Help in Ages Past" (ELW 632).

November 27, 2014

Day of Thanksgiving (U.S.A.)

At harvest time we join the psalmist in offering thanksgiving to God: "You crown the year with your goodness, and your paths overflow with plenty." We are grateful for the abundance of the good things of God's creation. Paul reminds us that our thanksgiving overflows into generosity. As the body of Christ in the world, we give ourselves away as bread for the hungry.

Prayer of the Day

Almighty God our Father, your generous goodness comes to us new every day. By the work of your Spirit lead us to acknowledge your goodness, give thanks for your benefits, and serve you in willing obedience, through Jesus Christ, our Savior and Lord.

Gospel Acclamation

Alleluia. God is able to provide you with every blessing ¹ in abundance,* so that by always having enough of everything, you may share abundantly in ev- ¹ 'ry good work. *Alleluia.* (2 Cor. 9:8)

Readings and Psalm

Deuteronomy 8:7-18

Times of abundance tempt us to forget the Lord and rely on our own power and resources. But the Lord is the one who took Israel out of Egypt, led and fed them in the wilderness, brought them into the land, and gave them power to be productive. To thank this God is to remember and proclaim God's deeds.

Psalm 65

You crown the year with your goodness, and your paths overflow with plenty. (Ps. 65:11)

2 Corinthians 9:6-15

Christian fellowship involves sharing with those in need. Here Paul is gathering a collection for the church in Jerusalem from all the Gentile churches he helped found. We can be extravagant in our giving because God is extravagant, not stingy, in providing for our lives.

Luke 17:11-19

A Samaritan leper becomes a model for thanksgiving. He does not take for granted the kindness shown to him, but takes time to thank Jesus and glorify God.

Preface   Weekdays

Color   of the season

Prayers of Intercession

The prayers are prepared locally for each occasion. The following examples may be adapted or used as appropriate.

Remembering the saints who have gone before us and giving thanks for God's blessings, we pray for the church, all in need, and God's good creation.

A brief silence.

For the church, that its generosity produces thanksgiving and continues to supply the needs of the saints, let us pray.

Have mercy, O God.

For the restoration of an abundant creation that produces food enough for all to eat their fill and have leftovers to share, let us pray.

Have mercy, O God.

For nations to come to ways of governing that produce peace, prosperity, and safety, let us pray.

Have mercy, O God.

For your Spirit to use our hands and lives to produce healing, comfort, and hope, let us pray.

Have mercy, O God.

For our congregation's faith in action, inviting all to share your indescribable gift in Christ's love, let us pray.

Have mercy, O God.

Here other intercessions may be offered.

With thanksgiving for all the saints, that as we live in the light of their witness, our lives produce praise and mercy, let us pray.

Have mercy, O God.

Receive our prayers and hopes, Good Shepherd, and bring us safely into all joy and peace, through Christ our Lord. **Amen.**

Images in the Readings

We are **lepers**, this is true: our very bodies are dying, little by little. Most of us are also **Samaritans**, this is true: we are seen by at least some others as not religiously pure enough. So in this worship service and with our entire lives, we are to praise God with a loud voice.

Paul's use here of the image of the **seed** can be applied to the New Testament's metaphor of the word of God as seed. God provides the seed in the hearts of the baptized, and that seed grows in order for its fruit to be shared with others.

The **good land**, as the Deuteronomy passage calls the promised land, has been interpreted in the church as our life together in the faith. The land with the flowing streams, vines, and wheat: these can have not only literal reference to a contemporary life of plenty, but to the gifts of God that are realized in faith. But millions of people in the world, many Christians, and perhaps some worshipers present are not "eating their fill."

Ideas for the Day

◆ On the tenth anniversary of the 9/11 terrorist attacks, "the plane people" returned to a small town in Newfoundland to thank the locals for their care and hospitality. About 6,700 people were stranded in Gander when U.S. airspace was closed after the attacks. There weren't enough hotel rooms to accommodate everyone, so people in the town welcomed strangers into their homes. Read "'Plane People' From 9/11 Return to Newfoundland to Give Thanks," *New York Times*, Sept. 11, 2011(www.nytimes.com/2011/09/12/world/americas/12canada.html?_r=1).

◆ Where does food come from? Who "supplies seed to the sower and bread for food" (2 Cor. 9:10)? Search online or interview food growers, processors, and sellers in your area to re-create the journey your Thanksgiving meal took to get to your table. How is God active in today's harvests and feasts?

◆ StoryCorps, a nationwide effort to encourage people to interview each other and record the real-life stories of everyday Americans, organizes and promotes the day after Thanksgiving as a national day of listening. In 2011, the focus of the day was giving thanks for teachers. People in every state recorded messages of thanks to favorite teachers, telling the stories of the impact those teachers had on their lives, and also recorded interviews with teachers as a way of honoring and thanking them for their work. Archived thanks-giving stories, and information about the current National Day of Listening project, are available at national-dayoflistening.org.

◆ "He made water flow for you from flint rock, and fed you in the wilderness with manna that your ancestors did not know, to humble you and to test you, and in the end to do you good" (Deut. 8: 15b-16). What experiences from your life do you associate with the words "it'll do you good"?

Connections with the Liturgy

The Greek name for holy communion is *eucharist*, "thanksgiving." Heeding Paul's admonition, assemblies continue to take up a collection for the poor at every gathering. Recent patterns of direct withdrawal from the bank accounts of members ought not confuse this essential Christian calling with a kind of dues owed to the parent organization.

Let the Children Come

Even though Thanksgiving happens once a year, every Sunday is thanksgiving at church for at least three reasons. First, every Sunday we sing a song of praise. We sing, "Thanks God!" Second, every Sunday we gather up the gifts of food and money that we brought for those in need. Finally, every Sunday we pray our thanks to God with our hearts. Invite children to put their hands on their heart and feel it beating. Children then echo this prayer: "Thank you, God, for giving me life. Amen."

Assembly Song
Gathering

Sing to the Lord of harvest   ELW 694, LBW 412
We praise you, O God   ELW 870
Come, ye thankful people, come   ELW 693

Psalmody

Hopson, Hal H. "Psalm 65" from TPP.
Schutte, Daniel L. "Glory and Praise to Our God" from PAS 65D.
Dudley-Smith, Timothy. "Every Heart Its Tribute Pays" (ST. GEORGE'S WINDSOR) from PAS 65E.

Hymn of the Day

For the fruit of all creation   ELW 679, WOV 760   AR HYD Y NOS
Great is thy faithfulness   ELW 733, WOV 771   FAITHFULNESS
Soli Deo Gloria   ELW 878   SOLI DEO GLORIA

Offering

We plow the fields and scatter   ELW 680/681, LLC 492
Praise and thanksgiving   ELW 689, LBW 409

Communion

Great is thy faithfulness   ELW 733, WOV 771
God of the sparrow   ELW 740
How Great Thou Art   ELW 856

Sending

Now thank we all our God   ELW 839/840, LBW 533/534
Let all things now living   ELW 881, LBW 557

Additional Assembly Songs

Give thanks   TFF 292, W&P 41
Jesus in the morning   TFF 167

Solis, Melchizedek M. Philippines. "In Great Thanksgiving" from *Sound the Bamboo*. 2 pt. GIA G-6830.

Trad. Southern/East Africa. "Siyabonga/Thank You, Jesus" from *Sing With Me*. SATB. Faith Alive/Calvin Institute of Christian Worship. 9781592552153.

Brown, Brenton/Paul Baloche. "Because of Your Love" from WT.

Houston, Joel/Jonathon Douglass/Marty Sampson. "Tell the World" from CCLI.

Ingram, Jason/Matt Hammitt/Chris Rohman. "Lead Me" from WT.

Mooring, Leeland/Marc Byrd/Steve Hindalong. "Carried to the Table" from CCLI.

Nifong, Alex. "Jesus Paid It All" from WT.

Redman, Matt. "I Will Offer Up My Life" from CCLI.

Music for the Day
Choral

Haugen, Marty/Jeremy Bankson. "Soli Deo Gloria." SATB, org, opt br qnt, timp, assembly. AFP 9780800678852.

Homilius, Gottfried August. "Deo Dicamus Gratias." SSATBB. GIA G-3985.

Neswick, Bruce. "Let the Peoples Praise Thee." SATB/S solo, org. Vivace 518.

Ridout, Alan. "Let Us with a Gladsome Mind." SATB, org. ECS 1.5077.

Schalk, Carl. "All Things Are Yours, My God." SATB, org. MSM 50-9032.

Young, Ovid. "Great Is Thy Faithfulness." SATB, pno. AFP 9781451423976.

Children's Choir

Bedford, Michael. "Let All the Peoples Praise You, O God." 2 pt, pno, fl. CG CGA933.

Kremser, Eduard. "We Gather Together." U, desc, kybd. ECS 1579.

Mayo, Becki Slagle. "All Good Gifts Around Us." U/2 pt, pno. ALF 00-29387.

Moore, Donald. "Thanks Canon." U/2 pt, kybd, opt fl/C inst. ALF 00-23646.

Keyboard / Instrumental

Leavitt, John. "Ar hyd y nos" from *A Mighty Fortress: Sacred Reflections for Piano*. Pno. CPH 97-7254.

Karg-Elert, Sigfrid. "Now Thank We All Our God: Marche Triomphale." Org. Various editions.

Near, Gerald. "Ar hyd y nos" from *Two Preludes for Evening Service*. Org. AUR AE40.

Wagner, Douglas E. "Great Is Thy Faithfulness" from *Seek Ye First: For Piano*. Pno. HOP 8118.

Handbell

Handley, Andrea. "Great Is Thy Faithfulness." 3-5 oct hb, opt 3 oct hc, L3. RR BL5037. Pno/synth. RR BP5037. Full score. RR FS5037.

Honoré, Jeffrey. "Go, My Children, with My Blessing." 3 or 5 oct hb, opt 3 or 5 oct hc, L2. CPH 97-7344.

Kellermeyer, David. "Thanksgiving Festival." 3-5 oct hb, opt 3 oct hc, L3. MSM 30-601.

= global song
= praise song
= relates to hymn of the day

Resources

Lectionaries

Lectionary for Worship Year A. Augsburg Fortress, 2007. The Revised Common Lectionary. Each reading is "sense-lined" for clearer proclamation of the scriptural texts. New Revised Standard Version. Available in study (includes reader helps) and ritual editions.

§ *Revised Common Lectionary Daily Readings.* Consultation on Common Texts. Fortress Press, 2005.

Readings for the Assembly (A). Gordon Lathrop and Gail Ramshaw, eds. Augsburg Fortress, 1995. The Revised Common Lectionary. Emended NRSV with inclusive language.

§ The Revised Common Lectionary: Twentieth Anniversary Annotated Edition. Consultation on Common Texts. Fortress Press, 2012. The most definitive source for the RCL and the most authoritative explanation of how it came to be developed. Includes marginal notes that identify sources and rationale for lectionary choices. With a foreword by Gordon Lathrop and a new historical introduction.

Worship Books

Evangelical Lutheran Worship. Augsburg Fortress, 2006. Available in pew, leaders ritual, leaders desk, gift, pocket, and enlarged print editions.

Evangelical Lutheran Worship Accompaniment Edition: Liturgies. Augsburg Fortress, 2006. Complete keyboard accompaniments for all ten holy communion settings and additional music within liturgies. Simplified edition also available.

Evangelical Lutheran Worship Accompaniment Edition: Service Music and Hymns (2 vols; Compact Edition, 1 vol.). Augsburg Fortress, 2006. Full accompaniments to all hymns and songs in the pew edition, #151–893. Simplified Keyboard and Guitar editions for service music and hymns also available.

* ∞ *Evangelical Lutheran Worship* Hymns in Braille. Augsburg Fortress, 2013. Texts of service music and hymns (#151–893) in a braille version. Digital edition includes .brf files suitable for local production using a braille embosser. Hard copy edition includes three-hole drilled loose-leaf sheets packaged in storage boxes.

§ *Evangelical Lutheran Worship Occasional Services for the Assembly.* Augsburg Fortress, 2009. Rites and prayers for use on particular occasions in the worshiping assemblies of congregations and synods, such as ministry rites, dedications, and blessings.

§ *Evangelical Lutheran Worship Pastoral Care:* Occasional Services, Readings, and Prayers. Augsburg Fortress, 2008. An essential tool for caregivers conducting the church's ministry of care outside the worshiping assembly.

* *Evangelical Lutheran Worship Prayer Book for the Armed Services:* For Chaplains and Other Military Personnel. Augsburg Fortress, 2013. Pocket-sized edition includes resources for individual daily devotion, prayers for various circumstances selected and composed especially for use by service members, several assembly service orders featuring ecumenical texts, and the texts of 26 psalms and 65 hymns and national songs. Intended for use by active and reserve service members and their families and friends, pastors and congregations who minister to them, chaplains, and veterans.

Libro de Liturgia y Cántico. Augsburg Fortress, 1998. A complete Spanish-language worship resource. Leader edition (2001) includes additional psalms and indexes.

New Hymns of Praise. Taosheng Publishing House, Hong Kong, 2011. This joint venture of the ELCA and the Evangelical Lutheran Church in Hong Kong is intended for North American congregations with Chinese language ministries. The majority of the 143 hymns and songs can be sung in either Mandarin or Cantonese and all include an English text. Keyboard accompaniments for all the hymns are also provided.

Ritos Ocasionales. Augsburg Fortress, 2000. Spanish language version of rites and prayers for various occasions and circumstances.

* *Santa Comunión / Holy Communion.* Augsburg Fortress, 2013. Bilingual Spanish/English edition of Setting Seven from Evangelical Lutheran Worship, including complete leader and assembly texts in both languages.

This Far by Faith: An African American Resource for Worship. Augsburg Fortress, 1999. A supplement of worship orders, psalms, service music, and hymns representing African American traditions and developed by African American Lutherans.

Worship Planning Tools, Indexes, Calendars

* ∞ www.preludemusicplanner.com. A subscription-based online music planning tool. Create comprehensive plans. Browse, preview, and download music from multi-publisher library. Search music based on lectionary days, keywords, skill level and more. Store your usage history. Upload and organize your own library.

∞ www.sundaysandseasons.com. A subscription-based online worship planning tool. Browse, select, and download content for worship planning and worship folder preparation.

∞ *Evangelical Lutheran Worship* Liturgies CD-ROM. Augsburg Fortress, 2006. Liturgical material from pew edition in editable text files; assembly singing lines provided as graphics.

Indexes to Evangelical Lutheran Worship. Augsburg Fortress, 2007. Indexes the hymns and songs in *Evangelical Lutheran Worship.* Includes extensive lectionary, scripture, and topical indexes.

Choral Literature for Sundays and Seasons. Bradley Ellingboe, ed. Augsburg Fortress, 2004. A comprehensive listing of time-tested choral works, indexed to the readings for each

* denotes new or newer print resource
∞ denotes electronic or Web resource
344 § denotes print resource also available as an ebook

Sunday and principal festival of the three-year lectionary. Includes information on voicing, instrumentation, composers, and publishers.

* *Calendar of Word and Season 2014: Liturgical Wall Calendar.* Augsburg Fortress, 2013. Features artwork by *Wayne Lacson Forte.* A reference tool for home, sacristy, office.

* *Church Year Calendar 2014.* Augsburg Fortress, 2013. A one-sheet calendar of lectionary citations and liturgical colors for each Sunday and festival of the liturgical year. Appropriate for bulk purchase and distribution. Also available in downloadable format.

* ∞ *Words for Worship: 2014, Year C.* Augsburg Fortress, 2013. CD-ROM includes lectionary readings, worship texts, seasonal rites, and more for use in worship folders and other self-published materials.

* *Worship Planning Calendar 2014.* Augsburg Fortress, 2013. A two-page per week calendar helpful for worship planners, with space to record appointments and notes for each day. Specially designed to complement *Sundays and Seasons.* Features the CCT daily lectionary.

Westermeyer, Paul. *Hymnal Companion to Evangelical Lutheran Worship.* Augsburg Fortress, 2010. Background and insightful commentary on all 650 hymns, both text and music, together with biographical information on hymn writers and composers. Expanded indexes.

Worship Support

Boesenecker, Andrew, and James Graeser. *A Field Guide to Contemporary Worship: How to Begin and Lead Band-Based Worship.* Augsburg Fortress, 2011. A guide for anyone thinking about starting a contemporary worship service and an essential reference work for those wondering about the nuts and bolts of instrumentation, arranging, working with microphones and speakers, and much more.

§ Brugh, Lorraine, and Gordon Lathrop. *The Sunday Assembly.* Augsburg Fortress, 2008. A resource to guide leaders in their understanding and interpretation of the *Evangelical Lutheran Worship* resources. Focuses on holy communion.

§ Bushkofsky, Dennis, and Craig Satterlee. *The Christian Life: Baptism and Life Passages.* Augsburg Fortress, 2008. Contains detailed information on holy baptism and its related rites, as well as marriage, healing, and funeral.

∞ *Fed and Forgiven: Communion Preparation and Formation.* Augsburg Fortress, 2009. A comprehensive set of resources for leading children, youth, and adults into the sacrament of holy communion. Leader Guide with CD-ROM for all ages. Learner Resources for PreK-K, Grades 1-3, Grades 4-6, and adults. Supplementary DVD.

* ∞ *Go Make Disciples: An Invitation to Baptismal Living.* Augsburg Fortress, 2012. An ecumenical handbook offering a basic "how to" and a collection of updated resources for preparing adults for baptism or affirmation of baptism, and for Christian discipleship. Appropriate for a wide range of Protestant denominations, especially Lutheran, Episcopal, Anglican, United Methodist, Presbyterian, and Reformed. Supplementary CD-ROM available separately.

*§ Hoyer, Christopher G. *Getting the Word Out: A Handbook for Readers.* Practical helps and spiritual wisdom for those who serve as lectors in the assembly. Augsburg Fortress, 2013.

Huffman, Walter C. *Prayer of the Faithful: Understanding and Creatively Leading Corporate Intercessory Prayer,* rev. ed. Augsburg Fortress, 1992. A helpful treatment of communal prayer, the Lord's Prayer, and the prayers of the people.

* ∞ *Leading Worship Matters: A Sourcebook for Preparing Worship Leaders* with companion DVD and CD-ROM. Augsburg Fortress, 2013. Practical, succinct, easy-to-use tools and resources to plan, execute, and evaluate worship leadership training. Covers assisting ministers, readers/lectors, altar guild/sacristans, intercessors, acolytes, ushers, greeters, communion ministers, and more.

§ Ramshaw, Gail, and Mons Teig. *Keeping Time: The Church's Years.* Augsburg Fortress, 2009. Contains detailed information on Sundays, seasons, festivals, and commemorations, as well as daily prayer.

*§ Scharen, Christian. *A Handbook for Assisting Ministers.* Practical helps and spiritual wisdom for those who serve as assisting ministers in the assembly. Augsburg Fortress 2013.

∞ *Washed and Welcome: A Baptism Sourcebook.* Augsburg Fortress, 2010. Resources to support a congregation's total baptismal ministry and the participation of God's people in the lifelong gift of baptism. Includes CD-ROM.

Choral Collections

Assembly Required. Augsburg Fortress, 2010. Volume 1 includes four liturgical songs for choir and assembly. Volume 2 includes four songs for the Easter Vigil.

Augsburg Choirbook, The. Augsburg Fortress, 1998. Kenneth Jennings, ed. Sixty-seven anthems primarily from twentieth-century North American composers.

Augsburg Choirbook for Advent, Christmas, and Epiphany. Augsburg Fortress, 2007. Thirty-three anthems, mostly easy-to-medium difficulty, for the Christmas cycle.

Augsburg Choirbook for Men. Augsburg Fortress, 2004. Fourteen anthems for two- to four-part male chorus.

Augsburg Choirbook for Women. Augsburg Fortress, 2006. Diverse selections for choirs of all ages and abilities from high school through adult.

Augsburg Easy Choirbook, vol. 1. Augsburg Fortress, 2003. Fourteen unison and two-part mixed anthems for the church year.

Augsburg Easy Choirbook, vol. 2. Augsburg Fortress, 2005. Sixteen anthems for the church year; accessible, quality music for the smaller, less-experienced choir.

* *Augsburg Motet Book.* Augsburg Fortress, 2013. Zebulon M. Highben, ed. Over thirty classic anthems and new motets, edited with optional accompaniments.

Bach for All Seasons. Augsburg Fortress, 1999. Richard Erickson and Mark Bighley, eds. Offers movements from cantatas and oratorios presented with carefully reconstructed keyboard parts and fresh English texts. Instrumental parts available.

---

* denotes new or newer print resource
∞ denotes electronic or Web resource
§ denotes print resource also available as an ebook

Chantry Choirbook. Augsburg Fortress, 2000. Choral masterworks of European composers spanning five centuries, many with new English translations, and indexed for use in the liturgical assembly throughout the year.

Choral Stanzas for Hymns. 2 vols. Augsburg Fortress, 2010–2011. More than 150 reproducible arrangements of selected hymn stanzas for choirs to sing in alternation with assemblies.

GladSong Choirbook. Augsburg Fortress, 2005. Eleven titles for fall, Advent, and Christmas use, plus Reformation, Thanksgiving, All Saints, Christ the King, Epiphany, and communion.

Hear Our Prayer. Augsburg Fortress, 2007. A collection of sung prayer responses to be used between the petitions of the prayers of intercession or as a call or closing to prayer.

* *The New Gloria Deo: Music for Small Choirs.* Augsburg Fortress, 2010 (vol. 1), 2012 (vol. 2). Twelve anthems written with small ensembles in mind by Aaron David Miller and Thomas Keesecker.

Vocal Descants for the Church Year. Based on hymns in *Evangelical Lutheran Worship.* Augsburg Fortress, 2008. 250 descants, mostly reproducible, for adding color and brilliance to hymn singing.

Wade in the Water: Easy Choral Music for All Ages. Augsburg Fortress, 2007. A collection of two- and three-part choral music for the less-experienced singer.

Hymn and Song Collections

As Sunshine to a Garden: Hymns and Songs. Rusty Edwards. Augsburg Fortress, 1999. Forty-six collected hymns from the author of "We all are one in mission."

Come, Beloved of the Maker: Hymns of Susan Palo Cherwien. Augsburg Fortress, 2010. Thirty-four hymn texts by Cherwien, following up on her previous collection, *O Blessed Spring (Augsburg Fortress, 1997).* Each text is presented with a harmonized tune.

Earth and All Stars: Hymns and Songs for Young and Old. Herbert F. Brokering. Augsburg Fortress, 2003. A collection of hymn texts by the popular writer.

Justice like a Base of Stone. Bret Hesla. Augsburg Fortress, 2006. A collection of peace and justice songs in a variety of styles, easily taught to the congregation. Audio CD also available.

Pave the Way: Global Songs 3. Bread for the Journey. Augsburg Fortress, 2004. Eighteen songs from around the world, with performance notes. Also available: Audio CD; Global Songs Local Voices (1995); and Global Songs 2 (1997).

∞ *Singing Our Prayer: A Companion to Holden Prayer Around the Cross. Shorter Songs for Contemplative Worship.* Augsburg Fortress, 2010. A collection of short, simple songs for worship. Available in full score and assembly editions, and audio CD.

Worship & Praise. Augsburg Fortress, 1999. A collection of songs in various contemporary and popular styles, with helps for using them in Lutheran worship.

Instrumental Collections

* Augsburg Organ Library. Augsburg Fortress, 2000–2013. Ten volumes of carefully selected organ music classics of the 20th and 21st centuries from a variety of publishers, organized according the seasons of the church year and primary liturgical contexts. Volume ten, Healing and Funeral (2013), is particularly useful for funerals, memorial services, services of healing, as well as Sundays when the lectionary explores themes of healing, death, and dying.

Evangelical Lutheran Worship Festival and Enhanced Settings of Communion Liturgies. Augsburg Fortress, 2008–2013. Additional instrumentation and choral elaboration for *Evangelical Lutheran Worship* Settings One, Two, Six, Seven, Eight, Nine.

Hymn Accompaniments for Handbells: Advent and Christmas. Augsburg Fortress, 2010. Fourteen settings by Lee J. Afdahl to introduce and accompany hymns.

Hymns for Ensembles: Instrumental Accompaniments for Ecumenical Hymns. 2 vols. Augsburg Fortress, 2010–2011. More than 100 orchestrations of hymns old and new. Full score with keyboard part; parts for various instruments on CD-ROM, included.

In Heaven Above: Piano Music for Funerals and Memorials. Augsburg Fortress, 2011. More than fifty arrangements by various composers of favorite hymns of comfort, hope, and celebration of the saints.

Introductions and Alternate Accompaniments. Augsburg Fortress, 2007–2009. Two 10-volume series, one for organ and one for piano, covering every *Evangelical Lutheran Worship* hymn and song. Various composers.

Let It Rip! at the Piano (2 vols.) and *Pull Out the Stops* (2 vols.). Augsburg Fortress, 2000–2005. Collections for piano and organ respectively, each containing introductions and varied musical accompaniments by various composers for more than 100 widely used hymns and songs.

* *Organ Plus Anthology,* vol. 1. Augsburg Fortress, 2012. Hymn arrangements by various composers for organ and one or two instruments.

Piano Plus: Hymns for Piano and Treble Instrument, Advent/ Christmas. Augsburg Fortress, 2006. *Through the Year,* 2009. Arrangements by various composers that range in difficulty from simple cradle songs to jazz, and span numerous world cultures and several centuries.

Psalm Collections

See p. 351.

Preparing Music for Worship

* ∞ www.preludemusicplanner.com. A subscription-based online music planning tool. Create comprehensive plans. Browse, preview, and download music from multi-publisher library. Search music based on lectionary days, keywords, skill level and more. Store your usage history. Upload and organize your own library.

* denotes new or newer print resource
∞ denotes electronic or Web resource
346 § denotes print resource also available as an ebook

Boesenecker, Andrew, and James Graeser. *A Field Guide to Contemporary Worship: How to Begin and Lead Band-Based Worship*. Augsburg Fortress, 2011. A guide for anyone thinking about starting a contemporary worship service and an essential reference work for those wondering about the nuts and bolts of instrumentation, arranging, working with microphones and speakers, and much more.

Cherwien, David. *Let the People Sing! A Keyboardist's Creative and Practical Guide to Engaging God's People in Meaningful Song*. Concordia, 1997. Emphasis on the organ.

Bradley Ellingboe, ed. *Choral Literature for Sundays and Seasons*. Augsburg Fortress, 2004. A comprehensive listing of time-tested choral works, indexed to the readings for each Sunday and principal festival of the three-year lectionary. Includes information on voicing, instrumentation, composers, and publishers.

∞ *Evangelical Lutheran Worship* Liturgies Audio CD, vols. 1, 2, 3. Augsburg Fortress, 2006, 2010. Complete recordings of Holy Communion Settings One–Ten and Daily Prayer.

∞ *Evangelical Lutheran Worship* Hymns Audio CD, vols. 1 and 2. Augsburg Fortress, 2006, 2007. Recordings of four dozen hymns and songs from *Evangelical Lutheran Worship*, both new and familiar. Performed by choirs from St. Olaf and Lenoir Rhyne colleges.

Farlee, Robert Buckley, ed. *Leading the Church's Song*. Augsburg Fortress, 1998. Various contributors, with musical examples and audio CD, giving guidance on the interpretation and leadership of various genres of congregational song.

∞ *Favorite Hymns Accompanied*. John Ferguson, organist. Augsburg Fortress, 2005. A 2-CD set of 52 widely known hymns played without singing.

Highben, Zebulon M., and Kristina M. Langlois, eds. *With a Voice of Singing: Essays on Children, Choirs, and Music in the Church*. Minneapolis: Kirk House Publishers, 2007.

Musicians Guide to Evangelical Lutheran Worship. Augsburg Fortress, 2007. An introduction to the music, including specific suggestions for each liturgical music item, service music item, and hymn.

Soli Deo Gloria: Choir Devotions for Year A (Craig Mueller), *Year B* (Jennifer Baker-Trinity), and *Year C* (Wayne L. Wold). Augsburg Fortress, 2009–2011.

Weidler, Scott, and Dori Collins. *Sound Decisions*. Evangelical Lutheran Church in America, 1997. Theological principles for the evaluation of contemporary worship music.

§ Westermeyer, Paul. *The Church Musician*, rev. ed. Augsburg Fortress, 1997. Foundational introduction to the role and task of the church musician as the leader of the people's song.

§ ———. *Te Deum: The Church and Music*. Fortress Press, 1998. A historical and theological introduction to the music of the church.

§ Wold, Wayne L. *Preaching to the Choir: The Care and Nurture of the Church Choir*. Augsburg Fortress, 2003. Practical helps for the choir director.

Preparing Environment and Art

Chinn, Nancy. *Spaces for Spirit: Adorning the Church*. Chicago: Liturgy Training Publications, 1998. Imaginative thinking about ways to treat visual elements in the worship space.

§ Christopherson, D. Foy. *A Place of Encounter: Renewing Worship Spaces*. Augsburg Fortress, 2004. An exploration of principles for planning and renewing worship spaces.

Crowley, Eileen D. *A Moving Word: Media Art in Worship*. Augsburg Fortress, 2006. An exploration of how visual elements in worship can enhance the assembly's understanding of the gospel.

∞ *Evangelical Lutheran Worship* Graphics CD-ROM. Augsburg Fortress, 2011. Contains more than 100 graphic images that appear in the *Evangelical Lutheran Worship* family of resources, including the pew edition, Pastoral Care, Occasional Services for the Assembly, and more. Color images are provided as both TIFF and JPG files; black-and-white versions of the images are provided as TIFF files.

Giles, Richard. *Re-Pitching the Tent: Reordering the Church Building for Worship and Mission*. Collegeville, MN: The Liturgical Press, 1999.

Huffman, Walter C., S. Anita Stauffer, and Ralph R. Van Loon. *Where We Worship*. Minneapolis: Augsburg Publishing House, 1987. Study book and leader guide.

Mazar, Peter. *To Crown the Year: Decorating the Church through the Seasons*. Chicago: Liturgy Training Publications, 1995.

§ Stauffer, S. Anita. *Altar Guild and Sacristy Handbook*. Augsburg Fortress, 2000. Revised and expanded edition of this classic on preparing the table and the worship environment.

Seasons and Liturgical Year

* *Of the Land and Seasons*. Assembly and leader/accompaniment editions. Augsburg Fortress, 2013. A worship service connected to the change of the seasons in farming, orchards, or natural settings. Intended for quarterly use. This is a revised edition of the resource first published in 1990. The pattern and language have been reshaped to coordinate with the liturgies of Evangelical Lutheran Worship.

Worship Guidebook for Lent and the Three Days. Augsburg Fortress, 2009. A collection of insights, images, and practical tips to help deepen your congregation's worship life during the days from Ash Wednesday to Easter. A companion to *Music Sourcebook for Lent and the Three Days*.

Music Sourcebook for Lent and the Three Days. Augsburg Fortress, 2010. This collection includes 100 assembly songs, many of them reproducible, greatly expanding the repertoire for the assembly and its leaders during the days from Ash Wednesday to Easter.

* *Music Sourcebook for All Saints through Transfiguration*. Augsburg Fortress, 2013. This collection offers a rich selection of assembly songs, mostly newly composed and many of them reproducible, for use during the days of November, Advent, Christmas, Epiphany, and the Time after Epiphany.

§ Pfatteicher, Philip. *New Book of Festivals and Commemorations: A Proposed Common Calendar of the Saints*. Fortress Press, 2008.

---

* denotes new or newer print resource
∞ denotes electronic or Web resource
§ denotes print resource also available as an ebook

§ Ramshaw, Gail. *The Three-Day Feast: Maundy Thursday, Good Friday, Easter.* Augsburg Fortress, 2004. A little history and a lot of suggestions about how these services can enrich the assembly's worship life.

Children

* *ChildrenSing in Worship.* Augsburg Fortress, 2011–2013. Three volumes of anthems by various composers. Reproducible choral parts.

ChildrenSing Psalms. Marilyn Comer, ed. Augsburg Fortress, 2009. Collection of psalms for all seasons keyed to the lectionary.

∞ *Fed and Forgiven: Communion Preparation and Formation.* (See Worship Support)

Kids Celebrate Worship Series. Augsburg Fortress, 2006–2007. A series of seasonal and topical 8-page booklets that introduce children and their families to worship and *Evangelical Lutheran Worship.* Pre-reader and young reader versions. Includes ideas and helps for parents, pastors, educators, and children's choir directors.
Our Worship Book (2006). A kid-friendly introduction to *Evangelical Lutheran Worship.*
Sunday Worship (2006). Focuses on the gathering, word, meal, sending pattern of Holy Communion.
Advent & Christmas (2006). Introduction to the Advent-Christmas season with activities.
Lent & Easter (2006). Introduction to the seasons of Lent and Easter with activities.
Three Amazing Days (2006). Introduction to Maundy Thursday, Good Friday, and the Easter Vigil.
Holy Communion (2007). Introduction to the sacrament of holy communion.
Baptism (2007). Introduction to the sacrament of holy baptism and baptismal living.
Our Prayers (2007). Focuses on how and when the assembly prays in worship, and prayer in the home.
The Bible (2007). Introduction to the ways in which scripture is used in worship.

LifeSongs (children's songbook, leader book, and audio CDs). Augsburg Fortress, 1999. A well-rounded selection of age-appropriate songs, hymns, and liturgical music that builds a foundation for a lifetime of singing the faith.

Living the Promises of Baptism: 101 Ideas for Parents. Augsburg Fortress, 2010. Concrete ideas for celebrating with children (infant to upper elementary) the gifts of baptism in daily living.

Patterson, Mark. *Young ChildrenSing, ChildrenSing, and ChildrenSing with Instruments.* Augsburg Fortress, 2004–2006. Short anthems for young singers.

Ramshaw, Gail. *Every Day and Sunday, Too.* Augsburg Fortress, 1996. An illustrated book for parents and children. Daily life is related to the central actions of the liturgy.

———. *Sunday Morning.* Chicago: Liturgy Training Publications, 1993. A book for children and adults on the primary words of Sunday worship.

∞ *Washed and Welcome: A Baptism Sourcebook.* (See Worship Support)

Ylvisaker, Anne. Illustrated by Claudia McGehee. *Welcome, Child of God.* Augsburg Fortress, 2011. A board book about baptism for infants and toddlers.

Daily Prayer Resources

Briehl, Susan, and Tom Witt. *Holden Prayer Around the Cross: Handbook to the Liturgy.* Augsburg Fortress, 2009. Practical suggestions for planning and leading flexible orders for contemplative prayer. Includes fourteen liturgies in the Prayer Around the Cross format.

∞ *Singing Our Prayer: A Companion to Holden Prayer Around the Cross. Shorter Songs for Contemplative Worship.* (See Hymn and Song Collections)

*§ *Bread for the Day 2014: Daily Bible Readings and Prayers.* Augsburg Fortress, 2013. Daily scripture texts for individual or group prayer based on the daily lectionary in *Evangelical Lutheran Worship.*

Cherwien, David. *Stay with Us, Lord: Liturgies for Evening.* Augsburg Fortress, 2001. Settings for Evening Prayer and Holy Communion, full music and congregational editions.

Haugen, Marty. *Holden Evening Prayer.* Chicago: GIA, 1990.

Haugen, Marty, and Susan Briehl. *Unfailing Light.* Chicago: GIA, 2004.

Makeever, Ray. *Joyous Light Evening Prayer.* Augsburg Fortress, 2000.

* Miller, Aaron David. *Behold Our Light: Music for Evening Worship.* Augsburg Fortress, 2013. Settings of the musical selections needed for evening prayer or an evening communion service, scored for cantor, assembly, piano, and optional C instrument. Includes a service of light, setting of Psalm 139, Magnificat, intercessory prayers, and blessing, as well as a gospel acclamation, Sanctus, and Nunc dimittis.

§ *Revised Common Lectionary Daily Readings.* Consultation on Common Texts. Fortress Press, 2005.

Worship Studies, series

Worship Matters Series. Augsburg Fortress, 2004–2011. The series explores a range of worship-related topics.
§ Christopherson, D. Foy. *A Place of Encounter: Renewing Worship Spaces* (2004).
Crowley, Eileen D. *A Moving Word: Media Art in Worship* (2006).
§ Dahill, Lisa. *Truly Present: Practicing Prayer in the Liturgy* (2005).
§ Lathrop, Gordon. *Central Things: Worship in Word and Sacrament* (2005).
§ Quivik, Melinda. *A Christian Funeral: Witness to the Resurrection* (2005).
Ramshaw, Gail. *A Three-Year Banquet: The Lectionary for the Assembly* (2004).
§ ———. *The Three-Day Feast: Maundy Thursday, Good Friday, Easter* (2004).
§ Rimbo, Robert A. *Why Worship Matters* (2004).

* denotes new or newer print resource
∞ denotes electronic or Web resource
348 § denotes print resource also available as an ebook

Stewart, Benjamin. *A Watered Garden: Christian Worship and Earth's Ecology* (2011).

Torvend, Samuel. *Daily Bread, Holy Meal: Opening the Gifts of Holy Communion* (2004).

———. *Flowing Water, Uncommon Birth: Christian Baptism in a Post-Christian Culture* (2011).

Wengert, Timothy, ed. *Centripetal Worship: The Evangelical Heart of Lutheran Worship* (2007).

Ylvisaker, John. *What Song Shall We Sing?* (2005).

Worship Studies, individual titles

* *Worship Matters: An Introduction to Worship.* Multiple authors. Augsburg Fortress, 2012. A 5-session adult course that illuminates the whys and hows of Christian worship so that worshipers might experience a deeper appreciation of their community's worship. Leader guide and participant book.

* ∞ *Go Make Disciples: An Invitation to Baptismal Living.* Multiple authors. Augsburg Fortress, 2012. An ecumenical handbook offering a basic "how to" and a collection of updated resources for preparing adults for baptism or affirmation of baptism, and for Christian discipleship. Appropriate for a wide range of Protestant denominations, especially Lutheran, Episcopal, Anglican, United Methodist, Presbyterian, and Reformed. Supplementary CD-ROM available separately.

§ *The Christian Life: Baptism and Life Passages.* Augsburg Fortress, 2008.

§ *Keeping Time: The Church's Years.* Augsburg Fortress, 2009.

§ *The Sunday Assembly.* Augsburg Fortress, 2008.

§ *Inside Out: Worship in an Age of Mission.* Thomas Schattauer, gen. ed. Fortress Press, 1999. Lutheran seminary teachers address the mission of the church as it pertains to various aspects of worship.

§ Lathrop, Gordon. *The Four Gospels on Sunday: The New Testament and the Reform of Christian Worship.* Fortress Press, 2011. Lathrop demonstrates that the Gospels can remain a true catalyst for liturgical theology and liturgical renewal, as well as an inspiring link to the faith and convictions of the earliest followers of the Christian way.

§ ———. *Holy Ground: A Liturgical Cosmology.* Fortress Press, 2003.

§ ———. *Holy People: A Liturgical Ecclesiology.* Fortress Press, 1999.

§ ———. *Holy Things: A Liturgical Theology.* Fortress Press, 1998.

Principles for Worship. Renewing Worship, vol. 2. Augsburg Fortress, 2002. Principles for language, music, preaching, and worship space in relationship to the Christian assembly. Also available in Spanish.

Ramshaw, Gail. *Christian Worship.* Fortress Press, 2009. An engaging textbook on 100,000 Sundays of Christians at worship.

Senn, Frank. *Christian Liturgy: Catholic and Evangelical.* Fortress Press, 1997. A comprehensive historical introduction to the liturgy of the Western church with particular emphasis on Lutheran traditions.

§ ———. *Introduction to Christian Liturgy.* Fortress Press, 2012.

This general introduction explores the meaning, history, and practice of worship in Eastern and Western, Catholic and Protestant traditions: the theology of worship, the historical development of the eucharist and the prayer offices, the lectionary and customs of the church year, other sacramental rites, and the use of music and the arts.

§ ———. *The People's Work: A Social History of the Liturgy.* Fortress Press, 2006. The first book to document the full history of ordinary Christians' liturgical expression.

Use of the Means of Grace: A Statement on the Practice of Word and Sacrament, The. Evangelical Lutheran Church in America, 1997. Also available in Spanish and Mandarin versions.

Web Sites

* ∞ www.preludemusicplanner.com. A subscription-based online music planning tool. Create comprehensive plans. Browse, preview, and download music from multi-publisher library. Search music based on lectionary days, keywords, skill level and more. Store your usage history. Upload and organize your own library.

∞ www.sundaysandseasons.com. A subscription-based online worship planning tool. Browse, select, and download content for worship planning and worship folder preparation. Complements *Sundays and Seasons.*

∞ www.alcm.org. Association of Lutheran Church Musicians. Links to conferences and resources available through this pan-Lutheran musicians' organization. Also a bulletin board and placement service.

∞ www.elca.org/worship. Evangelical Lutheran Church in America. Contains links to articles and essays on a variety of worship-related topics. Includes a section on frequently asked questions about church year, language, lectionary, liturgy, worship planning, worship space, and many other topics. Monthly WorshipNews e-newsletter.

∞ www.newproclamation.com. An online sermon preparation resource that combines in-depth exegesis with homiletic advice from practicing preachers.

∞ www.theworkofthepeople.com. Visual media for worship based on the Revised Common Lectionary, including videos, loops, and stills.

∞ www.worship.ca. Lift Up Your Hearts: The worship and spirituality site of the Evangelical Lutheran Church in Canada. Contains a variety of resources and news about events related to Lutheran worship.

Preaching Resources

*§ Brueggemann, Walter. *The Practice of Prophetic Imagination: Preaching an Emancipating Word.* Fortress Press, 2012.

Craddock, Fred, et al. *Preaching through the Christian Year.* Three volumes for Cycles A, B, C. Valley Forge, PA: Trinity Press International, 1992, 1993. Various authors comment on the Sunday readings, psalms, and various festival readings.

§ Elements of Preaching series. O. Wesley Allen, series editor. Fortress Press, 2008–. Guides to the art and craft of preaching. Authors include Ronald Allen, Teresa Fry Brown, Mary Foskett, Jennifer Lord, Marvin McMickle, James Nieman, Melinda Quivik.

* denotes new or newer print resource
∞ denotes electronic or Web resource
§ denotes print resource also available as an ebook

*§ Fortress Biblical Preaching Commentaries series. Fortress Press, 2013–. With their focus on the biblical books themselves and working with the realities of the lectionary, these volumes are useful in tandem with more extensive commentaries as well as with seasonal lectionary materials.

*§ Hedahl, Susan K. *Proclamation and Celebration: Preaching on Christmas, Easter, and Other Festivals.* Fortress Press, 2012.

§ Pagitt, Doug. *Preaching in the Inventive Age.* Sparkhouse, 2011.

§ Ramshaw, Gail. *Treasures Old and New: Images in the Lectionary.* Fortress Press, 2002. A creative unfolding of forty images drawn from the lectionary readings.

§ Rhodes, David, H. Paul Santmire, and Norman C. Habel, eds. *The Season of Creation: A Preaching Commentary.* Fortress Press, 2011. Scholars who have pioneered the connections between biblical scholarship, ecological theology, liturgy, and homiletics provide here a comprehensive resource for preaching and leading worship in this new season.

∞ Sloyan, Gerard. *Preaching from the Lectionary: An Exegetical Commentary with CD-ROM.* Fortress Press, 2003. Exegetical analysis of each text from the RCL.

§ Stiller, Brian. *Preaching Parables to Postmoderns.* Fortress Press, 2005. An introduction to postmodern sensibilities and how it informs preaching the parables.

∞ www.homileticsonline.com. An online sermon preparation resource including illustrations and visuals.

∞ www.newproclamation.com. An online sermon preparation resource that combines in-depth exegesis with homiletic advice from practicing preachers.

∞ www.thehardestquestion.com. A preaching blog with multiple contributors.

∞ www.workingpreacher.org. A resource for preachers from the Center for Biblical Preaching at Luther Seminary.

Periodicals

Catechumenate: A Journal of Christian Initiation. Chicago: Liturgy Training Publications. Published six times a year with articles on congregational preparation of older children and adults for the celebration of baptism and eucharist.

CrossAccent. Journal of the Association of Lutheran Church Musicians. Publication for church musicians and worship leaders in North America. www.alcm.org.

Faith & Form. Journal of the Interfaith Forum on Religion, Art and Architecture. www.faithandform.com.

Liturgy. Quarterly journal of The Liturgical Conference. Each issue explores a worship-related issue from an ecumenical perspective. customerservice@taylorandfrancis.com.

Worship. Collegeville, MN: The Order of St. Benedict, published through The Liturgical Press six times a year. One of the primary journals of liturgical renewal among the churches.

Key to Hymn and Song Collections

* Indicates resources whose hymns or psalm refrains are, at least in part, included in the online worship planning tool Sundays and Seasons.com.

ASG*	As Sunshine to a Garden. Augsburg Fortress.	
CBM	Come, Beloved of the Maker. Augsburg Fortress.	
DH*	Dancing at the Harvest. Augsburg Fortress.	
ELW*	Evangelical Lutheran Worship. Augsburg Fortress.	
GS2*	Global Songs 2: Bread for the Journey. Augsburg Fortress.	
GS3	Global Songs 3: Pave the Way. Augsburg Fortress.	
LBW*	Lutheran Book of Worship. Augsburg Fortress.	
LLC	Libro de Liturgia y Cántico. Augsburg Fortress.	
LS*	LifeSongs. Augsburg Fortress.	
Music Sourcebook*	Music Sourcebook for Lent and the Three Days. Augsburg Fortress.	
OBS*	O Blessed Spring: Hymns of Susan Palo Cherwien. Augsburg Fortress.	
SP	Singing Our Prayer: A Companion to Holden Prayer Around the Cross. Augsburg Fortress.	
TFF*	This Far by Faith. Augsburg Fortress.	
W&P*	Worship & Praise. Augsburg Fortress.	
WOV*	With One Voice. Augsburg Fortress.	

Key to Psalm Collections

The psalm collections included in this year's musical recommendations are by no means comprehensive, but were chosen for their variety in presentation as well as their ease of use. The refrains included in each of the resources below may be reprinted with a OneLicense .net copyright license. The one exception to this is *Psalms for All Seasons*, which is a compilation of psalm settings from a variety of publishers, some, but not all, of which are covered under the OneLicense .net license.

With the recent approval of "The Revised Grail Psalter" as the official English psalm translation in the Roman Catholic Church, several new volumes for psalm singing have been published. The Revised Common Lectionary does not follow exactly the Roman lectionary, but there is sufficient overlap to make these Catholic volumes very useful. Psalm collections below that follow the Roman lectionary are marked with [RL].

ChildrenSing Psalms. Marilyn Comer, ed. Augsburg Fortress. This collection of 15 of the more well-known psalms is a must-have for anyone working with children's choirs. Reproducible singer pages and assembly refrains.

DH   Ray Makeever. *Dancing at the Harvest.* Augsburg Fortress. This collection of songs includes lyrical settings of selected psalms with refrains and through-composed verses.

LP:LG   *Lectionary Psalms: Lead Me, Guide Me.* GIA. Refrains and psalm verse accompaniments composed in gospel style. These settings work well with *Evangelical Lutheran Worship* Holy Communion Setting Six or another gospel setting of the liturgy. [RL]

LP:W4   *Lectionary Psalms: Joseph Gelineau, SJ and Michel Guimont* (as found in *Worship, Fourth Edition*). GIA. Psalms in this volume are presented with a single refrain that may be used with a Gelineau tone or a tone by Michel Guimont. [RL]

PAS   *Psalms for All Seasons: A Complete Psalter for Worship.* Calvin Institute of Christian Worship, Faith Alive Christian Resources, and Brazos Press. In addition to each of the 150 psalms and several canticles presented in multiple sung settings, this volume contains a comprehensive introduction to psalmody, several services of prayer, and extensive appendixes and indexes.

PCY   Marty Haugen/David Haas. *Psalms for the Church Year, Vol. 1.* GIA. Part of a multi-volume set, this volume includes 24 of the most well-known psalm settings by these two composers.

PP   *The Portland Psalter.* Robert A. Hawthorne. 2 vols. Church Publishing. Book One contains settings for RCL psalms; Book Two, settings for lesser festivals and the Easter Vigil.

PRCL   Michel Guimont. *Psalms for the Revised Common Lectionary.* GIA. Responsorial psalms. May be accompanied by organ, piano, or guitar.

PS1   *Psalm Songs 1: Advent–Christmas–Epiphany.* Augsburg Fortress. This 3-volume set provides interesting settings of more common psalms. All settings include guitar chords and many have parts for other solo instruments.

PS2   *Psalm Songs 2: Lent–Holy Week–Easter.*

PS3   *Psalm Songs 3: Ordinary Time.*

Psallite   *Psallite: Sacred Song for Liturgy and Life.* Liturgical Press. This set of resources includes an accompaniment edition for each lectionary year and one volume for cantor/choir. In addition to lectionary psalms, provides biblically based songs that can be used at other times in the liturgy. [RL]

PSCY   *Psalm Settings for the Church Year.* 2 vols. Mark Mummert, ed. Augsburg Fortress. A collection of psalm settings in a wide variety of styles and structures. Includes all psalms used in the RCL.

PWA   *Psalter for Worship: Year A.* Augsburg Fortress. The first of three volumes of psalm refrains by various composers with *Evangelical Lutheran Worship* psalm tones. Coordinates with Celebrate and Today's Readings inserts. Includes a CD-ROM with reproducible psalm texts, refrains, and tones.

PWC   *Psalter for Worship: Year C.*

SJ   Richard Bruxvoort Colligan. *Shout for Joy: The Psalm Project, Vol. 2.* Augsburg Fortress. Selected psalms for congregational singing for Advent and Christmas.

SMP   Thomas Pavlechko, arr. *St. Martin's Psalter.* Augsburg Fortress. Refrains and psalm tones based on familiar hymns in Anglican chant style. Published on CD-ROM, it includes reproducible parts for choir.

SR   Richard Bruxvoort Colligan. *Sharing the Road: The Psalm Project, Vol. 1.* Augsburg Fortress. Psalm settings for congregational singing for Lent and Psalm 118 appointed for Easter.

TLP:A   Tony Alonzo/Marty Haugen. *The Lyric Psalter: Year A.* GIA. This set contains four editions, one for each of the three years of the lectionary and one for solemnities, feasts, and special occasions. Each has a companion volume of descants for C-instrument. Psalm verses are through-composed and can be sung by a cantor. [RL]

TLP:S   *The Lyric Psalter: Solemnities, Feasts, and Other Occasions.* [RL]

TP   *The Psalter: Psalms and Canticles for Singing.* Westminster/John Knox. An eclectic collection of psalm settings drawing from a variety of sources. Includes all psalms appointed in the RCL.

TPP   *The People's Psalter.* MorningStar. Responsorial psalm settings that makes use of folk tunes from around the world. Includes settings for every psalm in the three-year lectionary.

Key to Music for Worship

acc	accompaniment	eng hrn	English horn	narr	narrator	tamb	tambourine
bar	baritone	fc	finger cymbals	ob	oboe	tba	tuba
bng	bongos	fl	flute	oct	octave	tbn	trombone
br	brass	glock	glockenspiel	opt	optional	tpt	trumpet
bsn	bassoon	gtr	guitar	orch	orchestra	timp	timpani
cant	cantor	hb	handbells	org	organ	trbl	treble
ch	chimes	hc	handchimes	perc	percussion	tri	triangle
cl	clarinet	hp	harp	picc	piccolo	U	unison
cont	continuo	hpd	harpsichord	pno	piano	UE	upper elementary
cym	cymbal	hrn	horn	pt	part	vc	violoncello
DB	double or string	inst	instrument	qnt	quintet	vcs	voices
	bass	kybd	keyboard	qrt	quartet	vla	viola
dbl	double	LE	lower elementary	rec	recorder	vln	violin
desc	descant	M	medium	sax	saxophone	wch	windchimes
div	divisi	MH	medium high	sop	soprano	ww	woodwind
drm	drum	ML	medium low	str	strings	xyl	xylophone
		mxd	mixed	synth	synthesizer		

Key to Music Publishers

AFP	Augsburg Fortress	FB	Fred Bock Music	LOR	Lorenz	SEL	Selah
AGEHR	(Lorenz)	FLG	Flagstaff Publications	MSM	MorningStar Music	SF	SoundForth
ALF	Alfred	FTT	From the Top Music	NOV	Novello		Publications
AUR	Aureole	GIA	GIA Publications	OCP	Oregon Catholic Press	SHW	Shawnee
BAR	Bärenreiter	HAL	Hal Leonard	OXF	Oxford University Press	WAL	Walton
BP	Beckenhorst Press	HIN	Hinshaw Music Co.	PAR	Paraclete Press	WLP	World Library
CG	Choristers Guild (Lorenz)	HOP	Hope	PRE	Presser		Publications
CPH	Concordia	JEF	Jeffers	RR	Red River Music	WT	WorshipTogether.com
ECS	E. C. Schirmer	KJO	Kjos	RW	Ringing Word Publications		

A Note on Music Listings

Please note that some choral and instrumental music in the day listings may be out of print. We are unable to research whether musical pieces from other publishers are still available. Why do we still list music if it is out of print? Primarily because many music planners may have that piece in their files, and can consider it for use. If a planner wishes to use a piece that has gone out of print, that may still be possible. For Augsburg Fortress resources, call 800/421-0239 or e-mail copyright@augsburgfortress.org to inquire about onetime reprint rights or to see whether a piece may be available by print on demand.